MACHINE TOOL ENGINEERING

[*A Textbook for Engineering Students*]

G.R. NAGPAL

B.Sc., Engineering (Mechanical)
M.Tech. (Mechanical)
Assistant Professor Mech. Engineering Department
Y.M.C.A. Insitute of Management
Faridabad (Haryana)

KHANNA PUBLISHERS

Operational Office
4575/15, Onkar House, Ground Floor,
Darya Ganj, New Delhi 110 002
Phones : 011-23243042, 011-23243043 & Mob. 9811541460
E-mail : contactus@khannapublishers.in

Published by :

Romesh Chander Khanna & Vineet Khanna
for **KHANNA PUBLISHERS**
2-B, Nath Market, Nai Sarak
Delhi- 110 006 (India)

Website : www.khannapublishers.in

Hologram & Description

To all readers of our books, from yourself if being defrauded by pirates to prevent, please make sure that there is an Hologram on the cover of our books with the below specifications. If you find any book without Hologram and Description, please mail us at **contactus@khannapublishers.in**

Thanking you

ISBN No. 978-81-7409-046-0

First Edition : 1999
Eighth Edition
Eleventh Reprint : 2013

***Price :* ₹ 299.00**

Preface

The author is glad to present this book in a new revised format. This thoroughly revised edition is outcome of various suggestions and comments received from readers and professors of various universities from all over India for which I am really thankful for their suggestions and comments. I think this book will be now more useful for the students of Degree, Diploma and other similar courses. The purpose of this book is to provide a comprehensive knowledge of various aspects of the following :

(*i*) Method of metal cutting
(*ii*) Cutting tools
(*iii*) Machine tools.

Every effort has been made to present the subject matter in a simple language. The study and recitation is given in to develop the applications of the principles studied. Numerous examples and problems have been included, followed by a separate chapter on objective type questions to make topics more clear and prepare students for any type of examination.

Suggestions for improvement of the book shall be gratefully received and appreciated.

The author is thankful to the Publisher for the most painstaking and co-operative attitude for bringing out this book in a very short period.

G.R. NAGPAL

By the same Author :

(*i*) Power Plant Engineering
(*ii*) Machine Drawing
(*iii*) Machine Design
(*iv*) Material Science
(*v*) Metal Forming Process
(*vi*) Tool Engineering and Design

Introduction

Today metal-cutting is a very segment indeed of our industry. The motor car industry, electrical engineering, railways, shipbuilding, aircraft manufacture, production of domestic equipment and the machine tool industry itself—all these have large machine shops with many thousands of employees engaged in machining.

The technology of metal cutting has been improved by contributions from all the branches of industry with an interest in machining. The replacement of carbon tool steel by high speed steels and cemented carbides has allowed cutting speeds to be increased by many times. Machine tool manufacturers have developed machines capable of making full use of the new tool materials, while automatic machines, numerically controlled (NC) machines, often with computer control (CNC), and transfer machines greatly increase the output per worker employed. Tool designers and machinists have optimised the shapes of tools to give long tool life at high cutting speed. Lubricant manufacturers have developed many new coolants and lubricants to improve surface finish and permit increased rates of metal removal.

On the other hand, metal producers have responded to the demands of production engineers for metals which can be cut faster. New heat treatments have been devised, and the introduction of alloys like the free-machining steels and leaded brass has made great savings in production costs.

Metal removal rate during metal cutting is affected by quality of machine tool, quality of cutting tool and type of machining method. Modern machine tools such as NC, CNC machines have proved to be quite useful for increasing productivity. Coated cemented carbide tools have longer life, can cut harder materials and produce accurate components. The cutting tools used should be able to resist :

(*i*) wear
(*ii*) deformation
(*iii*) corrosion
(*iv*) high temperature
(*v*) high pressure.

Continuous or intermittent cutting is effected by plunging tool cutting elements into the work material and by displacing these elements relatively to the work.

Considerable efforts, which have to be applied to the cutting tool in the process of machining, cause failure of the work material owing to the occurrence of a complex deformation. The latter is accompanied by ample generation of heat, which raises the temperature of the tool cutting elements to a very high level (600—1,000°C and even more). Hence, the material of cutting tools must be hard, strong, and wear-resistant.

Depending on the type, purpose, and conditions of the machining operations to be done, cutting tools are shaped to a certain geometry and dimensions that would suit most efficiently the cutting process.

Correct sharpening and lapping of cutting tools is of great importance for attaining their high quality and stability of their cutting properties. At an earlier stage of industrial development, tools were sharpened by hand with the aid of primitive grinding appliances. The enlargement of the range of tools, complication of tool shapes, and growing demand for tools have necessitated the employment of special tool-and-cutter grinding machines.

Contents

1

Process of Metal Cutting

1.0. Metal Cutting

Metal cutting process consists in removing a layer of metal from blank to obtain a machine part of the required shape and dimensions and with the specified quality of surface finish.

A metal cutting tool is the part of a metal cutting machine tool that, in the cutting process, acts directly on the blank from which the finished part is to be made. The metal cutting process accompanied by deformation in compression, tension and shear by a great deal of friction and heat generation is governed by definite laws. In order to cut the material from blank the cutting tool should be harder than material to be cut, the tool should penetrate the blank and the tool should be strong enough to withstand the forces developed in cutting.

Metals are given different usable forms by various processes. These processes are of two types :

(*a*) Chip removal processes.

(*b*) Non-chip removal processes (Chipless processes).

1.1. Chip Removal Processes

In chip removal processes the desired shape and dimensions are obtained by separating a layer from the patent workpiece in the form of chips. The various chip forming processes are as follows :

(*i*) Turning
(*ii*) Shaping
(*iii*) Boring
(*iv*) Drilling
(*v*) Milling
(*vi*) Honing
(*vii*) Grinding.

During the process of metal cutting there is a relative motion between the workpiece and cutting tool. Such a relative motion is produced by a combination of rotary and translatory movements either of the workpiece or of cutting tool or of both. This relative motion depends upon the type of metal cutting operation. Table 1.0

indicates the nature of relative motion for various continuous cutting operations.

Table 1.0

Operation	*Motion of Workpiece*	*Motion of Cutting Tool*
Shaping	Fixed	Translatory
Turning	Rotary	Translatory
Drilling	Fixed	Rotary as well as translatory
Milling	Translatory	Rotary

In any metal cutting process the following aims should be achieved :

(*i*) Work piece surface finish should be of desired quality.

(*ii*) Metal removal rate should be high.

(*iii*) Power consumed during the process should be low.

(*iv*) Cutting tool life should be more.

1.2. Chipless Processes

In chipless processes the metal is given the desired shape without removing any material from the parent workpiece. Some of the chipless processes are as follows :

(*i*) Rolling (*ii*) Forging

(*iii*) Spinning (*iv*) Stamping.

1.3. Metal Cutting Principle

Metal cutting is one of the most important processes carried out in an industry. The purpose of any metal cutting operation commonly called machining is to produce a desired shape, size and finish of a component by removing the excess metal in the form of chips from a rough block of material. Consequently the primary objective in metal cutting is the production of chips, although these chips are only a means to an end and are discarded. They may constitute more than 50% of the initial workpiece material. The machining process should be carried at high speeds and feeds and least cutting effort and at lowest cost. The cutting operation whether being carried out on lathe, milling machine or any other machine tool is based on theory which is same for all processes. Number of inter-related factors affect metal cutting, the more important factors being as follows :

(*i*) The properties of work material.

(*ii*) The properties and geometry of the cutting tool.

(*iii*) The interaction between the tool and the work during metal cutting.

The exact mechanism of metal cutting briefly stated is that a cutting tool exerts a compressive force on the workpiece. Under this compressive force the material of the workpiece is stressed beyond its yield point causing the material to deform plastically and shear off. The plastic flow takes place in a localised region called shear plane (Fig. 1.1) which extends from the cutting obliquely up to the uncut surface ahead of tool (Fig. 1.2). The sheared material begins

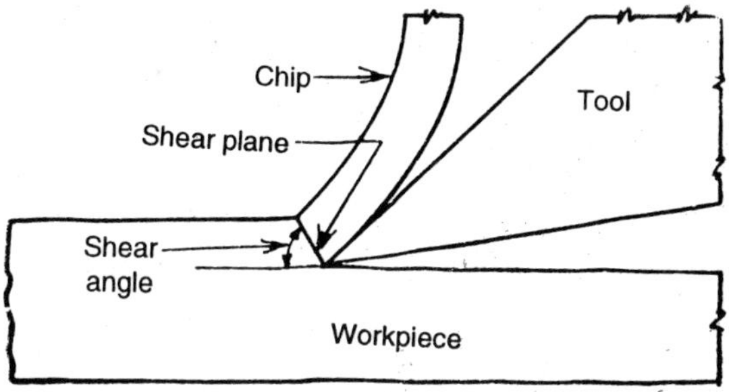

Fig. 1.1

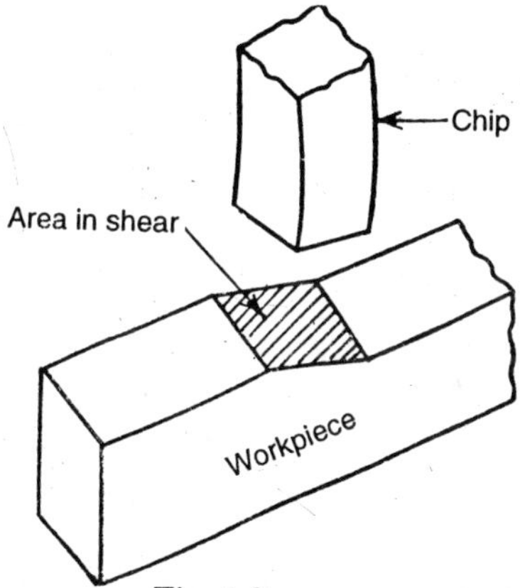

Fig. 1.2

to flow along the cutting tool face in the form of small pieces called chips. The compressive force applied to form the chips is called cutting force. The flowing chips cause wear of cutting tool. Heat is produced during shearing action. The heat generated raises the temperature of the work, cutting tool and chips. The temperature rise in the cutting tool tends to soften it and causes loss of keenness in the cutting edge leading to its failure. The cutting force, heat and abrasive wear are thus the basic features of the material cutting process.

During cutting process the following properties of the workpiece material are quite important :

(i) Hardness

(ii) Toughness

(iii) Inherent hard spots and surface inclusions

(iv) Abrasive qualities

(v) Tendency to weld.

On the other hand the tool material should be hard, strong, tough and wear resistant.

One of the basic requirements for metal cutting operations is that the tool is harder than the work piece. Both are held rigidly and the tool tends to penetrate into the work piece and this is how a small portion of work piece material is removed called as chip.

There are two distinct methods of producing surfaces by cutting tools :

(i) Generating (ii) Forming.

In generating the shape of the surface depends on the direction of motion of the tool with relation to the work. As shown in Fig. 1.2.1 (a) in generating a cylinder the work rotates about an axis and the cutting tool moves in a direction parallel to the axis. In forming a cylinder as shown in Fig. 1.2.1 (b) the work is stationary and the cutting tool moves in the direction of the axis of the cylinder.

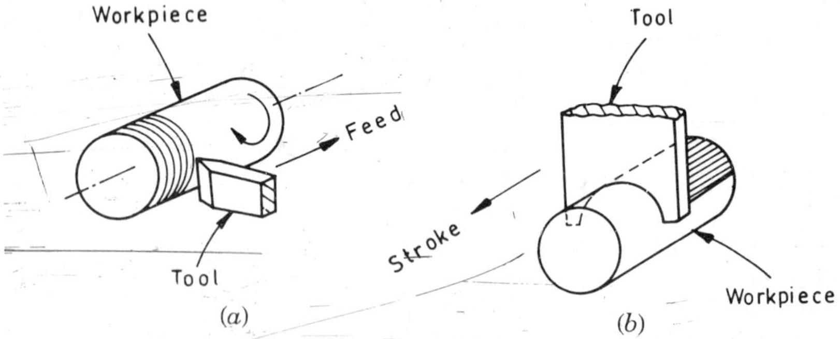

Fig. 1.2.1

1.3.1. Basic elements of machining

The basic elements of all machining operations are as follows :

(i) Workpiece (ii) Cutting tool

(iii) Chip.

The workpiece provides the parent metal from which the unwanted material is removed by the cutting action of tool to obtain desired size and shape. For providing the cutting action a relative motion between tool and workpiece is necessary.

1.4. Classification of Cutting Tools

Depending upon the number of cutting edges the cutting tools used in metal cutting are classified as follows :

(*i*) Single point cutting tool
(*ii*) Multipoint cutting tool.

(*i*) **Single point cutting tool.** This type of tool has an effective cutting edge and removes excess material from the workpiece along the cutting edge. Single point cutting tool is of the following types :

(*a*) Ground type (*b*) Forged type
(*c*) Tipped type (*d*) Bit type.

In ground type the cutting edge is formed by grinding the end of a piece of tool steel stock whereas in forged type the cutting edge is formed by rough forging before hardening and grinding. In tipped type cutting tool the cutting edge is in the form of a small tip made of high grade material which is welded to a shank made up of lower grade material. In bit type, a high grade material of a square, rectangular or some other shape is held mechanically in a tool holder. Single point tools are commonly used in lathes, shapers, planers, boring machines and slotters.

Single point cutting tool may be left-handed or right-handed type. A tool is said to be right/left hand type if the cutting edge is on the right or left side when viewing tool from the point end. Lathe tools, shaper tools, planer tools and boring tools are single point tools.

(*ii*) **Multipoints cutting tools.** They have more than one effective cutting edge to remove the excess material from the workpiece. Milling cutters, drills, reamers broaches and grinding wheels are multipoint cutting tools.

1.5. Tool Geometry

The desirability of getting the maximum use from a tool before it needs regrinding is one of the objectives of tool technology. Tool life is defined as the length of time, a tool will operate before its failure occurs. There are many factors that contribute to cutting tool efficiency. Among the most important of these are the following :

(*i*) The shape of the cutting edge that removes the excess material.

(*ii*) The correct selection of the type of cutting tool for the material to be machined.

(*iii*) The correct choice of cutting speed and feed.

(*iv*) The proper setting of cutting tool relative to work.

(*v*) The correct choice and proper application of coolants.

Unless the cutting tools is ground to the correct shape with correct angles and unless it is ground with a keen, smooth cutting edge, time will be wasted, accuracy will be impossible and a poor finish will result.

The optimum tool geometry depends upon the following factors :

(*i*) Workpiece material

(*ii*) Machining variables :

(*a*) Cutting speed (*b*) Feed

(*c*) Depth of cut

(*iii*) Material of the tool point

(*iv*) Type of cutting.

Tool geometry refers to the tool angles, shape of the tool face and the form of the cutting edges.

Fig. 1.3 shows a typical single point tool. The most important features are the cutting edges and adjacent surfaces.

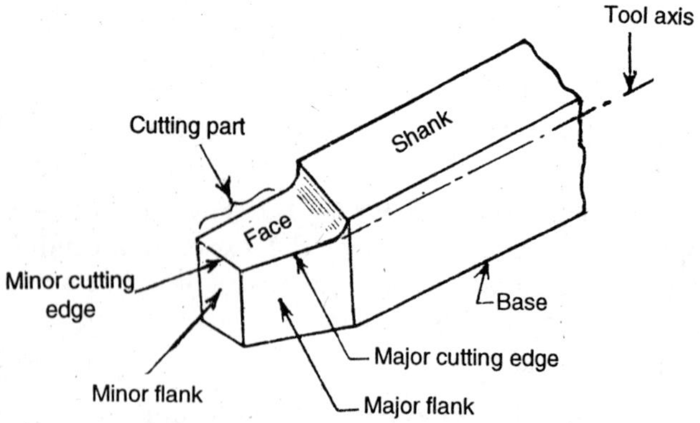

Fig. 1.3

Fig. 1.4 shows the principal plane and cutting plane with reference to a single point cutting tool with respect to velocity taken along. Z axis whereas Fig. 1.5 shows principal and cutting planes in relation to working surface.

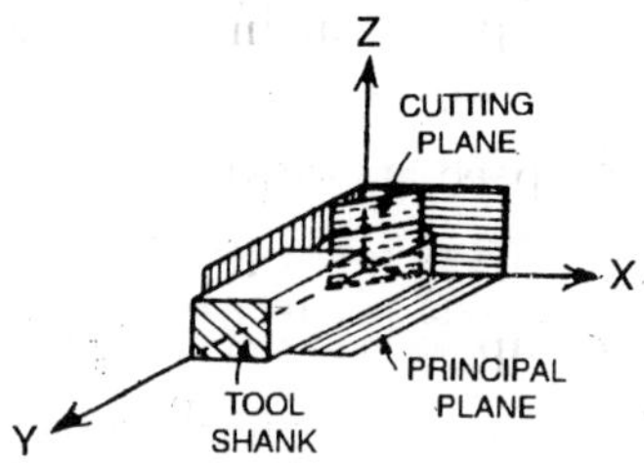

Fig. 1.4

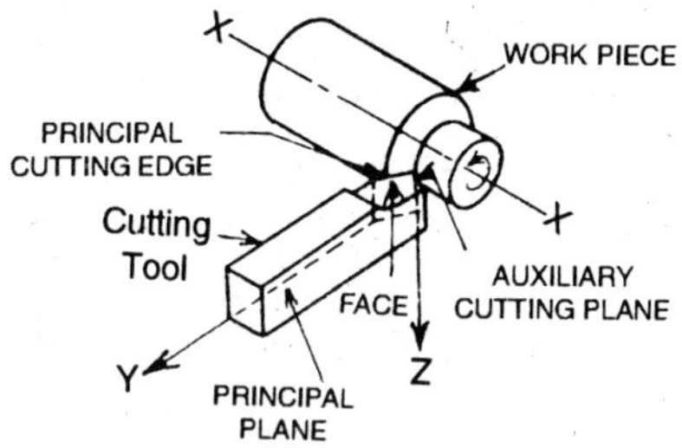

Fig. 1.5

Fig. 1.6 shows the geometry of a single point tool.

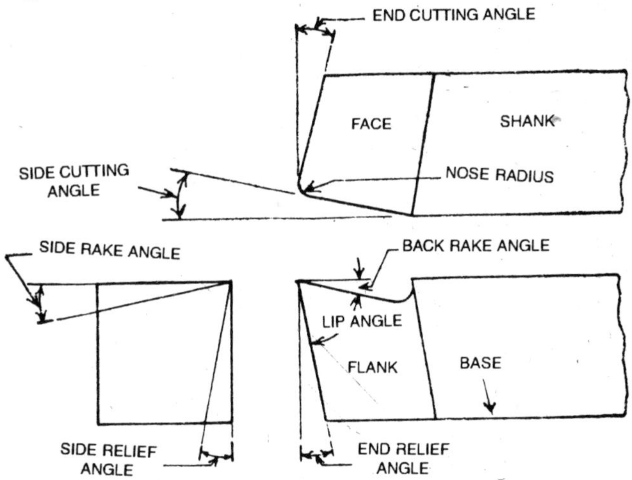

Fig. 1.6

1.5.1. Terms and definitions

(*i*) **Face.** The face is the surface over which the chip flows.

(*ii*) **Cutting edge.** The cutting edge carries out the cutting.

(*iii*) **Nose.** The nose is the corner, arc or chamfer at the junction of the major and minor cutting edges.

(*iv*) **Flank.** Flank of the tool is the surface below the cutting edge.

(*v*) **Tool angles.** The various angles influence tool performance to a considerable extent and therefore their value should be selected with great care and consideration.

The various functions of the rake or slope of the tool face are as follows :

(i) It allows the chip to flow in a convenient direction.

(ii) It gives sharpness to the cutting edge.

(iii) It increases tool life.

(iv) An improved surface finish is obtained.

(v) The cutting force required to shear the metal is reduced, and therefore power required during cutting is reduced.

The amount of rake angle to be provided on a cutting tool depends upon the following factors :

(i) Material of the workpiece

(ii) Material of cutting tool

(iii) Rigidity of the machine tool

(iv) Depth of cut.

(vi) **Back rake angle.** It measures the downward slope of the top surface of the tool from the nose to the rear along the longitudinal axis. Its purpose is to guide the direction of the chip flow. It also serves to protect the point of the cutting tool (Fig. 1.7). The size of

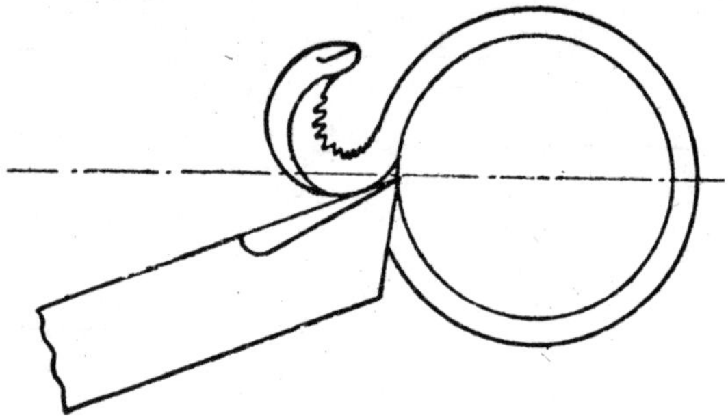

Fig. 1.7

the angle depends upon the material to be machined, the softer the material the greater should be positive rake angle. Aluminium requires more back rake angle than cast iron or steel. Back rake angle may be positive, neutral or negative. Fig. 1.8 shows a tool with

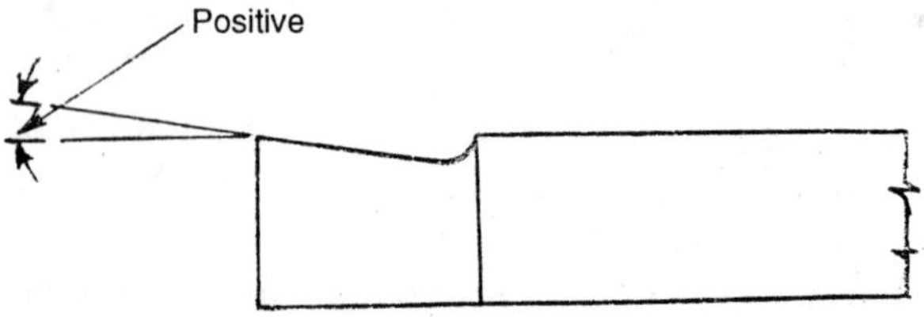

Fig. 1.8

a positive back rake angle. Fig. 1.9 shows a tool with a neutral back rake angle and Fig. 1.10 shows a tool with a negative back rake angle.

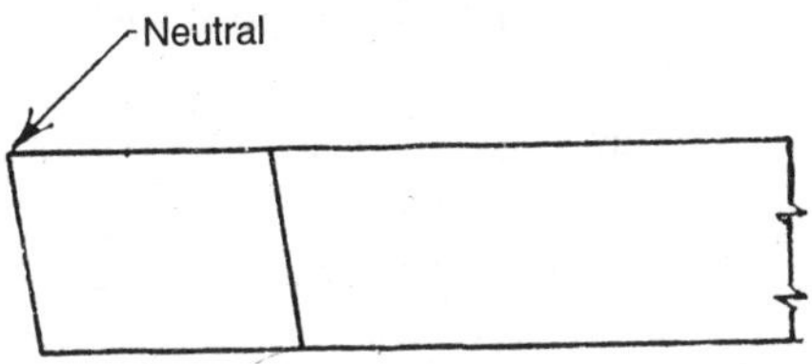

Fig. 1.9

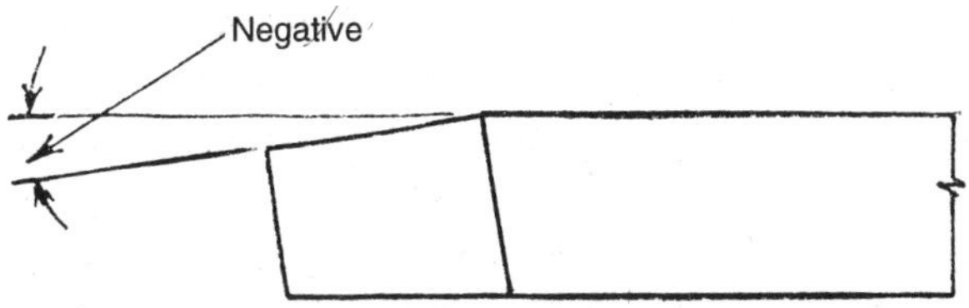

Fig. 1.10

Higher value of rake angle weakens the cutting edge. A negative rake angle increases tool forces to some extent but this minor disadvantage is offset by the added support to the cutting edge. This is particularly important in making intermittent cuts and in absorbing the impact during the initial engagement of the tool and work.

The inherently tough H.S.S. tools are used with positive rake mainly for reducing the magnitude of cutting forces, power, consumption and cutting temperature.

Positive rakes are used when cutting low tensile strength and non-ferrous materials, materials which work harden while being machined.

Negative rake angles are used for machining high tensile strength materials, heavy feeds and interrupted cuts. It is the rare case that a negative rake will be used that high speed or cast tool bits. They are generally used for carbide tool cutting materials such as grey, malleable cast iron, cast steels, hot work die steels, and tool steels.

Excessive positive rake weakens the cutting edge.

Cemented carbide cutting tools are normally given negative rake because cemented carbide possess very high compressive strength and comparatively very low tensile and shear strength.

The advantages of negative rake cutting when using sintered carbide or ceramics tool under suitable conditions are as follows :

(*i*) Higher cutting speeds may be used.

(*ii*) There is a less tendency for a built-up edge to form on the tool.

(*iii*) The heat conductivity of the working part of the tool is improved.

(*iv*) Favourable combination of conditions is that at high cutting speeds and corresponding high chip velocity, heat is carried away rapidly by the chip. Negative rake cutting with sintered carbide cutting tools can be applied with advantage on ductile steels. The machine tools using such tools must possess considerable rigidity and be equipped with high quality bearing.

(*v*) The main cutting force is directed towards strongest part of the tool.

A cutting tool with positive rake (Fig. 1.11) results in a force component in the direction of arrow *A* which tends to shear the edge

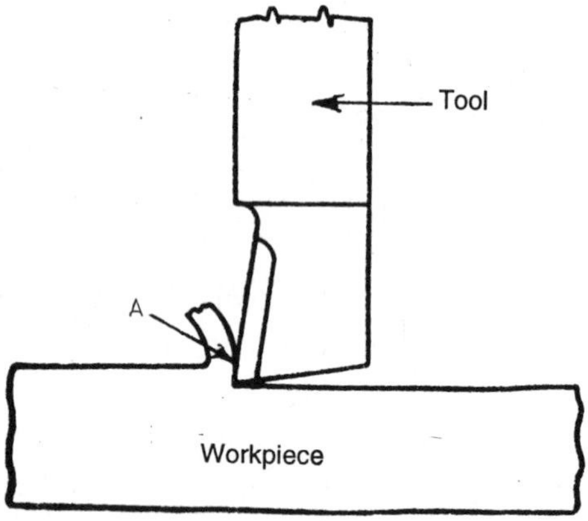

Fig. 1.11

of tool. When the cutting tool is provided with a negative rake (Fig. 1.12), the main force component is directed at the strongest rake section of the tool, as shown by arrow *B*. Cutting tools with negative rake angle are stronger and are used to cut high strength alloys.

However the use of an increased negative rake angle leads to increased cutting force during machining. This causes vibrations, reduces machining accuracy and raises power consumed in cutting. Therefore tools with negative rake should be used only when absolutely necessary.

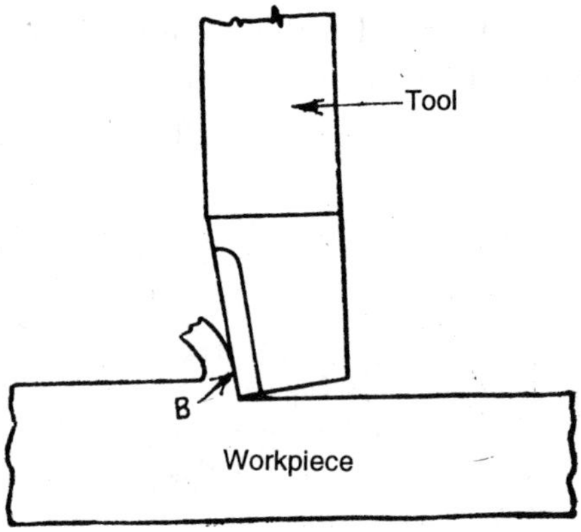

Fig. 1.12

(*vii*) **Side rake angle.** It measures the slope of the top surface of the tool to the side in a direction perpendicular to the longitudinal axis. It also guides the direction of the chip away from the job. The amount that a chip is bent depends upon this angle. With increase in side rake angle, the amount of chip has to bend decreases and hence the power required to part and bend the chip decreases. Larger side rake angle produces smooth surface finish. Fig. 1.13 shows side rake angle.

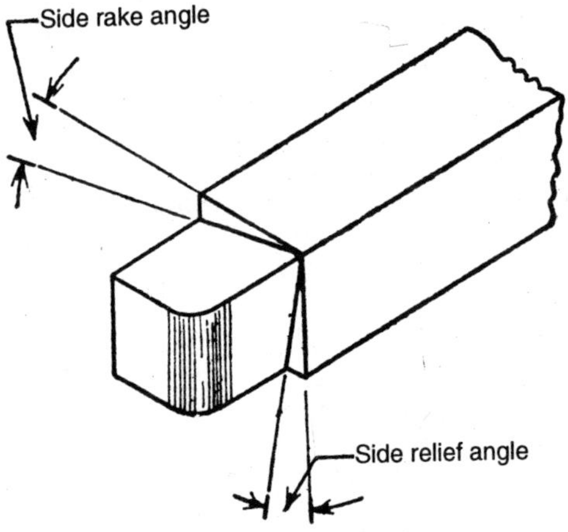

Fig. 1.13

(*viii*) **End cutting edge angle.** It is the angle between the face of the tool and a plane perpendicular to the side of the shank. It acts as a relief angle that it allows only small section of the end cutting edge to contact the machined surface and prevents chatter and vibration. Normally it varies from 5 to 15°.

(*ix*) **Side cutting edge angle.** It is the angle between the side cutting edge and the longitudinal axis of the tool. It avoids formation of built up edge, controls the direction of chip flow and distributes the cutting force and heat produced over larger cutting edge.

(*x*) **Side relief angle.** It is the angle made by the flank of the tool and a plane perpendicular to the base just under the side cutting edge. This angle permits the tool to be fed side-ways into the job so that it can cut without rubbing. If the side relief angle is very large the cutting edge of the tool will break because of insufficient support whereas if the side relief angle is very small the tool can not be fed into the job, it will rub against the job and will get overheated and become blunt and the finish obtained on the job will be rough.

(*xi*) **End relief angle.** It is the angle between a plane perpendicular to the base and the end flank. This angle prevents the cutting tool from rubbing against the job. If the angle is very large, the cutting edge of tool will be unsupported and will break off. Whereas, if this angle is very small the tool will rub on the job, cutting will not be proper and poor finish will be obtained on the job. Its value varies from 6 to 10°.

(*xii*) **Nose radius.** The nose radius is provided to increase finish and strength of the cutting tip of the tool. Small radii will produce smooth finishes and are used on thin cross-section of work. Large radii strengthen the tool and are used on cast iron and castings, where the cuts are interrupted.

Recommended tool angles for H.S.S. single point tools for some of the commonly used materials are indicated in Table 1.1.

Table 1.1

Material	*Relief Angle (degrees)*		*Rake Angle (degrees)*	
	Side	*End*	*Back*	*Side*
Aluminium	12—14	8—10	30—35	14—16
Brass (Free cut)	10—12	8—10	0	1—3
Cast Iron (Gray)	8—10	6—8	3—5	10—12
Copper (Commercial)	12—14	12—14	14—16	18—20
Steel	7—9	6—8	5—7	8—10

Recommended tool angles for carbide single point tool are indicated in Table 1.2.

Table 1.2

Material	*Relief Angle (degrees)*		*Rake Angle (degrees)*	
	Side	*End*	*Back*	*Side*
Aluminium	6—10	6—10	0—10	10—20
Copper	6—8	6—8	0—4	15—20
Brass	6—8	6—8	0—(– 5)	8—(– 5)
Cast Iron	5—8	6—8	0—(– 7)	6—(– 7)
Steel	5—10	5—10	0—(– 7)	6—(– 7)

1.5.2. Methods of holding tool

There are different ways of holding single point cutting tools. Tool directly fitted into tool holder is shown in Fig. 1.14 whereas Fig. 1.15 shows a tool fitted in a tool post.

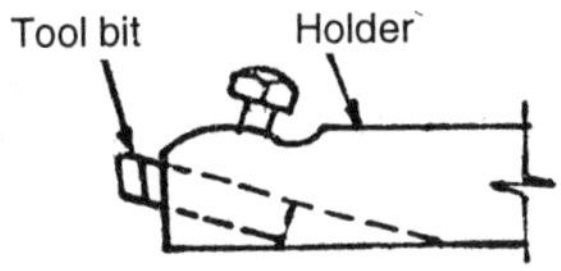

Fig. 1.14

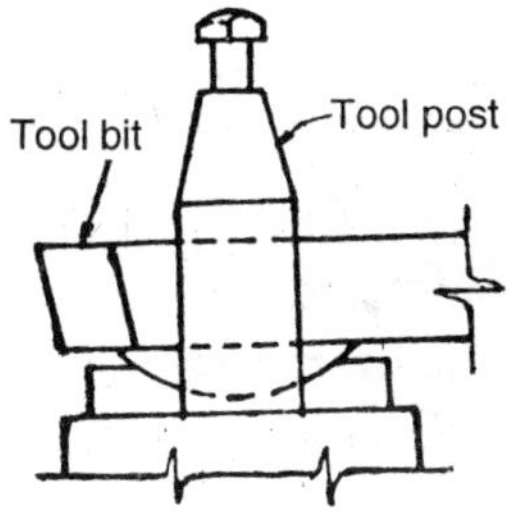

Fig. 1.15

The tool held by a clamp is shown in Fig. 1.16 and tool insert brazed to a tool shank is shown in Fig. 1.17.

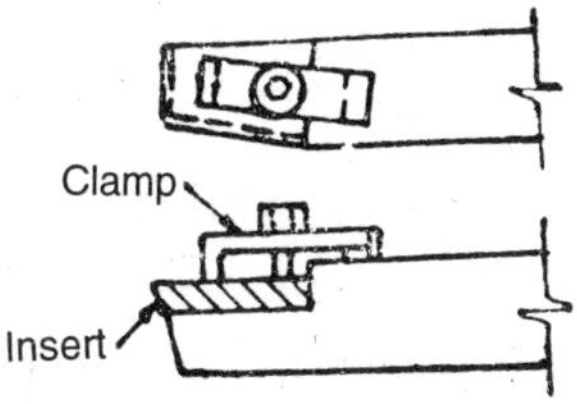

Fig. 1.16

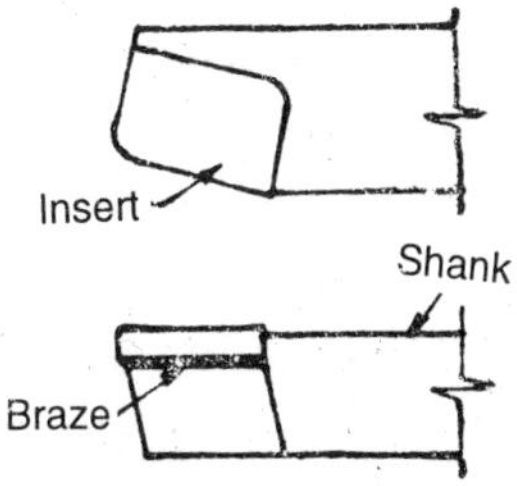

Fig. 1.17

1.5.3. Carbide inserts clamping methods. Fig. 1.17.1 shows types of seats for cemented carbide inserts.

1.5.4. High speed steel (H.S.S.) tools bits. The hardened and ground H.S.S. bits are available in the following general sizes :

$6 \times 6 \times 100$ mm ; $8 \times 8 \times 100$ mm ;
$10 \times 10 \times 100$ mm ; $12 \times 12 \times 150$ mm ;
$16 \times 16 \times 150$ mm ; $20 \times 20 \times 150$ mm ;
$25 \times 25 \times 150$ mm.

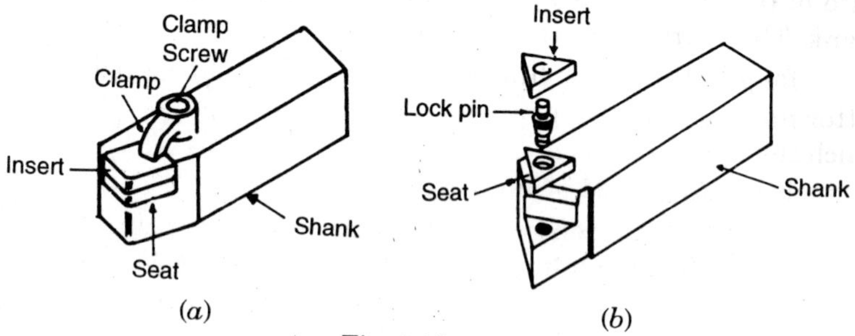

Fig. 1.17.1

H.S.S. tool bits have an average chemical composition as follows :

C = 0.75%

W (Tungsten) = 18%

Cr (Chromium) = 4%

V (Vanadium) = 1%

Cobalt = 5 or 10%

(5% cobalt H.S.S. is used for free machining steel whereas 10% cobalt H.S.S. is used for high tensile steel).

1.5.5. Specifying a single point tool. The following details should be specified while ordering a single point tool :

(*i*) Shape of the tool (*ii*) Size of the shank

(*iii*) Grade of the carbide tip

(*iv*) Direction of cutting :

(*a*) Right Hand (R.H.) (*b*) Left Hand (L.H.).

1.5.6. Brazing of carbide tools. For carbide tools a suitable shank material is carbon steel with a tensile strength of about 70 kg/mm^2. So that the least possible stresses shall occur, the ratio between the thickness of the carbide tip and the height of the shank material beneath the tip should be about 1 : 3 as shown in Fig. 1.17.2.

Grind the brazing areas of the tip on a silicon carbide or diamond wheel. Another reliable method is hard blasting with steel shot. De-grease the tip, and when necessary the tip-seating of the shank as well, with, for instance, trichlorethylene, acetone or carbon tetrachloride.

Arrange the seating of the tip so that the brazing stresses are as small as possible. 'Open' seatings of the tip generally give the best result. Only the underside of the tip and one side face (max. one third of the tip's thickness) should come into contact with the tool shank. Then carbide tip is brazed on the seat.

Re-grinding is facilitated and the carbide tip's thickness is better preserved if the tip is set at an inclination greater than that which the top-rake angle requires. Tip-seating angle for most turning tools is greater by 2° than the top rake angle.

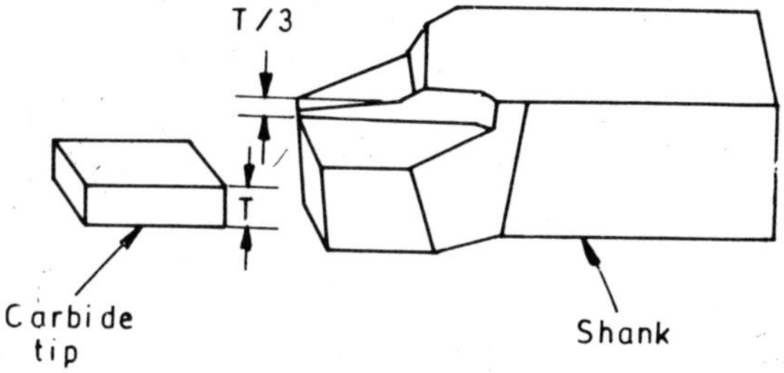

Fig. 1.17.2

The brazed joint has two functions. It has to hold the carbide tip in position despite heavy shearing forces and high temperatures. It must also be capable of minimizing the stresses which occur during the heating and cooling of the tool material.

1.6. Tool Signature

The tool angles have been standardised by the American Standards Association (A.S.A.). The seven important elements comprise the signature of the cutting tool and are stated in the following order.

Back rake angle, side rake angle, end relief angle, side relief angle, end cutting edge angle, side cutting end angle and nose radius. It is usual to omit the symbols for degrees and mm, simply starting the numerical value of each element. For example, a tool having tool signature as 10, 10, 6, 6, 8, 8, 2 will have the following angles :

Back rake angle = 10°

Side rake angle = 10°

End relief angle = 6°

Side relief angle = 6°

End cutting edge angle = 8°
Side cutting edge angle = 8°
Nose radius = 2 mm.

1.6.1. Requirements of a cutting tool

A cutting tool intended for high production machining should possess the following requirements :

(*i*) It should be amply strong and rigid.

(*ii*) It should be kneely sharpened with a high class finish.

(*iii*) It should have optimum geometry.

(*iv*) It should be producible in manufacture and convenient in use.

The performance and economy of cutting tool mainly depend on the following :

(*i*) Cutting tool material properties.

(*ii*) Geometry of cutting tool.

(*iii*) Methods used for mounting, clamping, indexing and change over for cutting tools.

The operational characteristics of a cutting tool are described by machinability produced. There are three main aspects of machinability :

(*i*) Tool life (*ii*) Surface finish

(*iii*) Power required to cut.

1.6.2. Types of Single point tools

A single point cutting tool is quite commonly used in metal cutting. It is employed for machining flat surfaces, solids of revolution, profile surfaces, and threads for cutting of different materials etc.

All single point tools are divided into a number of groups according to

(*i*) Direction of feed such as

(*a*) right hand tools (*b*) left hand tools.

Right hand tools are to be fed from right to left.

(*ii*) Shank form such as

(*a*) straight (*b*) bent
(*c*) offset (*d*) necked tools.

(*iii*) Application on a certain type of machine tool such as turning, planing, shaping, slotting and boring tools and tools for special purpose machine tools.

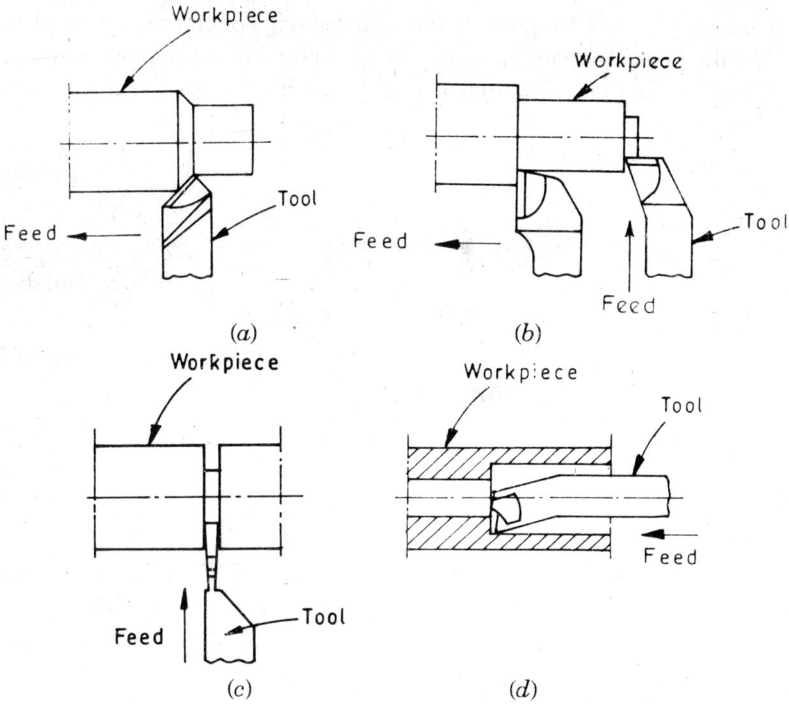

Fig. 1.17.3. Figure shows lathe tools for various machining operations such as turning (Fig. 1.17.3 (*a*)), facing (Fig. 1.17.3 (*b*)), parting (Fig. 1.17.3 (*c*)) and boring (Fig. 1.17.3 (*d*)).

(*iv*) Machining processes.

(*v*) Shank cross section such as

(*a*) rectangular (*b*) square (*c*) round.

(*vi*) Tool position relative to work such as

(*a*) radial (*b*) tangential.

(*vii*) Cutting material such as

(*a*) high speed steel tools (*b*) carbide tipped tools

(*c*) ceramic tools.

(*viii*) Method of manufacturing such as

(*a*) solid (*b*) tipped.

1.7. Two systems of Defining the cutting Angles of a Single Point Tool

The cutting angles of a single point tools are commonly defined in two systems called *L-M-N* planes and *X-Y-Z* planes. The *L-M-N* plane system is chosen in reference to three mutually perpendicular planes. The plane *L* called as cutting plane being a vertical plane is tangent to the cutting edge of the tool. The plane *M* called as orthogonal plane being a vertical plane is perpendicular *L* plane. The plane *N* called as base plane is a horizontal plane being

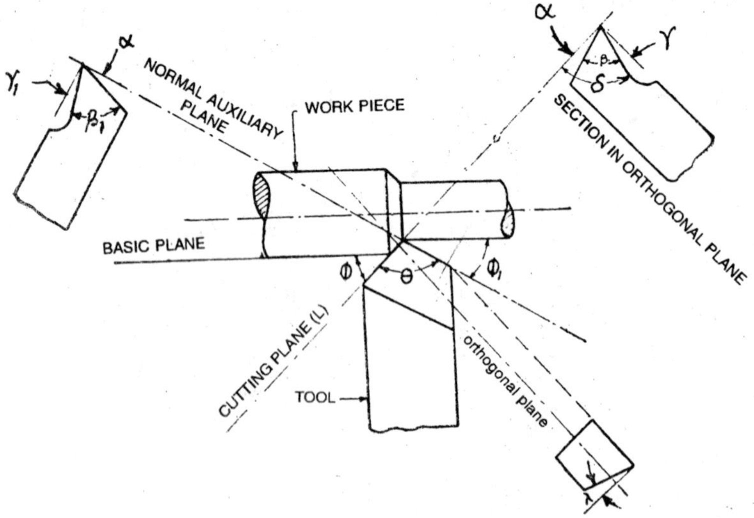

Fig. 1.18. Tool angles in *L-M-N* plane.

perpendicular to *L* and *M* planes. The various angles according to this shown in Fig. 1.18 are as follows :

α = Side relief angle.

β = Wedge angle.

γ = Orthogonal rake angle.

δ = Cutting angle = $\alpha + \beta$.

ϕ_1 = Auxiliary cutting edge angle.

θ = Nose angle.

ϕ = Plane approach angle. (Principal cutting edge angle).

λ_1 = Inclination angle.

α_1 = End relief angle.

β_1 = Side wedge angle.

γ_1 = Side rake angle.

This system is also known as International Orthogonal System of designating tool angles.

The various angles in *X-Y-Z* systems are shown in Fig. 1.19. The system is the most popular system. This system is also called American system of tool nomenclature.

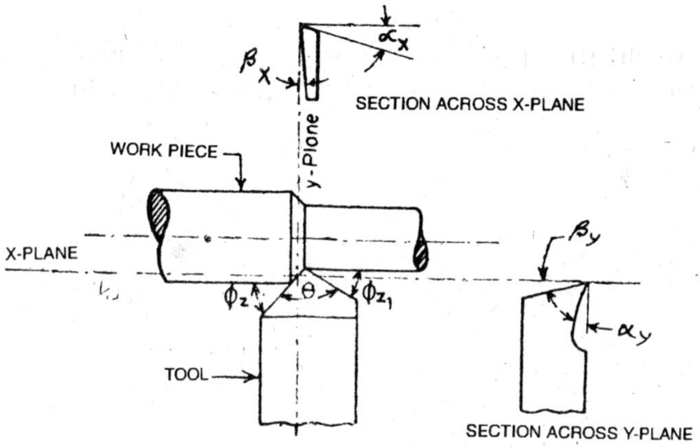

Fig. 1.19. Tool angles in *X-Y-Z* planes.

α_y = Back rake angle.

β_y = End relief angle.

α_x = Side rake angle.

β_x = Side rake angle.

θ = Nose angle.

ϕ_z = Side cutting edge angle.

ϕ_{z1} = End cutting edge angle.

Inter-relationship between different angles of system *L-M-N* and system *X-Y-Z* is as follows :

$$\tan \lambda = \tan \alpha_y \sin \phi - \tan \alpha_x \cos \phi$$

$$\tan \alpha_x = \sin \phi \tan \gamma - \cos \phi \tan \lambda$$

$$\tan \alpha_y = \cos \phi \tan \gamma + \sin \phi \tan \lambda$$

$$\tan \gamma = \tan \alpha_y \cos \phi + \tan \alpha_x \sin \phi$$

Normal rake angle (γ_n) is given by

$$\tan \gamma_n = \tan \gamma \cos \lambda.$$

1.8. Types of Metal Cutting Process

The metal cutting processes are of two types :

(*i*) Orthogonal cutting process (two dimensional cutting).

(*ii*) Oblique cutting process (three dimensional cutting).

Orthogonal cutting. Orthogonal (two dimensional) cutting occurs when the major cutting edge of the tool is presented to the work piece perpendicular to the direction of feed motion. Orthogonal cutting involves only two forces and this makes the analysis of cutting motion much easier (Fig. 1.20).

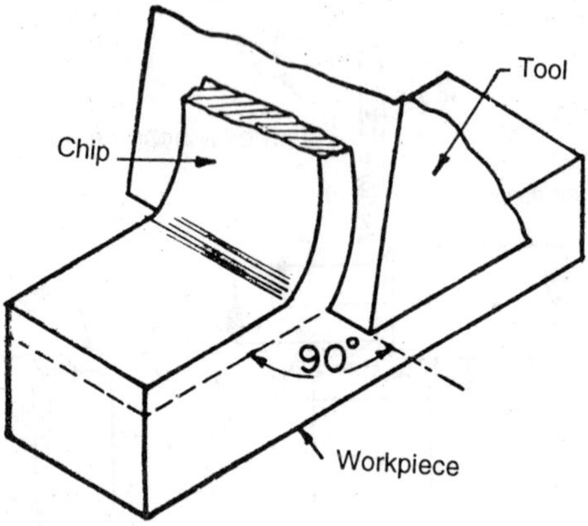

(a)

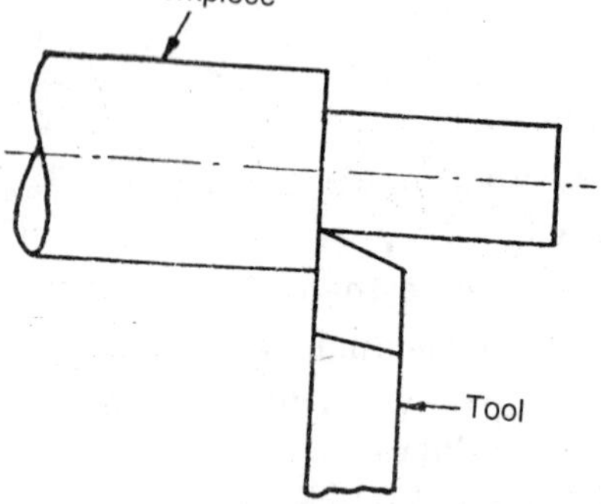

(b)

Fig. 1.20. Orthogonal cutting.

Oblique cutting. This form of cutting occurs when the major

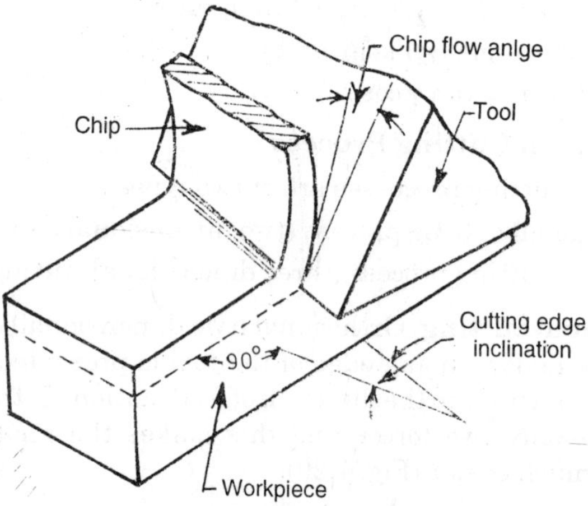

(a)

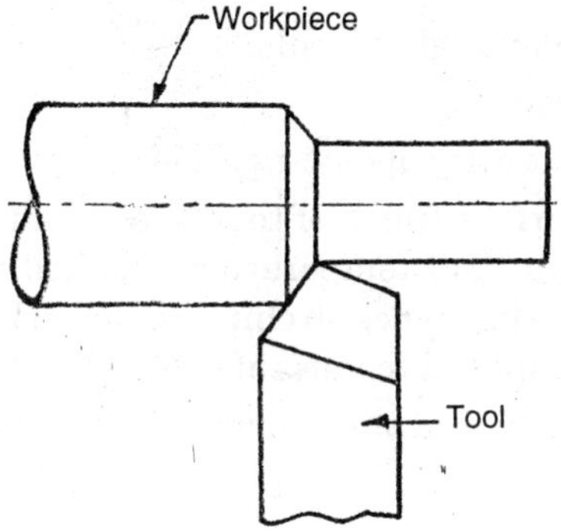

(b)

Fig. 1.21. Oblique cutting.

edge of cutting tool is presented to the work piece at an angle which is not perpendicular to the direction of feed motion (Fig. 1.21).

1.8.1. Comparison of orthogonal and oblique cutting

These two methods are compared as follows :

Orthogonal cutting	*Oblique cutting*
(i) The cutting edge of the tool remains normal to the direction of tool feed.	The cutting edge of the tool is inclined at an acute angle to the direction of tool feed.
(ii) The direction of chip flow velocity is normal to the cutting edge of the tool.	The direction of ship flow velocity is at an angle with the normal to the cutting edge of the tool.
(iii) The cutting edge clears the width of the workpiece on either ends.	The cutting edge may or may not clear the width of the workpiece.
(iv) Only two components of cutting forces act on the tool. These two components are perpendicular to each other.	Three mutually perpendicular components of cutting forces act at the cutting edge of the tool.

1.9. Chip Formation

The type of chip produced during metal cutting depends upon the machining conditions and material being cut. The variable which influence the type of chip produced are as follows :

(i) Properties of material cut especially ductility

(*ii*) depth of cut

(*iii*) feed rate

(*iv*) effective rake angle of tool

(*v*) cutting speed

(*vi*) type and quantity of cutting fluid.

Factors like surface finish of tool faces, coefficient of friction between tool and chip, and temperature reached in the region of cutting also have some influence on chip formation but are generally less significant as compared to variables listed above.

Three different type of chips formed during metal cutting are as follows :

(*i*) Continuous chip

(*ii*) Discontinuous chip

(*iii*) Continuous chip with a built-up edge.

1.9.1. Continuous chip

A continuous chip is obtained when cutting ductile materials such as low carbon steel, aluminium and copper. This chip is severely deformed and either comes off in the form of a long string, or curls into a tight roll (Fig. 1.22).

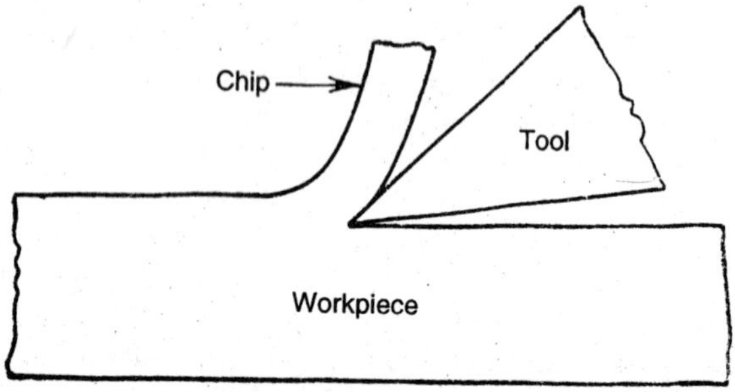

Fig. 1.22. Continuous chip.

Some very soft and ductile materials with a low strength tend to tear away from the parent metal of the workpiece rather than shear clearly. This results in a rough surface that has to be cleaned up by a very keen cutting edge. In addition to ductile workpiece material the other conditions which favour their formation are fine feed, sharp cutting edge, higher cutting speeds and larger rake angles.

The factors responsible for the formation of continuous chips are given below :

(*i*) Ductile material (*ii*) High cutting speed
(*iii*) Large rake angles (*iv*) Sharp cutting edge
(*v*) Efficient cutting fluids (*vi*) Low friction

The tool life increases and the power consumption reduces, in case of continuous chips. However, they may interface with the finished job surface and may spoil it. Disposal is also a problem.

1.9.2. Discontinuous chip

Brittle materials such as grey cast iron, lack the ductility necessary for appreciable plastic chip formation. Consequently the compressed material ahead of tool fails in a brittle manner along the shear zone producing small fragments. Such chips are called discontinuous chips (Fig. 1.23). Lower cutting speeds and insufficient rake angles cause the formation of such chips.

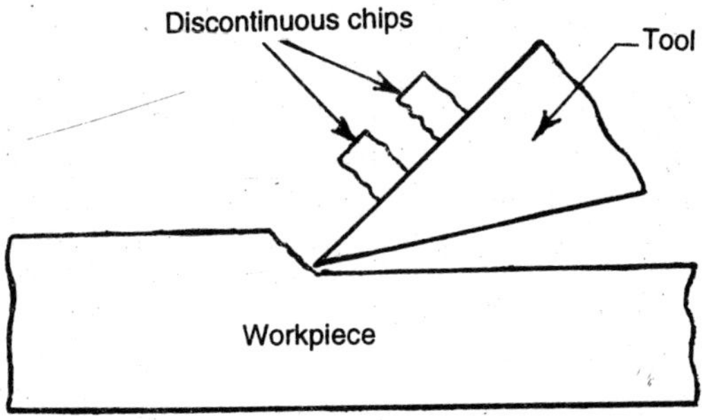

Fig. 1.23. Discontinuous chip.

Since brittle materials, such as cast iron, form a discontinuous chip with a constant shear plane angle, little advantage is gained from giving the tool a rake angle. Therefore brittle materials are usually cut with a zero rake angle. This permits the maximum possible wedge angle which results in an appreciable increase in tool life.

Discontinuous chips are associated with brittle materials such as cast iron and free cutting brass. Low cutting speeds and lack of rake can also cause discontinuous chips to be formed when cutting ductile materials such as mild steel.

1.9.3. Continuous chips with a built up edge

When during cutting, the temperature and pressure is quite high it causes the chip material to weld itself to the tool face near the nose (Fig. 1.24). This is called "Built up edge". This accumulated build up of chip material will then break away, part adhearing to

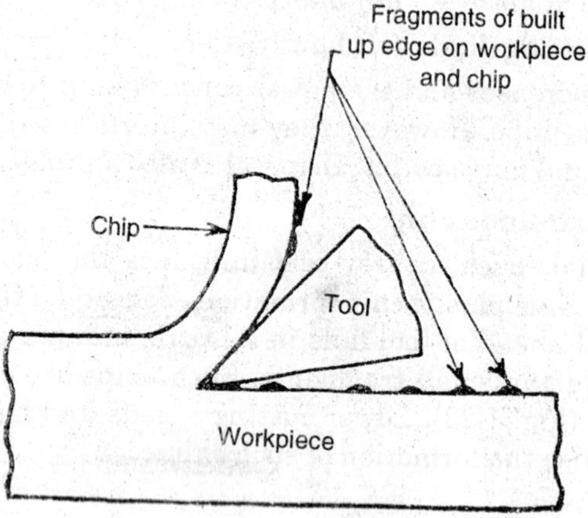

Fig. 1.24

the underside of the chip and part to the workpiece. This process gives rise to a poor finish on the machined surface and accelerated wear on the tool face. High friction at tool face, coarse feed, low rake angle and ineffective use of cutting fluid produce such chips.

Various factors responsible for the production of continuous chips with built-up edges are as follows :

(*i*) Ductile work-piece material
(*ii*) Small rake angle
(*iii*) Low cutting speed
(*iv*) Dull cutting edge
(*v*) Insufficient cutting fluid
(*vi*) High friction at the tool-chip interface
(*vii*) Coarser feed.

The extra metal, welded to the nose or point of the tool is called '*Built-up-Edge*' (BUE). This metal is highly strain hardened and brittle with the result, as the chip flows up the tool, BUE is broken and carried away with the chip, while the rest of it adheres to the surface of the workpiece, making it rough.

1.9.4. Areas in metal cutting

The important areas of interest in metal cutting are shown in Fig. 1.24 (*a*). First area (A_1) extends along the shear plane and is the boundary between the deformed and undeformed material or the chip and the workpiece. The second area (A_2) includes the interface between the chip and the tool face. While the third area

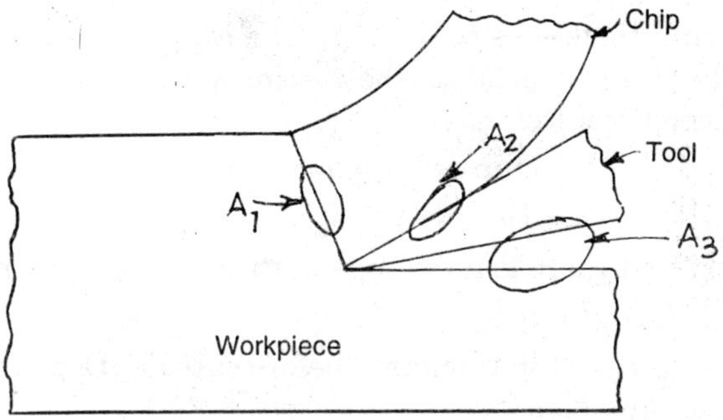

Fig. 1.24 (*a*)

(A_3) includes the finished or machined surface and the material adjacent to that surface.

The important aspect in first area (A_1) is the plastic deformation characteristics of the material cut, whereas in second area (A_2) the friction and wear characteristics of the tool workpiece combination and the important aspect in third area (A_3) is the surface roughness produced and the residual stresses involved in the surface constituting the area.

1.10. Chip Thickness Ratio

The outward flow of the metal causes the chip to be thicker after separation from the parent metal. Metal prior to being cut is much longer than the chip which is removed (Fig. 1.25).

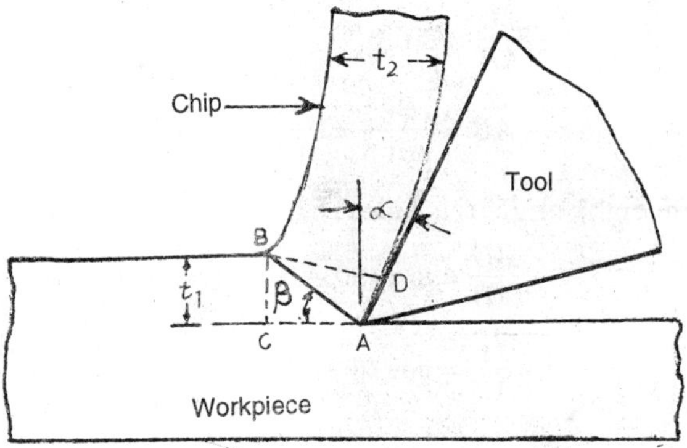

Fig. 1.25

Let t_1 = chip thickness before cutting

t_2 = chip thickness after cutting

chip thickness ratio, $r = \dfrac{t_1}{t_2}$.

The chip thickness ratio or cutting ratio is always less than unity. If the ratio r is large, the cutting action is good. A ratio of 1 : 2 yields good results.

$$k = \text{chip reduction coefficient}$$
$$= 1/r$$

when metal is cut there is no change in the volume of the metal cut.

$$t_1.b_1.l_1 = t_2.b_2.l_2$$

t_1 = chip thickness before cutting (Depth of cut)

where b_1 = width of cut

l_1 = length of chip before cutting

t_2 = chip thickness after cutting

b_2 = width of chip after cutting

l_2 = length of chip after cutting

It is observed that $b_1 = b_2$

$$\therefore \quad t_1.l_1 = t_2.l_2$$

$$\frac{t_1}{t_2} = \frac{l_2}{l_1} = r.$$

Although chip thickness ratio can be obtained by measuring chip thickness (t_2) and depth of cut (t_1) this is not the most precise procedure. Chip thickness ratio can be easily obtained by measuring l_1 and l_2.

From the right angle triangle ABC (Fig. 1.25), we have

$$\frac{BC}{AB} = \sin\beta$$

$$AB = \frac{BC}{\sin\beta} = \frac{t_1}{\sin\beta} \quad ...(i)$$

From right angle triangle ABD

$$\frac{BD}{AB} = \sin(90 - \beta + \alpha) = \cos(\beta - \alpha)$$

or

$$\frac{t_2}{AB} = \cos(\beta - \alpha)$$

$$\frac{t_2}{\cos(\beta - \alpha)} = AB \quad ...(ii)$$

From (*i*) and (*ii*), we get

$$\frac{t_1}{\sin\beta} = \frac{t_2}{\cos(\beta - \alpha)}$$

$$\frac{t_1}{t_2} = r = \frac{\sin \beta}{\cos(\beta - \alpha)}$$

$$= \frac{\sin \beta}{\cos \beta \cos \alpha + \sin \beta \sin \alpha}$$

$$r = \frac{\sin \beta}{\cos \beta \cos \alpha + \sin \beta \sin \alpha}$$

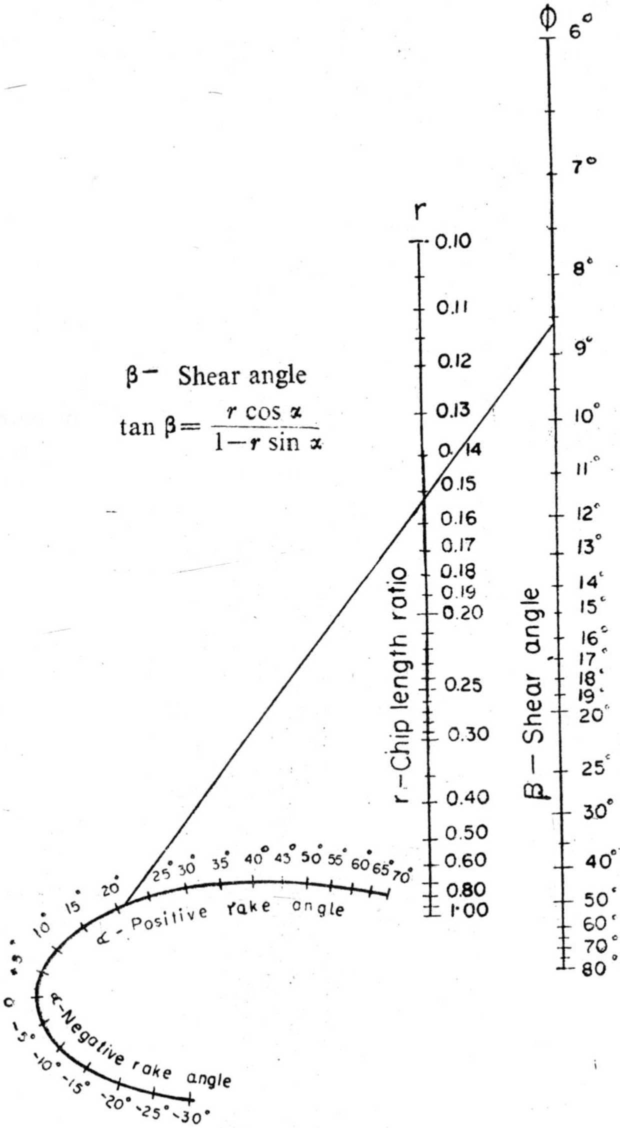

Fig. 1.26. Nomograph for Shear Angles.

$$\frac{r \cos \beta \cos \alpha}{\sin \beta} + \frac{r \sin \beta \sin \alpha}{\sin \beta} = 1$$

$$\frac{r \cos \alpha}{\tan \beta} + r \sin \alpha = 1$$

$$\frac{r \cos \alpha}{\tan \beta} = 1 - r \sin \alpha$$

$$\tan \beta = \frac{r \cos \alpha}{1 - r \sin \alpha}.$$

Shear angle can be measured by measuring chip thickness, depth of cut and rake angle of tool. This can be most conveniently solved with the help of nomograph shown in Fig. 1.26 for determining shear angles.

1.11. Chip Breaker

Chip breakers are provided to control the continuous ribbon-like chips that are formed at high cutting speeds. Continuous chips are dangerous to the operator of the machine. These chips are hard, sharp and hot. They become entangled around the revolving job and the cutting tool. The chip breaker deflects the chip at a sharp angle and causes it to break into small pieces. So that they are easily removed by the coolant or air or simply allowed to fall into the chip pan of the machine.

There are basically two types of chip breakers :

(*i*) Groove type (*ii*) Obstruction type.

Fig. 1.27 shows the groove type chip breaker.

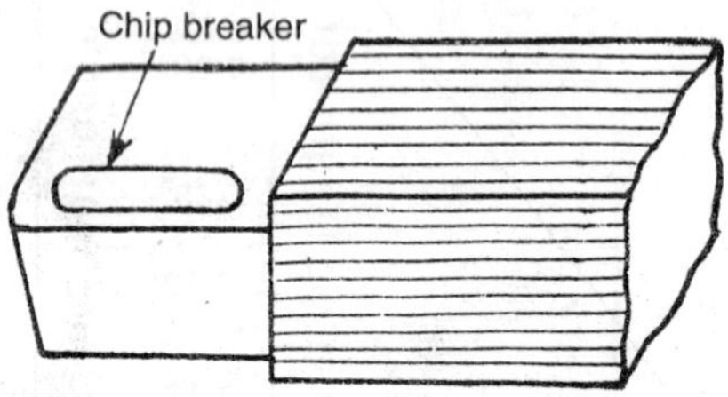

Fig. 1.27

Fig. 1.28 shows an obstruction type chip breaker.

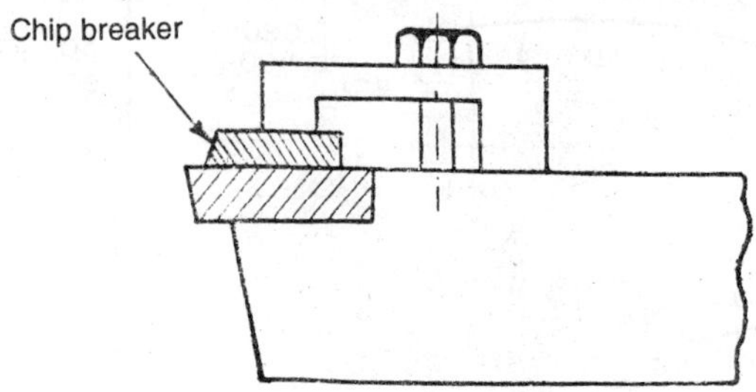

Fig. 1.28

1.12. Radius of Chip Curvature

In an obstruction type chip breaker the chip starts to curl away from the tool face at the end of chip tool contact region and that the chip then maintains a constant radius of curvature until it

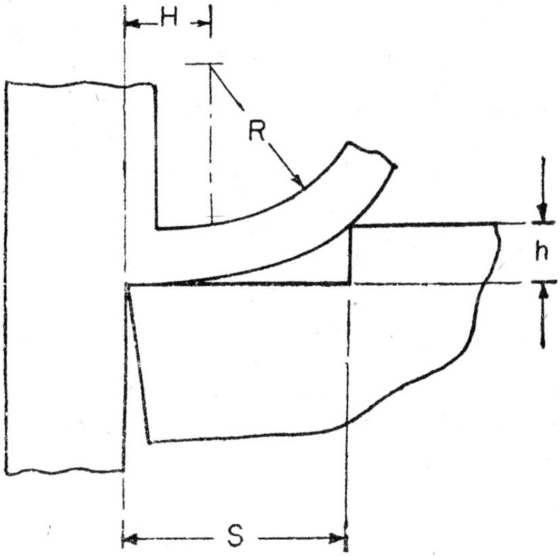

Fig. 1.29

clears the chip breaker (Fig. 1.29). The radius of the chip curvature can be found by the following formula :

$$R = \frac{(S - H)^2}{2h} + \frac{h}{2}$$

where R = Radius of chip curvature

S = Chip breaker distance

H = Length of chip tool contact

h = Chip breaker height.

It is observed that larger shear angles require less cuttings forces than smaller shear angles because smaller the shear angle the greater thickness of the material which the fracture plane need to traverse (Fig. 1.30). The shear angle is a function of the rake of the tool, the material being cut and the friction at the face of the tool. As shown $t_3 > t_2 > t_1$ and shear angle $\beta_2 < \beta_1$. The chip thickness is t_2 when shear angle is β_1 and chip thickness is t_3 when shear angle is β_2.

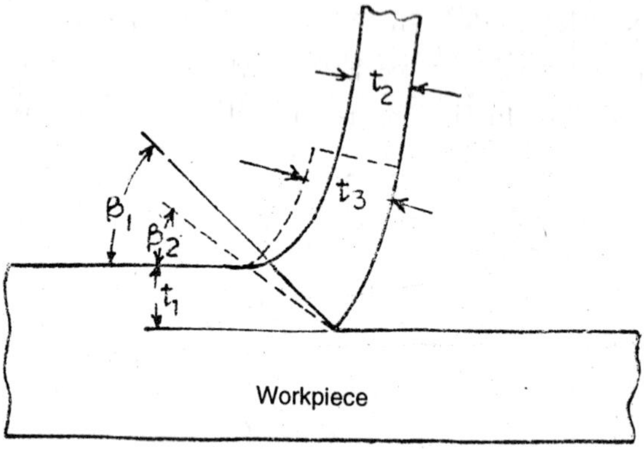

Fig. 1.30

1.12.1. Curling of Chip

The chip curls into a spiral because the layer adjoining the tool is deformed. It can be seen in Fig. 1.31 that on the side facing

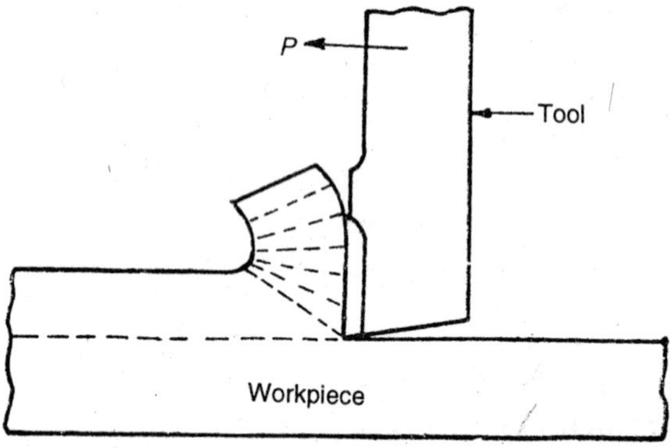

Fig. 1.31

the force *P* the layer becomes thicker and acquires a wedge shape as a result of which the curvature (curling) is produced. Another reason for curling the chip is that in meeting the tool face a change in its direction of flow away from tool face takes place curling is also produced by the non-uniform cooling of the chip throughout its thickness. Depending upon the machining conditions the chip may cut into a flat (logarithmic) spiral or into a helix.

1.13. Chip Reduction Coefficient

The chip produced during metal cutting turns out to be shorter than the part of the work from which it has been cut (Fig. 1.32) because of the plastic compression of the layer of metal being

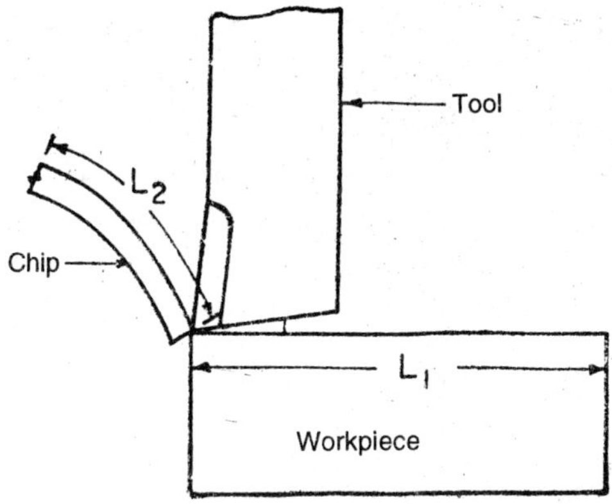

Fig. 1.32. Chip contraction.

cut. This shortening of the chip is known as longitudinal chip contraction and its magnitude is characterised by the coefficient of contraction.

Let, K = Chip reduction co-efficient

L_1 = Length of the section of the work from which chip was removed in mm

L_2 = Length of chip cut from the section in mm

$$K = \frac{L_1}{L_2}.$$

The value of K may be as high as 6 to 8 depending upon the machining conditions. The coefficient of chip contraction is a certain quantitative measure of the degree of plastic deformation in metal cutting smaller value of chip contraction coefficient indicates less plastic deformation in cutting process and this will require less power consumption to machine the given workpiece. Chip contraction depends upon the following factors :

(*i*) Cutting variables such as cutting speed, feed and depth of cut.

(*ii*) Geometry of cutting tool.

(*iii*) Type of cutting fluid used.

(*iv*) Type of material of work piece and its mechanical properties.

It is observed that the greater the cutting angle (or the smaller the positive rake angle) the greater the contraction. An increase in nose radius leads to greater chip contraction. Fig. 1.33 shows the effect of cutting speed (*V*) on chip reduction coefficient *K*. With an increase in cutting speed contraction is first reduced, reaching a minimum and then increases reaching a maximum after which it drops again. Fig. 1.34 shows variation of chip reduction coefficient with feed upon an increase in feed coefficient of chip reduction is usually reduced.

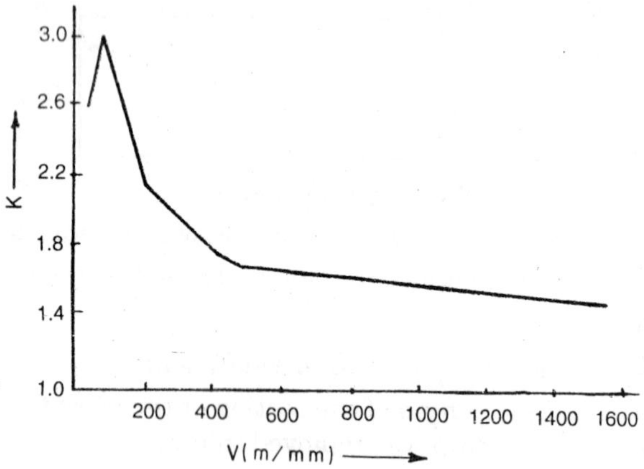

Fig. 1.33

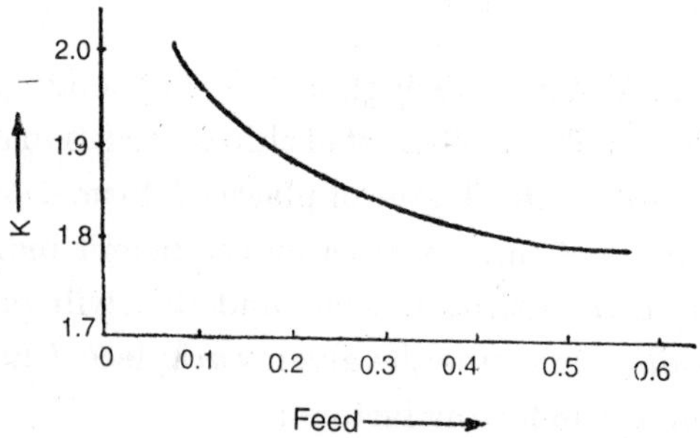

Fig. 1.34

The effect of surface active cutting fluids is clearly manifested is the reduction of chip contraction (Fig. 1.35).

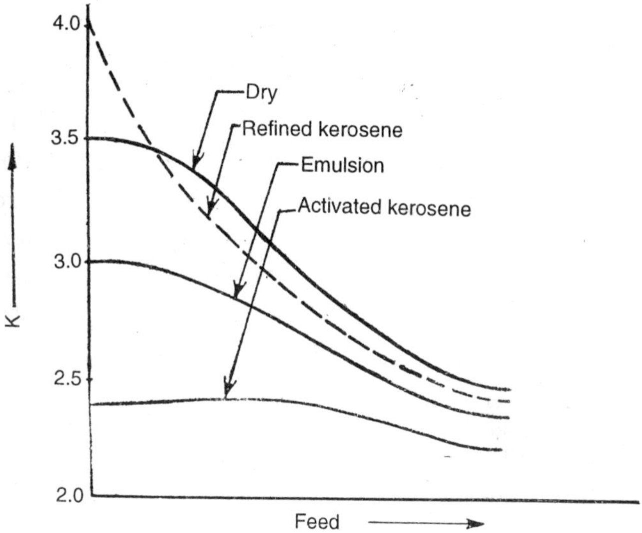

Fig. 1.35

1.14. Cutting Speed, Feed and Depth of Cut

Cutting speed. It is the travel of a point on the cutting edge relative to the surface of cut in unit time in the process of accomplishing the primary cutting motion. For example in lathe work when a workpiece of diameter D rotates at a speed N revolutions per minute the cutting speed (V) is given by the relation

$$V = \frac{\pi \cdot D \cdot N}{1000} \text{ m per min.}$$

where D = Diameter of workpiece in mm.

From surface finish consideration, higher speed is better, but it reduces tool life. So optimum speed can be decided only after taking into account various costs. Machining at higher speeds gives better surface finish and also lesser cutting force, provided adequate cutting power and rigidity of the machine tool is available.

Table 1.3 indicates cutting speed and feed for turning some of the materials with H.S.S. cutting tool.

Table 1.3. Cutting speeds and feeds for H.S.S. turning tools

Material being turned	*Feed (mm/rev)*	*Cutting speed (m/min)*
Aluminium	0.2—1.00	70—100
Brass (alpha) (ductile)	0.2—1.00	50—80
Brass (free-cutting)	0.2—1.5	70—100
Bronze (phosphor)	0.2—1.0	35—70
Cast iron (grey)	0.15—0.7	25—40
Copper	0.2—1.00	35—70
Steel (mild)	0.2—1.00	35—50
Steel (medium carbon)	0.15—0.7	30—35
Steel (alloy-high tensile)	0.08—0.3	5—10
Thermo-setting plastic	0.2—1.0	35—50

Fig. 1.35 (*a*) shows feed and depth of cut for a workpiece being turned.

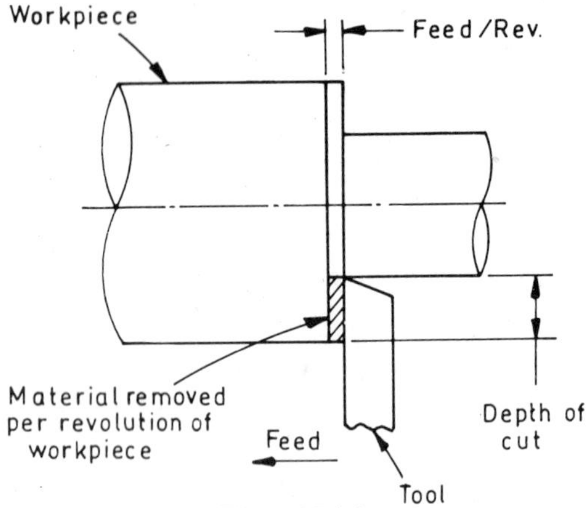

Fig. 1.35 (*a*)

Feed. The feed or more precisely rate of feed is the amount of tool advancement per revolution of job parallel to the surface being machined. Feed is expressed either as the distance moved by the tool in one minute. It is expressed in millimetres per revolution. On a shaper feed is the distance the work is moved relative to the tool for each cutting stroke. Feed is expressed as millimetres per tooth for milling cutters and broaches. Feed depends on depth of cut, rigidity of cutting tool and type of cutting tool material. Higher feeds are used in roughing cuts, rigid set-ups, soft materials, rugged cutters and heavy machine tools. Lower feeds are used for finishing cuts, frail set-ups, hard work materials and weak cutters. Normally feed varies from 0.1 to 1.5 mm.

In milling a good commercial surface finish can be obtained by using a feed rate of 0.75 mm to 1.25 mm per revolution of the cutter. Finer feeds such as 0.4 mm per revolution of cutter will result in an excellent surface finish.

Table 1.3 (A) shows cutting speed and feed for H.S.S. turning tools for machining some of the materials.

Table 1.3 (A)

Material to be machined	*Cutting speed (m / min)*	*Feed (mm / rev)*
Aluminium	70—100	0.2—1.00
Brass (Free cutting)	70—100	0.2—1.5
Copper	35—70	0.2—1.00
Grey Cast Iron	25—40	0.15—1.7
Mild Steel	35—50	0.2—1.00

In lathe work distinction is made between longitudinal feed when the tool travels in a direction parallel to the work axis and cross feed when the tool travels in a direction perpendicular to the work axis.

Feed of a lathe and similar machine tools is the distance the cutting tool is fed for each revolution of work. The feed of drilling machine is the rate at which drill is advanced into the work piece per revolution of drill. The feeds for reaming operation is usually higher than that used for drilling because reamers have more teeth and a reaming operation is used for sizing and finishing. The feed of shapers and planers is the distance the cutting tool advances at the end of each cutting stroke. Feed of a milling machine is expressed in millimeter per minute of table movement.

The maximum feed is limited by the following factors :

(*i*) Cutting edge strength

(*ii*) Rigidity and allowable deflection

(*iii*) Surface finish required

(*iv*) Tool chip space.

Use of proper cutting fluid permits higher feeds and increased cutting speeds as well as attainment of better surface finish.

Feed is measured in different units as follows :

(*i*) mm/Rev in machine tools with rotary drive motion such as lathes, boring machines.

(*ii*) mm/stroke in machine tools with reciprocating drive motion such at shaper, planer.

(*iii*) mm/tooth in machine tools using multiple tooth cutters such as milling machine.

Let, f = Feed per revolution or feed per stroke

f_m = Feed per minute

$= f \times N$

where N = Number of revolutions or strokes per minute.

Feed per tooth in multiple tooth cutters is related to the feed per revolution as follows :

$$f = f_t \times z$$

where f_t = feed per tooth of cutter

z = Number of teeth on cutter.

The machining time to carry out any operation on a machine tool is determined as follows :

$$T = \text{Machining Time (minutes)} = \frac{L}{f_m}$$

where L = length of machine surface (millimetre)

f_m = Feed per minute.

Depth of cut. It is the thickness of the layer of metal removed in one cut or pass measured in a direction perpendicular to the machined surface. The depth of cut is always perpendicular to the direction of the feed motion.

In external longitudinal turning it is half the difference between the work diameter (D_1) and the diameter of the machined surface (D_2) obtained after one pass.

$$t = \text{Depth of cut} = \frac{D_1 - D_2}{2} \text{ mm.}$$

Fig. 1.36 shows cutting speed (v), depth of cut (i) and feed (f) for lathe, milling machine, drill machine and shaper.

In general speed and feed depend upon the following factors :

(*i*) Type of material of workpiece.

(*ii*) Type of material of cutting tool.

(*iii*) Quality of finish desired.

(*iv*) Type of coolant used.

(*v*) Rigidity of the machine tool.

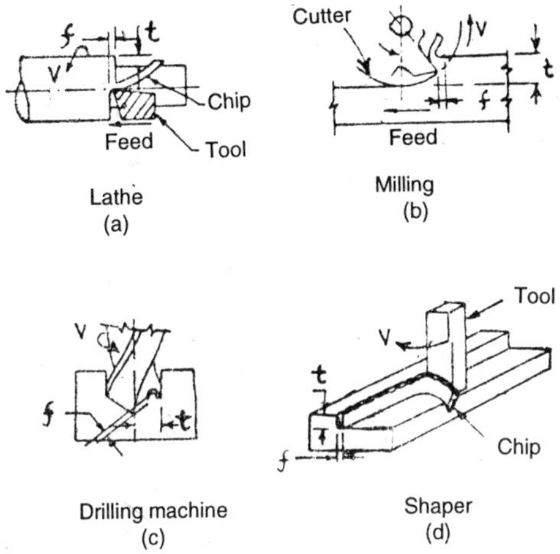

Fig. 1.36

Table 1.4 shows typical lathe turning speeds for ceramic tools.

Table 1.4

Material to be cut	*Roughing (m / min)*	*Finishing (m / min)*
Upto 0.2 Carbon Steel	130—260	320—240
0.2 to 0.3 Carbon Steel	100—200	260—320
0.3 to 0.4 Carbon Steel	80—160	230—300
0.4 to 0.6 Carbon Steel	65—100	130—200
Cast Iron (BHN 217)	160—320	320—500

To achieve higher machining efficiency it is desired to use high feed that will allow :

(*a*) Required surface finish.

(*b*) Use of maximum depth of cut consistent with available power and rigidity of machine tool.

(*c*) Maximum cutting speed depending on tool life.

1.14.1. Economical Cutting Speed

The best cutting speed is which reduces the total cost of machining and at the same time gives maximum production rate. Fig. 1.36.1 shows a graph between cutting speed (V) and production rate and production cost. It is observed that at point M production cost is minimum and at point N production rate is maximum. Therefore the best cutting speed will be between point M and point N.

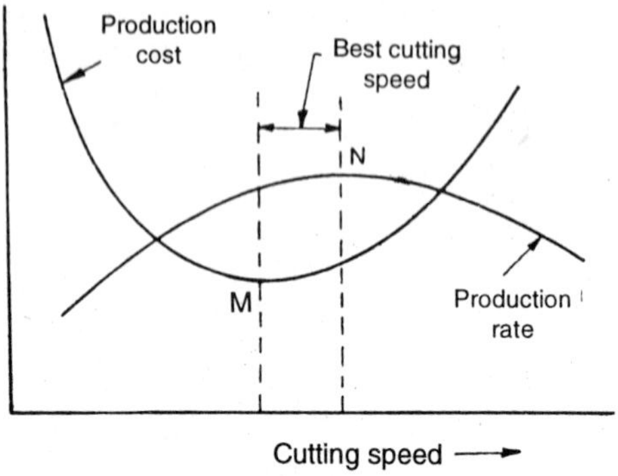

Fig. 1.36.1

Tool design depends on the following factors :

(1) Type of machining operation such as

(*i*) Turning (*ii*) Milling

(*iii*) Drilling (*iv*) Shaping

(*v*) Slotting etc.

(2) Type of material of tool such as

(*i*) H.S.S. (*ii*) Cemented Carbide

(3) Type of work piece material

(4) Machining variables such as

(*i*) Cutting speed (*ii*) Feed

(*iii*) Depth of cut

(5) Cutting force

(6) Accuracy to be obtained on work piece.

(7) Heat treatment and surface finish of tool.

1.15. Objectives of a Good Tool Design

A cutting tool should be made up of proper material and should be accurately designed in order to achieve the following objectives :

(*i*) Easy chip flow.

(*ii*) Proper surface finish and accuracy.

(*iii*) High productivity.

(*iv*) Less amount of input power.

(*v*) Minimum overall cost.

The tool designed should have sufficient strength to maintain a sharp cutting edge during cutting and should have sufficient hardness to prevent picking up the chips.

During machining the cutting forces should be low and the cost of production should be minimum. As shown in Fig. 1.36.2.

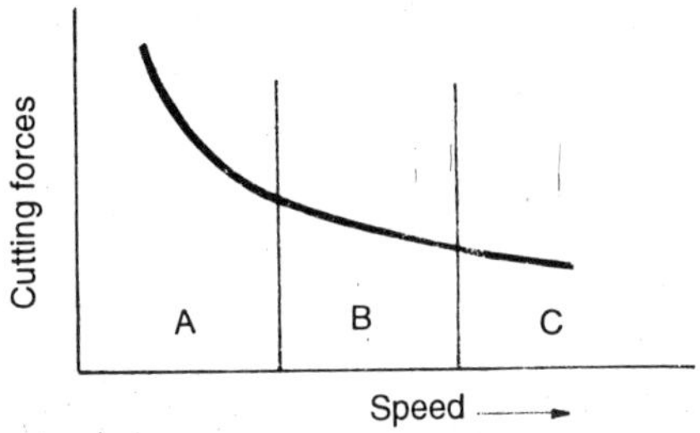

Fig. 1.36.2

In zone A cutting forces are very high due to the low cutting speed. Therefore cutting edges of brittle material like carbide may break. In zone C the cutting edge temperature will be very high due to the high cutting speed which will lead to rapid plastic deformation of the cutting edge. Zone B is, therefore, ideal for working with carbides where cutting forces are more or less independent of change in cutting speed. Cutting speeds vary with the machineability factor of the material being machined. Normally we employ higher cutting speeds for softer, and lower cutting speeds for harder materials. Therefore, it is advisable to use lower speeds within Zone B combined with higher feeds to achieve low cutting tool costs.

Though the tool life can be increased by using lower cutting speeds, the objective generally is to have that cutting speed which will give us the lowest cost of production. The cutting speed so selected is called economical cutting speed as shown in Fig. 1.36.3.

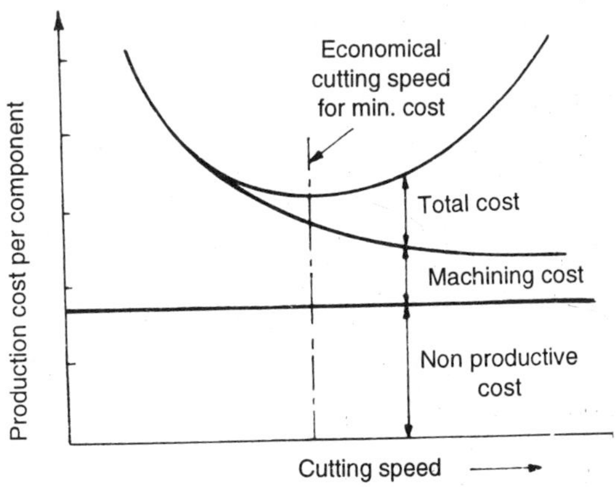

Fig. 1.36.3

1.15.1. Re-sharpening Allowance

Allowance for re-sharpening of single point tools is indicated in Table 1.4A.

Table 1.4A

			Resharpening allowance, millimeters						
Tool Types	*Tool material*	*Surface to be ground*	*Tool cross section, mm × mm*						
			10×16	*12×20*	*10×25*	*20×30*	*25×40*	*30×45*	*40×60*
For single tool lathes	Cemented carbide	Face and flank	0.2	0.2	0.3	0.4	0.4	0.4	0.5
	High speed steel	Face and flank	0.3	0.4	0.5	0.5	0.6	0.6	0.6
For multi-tool lathes	Cemented carbide	Flank	0.6	0.6	0.7	0.7	0.8	0.9	—
	High-speed steel	Flank	—	0.7	0.8	0.8	0.9	—	—
For circular foming tools	High-speed steel	Face	1.1	1.1	1.1	1.1	1.1	1.1	1.1

Tools used on multiple lathes are ground only on flanks whereas forming tools are ground on their faces.

1.16. Cutting Tools Materials

The purpose of cutting tool material is to remove metal under controlled conditions. Therefore the tool must be harder than the material which it is to cut. The cutting tools are made up of different materials. The cutting tool material should possess the following requirements :

(*i*) It should be strong enough to withstand the forces being applied due the cutting *i.e.* bending compression, shear etc.

(*ii*) It should be tough (resistant to shock loads). It is quite important when tool is used for intermittent putting.

(*iii*) It should be sufficient harder (resistant to wear, abrasion and indentation) the material being cut.

(*iv*) It should be able to resist high temperature.

(*v*) It should be capable of withstanding the sudden cooling effect of coolant used during cutting.

(*vi*) The coefficient of friction between the chip and the tool should be as low as possible in the operating range of speed and feed.

(*vii*) It should be easily formed to the required cutting shape.

Material chosen for a particular application will depend on the material being machined, the quantity of components to be produced, the cost of cutting tool materials, the type of machining operation (intermittent or continuous roughing or finishing, high or low speed etc.), the tool design details (cutting and clearance angles method of holding rigidity etc.) and the general conditions of machine tool.

Several materials exhibiting above properties in varying degrees have been developed for use in cutting tools.

The following metals suitably heat treated wherever required (tungsten carbide and ceramics are not heat treatable) are used in the manufacture of cutting tools :

(*a*) Carbon tool steel. (*b*) High speed steel.

(*c*) Cemented carbides. (*d*) Ceramics.

(*e*) Diamonds.

1.16.1. Carbon tool steels

Carbon steels are limited in use to tools of small section operating at lower speeds. A typical plain carbon steel used for cutting tool has the following composition.

C = 0.8 to 1.3%, SI = 0.1 to 0.4%, Mn = 0.1 to 0.4%.

Such steels when hardened and tempered have good hardness, strength and toughness and can be given a keen cutting edge. Tools made up of plain carbon steel can be used for machining soft materials such as free cutting steels and brass. This material starts loosing its hardness at about 250°C and is therefore not used when the operational temperature is more.

Table 1.5 (*a*) indicates percentage composition of typical medium alloy tool steels.

Table 1.5 (a)

Ca	*Mn*	*Si*	*Cr*	*W*	*Mo*
1.2	0.6	0.3	0.5	—	—
1.2	0.7	0.3	0.5	—	0.5
1.2	0.3	0.3	0.7	1.5	0.3
1.3	0.3	0.3	0.7	4.0	—

Medium alloy tool steels are similar to carbon tool steel. However in medium alloy tool steels elements like chromium, molybdenum and tungsten are added. Chromium and molybdenum are added to increase hardenability of steel whereas tungsten is added to improve wear resistance.

1.16.1. (a) Alloys and their effect on tool steels

Plain carbon steels when used as cutting tools lack certain necessary characteristics such as

(*i*) Red hardness (*ii*) Impact strength
(*iii*) Abrasive resistance.

Addition of alloying elements such as

(*i*) Chromium (*ii*) Vanadium
(*iii*) Tungsten (*iv*) Cobalt
(*v*) Titanium (*vi*) Molybdenum
(*vii*) Nickel (*viii*) Manganese
(*ix*) Silicon.

Helps in achieving the following properties :

(*i*) Improving toughness
(*ii*) Improving tensile and impact strength
(*iii*) Improving wear resistance
(*iv*) Improving hardenability
(*v*) Increasing high temperature resistance (red hardness)
(*vi*) Improving corrosion resistance.

Table 1.5 (*b*) indicates case hardening temperature (T) and hardness (HRC) obtainable for some of Die Steels.

Table 1.5 (b)

Type	*T(°C)*	*HRC*
En—8	830—840	38—48
En—9	830—860	45—55
En—24	850—870	55—60
En—30	900—920	50—60
En—31	850—860	58—60
En—36	900—920	50—60
En—56	860—870	55—58
Spring steel	840—850	60—64
OHNS	860—880	60—62

1.16.2. High speed steels

High speed steel tools give improved cutting performance and higher metal removal rates. High speed steel is widely used for drills, many types of general purpose milling cutters and single-point tools.

Although several types of high speed steels are in use but 18-4-1 high speed steel containing tungsten 18%, chromium 4% and vanadium 1% is quite commonly used. This type of material gives excellent performance over a great range of materials and cutting speeds and it retains its hardness upto around 600°C. The coolant should be used freely to increase tool life. The chief characteristics of high speed steels are superior hardness and wear resistance.

Sometimes, the surface of high speed steel tools are treated by the following methods to reduce friction and to increase wear resistance.

(*i*) Super finishing (to reduce friction).

(*ii*) Chromium of electrolytic plating (to reduce friction).

(*iii*) Oxidation (to reduce friction).

(*iv*) Nitriding (to increase wear resistance).

Table 1.5 indicates some of the carbon tool steels. (*Table on next page*)

Table 1.6 shows some of popular grades of high speed steels used for making tools. (*Table on next page*)

1.16.3. Cemented carbides

They consist of tungsten, tantalum and titanium carbides together with a binder usually cobalt all mixed together as fine powders. These powders are compacted (compressed) into the required shape and subjected to a high temperature treatment known as sintering. During this process the cobalt binder is fused to the carbides, producing a hard, dense substance.

Tools made up of cemented carbides are extremely hard having Rockwell hardness varying from 90—93 HRC. They can be used at cutting speeds 200 to 500% greater than those used for high speed steel. They have virtually replaced high speed steels in high speed and high producing machining. Cemented carbides are very hard and the usual practice is to confine the size to a relatively small shape known as an "insert" which is clamped to a tough steel shank or holder. This has the advantage that the tool bit is well supported to resist the cutting forces. This insert may have three to eight edges and is so designed that each of its cutting edges can be used in turn. It may then be discarded and replaced with a new tool bit giving low maintenance and breakdown time.

Table 1.5. Carbon Tool Steels

IS : 1570 / 1961	*Nominal Chemical Composition*						
Designation	*C%*	*Mn%*	*Si%*	*S%*	*P%*	*Cr%*	*V%*
T 70	0.70	0.25	0.20	0.03	0.03	—	—
T 80	0.80	0.25	0.20	0.03	0.03	—	—
T 90	0.90	0.25	0.20	0.03	0.03	—	—
T 103	1.00	0.25	0.20	0.03	0.03	—	—
T 118	1.15	0.25	0.20	0.03	0.03	—	—
T 133	1.30	0.25	0.20	0.03	0.03	—	—

Table 1.6. High Speed Steel

IS : 1570 / 1961	*Nominal Chemical Composition*										
Designation	*C%*	*Mn%*	*Si%*	*S%*	*P%*	*Cr%*	*Ni%*	*Mo%*	*W%*	*V%*	*CO%*
T70W18Cr4VI	0.70	0.40	0.35	0.25	0.025	4.15	—	—	18.25	1.20	—
T75W18Co6 Cr4VIMo75	0.75	0.40	0.35	0.25	0.025	4.20	—	0.75	18.25	1.25	5.50
T83Mo6W6Cr4 V2	0.83	0.40	0.35	0.25	0.025	4.10	—	5.50	6.00	1.90	—

The general characteristics of carbide tools are as follows :

(*i*) They have high thermal conductivity, low specific heat and low thermal expansion.

(*ii*) They have high hardness over a wide range of temperature (up to 900°C).

(*iii*) Their compressive strength is more than tensile strength.

(*iv*) They are very stiff. Their Young's modulus is about three times than steel.

Tungsten carbide cutting tools containing only tungsten carbide and cobalt with no other elements added are referred to as the straight grades. The only variables in this case are the grain size of the tungsten carbide particles and the percentage of cobalt. Any change of these variables affects the hardness and transverse rupture strength (toughness) of the carbide insert. In turn, any reduction of hardness would reduce the abrasion resistance of the tool, and a reduction in toughness would result in a more brittle tool. In other words, the tougher the grade, the lower its wear resistance and vice versa.

The effect of the variables in the straight carbide grades is as follows :

An increase in grain size

(*a*) lowers the hardness

(*b*) increases the transverse rupture strength (toughness).

An increase in cobalt content

(*a*) lowers the hardness

(*b*) increases the transverse rupture strength.

Maximum wear resistance is obtained from using a small grain size and a low cobalt content. When chipping of the tool occurs, the toughness is increased by increasing the grain size and cobalt content at the expense of wear resistance.

Appropriate reliefs and clearances are ground on carbide inserts as shown in Fig. 1.37.1.

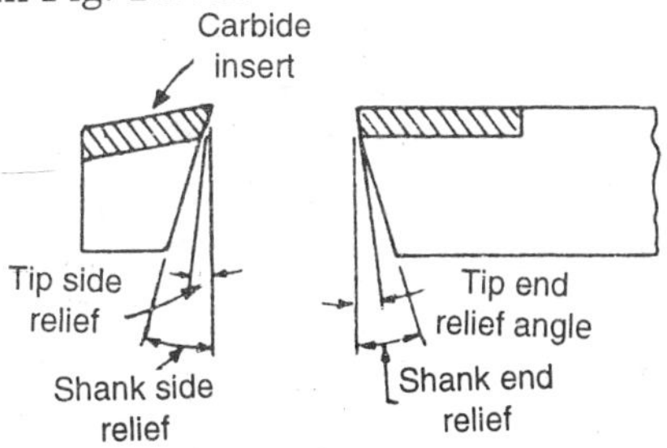

Fig. 1.37.1

Shank sizes for single point carbide tools vary from 12 mm to over 50 mm. The shank size should be large enough to support the load of the tool for a given tool over hang. A typical shank size for a single point carbide tool is as follows :

Shank size	= 12 mm × 24 mm.
when depth of cut	= 3 mm.
Feed	= 0.375 mm.
Over hang	= 36 mm.

The tool flank must be designed in such a way as to minimise sharpening costs. The flanks of almost all carbide tips are bevelled to an angle of 20°. Brazed tips are positioned at an angle varying between 12—18°. Fig. 1.37 (*a*) shows a carbide tip embedded in the shank. The flank can be shaped to three angles namely angle α on chamber, angle α + 3° on the rest of the tip and angle α + 5° on the shank as shown in Fig. 1.37 (*b*) for a tip without overhang and Fig. 1.37 (*c*) for a tip with overhang.

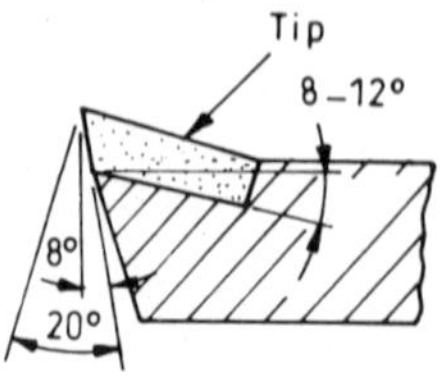

Fig. 1.37 (*a*)

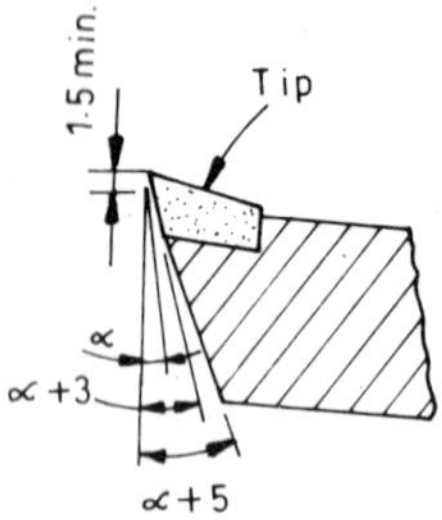

Fig. 1.37 (*b*)

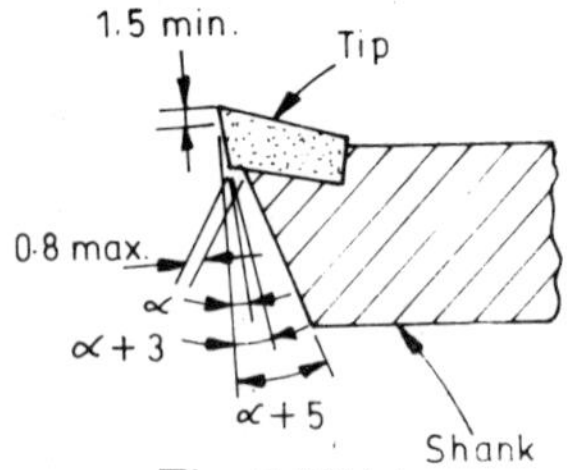

Fig. 1.37 (*c*)

Tipped tools are preferable when expensive cemented carbides or high speed steels are used : then, the point is made of a metal-cutting material, while the shank is of structural carbon steel.

Cemented-carbide tips are brazed or clamped mechanically, while tips of highspeed steel are clamped.

An as-brazed tip may protrude from the shank for as much as 1.5 millimetres, but in tool sharpening this over-hang should be reduced to within 0.8 millimetre. This will enable carbide tips to be sharpened by diamond wheels, keeping the latter out of touch with the shank.

Fig. 1.37 (*d*) shows a turning tool whereas a facing tool is shown in Fig. 1.37 (*e*). A parting tool used to cut off the material is shown in Fig. 1.37 (*f*). A boring tool is shown in Fig. 1.37 (*g*).

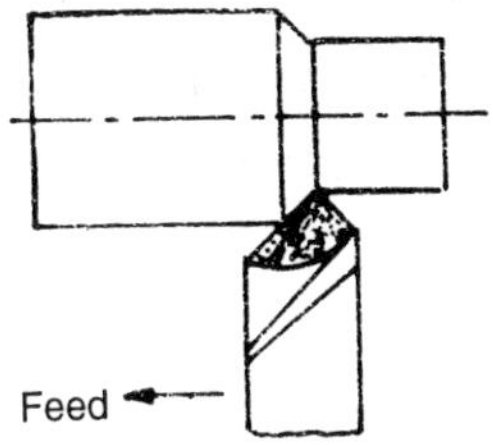

Fig. 1.37 (*d*)

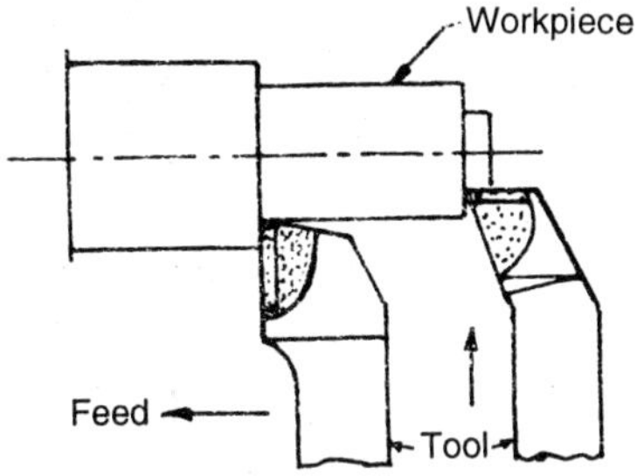

Fig. 1.37 (*e*)

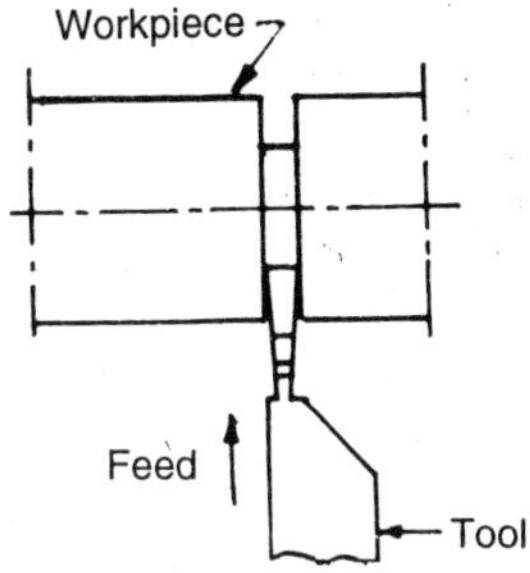

Fig. 1.37 (*f*)

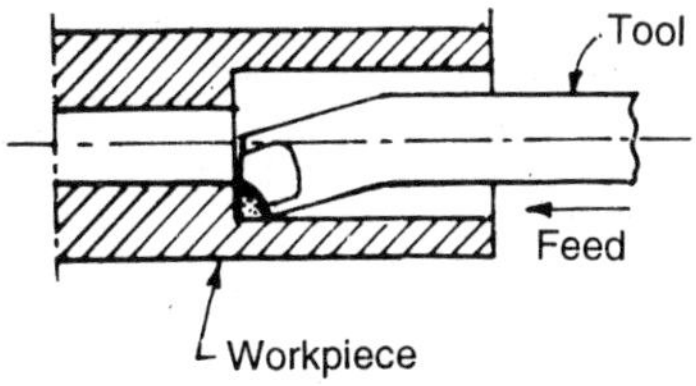

Fig. 1.37 (*g*)

1.16.4. Ceramics

Aluminium oxide and boron nitride powders mixed together and sintered at 1700°C form the ingredients of ceramic tools. These materials are very hard with good compressive strength. Ceramics are usually in the form of disposable tips. They can be operated at from two to three times the cutting speeds of tungsten carbide and cutting speeds on cast iron in the order of 1000 m/min are not uncommon. They resist cratering, usually require no coolant. However in order to take full advantage of their capabilities special and more rigid machine tools are required.

Ceramic and cemented carbide cutting tools should be sharpened to a high degree of surface finish to minimise friction between tool and chip. This will improve to efficiency of the cutting process and less power will be absorbed and there will be a less tendency for a built up edge to form on the cutting face of the tool.

Cemented carbide or ceramic tips can be brazed to medium carbon steel shank and resharpened by grinding when necessary. For many applications it is more economical to clamp the tip to the shank (Fig. 1.37). The technique enables a tip to be thrown away (called throw away tips) at the end of its useful life and new tip to be clamped to the existing shank.

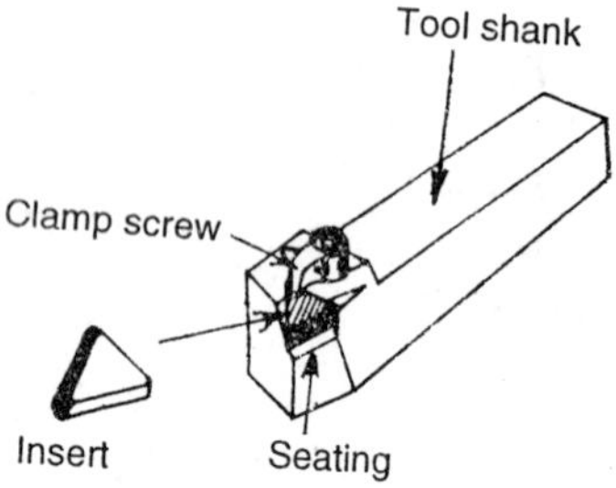

Fig. 1.37

The various conditions for the effective use of carbide or ceramic tool are as follows :

(*i*) Rigidity of tool and workpiece.

(*ii*) Highly finished surface on cutting tool.

(*iii*) High cutting speeds.

(*iv*) Use of machine tool having high quality bearings.

(*v*) Use of effective chip bearings.

(*vi*) Elimination of any unbalanced forces.

(*vii*) Chip guards are essential when using these tools.

Ceramic tools can cut at top speeds, upto 1500 m/min, but their tool life, is less than that of tools made of other materials. Their mode of failure is brittle fracture at random locations of point defects.

Three types of ceramic cutting tools are mainly used, Al_2O_3, Sialon (a combination of silica, aluminium, oxygen and nitrogen), and silicon nitride (Si_3N_4).Al_2O_3 is the most common and performs best for finishing and semi-finishing, with non-interrupted cuts. Sialon offers greater resistance to mechanical shock and possesses the ability to withstand the thermal shocks that arise from the use of coolants. Si_3N_4 tools have attributes, similar to sialon, but with improved toughness and ability to withstand high temperatures and loads.

1.16.5. Diamonds

Diamond is the hardest material known. It has a low coefficient of friction, high compressive strength and is extremely wear resistant. It is used mainly for cutting very hard materials, such as glass, plastics, ceramics etc. Diamond tools produce a very good surface finish at high speeds with good dimensional accuracy. Diamond tools are small and are best suited for light cuts and finishing operations. Other application for diamond is that it is used for truing the grinding wheels. The general properties of diamond may be summarised as follows :

1. It is the hardest known substance.
2. It has lowest thermal expansion of any pure substance.
3. It has high heat conductivity.
4. It is poor electrical conductor.
5. It has very low coefficient of friction against metals.

Since very high hardness is always accompanied by brittleness, a diamond tool must be cautiously used to avoid rupturing the point. This usually limits the use of diamond tools to light continuous cut in relatively soft metals and low values of rake angle are usually used to provide a stronger cutting edge.

The main disadvantages of diamonds are their brittleness and high cost.

1.16.6. Multi-coated cemented carbide inserts

Cemented carbide inserts coated with layers of optimum thickness of Titanium Carbide, Titanium Carbonitride, and Titanium nitride have more life. Layer coating is carried out by chemical vapour deposition process.

Various advantages of multiple coatings are as follows :

1. A hard, binderless layer of TIN, acts as a diffusion barrier and eliminates the possibility of chip welding and chemical diffusion on insert Rake face, thereby **increasing crater resistance**.
2. Reduced flank wear.
3. Lower frictional resistance and reduction in cutting forces upto 10—15%. This also allows higher cutting speed.
4. Higher thermal conductivity.
5. Superior surface finish on machined parts.

1.16.7. Cutting alloys

They are used on tools that operate at very high cutting speeds with high temperatures developing on the cutting edges (up to 1000—1100°C). Since they cannot be machined by ordinary methods, they are applied to cutting tools either by means of hard-facing techniques (as a weld deposit) or as tips brazed to the tool shank or body.

Depending upon method of manufacture, they are classified into two groups :

1. Cast cutting alloys.
2. Cemented carbides.

Cast cutting alloys or Stelites. They contain large amounts of the critical metals, cobalt and tungsten, have a high hardness (R_c = 60—65) and melt at very high temperatures. Tips or rods from 5 to 10 mm thick, cast of these alloys, are used in the hard-facing of tools by welding techniques to increase the life of the cutting edges. Dies and wear surfaces of various machine parts are hard-faced in the same manner.

Cemented carbides. They are made of a powdery mixture of tungsten and titanium carbides and metallic cobalt.

In their finished form cemented carbides consist of extremely fine grains of tungsten and titanium carbides with a cobalt binder. These alloys are extremely hard—with a Rockwell hardness number up to 85 and even higher—and they retain this hardness at temperatures up to 1000°C.

1.17. Variation of Hardness with Temperature

Fig. 1.38 shows the variation of hardness with temperature for the tools made up of different materials.

1. A plain carbon tool steel tool.
2. An 18-4-1 high speed steel tool.
3. A cast alloy tool.
4. A cast iron grade cemented tungsten carbide tool.

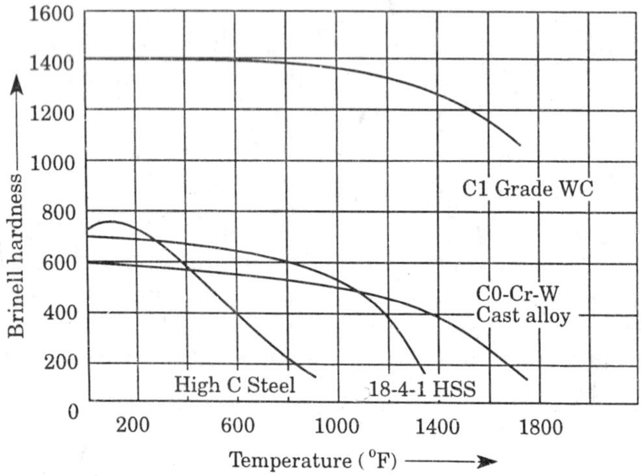

Fig. 1.38

1.18. Economic Comparison of Tool Materials

The principal tool materials are high speed steel, cemented carbide and ceramics in increasing order of hardness and reducing order of toughness. High speed steel is quite commonly used as it can be used to manufacture complicated shaped cutting tools such as drills, taps, reamers, dies and milling cutters. Cemented carbide because of its high cost and need to form it in its final shape has limited applications and is generally used for rough or finish turning and face milling operations. Ceramic tool material is brittle, cannot withstand high force and is generally used in finish turning operations.

Properties of tool materials are basically governed by the following:

(*i*) Chemical composition of the materials.

(*ii*) Type and size of grains of materials before manufacture.

(*iii*) Manufacturing process.

(*iv*) Finishing treatments.

1.19. Multi-edge Cutting Tools

Multi-edge cutting tools present more than one cutting edge to the work. They have a higher metal removal rate than single edged cutting tools and also the life of the multi-edge cutting tool is raised by increasing the number of cutting edges. The different multi-edge cutting tools are divided into two groups as shown in Table 1.7. A grinding wheel is also a form of multi-edge cutting tool.

Table 1.7

Group	*Machines*	*Cutting Tools*
A	Drills Capstan Lathe Turret Lathe	Twist drills Reamers Multi-flute core drills Counter bores spot Facing cutters.
B	Milling Machines	Saws and slotting cutters Side and face cutters Slab mills End mills Face mills Form-relieved cutters.

The tools in group *A* have their cutting edges in continuous engagement with the work and are fed axially at a uniform feed per revolution. The underformed chip thickness is therefore constant and directly proportional to the feed/rev. The geometry and mechanics of cutting are then identical with those discussed for single point tools. The various tools in group *B* have their cutting edges intermittently engaged with the work and are fed in a plane parallel or perpendicular to the cutter axis of rotation.

1.20. The Twist Drill

It is used to produce a hole in the workpiece. Its sole purpose is to remove the maximum volume of metal in a minimum period of time. The finish obtained by a drill is not so fine. If a hole of accurate size and good finish is required, the drilled hole should be finish machined by means of a reamer or by single point boring tool. Twist drills are usually made of high speed steel. High carbon steel can also be used to manufacture drills. Drills with cemented carbide cutting tips (tips are brazed) are used at very high speeds for drilling operations on non-ferrous metals but are not recommended for ferrous metal particularly steels because the tips are not supported as effectively as in case of single point cutting tools or milling cutters. A twist drill consists of a cylindrical body carrying two helical grooves into it to from the flutes. The flutes run the full length of body of twist drill and perform the following functions :

(*i*) They provide the rake angle.
(*ii*) They form the cutting edges.
(*iii*) They provide a passage to the coolant.
(*iv*) They facilitate swarf removal.

1.21. Elements of a Twist Drill

A twist drill is shown in Fig. 1.39. The various elements of a twist drill are as follows :

(*i*) **Body.** It is the part of the drill that is fluted and relieved.

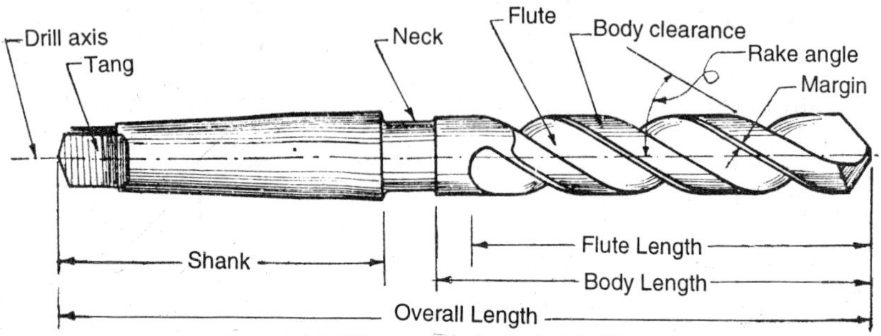

Fig. 1.39. Elements of a twist drill.

(*ii*) **Shank.** It is the part held in the holding device.

The most common types of shanks are the taper shank and the parallel shanks. Small drills up to about 12.7 mm diameter are provided with parallel shanks and the larger size drill have tapered shanks. Tapered shank drill carry a tang at the end of the shank to ensure a positive grip. The straight shank drills are held in a drill machine by a chuck. The jaws of the chuck are tightened around the drill by means of a key or wrench. The point of a drill is the entire cone shaped surface at the cutting end of the drill (Fig. 1.40).

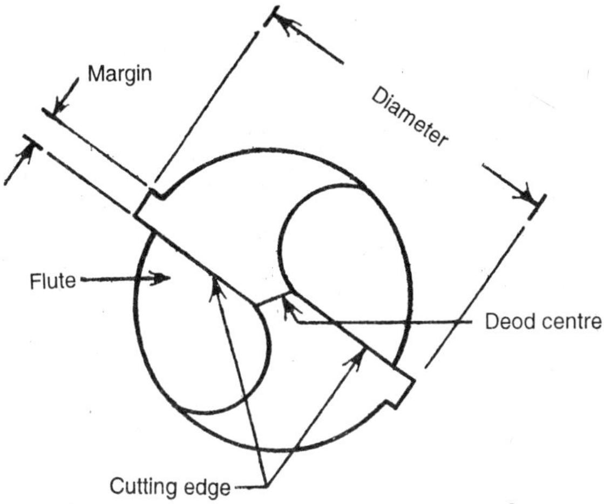

Fig. 1.40. The point of twist drill.

(*iii*) **Dead centre.** The dead centre or chisel edge of the drill is the sharp edge at the extreme tip end of the drill. It should always be in the exact centre of the axis of the drill.

(*iv*) **Lip.** Lip or cutting edge is formed by the intersection of the flank and face. Both the lips of the drill should be of equal length and should be at the same angle of inclination with the drill. axis. This will enable to produce a perfectly round smooth and accurate hole. Unequal lips will result in an oversize hole.

(*v*) **Flank.** Flank is the surface on a drill point which extends behind the lip to the following flute.

(*vi*) **Chisel edge corner.** The corner formed by the intersection of a lip and the chisel edge is called chisel edge corner.

(*vii*) **Flutes.** The grooves in the body of the drill which provides lips.

Twist drill angles. Lake any other cutting tool the twist drill is provided with correct tool angles (Fig. 1.41). The various angles are as follows :

(*i*) **Rake angle or helix angle.** It is the angle of flute in relation to the work.

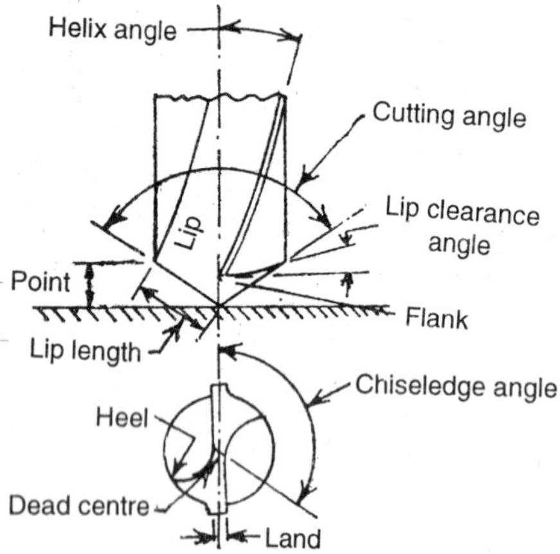

Fig. 1.41

Smaller the rake angle greater will be the torque required to drive the drill at a given speed. Its usual value is 30° although it may vary up to 45° for different materials.

The rake angle also partially governs the tightness with which the chips curl and hence the amount of space which the chips occupy. Other conditions being the same, a very large rake angle makes a tightly rolled chip, while a rather small rake angle makes a chip tend to curl into a more loosely rolled helix.

(*ii*) **Lips clearance angle.** It is the angle formed by the flank and a plan at right angle to the drill axis. Lip clearance is the relief that is given to the cutting edges in the order to allow the drill to enter the metal without interference. This angle is 12° in most cases. In order to allow strength and rigidity to the cutting edge the clearance angle should be kept minimum.

(*iii*) **Cutting angle or point angle.** It is the angle included between the two lips projected upon a plane parallel to the drill axis and parallel to the two cutting lips. It is observed that the best point angle is 118°.

(*iv*) **Chisel edge angle.** It is the angle included between the chisel edge and the lip as seen from the end of the drill.

The various angles for a drill are shown in Table 1.8.

Table 1.8

Material	*Point angle (Degrees)*	*Lip clearance angle (Degrees)*	*Chisel edge angle (Degrees)*	*Helix angle (Degrees)*
Aluminium	90—140	8—12	120—135	24—48
Brass	111	8—15	120—135	0—27
Copper	100—118	8—15	120—135	28—40
Cost iron hard	118	8—12	120—135	24—40
Steel	118	8—12	120—135	24—32
Stainless Steel	125—135	10—12	120—135	24—32

1.22. Cutting Fluids for Drilling

Cutting coolants and oils are used during drilling to carry away the heat from the drill point preventing it from overheating. This permits higher cutting speeds and longer drill life. The action of chips coming out of the hole tends to restrict the entry of the fluid. A continuous supply of cutting fluid should be maintained in order to obtain proper cooling. For severe conditions drills containing oil holes have a considerable advantage. In such case not only the fluid is supplied near the cutting edges but the flow of fluid aids in chip removal from the hole.

Practically all metals require the use of coolant when being drilled except cast iron which may be machined dry.

1.23. Twist Drill Grinding

It is very important that drills ore properly ground. The drill point must be in the centre of rotation of the drill. The lips should be of equal length and at correct angle with the axis. The twist drill is ground on the side of grinding wheel of the grinding machine as shown in Fig. 1.42 (*a*). The flat surface that this provides makes it much easier to generate a true point. The straight cutting lip should lie vertically against the side of the wheel when the drill has been ground it should be checked on a point gauge. Fig. 1.42 (*b*) shows a twist drill point angle and lip length gauge. If the lips are of unequal length, the result will be that both the point and lip will be off-centre (Fig. 1.43). This will cause the hole to be large than the drill. If a drill is ground with its tip on the centre but with the cutting edges at different angles, the drill will bend on one side of the hole (Fig. 1.44). Only one lip or cutting edge will do the work resulting in rapid wear on that edge and the hole will be larger than drill.

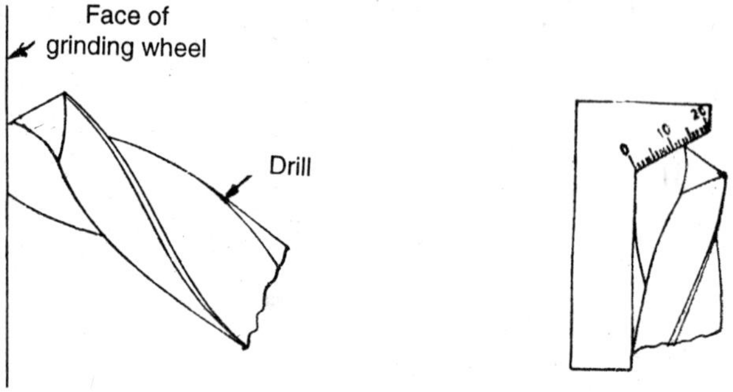

(a) (b)

Fig. 1.42

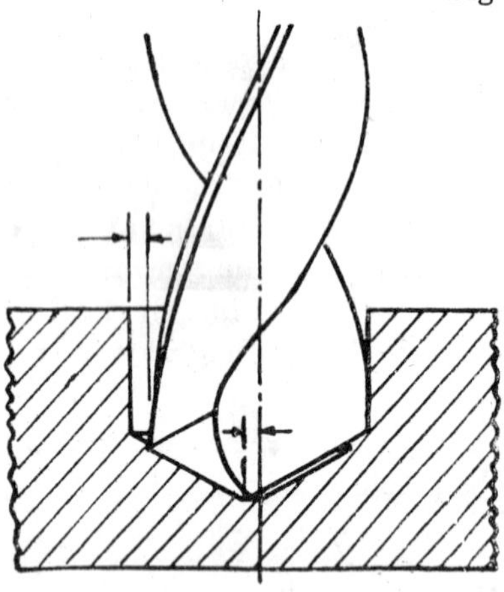

Fig. 1.43

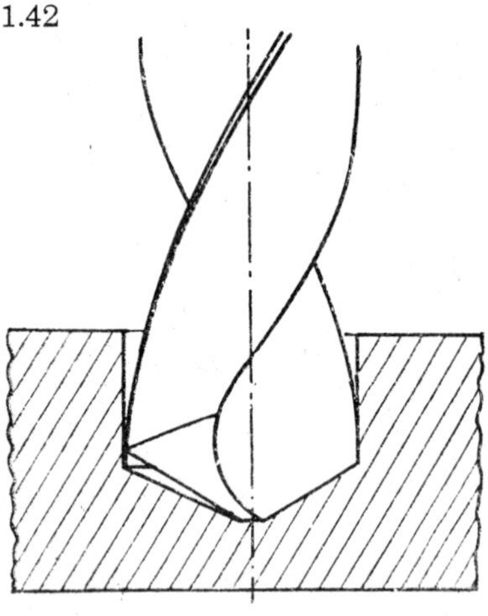

Fig. 1.44

1.23.1. Twist drill failure

A twist drill will suffer an early failure or produce holes that are dimensionally inaccurate, out of round and poor finish for the following general reasons :

(i) Incorrect speed and feeds

(ii) Incorrect grinding of the point

(iii) Mishandling.

1.24. Rake and Relief Angles of a Twist Drill

Rake Angle. The rake angle (α) is the angle between the tangent to the face (in the flute) at the point of lip (cutting edge) being referred to and the normal at the same point to the surface of revolution described by the lip about the drill axis. The rake angle is measured in a plane perpendicular to the lip (plane mm in Fig. 1.45). This angle varies gradually along the lip. It can be found by using the following relation :

$$\tan \alpha_x = \frac{r_x \tan \beta}{R \sin \theta}$$

where β = Helix angle of flutes.

R = Radius of drill.

θ = One half of the point angle.

r_x = Radius of the circle on which the point being considered is located.

R = Radius of the drill.

Angle α acquires its maximum value at the periphery of the drill. The variation of rake angle along the lip is shown by a graphical construction.

Refer Fig. 1.46. When a helix is developed on a plane, it will become the hypotenuse of a tight triangle of which one side is the lead (pitch) of the flutes and the other side is the circumference of a circle of a diameter (D) on which the helix was formed.

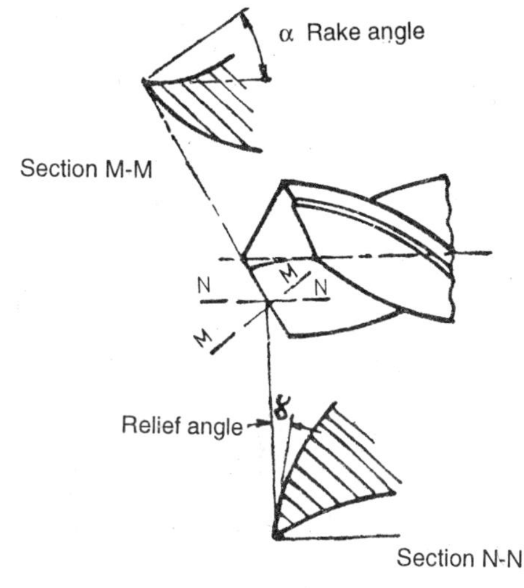

Fig. 1.45

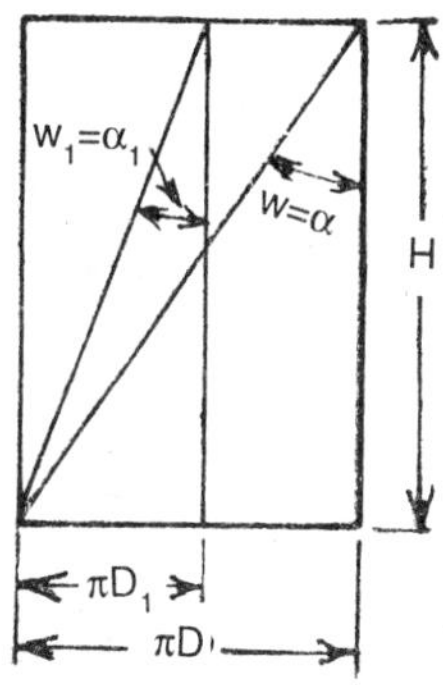

Fig. 1.46

Relief Angle γ. It is the angle between a tangent to the flank or lip relief surface at the point being considered on the lip and a tangent at the same point to the circle the point describes as it rotates about the drill axis. This angle is measured in plane NN (Fig. 1.45) which is tangent to the cylindrical surface on which the above mentioned point on the lip lies.

1.25. Drill Specifications

According to Indian Standard System, twist drills are specified by the diameter, the I.S. number, the material and the series to which they belong. The drills are made in three types :

(*i*) Type *N*—for normal low carbon steel.

(*ii*) Type *H*—for hard materials.

(*iii*) Type *S*—for soft and tough materials.

For example, a parallel shank twist drill 12 mm diameter and made up of high speed steel and conforming to IS : 5101 with a point angle of 118° and of N-type is designated as 12.00—IS : 5101 HS-N-118.

Unless otherwise mentioned in the designation it should be assumed that drill type is N and point angle is 118°.

Drill Size. In metric system the drills are made in diameters from 0.2 mm to 100 mm.

1.26. Cutting Speed, Feed and Depth of Cut

Cutting speed. It is the peripheral speed of a point on the surface of the drill in contact with the work piece. It is usually expressed in metres per minute.

Let D = Diameter of drill in mm.

N = R.P.M. of drill spindle.

V = Cutting speed in metre per minute.

$$V = \frac{\pi DN}{100} \text{ metre per minute.}$$

Cutting speed mainly depends upon the following factors :

(*i*) Type of material to be drilled.

(*ii*) Type of material of drill. Twist drill made of high speed steel can be operated at about twice the speed of drill made of high carbon steel.

(*iii*) Type of finish required.

(*iv*) Type of coolant used.

(*v*) Capacity of machine and tool life.

Table 1.9 shows cutting speed for high speed steel drill.

Table 1.9

Material being drilled	*Cutting speed (m / min)*
Aluminium	70—100
Brass	35—50
Phosphor Bronze	20—35
Grey Cast Iron	25—40
Copper	35—45
Mild Steel	30—40
Alloy Steel (High tensile)	5—8

Feed. It is the distance the drill moves into the work at each revolution of the spindle. It is expressed as millimeter per revolution.

It may also be expressed as feed per minute.

Let N = R.P.M. of drill spindle.

f = feed in mm/rev.

f_1 = feed in mm per minute.

$= N.f.$

Table 1.10 shows feed for high speed steel drill of various diameters.

Table 1.10

Drill diameter (mm)	*Feed (mm / rev.)*
1.0—2.5	0.04—0.06
2.6—4.5	0.05—0.10
4.6—6.0	0.075—0.15
6.1—12.00	0.75—0.25
12.1—15.0	0.20—0.30
15.1—18.0	0.23—0.33
18.1—21.0	0.26—0.36
21.1—25	0.28—0.39

A twist drill gives satisfactory performance if it is run at correct cutting speed and feed. The following factors help in running the drill at correct cutting speed and feed :

(*i*) The work is rigidly clamped.

(*ii*) The machine is in good condition.

(*iii*) A coolant is used if required.

(*iv*) The drill is correctly selected and ground for the material being cut. The selection of drill depends upon the following :

(*a*) Size of drill hole

(*b*) Material of workpiece

(*c*) Point angle of drill.

The rates of feed and cutting speed for twist drill are lower than most other machining operations because of the following reasons :

(*i*) The twist drill is weak compared with other cutting tools.

(*ii*) It is relatively difficult for the drill to eject chips.

(*iii*) It is difficult to keep the cutting edges cool when they are enclosed in the hole.

Depth of cut. It is equal to one half of the drill diameter.

D = Diameter of drill in mm.

t = Depth of cut in mm.

$= \frac{D}{2}$ mm.

1.27. Machining Time

Machining time in drilling is calculated as follows (Fig. 1.47).

Let T = Machining time in minutes

l = Thickness of workpiece in mm.

h = Approach of drill = 0.3 D in mm

D = Diameter of drill in mm.

L = length of axial travel of drill = $l + h$.

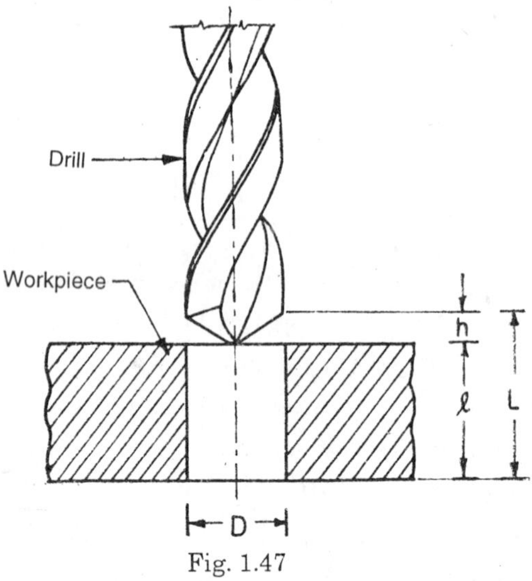

Fig. 1.47

f = feed/rev. in mm.

$$T = \frac{L}{N \times f}.$$

1.28. Forces Acting on a Drill

The various forces acting on a drill are shown in Fig. 1.48. All the elements of a drill are subject to certain forces in drilling. Resolving the resultant forces of resistance to cutting at each point of the lip we obtain three forces F_Z F_V, and F_H acting in directions mutually perpendicular to each other. The horizontal forces F_H acting on both lips are considered to counter balance each other. The vertical force F_V also called as thrust force comprises of the forces F_{V_1}, F_{V_2}, F_C and F_m. (The forces F_C and F_m are not shown). The force F_{V_1}, acts on the web. This force is quite large and is about 60% of the total thrust force. This force F_{V_2} act on each of the two lips and forms the real cutting force which depends upon the work material, cutting variables and cutting point geometry and is about 37% of total thrust force. The F_C and E_m are of smaller magnitude. The force F_C is due to the rubbing of the chips, flow from the hole against the sides of the hole and flutes on the drill. This force is about 1% of the total thrust force. The force F_M is due to the rubbing action of margin of the drill against the sides of the hole and is about 2% of thrust force.

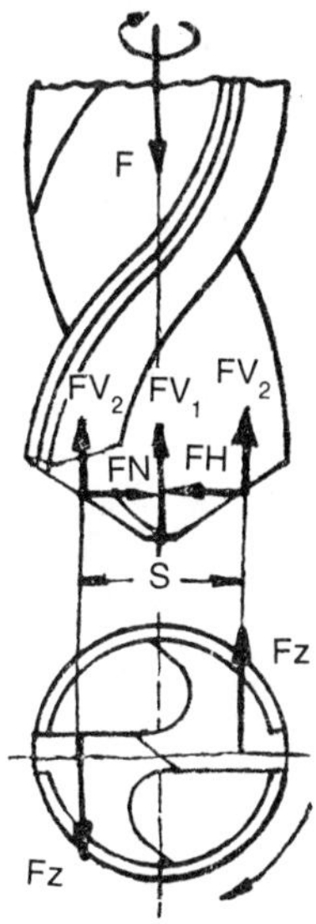

Fig. 1.48

In order that the drill to penetrate into the work piece the thrust force F applied to it by the machine must overcome the sum of resistances acting along the drill axis.

$$F > \Sigma(F_{V_1} + 2\,F_{V_2} + F_C + F_m)$$

The force F_Z sets up the moment of resistance (M_r)

$$M_r = F_Z.S$$

The total moment of the forces of resistance (M) to cutting is made up of the following moments :

(*i*) Moment of forces F_Z *i.e.* M_r

(*ii*) Moment of forces due to scraping and friction on the chisel edge (M_c)

(*iii*) Moment of the friction forces on the margins (M_m)

(*iv*) Moment of the forces of friction of the chip on the drill and on the machined surface (M_d)

$$M = M_r + M_c + M_m + M_d.$$

The total moment of resistance should be overcome by the available torque of the drilling machine.

1.29. Power of Drilling

When a drill is cutting, it has to overcome the resistance offered by the metal and a twisting effort is necessary to turn it. The effort is called turning moment or torque on the drill. The torque required to operate a drill depends upon various factors. The relationship between torque, diameter of drill and feed is as follows :

$$T_1 = C.f^{0.75}\, D^{1.8} \text{ newton metres}$$

where T_1 = Torque in newton metre

f = Drill feed in mm/rev.

D = Diameter of drill in mm.

C = Constant depending upon the material being drilled. The values of C are given in Table 1.11 for different materials.

Table 1.11

Material to be drilled	*Value of C*
Aluminium	0.11
Soft brass	0.084
Cast Iron	0.07
Mild steel	0.36
Carbon tool steel	0.4

$$\text{Power} \quad (P) = \frac{2\pi N T_1}{60{,}000} \text{ kW}$$

where N = Drill speed in R.P.M.

1.29. (a) Effect of Various Factors on the Axial Thrust and Torque in Drilling

The various factors which have effect on axial thrust F (see Fig. 1.48) and torque (T_1) are as follows :

(*i*) **Composition and hardness of material.** The greater the tensile strength and hardness of work piece material the greater the axial the thrust and the moment of forces of resistance to cutting in drilling.

(*ii*) **Rake angle.** The larger the rake angle of drill, the smaller the axial thrust and moment (M) of forces of resistance.

(*iii*) **Drill diameter and feed.** The larger the drill diameter and feed the greater the axial thrust and torque.

(*iv*) **Cutting fluid.** Axial thrust and torque is reduced by the use of suitable cutting fluids.

(*v*) **Cutting speed.** The torque and axial thrust first increase with the increase in cutting speed and then decrease with the increase in cutting speed.

(*vi*) **Drilling depth.** The axial thrust and torque are increased with an increased in depth of hole being drilling because removal of chip becomes difficult and also more heat is produced which can not be efficiently removed by the coolant.

1.30. Milling Cutters

Milling is an operation in which metal cutting is carried out by means of multi-teeth rotating tool called cutter. The cutters are manufactured in a variety of shapes and size each made for a specific purpose. In milling cutters each tooth after taking a cut comes into operation again after some interval of time. This allows the tooth to cool down before the next cutting operation is done by it. This minimises the effect of heat developed in cutting on cutting edges. A coolant helpful when milling steel for producing a good surface finish. The coolant may be oil or an emulsion of oil and water. The form of each tooth of cutter is same as that of a single point tool.

Many types of milling cutters are used on a milling machine. Most of them are considered standard and are available in many sizes. High speed steel is the material commonly favoured for cutters. They are also available with carbide tips as cutting edges. Cutters should be kept sharp. Cutters which are sharpened frequently usually last longer than those which are allowed to become dull.

A milling cutter is a multiple tooth tool and therefore higher requirements are made to its construction, sharpening and operation. The cutter should be reliably and rigidly clamped on the spindle. Milling cutters may be solid, inter-locking, carbide tipped solid cutters and inserted blade cutters with high speed steel or carbide tipped blades.

The various advantages of carbide tipped cutters either solid or inserted blade type are as follows :

(*i*) They have high production capacity.

(*ii*) They produce surface finish of high quality.

(*iii*) They can machine hardened steels.

(*iv*) Their use leads to reduction in machining costs.

With cylindrical cutters the two methods of milling operation commonly used are as follows :

1.30.1. Milling operations

With cylindrical cutters the two methods of milling operations commonly used are as follows :

(*i*) **Up or conventional milling.** In this process the cutter rotates against the direction in which the work is feeding (Fig. 1.49).

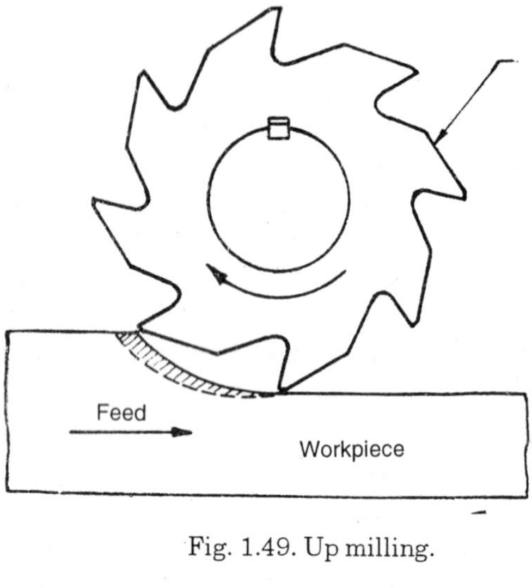

Fig. 1.49. Up milling.

(*ii*) **Down milling or Climb milling.** In this process the cutter rotates in the same direction as that in which the work is feeding (Fig. 1.50). The machine in which high velocity milling is to done should not only be capable of operating at high speeds and feeds but should also possess ample rigidity. The cutter should be reliable and rigidity clamped on the spindle.

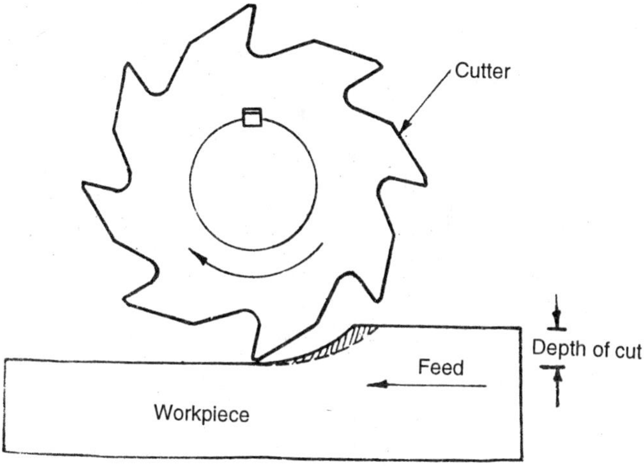

Fig. 1.50. Down milling.

1.31. Elements of a Plain Milling Cutter

A milling cutter may have either straight teeth *i.e.* parallel to the axis of rotation or in helical shape. A milling cutter can be considered as a built up unit of a number of single point cutting tools such that each tooth of the cutter is a single point cutting tool. Fig. 1.51 shows a plain milling cutter. The various parts of the cutter teeth are face, cutting edge, fillet, and body.

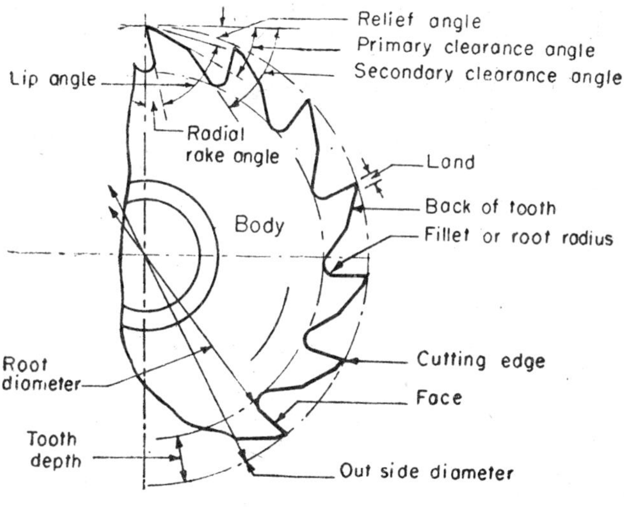

Fig. 1.51. Elements of plain milling cutter.

The various elements of the cutter are as follows :

(*i*) **Lip angle.** It is the angle included between the land and the face of the tooth or it is the angle between the tangent to the back at the cutting edge and the face of the tooth.

(*ii*) **Relief angle.** The angle in a plane perpendicular to the axis which is the angle between the land of a tooth and the tangent to the outside diameter of cutter at the cutting edge of that tooth.

The main function of relief angle is to prevent interference between land and work surface. The relief angle varies with the type of material being milled. Table 1.12 indicates the relief angles for different materials.

Table 1.12

Material	*Relief angle (Degrees)*
Cast Iron	4—7
Mild Steel	3—6
Brass	10—12
Aluminium alloys	10—12

(*iii*) **Rake angle (Radial).** It is the angle measured in the diameteral plane between the face of the tooth and radial line passing through the tooth cutting edge. It facilitates free cutting by tool allowing the chip to flow smoothly. This ensures less power consumption and better surface finish, less wear and hence more life of tool. It may be positive, negative or zero.

Table 1.13 indicates the rake angles in degrees for different materials to be milled.

Table 1.13

Material	*Cemented carbide cutter*	*H.S.S. Cutter*
Aluminium alloys	10—20	20—35
Cast Iron		
Hard	0—3	8—10
Soft	3—6	10—15
Mild Steel	0—(– 5)	10—15
Brass	3	10

(*iv*) **Primary clearance angle.** It is the angle between a line passing through the surface of the land and a tangent to the periphery at the cutting edge. This angle is provided to prevent the back of tooth from rubbing against the work. It is 4 to 7° for C.I. and 10 to 12 degrees for aluminium and brass.

(*v*) **Secondary clearance angle.** This angle is generally ground back of the land to keep the width of land within proper limits. It is usually 3 degrees greater than primary clearance angle.

(*vi*) **Land.** It is the narrow surface back of the cutting edge resulting from providing a clearance angle.

(*vii*) **Face.** Tooth face is the surface upon which the chip if formed when the cutter is cutting. It is may be flat or curved.

(*viii*) **Back of tooth.** It is created by the gullet and secondary clearance angle.

A milling cutter is a multiple tooth tool and therefore higher requirements are made to its construction, sharpening and operation. The cutter should be reliably and rigidly fixed on the spindle. The machine in which high velocity milling is to be done should not only be capable of operating at high speeds and feeds but possess ample rigidity.

Fig. 1.52 (*a*) shows a high speed steel milling cutter with teeth with positive rake angle. Teeth with zero rake is shown in Fig. 1.52 (*b*) and teeth with negative rake is shown in Fig. 1.52 (*c*).

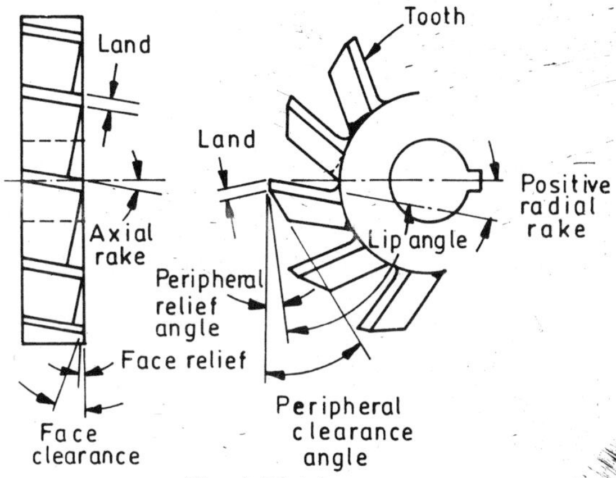

Fig. 1.52 (*a*)

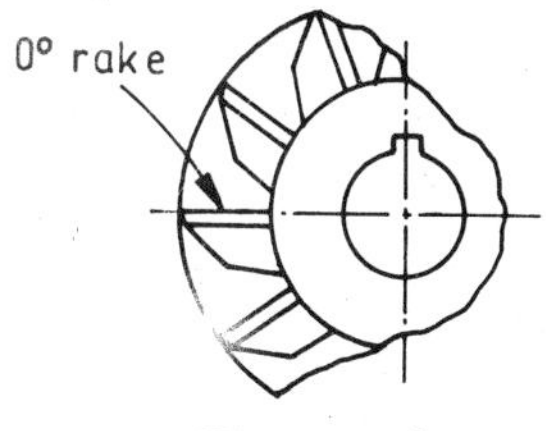

Fig. 1.52 (*b*)

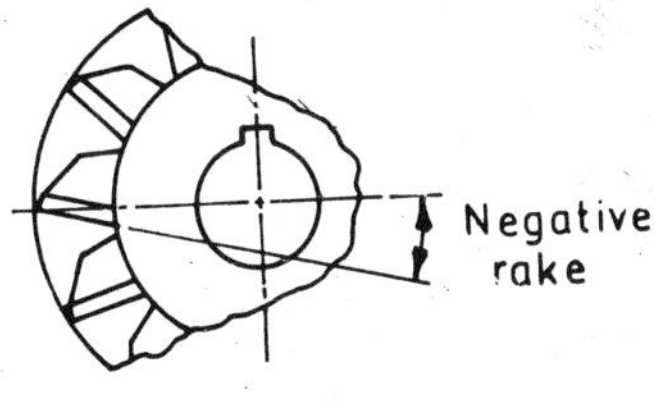

Fig. 1.52 (*c*)

Relief and rake angles are applied to milling cutters in the same manner in which they were applied to tool bits. The milling cutter is actually a multiple tool bit arrangement.

Table 1.13 (*a*) shows the approximate equivalents of tool geometry.

Table 1.13 (a)

Lathe and planer	*Milling cutter*	*Drill*	*Broach*
Back rake	Axial rake	Helix Angle	Hook angle
Side rake	Radial rake	Radial rake	Side rake
Side cutting edge angle	Corner Angle	Half point Angle	
End cutting edge angle	End cutting angle		
Side relief	Peripheral relief		Clearance
End relief	End relief	Lip relief	Clearance

1.31.1. Forces acting on a milling cutter

Fig. 1.52 (*d*) shows the forces acting on the tooth point of a plain slab cutter.

R = Resultant force

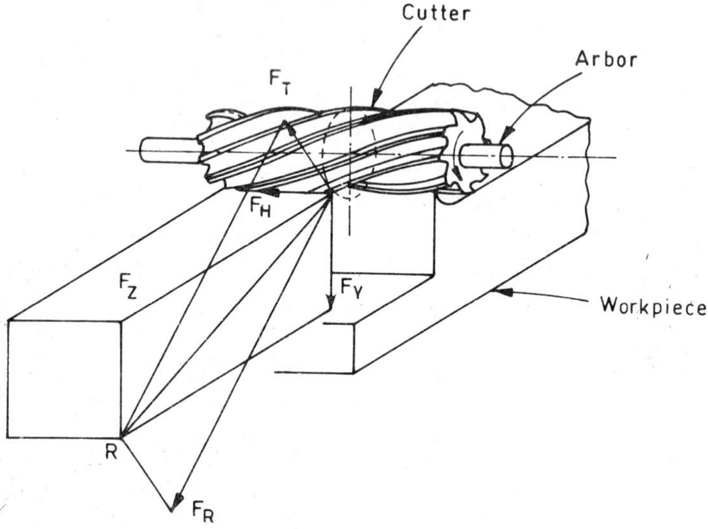

Fig. 1.52 (*d*)

It has three components as follows :

$$F_H = \text{Axial thrust}$$

$$F_y = \text{Vertical force}$$

$$F_Z = \text{Horizontal force}$$

$$R = \sqrt{F_H^2 + F_y^2 + F_Z^2}$$

$$F_T = \text{Power component}$$

It provides torque on arbor of milling cutter.

$$F_T = F_Z \cos \psi + F_y \sin \psi$$

$$F_r = \text{Radial thrust}$$

$$= F_Z \sin \psi - F_y \cos \psi$$

where ψ = Angle made by number of teeth in simultaneous engagement as shown in Fig. 1.52 (*e*)

Z_S = Number of teeth in simultaneous engagement

$$= \frac{\psi}{\psi_0}$$

where $\psi_0 = \dfrac{360}{Z}$ as showing Fig. 1.52 (*e*).

where Z = Total number of teeth.

Let d = Depth of cut, mm

D = Cutter diameter, mm

v = Feed rate, mm/min

Z = Number of teeth in cutter

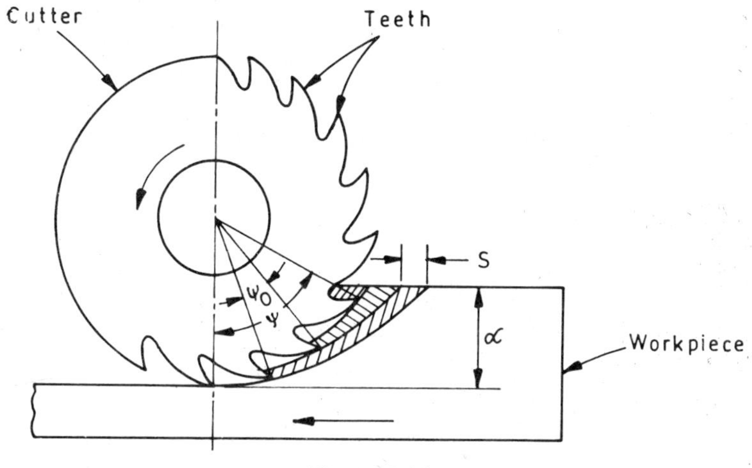

Fig. 1.52 (*e*)

N = R.P.M. of cutter

V = Cutter velocity, mm/min.

Then $\cos \psi = 1 - \frac{2d}{D}$, radians.

a_m = maximum undeformed chip thickness as shown in Fig. 1.52 (*f*).

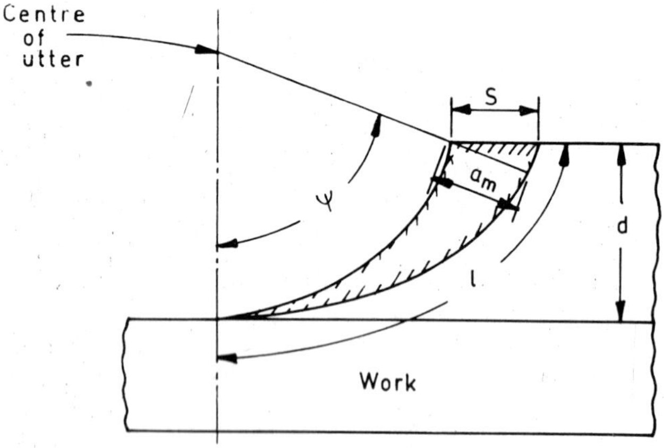

Fig. 1.52 (*f*)

$$S = \frac{v}{N.Z} \text{ feed, mm per tooth.}$$

θ = Helix angle of cutter

$$a_m = S \cdot \sin \psi \cdot \cos \theta$$

Now, l = Length of undeformed chip

$$= \frac{D}{2} \cos \theta \pm \frac{S}{2}$$

A = Maximum uncut area at any instant

$$= 2 \cdot B \cdot S \sqrt{\frac{d}{D} - \frac{d^2}{D^2}}$$

where B = Width of workpiece.

1.31.2. Milling cutter teeth

Following formula may be used to find number of teeth on a milling cutter $Z = \frac{D}{12} + 8$ provided D is more than 50 mm.

where D = cutter diameter in mm.

1.31.3. Feed for milling cutter

Feed per tooth for milling steel with H.S.S. cutters and cemented carbide cutters is indicated in Table 1.13 (*b*). The feed can be increased 1.5 to 2 times the feed values for milling steel.

Table 1.13 (b)

	Feed in mm. tooth for a depth of cut			
Types of cutter		up to 3 mm	3 to 5 mm	5 to 8 mm
Plain milling cutter	H.S.S.	0.08—0.05	0.08—0.05	0.05—0.03
	Carbide	0.15—0.12	0.12—0.10	0.10—0.05
Face milling cutter	H.S.S.	0.12—0.10	0.10—0.05	0.06—0.03
	Carbide	0.25—0.20	0.20—0.15	0.10—0.12
End milling cutter	H.S.S.	0.05—0.10	0.02—0.050	0.08—0.04
	Carbide	0.06—0.04	0.05—0.03	0.04—0.03

Milling machine feed mechanism is used for

(*i*) Logitudinal motion.

(*ii*) Cross motion.

(*iii*) Vertical up and down motion.

(*iv*) Rapid traverses for all the above motions.

Feed motions may be provided from

(*i*) the main motor through a telescopic shaft.

(*ii*) a sparate motor placed at the knee.

1.32. Milling Cutter Sharpening

Milling cutters are usually sharpened on universal tool and cutter grinder. During grinding the cutter should be so set that the tooth can be advanced to the grinding wheel. Grinding is done with the face of a cup wheel. The cutter tooth should be positioned in respect to the wheel so that required relief angle (γ) is obtained. The tooth face bears on a stationary tooth rest. Fig. 1.52 shows sharpening a face milling cutting by grinding the tooth flanks. The amount of offset (S) is determined by using the following relation :

$$S = \frac{2}{D} \sin \gamma$$

where D is the cutter diameter.

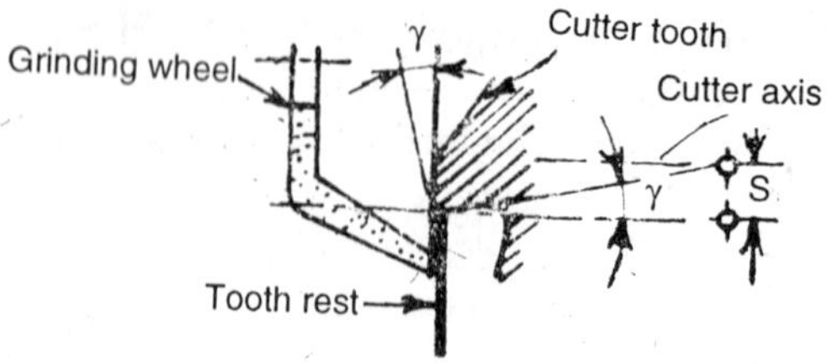

Fig. 1.52

1.33. Material for Milling Cutters

The common materials used for manufacturing milling cutters are as follows :

(*i*) High carbon steel (*ii*) High speed steel
(*iii*) Cemented carbides (*iv*) Stellite
(*v*) Ceramics.

High carbon steel is not commonly used except for a few cutters used for small scale production. High speed steel containing 18% tungsten is quite commonly used. Cemented carbides are very commonly used when milling cutters are to be run at higher speeds. Stellite is very useful material for milling cutters when particularly machining hard metals, forgings and castings. Tips made of ceramics are also used in milling cutters. Such cutters, because of their brittleness, are used for finishing operations and smaller cuts. They are commonly used to machine cast iron and bronze.

Cemented carbide tipped cutters have the following advantages :

(*i*) Their production capacity is high.
(*ii*) They can produce surface finish of high quality.
(*iii*) Hardened steels can be machined by them.
(*iv*) Their use leads to reduction in machining cost.

1.34. Number of Teeth in a Cutter

Milling cutters may be coarse tooth *i.e.* cutters with a large pitch and a small number of teeth or fine tooth *i.e.* cutters with a small pitch and a large number of teeth. The teeth are stronger in cutters with a coarse pitch. Coarse tooth straight flute cutters do not operate smoothly. Fine tooth cutters remove chips of relatively less thickness and are commonly used for finishing operation whereas coarse tooth remove thicker chip, resulting in removal of more metal in each cut and are used for roughing milling operation various empirical formulas are used to determine number of teeth in a cutter. A typical formula for calculating the number of teeth suitable for a cutter is as follows :

$$Z = A\sqrt{D}$$

where Z = Number of teeth

D = Diameter of cutter

A = Constant.

It depends upon the construction of cutter and machining conditions. Values of A are given in Table 1.14.

Table 1.14

Type of cutter	θ (*Helix angle*)	*A*
Solid cutters		
(*a*) Fine tooth	15 to 20°	2
(*b*) Coarse tooth	Upto 30°	1
Inserted blade cutters		
(*a*) Fine tooth	20°	0.9
(*b*) Coarse tooth	45°	0.8

1.35. Cutting Speed and Feed for Milling Cutter

Cutting Speed. It is the distance travelled per minute by the cutting edges of the cutter. It is expressed in metre per minute.

The cutting speed for milling cutter is found in the same way as for turning and drilling.

Let, D = Diameter of cutter in mm.

N = R.P.M. of cutter

V = Cutting speed

$$= \frac{\pi DN}{1000} \text{ metre/minute}$$

The cutting speed should be as high as possible constant with economics cutter life before it needs regrinding.

Feed. It is the rate at which the workpiece advances past the rotating cutter. Three types of feed are distinguished :

(*a*) Feed per tooth (f_1)

(*b*) Feed per cutter revolution (f_2).

(*c*) Table feed per minute (f_3).

These feeds are related by following equations.

Let T = Number of teeth on cutter

N = R.P.M. of cutter

f_1 = feed per tooth in mm

$f_2 = f_1 \times T$

$f_3 = f_2 \times N = f_1 \, . \, T \, . \, N$ mm/min.

Table 1.15 shows feed per tooth possible with various types of milling cutters.

Table 1.15. Feed for H.S.S. cutters

Cutter	*Feed per tooth (mm)*
Form cutter	0.05 to 0.2
Slotting cutter	0.5 to 0.15
End mill	0.1 to 0.25
Face mill	0.1 to 0.5
Spiral mill	0.05 to 0.2

The average value of cutting speed in metre per minute for H.S.S. cutter and cemented carbide cutter are shown in Table 1.16.

Table 1.16

Material to be machined	*Tool material*	
	H.S.S.	*Cemented carbide*
Aluminium	180—240	400—450
Brass soft	45—55	140
Copper	45—55	140
Gray cast iron	18—24	60
Cast iron hard	10—12	45
Mild steel	18—25	60
Hard steel	10—12	30

For a multipoint cutting tool such as milling cutter, the maximum feed per tooth is limited by the following factors :

(*i*) Cutting edge strength.

(*ii*) Rigidity and allowable deflection.

(*iii*) Surface finish required.

(*iv*) Tool chip space.

With increase in feed, the cutting force gets increased and this causes greater deflection between tool and work piece. Accuracy can not be maintained if deflection is large. Proper cutting fluid can permit higher feeds and increased speeds as well as attainment of better surface finish. Cutting fluid should be directed to the exact point where cutting is taking place.

For setting up the operating conditions for any multipoint cutting tool there are three important variable that can be adjusted. They are as follows :

(*i*) Cutting speed. (*ii*) Feed per cutting edge.
(*iii*) Cutting fluid.

1.36. Power Required at the Cutter

The horse power ($H.P_c$) required at the cutter depends on the volume of metal to be removed by the cutter per minute and varies for different materials.

$$H.P_c = \frac{Kfdb}{1,00,00}$$

where f = Feed in mm/min, d = Depth of cut in mm.
b = Width of cut in mm.
K = Constant varying according to the material being cut.

The values of K are shown in Table 1.17.

Table 1.17

Material to be cut	*Constant (K)*
Light alloy (Positive rake)	1.3
Copper (Positive rake)	2.6
Brass (Positive rake)	3.0
Cast iron (Positive rake)	3.0
Bronze (Positive rake)	5.0
Steel (Negative rake)	
Low carbon	5.0
High carbon	8.5

$$H.P_m = \text{Horse power at motor} = \frac{HP_c}{\eta}$$

The efficiency (η) of various milling machines is shown in Table 1.18.

Table 1.18

H.P. of the machine	*Efficiency (%)*
3	40
5	48
10	52
15	52
20	60
25	65
30	70
40	75

1.37. Machining Time

The machining time for plain milling and face milling is calculated at follows :

(*i*) **Plain Milling.** Fig. 1.53 shows milling operation being carried out by using plain milling cutter.

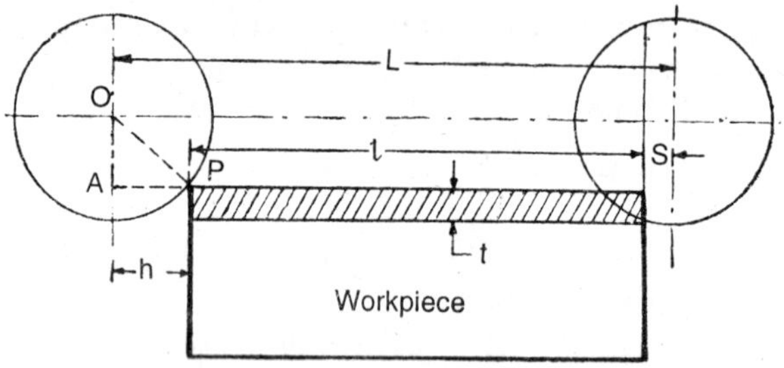

Fig. 1.53

Let h = Approach in mm.

l = Length of workpiece in mm.

s = Overrun of cutter in mm.

L = Total cutter travel in mm = $h + l + s$

D = Diameter of cutter ; t = Depth of cut

f = Feed/rev. in mm. ; N = R.P.M.

Then T = Machining time.

$$= \frac{L}{N \times f}$$

The approach h can be calculated as follows.

In triangle AOP

$$OP^2 = (OA)^2 + AP^2$$

$$\left(\frac{D}{2}\right)^2 = \left(\frac{D}{2} - t\right)^2 + h^2$$

$$h = \sqrt{t(D - t)}$$

(*ii*) **Face milling.** Fig. 1.54 shows milling operation being carried out by face milling cutter.

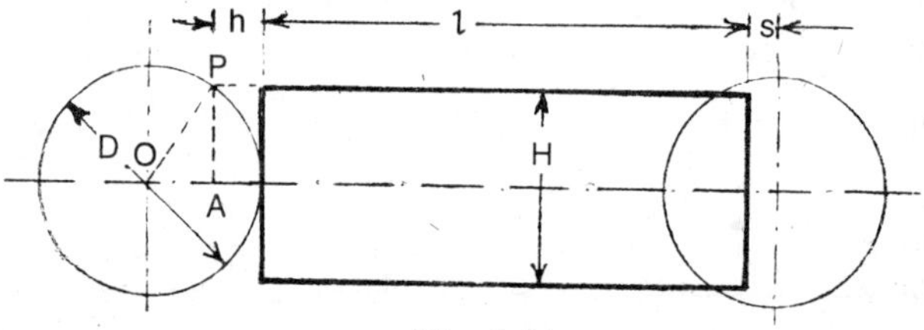

Fig. 1.54

l = Length of workpiece in mm.

h = Approach in mm. ; s = Overrun of cutter

$L = l + h + s$; f = Feed in mm/rev.

N = R.P.M.

$$T = \frac{L}{f \cdot N}$$

The approach h can be calculated as follows.

H = Width of workpiece, D = Diameter of cutter

$$OP^2 = OA^2 + AP^2$$

$$\left(\frac{D}{2}\right)^2 = \left(\frac{D}{2} - h\right)^2 + \left(\frac{H}{2}\right)^2$$

$$h = \frac{1}{2}[D - \sqrt{D^2 - H^2}].$$

1.37. (a) Turning/Milling data sheet

This data sheet indicates the following details of machine tool such as lathe, milling machine and cutting tool, workpiece etc.

1. Machine tool details

(*i*) Type (*ii*) Make

(*iii*) Power

(*iv*) Rigidity (*a*) Good (*b*) Fair (*c*) Poor

(*v*) Stiffness (*vi*) Coolant.

2. Workpiece details

(*i*) Material (*ii*) Strength

(*iii*) Hardness (*iv*) Dimensions

(*v*) Tolerance (*vi*) Surface conditions.

3. Tool details

(*i*) Material (*a*) Insert being used

(*ii*) Tool geometry/approach angle

(*iii*) Tool holder condition

(*a*) Good (*b*) Fair (*c*) New

(*iv*) Tool overhang

(*a*) Normal (*b*) Excessive.

4. Operation details

(*i*) Nature

(*a*) Turning (*b*) Copy turning

(*c*) Face milling (*d*) End milling etc.

(*ii*) Stage

(*a*) Roughing (*b*) Semi-finishing

(*c*) Finishing.

5. Machining data

(*i*) Spindle speed (*ii*) Cutting speed

(*iii*) Feed (*a*) Handfeed (*b*) Autofeed

(*iv*) Depth of cut (*v*) Metal removal rate

(*vi*) Surface finish (*vii*) Machining time

(*viii*) Number of parts made for insert

(*ix*) Wear pattern.

6. Chips

(*a*) Type

(*i*) Short (*ii*) Long

(*iii*) Broken (*iv*) Curved

(*v*) Ribbon type.

(*b*) Colour

(*i*) Grey (*ii*) Blue

(*iii*) Burnt.

1.37. (b) Broaching

Broaching is an operation in which a cutting tool with multiple *transverse* cutting edges (a broach) is pulled or pushed over a surface or through a hole. Each successive cutting edge removes a layer of metal, giving a steady approach to the required final shape. It is an operation designed to produce high-precision forms and the complex tools are expensive. The shapes produced may be flat surfaces but more often are holes of various forms or grooved components or the shaft of gears. Cutting speeds and feeds are low in this operation and adequate lubrication is essential.

In comparison with other types of machine tools, broaching machines are notable for their simple construction and operation. This is due to the fact that the shape of the surface produced in broaching depends upon the shape and arrangement of the cutting edges on the broach.

The primary cutting motion in broaching is a straight-line motion of either the broach, having cutting edges of a shape corresponding to the contour of the required surface, or of the work while the tool is held stationary. Broaching machines have no feed mechanisms since the feed feature is provided for by the gradual increase in height of the broach teeth (each tooth from the roughing to the finishing end is slightly larger than the preceding tooth).

Broaching machines are designed for machining external and internal surfaces of various contours in mass and large-lot production. These machines are distinguished for their exceptionally high output. They produce surfaces that are highly accurate in shape and size. Fig. 1.54 (*a*) shows typical internally broached shapes.

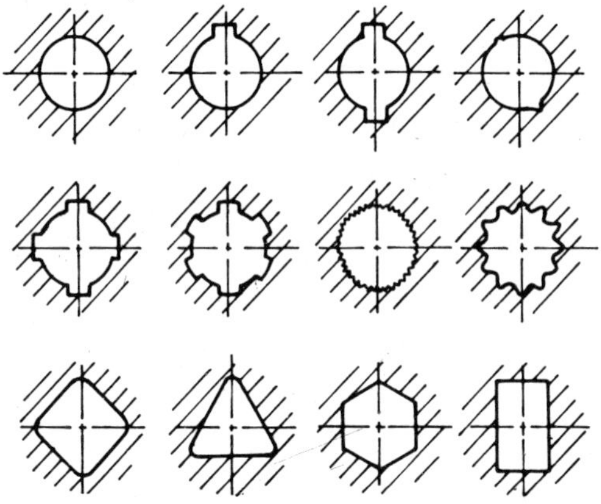

Fig. 1.54 (*a*)

1.37.1. Broaching Tool

A broaching tool or a broach has a series of multiple teeth. The main elements of a broaching tool are shown in Fig. 1.55. The first teeth are designed to do the heaviest cutting and are called roughing teeth. Next teeth are semi-finishing teeth which are followed by finishing teeth. The finishing teeth carry out finishing operation. Fig. 1.56 shows teeth details. The rake angle (face angle) of the tooth depends on the material to be cut and its hardness, toughness and ductility.

The values of face angle for different materials are as follows :

Material	*Face angle (Degrees)*
Aluminium	10
Brass	– 5—5
Cast iron	6—8
Steel (hard)	8—12
Steel (soft)	16—20

The land of tooth determines its strength. The pitch determines the length of cut and chip thickness which a broach can handle.

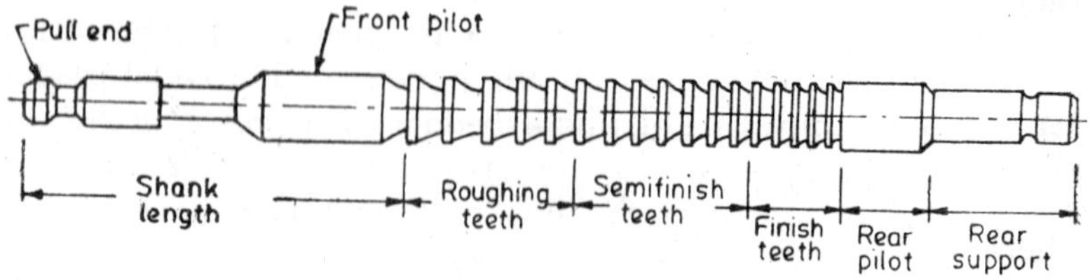

Fig. 1.55

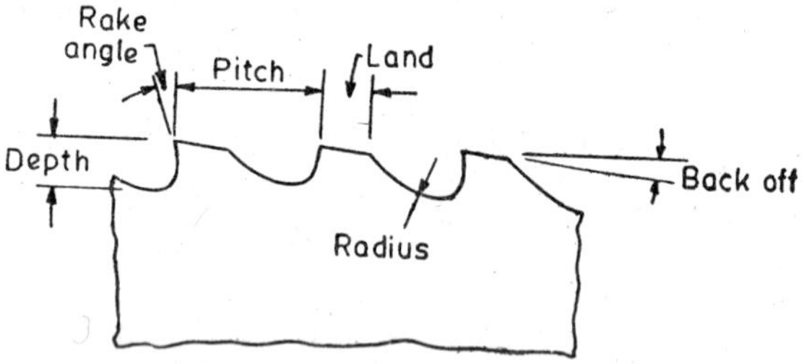

Fig. 1.56

During broaching operation the broach is either pulled or pushed by the broaching machine past the surface of the workpiece. In doing so each tooth of broach takes a small cut through the metal surface. Most broaches are made from 18-4-1 high speed steel, ground after hardening. Carbide broaches are used extensively in broaching cast iron.

1.37.2. Design elements

(*i*) **Length of broach.** The length of broach is calculated as follows :

$$L = L_1 + L_2 + L_3 + L_4 + L_5$$

where L_1 = Length of cutting portion = $p_1 \cdot Z_1$

where p_1 = Pitch of cutting teeth

Z_1 = Number of cutting teeth

L_2 = Length of finishing teeth = $p_2 \cdot Z_2$

where p_2 = Pitch of finishing teeth

Z_2 = Number of finishing teeth

L_3 = Length of pull end

L_4 = Length of neck

L_5 = Length of rear pilots

Values of L_3, L_4, L_5 depend on the standards, broaching fixture and work piece.

(*ii*) **Number of teeth.** The teeth provided on a broach are calculated as follows :

$$Z = \text{Total number of teeth}$$
$$= \frac{A}{d} + Z_1 + Z_2$$

where A = Amount of material to be removed
d = Depth of cut
Z_1 = Number of finishing teeth = 3 or 4
Z_2 = Number of safety teeth.

(*iii*) **Pitch of teeth.** It is determined as follows

$$p = \text{pitch}$$
$$= (1.25 \text{ to } 1.50)\sqrt{L} \text{ for plain broach}$$
$$= (1.45 \text{ to } 1.90)\sqrt{L} \text{ for progressive broach}$$

where L = Length of broached surface in mm.

(*iv*) **Cutting force (P_C).** The cutting force in broaching is found as follows

$$P_C = F\,\Sigma M$$

where P_C = Cutting force
F = Cutting force per mm of cutting edge length (kgf/mm)
ΣM = Total length of cutting edges of all the teeth in operation simultaneously (mm)

$$\Sigma M = \frac{\pi D Z_s}{Z_g} \text{ for cylindrical holes}$$

where D = Maximum diameter of teeth in mm
Z_g = Number of teeth in a group
Z_s = Number of teeth in operation simultaneously

$$\Sigma M = \frac{BN}{Z_g} \text{ for spline holes and key ways}$$

where B = Width of broached surface on work piece in mm
N = Number of splines on key ways.

The maximum broaching force is found as follows

$$P_{max} = k_1 \,.\, k_2 \,.\, d \,.\, b \,.\, \frac{l}{p}$$

where k_1 = Coefficient that takes into account friction = 1.1 to 1.3
k_2 = Specific cutting resistance (kg/cm^2)
d = Depth of cut per tooth in cm
b = Width of cut in cm
l = Length of tool entry in cm
p = Pitch of cutting edges in cm

(*v*) **Power required for broaching.** The power required during broaching is determined as follows

$$P = \text{Power}$$

$$= \frac{P_C V}{7200} \text{ k. Watt.}$$

where P_C = Cutting force in N

V = Cutting speed in m/min.

(*vi*) **Cutting speed.** The cutting speed is the speed of broach movement. It depends on material and type of surface being broached.

$$V = \frac{EK}{T^x S^y} \text{ m/min.}$$

where E = Co-efficient characterising the processing conditions

K = Co-efficient that takes into account broach material

T = Tool life in minutes

S = Cut per tooth in mm.

Values of x, y depend on broach material and other processing conditions.

For broaching round holes in steel

$$E = 12, x = 0.6, y = 0.6$$

$$K = 1 \text{ to } 1.5 \text{ and } T = 80 \text{ to } 100 \text{ minutes.}$$

Value of cutting speed in broaching usually varies from 1.5 m to 20 m per minute.

(*vii*) **Rise per tooth.** Rise per tooth depends on the following factors :

(*a*) Shape of hole

(*b*) Type of material of work piece

(*c*) Force available at the machine

(*d*) Size of hole.

$$h = \text{Rise per tooth.}$$

$$= 0.025 \text{ mm to } 0.16 \text{ mm.}$$

(*viii*) **Depth of tooth (H)**

$$H = 1.13 \sqrt{fLk}$$

where f = Difference in height between two successive cutting teeth

= 0.02 to 0.12 mm.

L = Length of work piece

K = Constant
= 3 to 5 for surface broaches
≐ 6 to 10 for internal broaches.

(*ix*) **Neck diameter.** It is 0.3 to 1.0 mm less than shank diameter.

(*x*) **Width of land.** It varies between 2.5 to 4.5 mm.

(*xi*) **Groove radius.** It varies between 2.5 to 5 mm.

(*xii*) **Broaching allowance.** It is calculated as follows

$$A = \text{Broaching allowance} = 0.005D + (0.1 \text{ to } 0.2)\sqrt{L}$$

where D = Basic diameter of hole in mm.
L = Length of hole to be broached in mm.

In terms of pitch the following commonly used values may be adopted.

Tooth height	= (0.35 to 0.40) p.
Land width	= (0.3 to 0.4) p.
Groove radius	= (0.2 to 0.25) p.
Flute angle	= 30° to 36°
Groove angle	= 45° to 50°.

1.37.3. Broaching machines

Broaching machines are classified into the principal types as follows : (*a*) according to their application—as general- purpose and special machines ; (*b*) according to their purpose—as internal and surface broaching machines ; (*c*) according to the direction and nature of the primary cutting motion—as horizontal, vertical and continuous broaching machines ; and (*d*) according to the number of main slides or stations—as single-, double- or multiple-slide machines.

1.38. Improving Cutting Efficiency

The cutting efficiency during machining can be improved by using following methods :

(*i*) Reduction of tool-face friction.

(*ii*) By reducing chip length by means of chip breakers.

(*iii*) By improving surface finish of tool face by honing or chrome plating.

(*iv*) By increasing cutting speeds.

(*v*) Increased depth of cut increases cutting efficiency by a small amount.

1.39. Power Distribution

Out of total power supplied to the machine tool the power available at the cutter depends upon the type of machine tool. A typical power distribution for a milling machine and a lathe is as follows.

Milling Machine

Electrical power input	= 100%
Losses in motor	= 16%
Losses in spindle transmission	= 18%
Power to feed	= 21%
Power available at cutter	= 45%

Lathe

Electrical power input	= 100%
Losses in motor	= 11%
Losses in machine	= 18.5%
Power to feed	= 0.5%
Power available at tool	= 70%.

1.40. To Determine Power Rating of Electric Motor

The required power of main drive is determined on the basis of useful power calculated for the most effective cutting conditions. In designing general purpose machine tools the useful power is calculated for the maximum cutting speeds and feeds.

$$N_m = \text{Required power rating of electric motor}$$
$$= N + N_f$$

where N = Useful power

N_f = Power lost in overcoming friction

η = Efficiency of main drive.

$$= \frac{N}{N_m}$$

The efficiency (η) may range from 0.7 to 0.85 for machine tools with a rotary primary motion having a single motor drive.

1.41. Cutting Tool Design

The design of a cutting tool means determination of all the dimensions and shapes of all the elements of a cutting tool by carrying out calculations and graphical construction. The cutting of metals with a single point cutting tool is fully applicable to any kind of cutting tool since all tools remove a certain layer of stock and impart the required shape, size and surface finish to the machined part. The cutting teeth of all cutting tools whatever may be their shapes and purpose resemble to the point of single point tool.

The common procedure carried out during the design of cutting tool consists of following calculations :

(*i*) To determine forces acting on cutting surface of the tool.

(*ii*) To find out optimum tool geometry.

(*iii*) To select suitable material for making cutting elements of the tool.

(*iv*) To find suitable shapes of cutting and mounting elements of tool and to determine the tolerance on the dimensions of cutting and mounting elements of tool depending on machining accuracy required on work piece.

(*v*) To determine strength and rigidity of mounting and cutting elements to tool.

(*vi*) To prepare a working drawing of tool.

Cutting tool design depends on the following factors :

(*i*) Workpiece material

(*ii*) Cutting tool material

(*iii*) Machining variables such as

(*a*) cutting speed (*b*) feed

(*c*) depth of cut

(*iv*) Cutting force

(*v*) Accuracy desired

(*vi*) Surface treatment of cutting tool.

1.42. Friction between Chip and Tool

Friction between the chip and tool plays a significant role in cutting process. It should be as low as possible friction can be reduced in the following ways :

(*i*) Improved tool finish and sharpness of the cutting edge.

(*ii*) Use of low friction tool material.

(*iii*) Improved tool geometry.

(*iv*) Use of cutting fluids.

(*v*) High sliding speeds.

1.43. Friction in Metal Cutting

During metal cutting the mean co-efficient of friction between the chip and the tool can vary considerably and is affected by changes in cutting speed, rake angle etc. This variance of mean co-efficient of friction results from the very high normal pressures that exist at the chip-tool interface.

Metallic surfaces consist of numerous hills and valleys. When cutting tool and metallic surfaces come in contact, the contact is established at the summits of only a few irregularities in each surface as shown in Fig. 1.56 (*a*).

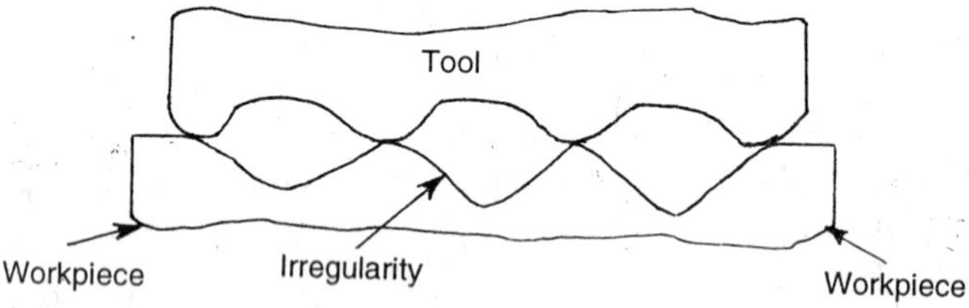

Fig. 1.56 (*a*)

When a normal load is applied, yielding occurs at the tips of the contacting asperities and the real area of contact increases until it is capable of supporting the applied load. Usually the real area of contact is only a small fraction of the apparent area of contact.

$$A_r = \frac{N}{\sigma y} \quad ...(1)$$

where A_r = Real area of contact

N = Normal force

σy = Yield stress of softer metal.

The adhesion resulting from the intimate metallic contact of these asperities has been termed as welding process and when sliding takes place, a force is required for the continuous shearing of the welded junctions at the tips of these asperities. Frictional force is given by

P = Frictional force

$$A_r = \frac{P}{f_s} \quad ...(2)$$

where f_s = Shear strength of softer metal.

From equation (1) and equation (2), we get

$$\frac{N}{\sigma y} = \frac{P}{f_s}$$

$$\mu = \frac{P}{N} = \frac{f_s}{\sigma y}$$

where μ = co-efficient of friction. This shows that co-efficient of friction is independent of the apparent contact area.

Since ratio $\frac{f_s}{\sigma y}$ is nearly constant for a given metal therefore co-efficient of friction will also remain constant.

1.44. Types of Tool Bits

The various types of tool bits shown in Fig. 1.56 (*b*), are as follows :

1. Parting tool.
2. Turning tool.
3. Right hand turning tool.
4. Left hand turning tool.
5. Radius tool.
6. Threading tool.
7. Chamber tool.

A right hand turning tool operates from right to left and that a left hand turning tool operates from left to right. Only those edges of tool which are involved in the cutting operation should touch the workpiece. All other faces should be ground to recede so that they do not interfere with the cutting action.

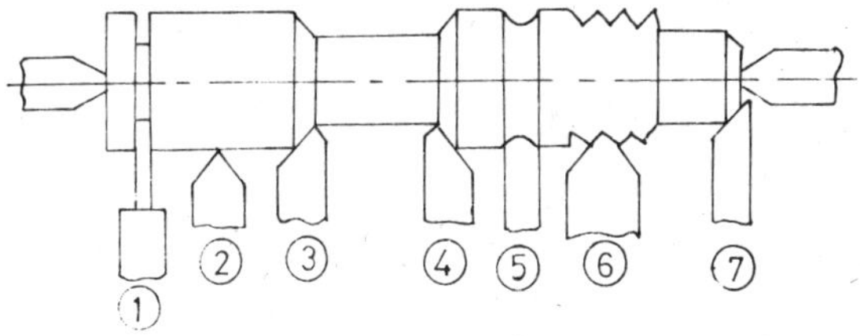

Fig. 1.56 (*b*)

1.45. High Speed Steel (H.S.S.) Tools Bits

The hardened and ground H.S.S. bits are available in the following general sizes :

6 × 6 × 100 mm. 8 × 8 × 100 mm.

10 × 10 × 100 mm. 12 × 12 × 150 mm.

16 × 16 × 150 mm. 20 × 20 × 150 mm.

25 × 25 × 150 mm.

H.S.S. tool bits have an average chemical composition as follows :

C = 0.75%

W (Tungsten) = 18%

Cr. (Chromium) = 4%

V (Vanadium) = 1%

Cobalt = 5 or 10%

(5% cobalt H.S.S. is used for free machining steel whereas 1% cobalt H.S.S. is used for high tensile steel).

1.46. Specifying a Single Point Tool

The following details should be specified while ordering a single point tool :

(*i*) Shape of the tool

(*ii*) Size of the shank

(*iii*) Grade of the carbide tip

(*iv*) Direction of cutting

(*a*) Right Hand (R.H.)

(*b*) Left Hand (L.H.).

1.47. Care and Maintenance of Cutting Tools

A properly maintained cutting tools has more life. The main causes of deterioration of a tool are as follows :

(*i*) *Damaging during use.* It is always desired to use tool properly. Wrong application of tool damages the tool.

(*ii*) *Deterioration when not in use.* The tools are deteriorated because of corrosion when not in use keeping a light film of oil on tools prevents the tools from rusting.

(*iii*) *Damage during storage.* Damage during storage usually results when cutting tools are piled up together in a tool box or drawer. Edged tools are best storaged on a panel in clips or racks tool remaining separate from the next.

(*iv*) *Loss of sharpness.* When the tool looses sharpness at the cutting edge, it should be sharpened in time.

1.48. Surface Treatment of Tools

Steel tools are given surface treatment to reduce sliding friction and to increase abrasion resistance by physically and chemically altering the surface of the tool.

The various surface treatment processes are as follows :

(*i*) *Nitriding.* In this surface treatment a surface layer of about 0.025 mm thick that is high in complex iron nitrides can be produced by treating a finished tool in a NaCN—kCN bath at about 1000°F for about $\frac{1}{2}$ hour. Surface layer so produced can have hardness up to 1000 Brinell hardness. This surface treatment is generally used for tools taking light cuts such as broaching bits and taps.

(*ii*) *Lapping and super finishing.* These surface treatment processes produce a fine finish of the order of 1 to 2 microns. Tools with such surface finishes are found to perform better.

(*iii*) *Chromium plating.* By this surface treatment process a layer of about 0.003 mm can be produced on tool surface. The hardness of such layer is estimated to be nearly 800 Brinell.

(*iv*) *Carburising.* By this surface treatment process a high carbon layer of nearly one millimeter thick can be produced by heating the tool surround by charcoal at 1950°F for about 30 minutes. The layer so produced is very hard. However the layer is brittle and the tool performance is not much improved.

(*v*) *Oxidation.* In this surface treatment process the tool is treated in an aqueous bath of NaOH and $NaNO_2$ at 285°F from 5 to 10 minutes. The layer of black Fe_3O_4 so produced is nearly 0.005 mm thick and provides a lower coefficient of friction because the oxide layer can hold oil better than polished surface.

During the last three decades surface enhancement technologies like

(*i*) Chemical vapor deposition (CVD)

(*ii*) Physical vapor deposition (PVD)

(*iii*) Carbide sputtring etc. have been commonly used.

These processes increase tool life and enhance performance of cutting tools. However these surface treatment methods are quite expensive.

A low cost high performance surface enhancement technology for improving performance and extending the life of cutting tool is molybdenum.

Di-sulphide (MOS_2) spray coating. This coating has a very low coefficient of friction and high wear resistance.

While applying the MOS_2 spray coating following method should be adopted.

(*i*) Surface to which coating is to be applied should be absolutely clean and dry.

Oil and grease films should be removed by solvent cleaning.

(*ii*) Burrs on the cutting edges should be removed.

(*iii*) Apply a single coat of spray from spray bottle uniformly so that the entire cutting portion of the tool is coated.

The film thickness is nearly 2 to 4 microns. Allow the tool to cure MOS_2 film at ambient temperature for about 30 minutes.

(*iv*) Whenever the tool is reground, this produce should be repeated for recoating of tool.

1.49. Measurement of Tool-chip Interface Temperature

Several methods have been used to measure temperature at the chip tool interface.

Commonly used methods are as follows :

1. Tool-work thermocouple method

In this method the tool-work contact area serves as the hot junction in a thermo-electric circuit and the e.m.f. generated is proportional to its temperature. The e.m.f. developed is measured by a suitable millivoltmeter.

The e.m.f. in the thermoelectric circuit depends only on the difference in temperature between the hot and cold functions. Fig. 1.56 (*c*) shows the thermocouple technique to measure the tool chip interface temperature for a work piece fitted on a lathe in which the chip and tool junction constitutes the hot junction while *A* and *B* the cold junction remain at room temperature.

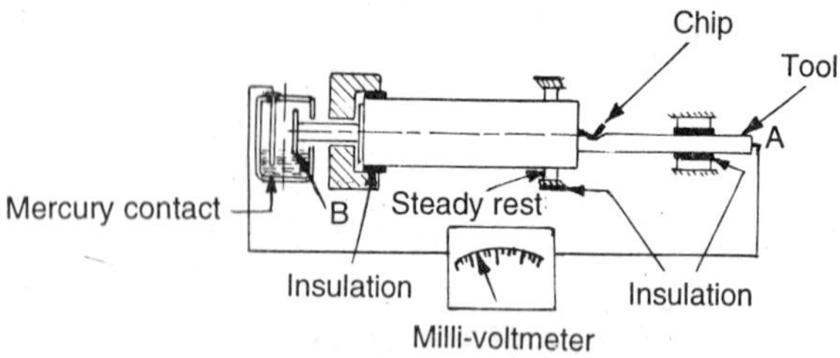

Fig. 1.56 (*c*)

Tool life is more dependent upon the temperature reached at the tool chip interface than the total amount of heat following into the tool or work.

The rate of tool wear is generally observed to increase with increased tool temperature.

2. Embedded thermocouple method

Fig. 1.56 (*d*) shows the embedded thermocouple for an H.S.S. tool. The hole in the tool bit is produced using a copper wire in a spark erosion machine. A miniature thermocouple element of commercial make is used. For the welding of thermocouple to the root of the hole, a spark welding set up is used. The principle of this method is to strike a high voltage between the thermocouple leads and underside of the hole, made in the tool to produce a spark at the contract point. Thus, the thermocouple gets automatically welded.

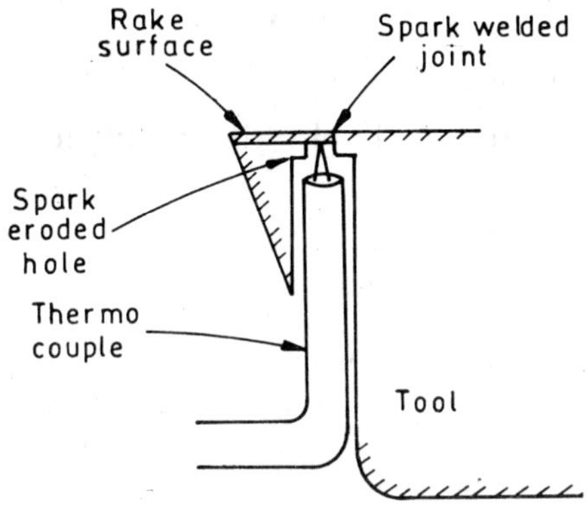

Fig. 1.56 (*d*)

Fig. 1.56 (*e*) shows typical variation of e.m.f. in millivolt (mv) and temperature in °C for chromel constantant thermocouple.

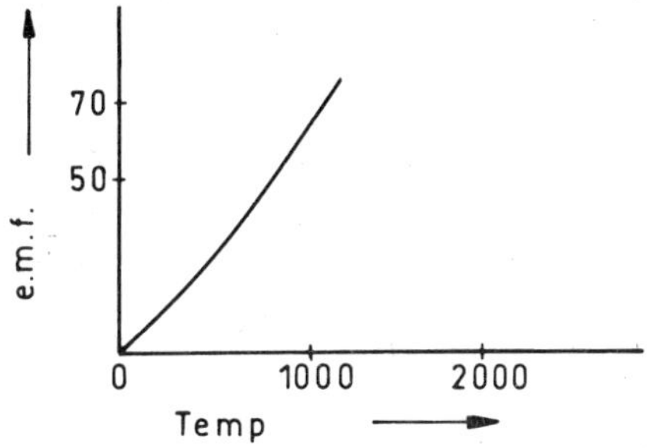

Fig. 1.56 (*e*)

3. Infrared photographic method

Fig. 1.56 (*f*) shows this method. This technique of infrared photography is a field method, which gives the temperature

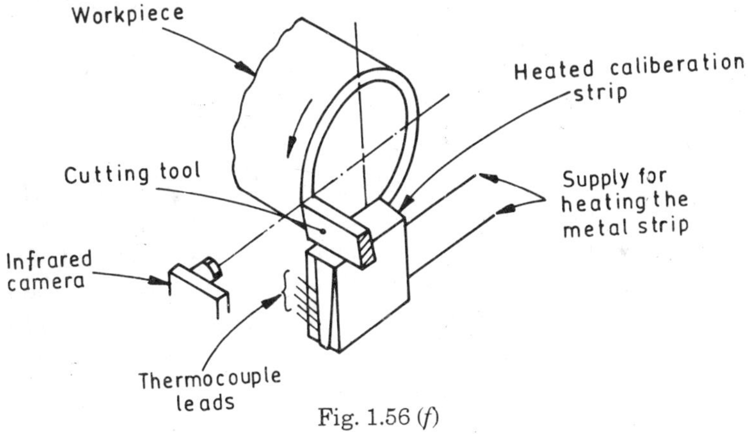

Fig. 1.56 (*f*)

distribution in the whole field, although the final interpretation may be done point by point.

Boothroyd photographed simultaneously a preheated tubular workpiece during orthogonal cutting in a lathe along with the tool used and a heated strip of metal (for calibration purpose).

In this method a tapered strip of Cu—Ni alloy through which a heavy current was passed, giving a linear variation of temperature. The strip temperature was measured using a set of eight standard thermocouples in the temperature range 300—800°C. Infrared photographs were taken and as the temperature distribution along the heated strip can be obtained by thermocouple readings, the optical density of the exposed plates after processing can be calibrated against temperature. Using a micro-densitometer (0.01 mm diameter aperture) the variation in optical density was explored and it was possible to plot the temperature distribution in the tool, chip and workpiece.

4. Calorimetric method

This method is shown in Fig. 1.56 (*g*). It is a simple method for the overall evaluation of heat flow rather than for the accurate measurement of temperature. It is based upon the conservation equation.

As shown for drilling operation

$$T_h = \frac{T + m_w (T - T_w)}{m_h C_h}$$

where T_h = Average chip temperature (°C)

T = Temperature of the calorimeter system with water and chip (°C)

T_w = Initial temperature of water (°C)

m_w = Weight of water (gms)

m_h = Weight of chip (gms)

C_h = Thermal capacity of chip.

This method has been successfully used by Schmidt during the drilling of metals. Here, the experiments were conducted in three stages using three setups, to evaluate the total heat generated in drilling, heat dissipation by the drill, and, lastly, the heat carried away by the chip. From these three data, it is possible to find separately the average tool, chip, and work temperatures.

Fig. 1.56 (*g*) (*i*) shows total heat generated, Fig. 1.56 (*ii*) shows heat of tool and Fig. 1.56 (*iii*) shows heat of chips.

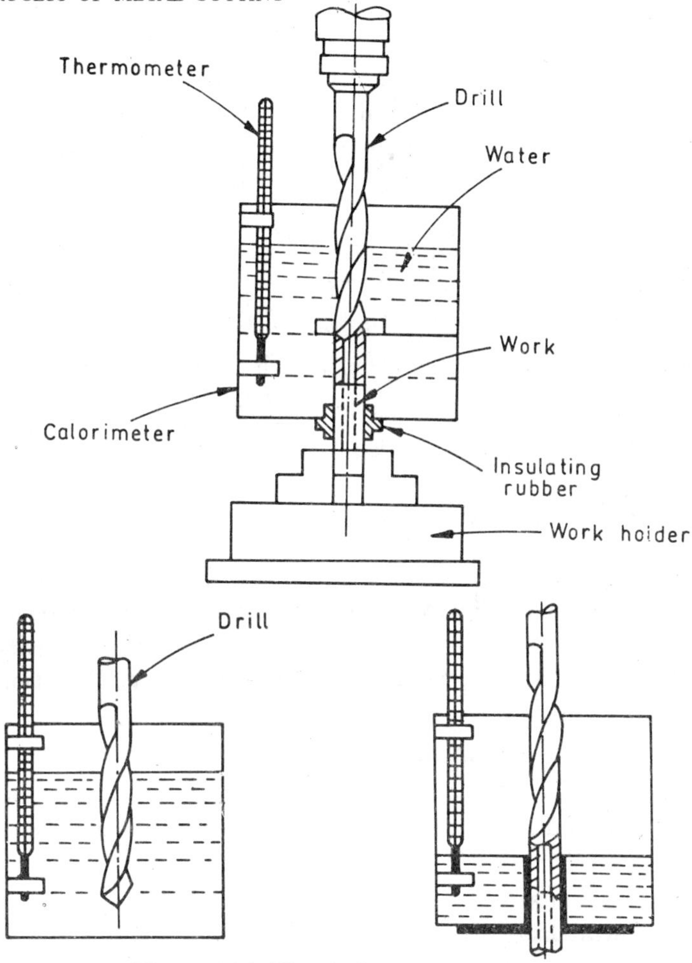

Fig. 1.56 (*g*). Fig. (*i*) shows total heat generated,
Fig. (*ii*) shows heat of tool and Fig. (*iii*) shows heat of chips.

1.50. Design of a Single Point Lathe Tool

The design on the cutting tool depends upon the cutting forces acting on the cutting surfaces of the tool and rigidity of the machine on which cutting tool is used. The shank of a single point tool may be rectangular, square or rounding cross-section. The rectangular cross-section is commonly used because the reduction in strength of shank (at section YY of a single point cutting tool as shown in Fig. 1.56 (*h*)) is less than for a square shank when a seat is cut for a tip.

F_H = Cutting force

Let B = Width of shank

H = Height of shank.

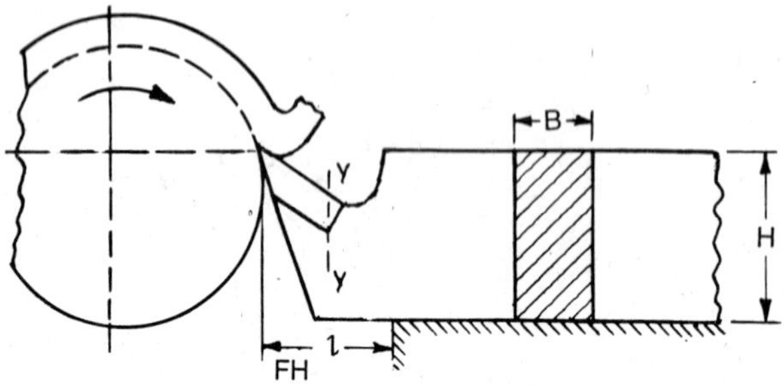

Fig. 1.56 (*h*)

For rectangular cross-section the relations between B and H are as follows :

$$\frac{H}{B} = 1.25 \text{ for roughing operations}$$

$$\frac{H}{B} = 1.6 \text{ for semifinishing and finishing operations.}$$

The minimum permissible size of the shank cross-section on strength basis is calculated by equating the actual bending moment to the maximum moment permitted by cross-section of the shank.

M_1 = Bending moment due to cutting force F_H

$= F_H \times l$

where l = Cutting tool overhang.

(l = 1 to 1.5 H)

M_2 = Maximum moment permitted by the cross-section of the shank

$= f \times Z$

where f = Permissible bending stress for the shank material

Z = Section modulus of the tool shank

$$\therefore \quad M_1 = M_2$$

$$F_H \times l = f \times Z$$

For rectangular cross-section of tool shank

$$Z = \frac{BH^2}{6}$$

$$\therefore \quad F_H \times l = f \times \frac{BH^2}{6}$$

$$BH^2 = \frac{6F_H \, . \, l}{f}$$

$$H = \sqrt{\frac{6F_H \, . \, l}{f \, . \, B}}$$

For square cross-section shank

$$B = H.$$

$$F_H \times l = f \cdot \frac{BH^2}{6} = f \cdot \frac{B \cdot B^2}{6}$$

$$B^3 = \frac{6F_H\, l}{f}$$

$$B = \sqrt[3]{\frac{6F_H \cdot l}{f}}$$

For round cross-section shank

$$Z = \frac{\pi}{32} D^3$$

where D = Diameter of shank.

$$l \times F_H = fZ = f \cdot \frac{\pi}{32} D^3$$

$$D^3 = \frac{32 \cdot F_H \cdot l}{\pi \times f}$$

$$D = \sqrt[3]{\frac{32F_H \cdot l}{\pi f}}$$

Square shank tools are commonly used for boring machines, screw machines and turret lathes. Round shank tools are generally used for boring and thread cutting operations.

Example 1.0. *In orthogonal cutting of a mild steel bar on a lathe the feed (f_1) used is 0.3 mm per revolution and the depth of cut (t) is 2 mm. Determine the cross-section of a rectangular tool shank if the allowable stress in the shank material is 7 kg/m² and the cutting force (F_H) can be calculated by the relation $F_H = 200 \times f_1^{0.75} \times t$.*

Solution. Let H = Height of a shank

B = Width of shank

$$\frac{H}{B} = 1.16 \text{ (assume)}$$

we know
$$H = \frac{\sqrt{6F_H \cdot l}}{f \cdot B}$$

where F_H = cutting $= 200 \times f_1^{0.75} \times t$

$= 200 \times 0.3^{0.75} \times 2 = 170$ kg.

l = Cutting tool overhang = 1.25 H (assume)

$f = 7$ kg/mm²

$$H = \sqrt{\frac{6 \times 170 \times 1.25H}{7 \times \dfrac{H}{1.6}}}$$

$$H = 17 \text{ mm.}$$

$$B = \frac{H}{1.6} = \frac{17}{1.6} = 10.6 \text{ mm.} \quad \textbf{Ans.}$$

Example 1.1. *Determine the spindle speed for a high steel drill 12 mm diameter cutting medium carbon steel at 28 m/min.*

Solution. $V = 28$ m/min

D = Diameter of drill = 12 mm.

N = R.P.M. of spindle

$$V = \frac{\pi DN}{1000}\ ;\ 28 = \frac{\pi \,.\, 12 \,.\, N}{1000}$$

N = 743 R.P.M. **Ans.**

Example 1.2. *Determine the machining time to drill a hole of 20 mm diameter in a workpiece 25 mm thick by a drill at a cutting speed of 30 metre/min with a feed of 0.2 mm/rev.*

Solution. L = Length of axial travel of drill in mm

= Thickness of workpiece + 0.3 D

where D = Hole diameter

$L = 25 + 0.3 \times 20 = 25 + 6 = 31$ mm

V = Cutting speed = 30 metre per min

$$V = \frac{\pi DN}{1000}\ ;\ 30 = \frac{\pi \times 20 \times N}{1000}$$

N = 477 R.P.M.

T = Machining time

f = feed /rev = 0.2 mm/rev.

$$T = \frac{L}{N \times f} = \frac{31}{477 \times 0.2} \text{ minute}$$

$$= \frac{31}{477 \times 0.2} \times 60 = 19.5 \text{ seconds.} \quad \textbf{Ans.}$$

Example 1.3. *A 30 mm H.S.S. drill is used to drill a hole in a cast iron block 100 mm thick. Determine the time required to drill the hole if feed is 0.3 mm/rev. Assume an over travel of drill as 4 mm. The cutting speed is 20 metre/min.*

Solution. D = diameter of drill = 30 mm

$$V = \text{cutting speed} = \frac{\pi DN}{1000}$$

$$20 = \frac{\pi \,.\, 30 \,.\, N}{1000}$$

N = 202 R.P.M. ; h = approach

= 0.3 D (assume) = 0.3 × 30 = 9 mm

s = Over-travel = 4 mm ; L = Total length

= h + S + Thickness of work piece

= 9 + 4 + 100 = 113 mm.

T = Machining Time

$$= \frac{L}{fN} = \frac{113}{0.3 \times 203} \quad \text{where } f = \text{feed}$$

= 1.85 minutes.

Example 1.4. *Calculate the power required to drill 20 mm diameter hole in mild steel at a feed of 0.25 mm / rev and at a drill speed 300 R.P.M. Determine also the volume of metal removed per unit of energy.*

Solution. D = hole diameter = 20 mm

f = feed = 0.25 mm/rev.

N = 300 R.P.M.

T_1 = Torque = $C.\, f^{0.75}\, D^{1.8}$

where, C = Constant = 0.36 for mild steel.

$$T_1 = 0.36 \times 0.25^{0.75} \times 20^{1.8} = 27.96 \text{ newton-m.}$$

P = Power

$$= \frac{2\pi N T_1}{60{,}000} = \frac{2\pi \times 300 \times 27.96}{60{,}000} = 0.879 \text{ kW.}$$

Volume of metal removed per minute

= Area of hole × Feed × Speed

$$= \frac{\pi}{4} \times 20^2 \times 2.25 \times 300 = \mathbf{23550\ mm^3.}$$

$$\text{Energy consumption } = \frac{23550}{879} = 21 \text{ mm}^2\text{/watt minute. } \textbf{Ans.}$$

Example 1.5. *(a) A carbide face milling cutter of 200 mm diameter is used take one cut across the face of a block of aluminium which is 200 mm wide. The length of block is 450 mm. If a feed of 0.75 mm / rev is used how long will it take to machine one cut on the block. The total travel is 12 mm. The cutting speed is 320 meter / minute.*

(b) Calculate the time taken if the diameter of cutter is 300 mm.

Solution.

(*a*) D = Diameter of cutter = 200 mm

H = Width of block = 200 mm

l = Length of block = 450 mm

f = Feed = 0.75 mm-rev.

s = Overrun of cutter = 12 mm.

As the diameter of cutter is equal to width of block, (Fig. 1.57).

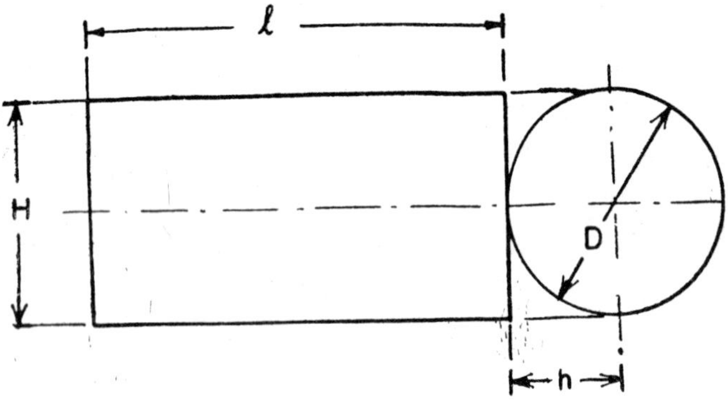

Fig. 1.57

$\therefore$ h = Approach

$$= \frac{D}{2} = \frac{200}{2} = 100 \text{ mm.}$$

N = R.P.M. of cutter

$$V = \text{cutting speed} = \frac{\pi DN}{1000}$$

$$320 = \pi \times \frac{200}{1000} \times N$$

N = 510 R.P.M.

Total length, $L = l + H + s = 450 + 100 + 12 = 562$ mm.

$$T = \text{machining time} = \frac{562}{0.75 \times 510}$$

= 1.45 minutes. **Ans.**

(*b*) D = Diameter of cutter = 300 mm.

In this case the diameter of cutter is more than the width of block

$$\therefore \quad h = \text{Approach} = \frac{1}{2}[D - \sqrt{D^2 - H^2}]$$

$$= \frac{1}{2}[300 - \sqrt{300^2 - 200^2}] = 38 \text{ mm.}$$

$$\therefore \quad L = \text{Total length} = l + h + S$$

$$= 450 + 38 + 12 = 500 \text{ mm.}$$

$$V = \frac{\pi DN}{1000}$$

$$320 = \frac{\pi \times 300 \times N}{1000}$$

$$N = 340$$

$$T = \text{Machining time}$$

$$T = \frac{L}{f \,.\, N} = \frac{500}{0.75 \times 340} = 1.97 \text{ minutes. } \textbf{Ans.}$$

Example 1.6. *A carbide milling cutter 250 mm in diameter is used to cut a block of mild steel with a plain cutter. The block is 500 mm long. If the feed is 0.50 mm / rev and depth of cut is 1.2 mm, determine the time required to take one cut. The over travel is 16 mm. The cutting speed is 80 metre per minute.*

Solution. D = Diameter of cutter = 250 mm.

f = feed = 3.5 mm/rev.

l = Length of block = 500 mm.

t = Depth of cut = 1.2 mm

s = Over-travel = 16 mm.

V = Cutting speed = 80 metre/minute

N = R.P.M.

$$V = \frac{\pi DN}{1000}$$

$$80 = \frac{\pi \,.\, 250 \,.\, N}{1000}$$

$$N = 102 \text{ R.P.M.}$$

$$h = \text{Approach} = \sqrt{t\,(D - t)}$$

$$= \sqrt{1.2\,(250 - 1.2)} = 17.3 \text{ mm.}$$

$$L = \text{Total length} = l + h + s$$

$$= 500 + 17.8 + 16 = 533.3 \text{ mm.}$$

$$T = \text{Machining time}$$

$$= \frac{L}{f \,.\, N} = \frac{533.3}{0.5 \times 102} = 10.45 \text{ minutes. } \textbf{Ans.}$$

Example 1.7. *Determine the horse power required to face mill a block of grey cast iron 125 mm wide, using a tungsten carbide cutter 150 mm in diameter and having eight tooth. The depth of cut is*

3 mm and a chip thickness of 0.25 mm is to be used. The cutting speed is 60 m / min and the specific horse power required for cast iron is 0.03 H.P. / cm^3 / min.

Solution. V = cutting speed = 60 m/min.

Now $$V = \frac{\pi DN}{1000}$$

$$60 = \frac{\pi \times 150 \times N}{1000}$$

where D = cutter diameter

N = R.P.M. of cutter

$\therefore$ $N = 128$

Now f_1 = feed per tooth (chip thickness) = 0.25 mm.

f_2 = feed per cutter revolution

$= f_1 \times$ Number of teeth $= f_1 \times 8 = 0.25 \times 8$

f_3 = feed per minute $= f_2 \times N$

$= 0.25 \times 8 \times 128$ mm/minute

= 256 mm/minute = 25.6 cm/minute.

The metal removal rate (w)

w = Width of workpiece × Depth of cut × Feed per minute

$= 125 \times 0.3 \times 25.6$ cm^3/minute

= 96 cm^3/minute

Horse power required = $96 \times 0.03 = 2.88$. **Ans.**

Example 1.8. *The feed of an 8-tooth face mill cutter is 0.325 mm per tooth at 200 R.P.M. The material cut is 300 BHN Steel.*

If the depth of the cut is 3 mm and width is 100 mm, calculate the following :

(a) B.P. at the cutter

(b) H.P. at the motor.

Solution. $$HP_c = \frac{K.f.d.b}{100000}$$

where K = Constant = 8.5 (From Table 1.11)

f = Feed = $0.325 \times 8 \times 200$ = 520 mm/minute.

d = Depth of cut in mm = 3 mm

b = Width of cut = 100 mm.

$$HP_c = \frac{85 \times 520 \times 3 \times 100}{10^5} = 12.48.$$ **Ans.**

Let the efficiency of the machine be 50%

$$HP_m = \text{Horse power at the motor}$$

$$= \frac{HP_c}{0.5} = \frac{12.48}{0.5} = 25. \textbf{ Ans.}$$

Example 1.9. *Determine the power required by a milling cutter to take a cut 100 mm wide × 3 mm deep at 75 mm / min feed for an alloy steel. If the cutter diameter is 100 mm and cutting speed is 15 metre / min, find the mean torque at the arbor.*

Solution. The horse power required at the cutter is given by

$$HP_c = \frac{K.f.d.b}{100{,}000}$$

Now $K = 8.5$ (From Table 1.11).

$f = 75$ mm/min.

$a = 100$ mm.

$d = 3$ mm.

$$HP_c = \frac{8.5 \times 75 \times 100 \times 3}{100{,}000} = 1.9.$$

Mean force at the periphery of the cutter,

$$F = \frac{HP_c}{V} \times 4500$$

where V = cutting speed = 15 metre/min.

$$F = \frac{1.9 \times 4500}{15} = 570 \text{ kg.}$$

Mean torque at the arbor,

$$T = F \times \text{Radius of cutter}$$

$$T = 570 \times \frac{50}{1000} = 28.5 \text{ kg-m.} \textbf{ Ans.}$$

Example 1.10. *During turning a mild steed component with a 0—10—7—7—8,—9—1.5 mm shaped orthogonal shaped tool a depth of cut of 1.8 mm is used. If feed is 0.18 mm / rev. and a chip thickness of 0.36 mm is obtained, determine the following :*

(*a*) *Chip thickness ratio*

(*b*) *Shear angle.*

Solution. (*a*) r = Chip thickness ratio = t_1/t_2

where t_1 = chip thickness before cutting = 0.18 mm.

t_2 = chip thickness after cutting = 0.36 mm.

$$r = \frac{0.18}{0.36} = 0.5$$

(*b*) β = Shear angle

α = Back rake angle = 0° (given)

$$\tan \beta = \frac{r \cos \alpha}{1 - r \sin \alpha}$$

$$= \frac{0.5 \times \cos 0}{1 - 0.5 \sin 0} = \frac{0.5}{1} = 0.5$$

$$\beta = 26° - 34'.$$

Example 1.11. *Determine the power required for milling a mild steel workpiece with a cutter of 80 mm diameter having 9 teeth and rotating at 120 R.P.M. The workpiece has a width of 60 mm. Depth of cut is 4 mm and tooth load is 0.03 mm.*

Solution. P = Power in kW/cm^2/min. It is given by the following formula

$$P = \frac{C}{\left[f\sqrt{\frac{d}{D}} \right]^n}$$

where f = feed per tooth

C = Material constant

d = Depth of cut in mm.

The values of C and n depend upon material to be cut. The values are as follows :

Mild Steel : C = 0.02 to 0.03

n = 0.28

Bronze : C = 0.006 – 0.007

n = 0.4

Now C = 0.02 (say)

$$f = \text{Feed per tooth} = \frac{F}{T}$$

where F = Feed rate, mm/min.

T = Number of teeth on cutter

f = 0.03 min.

d = Depth of cut = 4 mm

D = Diameter of cutter = 80 mm

n = 0.28

$$P = \frac{0.02}{\left[0.03\sqrt{\frac{4}{80}} \right]^{0.28}} = 0.245$$

$$P_1 = \text{Power in kW} = P \times b.d.f.T.N$$

where b = width of workpiece = 6 cm

N = R.P.M. = 120

$$P^1 = 0.245 \times 6 \times 0.4 \times 0.003 \times 9 \times 120 = 1.9 \text{ kW}.$$

Example 1.12. *Determine the power required to cut a brass bar on a lathe when the cutting speed is 18 metres per minute, feed is 0.06 mm per revolution and depth of cut is 0.058 cm. Assume that the power lost in friction is 30%.*

Solution. H.P. = Total horse power required

$= P_1 + P_2$

where P_1 = Power required for cutting action

P_2 = Power lost in friction

$= 30\%$ of P_1

$\therefore$ H.P. $= 1.3\, P_1$

$$= \frac{1.3 \times K.d.f.V}{4500}$$

where K = constant = 12000 for brass

d = depth of cut in cm.

= 0.058 cm = 0.58 mm

f = 0.06 mm per revolution

V = cutting speed

= 18 metres per minute.

The value of K depends on material being machined. The values of K are as follows.

Metal to be cut	*K*
Aluminium	6700
Brass	12000
Cast iron	8600
Steel	11000

$$\text{H.P.} = \frac{1.3 \times 12000 \times 0.58 \times 0.06 \times 18}{4500} = 2.17. \textbf{ Ans.}$$

Example 1.13. *Estimate the power of electric motor for a drilling machine to drill a hole 15 mm diameter in cast iron (soft) work piece at 450 R.P.M. and 0.2 mm feed. The specific power is 0.03 kW and efficiency of motor is 80%.*

Solution. D = Hole diameter = 15 mm

N = 450 R.P.M.

f = feed = 0.2 mm/rev.

S = specific power

= Power required to remove material of one cubic centimetre per minute

= 0.03 kW

η = Efficiency of motor = 0.8

V = volume of metal to be cut during drilling

$$= \frac{\pi}{4} D^2 \times f \times N$$

$$= \frac{\pi}{4}\left(\frac{15}{10}\right)^2 \times \frac{0.2}{10} \times 450 = 15.9 \text{ cu. cm/min}$$

P_1 = Power required at the drill

$= V \times S = 15.9 \times 0.03 = 0.477$ kW

P = Power of electric motor

$$= \frac{0.477}{\eta} = \frac{0.477}{0.8} = 0.6 \text{ kW. } \textbf{Ans.}$$

Example 1.14. *A broach is used to cut a key way 8 mm wide, 5 mm deep in a boss 64 mm long. Determine*

(a) cutting length of broach

(b) number of teeth on broach.

Solution. L = Length to be broached in mm

= 64 mm

p = Pitch

$= 1.5\sqrt{64} = 12$ mm.

d = Depth of cut = 5 mm

h = Rise per tooth

= 0.0875 mm (Assume)

Z_1 = Number of teeth

$$= \frac{d}{h} = \frac{5}{0.0875} = 57$$

Z_2 = Number of finishing teeth

= 13 (say)

Z = Total number of teeth

$= Z_1 + Z_2 = 57 + 13 = 70.$

p_1 = Pitch for finishing teeth

$$= \frac{p}{2} = \frac{12}{2} = 6 \text{ mm}$$

(The pitch for finishing teeth is usually half of that adopted for cutting teeth)

$$L = \text{Total effective length (cutting length) of broach}$$
$$= L_1 + L_2$$

where L_1 = length of roughing teeth

L_2 = length of finishing teeth

$$L = 57 \times p + 13 \times p_1$$
$$= 57 \times 12 + 13 \times 6 = 762 \text{ mm.}$$

Example 1.15. *For a single point tool the following angles are given in degrees :*

Front relief angle	*= 5°*
Side relief angle	*= 7°*
Back rake angle	*= 10°*
Side rake angle	*= 15°*
End cutting edge angle	*= 12°*
Side cutting edge angle	*= 0°*
Nose radius	*= 2 mm.*

Determine (a) Lip angle (b) Cutting angle (c) Nose angle.

Solution. As shown in Fig. 1.58.

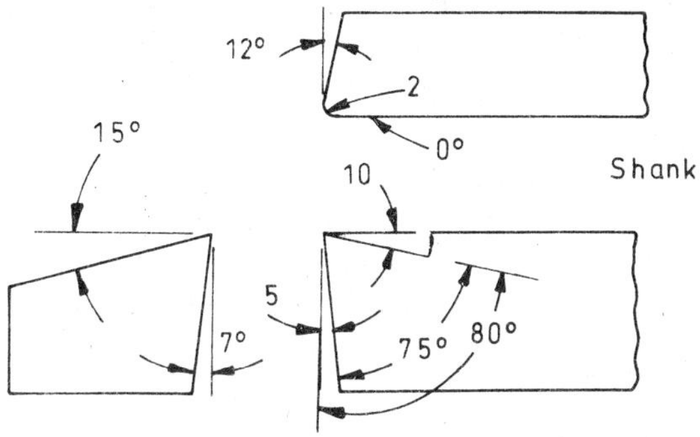

Fig. 1.58

(*a*) Lip angle = 90 – (Back rake angle + Front relief angle)

$= 90 - (10 + 5) = 75°$

(*b*) Cutting angle = 90 – Back rake angle

$= 90 - 10 = 80°$

(*c*) Nose angle $= 90 - (12 + 0) = 78°$.

Example 1.16. *Write a short note on brazing carbide tip on steel shank.*

Solution. Since carbide is an expensive material and because it is brittle in large cross-sections, it is usually brazed to a low-alloy carbon-steel shank.

The process of brazing a carbide tip to a steel shank usually requires that the shank be prepared with a recess [Fig. 1.59 (*a*)] into which the carbide tip is set, as shown in Fig. 1.59 (*b*).

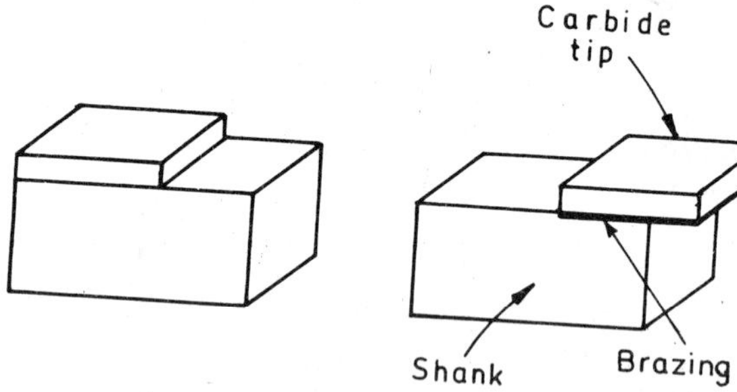

(*a*) (*b*)

Fig. 1.59

The recess must be chemically clean. The brazing material may be copper, Tobin bronze, or silver solder. A flux brazing foil is placed in the recess. The carbide slug is then placed on the foil in the recess. Heating may take place in a furnace or with an oxyacetylene flame. The underside of the shank, directly under the carbide slug, is heated until the braze material is liquid. The slug is pressed down and held until the braze solidifies.

Example 1.16(a). *(a) Sketch a single point cutting tool indicating back rake angle, lip angle (wedge angle) and clearance angle. State the importance of these angles.*

(b) State the typical values of rake angle for machining cast iron, brass, steel and plastic using high speed steel cutting tool.

Solution.

(*a*) Fig. 1.60 shows a single point tool.

α = Back rake angle

θ = Lip angle (wedge angle)

α_1 = Clearance angle.

With the clearance angle fixed within narrow limits the rake angle and wedge angle have to be balanced to form a compromise.

1. Increasing the *rake angle* increases the cutting efficiency of the tool but decreases the wedge angle.

2. Decreasing the *wedge angle* reduces the mechanical strength of the tool and reduces the mass of metal available at the

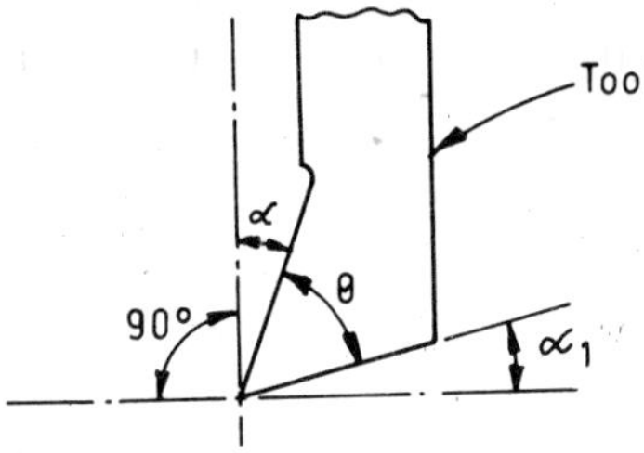

Fig. 1.60

cutting edge to conduct away the heat generated by the cutting process. This leads to a build up in the temperature of the tool at the cutting edge, softening of the tool and early failure.

Generally, therefore, low strength, ductile materials are cut with high rake tools to take advantage of the increased cutting efficiency. High strength, ductile materials are cut with low rake tools having a large wedge angle to give them adequate strength and heat dissipation capability at the cutting edge.

The clearance angle is generally fixed, depending upon the geometry of the surface being cut, at the following values :

(*a*) external cylindrical surface 5° to 7°

(*b*) flat surface 6° to 8°

(*c*) internal cylindrical surface 8° to 10°

(*b*) Table 1.19 shows typical rake angles for high speed tools cutting with positive rake. The values given are for roughing cuts and can be slightly increased, with advantage, for finishing cuts.

Table 1.19

Material being cut	*Rake*
Cast iron	0°
Free-cutting brass	0°
Ductile brass	14°
Tin bronze	8°
Aluminium alloy	30°
Mild steel	25°
Medium carbon steel	20°
High carbon steel	12°
'Tufnol' plastic	0°

Example 1.17. *Calculate the time required to turn a work-piece 160 mm long from 50 mm diameter to 44 mm diameter. The work piece rotates at 440 RPM, feed is 0.3 mm/rev. and maximum depth of cut is 1.8 mm.*

Solution. L = Workpiece length = 160

D = Initial diameter = 50 mm

d = Diameter after turning = 44 mm

$$\text{Total depth of cut} = \frac{D-d}{2} = \frac{50-44}{2} = 3 \text{ mm}$$

$$n = \text{Number of cuts required} = \frac{3}{1.8} = 1.67 = 2 \text{ (say)}$$

where 1.8 = Maximum depth of cut

L_1 = Total length = $L + S$

where S = Over-travel + Tool approach = 5 mm (say)

N = RPM = 440

$L_1 = 160 + 5 = 165$

f = Feed = 0.3 mm/Rev

T = Machining time per cut

$$= \frac{L_1}{f.N} = \frac{165}{0.3 \times 440} = 1.25 \text{ minutes}$$

Total time for two cuts = $2T = 2 \times 1.25 = 2.5$ minutes.

Example 1.18. *It is required to machine on a shaper a mild steel plate measuring 480 × 280 × 40 mm along its wider face. Calculate the machining time considering approach = 20 mm*

Feed/cycle	*= 1.2 mm*
Over-travel	*= 30 mm*
Cutting speed	*= 16 m/min*
Return speed	*= 25 m/min*
Allowance on sides	*= 5 mm.*

Solution. L = Length of plate = 480 mm

L_1 = Length of stroke = L + Tool approach + Over-travel

= 480 + 20 + 30 = 530 mm

V_1 = Cutting speed = 16 m/min

t_1 = Cutting stroke time

$$= \frac{L_1}{V_1} = \frac{530}{16 \times 1000} = 0.033 \text{ min}$$

V_2 = Return speed = 25 m/min

$$t_2 = \text{Return stroke time} = \frac{L_1}{V_2} = \frac{530}{25 \times 1000} = 0.021 \text{ min}$$

t = Time per cycle = $t_1 + t_2 = 0.033 + 0.021 = 0.054$ min

w = Shaping width
= Width of plate + 2 × Allowance
= 280 + 2 × 5 = 290 mm

f = Feed = 1.2 mm

N = Number of cycles required $= \frac{w}{f}$

$= \frac{290}{1.2} = 241.6 = 242$ (say)

T = Machining time $= t \times N = 0.054 \times 242 = 13.1$ minutes.

Example 1.19. *A mild steel plate 780 × 460 × 30 mm is to be shaped on a shaper along its wider face. Feed is 1.6 mm / cycle, tool over-travel and tool approach is 40 mm, cutting speed is 24 m / min and ratio of return time to cutting time is 2 : 3. The allowance on sides is 5 mm. Determine the machining time.*

Solution. L = Length of plate = 780 mm

L_1 = Length of stroke
= L + Tool approach + Tool travel
= 780 + 40 + 40 = 860 mm

w = Shaping width
= Width of plate + 2 × Allowance
= 460 + 2 × 5 = 470 mm

f = Feed = 1.6 mm/cycle

V_1 = Cutting speed = 24 m/min

T = Machining time

$$= \frac{w}{f} \times \frac{L_1}{V_1}(1 + R)$$

where R = Ratio of return time to cutting time $= \frac{2}{3}$

$$T = \frac{470}{1.6} \times \frac{860}{24 \times 1000}\left(1 + \frac{2}{3}\right) = 17.6 \text{ minutes.}$$

Example 1.20. *Discuss typical carbon tool steels.*

Solution. In carbon tool steels the carbon content varies from 0.8 to 1.3 per cent. Frequently, alloying elements such as vanadium, chromium, silicon manganese are added to improve its property.

Table 1.20 shows different percentages of the alloying elements.

Table 1.20

Tool material	*Percentage*				
	C	*Mn*	*Si*	*V*	*Cr*
Carbon steel	0.8–1.30	0.1–0.40	0.1–0.40	—	—
Carbon-vanadium steel	0.8–1.30	0.1–0.4	0.10–0.40	0.15–0.25	—
Carbon chromium steel	0.9–1.30	0.10–0.40	0.10–0.40	—	0.40–0.60

A typical composition would be carbon 1.0%, silicon 0.3% and manganese 0.2%.

Such steels have low hot hardness and poor hardenability. The tools made up of these types of steel cannot withstand cutting temperatures over 200 to 250°C. At temperatures higher than this they lose their hardness rapidly.

The carbon tools, therefore, are suitable for cutting relatively soft material at low cutting speeds. The materials cut are : wood, plastics and non-ferrous materials such as aluminium, copper etc. At low chip tool interface temperatures, carbon tool steels are harder than many of the high speed tool steels and can be used most economically under these following conditions :

(*i*) The carbon steels are used for making taps and core drills (for machining soft materials).

(*ii*) For making wood-working tools.

Example 1.21. *Calculate the cutting times for each of the following machining operations :*

(*a*) *Work piece-grey cast iron, cutting speed 20 m/min, depth of cut is 2.5 mm, dimensions of surface to be machined 50 mm long × 70 mm wide over run of cutter = 10 mm cutter (i) Helical mill 76 mm diameter and 45 degree helix (ii) Face mill 100 mm diameter.*

Solution. (*a*) *For helical milling*

D = Cutter diameter = 76 mm

α = Helix angle = 45°

d = Depth of cut = 2.5 mm

Z = Number of teeth in cutter

$$= \frac{4\pi D}{D + 4d} \times \cos\alpha = \frac{4\pi \times 76}{76 + 4 + 2.5} \times \cos 45 = 8$$

f = feed/tooth = 0.25 mm (From Table 1.15)

h = Approach = $\sqrt{d(D - d)}$

$$= \sqrt{2.5(76 - 2.5)} = 13.6 \text{ mm}$$

N = R.P.M. of spindle

V = cutting speed = 20

$$20 = \frac{\pi DN}{1000} = \frac{\pi \times 76 \times N}{1000}$$

N = 84 R.P.M.

S = over run of cutter = 10 mm

F = Table feed = $N \times Z \times f$

= 84 × 8 × 0.25 = 168 mm/min

L = length of cut

= length of workpiece + h + s

= 50 + 13.6 + 10 = 73.6 mm

$$T = \text{Time for one cut} = \frac{L}{F}$$

$$= \frac{73.6}{168} = 0.44 \text{ min.}$$

(*b*) *For face milling*

b = Width of component (cut) = 70 mm

$$Z = \frac{2\pi D}{b} = \frac{2\pi \times 100}{70} = 9$$

d = Depth of cut

= 0.3 mm (From table 1.15)

D = Cutter diameter = 100 mm

h = Approach

$$= \frac{D}{2} - \sqrt{\frac{D^2}{4} - \frac{b^2}{4}}$$

$$= \frac{100}{2} - \sqrt{\frac{100^2}{4} - \frac{70^2}{4}} = 14.3 \text{ mm}$$

$$V = 20 = \frac{\pi DN}{1000}$$

$$20 = \frac{\pi \times 100 \times N}{1000}$$

N = 64 R.P.M.

F = Table feed = $N \times Z \times f$

= 64 × 9 × 0.3 = 172.3 mm/min

L = Length of component + h + s
= 50 + 14.3 + 10 = 74.3 mm

T = Time for one cut

$$= \frac{L}{F} = \frac{74.3}{172.8} = 0.43 \text{ minutes.}$$

Example 1.22. *The bore of an alloy steel component is to be finish broached to* $21.75^{+0.01}$ *mm diameter, the bore prior to broaching being* $21.24^{+0.05}$ *mm diatermeter. Determine*

(a) Pitch of teeth

(b) Length of cutting portion

(c) Force to pull broach through work if length of hole is 36 mm and rise per tooth is 0.025.

Number of finishing teeth is 3 and force to remove 1 mm^2 *of metal is 4800 N.*

Sketch the broach.

Solution. L_1 = Hole length = 36 mm

p = Pitch

$= 1.5\sqrt{36} = 9$ mm

Z = Number of finishing teeth = 5

L = Length of cutting portion of broach

$$= P\left(\frac{T}{h} + Z\right)$$

where T = Metal to be removed by roughing teeth

$$= \frac{21.76 - 21.24}{2} = 0.26 \text{ mm}$$

h = Rise per tooth = 0.025 mm

$$L = p\left(\frac{T}{h} + Z\right) = 9\left(\frac{0.26}{0.025} + 5\right) = 144 \text{ mm.}$$

The first cutting tooth will be 21.24 mm diameter, second will be 21.26 mm diameter. The rest of cutting teeth will rise in steps of 0.05 mm on diameter and finishing teeth will be 21.76 mm diameter.

F = Force to pull broach = $\pi D Z_1 h K$

where D = Finish diameter = 21.76 mm

Z_1 = Maximum number of teeth cutting at a time = 3

K = Force required to remove 1 mm^2 of metal at given rise/tooth

= 4800 N

h = Rise per tooth = 0.025 mm

$F = \pi \times 21.76 \times 3 \times 0.025 \times 4800$

$= 25581$ N = 25.581 kN

Fig. 1.61 shows sketch of broach.

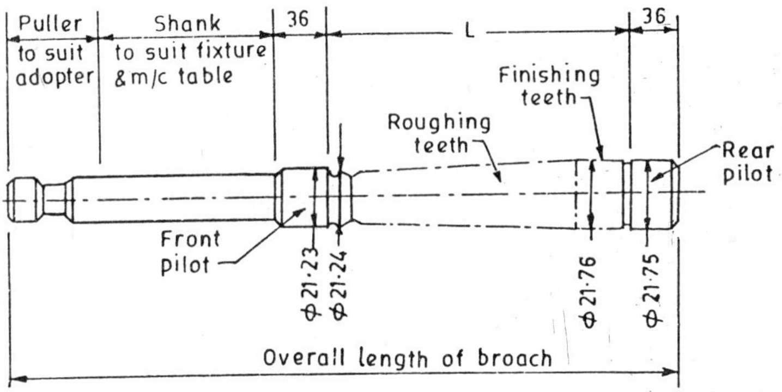

Fig. 1.61

Example 1.23. *A mild steel rod is machined on a lathe. Find power of motor using following data :*

Cutting speed = *90 m / min*

Feed = *0.5 mm / rev.*

Depth of cut = *2.54 mm*

Correction factor = *0.5.*

Solution. The formula for calculating power of motor is as follows :

$$P = \text{Power (kW)}$$

$$= \frac{v \,.\, f \,.\, d \,.\, F}{6000 \times \eta}$$

where v = cutting speed = 90 mpm

f = feed = 0.5 mm/rev.

F = specific resistance = 270 – 300 kg/mm^2 (assume) for steel

d = depth of cut = 2.54 mm

η = correction factor

$$p = \frac{90 \times 0.5 \times 2.54 \times 280}{6000 \times 0.5} = 10.7 \text{ kW.}$$

1.51. Screwing Tap

Fig. 1.62 shows various elements of a screwing tap. Fig. 1.63 shows flutes with right hand (RH) helix and flutes with spiral point. Fig. 1.64 shows various types of rake for the tap teeth.

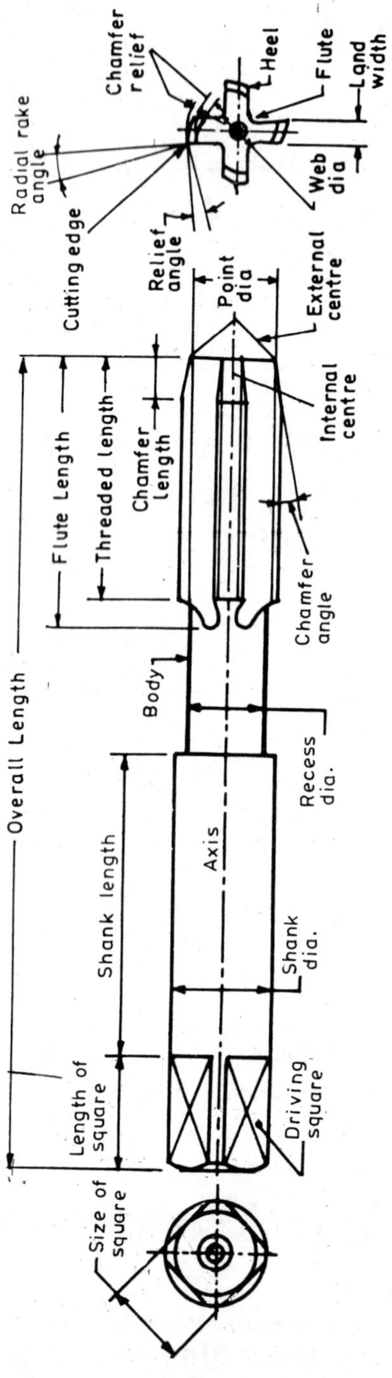
Chamfer relief
Heel
Flute
Land width
Radial rake angle
Cutting edge
Web dia
Relief angle
Point dia
External centre
Overall Length
Flute Length
Threaded length
Chamfer length
Internal centre
Chamfer angle
Body
Recess dia.
Axis
Shank length
Shank dia.
Length of square
Driving square
Size of square

Fig. 1.62

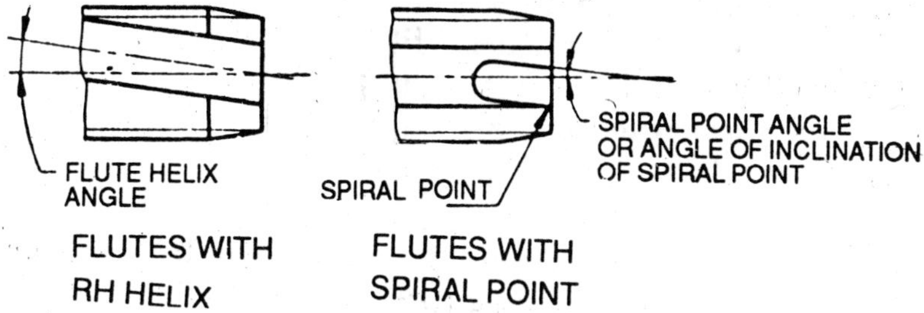

Fig. 1.63

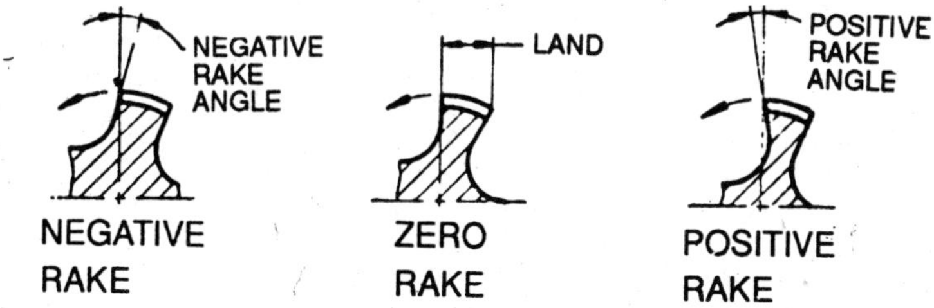

Fig. 1.64

1.52. Force and Torque during Drilling

The drilling thrust (P) and drilling torque (T) depend on the following factors :

(*i*) Workpiece material (*ii*) Hardness
(*iii*) Point angle of drill (*iv*) Drill diameter
(*v*) Feed rate

P = Thrust force during drilling as shown in Fig. 1.65.
$= 9.80665 \cdot C_1 \cdot K_1 \cdot K_2 \cdot d^x \cdot s^y$ Newton.

where C_1 = Material constant.
K_1 = Brinell hardness coefficient.

Fig. 1.65

K_2 = Drill point angle coefficient.
d = Drill diameter in mm.
S = Feed rate in mm/Rev.
T = Drilling torque.
$= 9.80665 \cdot C_2 \cdot K_1 \cdot K_2 \cdot d^m s^n$ (N-mm)

where x, y, m and n are constants.

The values of c_1, c_2, x, y, m and n are shown in Table 1.19.

Table 1.19

Materials	C_1	C_2	x	y	m	n
Carbon steel :						
$\sigma_u = 735$ N/mm^2	85	34	1	1.9	0.7	0.8
C.I. HB = 190	52	20	1	1.9	0.8	0.8
Bronze	31	12	1	1.9	0.8	0.8
Alloy steel :						
$\sigma_u = 112$ N/mm^2	270	75	1.15	2.1	0.77	0.76
$\sigma_u = 686$ N/mm^2	163	55	1.0	2.0	0.62	0.76

The values of K_1 is indicated in Table 1.20.

Table 1.20

HB	130	150	170	190	210	220	250	270
K_1	0.80	0.87	0.94	1.00	1.96	1.23	1.18	1.25

The values of K_2 are indicated in Table 1.21.

Table 1.21

1/2 point angle degree	*P*			*T*		
	45	60	75	45	60	75
Steel	0.97	1.0	1.04	1.23	1.0	0.82
Cast iron (K_2)	0.73	1.0	1.27	1.25	1.0	0.88

1.53. Cutting Tool Wear

For a given metal cutting operation the metal removal rate and the tool life are controlled by cutting parameters. By a judicious selection of cutting data one could get the maximum rate of metal removal and optimum tool life.

Under usual cutting conditions when the form stability of the cutting edge has been achieved, wear due to interaction between the chip and the tool and between the workpiece and the tool are the main processes by which the cutting tool wears out. These types of wear are called crater wear and flank wear respectively.

1.53.1. Tool wear mechanism

Tool wear is a complex phenomenon in which the following actions take place simultaneously :

(*i*) Molecular diffusion between workpiece material and tool material. Carbon and cobalt move from tool surface to flow zone of the workpiece. Iron moves from work material to tool surface. Structural changes in the surface region of a carbide tool lead to its deterioration. By providing thin diffusion barriers the wear can be reduced.

(*ii*) Chemical affinity between the nascent layer of the workpiece material and the cutting tool material.

(*iii*) Mechanical abrasion between the micro constituents and matrix of the workpiece material and the layer of the cutting tool.

(*iv*) Pressure welding of workpiece material to cutting tool surface followed by micro transfer of small particles from the cutting tool matrix adhering to workpiece material.

All the above actions in tool wear phenomena result in two predominant types of tool wear-crater wear and flank wear.

1.53.2. Tool wear types

(*i*) *Flank Wear*. This occurs on the relief side and nose radius of the cutting edge. It is due to the action of abrasion and resultant heat generated between the tool and the workpiece. This increases the cutting forces, ruins the surface finish and dimensional accuracy.

(*ii*) *Crater Wear*. When turning long chipping materials like steel, the hot chips under pressure have a tendency to weld to the top face as the chip moves over it. These welded granules in turn get loosened along with some carbide particles and are carried away by passing chips. This triple action of welding, uprooting and carrying away leads to cratering. The development of a crater results in premature cutting edge failure. Higher cutting speed wear out tools faster than higher cutting feeds.

1.54. Carbide Tool Failures and Remedies

Premature tool failure problems should be checked to increase tool life. Some of the commonly observed problems and their solutions are as follows :

Problem	Recommended Solution
1. Wear	(*i*) Decrease speed
	(*ii*) Increase feed
	(*iii*) Decrease lead angle
	(*iv*) Check that tool is not above centre height.
	(*v*) Tool should be of proper grade and hardness.
	(*vi*) Increases one or both relief and clearance angle.
2. Poor surface finish	(*i*) Increase nose radius
	(*ii*) Increase lead angle
	(*iii*) Tool should be properly clamped
	(*iv*) Increase speed
	(*v*) Decrease feed
3. Chatter	(*i*) Decrease nose radius
	(*ii*) Decrease rake angle
	(*iii*) Increase relief and clearance angle
	(*iv*) Decrease overhang
	(*v*) Check the condition of spindles and slides of the machine
	(*vi*) Decrease cutting speed
	(*vii*) Increase feed
	(*viii*) Check that workpiece is properly held and clamped.

4. Crater	(*i*) Use coolant of good lubricating qualities
	(*ii*) Use harder grade tool
	(*iii*) Increase speed
	(*iv*) Decrease feed
	(*v*) Positive rake angle may be used.
5. Built up edge	(*i*) Increase speed
	(*ii*) Use positive rake
	(*iii*) Use coolant with good lubricating properties.
6. Chipping Cracking and Breakage	(*i*) Increase nose radius
	(*ii*) Increase lead angle if possible
	(*iii*) Use negative rake
	(*iv*) Increase speed
	(*v*) Decrease feed
	(*vi*) Check the tool for looseness
	(*vii*) Check rigidity of workpiece
	(*viii*) Decrease tool overhang.

Only one solution or number of solutions listed above may be used to run the tool smoothly to increase life of tool, to obtain proper surface finish, production rate etc.

1.55. Cast Alloy Tools

They contain no iron and are cast into their final shape. They consists of cobalt, chromium, tungston, and carbon, the carbide phase being about 25 to 30 per cent by volume of the matrix. These tools can be used at slightly higher speeds than high speed steels and have less tendency to form a built up edge during machining. They are commonly used in machining of cast iron, malleable iron and hard bronzes.

1.56. Reamer

It is used to produce an accurate hole. Reaming is carried out after drilling.

Fig. 1.66 shows various elements of a reamer. The various terms relating to cutting geometry of reamers are shown in Fig. 1.67.

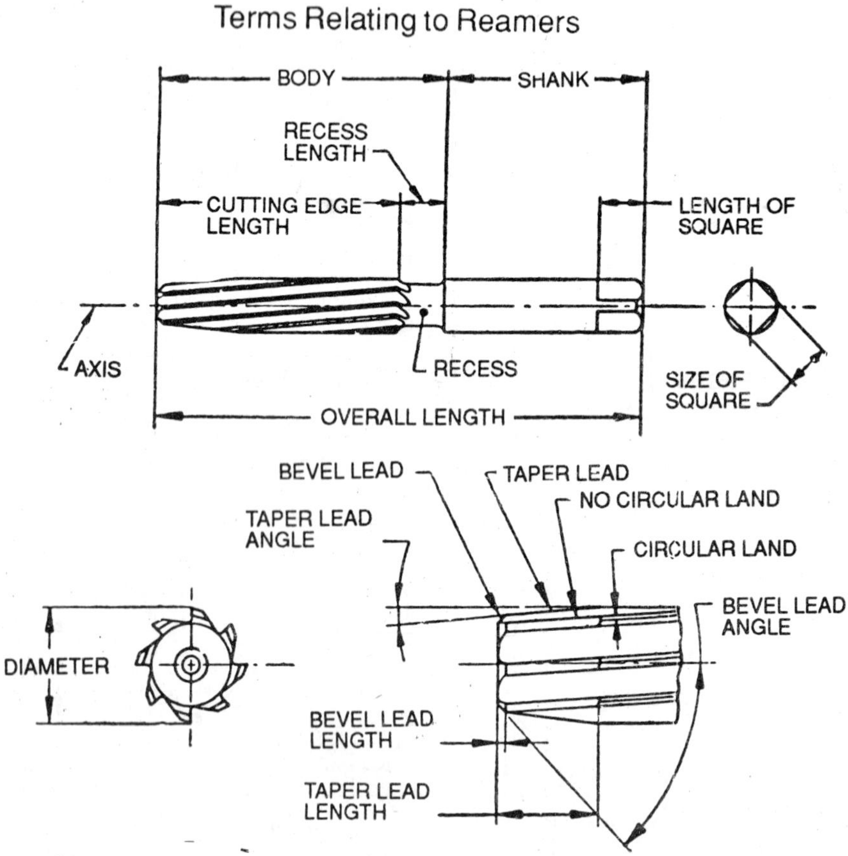

Fig. 1.66

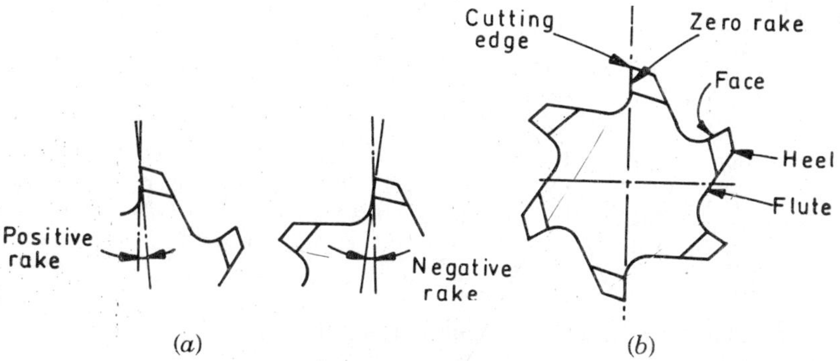

Fig. 1.67

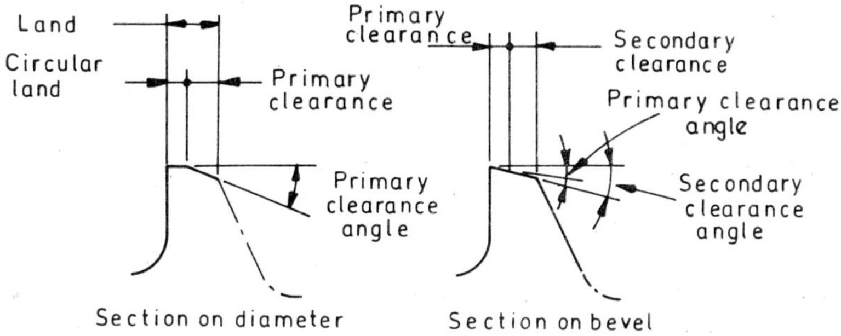

(c) (d)

Fig. 1.67

PROBLEMS

1.1. (*a*) What is metal cutting ? Define chip removal and non-chip removal process. Give examples.

(*b*) Discuss basic elements of metal cutting.

1.2. Explain orthogonal cutting and oblique cutting.

1.3. (*a*) How are tools classified ? State three examples of each.

(*b*) Explain with the help of neat sketch the complete geometry of a single point cutting tool.

1.4. (*a*) Define 'tool signature'.

(*b*) Explain each term of a tool designated as 8, 12, 10, 7, 0, 15, 1.5 mm.

1.5. (*a*) What is chip formation ?

(*b*) Name the different types of chips formed in metal cutting. Describe each type with the help of neat sketches.

State the conditions which favour the production of each type.

1.6. (*a*) List the main requirements of cutting tool material.

(*b*) Name and explain the various materials used for cutting tools.

1.7. Write short notes on the following :

(*a*) Chip breakers

(*b*) Advantages of negative rake angle

(*c*) Curling of chip (*d*) Cutting speed

(*e*) Feed (*f*) Depth of cut

(*g*) Throw-away tips.

1.8. (*a*) What is chip reduction coefficient ?

(*b*) What are the effects of cutting variable on the chip reduction coefficient.

1.9. (*a*) What is a multipoint cutting tool ?

(*b*) Sketch a twist drill and describe its various elements.

1.10. (*a*) Make a neat sketch of a twist drill, showing various angles.

(*b*) Define the following angles of a twist drill :

(*i*) Rake angle

(*ii*) Lip clearance angle

(*iii*) Point angle

(*iv*) Chisel edge angle.

1.11. Write short notes on the following :

(*a*) Cutting fluids for drilling (*b*) Twist drill grinding

(*c*) Twist drill failure (*d*) Drill specifications.

1.12. Analyse the forces acting on a drill.

1.13. What are the parameters which affect the drilling torque.

1.14. What factors decide the cutting speed of a drill ?

1.15. (*a*) What is a milling cutter ?

(*b*) Sketch and explain

(*i*) Up milling

(*ii*) Down milling.

1.16. Sketch a plain milling cutter and explain the various elements of the cutter.

1.17. Write short notes on the following :

(*a*) Milling cutter sharpening (*b*) Number of teeth on a cutter

(*c*) Cutting speed

(*d*) Coarse tooth and fine tooth milling cutters.

1.18. Explain how to calculate machining time in

(*a*) Plain milling (*b*) Face milling.

1.19. A stab milling operation is carried out with a 60 inch diameter inserted carbide tooth cutter having 10 teeth at a cutting speed of 400 feet/min and a feed of 40 inches per minute. If the depth of cut is 0.02 inch and width of cut is 4.5 inch and the following relation is assumed :

$$F = -\,32000\; b.d^{0.8}\, f^{0.7}$$

where F = Tangential force on cutter

d = Depth of cut in inch

b = Width of cut in inch

f = Feed in inches per tooth.

Determine the following :

(*a*) Tangential force exerted by the cutter.

(*b*) Torque transmitted by the cutter.

(*c*) Total H.P. required at the drive end of milling machine at a mechanical efficiency of 7%.

(*d*) Specific H.P. required at the arbor.

1.20. Determine the depth of cut taken on a lathe while turning brass at a feed of 0.625 mm per revolution and cutting speed of 24 metre/min if 3 horse power is available and 20% of power is lost in friction.

1.21. Estimate the time required for a single cut in each of the following machining operations :

(*a*) To turn 25 mm dia × 1.0 mm long with cutting speed 30 m/min and a feed of 0.25 mm/rev.

(*b*) To turn 3 mm deep recess in a 50 mm dia and shaft using a 6 mm wide from tool with a cutting speed of 12 m/min and a feed of 0.05 mm.

1.22. (*a*) State the characteristics of carbide tools.

(*b*) Describe the power distribution in a milling machine and a lathe.

1.23. Write short notes on the following :

(*a*) Requirements of cutting tool.

(*b*) Power required at milling cutter.

1.24. Write short notes on the following :

(*a*) Improving metal cutting efficiency.

(*b*) Power distribution in the following machines.

(*i*) Lathe (*ii*) Milling machine.

1.25. Discuss the design of a cutting tool.

1.26. Explain the following terms with reference to a plain milling cutter :

(*i*) Radial rake angle (*ii*) Lip angle

(*iii*) Relief angle (*iv*) First clearance angle

(*v*) Second clearance angle. (*A.M.I.E. 1982*)

1.27. Sketch a broaching tool and describe its construction.

1.28. Write short notes on the following :

(*a*) Friction between chip and tool.

(*b*) Power rating of electric motor.

(*c*) Improvement of cutting efficiency during machining.

(*d*) Care and maintenance of cutting tools.

1.29. State the factors which affect thrust and torque during drilling.

1.30. A mild steel plate 980 × 470 × 180 mm is to be machined on a shaper to a size 700 × 400 × 150 mm. If the cutting speed is 24 m/min, tool approach is 50 mm and tool over-travel is 40 mm, return speed is 30 m/min and feed is 1.3 mm/cycle, determine machining time.

1.31. Describe the following :

(*i*) Design of a single point cutting tool.

(*ii*) Common sizes of H.S.S. tool bits.

(*iii*) Specification of a single point tool.

1.32. Determine the total production time for a batch of 400 components to be milled two at a time in a fixture on a horizontal milling machine given that :

Length of workpiece	= 180 mm
Approach	= 25 mm
Over run	= 10 mm
Feed/tooth	= 0.25 mm
Number of teeth on cutter	= 10
R.P.M. of cutter	= 80

Time allowed for loading, unloading and cleaning is 1 ½ min/cycle and other allowances amount to 1/2 min/cycle.

1.33. Determine the production quantity at which the manufacturing costs of the following two alternative manufacturing methods break-even :

Numerically controlled miller and Conventional miller

(*i*) Computer cost Rs. 80,

(*ii*) Programming cost Rs. 60,

(*iii*) Machining time $\frac{1}{2}$ h and $1\frac{1}{2}$ h

(*iv*) Setter operator rate Rs. 12/h and Rs. 10/h

(*v*) Set up time $\frac{1}{2}$ h and 1 h

(*vi*) Over heads Rs. 9/h and Rs. 7/h

(*vii*) Depreciation Rs. 15/h and Rs. 8/h.

1.33. Write short notes on the following :

(*i*) Tool wear

(*ii*) Carbide tool failure and remedies

(*iii*) Cast alloy tools

(*iv*) Sketch a reamer and name its parts

(*v*) Brazing of carbide tools

(*vi*) Screwing tap

(*vii*) Surface treatment of cutting tools.

1.35. Describe the various methods of measuring Tool-chip interface temperature.

2

Mechanics of Metal Cutting

In any metal cutting process, considerable forces are involved and in order to design machine tool holders and work holders that will withstand these forces, it is important to establish the magnitude of these forces and the directions in which they act. According to Ernst and Merchant the chip is assumed to behave as a rigid, body held in equilibrium by the action of the forces transmitted across the chip tool interface and across the shear plane. A number of attempts have been made to study the mechanics of the cutting process starting with Mallock in 1881. The theory suggested by Ernst and Merchant and later developed by Merchant considers orthogonal cutting with a flow type having no built up edge. The mode of plastic deformation is considered to be one of simple shear across a plan extending from the tool cutting edge to the junction of the chip with the original work surface. Lee and Shaffer in 1949 obtained a solution to the problem of the mechanics of metal cutting by using the slip-line field theory which was developed for studying the stress distribution in a body undergoing plastic deformation in two dimensions.

2.1. Cutting Forces in Orthogonal Cutting

The forces acting on a single point cutting tool are of fundamental importance in the design and of cutting and machine tools. For a conventional turning process the force system is shown in Fig. 2.1. The resultant cutting force P represented by OA acting on the tool is considered to be as vector sum of three component cutting forces mutually at right angles.

(*i*) Feed force F_x acts in a horizontal plane but in the direction opposite to the seed.

(*ii*) Thrust force F_y acting in the direction perpendicular to the generated surface.

(*iii*) Cutting forces F_z in the direction of the main cutting motion.

The relationships between forces, F_x, F_y and F_z depend upon the cutting variables, geometry of the tool point, the work material, tool wear etc.

$$R = \text{Resultant force} = \sqrt{F_x^2 + F_y^2 + F_z^2}$$

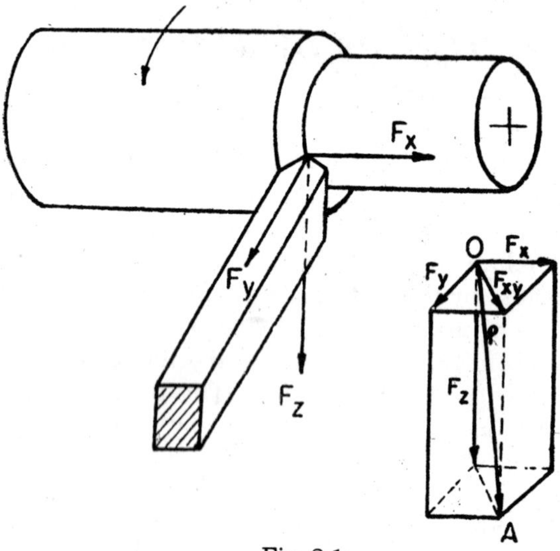

Fig. 2.1

This three dimensional force system can be reduced to a two dimensional force system if in the orthogonal plane M the forces are considered in such a way that the entire force system is contained in the considered state, when

$$R = \sqrt{F_z^2 + F_{xy}^2}$$

$$F_{xy} = \sqrt{F_x^2 + F_y^2}$$

For this $\lambda = 0$ and F_{XY} is contained in orthogonal plane M. This system is then known as orthogonal system of first kind for which the conditions are as follows :

(*i*) $\lambda = 0$

(*ii*) $0 < \phi < 90$

(*iii*) Chip flow deviations are small.

The various forces for the orthogonal system of first kind is shown in Fig. 2.2 (a).

where ϕ = Principal cutting edge angle

λ = Inclination angle.

In orthogonal system of first kind

$$F_x = F_{xy} \sin \phi$$
$$F_y = F_{xy} \cos \phi$$

There is other orthogonal system known as orthogonal system of second kind in which F_y is make zero by having $\lambda = 0$ and $\phi = 90°$ when two dimensional force system is

$$R = \sqrt{F_z^2 + F_x^2}$$
$$F_{xy} = \sqrt{F_x^2 + F_y^2}$$
$$= \sqrt{F_x^2 + 0} = F_x.$$
$$F_{xy} = F_y \quad \text{when } \phi = 0 \text{ and } \lambda = 0$$

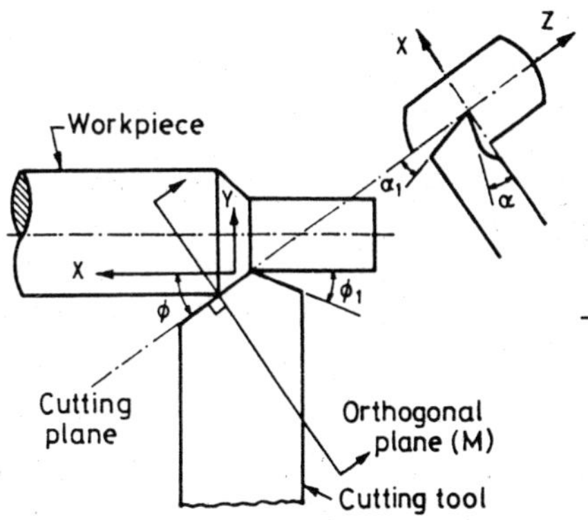

Fig. 2.2 (*a*)

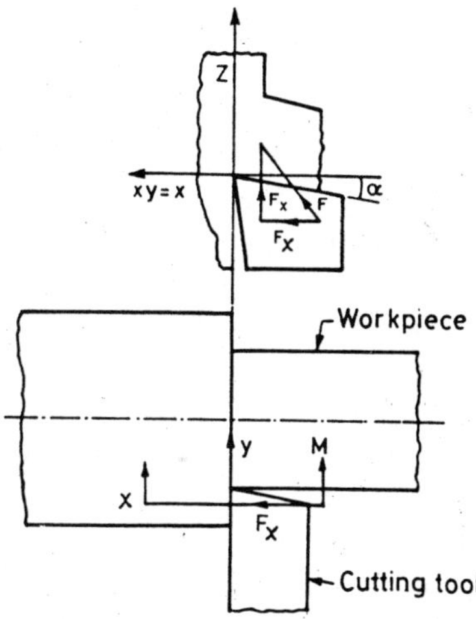

Fig. 2.2 (*b*)

Fig. 2.2 (*b*) shows two dimensional force system in plane *M* for orthogonal system of second kind.

In orthogonal system the tool shape is specified by the following terms stated in order.

(*i*) Inclination angle.
(*ii*) Orthogonal rake angle (α).
(*iii*) Orthogonal clearance angle (α_1).
(*iv*) Auxiliary orthogonal clearance angle.
(*v*) Auxiliary cutting edge angle (ϕ_1).
(*vi*) Principal cutting edge angle (ϕ).
(*vii*) Nose radius in millimetres.

The chip may be considered as a separate body held in equilibrium by the various forces shown in Fig. 2.2.

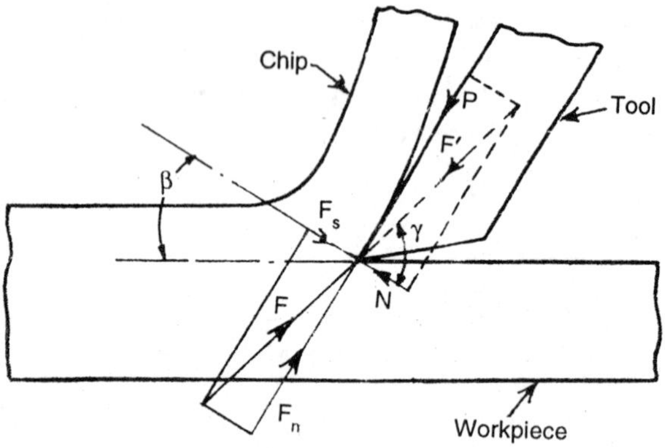

Fig. 2.2

Force F_s acts along the shear plane and is the resistance to shear of the metal in forming the chip. Force F_n is normal to shear plane. This is a backing up force on the chip provided by the work piece. F is the resultant of F_s and F_h. Force P is the frictional resistance of the tool acting downward against the motion of chip as it moves along the tool face. The normal force N is normal to the tool face and is provided by the tool. The resultant of these two forces is F' and is the force exerted by the tool on the workpiece. The force F and F' are equal in magnitude, opposite in direction and collinear.

$$\vec{F} = \vec{F_s} + \vec{F_n}$$

$$F' = \vec{P} + \vec{N}$$

The relation between various forces have been worked out by Merchant with a large number of assumptions as follows :

(*i*) The chip behaves as a free body in stable equilibrium under the action of two equal, opposite and collinear resultant forces.

(*ii*) Continuous chip without built up edge is produced.

(*iii*) The cutting velocity remains constant.

(*iv*) The cutting tool has a sharp cutting edge and it does not make any flank contact with the workpiece.

Merchant suggested a compact and easiest way of representing the various forces inside a circle having the vector F as diameter. Fig. 2.3 shows Merchant circle diagram which is convenient to determine the relation between the various forces and

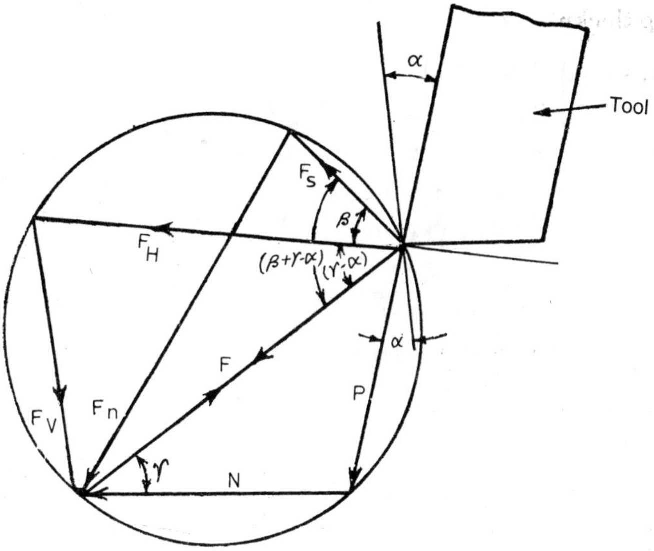

Fig. 2.3. Merchant circle diagram.

angles. The circle has a diameter equal to F or F' passing through the tool point.

α = Rake angle of tool.

β = Shear angle.

γ = Friction angle of the tool face.

From the Merchant circle it is found that

$$\frac{F_V}{F_H} = \tan(\gamma - \alpha)$$

where F_V = Feed force

F_H = Cutting force.

As the chip slides over the tool face under pressure therefore the kinetic coefficient of friction (μ) may be expressed as

$$\mu = \frac{P}{N} = \tan \gamma$$

The cutting force F_H and feed force F_V can be measured with a cutting tool dynamometer and then the other forces can be determined in terms of F_H and F_V. Shear angle β can be obtained from the equation

$$\tan \beta = \frac{r \cos \alpha}{1 - r \sin \alpha}.$$

Chip thickness ratio, $r = \dfrac{t_1}{t_2}$

where t_1 = Chip thickness before cutting

t_2 = Chip thickness after cutting

P = Friction resistance

$= F_H \sin \alpha + F_V \cos \alpha$

N = Normal force

$= F_H \cos \alpha - F_V \sin \alpha.$

$$F = \sqrt{F_H^2 + F_V^2}$$

F_H = Cutting force

$= F \cos (\gamma - \alpha)$

Also $F_S = F \cos \theta$

$\therefore \quad F = \dfrac{F_S}{\cos \theta}$

where $\theta = \beta + \gamma - \alpha$

$$\therefore \quad F_H = \frac{F_S \,.\, \cos (\gamma - \alpha)}{\cos \theta} = \frac{F_S \cos (\gamma - \alpha)}{\cos (\beta + \gamma - \alpha)}$$

μ = Coefficient of friction

$= \tan \gamma = \dfrac{P}{N}$

$$= \frac{F_H \sin \alpha + F_V \cos \alpha}{F_H \cos \alpha - F_V \sin \alpha} = \frac{F_H \,.\, \tan \alpha + F_V}{F_H - F_V \tan \alpha}$$

The relationships for F_S and F_n are as follows :

$$F_S = F_H \cos \beta - F_V \sin \beta.$$

$$F_n = F_V \cos \beta + F_H \sin \beta.$$

These forces are determised as follows :

(*i*) *Shear Plane forces*

The various forces are shown in Fig. 2.3. (*a*).

AB represents the force F_H

BC represents the force F_V

BC is at right angle to *AB*

AD represents shear force F_S

F_H = Cutting force

F_V = Feed force

F_N = Force normal to shear force

β = Shear angle.

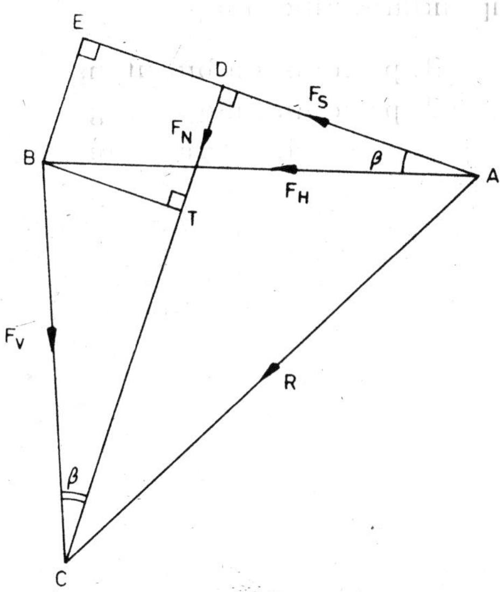

Fig. 2.3 (*a*)

Draw BE perpendicular to AD produced

α = Back rake angle of tool

Draw BT perpendicular to CD.

$$R = \text{Resultant force}$$

$$F_S = AD = AE - ED = AE - BT$$
$$= AB \cos \beta - BC \sin \beta$$
$$= F_H \cos \beta - F_V \sin \beta.$$

Now $F_N = CD = CT + TD = CT + BE$

$$= CB \cos \beta + AB \sin \beta$$
$$= F_V \cos \beta + F_H \sin \beta$$

(*ii*) *Tool Plane Forces*

The various forces are shown in Fig. 2.3 (*b*).

Force P makes an angle α with vertical line at A.

Draw AS at angle α with AB.

CK is parallel to AS.

Force P and force N are mutually at right angle.

$$P = \text{Frictional resistance}$$
$$= AK = CM$$
$$= CT + TM = CT + BS$$
$$= CB \sin (90 - \alpha) + AB \sin \alpha$$

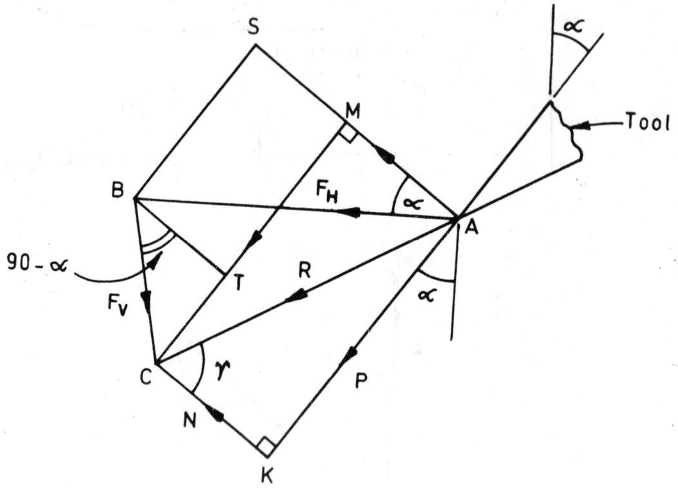

Fig. 2.3 (*b*)

$= F_V \cos\alpha + F_H \sin\alpha$

N = Normal force to frictional resistance

$= CK = AM = AS - SM$

$= AS - BT = AB \cos\alpha - BC \cos(90 - \alpha)$

$= F_H \cos\alpha - F_V \sin\alpha.$

Cutting force depends on the following :

(*i*) Material to be cut

(*a*) Hardness of material

(*b*) Strength of material

(*ii*) Depth of cut (*iii*) Feed

(*iv*) Tool geometry.

2.1.1. Stresses on tool

In simple turning operation, two types of stresses act on the tool :

1. Compressive stress. This is due to the cutting force.

f_C = Mean compressive stress

$$= \frac{F_H}{A}$$

where F_H = Cutting force

A = Contact area.

2. Shear stress. In a twist drill the stresses are mainly torsional.

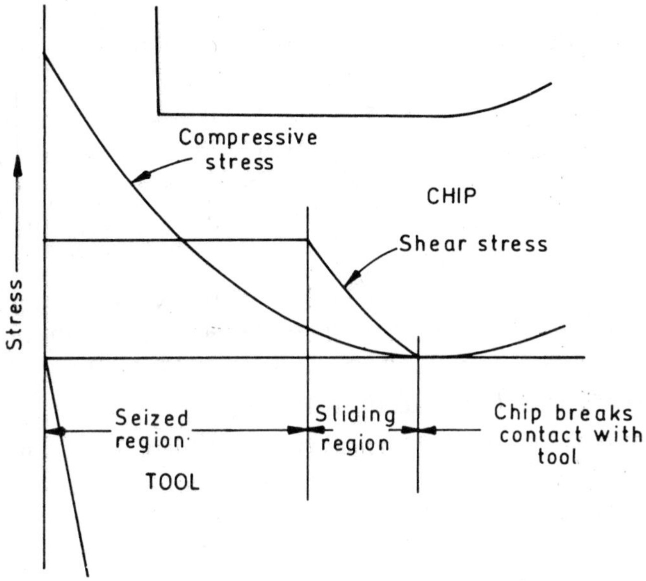

Fig. 2.3 (*c*)

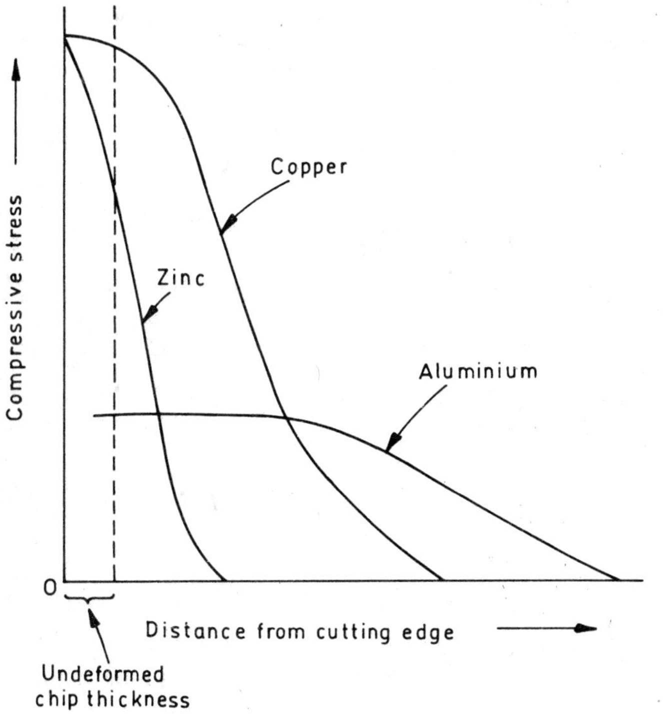

Fig. 2.3 (*d*)

Fig. 2.3 (*c*) shows model of stress distribution on tool during metal cutting.

The compressive stress varies as follows :

$$f_C = \text{Compressive stress} = k \cdot x^y$$

where k and y are constants.

x = Distance from the point B where the chip breaks contact with the tool.

Fig. 2.3 (*d*) shows typical variation of compressive stress on tool with respect to distance from cutting edge when high speed steel tool has been used to cut zinc, copper and aluminium.

2.2. Stress and Strain in the Chip

During machining the chips are produced due to the plastic deformation of the metal and are subjected to stress and strain.

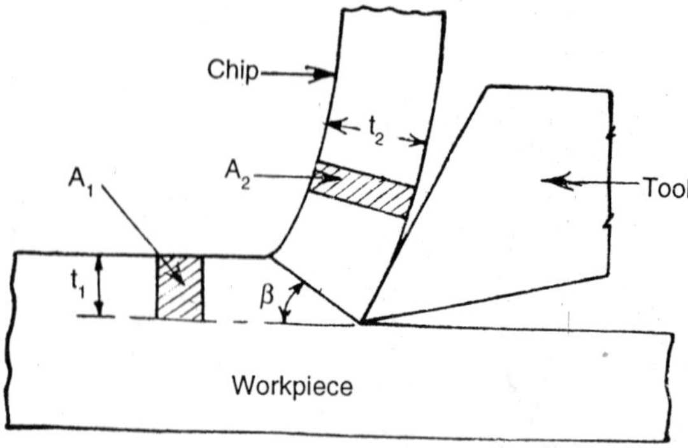

Fig. 2.4

Let F_S = Shearing force.

f_S = Shear stress in the shear plane.

A_1 = Cross sectional area of chip before cutting.

A_2 = Area of shear plane.

Now
$$f_S = \frac{F_S}{A_2}$$

$$A_2 = \frac{A_1}{\sin \beta}$$

$$\therefore \quad f_S = \frac{F_S}{A_1} \sin \beta$$

$$= \frac{(F_H \cos \beta - F_V \sin \beta) \sin \beta}{A_1}$$

$$= \frac{F_H \cos \beta \sin \beta - F_V \sin^2 \beta}{A_1}$$

where $A_1 = b_1 . t_1$.

and b_1 and t_1 indicate width and thickness of chip respectively (Fig. 2.4).

In the chip formation mechanics the resistance to deformation during chip formation is dependent upon the following :

(*i*) Dynamic shear stress in the conventional shear plane.

(*ii*) Frictional stresses at the chip tool interface.

2.3. Shear Strain

The chip is considered to be consisting of series of plate like elements of thickness Δy and displaced through a distance ΔS relative to each other as shown in Fig. 2.5. Strain is defined as the deformation per unit length.

$$e = \text{Shear strain} = \frac{\Delta S}{\Delta y}$$

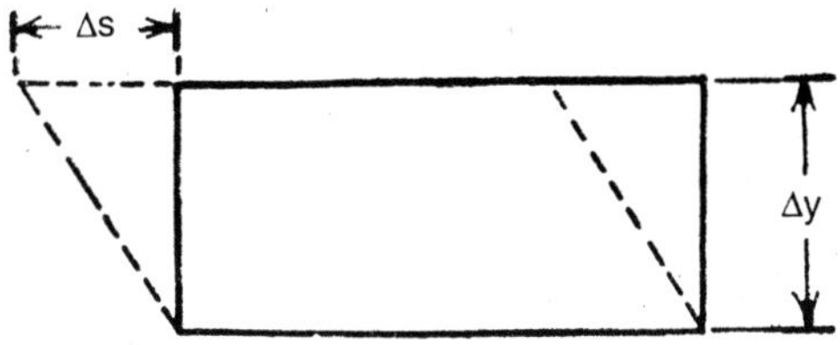

Fig. 2.5

Fig. 2.6 shows elements of chips in the strain state.

Now $\qquad e = \frac{\Delta S}{\Delta y} = \frac{AB}{CD}$

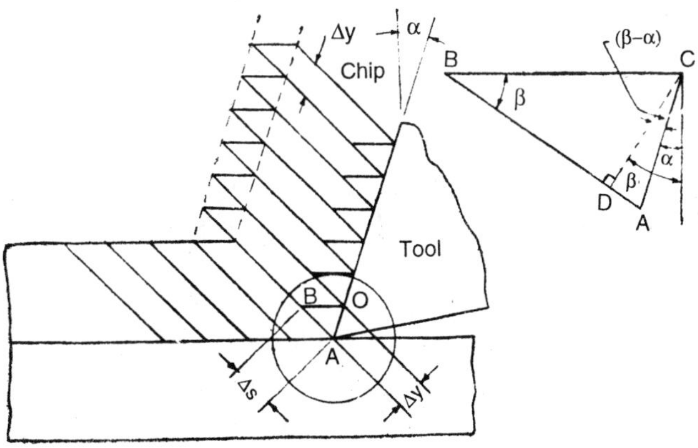

Fig. 2.6

$$= \frac{BD}{CD} + \frac{AB}{CD}$$

$$= \cot \beta + \tan (\beta - \alpha). \qquad ...(1)$$

$$= \frac{1}{\tan \beta} + \frac{\tan \beta - \tan \alpha}{1 + \tan \beta \tan \alpha}$$

$$= \frac{1 + \tan^2 \beta}{\tan \beta + \tan^2 \beta \tan \alpha}$$

$$= \frac{\sec^2 \beta}{\tan \beta (1 + \tan \beta \tan \alpha)} = \frac{\cos \alpha}{\sin \beta \,.\, \cos (\beta - \alpha)}$$

2.3. (*a*) **To prove that**

$$e = \frac{K^2 - 2K \sin \alpha + 1}{K \cos \alpha}$$

We know from equation (1)

$$e = \cot \beta + \tan (\beta - \alpha)$$

$$\tan \beta = \frac{r \cos \alpha}{1 - r \sin \alpha} = \frac{\cos \alpha}{\frac{1}{r} - \sin \alpha}$$

$$= \frac{\cos \alpha}{K - \sin \alpha}$$

Now $\quad e = \cot \beta + \tan (\beta + \alpha)$

$$e = \frac{\cot \beta + \tan \beta - \tan \alpha}{1 + \tan \beta \,.\, \tan \alpha}$$

Substitute the values of $\tan \beta$

$$e = \frac{K - \sin \alpha}{\cos \alpha} + \frac{\frac{\cos \alpha}{K - \sin \alpha} - \tan \alpha}{1 + \frac{\cos \alpha}{K - \sin \alpha} \times \tan \alpha}$$

$$= \frac{K - \sin \alpha}{\sin \alpha} + \frac{\cos \alpha - \tan \alpha \times (K - \sin \alpha)}{K - \sin \alpha + \cos \alpha \,.\, \tan \alpha}$$

$$= \frac{K - \sin \alpha}{\cos \alpha} + \frac{\cos^2 \alpha - K \sin \alpha + \sin^2 \alpha}{K \sin \alpha}$$

$$= \frac{K - \sin \alpha}{\cos \alpha} + \frac{1 - \sin \alpha \times K}{K \cos \alpha}$$

$$= \frac{K^2 - K \,.\, \sin \alpha + 1 - K \sin \alpha}{K \cos \alpha} = \frac{K^2 - 2K \sin \alpha + 1}{K \cos \alpha}$$

where K = Chip reduction coefficient.

Fig. 2.6 (*a*) shows how the strain increases when a layer undergoes deformation in the shear zone. In this figure

e = strain.

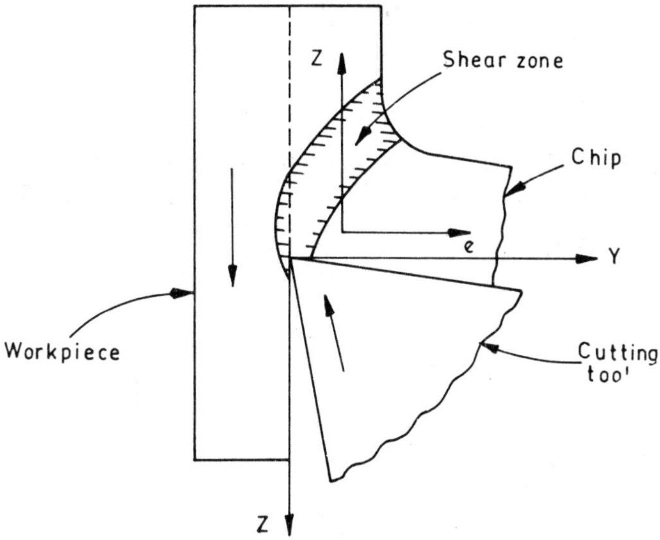

Fig. 2.6 (*a*)

Plastic deformation involved in the formation of chips affects the hardness of material. Hardening is usually characterised by a decrease of ductility or loss of plasticity. During this process, material undergoes strain-hardening. Amount of strain-hardening of the chip is a characteristic of the intensity of plastic deformation undergone by work material.

2.4. Work Done and Power Required

The work done and power required in metal cutting is calculated as follows.

Let V = Cutting speed (metre/minute)

F_H = Cutting force (kg)

W = Total work done in cutting

$= F_H \times V$ kg-m/min

W_1 = Work done in shear.

$= F_S \times V_S$ kg-m/min.

where. V_S = Velocity of the chip relative to work in metre minute.

F_S = Shear force in kg.

W_2 = Work done in friction

$$= P \times V_C. \text{ kg-m/min}$$

where V_C = Velocity of the chip relative to the cutting tool in metre/min.

$$W = W_1 + W_2$$

$$F_H \times V = F_S \times V_S + P \times V_C.$$

$$\text{H.P.} = \frac{F_H \times V}{4500}.$$

2.5. Power Consumed in Metal Cutting

Specific power means power required to remove unit volume of metal.

During two dimensional metal cutting operation the total energy (power) consumed is found as follows :

U = Total energy (power) consumed per unit time

$$= F_H \times V$$

where F_H = Cutting force (kg)

V = Cutting speed (mpm)

$$P = \text{Power} = \frac{F_H \times V}{4500}$$

E = Energy consumed per unit volume

$$= \frac{U}{V \,.\, b \,.\, t} = \frac{F_H \times V}{V \,.\, b \,.\, t} = \frac{F_H}{b \,.\, t}$$

where b = Width of cut

t = Depth of cut

Energy consumed per unit volume is utilised as follows.

(*i*) Shear energy per unit volume (E_S) on shear plane

$$E_S = \frac{F_S \,.\, V_S}{V \,.\, b \,.\, t} = f_S \left[\frac{V_S}{V \sin \beta} \right]$$

where F_S = Shear force.

V_S = Shear velocity

f_S = Shear stress

β = Shear angle.

(*ii*) Friction energy per unit volume (E_f) on the tool face.

$$E_f = \frac{F \,.\, V_C}{V \,.\, b \,.\, t}$$

where F = Force along tool face.

V_C = Chip velocity.

(*iii*) Surface energy per unit volume (E_A) due to the formation of new surface area in cutting.

(*iv*) Momentum energy per unit volume (E_m) due to the momentum change associated with the metal as it crosses the shear plane

$$E_m = \rho V^2 e^2 \sin^2 \beta$$

where ρ = Mass density of metal

e = Shear strain.

It is observed that the surface energy per unit volume (E_A) and momentum energy per unit volume (E_m) are relatively very small and can be neglected and therefore to a good approximation, we have

$$E = E_S + E_f$$

In general the friction energy is found to be about $\frac{1}{3}$th shear energy in turning.

It is important to reduce coefficient of friction between tool and chip in metal cutting because when the coefficient of friction is decreased in metal cutting not only a decrease in friction work will result but a decrease in the shear work as well.

2.6. Machine Tool Efficiency

H.P. used in metal cutting is estimated by measuring the gross horse power (HP_g) and t are horse power (HP_t).

H.P. cutting (HP_c) = $HP_g - HP_t$.

$$\eta = \text{Machine tool efficiency} = \frac{HP_c}{HP_g}.$$

2.7. Metal Removal Rate (w)

It is the volume of metal removed in unit time. It helps to calculate time required to remove specified quantity of material from the workpiece.

Let, t = Depth of cut in centimetres

f = Feed/revolution in cm.

V = Cutting speed in cm/minute.

$w = t.f.v$ cm^3/min.

The metal should be removed by the cutting rapidly to reduce the machining cost. To achieve this the following factors should be considered.

(*i*) The cutting tool should be made up of proper material.

(*ii*) The cutting tool should be properly ground.

(*iii*) Tool should be held rigidly and there should be no vibrations.

(*iv*) Depending upon the rigidity of the machine maximum speed and feed should be used.

The material removed per minute is calculated as indicated in Table 2.1 for various operations.

Table 2.1

Operation	*Volume (cm^3/min)*
Turning	$f \times t \times V$
Face milling	$B \times t \times T$
Slot milling	$B \times t \times T$
Planning or shaping	$t \times f \times L \times S$

where f = Feed (cm/rev.)

t = Depth of cut in cm.

V = Cutting speed in cm/min.

B = Width of cut in cm.

T = Table travel cm/min.

L = Length of work piece in cm.

S = Strokes per minute.

2.7.1. Specific horse power

Specific horse power means power required to remove unit volume of metal.

Total energy required for unit volume of metal cut is function of the following variables :

(*i*) Work piece material

(*ii*) Friction condition on tool face

(*iii*) Tool sharpness

(*iv*) Cutting speed, feed and depth of cut

(*v*) Rake angle

(*vi*) Clearance angle

(*vii*) Cutting fluid used.

2.8. Ernst-Merchant Theory

According to this theory the relation between rake angle α, shear angle β and friction angle γ is as follows :

$$\beta = \frac{\pi}{4} - \frac{\gamma}{2} + \frac{\alpha}{2}$$

(*i*) Shear will take place in a direction in which energy required for shearing is minimum.

(*ii*) Shear stress is maximum at the shear plane and it remains constant.

We have proved that

$$F_H = \frac{F_S \, . \cos(\gamma - \alpha)}{\cos(\beta + \gamma - \alpha)}$$

Now $F_S = f_S . A_2$

where f_S = Shear stress

$$A_2 = \text{Area of shear plane} = \frac{b_1 t_1}{\sin \beta}$$

$$\therefore \quad F_H = f_S . \frac{b_1 t_1}{\sin \beta} \frac{\cos(\gamma - \alpha)}{\cos(\beta + \gamma - \alpha)}$$

Differentiating w.r.t. β.

$$\frac{dF_H}{d\beta} = -f_S \, . \, b_1 t_1 \cos(\gamma - \alpha)$$

$$\times \left[\frac{\cos \beta \, . \cos(\beta + \gamma - \alpha) - \sin \beta \sin(\beta + \gamma - \alpha)}{\sin^2 \beta \cos^2(\beta + \gamma - \alpha)} \right]$$

= 0 in order that β will assume that value which required a minimum force to cut the material.

$$\therefore \quad \cos \beta \cos(\beta + \gamma - \alpha) - \sin \beta \sin(\beta + \gamma - \alpha) = 0$$

$$\cos(\beta + \beta + \gamma - \alpha) = 0$$

$$\cos(2\beta + \gamma - \alpha) = 0$$

$$2\beta + \gamma - \alpha = \frac{\pi}{2}$$

$$\beta = \frac{\pi}{4} - \frac{\gamma}{2} + \frac{\alpha}{2}.$$

2.9. Lee and Shaffer's Theory

The theory of Lee and Shaffer was the result of an attempt to apply the plasticity theory to the problem of orthogonal metal cutting. The assumptions made in this theory are follows :

(*i*) The work material ahead of the tool behaves as ideal plastic mass.

(*ii*) There exists a shear plane which separates the chip and workpiece.

(*iii*) No hardening in chip occurs. On the basis of above assumptions the following relationship was obtained :

$$\beta + \gamma - \alpha = \frac{\pi}{4}.$$

Lee and Shaffer realised that the above equation could not apply for all values of γ and α such as when γ in $\frac{\pi}{4}$ and α is zero, this will give β as zero. Therefore they modified the above equation by including the effect of built up edge by using addition angle θ depending on the size of built up edge and arrived at the following solution :

$$\beta + \gamma - \alpha - \theta = \frac{\pi}{4}.$$

2.10. Velocities in Metal Cutting

There are three velocities in a metal cutting process :

(*i*) **Cutting velocity (V).** It is the velocity of the tool relative to the workpiece and directed parallel to the cutting force.

(*ii*) **Chip velocity (V_C).** It is the velocity of the chip relative to the tool and is directed along the tool face.

(*iii*) **Shear velocity (V_S).** It is the velocity of the chip relative to the workpiece and is directed along the shear plane.

2.10.1. Velocity relationship

The velocity relationship in orthogonal cutting are shown in Fig. 2.7. The various velocities are the cutting velocity *V*, chip

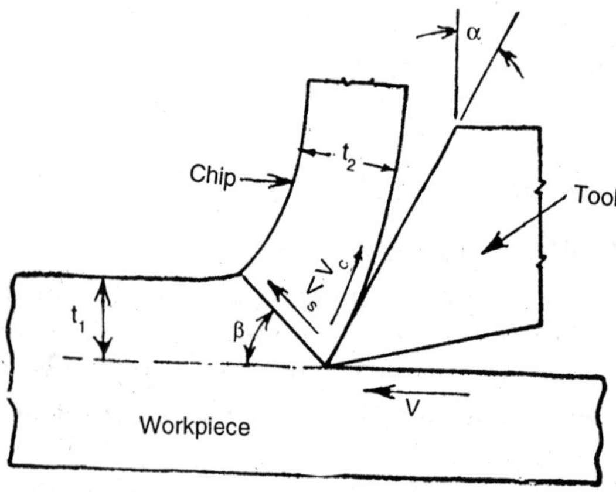

Fig. 2.7

velocity V_C and shear velocity V_S. Velocity V_C is the velocity of chip relative to tool and is directed along tool face and V_S is velocity of chip relative to workpiece and is directed along shear plane (Fig. 2.8).

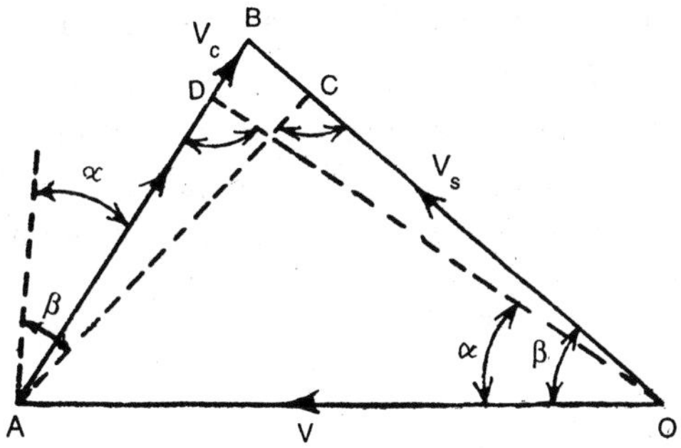

Fig. 2.8

In Fig. 2.8, from right angle triangle *OCA*

$$AC = OA \sin \beta$$

$$AC = V \sin \beta$$

From right angled triangle *BAC*.

$$AC = AB \cos (\beta - \alpha)$$

$$AC = V_C \cos (\beta - \alpha) \quad ...(ii)$$

∴ From (*i*) and (*ii*)

$$V \sin B = V_C \cos (\beta - \alpha)$$

$$V_C = \frac{V \sin \beta}{\cos (\beta - \alpha)}$$

Again from right angle triangle *ODA*

$$OD = OA \cos \sigma$$

$$= V \cos \alpha \quad ...(iii)$$

From right angled triangle *ODB*.

$$OD = V_S \cos (\beta - \alpha) \quad ...(iv)$$

∴ From (*iii*) and (*iv*)

$$V \cos \alpha = V_S \cos (\beta - \alpha)$$

$$V_S = \frac{V \cos \alpha}{\cos (\beta - \alpha)}.$$

2.10.2. To prove $V_C = rV$

We have proved that

$$V_C = \frac{V . \sin \beta}{\cos (\beta - \alpha)}$$

And it has also been proved in chapter one

$$r = \frac{\sin \beta}{\cos (\beta - \alpha)}$$

where, r = chip thickness ratio

$$\therefore \quad V_C = \frac{V . \sin \beta}{\cos (\beta - \alpha)} = V . r.$$

2.10.3. Effect of cutting variables on cutting forces

The cutting forces are direct functions of feed (f) and depth of cut (d) under conditions of other variables kept constant, the following relations may be used for machining steel :

$$F_z = C_1 d.f^{0.75}$$
$$F_y = C_2 d^{0.9} f^{0.75}$$
$$F_x = C_3 d^{1.2} f^{0.55}$$

For steel having ultimate strength 35 kg/mm^2 the values of C_1, C_2 and C_3 are as follows :

$$C_1 = 14$$
$$C_2 = 27$$
$$C_3 = 20$$

For machining cast iron (BHN = 150) the following relations may be used :

$$F_z = K_1 d.f^{0.78}$$
$$F_y = K_2 d^{0.9} f^{0.75}$$
$$F_x = K_3 d^{1.1} f^{0.65}$$

The values of constants K_1, K_2 and K_3 are follows :

$$K_1 = 80$$
$$K_2 = 59$$
$$K_3 = 28.$$

2.11. Improvement of Cutting Efficiency

It is desirable that the metal cutting should be economical.

Cutting efficiency can be improved by following factors :

(*i*) By reducing chip length by means of chip breakers.

(*ii*) By improving surface finish of the tool face by honing or chrome plating.

(*iii*) Increased depth of cut increases the cutting efficiency by a small amount.

(*iv*) By effective removal of heat produced during cutting.

2.12. Requirements Made to the Cutting Tool

A tool intended for high production machining should be amply strong and rigid, it should have optimum geometry, be keenly sharpened with a high class finish, producible in manufacture and convenient in use.

2.13. Cutting Tool Design

Proper cutting tool design is essential in order to achieve desired accuracy, and to increase tool life. The cutting tool should be of proper material and should be able to resist the forces acting on it. Proper tool geometry leads to increased tool life, desired functioning of tool and to increased strength of tool.

2.13.1. Carbide tool failures and remedies

Premature tool failure problems should be checked to increase tool life. Some of the commonly observed problems and their solutions are as follows :

Problem	*Recommended Solution*
1. Wear	(*i*) Decrease speed
	(*ii*) Increase feed
	(*iii*) Decrease lead angle
	(*iv*) Check that tool is not above centre height
	(*v*) Tool should be of proper grade and hardness
	(*vi*) Increases one or both relief and clearance angle.
2. Poor surface finish	(*i*) Increase nose radius
	(*ii*) Increase lead angle
	(*iii*) Tool should be properly clamped
	(*iv*) Increase speed
	(*v*) Decrease feed.
3. Chatter	(*i*) Decrease nose radius
	(*ii*) Decrease rake angle

	(*iii*)	Increase relief and clearance angle
	(*iv*)	Decrease overhang
	(*v*)	Check the condition of spindles and slides of the machine
	(*vi*)	Decrease cutting speed
	(*vii*)	Increase feed
	(*viii*)	Check that workpiece is properly held and clamped.
4. Crater	(*i*)	Use coolant of good lubricating qualities
	(*ii*)	Use harder grade tool
	(*iii*)	Increase speed
	(*iv*)	Decrease feed
	(*v*)	Positive rake angle may be used.
5. Built up edge	(*i*)	Increase speed
	(*ii*)	Use positive rake
	(*iii*)	Use coolant with good lubricating properties.
6. Chipping cracking and breakage	(*i*)	Increase nose radius
	(*ii*)	Increase lead angle if possible
	(*iii*)	Use negative rake
	(*iv*)	Increase speed
	(*v*)	Decrease feed
	(*vi*)	Check the tool for looseness
	(*vii*)	Check rigidity of workpiece
	(*viii*)	Decrease tool overhang.

2.14. Dynamometry

It is a method of measuring cutting force during metal cutting. Dynamometer is the instrument used for measuring the cutting force.

A dynamometer should possess the following two requirements :

(*i*) Sensitivity

(*ii*) Rigidity

A dynamometer is said to be sensitive if the measurements are accurate to within ± 1%. During use some deformation is associated with the operation of every dynamometer. A dynamometer should be rigid enough so that the cutting operation is not influenced by the accompanying deflections. The main stiffness criterion is the natural frequency of the dynamometer. All machine tools operated with vibrations. Large amplitude of vibrations are experienced during machining operations like milling, grinding, shaping etc. In order that the cutting force is not influenced by any vibrating motion of the dynamometer its frequency should be high (about 4 times as high) as compared to the exciting vibration. The dynamometer can be compared to a spring-mass system for purpose of analysis of vibrations. The natural frequency of such system is given by

$$\omega_n = \frac{1}{2\pi}\sqrt{\frac{K}{m}}$$

where ω_n = Natural frequency in cycles per second (CPS)

K = Spring stiffness (kgf/cm)

m = Mass (kg)

(*iii*) Size

(*iv*) Ruggedness

(*v*) Adaptability to several jobs.

A dynamometer should be stable with respect to the following :

(*i*) Time

(*ii*) Temperature

(*iii*) Humidity

Once a calibration is made, the dynamometer should only have to be checked occasionally.

2.15. Types of Dynamometers

Various types of dynamometers are as follows :

(*i*) **Direct reading type.** These dynamometers use devices for the separation of force components which involve friction such as rollers, balls and sliding surfaces. However as friction conditions are usually variable due to dirt, temperature etc., such instruments are not commonly used.

(*ii*) **Recording or indicating dynamometers.** These dynamometers cost more than direct reading type. But these have the advantages of easy measurement and more life.

2.16. Force Measurement

A dynamometer should measure at least two force components in order to determine a two dimensional resultant cutting force. In a three dimensional cutting operation three force components are necessary while in drilling or tapping only a torque and a thrust are required.

Force measurement involves the measurement of a deflection with a suitable calibration between the force and deflection it produces. In most dynamometers the force is applied to some sort of spring and the deflection thus produced is measured.

Some of the devices used to measure small deflections in dynamometers are as follows :

(*i*) **Dial Indicator.** It can read deflections to about 25×10^{-4} mm.

However dial indicators are subject to sticking and are not to be relied upon for absolutely static readings. A lever system is frequently use in conjunction with a dial indicator.

The cutting forces are generally measured by an instrument called cutting tool dynamometer. There are different designs of dynamometers although their basic principle is same. The general principle used in deflection type cutting tool dynamometer is shown in Fig. 2.8 (*a*). A stiff member *M* resting on a solid pivot carries a

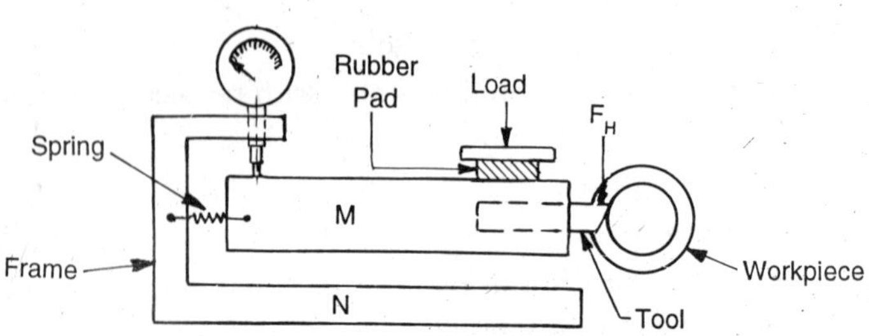

Fig. 2.8 (*a*)

cutting tool at one end and is attached to a frame N by means of a leaf spring at the other end. The cutting force F_H deflects the member M relative to N by an amount depending on the magnitude of F_H and stiffness of spring. The deflection so produced is taken up by the dial gauge which is calibrated to real the magnitude of F_H proportional to deflection. The feed force (F_V) can be measured by housing the frame in a further solid member so that it deflects in a plane perpendicular to the plane of the given projection.

(*ii*) **Hydraulic Dynamometer.** Hydraulic pressure cells are used in conjunction with pressure gauges to measure or record the force on a tool.

Fig. 2.9 shows basic principle of hydraulic dynamometer.

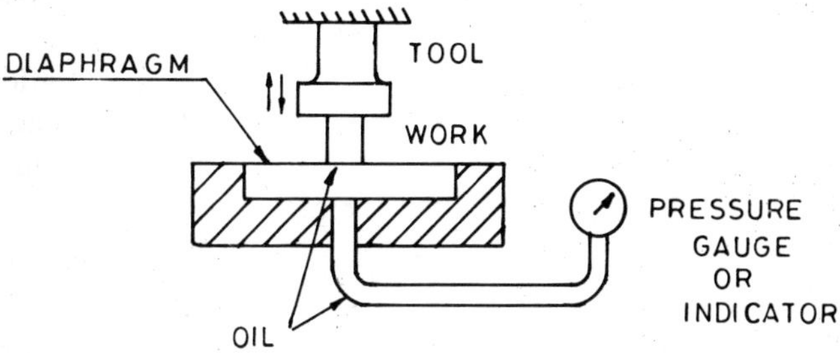

Fig. 2.9

(*iii*) **Pneumatic Dynamometer.** In such dynamometers the change in back pressure that occurs when a flat surface is brought into closer contact with a sharp edged orifice are some times used to measure deflections in tool dynamometers.

These dynamometers have the following advantages :

(*i*) Simple

(*ii*) Reliable if air supplied is clean with constant pressure of air.

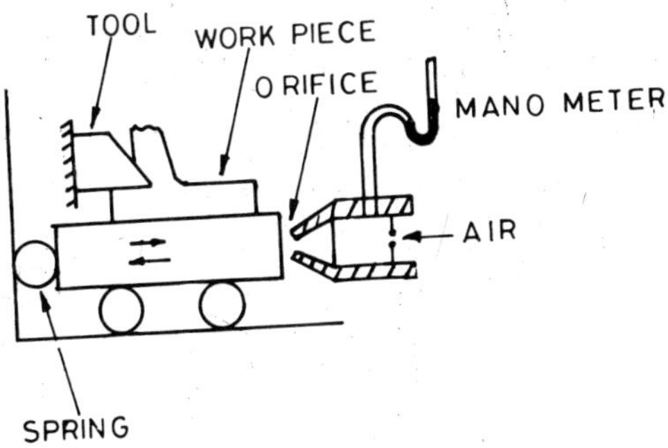

Fig. 2.10

However following drawbacks are observed in these dynamometers :

(*i*) There is a limited region over which they are linear.

(*ii*) They are generally bulky.

Basic principle of pneumatic dynamometer is shown in Fig. 2.10.

(*iv*) **Optical Dynamometer.** These dynamometers use two methods :

(*a*) Interferometric method can be used to give very precise measurements using the wave length of light as a yard stick. But it is difficult to apply this method to the measurement of the dynamic deflections obtained in metal cutting.

(*b*) Optical lever principle to measure small deflections. Fig. 2.11 shows principle of optical lever principle. A narrow beam of

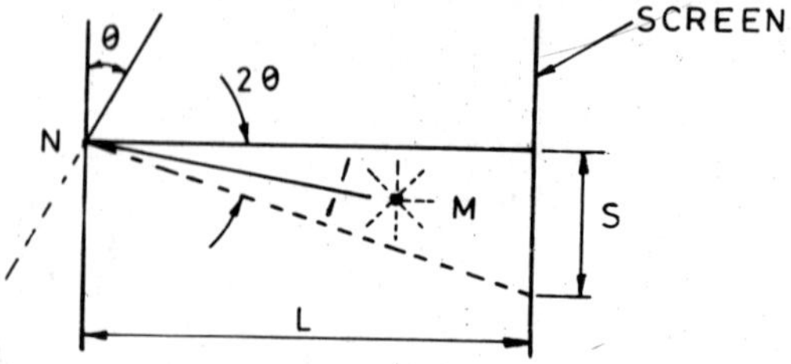

Fig. 2.11

light travels from M to N where it is reflected and hence travels to screen. When the surface N rotates through an angle (θ), the spot of light moves through a distance (S) on the screen.

$$\tan 2\theta = \frac{S}{L}$$

If angle θ is small

$$2\theta = \frac{S}{L}$$

$$S = 2\theta \times L$$

(*v*) **Electric Dynamometers**

(*a*) Piezo electric crystals may be used as force measuring units.

(*b*) The electric transducers provide more convenient electrical units in the construction of dynamometers.

Electric transducers commonly used are as follows :

(*i*) The electronic transducer tube.

(*ii*) The magnetic strain gauge.

(*iii*) The bonded wire resistance strain gauge.

(*iv*) The unbonded wire resistance strain gauge.

(*v*) The differential transformer.

Example 2.1. *During turning a mild steel component with an orthogonal tool a feed of 0.75 mm / rev is used at 50 R.P.M. If the chip thickness is 1.5 mm, determine the chip thickness ratio. Also find the length of chip removed in one minute, if the work diameter is 50 mm before the cut is taken. Assume a continuous chip.*

Solution. r = Chip thickness ratio

$$r = \frac{t_1}{t_2}$$

where $t_1 = 0.75$ mm and $t_2 = 1.5$ mm.

$$r = \frac{0.75}{1.5} = 0.5$$

L_1 = Length of chip before cutting

$= \pi DN$

where D = Diameter of work piece = 50 mm.

N = R.P.M. = 50.

$L_1 = \pi \times 50 \times 50 = 7850$ mm

L_2 = Length of chip removed per minute.

$$r = \frac{L_2}{L_1}$$

$$0.5 = \frac{L_2}{7850}$$

$L_2 = 3925$ mm. **Ans.**

Example 2.2. *In an orthogonal turning operation :*

Cutting speed	*= 80 m / min*
Cutting force	*= 20 kg.*
Feed force	*= 8 kg.*
Back rake angle	*= 15°.*
Feed	*= 0.2 mm / rev.*
Chip thickness	*= 0.4 mm.*

Determine the following :

(*a*) *Shear angle.*

(*b*) *Work done in shear.*

(*c*) *Shear strain.*

Solution. r = chip thickness ratio = t_1/t_2

where $t_1 = 0.2$ mm and $t_2 = 0.4$ mm

$$r = \frac{0.2}{0.4} = 0.5$$

β = shear angle.

α = rake angle = 15°

$$\tan \beta = \frac{r \cos \alpha}{1 - r \sin \alpha}$$

$$\tan \beta = \frac{0.5 \cos 15}{1 - 0.5 \sin 15} = 0.55$$

$\beta = 28°$.

F_S = Shear force

$= F_H \cos \beta - F_V \sin \beta$.

Now F_H = Cutting force = 20 kg.

F_V = Feed force = 8 kg.

$F_S = 20 \cos 28 - 8 \sin 28 = 13.84$ kg.

Now V = Cutting speed = 80 m/min.

$$V_S = \frac{V \cos \alpha}{\cos (\beta - \alpha)}$$

$$= \frac{80 \cos 15}{\cos (28 - 15)} = 79 \text{ m/min.}$$

Work done in shear

$= F_S \,.\, V_S = 13.84 \times 79$

$= 1093$ kg-m/min.

Shear strain $= \cot \beta + \tan (\beta - \alpha)$

$= \cot 28 + \tan (28 - 15) = 1.65.$

Example 2.3. *Calculate the power consumed during cutting of a low carbon steel bar 40 mm diameter if cutting force is 150 kg at 200 R.P.M.*

Solution. F_H = Cutting force

= 150 kg

V = Cutting speed

$$= \frac{\pi DN}{1000} = \frac{\pi \times 40}{10000} \times 200 = 25.12 \text{ m/min.}$$

Work done $= F_H \times V = 150 \times 25.12$ kg-m/min

$$\text{H.P.} = \frac{150 \times 25.12}{4500} = 0.83. \textbf{ Ans.}$$

Example 2.4. *Determine the time required to turn a brass component 50 mm diameter and 100 mm long at a cutting speed of 36 m / min. The feed is 0.4 m / revolution and only one cut is taken.*

Solution. D = Diameter of component = 50 mm

L = Length = 100 mm

V = Cutting speed = 36 m/min.

f = Feed = 0.4 mm/rev.

N = Spindle speed (R.P.M.)

$$V = \frac{\pi DN}{1000} \text{ m/min.}$$

$$36 = \frac{\pi \,.\, 50 \,.\, N}{10000}$$

N = 229 R.P.M.

T = Time required

$$= \frac{L}{f \,.\, N} = \frac{100}{0.4 \times 229} \text{ minutes.}$$

$$= \frac{100 \times 60}{0.4 \times 229} = 65 \text{ seconds. } \textbf{Ans.}$$

Example 2.5. *(a) In orthogonal cutting if the feed is 1.25 mm / rev. and chip thickness after cutting is 2 mm, determine the following :*

(i) Chip thickness ratio.

(ii) Shear angle.

The tool bit has a rake angle of 10°

(b) If shear strength = 6000 kg / cm²

Width of cut	*= 10 mm*
Cutting speed	*= 30 m / min.*
Coefficient of friction	*= 0.9.*

Determine the following :

(i) Shearing force.

(ii) Friction angle.

(iii) Cutting force.

(iv) Horse power at the cutting tool.

Solution. (*a*) Let r = chip thickness ratio = $\dfrac{t_1}{t_2}$

where t_1 = Chip thickness before cutting.

t_2 = Chip thickness after cutting.

Now $t_1 = 1.25$ mm.

$t_2 = 2$ mm.

$$r = \frac{1.25}{2} = 0.625$$

Let β = Shear angle

α = Rake angle = 10°

$$\tan \beta = \frac{r \cos \alpha}{1 - r \sin \alpha} = \frac{0.625 \cos 10}{1 - 0.625 \sin 10}$$

$$= \frac{0.625 \times 0.9848}{1 - 0.625 - 0.1736} = 0.65$$

$\beta = 33° 2'$. **Ans.**

(*b*) We know

$$F_S = \frac{f_S \cdot A_1}{\sin \beta}$$

where F_S = Shearing force

F_S = Shear stress

A_1 = Area of chip

= Width of chip × Depth of cut

= 1 cm × 0.125 cm

$$\therefore \quad F_S = \frac{6000 \times (1 \times 0.125)}{\sin 33° 2'}$$

$$= \frac{6000 \times 0.125}{0.545} = 1376 \text{ kg.}$$

Let γ = Friction angle

μ = Coefficient of friction

$\tan \gamma = \mu = 0.9$

$\gamma = 42°$.

F_H = Cutting force

$$= \frac{F_S \cdot \cos(\gamma - \alpha)}{\cos(\beta + \gamma - \alpha)}$$

$$= \frac{1376 \cos(42 - 10)}{\cos(33' - 2' + 42 - 10)}$$

$$= \frac{1376 \cos 32}{\cos 65° 2'} = 2778 \text{ kg.}$$

H.P. = Horse power at the tool

$$= \frac{F_H \times V}{4500}$$

where V = Cutting speed (metre/min)

$$\text{H.P.} = \frac{2778 \times 30}{4500} = 18.52. \textbf{ Ans.}$$

Example 2.6. *In orthogonal cutting of a material the feed force is 80 kg and cutting force is 150 kg. Calculate the following :*

(*i*) *Compression and shear forces on shear plane.*

(*ii*) *Coefficient of friction of the chip on the tool face.*

Take chip thickness ratio as 0.3 and rake angle as 8°.

Solution. We have proved that

F_n = Compressive force on shear plane.

$= F_V \cos \beta + F_H \sin \beta.$

F_S = Shear force on shear plane

$= F_H \cos \beta - F_V \sin \beta$

Now $F_H = 150$ kg.

$F_V = 80$ kg.

$\alpha = 8°$

β = Shear angle.

$$\tan \beta = \frac{r \cos \alpha}{1 - r \sin \alpha} = \frac{0.3 \cos 8}{1 - 0.3 \sin 8} = 0.3$$

$\beta = 17°$

$\therefore$ $F_n = F_V \cos \beta + F_H \sin \beta$

$= 80 \cos 17 + 150 \sin 17 = 121$ kg. **Ans.**

$F_S = F_H \cos \beta - F_V \sin \beta.$

$= 150 \cos 17 - 80 \sin 17 = 119.3$ kg. **Ans.**

μ = Coefficient of friction

$$\frac{F_H \tan \alpha + F_V}{P_H - F_V \tan \alpha} = \frac{150 \tan 8 + 80}{150 - 80 \tan 8} = 0.73. \textbf{ Ans.}$$

Example 2.7. *In orthogonal turning process the feed is 0.25 mm / rev. at 50 R.P.M. The thickness of the chip removed is 0.5 mm.*

(*a*) *What is the chip thickness ratio ?*

(*b*) *If the work diameter is 50 mm before the cut is taken, what is the approximate length of the chip removed in one minute. Assume a continuous chip.*

Solution. r = Chip thickness ratio = t_1/t_2

t_1 = Chip thickness before cutting

= 0.25 mm.

t_2 = Chip thickness

$$r = \frac{t_1}{t_2} = \frac{0.25}{0.5} = 0.5 \text{ Ans.}$$

Work diameter,

$$D = 50 \text{ mm} = 5 \text{ cm.}$$

$$N = \text{R.P.M.} = 50.$$

L_1 = Length of chip before cutting

$$= \pi \,.\, D \,.\, N$$

$$= \pi \,.\, 5.50 = 785 \text{ cm.}$$

L_2 = Length of chip after cutting.

$$r = \frac{L_2}{L_1}$$

$$0.5 = \frac{L_2}{785}$$

$$L_2 = 0.5 \times 785 = 392.5 \text{ cm. } \textbf{Ans.}$$

Example 2.8. *A medium carbon steel bar 40 mm diameter is turned on a lathe with a cutting tool having top rake angle 30° and with a cutting speed of 24 mpm (metre per minute). If the cutting force is 200 kg, feed force 80 kg and feed given to tool is 0.12 mm / rev. length of chip in one revolution = 70 mm, determine the following :*

(*a*) *Shear angle.*

(*b*) *Chip thickness.*

(*c*) *Velocity of chip along the tool face.*

Solution. F_H = Cutting force = 200 kg.

F_V = Feed force = 80 kg.

α = Rake angle = 30°

f = feed/revolution = 0.12 mm/rev.

β = Shear angle.

$$\tan \beta = \frac{r \cos \alpha}{1 - r \sin \alpha} = \frac{r \cos 30}{1 - r \sin 30}$$

$$r = \text{Chip thickness ratio} = \frac{L_2}{L_1}$$

L_1 = Length of chip before cutting.

$$= \pi D$$

where D = Diameter of workpiece = $\pi \times 40$ mm

L_2 = Length of chip after cutting = 70 mm (given).

$$r = \frac{70}{\pi \times 40} = 0.55$$

$$\tan \beta = \frac{0.55 \cos 30}{1 - 0.55 \sin 30}$$

$$\beta = 33° \, 6'. \textbf{ Ans.}$$

$$r = \frac{t_1}{t_2}.$$

where t_1 = Chip thickness before cutting = Feed.

t_2 = Chip thickness.

$$r = \frac{\text{Feed/rev.}}{\text{Chip thickness}}$$

Chip thickness

$$= \frac{\text{Feed/rev.}}{r} = \frac{0.12}{0.55}$$

$$= 0.218 \text{ mm. } \textbf{Ans.}$$

V_C = Velocity of chip along the tool face.

$$= \frac{V \sin \beta}{\cos (\beta - \alpha)} = V \times r$$

where V = Cutting speed.

$$\left[\text{As we have proved } r = \frac{\sin \beta}{\cos (\beta - \alpha)} \right]$$

$$V_C = 24 \times 0.55 = 13.2 \text{ mpm. } \textbf{Ans.}$$

Example 2.9. *To turn a mild steel component the power required is 0.1/cm³/min. The maximum power available at the machine spindle is 5 H.P. If the cutting speed is 35 metre/min and feed rate is 0.25 mm/rev., determine the following :*

(*a*) *Maximum metal removal rate.*

(*b*) *Depth of cut.*

(*c*) *Cutting force.*

(*d*) *Normal pressure on chip.*

Solution. w = Maximum metal removal rate.

$$= \frac{5}{0.1} = 50 \text{ cm}^3/\text{min.}$$

F_H = Cutting force (kg)

V = Cutting speed (mpm)

$$\frac{F_H \times V}{4500} = \text{Horse power} = 5.$$

$$F_H = \frac{4500 \times 5}{35} = 643 \text{ kg.}$$

t = Depth of cut in cm.

f = Feed in cm. = 0.025 cm/rev.

V = Cutting speed in cm.

$w = t \times f \times V$

$50 = t \times 0.025 \times 35 \times 100$

$$t = \frac{50}{35 \times 100 \times 0.25} = 0.55 \text{ cm} = 5.5 \text{ mm}.$$

Normal pressure on chip

$$= \frac{F_H}{\text{Chip Area}} = \frac{643}{\text{Feed} \times \text{Depth of cut}}$$

$$= \frac{643}{0.25 \times 5.5} = 468 \text{ kg/mm}^2. \textbf{ Ans.}$$

Example 2.10. *Following observations were made from a metal cutting test carried out on a lathe.*

Cutting force = 180 kg.

Feed = 5 cuts/mm.

Depth of cut = 5 mm.

Cutting speed = 30 mpm.

If overall efficiency of the machine is 70%, determine :

(a) Normal pressure on chip.

(b) Power required at the motor to turn the material.

Solution. F_H = Cutting force = 180 kg.

Feed $= \frac{1}{5} = 0.2$ mm/rev.

Normal pressure on chip

$$= \frac{F_H}{\text{Cross sectional area of chip}}$$

$$= \frac{180}{5 \times 0.2} = 180 \text{ kg/mm}^2.$$

(Cross sectional area of chip

= Depth of cut × Feed per revolution)

Power required for cutting

$$= \frac{F_H \times V}{4500}$$

$$= \frac{183 \times 30}{4500} = 1.2$$

Power required at the motor

$$= \frac{1.2}{0.70} = 1.7 \text{ H.P. } \textbf{Ans.}$$

Example 2.11. *The power required by a lathe when running idle is 300 watts. The power input rises to 2400 watts when an alloy steel is machined on lathe at 120 r.p.m. If the depth of cut is 3.50 mm, feed is 0.2 mm/rev and cutting speed is 24 metre/min. Calculate the following :*

(a) Cutting force and torque at the spindle.

(b) H.P./cm^3/min required to cut the material.

Solution. Power required for cutting

$$= 2400 - 300 = 2100 \text{ Watts.}$$

H.P. required for cutting

$$= \frac{2100}{735} = 2.87$$

$$T = \text{Torque at the spindle}$$

$$N = \text{r.p.m.} = 120$$

$$\text{H.P.} = \frac{2\pi NT}{4500}$$

$$2.87 = \frac{2\pi \times 120 \times T}{4500}$$

$$T = \frac{2.87 \times 4300}{2\pi \times 120} = 17 \text{ kg m}$$

$$F_H = \text{Cutting force}$$

$$V = \text{Cutting speed in metre per minute}$$

$$= 24 \text{ mpm}$$

$$\text{H.P.} = \frac{F_H \times V}{4500}$$

$$2.87 = \frac{F_H \times 24}{4500}$$

$$F_H = \frac{2.87 \times 4500}{24} = 538 \text{ kg}$$

$$w = \text{Maximum metal removal rate}$$

$$= f \times t \times V$$

where f = Feed = 0.2 mm/rev. = 0.02 cm/rev.

t = Depth of cut. = 3.5 mm = 0.35 cm

V = Cutting speed = 24 metre/min. = 2400 cm/min.

$$w = 0.02 \times 0.35 \times 2400 = 16.8 \text{ cm}^3/\text{min}.$$

$$\text{H.P./cm}^3/\text{min} = \frac{2.87}{16.8} = 0.17. \textbf{ Ans.}$$

Example 2.12. *During a metal cutting test under orthogonal conditions it was found that cutting force is 110 kg and feed force is 102 kg when cutting at 165 metre/min. The rake angle of tool is 10° and shear plane angle was found to be at 19°. Determine the following :*

(*i*) *Shear velocity.*

(*ii*) *Chip flow velocity.*

(*iii*) *Work done per minute in shearing the metal and work done against friction.*

(*iv*) *Show that the work input is equal to the sum of work done in shearing and against friction.*

Solution. Draw merchant circle diagram (Fig. 2.12).

$F_H = 110$ kg

$F_V = 102$ kg

α = Rate angle = 10°

β = Shear angle = 19°

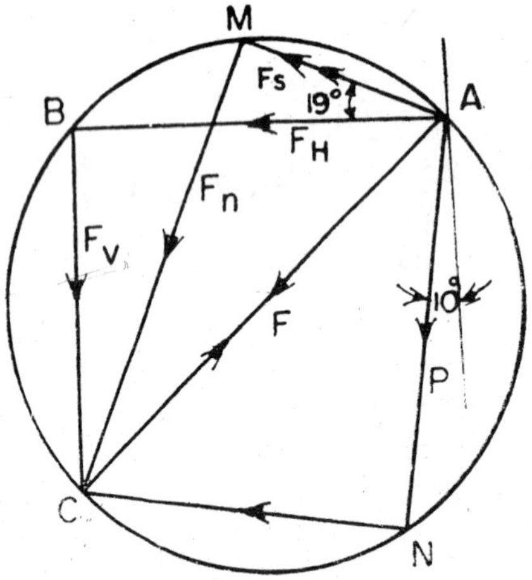

Fig. 2.12

Take $AB = F_H$ and $BC = F_V$ the two forces being at right angles. Draw a circle with AC diameter.

From the diagram, $F_S = 70$ kg

$P = 124$ kg

Now $V = 165$ m/min.

Draw the velocity diagram (Fig. 2.13).

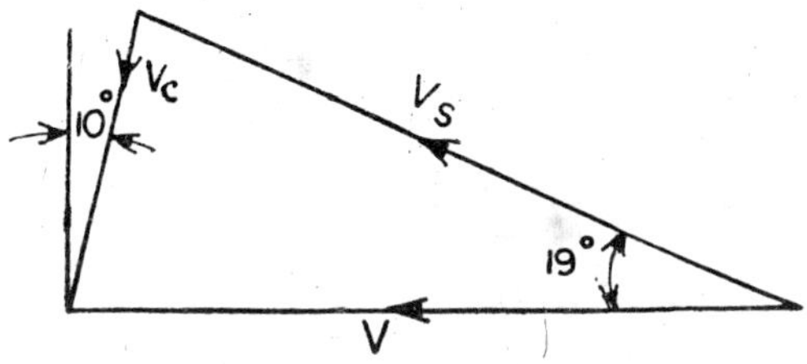

Fig. 2.13

From the diagram

Shear velocity, $V_S = 162$ m/min

Chip flow velocity, $V_C = 58$ m/min

(*W*) Work input

$$F_H \times V = 110 \times 165 = 18{,}150 \text{ kg-m/min}$$

Work done in shearing the metal (W_1)

$$= F_S \times V_H = 70 \times 162 = 11{,}340 \text{ kg-m}$$

Work done against friction (W_2)

$$= P \times V_C = 124 \times 58 = 71{,}292 \text{ kg-m.}$$

$$W_1 + W_2 = 11340 + 7192 = 18{,}532 \text{ kg-m. } \textbf{Ans.}$$

It shows that within limits of accuracy the work input is equal to the work done in shearing and work done against friction.

Example 2.13. *In orthogonal cutting of a mild steel tube of 150 mm diameter and 2 mm thick the cutting force was observed to be 130 kg and feed force 35 kg and chip thickness 0.3 mm. The orthogonal cut was taken at 60 mpm with a feed of 0.14 mm / rev. If the back rake angle of the cutting tool was – 8°, calculate the following :*

(*a*) *Shear strain,*

(*b*) *Strain energy per unit volume.*

Solution. Feed = 0.15 mm/rev.

Chip thickness = 0.3 mm

$$r = \text{Chip thickness ratio} = \frac{0.15}{0.3} = 0.5$$

For negative rake angle

$$\tan \beta = \frac{r \cos \alpha}{1 + r \sin \alpha}$$

where α = Rake angle

$$\tan \beta = \frac{0.5 \cos 8}{1 + 0.5 \sin 8} = 26.5°$$

Shear strain $= \tan (\beta - \alpha) + \cot \beta$

$= \tan [26.5 - (-8)] + \cot 26.5$

$= \tan 34.5° + \cot 26.5 = 2.68$

Shear stress : $f_s = \dfrac{F_H \cos \beta \sin \beta - F_V \sin^2 \beta}{b_1 \cdot t_1}$

Now $F_H = 130$ kg

$F_V = 35$ kg

$\beta = 26.5°$

$$f_s = \frac{130 \cos 26.5 \sin 26.5 - 35 \sin^2 26.5}{2 \times 0.15}$$

$= 145$ kg/mm^2

Shear energy per unit volume

= Shear stress × Shear strain

= 145 × 2.68 = 388.6 kg/mm^2. **Ans.**

Example 2.14. *During orthogonal turning operation the following data was obtained :*

Cutting force (F_z)	= *120 kg.*
Feed force (F_x)	= *30 kg.*
Rake angle	= *10°*
Feed	= *0.2 mm / revolution.*
Width of cut	= *2.3 mm.*
Chip thickness	= *0.4 mm.*
Cutting speed	= *120 m / min.*

Determine the following :

(*a*) *Chip thickness ratio*

(*b*) *Shear angle*

(*c*) *Shear stress.*

Solution. (*a*) r = Chip thickness ratio $= \dfrac{t_1}{t_2}$

t_1 = Chip thickness before cutting = 0.2 mm.

t_2 = Chip thickness = 0.4 mm

$$r = \frac{0.2}{0.4} = 0.5$$

(*b*) β = Shear angle

α = Back rake angle = 10°.

$$\tan\beta = \frac{r\cos\alpha}{1 - r\cos\alpha} = \frac{0.5\cos 10}{1 - 0.5\sin 10}$$

$$= \frac{0.5\times 0.9848}{1 - 0.5\times 0.1736} = 0.54$$

$$\beta = 28.4°$$

(c) F_H = Cutting force = F_z = 120 kg

F_V = Feed force = F_x = 30 kg

$$F_S = F_H\cos\beta - F_V\sin\beta$$

$$= 120\cos 28.4 - 30\sin 28.4$$

$$= 120\times 0.8796 - 30\times 0.4756 = 91.2 \text{ kg}$$

$$A = \text{Shear area} = \frac{t_1\times b_1}{\sin\beta}$$

where b_1 = Width of chip = 2.3 mm

t_1 = 0.2 mm.

$$A = \frac{0.2\times 2.3}{\sin 28.4} = \frac{0.2\times 2.3}{0.4756} = 0.97 \text{ mm}^2$$

$$f_S = \text{Shear stress} = \frac{F_S}{A} = \frac{91.2}{0.97} = 94 \text{ kg/mm.}$$

Example 2.15. *During machining of C 20 steel with a triple carbide cutting tool 0—8—6—7—10—70—1 mm ORS shape, the following data was obtained :*

Feed = *0.18 mm / revolution.*

Depth of cut = *2 mm*

Cutting speed = *120 m / min.*

Chip thickness = *0.4 mm.*

Determine : (a) Chip reduction coefficient

(b) Shear Angle.

Solution. In orthogonal turning

K = Chip reduction co-efficient

$$= \frac{t_2}{f.\sin\phi}$$

where t_2 = Chip thickness = 0.4 mm

f = Feed – 0.18 mm

ϕ = Principal cutting edge angle = 70°.

$$\therefore \quad K = \frac{0.4}{0.18\times\sin 70} = \frac{0.4}{0.18\times 0.9397} = 2.36$$

(*b*) β = Shear angle

α = Rake angle = 8°.

$$\tan \beta = \frac{\cos \alpha}{K - \sin \alpha}$$

$$\tan \beta = \frac{\cos 8}{2.36 - \sin 8} = \frac{0.99}{2.36 - 14} = 0.446$$

$\beta = 24° - 2'$.

Example 2.16. *During machining C 20 steel with a carbide cutting tool having a tool geometry given by 0—5—6—6—8—75—1 mm ORS, the following forces have been recorded by a two dimensional dynamometer :*

F_z = *130 kg*

F_x = *80 kg.*

Determine the following :

(*a*) *Radial component of force,* F_y

(*b*) *Frictional force P and normal force N*

(*c*) *Kinetic coefficient of friction,* μ.

Solution. (*a*) In this case ϕ is less than 90°.

It is a case of orthogonal system of first kind.

F_z = Feed force = 80 kg.

ϕ = Principal cutting angle = 75°

$F_x = F_{xy} \sin \phi$

$80 = F_{xy} \sin \phi$

$$F_{xy} = \frac{80}{\sin 75} = \frac{80}{0.9652} = 82.83 \text{ kg.}$$

$F_y = F_{xy} \cos \phi = 82.83 \times \cos 75$

$= 82.83 \times 0.2588 = 21.43$ kg.

(*b*) α = Orthogonal rake angle = 5°

P = Frictional force = $F_{xy} \cos \alpha + F_z \sin \alpha$.

$= 82.83 \cos 5 + 130 \sin 5$

$= 82.83 \times 0.9962 + 130 \times 0.0871$

$= 82.5 = 11.3 = 93.8$ kg.

N = Normal force

$F_z = F_H$ = Cutting force

$N = F_z \cos \alpha - F_{zy} \sin \alpha$

$= 130 \cos 5 - 82.83 \sin 5$

$= 130 \times 0.9962 - 82.83 \times 0.0871$

$= 129.5 - 7.2 = 136.7$ kg.

(c) μ = Kinetic coefficient of friction

$$= \frac{F_{zy} \cos \alpha + F_z \sin \alpha}{F_z \cos \alpha - F_{xy} \sin \alpha}$$

$$= \frac{82.83 \cos 5 - 130 \sin 5}{130 \cos 5 - 82.83 \sin 5}$$

$$= \frac{82.83 \times 0.9962 - 130 \times 0.0871}{130 \times 0.9962 - 82.83 \times 0.0871}$$

$$= \frac{82.5 - 11.3}{129.5 - 7.2} = \frac{71.2}{122.3} = 0.58.$$

Example 2.17. *During machining C 25 steel with 0—10—6—7—8—90—1 mm ORS shaped triple carbide cutting tool, the following observations have been made :*

Feed = *0.18 mm/rev.*

Depth of cut = *2 mm.*

Cutting speed = *150 m/min.*

F_z = *160 kg.*

F_x = *80 kg.*

Chip thickness = *0.4 mm.*

Determine :

(*i*) *Chip reduction coefficient.*

(*ii*) *Shear force and normal force at shear plane.*

(*iii*) *Kinetic coefficient friction.*

(*iv*) *Specific energy of friction.*

Solution. (*a*) ϕ = Principal cutting edge angle = 90°

$\lambda = 0.$

It is a case of orthogonal system of second kind

α = Orthogonal rake angle = 10°

K = Chip reduction coefficient

$$= \frac{t_2}{f \cdot \sin \phi}$$

where t_2 = Chip thickness = 0.4 mm.

f = Feed = 0.18 mm/rev.

$\sin \phi = \sin 90 = 1$

$$K = \frac{0.4}{0.18} = 2.22$$

(*b*) F_S = Shear force = $F_H \cos \beta - F_V \sin \beta$

where F_H = Cutting force = F_z = 160 kg.

$$F_V = \text{Feed force} = F_{xy} = F_x = 80 \text{ kg}$$

$$\beta = \text{Shear angle}$$

$$\tan\beta = \frac{r\cos\alpha}{1 - r\sin\alpha}$$

$$r = \text{Chip thickness ratio} = t_1/t_2.$$

where t_1 = Chip thickness before cutting = Feed = 0.18 mm

t_2 = Chip thickness after cutting = 0.4 mm.

$$r = \frac{0.18}{0.4} = 0.45$$

$$\tan\beta = \frac{r\cos\alpha}{1 - r\sin\alpha} = \frac{0.45\cos 10}{1 - 0.45\sin 10}$$

$$= \frac{0.45 \times 0.9848}{1 - 0.45 \times 1736} = 0.4782$$

$$\beta = 25.5°$$

$$F_S = F_H\cos\beta - F_V\sin\beta$$

$$= 160\cos 25.5 - 80\sin 25.5 = 110 \text{ kg.}$$

$$F_x = \text{Force normal to shear plane}$$

$$= F_V\cos\beta + F_H\sin\beta$$

$$= 80\cos 25.5 + 160\sin 25.5 = 140.8 \text{ kg.}$$

(c) μ = Kinetic coefficient of friction

$$= \frac{F_H\sin\alpha + F_V\cos\alpha}{F_H\cos\alpha - F_V\sin\alpha} = \frac{160\sin 10 + 80\cos 10}{160\cos 10 - 80\sin 10}$$

$$= \frac{160 \times 0.1736 + 80 \times 0.9848}{160 \times 0.9848 - 80 \times 0.1736} = \frac{106.55}{143.66} = 0.74.$$

(d) Specific friction energy $(E_f) = \dfrac{P}{kb_1t_1}$

where b_1 = Width of chip $= \dfrac{d}{\sin\phi} = \dfrac{2}{1} = 2$ mm.

d being depth of cut. P = Frictional force

$$= F_{xy}\cos\alpha + F_z\sin\alpha = 80\cos 10 + 160\sin 10$$

$$= 80 \times 0.9848 + 160 \times 0.1736 = 106.55 \text{ kg.}$$

$$E_f = \frac{106.55}{2.22 \times 2 - 0.18} = 133.3 \text{ kg/mm}^2.$$

Example 2.18. *A medium steel workpiece is turned on a lathe from 34 mm diameter to 31 mm diameter when depth of cut is 1.5 mm and cutting speed is 50 metre per minute. The lathe has a 5 kW motor whose efficiency is 0.85. If a power of 0.07 kW per cubic centimetre per minute is required for stock removal, find the feed.*

Solution. V = Volume of metal removed = $f \cdot t \cdot V$

where f = feed mm/rev.

$$t = \text{Depth of cut} = \frac{1.5}{10} \text{ cm.}$$

V_1 = cutting speed

= 50 metre per minute

= 50 × 100 cm per minute

$$V = \frac{f}{10} \times \frac{1.5}{10} \times 50 \times 100$$

$$N = 75 f. \text{ cu. cm/min.} \quad ...(1)$$

Now P = Power of motor = 5 kW

η = Efficiency of motor = 0.85

S = Power required for removing once cubic centimeter of material per minute

= 0.07 kW

V = volume of metal removed

$$= \frac{P \times \eta}{S} = \frac{5 \times 0.85}{0.07}$$

$$V = 60.7 \text{ cu. cm/min} \quad ...(2)$$

From (1) and (2)

$$75 f = 60.7$$

f = 0.81 mm/rev. **Ans.**

Example 2.19. *Design a lathe turning tool tipped with cemented carbide for making a shaft of steel of ultimate strength about 70 kgf/mm^2. The diameter of shaft is 75 mm, allowance per side (metal to be removed) is 3.6 mm, feed is 0.2 mm/rev. and tool over-hang is 60 mm.*

Solution. D = Shaft diameter = 75 mm

t = Allowance per side = 3.5 mm

f = Feed = 0.2 mm per revolution

L = Overhang = 60 mm

F_H = Cutting force = $k.f.t.\ k_w.\ k_r.$ kv

where k = Specific cutting resistance

= 200 – 300 kg/mm^2 for steel

f = Feed = 0.2 mm/revolution

t = Allowance per side = 3.6 mm

k_w = Correction factor for wear = 0.96 (say)

k_r = Correction factor for rake angle = 0.9 (say)

k_v = Correction factor for cutting speed = 0.92 (say)

$$F_H = 300 \times 0.2 \times 3.6 \times 0.96 \times 0.9 \times 0.92$$
$$= 171.7 \text{ kg}$$

For rectangular cross section of tool

B = Width of tool shank

$$= \sqrt[3]{\frac{6\,F_H\,.\,L}{2.56 \times \sigma}} \quad \text{where } H = 1.6\,B$$

where F_H = Cutting force = 171.7 kg.

L = Overhang = 60 mm

σ = Bending stress for tool material

= 20 – 30 kg/mm^2 for carbon steel tools

= 40 – 60 kg/mm^2 for H.S.S. tools

$$B = \sqrt[3]{\frac{6 \times 171.7 \times 60}{2.56 \times 20}} = 10.7 \text{ mm}$$

H = Height of shank

$$= 1.6 \times B = 1.6 \times 10.7 = 17.1 \text{ mm}$$

Check for tool strength

F_{HP} = Maximum load permitted by tool strength

$$= \frac{BH^2\sigma}{6L} = \frac{10.7 \times 17.1^2 \times 20}{6 \times 60} = 174 \text{ kg.}$$

F_{HR} = Maximum load permitted by tool rigidity

$$= \frac{3.C.E.I.}{L^3}$$

where C = Deflection

= 0.05 mm for finishing tool

= 0.1 mm for roughing tool.

E = Modulus of Elasticity

= 2 × 10^4 kg/mm^2 for carbon steel tools.

= 4 × 10^4 – 5 × 10^4 kg/mm^2 for H.S.S. tools

I = Moment of inertia

$$= \frac{BH^3}{12} = \frac{10.7 \times 17.1^3}{12} = 4458.5 \text{ mm}^4$$

$$F_{HR} = \frac{3 \times 0.1 \times 4 \times 10^4 \times 4458.5}{60^3} = 249 \text{ kg.}$$

Since F_{HP} and F_{HR} are more than F_H so the tool is safe.

Example 2.20. *A steel tube 42 mm outside diameter is turned on a lathe. The following data was obtained :*

Rake angle	= *32°*
Cutting speed	= *18 m / min.*
Feed	= *0.12 mm / rev.*
Length of continuous chip in one revolution	= *52 mm.*
Cutting force	= *180 kg*
Feed force	= *60 kg.*

Determine :

(a) Chip thickness ratio

(b) Chip thickness

(c) Shear plane angle

(d) Velocity of chip along tool face

(e) Coefficient of friction.

Solution.

D = Diameter of tube

L_1 = Length of continuous chip in one revolution
= 52 mm.

L_2 = Length of undeformed chip = $\pi \times D = \pi \times 42$

r = Chip thickness ratio

$$= \frac{L_1}{L_2} = \frac{52}{42\,\pi} = 0.394$$

t = Chip thickness

f = Feed = 0.12 mm/rev.

$$r = \frac{0.12}{t}$$

$$t = \frac{0.12}{0.394} = 0.3$$

β = Shear plane angle

α = Rake angle = 32°

$$\tan \beta = \frac{r \,.\, \cos \alpha}{1 - r \sin \alpha}$$

$$\tan \beta = \frac{394 \times 0.848}{1 - 0.394 \times 0.529}$$

β = 22.6°

V = Cutting speed = 18 m/min

V_C = Chip velocity = $r \times V = 0.394 \times 18$
$= 7.1$ m/min.
F_H = Cutting force = 180 kg
F_V = Feed force = 60 kg.
μ = Coefficient of friction

$$= \frac{F_V + F_H \tan \alpha}{F_H - F_V \times \tan \alpha} = \frac{60 + 180 \tan 32}{180 - 60 \tan 32}$$

$= 0.62.$

Example 2.21. (*a*) *Define working and auxiliary motions.*

(*b*) *Sketch the working motions of the lathe, milling machine, shaper, drilling machine and grinding machine.*

(*c*) *Name the parameters which define working motions of a machine tool.*

(*d*) *Define machining time.*

Solution. (*a*) In order to obtain the required shape on the workpiece, there should be relative movement between the workpiece and cutting edge of the cutting tool. These motions which are essential to impart the required shape to the workpiece are known as working motions.

Working motions are of two types :

(*i*) Rotary

(*ii*) Translatory.

The auxiliary motions do not participate in the process of formation of the required surface but are nonetheless necessary to make the working motions fulfill their assigned function.

Some of the auxiliary motions in a machine tool are as follows :

(*i*) Clamping and unclamping of workpiece.

(*ii*) Idle travel of the cutting tool to the position from where cutting is to proceed.

(*iii*) Changing the speed of the drive and feed motions.

(*iv*) Engaging and dis-engaging of working motions.

In machine tools the working motions are powered by an external source of energy (electrical or hydraulic motor) whereas auxiliary motions may be carried out manually or may be power operated depending upon the degree of automation of the machine tool.

(*b*) The working motions of the different machine tools are indicated in Fig. 2.14.

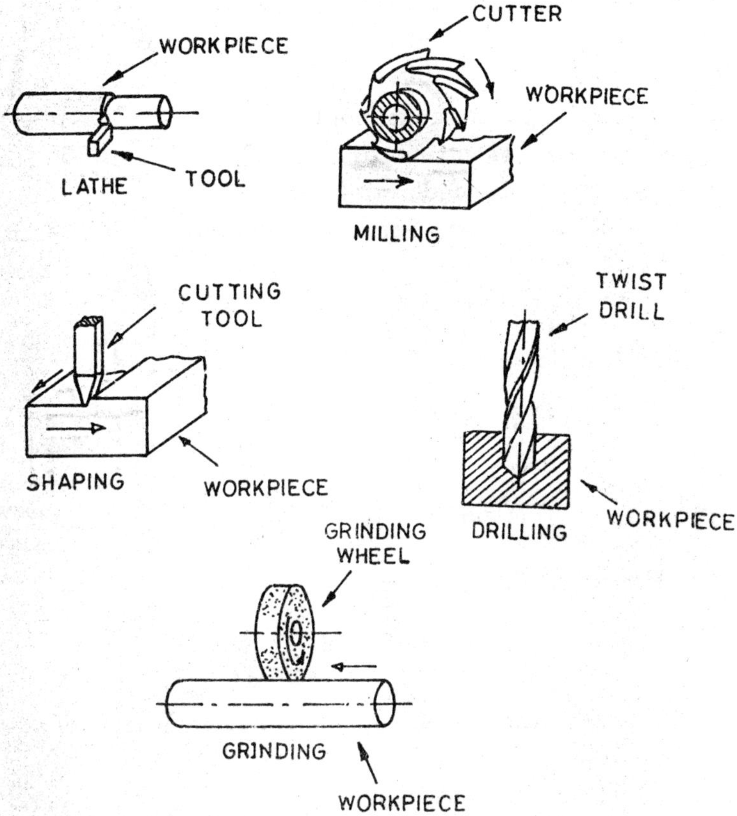

Fig. 2.14

(*c*) For a machine tool the working motions are numerically defined by their velocity. The velocity of primary cutting motion or drive motion is known as cutting speed while velocity of feed motion is known as feed.

In machine tools with rotary primary cutting motion the cutting speed is determined as follows :

$$V = \frac{\pi DN}{1000} \text{ m/min.}$$

where v = Cutting speed (m/min)

D = Diameter of work piece (as in lathe) and cutter (as in milling machine) in mm.

N = R.P.M. of workpiece or cutter.

In machine tools with reciprocating primary cutting motion the cutting speed is determined as follows :

$$V = \frac{L}{1000 \times T_1} \text{ m/min.}$$

where L = Length of stroke (mm)

T_1 = Time of cutting stroke (min.)

Let T_2 = Time of idle stroke (min.)

N = Number of strokes per minute

$$= \frac{1}{T_1 + T_2}$$

Further, let $k = \frac{T_1}{T_2}$

$$N = \frac{1}{T_1 + T_2} = \frac{1}{T_1 (1 + T_2/T_1)} = \frac{1}{T_1}\left(1 + \frac{1}{k}\right)$$

$$N = \frac{k}{T_1 (k + 1)}$$

Therefore, $T_1 = \frac{k}{N (k + 1)}$

Now $$V = \frac{L}{1000 \times T_1} = \frac{L \,.\, N \,.\, (k + 1)}{1000 \times k}$$

Generally time of idle stroke is less than time of cutting stroke.

Feed is indicated as follows :

(*i*) mm/revolution in machine tools with rotary drive motion such as lathes, boring machines etc.

(*ii*) mm/stroke in machine tools with reciprocating-drive motion such as shaper and planer.

(*iii*) mm/tooth in machine tools using multiple-tooth cutters such as milling machine.

Let f_m = Feed per minute

f = Feed per revolution or feed per stroke

n = R.P.M. or strokes per minute.

Then $$f_m = f \,.\, N$$

In multiple tooth cutters

$$f = f_1 \times Z$$

where f_1 = Feed per tooth of cutter

z = Number of teeth on the cutter.

(*d*) *Machine Time*. It is the time required to machine the given surface.

T = Machining time (min.)

f_m = Feed per minute (mm/min.)

L = Length of machined surface (mm)

$$T = \frac{L}{f_m}.$$

Example 2.22. *During orthogonal cutting of a mild steel workpiece, the following data was obtained :*

Cutting force	*= 900 N*
Thrust force	*= 670 N*
Cutting speed	*= 2 m / s*
Underformed chip thickness	*= 0.26 mm*
Width of cut	*= 2.8 mm*
Chip thickness ratio (cutting ratio)	*= 0.32*
Back rake angle of tool	*= 0 degree*
Length of contact between chip and tool	*= 0.8 mm*

Determine : (a) Heat generated due to shearing

(b) Maximum temperature along the tool face.

Solution. r = Chip thickness ratio = 0.32

α = Back rake angle = 0 degree

V = Cutting speed = 2 m/s

F_H = Cutting force = 900 N

F_v = Feed (Thrust) force = 670 N

b = Width of cut

= 2.8 mm = 0.0028 m

H = Total heat generated during cutting

$= F_H \times V = 900 \times 2 = 1800$ J/s

H_1 = Rate of heat generated by friction between chip and tool

$= P \times V_c$

where V_c = Velocity of chip relative to tool

$= r \times v$

$= 0.32 \times 2$

P = Frictional force

$= F_v$ as rake angle is zero

$H_1 = 670 \times 0.32 \times 2 = 428$ J/s

H_2 = Heat rate from shearing

$H = H_1 + H_2$

$$1800 = 428 + H_2$$

$$H_2 = 1372 \text{ J/s}$$

$$T = T_1 + T_2 + T_3$$

where T = Maximum temperature along tool face

T_1 = Temperature rise of material passing through primary deformation zone

T_2 = Temperature rise of material passing through the secondary deformation zone

T_3 = Initial temperature of the workpiece

R = Thermal number

L = Length of heat source divided by chip thickness

$$= \frac{L_1}{t_2}$$

where L_1 = Length of contact between chip and tool

$= 0.8$ mm

$$r = \frac{t_1}{t_2}$$

where t_1 = undeformed chip thickness = 0.26 mm

t_2 = chip thickness after cutting

$$t_2 = \frac{t_1}{r} = \frac{0.26}{0.32}$$

$$L = \frac{L_1}{t_2}$$

$$L = \frac{0.8 \times 0.32}{0.26} = 0.98$$

$$R = \frac{\rho \,.\, C \,.\, V \,.\, t_1}{k}$$

where ρ = Density of steel

$= 7200$ kg/m^3 (Assume)

C = Specific heat capacity = 500 J/kg K

k = Thermal conductivity = 43.5 J/s mk

$$t_1 = \frac{0.26}{1000} \text{ m} = 0.00026$$

$$R = 7200 \times 500 \times 2 \times \frac{0.26}{1000} \times \frac{1}{43.5} = 43$$

$$T_1 = \frac{(1-p) \times H_2}{\rho . C . V . t_1 . b}$$

where p = proportion of shearing heat conducted into the workpiece = 0.1

$$T_1 = \frac{(1-0.1) \times 1372}{7200 \times 500 \times 2 \times 0.00026 \times 0.0028}$$

$$= 235.5°C.$$

It is the mean temperature rise in the primary deformation zone and since it is a temperature difference can be expressed in either centigrade (°C) or degree Kelvin (°K)

T_4 = Average temperature rise of the chip resulting from secondary deformation (Frictional heat source)

$$= \frac{H_1}{\rho . C . V . t_1 . b}$$

$$= \frac{428}{7200 \times 500 \times 2 \times 0.00026 \times 0.0028}$$

$$= \frac{428}{5.24} = 81.7°C$$

Now $\frac{R}{L} = \frac{43}{0.98} = 43.87.$

The value of $\frac{T_2}{T_4}$ depends on the values of $\frac{R}{L}$ and width of secondary deformation zone.

A typical value of $\frac{T_2}{T_4} = 4.2$ when $\frac{R}{L} = 43.87$

$$\frac{T_2}{T_4} = 4.2$$

$$T_2 = 4.2 \times T_4$$

$$= 4.2 \times 81.7 = 343°C$$

T_3 = Initial temperature of work piece

= Room temperature

= 25°C (say)

$$T = T_1 + T_2 + T_3$$

$$= 235.5 + 343 + 25 = 603.5°C.$$

Example 2.23. *A mild steel rod is machined on a lathe. Find power of motor using following data :*

Cutting speed	*= 90 m / min*
Feed	*= 0.5 mm / rev.*
Depth of cut	*= 2.54 mm*
Correction factor	*= 0.5.*

Solution. The formula for calculating power of motor is as follows :

$$P = \text{Power (kW)}$$

$$= \frac{V\,.\,f\,.\,d\,.\,F}{6000 \times \eta}$$

where v = cutting speed = 90 mpm

f = feed = 0.5 mm/rev.

F = specific resistance

= 270 – 300 kg/mm^2 (assume) for steel

d = depth of cut = 2.54 mm

η = correction factor = 0.5

$$P = \frac{90 \times 0.5 \times 2.54 \times 280}{6000 \times 0.5} = 10.7 \text{ kW}.$$

Example 2.24. *(a) A carbide cutting tool lasted for 100 minutes while machining mild steel work material at a cutting speed of 40 m / min. Determine the tool life of the tool is used for machining mild steel at a 20% higher speed.*

(b) Also calculate the value of cutting speed of the tool is required to machine for 160 minutes without failing. Assume n = 0.26.

Solution.

(*a*) V_1 = cutting speed = 40 mpm

T_1 = tool life = 100 minutes

V_2 = cutting speed

$= 1.2 \times V_1 = 1.2 \times 40$

= 48 mpm

T_2 = tool life

$n = 0.26$

$$V_1\, T_1^n = V_2\, T_2^n$$

$$40 \times 100^{.0026} = 48 \times T_2^{0.26}$$

$$T_2 = 48.6 \text{ minutes}$$

T_3 = Tool life = 160 minutes

Now $V_1 T_1^n = V_3 T_3^n$

$$40 \times 100^{0.26} = V_3 \times 160^{0.27}$$

$$V_3 = 33.6 \text{ mpm.}$$

Example 2.25. *In an orthogonal cutting operation on a copper workpiece, following data has been obtained :*

Back rake angle	*= 20°*
Chip thickness before cutting	*= 0.12 mm*
Width of chip before cutting	*= 3.75 mm*
Width of chip after cutting	*= 4.1 mm*
Chip length before cutting	*= 130 mm*
Chip length after cutting	*= 50 mm*
Shear stress of work material	*= 20 kg / mm²*
Coefficient of friction	*= 0.55*
Cutting speed	*= 30 mpm.*

Determine the forces and power consumption.

Solution. α = back rake angle = 20°

t_1 = 0.12 = chip thickness before cutting

t_2 = chip thickness after cutting.

Chipwidth, (b_1) = 3.75 mm

b_2 = 4.1 mm

Chip length (L_1) = 130 mm

Chip length (L_2) = 50 mm

Now according to volume continuity equation

$$L_1 \,.\, b_1 \,.\, t_1 = L_2 \,.\, b_2 \,.\, t_2$$

$$130 \times 3.75 \times t_1 = 50 \times 4.1 \times t_2$$

$$\frac{t_1}{t_2} = 0.42 = r$$

where r = chip thickness ratio

Now let β = shear angle

$$\tan \beta = \frac{r \cos \alpha}{1 - r \sin \alpha}$$

$$= \frac{0.42 \times \cos 20}{1 - 0.42 \sin 20}$$

$$\beta = 24 \text{ degrees}$$

γ = Friction angle of tool face

$$\tan \gamma = \mu$$

where μ = coeff. of friction = 0.55

γ = 29 degrees

F_s = shear force

$$= f_s \times \frac{b_1 . t_1}{\sin \beta}$$

where f_s = shear stress

$= 20 \text{ kg/mm}^2$

[τ is also used as symbol for shear stress]

$$F_S = \frac{20 \times 3.75 \times 0.12}{\sin 24} = 22.5 \text{ kg}$$

$$F_H = \text{cutting force} = \frac{F_S \times \cos(\gamma - \alpha)}{\cos \theta}$$

where $\theta = \beta + \gamma - \alpha$

$= 24 + 29 - 20 = 33$ degrees

$$F_H = \frac{22.5 \cos(29 - 20)}{\cos 33} = 26.5 \text{ kg}$$

F_V = Feed force

From merchant circle diagram

$$\frac{F_V}{F_H} = \tan(\gamma - \alpha)$$

$$F_V = F_H \tan(\gamma - \alpha)$$

$$= 26.5 \tan(29 - 20) = 4.1 \text{ kg}$$

v = cutting speed = 30 mpm

$$\text{Power consumption } = \frac{F_H \times V}{4500} = \frac{26.5 \times 30}{4500}$$

$= 0.18$ H.P.

Example 2.26. *(a) State the forces to which a machine tool is subjected.*

(b) Name the variables which affect metal removal rate.

(c) Represent the cutting tool wear.

Solution. (*a*) Various types of forces to which a machine tool is generally subjected to are as follows :

(*i*) Cutting forces (*ii*) Friction forces

(*iii*) Inertia loads

(*iv*) Reaction at the supporting surfaces

(*v*) Forces due to starting and braking.

(*b*) Total energy required per unit volume of metal cut is function of the following variables :

(*i*) Workpiece material

(*ii*) Friction condition on tool face

(*iii*) Tool sharpness

(*iv*) Cutting speed, feed and depth of cut

(*v*) Rake angle

(*vi*) Clearance angle

(*vii*) Cutting fluid used.

(*c*) The cutting tool wear is represented as follows :

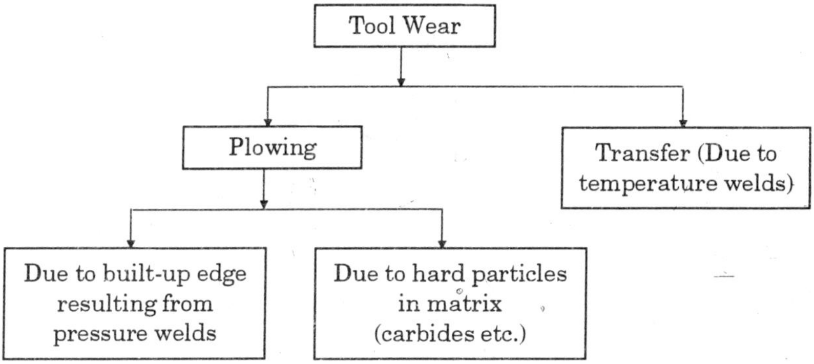

Tool wear at very low cutting speeds is due to the ploughing action of the built up edge debris and other hard particles in the matrix such as carbides while at high cutting speeds the wear takes place due to transfer resulting from temperature welds as well as the flowing action of hard particles.

Example 2.26. *A 90 mm diameter mild steel bar is being turned on a multi tool lathe having six tools at 2 rev./S. If the depth of cut is 4 mm and feed is 0.3 mm/rev. for all tools, determine* :

(*a*) *cutting speed*

(*b*) *total power required.*

Given specific cutting pressure is 1600 N/mm².

Solution. D = Bar diameter = 90 mm

d = Depth of cut = 4 mm

f = Feed = 0.3 mm/rev.

N = R.P.S. = 2

$$V = \pi DN = \frac{\pi \times 90 \times 2}{1000} = 0.56 \text{ m/s}$$

p = Specific cutting pressure

$= 1600 \text{ N/mm}^2 = 1.6 \text{ kN/mm}^2$

Z = Number of tools = 6

Total power $= Z \times p \times d \times f \times V$

$= 6 \times 1.6 \times 4 \times 0.3 \times 0.56 = 6.45$ kW.

Example 2.27. *During turning a steel rod 80 cm long and 10 cm in dia. on a lathe with a depth of cut of 5 mm and the feed of 0.4 mm, the tool life yielded the following equation :*

$$VT^{1.3} = 60$$

The following costs relate to the above operation :

Machine labour cost = Rs. 4/hr

Machine burden rate = Rs. 30% of labour

Grinding labour cost = Rs. 5/hr

Grinding burden rate = 350% of labour

Loading time = 5 min./part.

Two types of carbide tools were used i.e. Brazed insert and throw away inserts.

For Brazed inserts :

Original cost of tool Rs. 25

Grinding time 6 minutes

Tool changing time 2 minutes

(One cutting edge/grind, 5 grinds available per tool before rejection plus original cutting edge).

For throw away inserts (Square)

Original cost Rs. 20

Tool changing time 0.5 minutes

Determine which tool is economical ?

Solution.

For Brazed Inserts

C_1 = Machine labour cost + Burden cost/min.

$$= \frac{4 + 3 \times 4}{60} = \text{Re. } 0.266$$

$$C_2 = \text{Original cost/edge} + \frac{\text{Time}}{\text{grind}}\left(\frac{\text{Labour}}{\text{grind}} + \frac{\text{Burden}}{\text{grind}}\right)$$

$$= \frac{25}{6} + \frac{6\,(4 + 4 \times 3.5)}{60} = \text{Rs. } 5.96$$

where total cutting edges = 5 + 1 = 6

T_m = Tool life for minimum cost.

It is given by the following relation :

$$T_m = \left(\frac{1}{n} - 1\right)\left(\frac{C_1 T + C_2}{C_1}\right)$$

where T = Tool changing time (minutes)

and $n = 0.3$

$$= \left(\frac{1}{0.3} - 1\right) \times \left(\frac{0.266 \times 2 + 4.3}{0.266}\right) = 42.38 \text{ minutes}$$

Cutting speed,

$$V = \frac{C}{T_m^n} = \frac{60}{(42.38)\ 0.3} = \text{mpm}$$

$$N = \frac{19.6 \times 100}{\pi \times 10} = 62.4 \text{ rpm.}$$

Therefore

S_1 = Loading cost/piece = Loading time × C_1

= 5 × 0.266 = Rs. 1.33

S_2 = Cutting cost/piece = $C_1 \times \dfrac{\text{Length of cut}}{\text{Feed} \times \text{rpm}}$

$$= \frac{0.266 \times 90}{0.40 \times 62.4} = \text{Rs. } 9.6$$

S_3 = Tool grinding cost/piece

= C_1 × Tool failure per piece × Tool changing time

$$= \frac{0.266 \times 90 \times 2}{0.04 \times 62.4 \times 42.38} = \text{Rs. } 0.45$$

S_4 = Tool grinding cost/piece = C_2 × Tool failure/piece.

$$= \frac{5.96 \times 90}{0.04 \times 62.4 \times 42.38} = \text{Rs. } 5.07$$

S = Total cost per piece

= $S_1 + S_2 + S_3 + S_4$ = 1.33 + 9.6 + 0.45 + 5.07

= Rs. 16.45

For throw away inserts

Loading Time/piece = 5 min.

Tool changing time = 0.5 min.

C'_2 Original cost/edge = $\dfrac{20}{6}$ = 3.33

$$T_m = \left(\frac{1}{0.3} - 1\right)\left[\frac{0.5 \times 0.266 + 3.33}{0.266}\right] = 30.4 \text{ min.}$$

Now $VT_m^n = C$

$$V = \frac{60}{(30.4)\ 0.3} = 21.6 \text{ M/min.}$$

$$N = \frac{V}{\pi D} = \frac{21.6 \times 100}{3.14 \times 10} = 68.8 \text{ R.P.M.}$$

R_1 = Loading cost/piece = Loading time × C_1

$= 5 \times 0.266 =$ Rs. 1.3

R_2 = Cutting cost/piece

$$= \frac{0.266 \times 90}{0.04 \times 68.8} = \text{Rs. } 8.7$$

R_3 = Tool changing cost/piece

$$= \frac{0.266 \times 0.5 \times 90}{0.04 \times 68.8 \times 30.4} = \text{Re. } 0.14$$

R_4 = Tool cost/piece

$$= \frac{3.33 \times 90}{0.04 \times 68.8 \times 30.4} = \text{Rs. } 3.58$$

R = Total cost/piece = $R_1 + R_2 + R_3 + R_4$

$= 1.3 + 8.7 + 0.14 + 3.58 =$ Rs. 13.72

As total cost per piece for throw away inserts is less than the total cost for brazed inserts therefore it is economical to use throw away inserts.

Example 2.28. *Calculate the time required to turn a workpiece 140 mm long from diameter 50 mm to 44 mm. The machine is running at 300 R.P.M. and feed is 0.3 mm / rev. Maximum depth of cut is 1.8 mm.*

Solution.

d = Depth of cut = 1.8 mm

$$S = \text{Total depth of cut} = \frac{50 - 44}{2} = \frac{6}{2} = 3 \text{ mm}$$

n = Number of cuts

$$= \frac{S}{d} = \frac{3}{1.8} = 1.7 = 2 \text{ (say)}$$

L = Length of work piece = 140 mm

f = Feed = 0.3 mm/rev.

N = R.P.M. = 300

$$T = \text{Machining time} = \frac{L \cdot n}{f \cdot N} = \frac{140 \times 2}{0.3 \times 300}$$

$= 3.1$ minutes.

Example 2.29. *While machining a mild steel rod on a lathe, following results were obtained :*

Width of cut	*= 2.6 mm*
Uncut chip thickness	*= 0.28 mm*
Chip thickness	*= 0.8 mm*
Rake angle	*= 0 degree*
Cutting force	*= 900 N*
Thrust force	*= 480 N*

Determine : (a) Coefficient of friction between tool and chip.
(b) Ultimate shear stress of work material.

Solution.

F_H = Cutting force = 900 N

F_V = Thrust force = Feed force = 480 N

α = Rake angle = zero degree

t_1 = Uncut chip thickness = 0.28 mm

t_2 = Chip thickness = 0.8

$$r = \text{Chip thickness ratio} = \frac{t_1}{t_2} = \frac{0.28}{0.8} = 0.35$$

β = Shear angle

$$\tan\beta = \frac{r\cos\alpha}{1 - r\sin\alpha} = \frac{0.35\cos 0}{1 - 0.35\sin 0} = 0.35$$

$\beta = 19.3°$

(*a*) μ = Coefficient of friction

$$= \frac{F_H \tan\alpha + F_V}{F_H - F_V\tan\alpha}$$

$$= \frac{900\tan 0 + 480}{900 - 480\tan 0} = 0.53$$

(*b*) τ_S = Ultimate shear stress

$$= \frac{F_S}{A_S} = \frac{F_H\cos\beta - F_V\sin\beta}{A_S}$$

Now A_S = Shear area $= \dfrac{b_1 \cdot t_1}{\sin\beta}$

where b_1 = width of cut = 2.6 mm

$$A_S = \frac{2.6 \times 0.28}{\sin 19.3} = 2.2 \text{ mm}^2$$

$$\tau_S = \frac{900\cos 19.3 - 480\sin 19.3}{2.2} = 314 \text{ N/mm}^2.$$

PROBLEMS

2.1. Describe how to calculate the result force acting on a single point tool in turning.

2.2. Explain the relationship between various forces of orthogonal cutting.

2.3. Sketch Merchant's circle diagram and explain the different quantities involved.

2.4. (*a*) What are the three velocities of interest in the cutting process.

(*b*) Explain the relationship between cutting velocity and chipflow velocity and between shear velocity and cutting velocity.

2.5. Write short note on the following :

(*a*) Shear stress in shear plane. (*b*) Shear strain.

(*c*) Power required in metal cutting.

(*d*) Specific horse power. (*e*) Machine tool efficiency.

(*f*) Metal removal rate. (*g*) Lee and Shaffer's theory.

2.6. Prove that according to Ernst.

Merchant theory the relation between rake angle (α), shear angle (β) and friction angle (γ) is given by

$$\beta = \frac{\pi}{4} - \frac{\gamma}{2} + \frac{\alpha}{2}.$$

2.7. In orthogonal cutting of a mild steel component if the rake angle of tool is 10° and the shear angle is 30°. Calculate the chip thickness ratio.

2.8. (*a*) In orthogonal cutting of stainless steel depth of cut is 3.125 mm and rake angle of tool is 10° which results in a chip thickness of 4 mm, determine the following :

(*i*) Cutting Ratio.

(*ii*) Shear Angle.

(*b*) If Shear Strength = 8000 kg/cm^2

Width of cut = 12 mm

Cutting speed = 10 m/min.

Coefficient of friction = 0.11.

Determine the following :

(*i*) Shearing force.

(*ii*) Friction angle.

(*iii*) Cutting force.

(*iv*) Horse power.

2.9. Determine the cutting speed and machining time per cut when the work having 35 mm diameter is rotated at 200 R.P.M. The feed given is 0.2 mm/revolution and length of cut is 60 mm.

[**Ans.** 22 m/minute, 1.5 minute]

2.10. Determine the cutting speed (*V*) and feed (*f*) to be used for turning a mild steel component with a H.S.S. cutting tool under the following conditions :

Cutting force (F_H) = 280 kg.
Tool life (*T*) = 70 minutes
Depth of cut (t) = 2.1 mm.

Use the following relationships

$$F_H = 200\, f^{3/4} t$$

$$V_T^{0.125} \times f^{0.37} \times t^{0.78} = 37$$

Also determine the R.P.M. of the component if the diameter of the component is 30 mm.

2.11. What is the difference between orthogonal system of first kind and second kind ?

2.12. Prove that kinetic coefficient of friction (μ) is given by

$$\mu = \frac{F_H \sin \alpha + F_V \cos \alpha}{F_H \cos \alpha - F_V \sin \alpha}$$

where F_H is cutting force and F_V is feed force.

2.13. Prove that dynamic shear strain (e) is given by

$$e = \frac{k^2 - 2k \sin \alpha + 1}{k \, . \cos \alpha}$$

where k is chip reduction coefficient and α is orthogonal rake angle.

2.14. (*a*) Show the Merchant's circle diagram of forces and its utility.

(*b*) During machining of C-20 steel with a carbide tool having a shape of 0—(– 5)—6—9—8—75—1 mm (ISO) the following force have been measured by a two dimensional electro-mechanical dynamometer :

$$P_z = 140 \text{ kg}, \quad P_x = 15 \text{ kg}.$$

Calculate : (*i*) The radial force, P_y

(*ii*) The friction force, *F*

(*iii*) The normal force, *N*

(*iv*) The kinetic co-efficient, μ. (*A.M.I.E. 1977*)

2.15. A soft steel component is to be turned on a lathe from 40 mm diameter to 37 mm diameter when depth of cut is 1.5 mm and cutting speed is 40 m/min. If lathe has a motor of 4 kW whose efficiency is 0.8, find the feed assuming that a power of 0.05 kW is required for removing one cu. cm. of material per minute.

2.16. When turning a 400 mm diameter round bar on a lathe, the force exerted on the tool was found to be 50 N. If the machine is running at a speed of 300 R.P.M., find the work alone per minute.

[**Ans.** 18840 N-m]

2.17. Write short notes on the following :

(*a*) Velocities in metal cutting

(*b*) Power consumed in metal cutting.

2.18. (*a*) What is dynamometry in metal cutting ?

(*b*) What is a dynamometer ? Discuss various types of dynamometers used for force measurement during metal cutting ?

2.19. Write short note on :

(*i*) Measurement of tool-chip interface temperature

(*ii*) Design of single point tool.

2.20. A hollow cylinder of 35 mm outer dia is turned orthogonally on a lathe. The following data is available : rake angle 35°, cutting speed 15 m/min, feed 0.10 mm/rev, length of continuous chip in one revolution is 50 mm, cutting force 200 kg, feed force 80 kg. Find out shear plane angle, chip velocity along tool face and chip thickness.

3

Machinability

3.1. Machinability

Chips may be cut from some materials with relative case and from others with the greater difficulty. This difference may be attributed to the machinability of the respective materials. Machinability is defined as the case with which the metal is cut satisfactorily for the purpose intended. In general good machinability is associated with the removal of material with moderate forces, the formation of rather small chips, not excessive tool abrasion and good surface finish. It is commonly observed that high hardness gives poor machinability because of high temperature power consumption high tool wear.

Machinability depends upon the following factors :

(*i*) Chemical composition if workpiece material.

(*ii*) Micro-structure of workpiece material.

(*iii*) Physical properties such as tensile strength, ductility and hardness of workpiece material.

(*iv*) Rigidity of tool and work holding devices.

(*v*) Cutting conditions such as cutting speed, feed, etc.

The machinability of plain carbon steels falls steadity as its carbon content rises. Steels up to 300 H.B. hardness do not present great machining difficulty unless large amounts of alloying materials are present.

Fine grained materials take a good surface finish but have an increased resistance to machining. In general good machinability is associated with the removal of material with moderate forces, the formation of rather small chips, not excessive tool abrasion and good surface finish.

It is easier to machine fine grained steel than coarse grained steel and that the addition of small amount of certain elements (for example up to 0.1% S or up to 0.2% Pb) can improve the machinability of steel without appreciable changing mechanical properties. Heat resisting steels and super alloys have very poor machinability. Free cutting steels, non ferrous and light alloys can be easily machined at high cutting speeds. A dull cutting tool operating at too small a feed may fail to cut a chip and will work harden the surfaces of the material some of the plastics are much softer than most metals but are more difficult to machine because the abrasive nature of the material results in excessive tool wear. In evaluating the machinability the following criteria may be considered :

(*i*) Rate of metal removal per tool grind.

(*ii*) Tool life between grinds.

(*iii*) Magnitude of cutting forces.

(*iv*) Quality of surface finish.

(*v*) Shape and size of chips.

(*vi*) Temperature during cutting.

(*vii*) Power consumed during machining.

In case of a metal having high machinability,

(*a*) Good surface finish can be produced.

(*b*) Higher cutting speed can be used.

(*c*) Metal removal rate is high.

(*d*) Cutting tool wear is less.

(*e*) There is low power consumption.

Various criteria for machinability include the following :

(*a*) **Based on tool life.** The material which gives more life to the cutting tool is said to have higher machinability, as compared to the material which gives less tool life.

(*b*) **Criterion based on cutting forces.** The higher the cutting force induced under a set of cutting conditions during the machining of a material, the lower is its machinability.

(*c*) **Criterion based on surface finish**. The superior the surface finish obtained on a material, under a given set of conditions, the better is its machinability.

(*d*) **Criterion based on heat generation during cutting.** If the heat generated during machining of a material is more, it is said to possess less machinability.

The variables affecting machinability are given below :

(*a*) **Machine variables**

(*i*) Capacity of the machine, power, torque and accuracy of the machine ;

(*ii*) Rigidity of the machine and work holding devices.

(*b*) **Cutting tool variables**

(*i*) Tool materials ;

(*ii*) Tool geometry ;

(*iii*) Nature of engagement of tool with work-continuous or intermittent.

(*c*) **Cutting conditions**

(*i*) Cutting speed ; (*ii*) Feed ;

(*iii*) Depth of cut.

(*d*) **Work material variables**

(*i*) Hardness ; (*ii*) Microstructure ;

(*iii*) Tensile strength ; (*iv*) Chemical composition.

3.2. Machinability Index

It is used to compare the machinability of different metals. The rated machinability of two or more metals may vary for different processes of cutting such as heavy turning, light turning, forming, milling etc.

I = Machinability index.

V_i = Cutting speed of metal investigated for 20 minutes tool life.

V_S = Cutting speed of a standard steel for 20 minutes tool life.

$$I(\%) = \frac{V_i}{V_S}$$

Free cutting steel having carbon 0.13 (maximum) manganese 0.06 to 1.1 and sulphur 0.08 to 0.03 per cent is taken as standard steel. Its machining index is relatively fixed at 100 per cent, machinability index for some of the materials is shown in Table 3.1.

Table 3.1

Material	*Machinability Index (%)*
Low carbon steel	55—60
Stainless steel	25
Red Brass (Cu = 77 to 80%)	180
Aluminium alloy	390—1500
Magnesium alloy	500—2000

Table 3.1 (*a*) shows machinability rating of some of steels.

Table 3.1 (a)

Kind of Steel	*Designation*	*Machinability rating*
Free Cutting Steel	14 Mn $1s_{14}$	200
	St 32	160
St. Steels	St 50	125
	St 58	100
	C 14	160
	C 35	125
	C 40	125
Carbon Steels	C 45	100
	C 55	80
	C 85	50
Mn Steel	27 Mn 2	63
Mn-Cr Steel	105 Cr 1 Mn 60	63
Cr-V Steel	50 Cr 1 V 23	50
NI-Cr Steel	13 NI 9 Cr 80	63
High alloy Cr Steel	07 Cr 13	100
High alloy Cr Ni Steel	04 Cr 19 Ni 9 Ti	20—40

3.2.1. Effect of micro structure on machining

A high degree of homogeneity decreases the ease machinability giving tearing, poor finish and build up. Hence the difficulty of machining pure metals such as iron (ferrite) and copper and full solid solutions. Hetrogenous alloy whose components are segregated into bands or excessively large grains is also bad and so arises the bad machinability of wrought steel in which ferrite banding has occured. Hard and soft components uniformly dispersed tend to give good cutting properties. A uniformly heterogeneous structure gives best machining.

3.3. Basic Objectives of Economical Machining

The basic objectives of an efficient and economical machining are as follows :

(*i*) Quick metal removal. (*ii*) Low tool cost.

(*iii*) Good surface finish.

(*iv*) Minimum idle time of machine tools.

(*v*) Less power consumption.

In any machining operation the most important characteristics requiring due considerations are as follows :

(*i*) The life of a tool-workpiece combination.

(*ii*) The surface finish produced.

(*iii*) The type of chip produced.

(*iv*) The power consumed in the formation of chips.

The relative importance of each characteristic depends upon the application.

By using following techniques more efficient metal removal can be achieved :

(*i*) **Optimum cutting speed.** By using optimum cutting speed :

(*a*) tool costs are reduced

(*b*) production rate is increased.

(*ii*) **Highest feed rate and depth of cut.** By using highest feed rate and depth of cut

(*a*) productivity is increased

(*b*) tool life is not affected.

(*iii*) **Largest nose radius.** Use of largest nose radius of the cutting tool has following advantages :

(*a*) surface of the workpiece is improved

(*b*) heat dissipation is better

(*c*) tool has greater strength

(*d*) thinner chips are produced.

(*iv*) Optimum tool geometry

(*v*) Cemented tungsten and titanium carbide tips are quite commonly used for all metal cutting conditions for these inserts.

(*a*) Use largest side cutting or end cutting edge angle. This will

(A) protect nose radius

(B) heat dissipation rate

(C) produce thinner chips.

(*b*) Use largest tool holder shank. This will

(A) minimise deflection

(B) reduce overhang ratio.

(*c*) Use strongest insert shape such as triangular, rectangular etc.

(*d*) Use negative rake angle. By using negative rake angle

(A) cutting edges are doubled

(B) tool has better strength

(C) heat dissipation is better.

(*e*) Use of smallest insert size is better.

(*vi*) By using optimum quantity of cutting fluid.

(*vii*) By using optimum cutting tool angles, the following get increased :

(*a*) Cutting speed

(*b*) Feed

(*c*) Tool life

(*d*) Surface finish.

This will lead to increase in production rate.

3.4. Tool Failure

Cutting tools usually reach the end of their useful life either by breaking or by wearing. Breaking is usually caused by overloading or neglect. Tool wear refers to abrasion on the flank below the cutting edge and abrasion of tool face just back of cutting edge.

During cutting the tool should perform satisfactorily. Unsatisfactory performance of the cutting tool indicates tool failure. Tool failure may occur because of failure of the geometry of cutting tool or it results from tool wear. The following drawbacks are observed when the tool failure takes place :

(*i*) The tool ceases to produce the workpiece according to the required dimensions.

(*ii*) The tool gets over-heated.

(*iii*) Excessive surface roughness is observed.

(*iv*) Tool failure leads to increased cutting forces and therefore power requirement will be more,

(*v*) Some times a burnishing band will appear on the workpiece if the tool is failing.

It is a judgement decision as to how long a tool should be permitted to operate after preliminary indications that the tool is beginning to fail. The tool engineer must weigh the factors of the economics of stopping production and regrinding the tool versus allowing it to continue to operate.

Premature failure of cutting tools by mechanical breakage and plastic deformation can be successfully overcome by providing adequate strength toughness and hot hardness in tool materials and by controlling tool geometry. Hardness is essential so that the cutting edge can penetrate into workpiece material. Poor toughness causes breaking of the cutting edge. Heat resistance enables the cutting edge to maintain its hardness when it gets heated due to friction in chip removal.

The failure of tool may be classified in three general ways as follows :

(*i*) Temperature failure (*ii*) Rupture of tool point

(*iii*) Gradual wear at the tool point.

3.4.1. Temperature failure

Heat produced during metal cutting is mainly responsible for tool failure. When the temperature during cutting becomes very high, the tool becomes too soft to function properly and failure ensues. This type of failure occurs quite rapidly, is the frequently accompanied by sparkling and is easily recognised.

The various tool materials can withstand. Various heating temperature (critical temperatures) before they lose the required hardness.

Carbon tool steel	200 to 250°C
High speed steel	560 to 600°C
Cemented carbides	800 to 1000°C

3.4.2. Rupture of tool point

Because of high hardness required the tip of a cutting tool is mechanically weak and brittle. This type of tool failure is commonly observed in carbide and diamond tipped tools. This failure takes

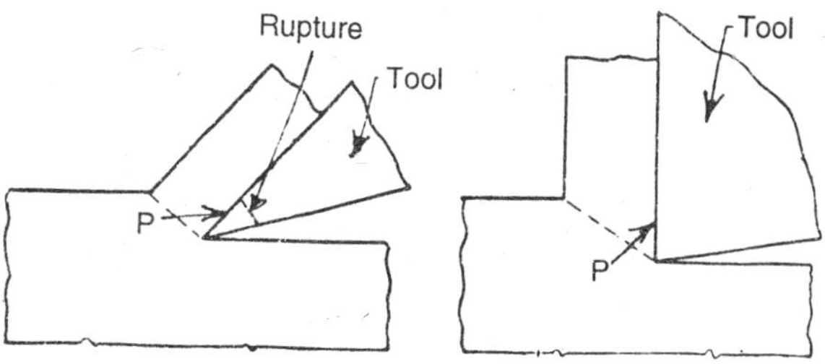

Fig. 3.1

place when the cutting forces exceed the critical value for a given tool when small portions of the cutting edge begin to chip off or the entire tip may break away in one piece. For a given tool material the tendency towards a rupture failure can be diminished either by reducing the causal forces, redirecting them or redesigning the tool to withstand them. Fig. 3.1 shows how a redesion of tool from (*a*) to (*b*) redirects the resultant force *P* so that the tendency for rupture is removed. The forces can also be reduced by increasing the rigidity of tool and workholder.

3.4.3. Gradual wear at the tool point

When a tool has been in used for some time, wear becomes evident. In metal cutting main causes of wear are as follows :

(*i*) Adhesion wear

(*ii*) Abrasion wear

(*iii*) Diffusion wear.

Adhesion wear. In metal cutting junctions between the chip and tool materials are formed as part of friction mechanism. When these junctions are fractured small fragments of tool material can be torn out and carried away on the underside of the chip or on the new workpiece surface.

Abrasion wear. This type of wear takes place when hard particles on the under-side of the chip pass over the tool face and remove total material by mechanical action.

Diffusion wear. This type of wear takes place due to diffusion process where atoms in a metallic crystal lattice move from a region of high atomic concentration to one of low concentration. During cutting when temperature is quite high at interface of tool and workpiece the atoms move from tool material to work piece material and thus weaken the surface structure of the tool.

3.4.4. Types of wear

Tool wear may be attributed to two basic causes :

(*i*) The plowing action of carbides and other hard constituents in the matrix of metal cut.

(*ii*) Wear which results from instantaneous welds which are formed when the finished surface (or chip) slides across a tool face.

The most prevalent type of wear are as follows :

(*i*) Crater wear

(*ii*) Flank wear.

3.4.4. (a) Crater wear. The major tendency for wear is due to the abrasion between the chip and the face of the tool, a short distance from the cutting edge. This results in a crater being formed in the tool face. The crater is formed on the surface of the tool by the action of chip particles flowing over it because of very high temperature. When cratering becomes excessive, the cutting edge may break from the tool. Cratering is commonly observed while machining ductile materials, which produce continuous chips. The maximum depth of the crater is usually a measure of the amount of the crater wear and can be determined by a surface measuring instrument.

3.4.4. (b) Flank wear. The second area in which wear takes place is on the flank below the cutting edge resulting from the abrasive contact with the machined surface. Brittle materials tend to cause excessive flank wear because tool cutting edge tends to scrape over the machined surface and due to low abrasive action of loose fractured chips on the tool face while the flank is in constant contact with the work.

The worn region at the flank is called wear land. The increased wear land means that frictional heat will cause excessive temperature of the tool at the cutting point and therefore the tool will rapidly loose its hardness and tool failure will take place. Flank wear result in a rough machined surface. Fig. 3.2 shows regions of tool wear in metal cutting.

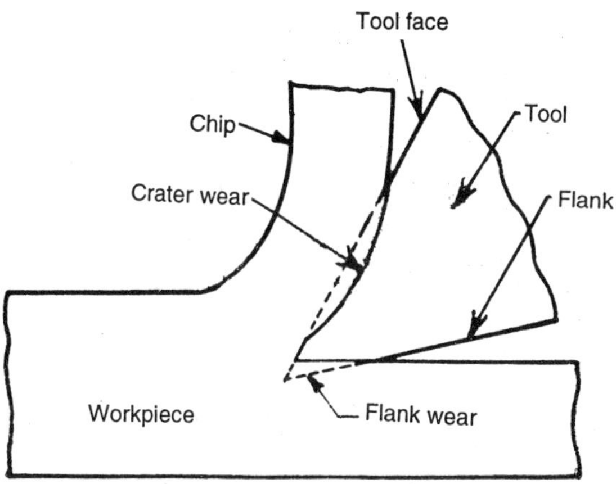

Fig. 3.2

In machining tough (ductile) metals tool wear will proceed in a more complex manner. Flank wear predominates at low cutting speeds when there is no built up edge because of sliding speed being higher on the flank than that of the chip on the tool face.

Whereas in case of heavy chip when pressure on the face is higher, a wear crater is formed. Both flank and crater wear take place when feed is more than 0.15 mm/rev. at low and moderate speeds. The dependence of wear on the time of tool operation is expressed by the wear and time curve (Fig. 3.3) that can be divided into three sections.

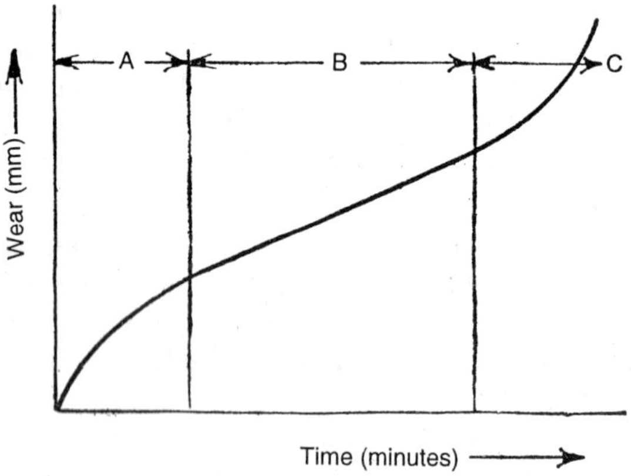

Fig. 3.3

Section A is wear in period (initial wear) during which heavy abrasion of the most salient parts of the surface occurs. Smoother friction surfaces will produce lower rate of wear. Section B is the period of normal wear. Section C is the period of rapid (destructive) wear.

Period of rapid wear is not observed with carbide tipped tool because of the high hardness of cemented carbides and very slight reduction in hardness at high temperatures.

The use of cutting fluids, reduces tool wear (especially face wear) because it cases chip formation, reduces friction force on sliding surface and lowers the temperature to which the tool is heated.

Tool failure depends on the following factors :

1. The normal force between the sliding surfaces and the apparent area of contact.

2. Temperature at the tool point because hardness is influenced by temperature.

3. Relative hardness of the chip and the tool.

4. The composition and structure of metal to be cut.

5. Cutting conditions such as (*i*) cutting fluid used (*ii*) feed (*iii*) depth of cut (*iv*) cutting speed.

The cutting tool wear is represented as follows :

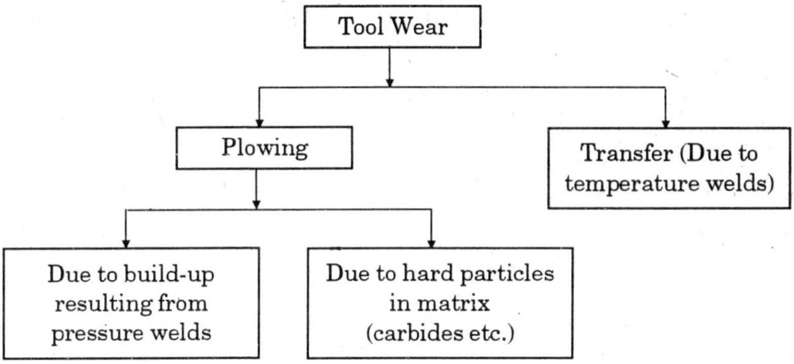

Tool wear at very low cutting speeds is due to the plowing action of the built up edge debris and other hard particles in the matrix such as carbides while at high cutting speeds the wear takes place due to transfer resulting from temperature welds as well as the plowing action of hard particles.

3.4.5. Tool failure process

A cutting tool may fail by following processes :

(*i*) **Plastic Deformation.** Due to plastic deformation the form of the tool is lost. Plastic deformation takes place because of the following reasons :

(*a*) High temperature (*b*) High stresses.

The maximum amount of bulging and the depression of the cutting edge are taken as index for degree of plastic deformation as shown in Fig. 3.3 (*a*).

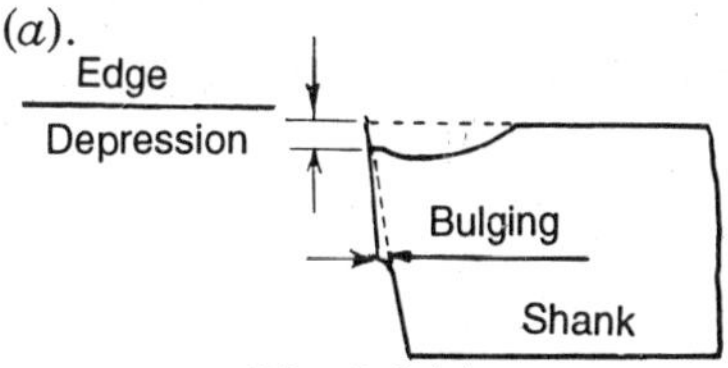

Fig. 3.3 (*a*)

(*ii*) **Mechanical Breakage.** A cutting tool gets broken due to following factors :

(*a*) Large cutting force.

(*b*) By developing fatigue cracks under chatter conditions.

(*c*) Weak tool material.

(*iii*) **Gradual Wear.** It is the result of interaction between the work and the tool material.

3.5. Tool Life

The life is defined as the time elapsed between two successive grindings of the tool. During this period the tool cuts efficiently and effectively.

The cutting tool life is one of the most important economic considerations in metal cutting. The cutting tool should have longer life. Conditions giving a very short tool life will be uneconomical because tool grinding and tool replacement costs will be high. Any tool or work material improvements that increase tool life will be beneficial.

There are number of ways of expressing tool life such as :

(*i*) Volume of metal removed.

(*ii*) Number of work pieces machined.

(*iii*) Time unit.

It is most commonly expressed in minutes. The life of cutting tool is affected by the various factors mentioned below :

1. Machining variables.

(*i*) Cutting speed.

(*ii*) Feed.

(*iii*) Depth of cut.

2. Type of cutting such as continuous and intermittent cutting.

3. Tool geometry.

4. Tool material.

5. Machining conditions.

(*i*) Temperature of the work and tool.

(*ii*) Type of cutting fluid used.

6. Properties of material being cut.

(*i*) Microstructure of workpiece materials.

(*ii*) Tensile strength and hardness of the material.

(*iii*) Degree to which the material cold works.

In order that a cutting tool should have long life it is essential that the face of the tool should be as smooth as possible. A blunt tool should not be used as it causes the following defects.

(*i*) It produces poor surface finish

(*ii*) It produces vibrations during machining

(*iii*) It increases the cutting forces and therefore power consumption is increased.

(*iv*) Tool gets over heated.

Tool life is said to be over when any one or more of following appear :

(*i*) Spoiled cutting edge.

(*ii*) Presence of chatter marks on the workpiece.

(*iii*) Sudden increase in power.

(*iv*) Over heating due to friction.

(*v*) Poor surface finish.

(*vi*) Dimensional unstability.

Expected tool life is as follows :

(*i*) Cast tool steel = 124 minutes.

(*ii*) High speed steel tool = 60 to 120 minutes.

(*iii*) Cemented carbides tool = 420 to 480 minutes.

3.6. Relationship between the Cutting Speed and Tool Life

There is a definite relationship between the cutting speed and tool life. The higher the cutting speed, the shorter is the tool life. The relation between cutting speed and tool life is given by Taylor formula as follows :

$$VT^n = C$$

where V = Cutting speed in metre/min.

T = Tool life in minutes.

n = an index closely related to the cutting tool material.

= 0.1 to 0.5 for high speed steel tools.

= 0.2 to 0.4 for tungsten carbide tool.

= 0.4 to 0.6 for ceramic tools.

C = Constant. It is numerically equal to cutting speed that gives a tool life of one minute.

The higher the cutting speed permitted by a tool for the same life, the better its cutting properties the more productive it will be.

Depending upon the circumstances there is a best economic tool life for every tool. If the cutting duty is made such as to allow the tool to last longer than the best economic time then it is cutting at an efficient rate. On the other hand if its performance is raised to a level such as to cause it to become blunted in less than economic time then undue expense and loss in time are being incurred in the additional sharpening and re-setting necessary.

In tool life testing tools are operated to failure at different cutting speeds and the test results are plotted. In general a parabolic decrease in tool life with increased cutting speeds is obtained (Fig. 3.4).

Such a relationship plots as a straight line on a log-log graph as shown in Fig. 3.5.

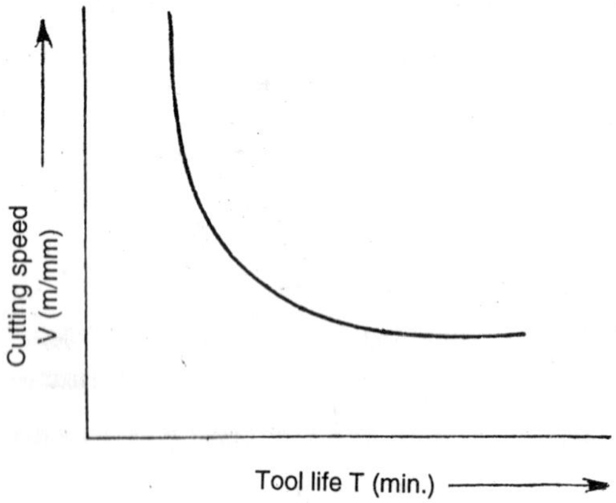

Fig. 3.4

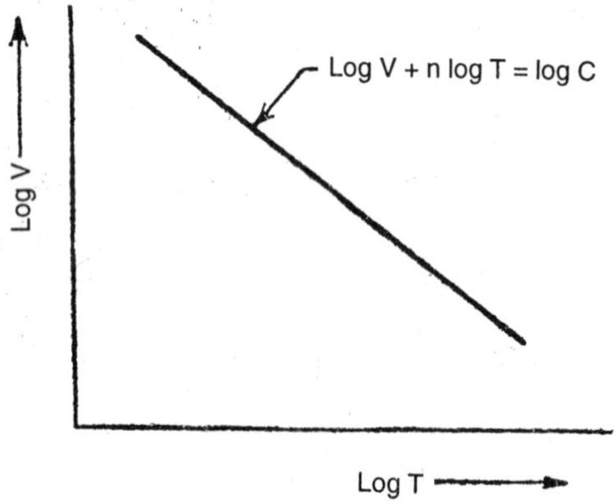

Fig. 3.5

Cutting tool life and efficiency can be improved by giving a surface finish of high quality to the cutting edge of the tool.

This is due to the reason that friction between tool and chip is minimised. Roughness of the tool's cutting edge could result in a concentration of stresses which may cause surface cracks and eventual chipping of tool.

The following factors influence the cutting speed permitted by a tool :

(*i*) Tool life.

(*ii*) Physico-mechanical properties of metal being machined.

(*iii*) Material of the cutting element of the tool.

(*iv*) Rate of feed and depth of cut.

(*v*) Tool geometry.

(*vi*) Size of the tool shank.

(*vii*) Cutting fluid used.

(*viii*) Maximum permissible amount of wear.

(*ix*) Type of machining process.

3.7. Effect of Feed and Depth of Cut on Tool Life

The effect of feed and depth of cut on tool life is given by the formula :

$$V = \frac{257}{T^{0.19} \times f^{0.36} \times t^{0.08}} \text{ m/min}$$

where V = Cutting speed in m/min.

T = Tool life in minutes.

f = Feed in mm/min.

t = Depth of cut in mm.

This relation is commonly applied for turning low carbon steel by a cemented carbide tool. Fig. 3.6 shows relation between permissible cutting speed (V) and depth of cut at different feed's for H.S.S. tool with tool life 20 minutes and rake angle 20°.

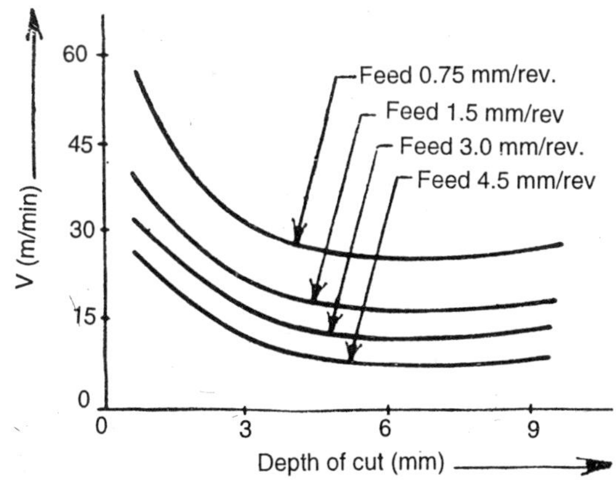

Fig. 3.6

Expected tool life for tools made up of different materials is as follows :

(*i*) Cemented carbides = 240 to 480 minutes.

(*ii*) High speed steel = 60 to 120 minutes.

(*iii*) Cast tool steel = 20 minutes.

Tool life excludes the following points :

(*a*) Removing. (*b*) Regrinding. (*c*) Resetting.

The time for the above three operations should be minimum to increase the productive time.

3.7. (*a*) Tool Life in Terms of Metal Removed

During tool wear studies it is convenient to express tool life in terms of metal removed.

For example in case of turning

Let, D = Diameter of workpiece (mm)

N = R.P.M. of workpiece

V = Surface speed $= \dfrac{\pi DN}{1000}$ m/min.

d = Depth of cut (mm)

f = Feed (mm/rev.)

T = Time to tool failure (minutes)

L = Tool life in terms of metal removal unit

Volume removed per revolution

$$= \pi D.d.f. \text{ mm}^3$$

Volume of metal removed per minute

$$= \pi D.\ d.f.\ N\text{mm}^3/\text{min.}$$

Volume removed in T minutes

$$= \pi D.d.f.N.T. \text{ mm}^3$$

Thus the volume of metal removed between tool regrinds

$$= \pi D.d.f.N.T. \text{ mm}^3$$

or

$$L = \pi\ D.d.f.N.T. \text{ mm}^3 = 1000.\ V.d.f.T. \text{ mm}^3$$

$$= V.d.f.T. \text{ cm}^3.$$

3.8. Effect of Type of Cutting

Tool life is more in case of continuous cutting as compared to intermittent cutting in which regular impacts on the tool lead to failure much earlier.

3.9. Effect of Tool Material

An ideal tool material is one which removes maximum volume of material at all cutting speeds.

For a given cutting speed work material removed by different tool materials in increasing order, is as follows :

(*a*) Cemented oxide. (*b*) Cemented carbide.

(*c*) H.S.S.

3.10. Effect of Tool Geometry on Tool Life

The larger the cutting angle the greater the deformation, heat generation and forces acting on the tool, the more intensive tool wear and shorter the tool life. When cutting angle is reduced (positive rake angle is increased), the cutting forces, deformation and heat generation are reduced and tool life is increased. The more the relief angle of the tool, the less the friction of the tool on the work, the less the tool wear and longer tool life larger values of end cutting edge angle give more life to tool. Similarly a higher values of side cutting edge angle gives longer life to tool. Increase in nose radius improves tool life as the smaller nose radius results in excess stress concentration and greater heat generation. The relationship between cutting speed, tool life (T) and nose radius (r) is given by

$$VT^{0.0927} = 331r^{0.244}$$

where V is the cutting speed in feet per minute, T is the tool life in minutes and r is the nose radius in inch.

Fig. 3.7 shows the tool life relationship with positive rake angle.

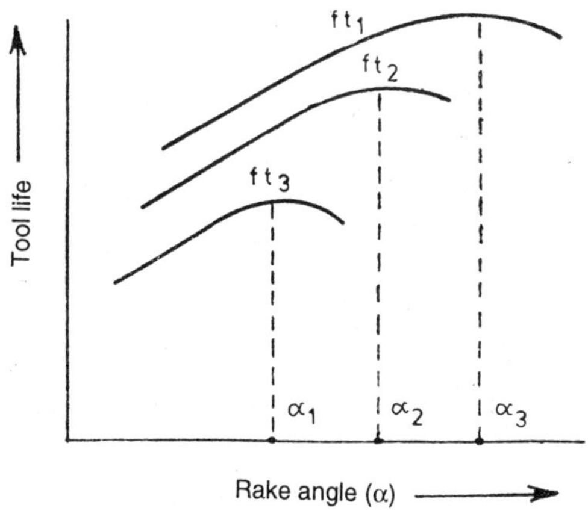

Fig. 3.7

The optimum value of rake angle (α) is more for smaller values of tensile stress (*ft*) of work material. The tensile stress $ft_3 > ft_2 > ft_1$. The optimum rake angle $\alpha_3 > \alpha_2 > \alpha_1$. The typical relationship between tool life and relief angle is shown in Fig. 3.8. The greater the relief angle of the tool the less the friction of tool on the work, less tool wear and tool will have longer life. The optimum relief angle for work material at different feed (*f*) is different. Feed $f_3 > f_2 > f_1$ and relief and $\alpha_3 > \alpha_2 > \alpha_1$.

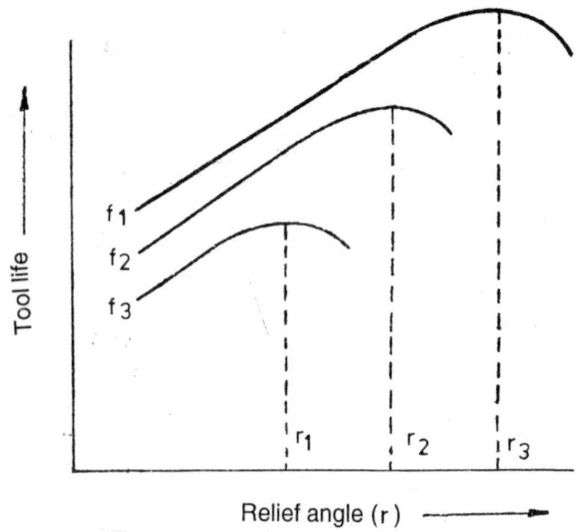

Fig. 3.8

3.11. Effect of Work-piece Material

The microstructure of the work-piece material affects tool life. Hard constituents in the structure result in poor tool life. On the basis of tool life the micro constituents have been placed in the order. Pearlite, Sorbite, Troostite, Bainite and Martansite.

3.12. Effect of Cutting Fluid

Heat produced during metal cutting is carried away from the tool and work by means of cutting fluids. This reduces the coefficient of friction and the cutting temperature. This will help the tool to maintain its hardness and therefore the tool life will be increased.

Cutting fluid which directly controls the amount of heat at the chip tool interface plays an important role in increasing tool life. Schallbroch, Schaumann and Wallich gave the following formula between tool life and temperature of cutting tool

$$T\theta^n = C$$

where T = Tool life (minutes)

θ = Temperature at chip tool interface (°C)

n = An exponent. Its value depends of material and shape of cutting tool

C = Constant.

Table 3.2 indicates the typical economic tool life in minutes for various types of tools.

Table 3.2

Type of tool	*Tool Material*		
	High Speed Steel	*Cemented Carbide*	
		Brazed	*Mechanical*
Single point tools	60	30	15
Drills, reamers	30	20	—
Taps and dies	90	—	—
Form tools	120	120	—
Milling cutters	60 × K	30 × K	15 × K

Where factor K for slab, slot or face milling is given by

$$K = \frac{ar\cos\left(1 - \frac{2y}{d}\right)}{360}$$

d = Milling cutter diameter

c = Depth of cut

$w = c = y.$

as indicated in Figs. 3.8 (a) and 3.8 (b).

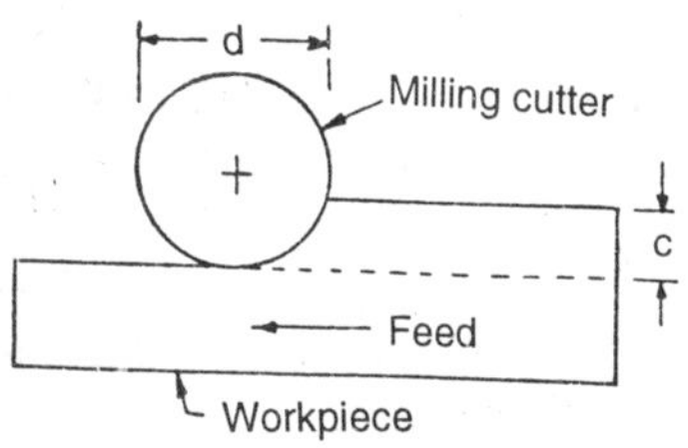

Figs. 3.8 (a)

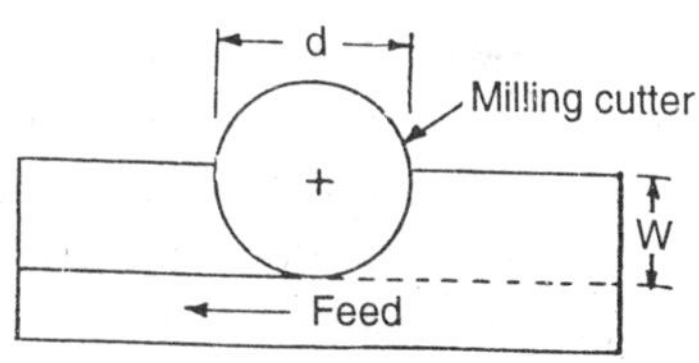

Figs. 3.8 (b)

3.13. Tool Grinding

Lathe and shaping machine tools are ground on the off-hand grinding machine.

When grinding carbide tipped tools it is important to ensure than the tool's steel shank does not come into contact with the grinding wheel cemented carbides may be ground with either silicon carbide grinding wheel or diamond impregnated wheels. Although diamond wheels are costly but they cut more effectively and last longer. Diamond impregnated wheels may be vitrified bonded, metal bonded or resinoid bonded. When off-hand grinding vitrified bonded wheels are used mainly for roughing operations whereas for fine grinding operation metal bonded wheels are preferred. Resinoid bonded diamond wheels are quite commonly used for machine grinding of multi-point cutters.

3.14. Cost Analysis

The production of a component involves several machining operations using a variety of machine tools. Production engineering is an economic function the manufacture of a component must be carried out, at the lowest cost consistent with quality and functional need of production. Production time is defined as the average time taken to produce one component and the production cost is defined as the total average cost of performing the machining operation on a component.

The production cost of a component includes :

(*i*) Cost of material of the work-piece.

(*ii*) Wages to labour.

(*iii*) Overhead charges.

3.14.1. Surface treatment of tools

Following types of treatments are carried out in order to increase the strength and hardness of cutting tools :

(*i*) Carburising (*ii*) Nitriding

(*iii*) Finishing (*iv*) Plating.

Carburising and nitriding are heat treatments processes by which tool surface lapers are saturated with carbon and nitrogen respectively. Processes like lapping and superfinishing may be carried out to improve strength. Hardness can be increased to considerable extent by chromium plating using electrolysis process.

Frictional wear of tools can be reduced by the application of very hard low friction layers to tools. These layers characterised by :

(*i*) high hardness ;

(*ii*) low coefficient of friction ;

(*iii*) high bond strength ;

(*iv*) antiweld behaviour ; and

(*v*) resistance to acids and bases.

can be applied to hot and cold working tools and cutting tools.

Steel tools are given surface treatment to reduce sliding friction and to increase abrasion resistance by physically and chemically altering the surface of the tool.

The various surface treatment processes are as follows :

(*i*) **Nitriding.** In this surface treatment a surface layer of about 0.025 mm thick that is high in complex iron nitrides can be produced by treating a finished tool in a NaCN-KCN bath at about 1000°F for about 1/2 hour. Surface layer so produced can have hardness up to 1000 Brinell hardness. This surface treatment is generally used for tools taking light cuts such as broaching bits and taps.

(*ii*) **Lapping and super finishing.** These surface treatment processes produce a fine finish of the order of 1 to 2 microns. Tools with such surface finishes are found to perform better.

(*iii*) **Chromium plating.** By this surface treatment process a layer of about 0.003 mm can be produced on tool surface. The hardness of such layer is estimated to be nearly 800 Brinell.

(*iv*) **Carburising.** By this surface treatment process a high carbon layer of nearly one millimetre thick can be produced by heating the tool surround by charcoal at 1950°C for about 30 minutes. The layer so produced is very hard. However the layer is brittle and the tool performance is not much improved.

(*v*) **Oxidation.** In this surface treatment process the tool is treated in an aqueous bath of NaOH and $NaNO_2$ at 285°F from 5 to 10 minutes. The layer of black Fe_3O_4 so produced is nearly 0.005 mm thick and provides a lower coefficient of friction because the oxide layer can hold oil better than polished surface.

During the last three decades surface enhancement technologies like

(*a*) Chemical vapor deposition (CVD)

(*b*) Physical vapor deposition (PVD)

(*c*) Carbide sputtring etc. have been commonly used.

These processes increase tool life and enhance performance of cutting tools. However these surface treatment methods are quite expensive.

A low cost high performance surface enhancement technology for improving performance and extending the life of cutting tool is

Molybdenum Di-Sulphide (MoS_2) spray coating. This coating has a very low coefficient of friction and high wear resistance.

While applying the MoS_2 spray coating following method should be adopted :

(*i*) Surface to which coating is to be applied should be absolutely clean and dry.

Oil and grease films should be removed by solvent cleaning.

(*ii*) Burrs on the cutting edges should be removed.

(*iii*) Apply a single coat of spray from spray bottle uniformly so that the entire cutting portion of the tool is coated.

The film thickness is nearly 2 to 4 microns. Allow the tool to cure MoS_2 film at ambient temperature for about 30 minutes.

(*iv*) Whenever the tool is reground this process should be repeated for recoating of tool.

3.15. Cost per Component

The cost of manufacturing a component is composed of the following elements :

(*i*) Tooling cost (*ii*) Machining cost

(*iii*) Non-productive cost.

3.15.1. Tooling Cost. This cost includes the following costs :

(*a*) Cost of tool (*b*) Tool changing cost

(*c*) Tool sharpening cost.

3.15.2. Machining Cost. It includes the following costs :

(*a*) Direct labour cost (*b*) Overhead cost.

Direct labour cost is the cost of direct labour expended for the work done directly on the workpiece. It depends upon the time required for actual machining of the component. The machining time is multiplied by the direct labour rate to obtain this cost.

Overhead cost is the cost of the activities which do not enter directly into the manufacture of the product, but which affect production cost. Overhead cost is composed of the following costs :

(*a*) Indirect labour cost

(*b*) Indirect material cost

(*c*) Fixed cost.

Indirect labour cost includes wages of managers, foremen, supervisors, office staff, and maintenance staff. Indirect material cost includes cost of lubricants, cotton wastes, lighting etc. Fixed cost includes the following :

(*a*) Interest on investment (*b*) Depreciation

(*c*) Taxes (*d*) Insurance.

3.15.3. Non-productive Cost. This cost is related to the activities which are necessary for preparing the machine tool. It is calculated taking into account the time required for the following activities :

(*i*) **Set up time.** It includes the time required to collect all the tools and materials, time required to set these into the machine tool, and make the necessary trial runs and adjustment.

(*ii*) Loading and unloading time.

(*iii*) Time required for inspection and gauging.

(*iv*) Time required for fatigue and personal needs.

(*v*) **Down time.** It includes the time required for unpredictable circumstance such as breakdown in machine tool, delay in supply of materials, tool etc.

Many techniques are available to reduce manufacturing costs and increase manufacturing productivity. These measures include using the following :

(*i*) Improved materials, tools and processes.

(*ii*) Automation wherever it improves efficiency.

(*iii*) More effective organisation and factory layout, assembly techniques and material handling.

3.15.4. Aim of speed and feed regulation

In order to ensure the minimum cost price of the machined component the machining operation should be carried out at optimum values of cutting speed, feed and depth of cut. Machining cost can be expressed as follows :

$$C = C_m + C_n + C_t + C_L$$

where C = Machining cost

C_m = Cost of machining time

$= (R + M)\, T_m$

where R = Wage rate per unit time

M = Cost of operating the machine tool per unit time

T_m = Machining time

C_n = Cost of non-productive time

$= (R + M)\, T_n$

where T_n = Total time of non-productive operations such as loading, unloading idle travel of cutting tool to provide for approach and overtravel etc.

C_t = Tool changing cost per component

$$= \frac{(R + M)\, T_c}{N}$$

where T_c = Time required for replacing, regrinding a tool and setting the new ground tool

N = Number of components machined during the period of tool life.

C_L = Cost of tool per component for a period equal to tool life

$$= \frac{\text{Cost of tool}}{N}.$$

This shows that by using optimum values of cutting speed feed and depth of cut, the machining time, the non-productive time, the time required for grinding, resetting etc. can be minimised which will lead to reduction in machining cost.

3.16. Objectives of Machining

Metal cutting is primarily an economic activity. The aim is to remove a particular volume of metal in minimum time or at minimum cost. The basic objectives of efficient and economical machining are as follows :

(*i*) High metal removal rate

(*ii*) Good surface finish

(*iii*) Low tool cost

(*iv*) Minimum idle time of machine tools

(*v*) Less power consumption.

3.17. Choice of Cutting Speed

The metal removal rate (w) is given by

$$w = f.t.V. \text{ cm}^3/\text{min.}$$

where f = Feed in cm/rev. ; t = Depth of cut in cm.

V = Cutting speed in cm/min.

Any increase in cutting speed for a particular combination of feed and depth of cut will give a directly proportional increase in metal removal rate. This will reduce the machining cost.

But an increase in cutting speed will decrease the tool life and tool and grinding cost will increase. The total cost of machining will be sum of separate costs. Fig. 3.9 shows the variation of costs and cutting speed. The cutting speed corresponding to minimum cost is called economical cutting speed and tool life at this speed is called economical tool life.

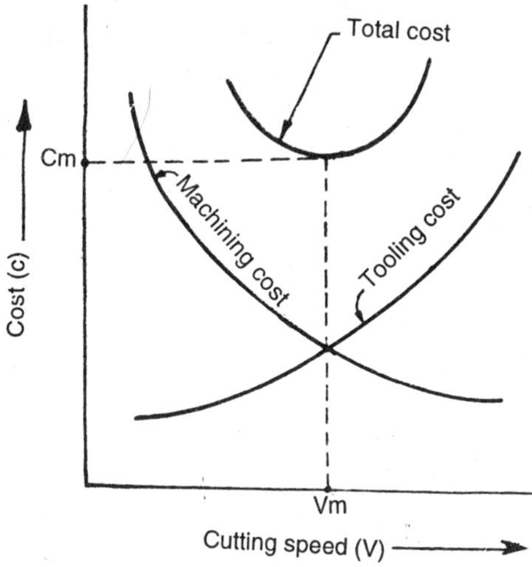

Fig. 3.9

The economical cutting speed is found as follows :

Let H = Machining cost/minute

= Labour cost/minute + Overheads/min.

E = Tooling cost

= Cost of changing tool + Cost of regrinding + Tool depreciation

S_1 = Cost of machining metal/unit volume of metal cut

S_2 = Cost of servicing tools/unit of volume of metal cut

S = total cost/unit volume of metal cut = $S_1 + S_2$

f = Feed

T = Total life

V = Cutting speed

t = Depth of cut.

Time to machine a unit volume of metal in minutes

$$= \frac{1}{t.f.V}$$

At t and f are constant

Let $\frac{1}{t.f} = K.$

$\therefore$ Time to machine a unit volume of metal in minutes.

$= K/V$ where K is constant.

$$\therefore \qquad S_1 = H\frac{K}{V}$$

Now number of tool change in $\frac{K}{V}$ minutes

$$= K/TV$$

$$\therefore \qquad S_2 = \frac{EK}{TV}$$

As the relation between cutting speed (V) and tool life (T) is given by

$$VT^n = C$$

$$T = \left(\frac{C}{V}\right)^{1/n}$$

$$S_2 = \frac{EK}{\left(\frac{C}{V}\right)^{1/n} . V} = \frac{EK}{C^{1/n}} . V\frac{1-n}{n}$$

$$S = S_1 + S_2 = \frac{HK}{V} + \frac{EKV\frac{1-n}{n}}{C^{1/n}}$$

Differentiating w.r.t. V, we get

$$\frac{dS}{dV} = \frac{-HK}{V^2} + \frac{1-n}{n}\frac{EK}{C^{1/n}}V\frac{1-2n}{n}$$

$$= 0 \text{ for the cost to be minimum.}$$

$$\frac{H}{V^2} = \frac{1-n}{n} . \frac{E}{C^{1/n}} . V\frac{1-2n}{n}$$

$$H = \frac{1-n}{n} . E . \left(\frac{V}{C}\right)^{1/n} \qquad \text{...(1)}$$

Let $\qquad Q = \frac{E}{H}$.

$$\therefore \qquad \frac{1}{Q} = \frac{1-n}{n}\left(\frac{V}{C}\right)^{1/n}.$$

$$V = C.\left[\frac{n}{Q\,(1-n)}\right]^n.$$

This will give the required economical speed at which the cost will be minimum.

From equation (1) $\frac{1}{Q} = \frac{1-n}{n} \times \frac{1}{T}$

as $$\left(\frac{V}{C}\right)^{1/n} = \frac{1}{T}$$

$$\frac{T}{Q} = \frac{1-n}{n} \quad \text{or} \quad \frac{HT}{E} = \frac{1-n}{n}$$

This will give economic tool life.

3.18. Trends in Conventional Machining (Metal Cutting)

Conventional manufacturing processes have been able to meet major requirements in the field of manufacturing because of the following reasons :

(*i*) due to improvement in cutting tool materials and tool geometry.

(*ii*) due to advent of very powerful, strong, rigid and highly automatic machine tools.

(*iii*) due to the introduction of very fast and accurate worktool handling systems.

(*iv*) integrated computerisation and flexible manufacturing system have added new dimension in machining.

Some or all of the following objectives should be fulfilled during machining by conventional machining methods in addition to basic dimensional requirements with maximum attainable machinability :

(*i*) Minimisation of machining time per component.

(*ii*) Minimisation of production rate.

(*iii*) Minimisation of machining cost per component.

Machining cost can be reduced with following ways :

(A) Reduction of actual cutting time

This is achieved by

(*a*) by using highly powerful, rigid and dynamically stable machine tools.

(*b*) by using machine-fixture-tool work system having high process capability.

(*c*) by using proper tool material and tool geometry.

(*d*) by using sufficiently strong and rigid work and tool holding devices.

(*e*) by using proper cutting fluids.

(*f*) by eliminating vibrations produced during machining.

(*g*) by compounding the processing operations and/or their sub-groups incorporating multi tool and multi spindle working systems.

(B) Reduction of idle time

This can be achieved by

(*a*) reducing the number of idle operations.

(*b*) mechanisation for flowless and quick handling operations like mounting, setting, indexing, unloading and transfer of blanks and cutting tools.

(*c*) using proper chip control and disposal methods.

(*d*) on-line inspection.

(C) Reduction of tool-change time

This is achieved by

(*a*) using cutting tools of longer life.

(*b*) using quick systems for the removal of worm out tools and for setting of new tools.

(D) Reduction of cutting tool cost

This is achieved by

(*a*) using durable cutting tools

(*b*) using in expensive but quality cutting tools.

(E) Maximisation of profit rate

This is achieved by

(*a*) minimising machining cost.

(*b*) minimising rejections through on-line inspection and gauging.

(*c*) proper replacement of in-effective cutting tools.

(*d*) minimisation of heavy breakdowns.

(*e*) incorporating proper maintenance schedule for machine tools etc.

Thus higher productivity and overall economy during machining methods can be achieved by using the following :

(*i*) High powerful and rigid machine tools.

(*ii*) Cutting tools of proper materials and strength.

(*iii*) On-line inspection.

(*iv*) Automation of motions, inspections, handling of tools, work pieces etc.

Example 3.1. *Determine the optimum cutting speed for an operation carried on a lathe machine using the following operations :*

Tool change time	*= 4 minutes*
Tool regrind time	*= 3 minutes*
Machine running cost	*= 20 paise per minute*
Depreciation tool regrind	*= Re 1.*

The tool life equation is given by

$$VT^n = C.$$

Assume $C = 60, n = 1/5.$

Solution. H = Machining cost = 20 paise/minute

E = Tooling cost

= Tool change cost + Cost of regrinding + Tool depreciation

Tool change cost	$= 4 \times 20 = 80$ paise
Tool regrinding cost	$= 3 \times 20 = 60$ paise
Tool depreciation	= Re. 1

E = Tooling cost = 80 + 60 + 100

= 240 paise

$$Q = \frac{E}{H} = \frac{240}{20} = 12$$

Now V = Optimum cutting speed

$$C \times \left[\frac{n}{Q(1-n)}\right]^n = 60\left[\frac{0.2}{12(1-0.2)}\right]^{0.2}$$

= 26.6 m/min. **Ans.**

Example 3.2. *Find the optimum cutting speed and tool life for minimum cost for machining medium carbon steel under the following conditions :*

Cost of operating the machine = 20 paise per minute.

Total cost of tool change = Rs. 8

The cutting speed is 40 metre per min. when the tool life is 50 minutes for the depth of cut and feed employed. Assume

n = 0.2 in the relation

$$VT^n = C.$$

Solution. H = Machining cost/minute = 20 paise

E = Tooling cost = Rs. 8

We know $\frac{HT}{E} = \frac{1-n}{n}$

where T = economic tool life and $n = 0.2$

$$\frac{20 \times T}{1 \times 100} = \frac{1 - 0.2}{0.2}$$

$$T = 160 \text{ minutes.}$$

Now the cutting speed is 40 metre/min when tool life is 50 minutes.

$$40 \times 50^{0.2} = C = VT^n$$

where V = economic cutting speed and T is economic tool life

$$40 \times 50^{0.2} = V.\ 160^{0.2}$$

$$V = 30 \text{ metre/min. } \textbf{Ans.}$$

Example 3.3. *Determine the tool cost of a batch of 4000 components made on a capstan lathe. Work rate per piece is 5 paise and the direct material cost is 10 paise per piece. Indirect costs are 500% of direct labour cost.*

Solution. N = Number of components = 400

C_1 = Direct cost

= N[Material cost + Labour cost]

$$= \frac{400\ [10 + 5]}{100} = \text{Rs. } 60$$

C_2 = Indirect cost

$$= \frac{500}{100} \times \frac{5 \times 400}{100} = \text{Rs. } 100$$

C = Tool cost + C_1 + C_2

= 60 + 100 = Rs. 160. **Ans.**

Example 3.4. *A tool will cut for 4 hours before it needs sharpening. Determine the time charged to one cycle if it takes 12 minutes to change the tool and tool can be sharpened 10 times before it is discarded.*

Solution. t = Time charged to one cycle

$$= \frac{T_1 \times T_2}{T}$$

where T_1 = Cutting time

= 4 × 60 = 240 minutes.

T_2 = Tool charge time = 12 minutes.

T = Tool life = 10 × 4 = 40 hours

= 40 × 60 = 2400 minutes

$$t = \frac{T_1 \times T_2}{T} = \frac{240 \times 12}{2400} = 1.2 \text{ minutes. } \textbf{Ans.}$$

Example 3.5. *It is desired to machine 20 costings in two set ups. What is the cost of production if the following data are used.*

Machining time = *15 minutes per casting*

Set up time = *20 minutes per set up*

Tool sharpening time = *0.5 minute per casting*

Tool change time = *0.8 minute per casting*

Overhead cost = *15 paise per casting*

Fatigue = *15%*

Personal need = *5%*

Check and gauging time

= *12 seconds and 5 checks per casting*

Direct labour cost = *5 paise per minute.*

Solution. H = Direct labour cost = 5 paise per minute

N = Number of castings = 20.

Tooling cost (C_1)

= Total changing cost + Total sharpening cost

= (Tool change time + Tool sharpening time) × N.H.

$$= (0.8 + 0.5) \times \frac{20 \times 5}{100} = \text{Rs. } 1.3.$$

Machining cost (C_2)

= Machining time × N × H + Over head cost × N

$$= 15 \times 20 \times \frac{5}{100} + \frac{15 \times 20}{100} = \text{Rs. } 18.$$

Set up time = 20 min. per set up × Number of set ups

= 20 × 2 = 40 minutes.

$$\text{Fatigue time} = \frac{15}{100} \times \text{machining time}$$

$$= \frac{15}{100} \times 15 = 2.25 \text{ minutes.}$$

Time of personal needs

$$= \frac{5}{100} \times \text{machining time}$$

$$= \frac{5}{100} \times 15 = 0.75 \text{ minute.}$$

Checking and gauging time

$$= \frac{12 \times 5}{60} - 1 \text{ minute.}$$

Non-productive cost (C_3)

= Set up time cost + Fatigue cost + Cost of personal needs + Cost of checking and gauging.

$$C_3 = 40 \times \frac{5}{100} + 2.25 \times 20 \times \frac{5}{100} + 0.75 \times 20 \times \frac{5}{100} + 1 \times 20 \times \frac{5}{100}$$

$$= 2 + 2.25 + 0.75 + 1 = \text{Rs. } 6$$

Total cost, $C = C_1 + C_2 + C_3 = 1.3 + 18 + 6$

= Rs. 25.3. **Ans.**

Example 3.6. *Determine the cost of manufacturing a component using the following data :*

Initial cost of the machine	*= Rs. 10,000*
Depreciation rate of machine	*= Rs. 2000 per year*
Labour rate	*= Rs. 3 per hour*
Operator and machine overloads	*= 100%*
Number of working days per year	*= 250*
Working hours per day	*= 8*
Machine time	*= 3 minutes*
Non-productive time	*= 2 minutes*
Tool changing and resetting time	*= 0.6 min per component*
Cost of regrinding the tool per component	*= 7 paise*
Total depreciation per component	*= 6 paise.*

Solution. Machine depreciation per minute

$$= \frac{2000 \times 100}{250 \times 8 \times 60} = 1.66 \text{ paise/min.}$$

Labour rate $= \dfrac{3 \times 100}{60} = 5$ paise/min.

Machine and operator overheads = 100%

∴ Machine and operator rate

= 1.66 + 1.66 + 5 + 5 = 13.32 paise/min.

Machining cost = 13.32 × 3 = 39.96 paise

Non-productive cost = 13.32 × 2 = 26.64 paise.

Total cost = Tool changing and resetting cost + Cost of grinding + Tool depreciation

= 0.6 × 13.3 + 7 + 6 = 21 paise.

Total cost = Machining cost + Non-productive cost + Tooling cost

= 39.26 + 26.64 + 21 = 87.60 paise. **Ans.**

Example 3.7. *Three different methods of production utilising three different grades of labour have been suggested for the manufacture of a component. The manufacturing information is as follows :*

Method	*Machining time per component (minutes)*	*Hourly Rate*	*Tool cost*	*Number of set up per year*	*Set up time (Hours)*	*Hourly rate for set up*
A	20	Rs. 4	Nil	10	2	Rs. 8
B	12	Rs. 6	Rs. 240	8	2.5	Rs. 6
C	9	Rs. 7	Rs. 960	4	3	Rs. 7

Assuming all time saved can be gainfully used, prepare a graph and show at what quantities methods A and B cease to be the most economic.

Solution.

Let C_1 = Total cost per year for method A

C_2 = Total cost per year for method B

C_3 = Total cost per year for method C

n = Number of components produced per year.

Method A

$$C_1 = \text{Tooling cost} + \text{Cost of set ups} + \text{Machining cost}$$

$$= 0 + 10 \times 2 \times 8 + \frac{20}{60} \times 4 \times n$$

$$= \text{Rs. } 160 + \text{Rs. } 1.33\, n$$

Method B

$$C_2 = \text{Tooling cost} + \text{Cost of set ups} + \text{Machining cost}$$

$$= 240 + 8 \times 2.5 \times 6 + \frac{12}{60} \times 6 \times n$$

$$= \text{Rs. } 360 + 1.2\, n$$

Method C

$$C_3 = \text{Tooling cost} + \text{Cost of set ups} + \text{Machining cost}$$

$$= 960 + 4 \times 3 \times 7 + \frac{9}{60} \times 7 \times n$$

$$= \text{Rs. } 1044 + 1.05\, n$$

The break even point between methods A and B occurs when

$$C_1 = C_2$$

$$160 + 1.33n = 360 + 1.2n$$
$$n = 1538$$

Now break even point between methods B and C occurs when $C_2 = C_3$

$$360 = 1.2n = 1044 + 1.05n$$
$$n = 4560.$$

Method A cease to be economic when more than 1438 components are required per year and method B cease to be economic when more than 4560 components are required. Fig. 3.10 shows cost quantity graph indicating break-even points.

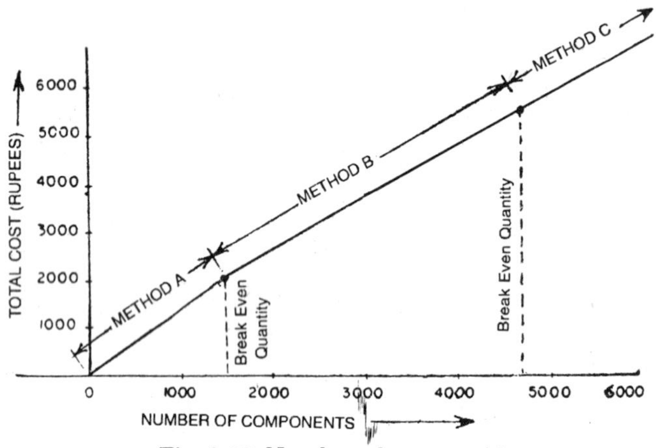

Fig. 3.10. Number of component.

Example 3.8. *A component is being manufactured by a manufacturing organisation. The manufacturing information is as follows :*

Cost of machine	*= Rs. 24,000*
Depreciation rate of machine	*= Rs. 2400 per year*
Cost of tools consumption	*= Rs. 8000 per year*
Fixture cost	*= Rs. 3000*
Depreciation reach of fixture	*= 600 per year.*
Production rate per day	*= 4 components.*
Number of working days per year	*= 300*
Working hours per day	*= 8*
Labour cost	*= 5 paise / min.*
Overhead cost	*= 6 paise / min.*
Machining time per component	*= 70 min.*

Tool changing and sharpening time = 10 min.
Handling time = 6 min.
Loading and unloading time = 24 min.
Gauging time = 10 min.
Determine the cost of manufacturing.

Solution. Fixed cost per year

= Depreciation rate of machine
+ Cost of tool consumption
+ Depreciation rate of fixture
= 2,400 + 8,000 + 600 = Rs. 11,000.

Fixed cost per minute

$$= \frac{11000 \times 100}{300 \times 8 \times 60} = 7.6 \text{ paise}$$

Labour cost = 5 paise/min.

Over head cost = 6 paise/min.

Total machine and operator rate

= 7.6 + 5 + 6 = 18.6 paise/min.

C = Total cost of manufacturing a component
= Machining cost + Non-productive cost
+ Tooling cost.

Machining cost

= Machining time × 18.6

$$= \frac{70 \times 18.6}{130} = \text{Rs. } 13.02$$

Non-productive cost

= 18.6 × [Loading and unloading time
= Gauging time]

$$= \frac{18.6[24 + 10]}{100} = \text{Rs. } 6.32$$

Tooling cost = [Tool sharpening and changing time
+ Handling time] × 18.6

$$= \frac{[10 + 6] + 18.6}{100} = \text{Rs. } 2.97$$

Tool cost of manufacturing a component

= 13.02 + 6.32 + 2.97 = Rs. 22.31. **Ans.**

Example 3.9. *For a cutting tool the tool life is expressed by the equation*

$$VT^n = C$$

In a certain tool test a single point cutting tool had a life of 10 minutes when operating at 240 metres / minute. At what speed should the tool have to be operated in order to have a tool life of 3 hours. Assume n = 0.2.

Solution. Tool life is expressed by the equation

$$VT^n = C$$

where V = Cutting speed (m/min)

T = Tool life (minutes)

n = 0.2

C = Constant.

Substituting these value in the given equation, we have

$$240(10)^{0.2} = C$$

$$C = 384$$

when T = 180 minutes, n = 0.2 and C = 384

then

$$VT^n = C$$

$$V(180)^{0.2} = 384.$$

$\therefore$ V = 137 metre-minute. **Ans.**

Example 3.10. *The tool life for a high speed steel (H.S.S.) tool is expressed by the relation* $VT^{1/7}$ *and for tungsten carbide (WC) is expressed as* $VT^{1/5} = C_2$. *If at a speed of 24 metres per minute the tool life 128 minutes, compare the life of the two tools at a speed of 30 metre / min.*

Solution. For high speed steel tool, $VT^{1/7} = C_1$

$$24 \times 128^{2/7} = C_1$$

$$C_1 = 48$$

For tungsten carbide tool, $24 \times 128^{1/5} = C_1$

$$C_2 = 62$$

when V = 30 metres/minute.

Let T_1 = Tool life for high speed steel tool

T_2 = Tool life for tungsten carbide tool.

For high speed steel tool.

$$\therefore \quad 30 \times T_1^{1/7} = 48$$

$$T_1 = 29 \text{ minutes.}$$

For tungsten carbide tool.

$$30 \times T_2^{1/5} = 62$$

$$T_2 = 38 \text{ minutes}$$

$$\therefore \qquad \frac{T_1}{T_2} = \frac{29}{38} = 0.7. \textbf{ Ans.}$$

Example 3.11. *A tool life of 80 minute is obtained at a speed of 30 mpm and 8 minute at 60 m.p.m. Determine the following :*

(a) Tool life equation.

(b) Cutting speed for 4 minute tool life.

Solution. $V_1 = 30$ m.p.m., $V_2 = 60$ m.p.m.

$T_1 = 80$ minutes, $T_2 = 8$ minutes.

Now the tool life equation is

$$VT^n = C$$

$$V_1 T_1^n = V_2 T_2^n$$

$$30(80)^n = 60(8)^n$$

$$\frac{30}{60} = \left(\frac{8}{10}\right)^n$$

$$\frac{1}{2} = \left(\frac{1}{10}\right)^n$$

$$n = 0.3$$

$\therefore$ The tool life equation is

$$VT^{0.3} = \text{constant.}$$

Let V_3 = cutting speed

T_3 = Tool life = 4 minutes

$$\therefore \qquad V_1 T_1^n = V_3 T_3^n$$

$$30(80)^n = V_3(4)^n$$

$$30(80)^{0.3} = V_3(4)^{0.8}$$

$$V_3 = 82 \text{ metres/minute. } \textbf{Ans.}$$

Example 3.12. *Determine the percentage change in cutting speed required to give 60% reduction in tool life (i.e. to reduce tool life to 2/5 of its former value). The speed/life relationship of cutting tool is given by $VT^n = C$. Take $n = 0.2$.*

Solution. V_1 = cutting speed, V_2 = cutting speed

T_1 = Tool life, T_2 = Tool life

$n = 0.2$

$$V_1 T_1^n = V_2 T_2^n$$

$$\frac{V_1}{T_2} = \left(\frac{T_h}{T_2}\right)^{0.2} = \left(\frac{1}{2/5}\right)^{0.2} = 1.2$$

Increase in cutting speed = **20%. Ans.**

Example 3.13. *The speed life relationship for a tool is given by $VT^{1/3} = 200$ for a given set of conditions and the time taken to change the tool is 6 minutes. Show that operating at a cutting speed of 75 metre per minute gives higher output than operating at either 110 metre/min or 50 metre per minute if other conditions remain unchanged.*

Solution. $VT^{1/3} = 200$

where V = cutting speed

T = tool life.

$\therefore$ when cutting speed $V = 50$, $T = 60$ minutes

$V = 75$, $T = 18$ minutes

$V = 110$, $T = 6$ minutes

The average cutting speed at different values of V can be calculated as follows :

Time taken to change the tool is 6 minutes.

when $V = 50$, Average cutting speed $= \dfrac{50 \times 64}{64 \times 6} = 45.7$ m/min

$V = 75$, Average cutting speed $= \dfrac{75 \times 18}{18 + 6} = 56.2$ m/min

$V = 110$, Average cutting speed $= \dfrac{110 \times 6}{6 \times 6} = 55$ m/min

Therefore on a time basis 75 metre/minute is the best of the three cutting speeds. **Ans.**

Example 3.14. *The cutting speed and tool life relationship for a tool is given by $VT^n = C$, where V is the cutting speed in metre per minute and T is tool life in minutes. During machining 18 mm bar on a lathe at a cutting speed of 110 metre per minute the life of tool is found to be 60 minutes. If n = 0.2, calculate the speed at which the spindle should be run to give a tool life of 5 hours. If a length of 50 mm per component is machined, what is the cutting time per piece and how many pieces can be produced between tool changes. The feed used is 0.15 mm/rev.*

Solution. V_1 = cutting speed = 110 mpm

$T_1 = 60$ minutes, $T_2 = 300$ minutes

$n = 0.2$

$$V_1 T_1^{\,n} = V_2 T_2^{\,n}$$

$$V_2 = V_1 \left(\frac{T_1}{T_2}\right)^{0.2} = 110\left(\frac{60}{300}\right)^{0.2} = 80 \text{ metre/min.}$$

Let N = spindle speed

D = diameter of bar = 1.8 cm.

$$\pi DN = 80$$

$$\pi \times \frac{1.8}{100} \times N = 80$$

N = 1415 R.P.M.

f = feed = 0.15 mm/rev

L = length of piece = 50 mm.

Cutting time per piece

$$= \frac{L}{f \times N}$$

$$= \frac{50}{0.15 \times 1415} \text{ minutes}$$

$$= \frac{50 \times 60}{0.15 \times 1415} = 14.2 \text{ seconds.}$$

Number of components produced in 5 hours

$$= \frac{5 \times 60 \times 60}{14.2} = 1267. \textbf{ Ans.}$$

Example 3.15. *During a tool life cutting test of H.S.S tool material used to cut a special die steel the following values were obtained :*

Cutting speed V (m / min)	*52*	*50*	*49*	*46*	*42*
Tool life (T) (minutes)	*3*	*4*	*4.9*	*10.5*	*30*

Use the above values to calculate the constants of the tool life equation $VT^n = C$.

Solution. $VT^n = C$

$$\log V + n \log T = \log C$$

In order to obtain satisfactory results a straight line graph should be plotted. This can be obtained by plotting the equation

$$\log V + n \log T = \log C$$

$$\log V = -n \log T + \log C.$$

$\log V$	1.7160	1.6990	1.6902	1.6638	1.6232
$\log T$	0.4771	0.6081	0.6902	1.0212	1.4771

The resulting graph between log V and log T is shown in Fig. 3.11.

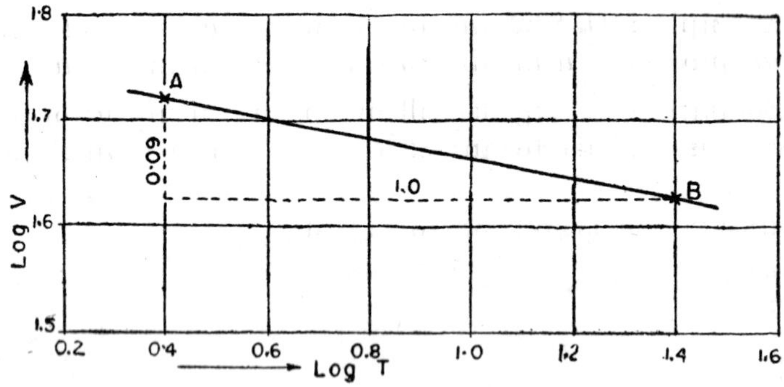

Fig. 3.11

To obtain the value of n consider any two points A and B on the graph slope = n = + 0.09

$$\therefore \quad n = 0.09$$

Now $\log V + n \log T = \log C$

$$1.72 + 0.09\,(0.4) = \log C$$

(For point A)

$$\log C = 1.756$$

$$C = 57$$

Therefore the tool life equation is

$$VT^{0.09} = 57. \textbf{ Ans.}$$

Example 3.16. *A tool cutting at 32 m/min has a life of 54 minutes when used for a rough cut. Determine tool life when used for a light finishing cut.*

Given n = 0.124 for rough cut

= 0.1 for finish cut.

Solution. Tool life equation is given by :

$$VT^n = C$$

For rough cut V = 32 m/min

$$T = 54 \text{ minutes}$$

$$n = 0.124$$

$$\therefore \quad 32 \times 54^{0.124} = C$$

$$C = 52.5$$

For finish cut V = 32 m/min

$$n = 0.1$$

$$32 \times T^{0.1} = 52.5$$

$$T = 141 \text{ minutes. } \textbf{Ans.}$$

Example 3.17. *State the conditions for a cutting tool to give maximum production with minimum maintenance and trouble.*

Solution. A cutting tool will give maximum production with least troubles and maintenance if it satisfies the following conditions :

(*i*) If the tool is made of proper material.

(*ii*) If the cutting tool geometry is properly designed.

(*iii*) If the tool is properly heat treated.

(*iv*) If proper cooling is used during the application of cutting tool.

Example 3.18. *A carbide tool while machining a mild steel workpiece was found to have a life of 1 hour and 40 minutes when cutting at 50 metre per minute. Find the tool life if the tool is to operate at speed 30% higher than previous one. Also calculate the cutting speed if tool is required to have a life of 2 hours and 45 minutes. Assume Taylor's exponent n = 0.28.*

Solution. (*a*) V = Cutting speed = 50 metre/min.

T = Life of cutting tool

= 100 minutes.

$$VT^n = C$$

$$50 \times 100^{0.28} = C \quad ...(1)$$

When speed is increased by 30%

V_1 = Cutting speed

$$= 50 + 50 \times \frac{30}{100} = 65 \text{ metre per minute}$$

T_1 = Tool life

$$V_1 T_1^n = C$$

$$65 \times T_1^{0.28} = C \quad ...(2)$$

From (1) and (2), we get

$$50 \times 100^{0.28} = 65 \times T_1^{0.28}$$

$$T_1 = 39 \text{ minutes. } \textbf{Ans.}$$

(*b*) T_2 = Tool life = 165 minutes

V_2 = Cutting speed

$$V_2 T_2^n = C$$

$$V_2 \times 165^{0.28} = C \qquad ...(3)$$

From (1) and (3)

$$50 \times 100^{0.28} = V_2 \times 165^{0.28}$$

$$V_2 = 43.4 \text{ metre per minute. } \textbf{Ans.}$$

Example 3.19. *(a) Define machining time in a lathe operation.*

(b) A mild steel pin is of 38 mm diameter and 400 mm length is to be turned on a lathe. Determine the turning time to reduce the pin to 36.5 mm is one pass when cutting speed is 30 metres per minute and a feed of 0.7 mm per revolution is used.

Solution. (*a*) Machining time in a lathe operation is defined as follows :

$$T = \text{machining time for one pass or cut}$$

$$= \frac{L}{f \, . \, N}$$

where L = Length of cut, mm

f = Feed, mm/revolution

N = R.P.M. of workpiece.

(*b*) V = Cutting speed

D = Diameter of workpiece = 38 mm

$$V = \frac{\pi DN}{1000}$$

$$30 = \frac{\pi \, . \, 38 \, . \, N}{1000}$$

$$N = 251 \text{ R.P.M.}$$

$$T = \text{Machining time}$$

$$= \frac{L}{f \, . \, N} = \frac{400}{0.7 \times 251} = 2.27 \text{ minutes.}$$

Example 3.20. *Calculate the time required to drill a 20 mm diameter hole in a workpiece having thickness of 60 mm. The cutting speed is 14 metres per minute and feed is 0.3 mm per revolution. Neglect the length of approach.*

Solution. $V = \text{Cutting speed} = \dfrac{\pi DN}{1000}$

$$14 = \frac{\pi \times 20 \times N}{1000}$$

$$N = 223 \text{ R.P.M.}$$

$$T = \text{Drilling time} = \frac{L}{f \,.\, N}$$

where L = Thickness of workpiece

$$= \frac{60}{0.3 \times 223} = 0.89 \text{ minutes.}$$

Example 3.21. *Derive an expression for optimum cutting speed and tool life for*

(*a*) *Minimum production cost*

(*b*) *Maximum production rate*

(*c*) *Also derive an expression for minimum cost of production.*

Solution. The cutting speed and tool life should be so chosen that following two objectives are achieved :

(*i*) Minimum production cost

(*ii*) Minimum production time and maximum production rate.

The optimum value of cutting speed for minimum production cost for cylindrical turning may be obtained as follows.

Let S = Number of components to be manufactured per batch

T_f = Time taken to load and unload each component and to return the tool to the beginning of the cut.

Thus, T_1 = Non-productive time = $S \,.\, T_f$

T_m = Machining time for each component

T_2 = Total machining time = $T_m \,.\, S$

N_t = Number of tools used in machining batch components

T_c = Tool changing time.

Therefore,

T_3 = Tool time for changing worn out tools

$T_3 = N_t \,.\, T_c$

R = Machine and operator rate (including overheads)

C_1 = Total machine and operator cost

$= R\,(T_1 + T_2 + T_3)$

$$C_1 = R\,(S \,.\, T_f + S \,.\, T_m + N_t \,.\, T_c) \qquad \ldots(1)$$

C_t = Cost of each tool.

Cost of tools used

$= N_t \,.\, C_t$

$C_2 = C_1$ + Cost of tools used

$= R\,(S \,.\, T_f + S \,.\, T_m + N_t \,.\, T_c) + N_t \,.\, C_t$

C_A = Average production cost for each component

$$= \frac{C_2}{S}$$

$$C_A = R \,.\, T_f + R \,.\, T_m + R \,.\, \frac{N_t}{S} \,.\, T_c + \frac{N_t \,.\, C_t}{S} \qquad ...(2)$$

Now according to Taylor equation

$$VT^n = C.$$

Thus it can be written as

$$\frac{V}{V_r} = \left(\frac{T_r}{T}\right)^n \qquad ...(3)$$

where V = Cutting speed

T = Tool life

n = Constant

T_r = Measured tool life for a given cutting speed V_r.

The value of T_r may be found for a particular workpiece and tool material and a particular feed either by experiment or from standard empirical data. The value of constant n depends mainly on tool material.

n = 0.125 for high speed steel

= 0.25 – 0.3 for carbide tools

= 0.5 to 0.7 for ceramics

For a particular situation

$$T = T_r \left(\frac{V_r}{V}\right)^{1/n} \qquad ...(4)$$

N_t = Number of tools used in machining the batch components

$$= \frac{S \,.\, T_m}{T}$$

$$\frac{N_t}{S} = \frac{T_m}{T} = \frac{T_m}{T_r}\left(\frac{V}{V_r}\right)^{1/n} \qquad ...(5)$$

Assuming that the tool is engaged with the workpiece during the entire machining.

Now $\quad T_m = \dfrac{K}{V} \qquad ...(6)$

where V = cutting speed

K = constant for a particular operation

$$= \frac{\pi d \cdot L}{f} \text{ for cylindrical turning}$$

where d = workpiece diameter

L = length to be turned

f = feed.

In general K can be regarded as the distance moved by the tool corner relative to the workpiece during the machining operation.

Substituting the value of N_t from equation (5) and value of T_m from equation (6) into equation (2), we get

$$C_A = RT_f + RKV^{-1} + \frac{K}{V_r^{1/n} \cdot T_r} [R \cdot T_C + C_t] V^{\frac{1-n}{n}} \quad ...(7)$$

To find cutting speed (V_O for minimum cost, equation (7) should be differenti: ted with respect to cutting speed V and equated to zero. This will give

$$V_O = V_r \left(\frac{n}{1-n} \times \frac{R \cdot T_r}{R \cdot T_C + C_t} \right)^n \quad ...(8)$$

The cutting speed that gives maximum production rate or minimum production time is determined as follows.

T_A = Average production time for one component

$$= T_f + T_m + \frac{N_t}{S} \times T_C \quad ...(9)$$

Substituting the values of N_t from equation (5) and value of T_m from equation (6) into equation (9) and differentiation gives the cutting speed (V_P) for minimum production time or maximum production rate as

$$V_P = V_r \left(\frac{n}{1-n} \times \frac{T_r}{T_C} \right)^n \quad ...(10)$$

$$= V_r \cdot T_r^n \left(\frac{n}{1-n} \times \frac{1}{T_C} \right)^n$$

$$= C \left(\frac{n}{1-n} \cdot \frac{1}{T_C} \right)^n \quad ...(11)$$

Tool life for economical production

Tool life based on

(*i*) minimum cost

(*ii*) minimum production time or maximum production rate is determined as follows :

The optimum value (T_O) of tool life for minimum cost and the optimum value (T_P) of tool life for minimum production time can be obtained by substitution of equation (8) and equation (10) respectively in Taylor tool life equation (4). This will give

$$T_O = \text{optimum tool life for minimum cost}$$

$$= \frac{1-n}{n}\left(T_C + \frac{C_t}{R}\right) \quad \text{...(12)}$$

and $$T_P = \text{optimum tool life for minimum production time}$$

$$= \left(\frac{1-n}{n}\right) T_C \quad \text{...(13)}$$

For example, for High speed Steel tool

$$n = 0.125 \text{ (say)}$$

$$T_O = \left(\frac{1-.125}{.125}\right)\left(T_C + \frac{C_t}{R}\right)$$

$$= 7\left(T_C + \frac{C_t}{R}\right)$$

and $$T_P = 7T_C.$$

(*c*) **To derive expression for minimum cost of production**

From equation (12)

$$T_O = \text{optimum tool life for minimum cost}$$

$$= \frac{1-n}{n}\left(T_C + \frac{C_t}{R}\right) \quad \text{...(14)}$$

and from equation (7)

$$C_A = \text{Average production cost of each component}$$

$$= RT_f + RKV^{-1} + \frac{K}{V_r^{1/n} \cdot T_r}[RT_C + C_t]\, V^{\frac{1-n}{n}} \quad \text{...(15)}$$

Combining these two equations the minimum cost will be

$$C_m = \text{Minimum cost of production of component}$$

$$= RT_f + \frac{RK}{(1-n)V_r}\left(\frac{T_O}{T_r}\right)^n \quad \text{...(16)}$$

In this equation (16) the first expression is the cost of non-productive time on the machine tool and will not be affected by the work material chosen or by the amount of machining carried out on the workpiece. The second term is the cost of actual machining operation and for a given machine tool and tool design depends on the values of n, V_r, T_r and K.

When choosing the material for a component the design engineer should consider the following factors :

(*i*) Applicability

(*ii*) Cost

(*iii*) Availability

(*iv*) Machinability

(*v*) Amount of machining required.

The applicability of various materials will depend on the component's eventual function and will be decided by factors like

(*i*) Strength

(*ii*) Resistance to wear

(*iii*) Appearance

(*iv*) Corrosion resistance etc.

Example 3.23. *A large batch of steel shafts are to be rough turned to 78 mm diameter for 320 mm of their length at a feed of 0.26 mm. A brazed carbide tip tool is used. The critical cost of the machine (lathe) is Rs. 28000 and the machine is to be amortised for 5 years.*

The operator wage	*= Rs. 18 per hour*
Salvage value of lathe	*= Rs. 4000*
Operator and machine overheads	*= 100%*
Tool changing and resetting time	*= 5 minutes*
Cost of regrinding tool	*= Rs. 6*
Initial cost of tool	*= Rs. 70*
Number of times tool can be ground	*= 10*
Non productive time for each component	*= 2 minutes.*

In Taylor's tool life equation n = 0.25 when cutting speed = 4 m/sec and tool life is 4 minutes.

Determine :

(*a*) *Machine and operator rate*

(*b*) *Cost of a sharp tool*

(*c*) *Tool life and cutting speed for minimum cost*

(*d*) *Tool life and cutting speed for minimum production time or maximum production*

(*e*) *Total production time.*

Solution.

(*a*) R = Machine and operator rate

$= R_1 + R_2 + R_3 + R_4$

where R_1 = operator wage rate = Rs. 18 per hour

R_2 = operator overheads

$$= \frac{\text{Percent overheads}}{100} \times R_1$$

$$= \frac{100}{100} \times 18 = \text{Rs. } 18$$

R_3 = Machine tool depreciation rate

$$= \frac{P - S}{N}$$

where P = Capital cost of machine tool (lathe) = 28000

S = Salvage value = Rs. 4000

N = Number of hours in amortisation period of 5 years

$= 5 \times 50 \times 6 \times 8 = 12000$

(Assuming 50 working weeks per year with 6 days a week and 8 hours per day of work)

$$R_3 = \frac{28000 - 4000}{12000} = \text{Rs. } 2$$

R_4 = Machine tool overheads

$$= \frac{\text{Percent machine overheads}}{100} \times R_3$$

$$= \frac{100}{100} \times R_3 = R_3 = \text{Rs. } 2$$

$R = 18 + 18 + 2 + 2 = \text{Rs. } 40$ per hour.

(*b*) C_t = Cost of a sharp tool

$$= \text{Cost of grinding the tool} + \frac{\text{Cost of tool}}{\text{Number of regrinds}}$$

$$= 6 + \frac{70}{10} = 6 + 7 = \text{Rs. } 13.$$

(*c*) For minimum cost

V_o = Cutting speed

T_o = Optimum tool life

$$= \frac{1 - n}{n}\left(T_C + \frac{C_t}{R}\right)$$

where T_C = Tool changing time = 5 minutes

$$= \frac{1 - 0.25}{0.25}\left(5 + \frac{13}{40}\right) = 16 \text{ minutes}$$

It is given that

when V_r = Cutting speed

$= 4$ m/sec $= 240$ m/min.

T_r = Cutting tool life

$= 4$ minutes

Now $V_o T_o^n = V_r T_r^n$

where $n = 0.25$

$$V_o = \left(\frac{T_r}{T_o}\right)^n \times V_r$$

$$= \left(\frac{4}{16}\right)^{0.25} \times 240 = 169.7 \text{ m/min.}$$

(*d*) For maximum production time

T_p = optimum tool life

$$= \frac{1-n}{n} \times T_C$$

$$= \frac{1 - 0.25}{0.25} \times 5 = 15 \text{ minutes}$$

V_p = optimum cutting speed

$$V_p T_p^n = V_r T_r^n$$

$$V_p = \left(\frac{T_r}{T_p}\right)^n \times V_r = \left(\frac{4}{15}\right)^{0.25} \times 240$$

$= 172$ m/min.

(*e*) T_1 = Non-productive time

$= 2$ minutes

T_m = Machining time for each component

$$= \frac{\pi d L}{V_o \cdot f}$$

where d = Workpiece diameter = 78 mm

L = Length of workpiece = 320 mm

V_o = Cutting speed = 169.7 m/min for minimum cost

f = Feed = 0.26 mm

$$T_m = \frac{\pi \times 78 \times 320}{169.7 \times 10^3 \times 0.26} = 1.77 \text{ minutes.}$$

N_t = Number of tools used = 1

S = Number of workpieces that can be produced using one tool

$$= \frac{T_o}{T_m} = \frac{16}{1.77} = 9$$

T_{C_1} = Net tool changing time $= \frac{N_t}{S} \times T_C$

$$= \frac{1}{9} \times 5 = 0.55 \text{ minutes}$$

T_A = Total production time

$= T_1 + T_m + T_{C_1}$

$= 2 + 1.77 + 0.55 =$ **4.32 minutes.**

Example 3.24. *A high speed steel tool is used to machine a component made of (a) mild steel (b) aluminium. The data supplied is as follows :*

For mild steel component

Machine and operator rate (R) = Rs. 20 / hour

Time to load and unload each component end to return the tool to the beginning of the cut (T_f) = 5 minutes

Tool life for minimum cost (T_o) = 50 minutes

Machining operation constant (K) = 185 m

Cutting Speed (V_r) = 48 m / min.

Tool life (T_r) = 12 minutes

For aluminium component

Cutting speed (V_r) = 86 m / min.

Tool life (T_r) = 18 minutes.

Determine minimum production cost of the component.

Solution. For M.S. Component

C_m = Minimum cost of production

$$= R \cdot T_f + \frac{RK}{(1-n)V_r}\left(\frac{T_o}{T_r}\right)^n$$

Now R = Rs. 20 per hour $= \frac{20}{60} = \frac{1}{3}$ per min.

T_f = 5 minutes

K = 185

n = 0.125 for high speed steel tool

V_r = 48 m/min.

T_o = 50 minutes

T_r = 12 minutes.

Substituting these values in above equation, we get

C_m = Rs. 3.4 per min.

For aluminium component

V_r = 86 m/min.

T_r = 18 min.

Substituting these values, we get

C_m = Rs. 2.59 per min.

Hence the cost of production of component made of aluminium is less.

Example 3.25. *(a) During turning operation on a lathe following information was obtained :*

Machine running cost	*= Rs. 0.5 per min.*
Tool regrinding and depreciation cost	*= Rs. 3.0*
Tool change time	*= 8 minute*
Tool regrind time	*= 4 minutes*

In Taylor's equation

$n = 0.3$

$c = 160$

Determine the optimum cutting speed.

(b) If 180 components with a machined length of 360 mm and 100 mm diameter are to be manufactured, determine :

(i) Total cost of machining

(ii) Time required to machine the parts.

Feed may be taken as 0.24 mm / rev.

Solution. Let V_T = Optimum cutting speed

M = Machining cost/minute

= Rs. 0.5

S_1 = Cost of changing tool

= Tool change time × M

= 8 × 0.5

= Rs. 4.0

S_2 = Tool regrind cost

= Tool regrind time × M

= 4 × 0.5 = Rs. 2.0

S_2 = Tool depreciation cost = Rs. 3.0

S = Tooling cost = $S_1 + S_2 + S_3$

= 4 + 2 + 3 = Rs. 9.0

$c = 160$

$n = 0.3$

$$R = \frac{S}{M} = \frac{9}{0.5} = 18$$

V_T = Optimum cutting speed

$$= c\left[\frac{n}{R(1-n)}\right]^n$$

$$= 160\left[\frac{0.3}{18(1-0.3)}\right]^{0.3}$$

= 47 metre/minute.

(b) N = R.P.M. of spindle

D = Workpiece diameter = 100 mm

V_T = Cutting speed

= 47 metre/min.

$$V_T = \pi DN$$

$$47 = \pi \times \frac{100}{1000} \times N$$

$N = 150$

f = feed = 0.24 mm/rev.

T_1 = Machining time per component

$$= \frac{L}{f \cdot N}$$

where L = length to be machined = 360 mm

$$= \frac{360}{0.24 \times 150} = 10 \text{ minutes}$$

T = Tool life at cutting speed 47 mpm.

$$V_T^n = c$$

$$47 \times T^{0.3} = 160$$

T = 59 minutes

N_1 = Number of parts/regrind

$$= \frac{T}{T_1} = \frac{59}{10} = 5.9$$

C_1 = Tool change cost per part

$$= \frac{S_1}{N_1} = \frac{4}{5.9} = \text{Re. } 0.68$$

C_2 = Tool regrind cost per part

$$= \frac{S_2}{N_1} = \frac{2}{5.9} = \text{Re. } 0.34$$

$$C_3 = \frac{S_3}{N_1} = \frac{3}{5.9} = \text{Re. } 0.51$$

C_4 = Machining cost per part

$$= M \times T_1 = 0.5 \times 10 = \text{Rs. } 5.0$$

C = Total cost per part = $C_1 + C_2 + C_3 + C_4$

$$= 0.68 + 0.34 + 0.51 + 5$$

$$= \text{Rs. } 6.53.$$

Total cost of 180 components

$$= 180 \times C = 180 \times 6.53 = \text{Rs. } 1175.$$

T_2 = Tool change time per part

$$= \frac{\text{Tool change time}}{N_1}$$

$$= \frac{8}{5.9} = 1.36 \text{ minutes}$$

T_3 = Tool regrind time per part

$$= \frac{\text{Tool regrind time}}{N_1}$$

$$= \frac{4}{5.9} = 0.68 \text{ minute}$$

r = Rate of production per hour

$$= \frac{60}{T_1 + T_2 + T_3}$$

$$= \frac{60}{10 + 1.36 + 0.68} = 4.98$$

Time required for 180 parts

$$= \frac{180}{r} = \frac{180}{4.98} = 36.2 \text{ hours.}$$

Example 3.26. *(a) What is cutting tool wear ? (b) Discuss tool wear mechanism and tool wear types.*

Solution. (*a*) **Cutting Tool Wear**

For a given metal cutting operation the metal removal rate and the tool life are controlled by cutting parameters. By a judicious selection of cutting data one could get the maximum rate of metal removal and optimum tool life.

Under usual cutting conditions when the form stability of the cutting edge has been achieved, wear due to interaction between the chip and the tool and between the workpiece and the tool are the main processes by which the cutting tool wears out. These types of wears are called crater wear and flank wear respectively.

(*b*) Tool Wear Mechanism

Tool wear is a complex phenomenon in which the following actions take place simultaneously :

(*i*) Molecular diffusion between workpiece material and tool material. Carbon and cobalt move from tool surface to flow zone of the workpiece. Iron moves from work material to tool surface. Structural changes in the surface region of a carbide tool lead to its deterioration. By providing thin diffusion barriers the wear can be reduced.

(*ii*) Chemical affinity between the nascent layer of the workpiece material and the cutting tool material.

(*iii*) Mechanical abrasion between the micro constituents and matrix of the workpiece material and the layer of the cutting tool.

(*iv*) Pressure welding of workpiece material to cutting tool surface followed by micro transfer of small particles from the cutting tool matrix adhering to workpiece material.

All the above actions in tool wear phenomena result in two predominant types of tool wear-crater wear and flank wear.

(*c*) Tool Wear Types

(*i*) *Flank Wear*. This occurs on the relief side and nose radius of the cutting edge. It is due to the action of abrasion and resultant heat generated between the tool and the workpiece. This increases the cutting forces, ruins the surface finish and dimensional accuracy.

(*ii*) *Crater Wear*. When turning long chipping materials like steel, the hot chips under pressure have a tendency to weld to the top face as the chip moves over it. These welded granules in turn get loosened alongwith some carbide particles and are carried away by passing chips. This triple action of welding, uprooting and carrying away leads to cratering. The development of a crater results in premature cutting edge failure. Higher cutting speed wear out tools faster than higher cutting feeds.

PROBLEMS

3.1. (*a*) What is machinability ? State the factors which come into play while evaluating machinability of any metal.

(*b*) Define machinability index.

3.2. (*a*) State the reasons responsible for tool failure.

(*b*) Explain

(*i*) Crater wear. (*ii*) Flank wear.

3.3. (*a*) Define tool life. State the factors which affect tool life.

(*b*) Explain the relationship between tool life and cutting speed ?

(*c*) Explain the effect of tool geometry and cutting variables on tool life.

3.4. If $VT^n = C$ is the tool-life equation, calculate the cutting speed that will give a tool life of 1 hour if $n = 0.2$ and $C = 90$.

3.5. Write short notes on the following :

(*i*) Causes of wear.

(*ii*) Tool grinding.

(*iii*) Treatments of tool.

3.6. When turning under certain conditions the relationship between cutting speed and tool life could be expressed as $VT^n = C$. In the tool test, a single point tool had a life of 10 minutes when operating at 200 metres/minute. At what speed would the tool have to be operated to have a tool life of 240 minutes. Assume $n = 0.2$.

[**Ans.** 106 m/min]

3.7. A tool cutting at 24 m/min gave a life of 50 minutes between regrinds when operating on rough cuts with medium carbon steel. What will be its probable life when engaged on light finishing cuts. Assume $n = 0.125$ for rough cutting and $n = 0.1$ for finishing cuts in the tool life and cutting speed relationship $VT^n = C$.

3.8. Define the following :

(*a*) Direct labour cost. (*b*) Overhead cost.

(*c*) Fixed cost.

3.9. List the cost items which are classified in the non-machining (non-productive) type. Explain each and give example.

3.10. State the basic objectives of efficient and economic machining.

3.11. Derive an expression for the optimum cutting speed at which the cost will be minimum.

3.12. (*a*) Discuss economic tool life.

(*b*) The time required to handle and machine a workpiece is 60 minutes. If the allowance for fatique is 20% and for personal needs is 5%, calculate the total time required for each workpiece.

3.13. A company is to manufacture 200 parts per set up and that the job calls for 6 set ups. Calculate the cost of production using the following data :

Machining time	= 24 minutes per component.
Non-machining time	= 16 minutes per component
Tool sharpening	= 2 minutes per component.
Set up time	= 80 minutes per set up.
Gauging and inspection	= 16 seconds and 8 checks per component
Tool change	= 13 minutes
Fatique	= 20%
Personal needs	= 4%
Tool life	= 12 hours
Direct labour cost	= Rs. 3 per hour.

3.14. A batch of 1200 components are to be rough turned to 70 mm diameter for 250 mm of their length using a feed of 0.23 mm per revolution. The tool life equation is given by

$$VT^{0.26} = 26$$

where V is the cutting speed in metres per second and T is tool life in seconds. If the cost per cutting edge including cost of tool depreciation and cost of resting the cutting edge is rupees six and total machine rate including operator cost is Rs. 62, calculate the following :

(*a*) Tool life to give minimum production costs.

(*b*) Cutting speed that will result in this optimum tool life.

(*c*) Total production time assuming time taken to reset the cutting edge of tool is 40 seconds, time taken to load and unload a components is 50 seconds and initial set up time for the batch is 45 minutes.

(*d*) Total production cost.

3.15. The Taylorian tool life equation for machining C-40 steel with 18-4-1 H.S.S. at a feed of 0.2 mm/min and a depth of cut of 2 mm is given by $VT^n = C$ where n and C are constants depending on cutting conditions and tool work combinations

The following V and T observations have been noted

Cutting speed (V) m/min	25	36
Tool-life (T) minute	88	20

Calculate the index n and constant C. Hence recommend the cutting speed for a desired tool life of 65 minutes.

3.16. Write short note on the following :

(*i*) Machining time in a lathe operation.

(*ii*) Machining time in drilling.

3.17. Discuss the trends in conventional machining (metal cutting).

4

Cutting Fluids

4.1. Cutting Fluids

During metal cutting heat is generated as a result of the work done. Heat is carried away from the tool and work by means of cutting fluids which at the same time reduce the friction between the tool and chip and between tool and work and also facilitates the chip formation. Cutting, fluids usually in the form of a liquid are applied to the chip formation zone to improve the cutting conditions compared to dry cutting conditions. If sufficient quantity of cutting fluid is properly applied, heat can be removed almost as fast as it is generated and the temperature of tool, workpiece and chip can be kept within limit. Cutting fluid is one of the 'important aids to improve production efficiency'.

Most practical cutting fluids have a mineral oil or vegetable oil base the mineral oil being the more widely used.

4.2. Sources of Heat in Metal Cutting

The main factors likely to cause excessive heat during a metal cutting operation are as follows :

(*i*) Cutting speed too high.

(*ii*) Poor surface finish on the cutting face of the tool.

(*iii*) Worn or incorrectly ground cutting tool.

(*iv*) Formation of a built up edge on cutting face of the tool.

(*v*) Friction between tool and work-piece.

4.3. Thermal Aspects of Metal Machining

During metal cutting considerable amount of heat is produced due to the friction between tool and work and plastic shearing of metal in the form of chips. This heat reduces the hardness of the cutting tool, makes it less wear resistant and changes its dimensions. Heat also leads to changes in the dimensions of machined surfaces. These temperature deformations of the tool and work reduce the machining accuracy.

The colour of the chip is frequently noted as a measure of the temperature obtaining at the tool point. A blue temper color on the surface of a chip formed in dry cutting is taken to mean that the tool point is hotter than when an uncolored silvery chip is obtained when cutting with a fluid.

There are three zones at which heat is generated :

(*i*) Shear zone (Primary deformation zone)

(*ii*) Friction zone (Secondary zone)

(*iii*) Work tool contact zone.

The heat produced at zone Z_1 (Shear zone) is maximum because of the plastic deformation of metal and practically all of this heat is carried away by the chips. Only a small portion of this heat (5—10%) is conducted to the workpiece. The heat is produced at zone Z_2 (Friction zone) due to the friction between moving chip and tool face. In zone Z_3 (work tool contact zone) the heat is generated due to burnishing friction and the heat in this zone goes on increasing with time as the wear land on the tool develops and goes on increasing. From these zones the maximum heat flows to work piece or chip as indicated by arrows (Fig. 4.1). However some heat flows in other directions also. A typical distribution of heat in chips tool and work piece versus cutting speed is shown in Fig. 4.2.

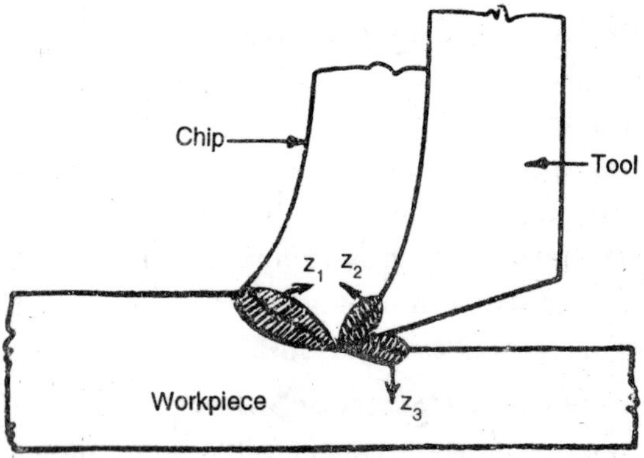

Fig. 4.1

It is observed that distribution of heat in chips, tool and work piece is nearly in the ratio 80 : 10 : 10. When carbide cutting tools are used at speeds about 30 mpm. In Fig. 4.2, V is the cutting speed in metre per minute and φ is total heat.

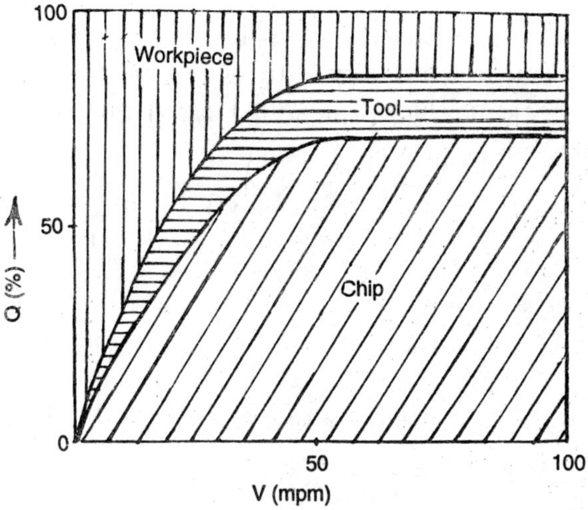

Fig. 4.2

Rate of energy consumption during metal cutting is found as follows

$$E = F_H \times V$$

where E = Rate of energy consumption

F_H = Cutting force

V = Cutting speed.

Conversion of this energy into heat occurs into various regions of plastic deformation such as shear zone (Primary deformation zone), secondary zone and tool and new workpiece surface zone. However the tool and new workpiece surface zone will be a very small heat source

$$E = E_S + E_f$$

where E_S = Rate of heat generation in primary deformation zone (Shear zone heat rate)

E_f = Rate of heat generation in the secondary deformation zone (Frictional heat rate)

$$E_f = P \times V_C$$

where P = frictional force on the tool face

V_C = velocity of chip flow.

4.3.1. Temperature in the primary deformation zone

Some of heat produced in the primary deformation zone is conducted into the workpiece and remainder is transported with the chip

$$\theta_S = \frac{(1-k)\,.\,E_S}{\rho \times S \times V \times t \times b}$$

where θ_S = Average temperature rise in the material passing through the primary deformation zone

K = Fraction of heat conducted into the workpiece

E_S = Rate of heat generation in the primary deformation zone

ρ = Density

S = Specific heat capacity

V = Velocity of the material relative to the heat source

t = Undeformed chip thickness

b = Width of chip.

4.3.2. Heat distribution in metal cutting

The maximum temperature occurs along the tool face some distance from the cutting edge.

$$E = E_c + E_w + E_t$$

where E = Total heat generation

E_c = Rate of heat transportation by the chip

E_w = Rate of heat conduction into the workpiece

E_t = Rate of heat conduction into the tool.

Since chip material near the tool face is flowing rapidly, it has a much greater capacity for the removal of heat than the tool. For this reason rate of heat conduction into the tool (E_t) usually forms a very small proportion of total rate of heat generation and may be neglected.

4.3.3. Temperatures in the secondary deformation zone

In secondary deformation zone the maximum temperature in the chip occurs where the material leaves the secondary deformation zone.

$$\theta_m = \theta_1 + \theta_2 + \theta_3$$

where θ_1 = Initial workpiece temperature

θ_2 = Temperature rise of material passing through the primary deformation zone

θ_3 = Temperatures rise of the material passing through the secondary zone.

4.4. Functions of Cutting Fluid

Most machining operations can be carried out advantageously by using a cutting fluid. During metal cutting heat and wear are inevitably produced due to friction and shearing action that takes place as the chip is being formed. Both heat and wear are undesirable in order to obtain a reasonable tool life and good surface finish. One way of improving metal cutting operation is by using a cutting fluid. The cutting fluids can benefit metal cutting in several ways but by far the most important is heat removal. The various functions of a cutting fluid are as follows :

(*i*) It cools the cutting tool and workpiece. The heat produced is carried away by the fluid by supplying adequate quantity of cutting fluid. This makes possible more accurate production and measurement.

(*ii*) It lubricates the cutting tool and thus reduces the coefficient of friction between the chip and tool. This increases tool life.

(*iii*) The use of a cutting fluid results in better surface finish.

(*iv*) As friction gets reduced, the tool forces are also reduced and therefore the power consumption during cutting is also reduced.

(*v*) It causes the chips to break up into small pieces.

(*vi*) It washes away the chips from the tool.

(*vii*) It prevents corrosion of work and machine.

(*viii*) Removal of heat from the cutting zone also reduces thermal distortion of the work and permits improved dimensional control.

In performing the above functions the cutting fluid enables the maximum possible cutting speed to be used thus reducing time and cost of production.

4.5. Properties of Cutting Fluid

A cutting fluid should possess the following properties :

(*i*) It should have a high specific heat, high heat conductivity and high film coefficient.

(*ii*) It should possess good lubricating properties to reduce frictional forces and to decrease the power consumption.

(*iii*) It should be odorless.

(*iv*) It should be non-corrosive to work and machine.

(*v*) It should be non-toxic to operating personnel.

(*vi*) It should have low viscosity to permit free flow of the liquid.

(*vii*) It should be stable in use and storage.

(*viii*) It should permit clear view of work which is specially desirable in precision work.

(*ix*) It should be safe particularly with regards to fire and accident hazards.

4.6. Types of Cutting Fluids

One way of improving the metal cutting operation is by using a cutting fluid. Cutting fluids mainly required to carry away heat and swarf are generally based on water. The additions of oils and emulsifying agents serves primarily to inhibit rusting although when the oil concentration is raised some lubrication effects are achieved. A cutting fluid mainly serves following functions :

(*i*) Cooling.

(*ii*) Lubrication.

(*iii*) Antiwelding.

4.6.1. Cooling

The cooling function is achieved by supplying an adequate volume of cutting fluid to carry away the heat generated during cutting.

4.6.2. Lubrication

Lubricating the cutting tool reduces the coefficient of friction between chip and tool. This reduces the temperature and tool wear and therefore the cutting process becomes more economical.

All the cutting fluids can be divided into two groups :

(*i*) Water based fluids.

(*ii*) Straight or neat oil based fluids. Many additives are used in conjunction with each of these fluids to accomplish a variety of specific objectives. The most common gaseous cutting fluids are the oxygen and the water vapours in the ordinary atmosphere. In some machining operations it also plays an important role. The best cutting fluid is one that possesses good oiliness in addition to its cooling properties.

4.6.3. Antiwelding

The cutting fluid prevents intimate contact between the surface of chip and tool face. In spite of the lubricating and cooling action of cutting fluids there always exists some metal to metal contact between the tool and the chip and temperature high enough to weld the contacting asperities of the metal. It is prevented by adding compounds of sulphur, chlorine etc. to the cutting fluids.

These compounds generate a soapy film which prevents particles of metal from welding.

4.6.4. Water based cutting fluids

Early attempts to improve cooling and lubricating properties of water included the addition of soft soap but there are now oils which have the desired effect and from emulsion with water. These oils are known as soluble oils. Water based cutting fluids are quite commonly used, the most popular being soluble oil (suds or slurry). Soluble oil (1 to 5%) is mixed with water to form an emulsion. This has excellent cooling properties at low cost and there is also some lubricating effect between tool and chip which reduces tool wear. Modern soluble oil contain corrosion inhibitor and a biocide to keep down the growth of bacteria that would otherwise become a health hazard. Less frequently used forms of water based cutting fluids are based on chemical solutions. Soda solutions are often used on grinding operations as it has good flushing action and cooling effect. Water itself is seldom used as its coolant as it causes rust and corrosion.

When water based fluids are used in conjunction with carbide tipped tools, a sufficient stream of cutting fluid should be maintained otherwise the tool may be unevenly cooled and the carbide inserts may fail soon by a thermally induced fatigue. Care should be taken that a sufficient flow of fluid is applied at all points of high speed carbide cutters to prevent the temperature at a given point on the cutter from fluctuating appreciably.

4.6.5. Straight or neat oil based cutting fluids

The term straight when applied to lubricants and coolants means undiluted. However most of the oils are not used straight but are mixtures of oils or oil with chemicals such as sulphur and chlorine added to them. Straight or neat oils are classified into following subgroups :

(*i*) Mineral oils.
(*ii*) Straight fatty oils.
(*iii*) Compounded or blended oils.
(*iv*) Sulphurised oils.
(*v*) Chlorinated oils.

1. **Mineral oils.** Mineral oils are primarily composed of hydro carbons of different structures and molecular weights. These oils are normally used for light machining operations such as turret and capstan lathes and single spindle automatics where free cutting brasses and steels are being machined.

2. **Straight fatty oils.** The most important variety of straight fatty oils is lard oil. These oils are not stable and rapidly lose their lubricating properties. Neither are they satisfactory coolants as they have a high viscosity. Lard oil is mainly used during thread cutting with taps and dies. These oils are more expensive and less plentiful than mineral oils.

3. **Compounded or blended oils.** These are mixtures of mineral and fatty oils. The film strength of fatty oils is retained ever when diluted with 75% mineral oil. As a result they are much cheaper and more fluid than neat fatty oils. They are suitable for heavier duty operations such as threading on capstan and turret lathes, thread milling and medium capacity automatic lathes.

4. **Sulphurised oils.** When sulphur (about 5%) is mixed in lard oil it is called sulphurised cutting oil. It is used for heavy duty lathe work, gear cutting and thread grinding.

Extreme pressure (E.P.) cutting oils are mineral oils containing extreme pressure additives like sulphur. Depending on the form in which sulphur is added there are mainly three types of sulphurised E.P. oils :

(*i*) Those containing combined sulphur

(*ii*) Those containing free sulphur

(*iii*) Those containing both combined and free sulphur.

The first type of E.P. oils are called "In active oils" because they do not stain yellow metals whereas second and third type of E.P. oils mentioned above are called "Active oils" since they stain yellow metals.

5. **Chlorinated oils.** When chlorine (about 3%) is added in mineral oils, it is called chlorinated cutting oil. When both chlorine and sulphur (upto 5%) are present in mineral oil, they give the oil and extreme pressure property and are suitable for severe cutting operations on strong and tough materials such as stainless steels and nickel alloys. In broaching operation also these oils are quite commonly used.

4.7. Lubricants

Solid lubricants are employed in a finely divided state and are kept in suspension in the liquid vehicle by means of a depressing agent. Under certain conditions during metal cutting the lubricant reduces the friction on the tool face and thus reduction in power consumption, increase in tool life and improvement in surface finish of the machined surface by reducing the occurrence of a build up edge is achieved. A lubricant used in metal cutting should possess the following properties :

(*i*) It should contain suitable reactive ingredients that on reaction with the work material forms a compound of lower shear strength that acts as a boundary lubricant.

(*ii*) It should be sufficiently unstable to be broken down under the temperature and pressure existing at the chip tool interface.

(*iii*) It should have a small molecular size in order to allow rapid diffusion and penetration to the chip tool interface. It should maintain a conventional hydrodynamic film between the chip and the tool face.

Carbon tetrachloride (CCl_4) chloroform ($CHCl_3$), trichloroethane (CH_3CCl_3) and certain other chlorinated hydrocarbons are quite commonly used lubricants when cutting metals at low speeds.

4.8. Selection of a Cutting Fluid

The cutting fluid should be carefully chosen. It is observed that each metal being machined and even each type of machining has its optimum cutting fluid. The selection of a particular type of cutting fluid depends on factors listed below :

(*i*) Cutting speed.

(*ii*) Feed rate.

(*iii*) Depth of cut.

(*iv*) Cutting tool material.

(*v*) Workpiece material.

(*vi*) Velocity of cutting fluid.

(*vii*) Expected cutting tool life.

(*viii*) Cost of cutting fluid.

(*ix*) The life of cutting fluid and loss of cutting fluid during operation.

Low speed and shallow cuts require little cooling or lubrication. A lubricant of considerable oiliness is required while machining tough metals at low speeds and heavy cuts. Shallow cuts at high speeds require good coolants, therefore, emulsions of soluble and sulphur base cutting oils are frequently employed a lubricant that excels as a coolent as well as a lubricant is used for heavy cuts at high speeds. Brittle materials like cast iron are often cut without the use of a lubricant although emulsions of soluble oil in water are sometimes used.

Cutting lubricants may be applied by hand from a can, by a gravity feed drops system or by some medium of forced circulation such as centrifugal pump. While using pump care should be taken to filter effectively the lubricant that is returned order to prevent the chips from damaging the pump.

Table 4.1 shows the cutting fluids used during machining for some of workpiece materials.

Table 4.1

Material	*Turning*	*Tapping*	*Drilling*
Cast Iron	Machined dry	Machined Dry or 25% lard oil + 75% mineral oil	Machined dry
Tool and low carbon steels	25% to 70% lard oil + mineral oil	20 to 40% lard oil + mineral oil	Soluble oil with 95% water
Alloy steel	25% Sulphur base oil + 75% mineral oil	30% lard oil + 70% mineral oil	Soluble oil with 80% water
Copper	Soluble oil with 90 to 95% water		
Aluminium	Mineral oil with 10% soluble oil	Lord oil	Soluble oil with 75 to 90% water

During metal cutting friction must be kept as low as possible to reduce the heat generated. Where the cutting operation is severe and the lubricant can not remove the heat rapidly enough, water soluble oils may be used. When mixed with a high concentration of water, the cooling effect is greatly increased with some lubricating properties retained. These mixtures do not corrode the steel parts with which they come into contact.

Generally following coolants and lubricants may be used for machining different metals :

(*i*) **For steel and wrought iron.** The water soluble oils or sulphur based and mineral oils may be used.

(*ii*) **For aluminium.** The mineral oils and fatty oils or soluble oils may be used.

(*iii*) **For brass, copper, bronze-monel metal and malleable iron.** The soluble oils may be used.

(*iv*) **Cast iron.** It is machined dry.

Lubricating oils are chiefly used to reduce friction and water soluble oils are used chiefly as coolants.

4.9. Cutting Fluid Penetration

The various properties of a cutting fluid which are considered to be essential for the penetration into the capillaries between the chip and tool are as follows :

(i) Wetting and spreading.

(ii) Surface tension.

(iii) Small fat molecules.

The molecules of the fluid should be more attracted to the surface than to each other so that cutting fluid spreads over the surface and wets the surface.

For efficient cooling it is necessary that the fluid penetrates as much as possible to the chip tool interface. Fig. 4.3 shows nature of chip tool interface where the hills and valleys that form a labyrinth of fine capillaries are shown to a greatly increased scale. Surface tension forces in the fluid and the action of pressure difference of one atmosphere due to the tendency to form a vacuous cavity as the tool penetrates the workpiece, will cause the fluid to flow between the capillaries and reach the tool point against the adverse motion of the chip. It would appear unlikely that the fluid can be in the form of a liquid as it penetrates the very fine labyrinth of capillaries. The material is probably carried to a point close to the tool point in the liquid state by capillary forces and is then converted to a vapour upon absorption of some of the heat generated by the cutting process. The vapour could then penetrate the capillaries, physically absorbing on the freshly cut nascent metal as it goes.

The field can enter at two pieces one at P and the other at Q as shown in Fig. 4.3. The motion of the chip across the tool face will tend to prevent fluid from reaching the tool tip from P and similarly

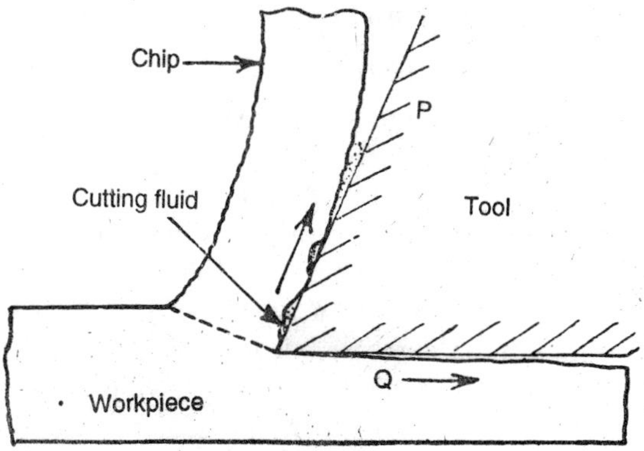

Fig. 4.3

the motion of the workpiece across the clearance surface of the tool will tend to prevent fluid from entering at Q. While the relative velocity of the surfaces at B will be more than that at P the distance of intimate contact to be traversed at Q will usually be much less than that at P. The net result is that there will usually be a greater tendency for penetration along the clearance surface than along the tool face.

The penetration of the cutting fluid to the tool chip interface becomes difficult at high cutting speeds because of high relative velocity of chip over the cutting face of the tool. This tends to retard the motion of the fluid. In order that a cutting fluid works effectively at higher cutting speed at high velocity stream of fluid is used. Nozzles of 3.3 mm to 0.375 mm diameter are used to obtain high velocity stream of cutting fluid. A fluid of smaller particle size and lower surface tension can enter the voids between tool and chip more readily than a fluid of larger particle size and higher surface tension.

The fluid that finds its way into asperities between chip and tool in the vicinity of tool point is subjected to the following unique combination of conditions :

(*i*) High local temperature

(*ii*) High local pressure approaching the hardness of the metal cut

(*iii*) Smooth surface produced

(*iv*) Highly stressed metal.

During cutting under above conditions the chip may be made to react with the fluid to form a low shear strength solid lubricant. The thin layer of solid so formed prevents the formation of a weld between the chip and tool. This helps in reducing the coefficient of friction between the chip and tool.

4.10. Application of Cutting Fluid

Most of the larger machine tools have an adequate coolant system usually enclosed within the body of the machine itself. The cutting fluid should be well filtered and stored in a cool area from where it is pumped through a piping system to the area of tool work contact. A continuous supply should be maintained at chip tool interface where heat and wear are produced. A intermittent supply of cutting fluid is not desirable because when the supply stops the temperature of the tool quickly rises and when the supply is maintained again it cools the tool which may lead to cracks at the cutting edge. It is preferable to direct a jet of cutting fluid to the cutting area. The stream of cutting fluid should be directed on the point of chip removal (Fig. 4.4) and delivered in a sufficient quantity (8 to

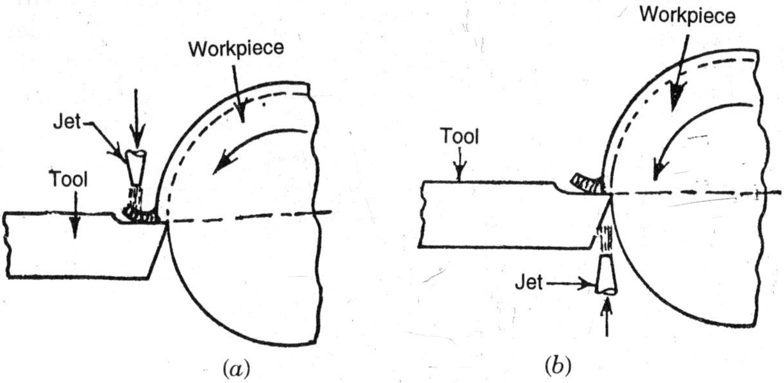

Fig. 4.4

12 and at high speeds up to 20 litres/min). A high lubricating and cooling effect is obtained if the cutting liquid is mixed with compressed air at a pressure of about 1.5 to 2 kg/cm^2 and supplied through a nozzle, directed at the tool flank. The liquid delivered thus in the atomised state not only reduces friction and facilitates chip formation but removes heat more intensively.

4.11. Effect of Cutting Fluid on Cutting Speed and Tool Life

Cutting fluids also affect the cutting speed permitted by the cutting tool. The cutting speed can be increased by about 40% in comparison to machining dry if the emulsion cutting fluid is cooled to + 2°C before used. Lower the temperature of the cutting fluid and the farther the curve is from the line representing dry machining the higher the cutting speed permitted by the tool for the same tool life. Fig. 4.5 shows relationship between the cutting speed and tool life at various temperature of the cutting fluid when structural steel having carbon 0.6% is being machined with a high speed steel tool.

The increase in tool life is about 50% in case of carbon tool steel when using cutting the fluid as compared to dry machining. Whereas the increase in tool life is 25% in case of high speed steel tools and 5 to 10% in case of carbide tools. (Fig. 4.6).

Tests made by Earnst and Merchant on a variety of cutting fluids shows that use of cutting fluids generally increases the chip thickness ratio (cutting ratio) but that the effect within the normal cutting speed range falls as the cutting speed is increased. A relationship between cutting ratio and cutting speed and various cutting fluids is shown in Fig. 4.7. It is observed from these results

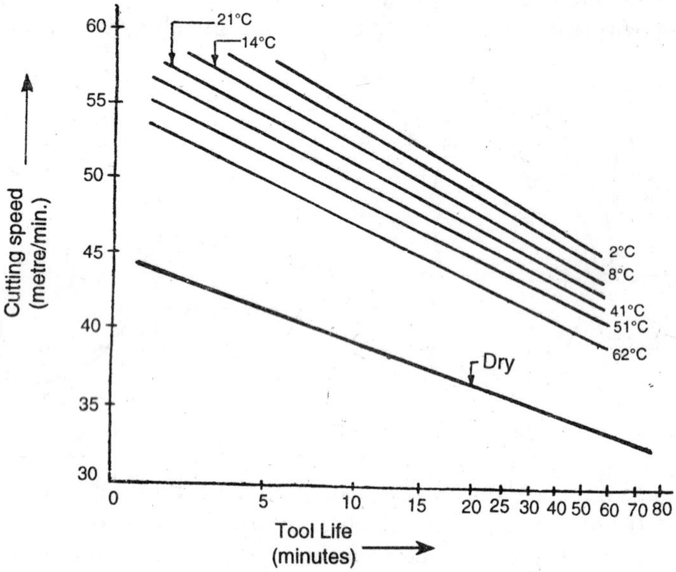

Fig. 4.5

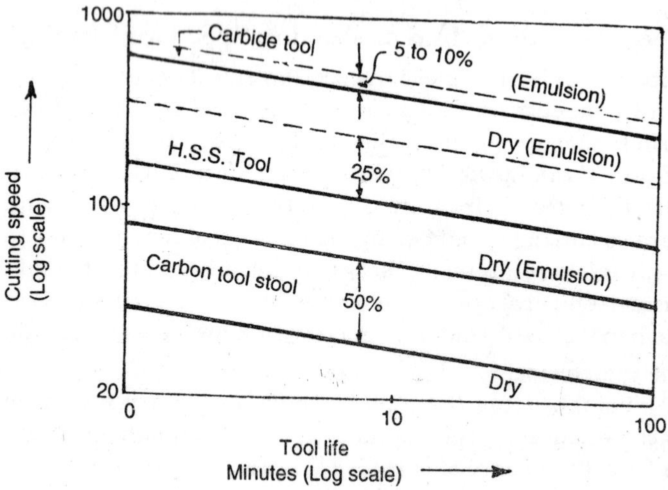

Fig. 4.6

that the depth of penetration of cutting fluid into the area of contact where friction occurs falls with the increase in cutting speed.

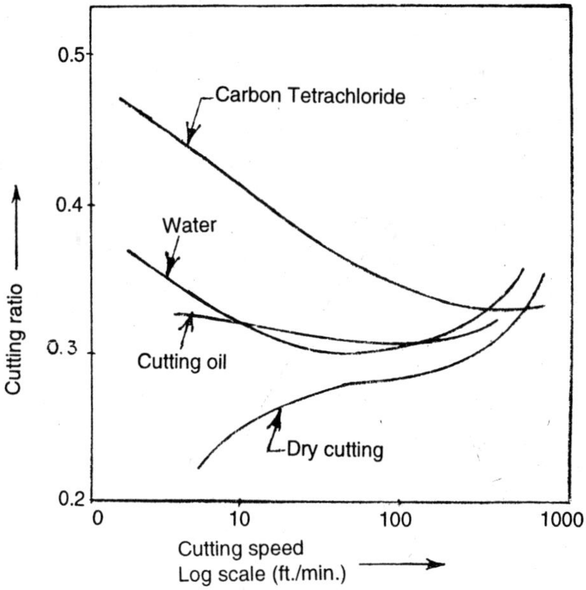

Fig. 4.7

4.12. Maintenance of Cutting Fluid

One of the important aspect of cutting fluid is its maintenance which is often neglected. From the point of view of both production efficiency and hygienic working conditions it is essential to pay due attention to the quality of water used, preparation of emulsion, concentration, control of emulsion, filtration, prevention of tramp oil etc. Poor maintenance of cutting fluids leads to bad odour and bacterial growth thereby spoiling the working environments. For effective and easy maintenance of cutting fluids centralised coolant systems are now finding wider acceptance. It is advisable to exercise greater care on control in disposing of used cutting fluids to preserve the ecology and water resources. Neat oils can be recycled and reused. Emulsions must be spilt into water and oil before they are disposed off.

4.13. Characteristics of a Lubricant

The various characteristics of an efficient lubricant used in metal cutting are as follows :

(*i*) It should have a small molecular size to allow rapid diffusion and penetration to the chip tool interface.

(*ii*) It should be sufficiently unstable to be broken down under the temperature and pressure existing at the chip tool interface.

(*iii*) The lubricant should have a suitable reactive ingredient which on reaction with the work material forms a compound of lower shear strength that as a boundary lubricant.

The commonly used lubricants are carbon tetrachloride (CCl_4) chloroform ($CHCl_3$) and trichloroethane (CH_3CCl_3).

4.14. Tool Friction

The surface finish of a machined surface is improved when coefficient of friction is decreased.

This is due to the decreased tendency to form a built up edge as the cutting forces and strain in the chip are reduced both of which result when the coefficient of friction is decreased. The coefficient of friction between chip and tool in metal cutting operation may be reduced in the following ways :

(*i*) By using fluids.

(*ii*) By improving surface finish of tool face.

(*iii*) By using free machining additions to steel.

(*iv*) Change of tool material.

(*v*) By increasing cutting speed (some times).

4.15. Effect of Cutting Fluid on Chip Concentration

Surface active cutting fluids greatly affect the chip formation by changing the stressed state in the deformation zone and facilitate disintegration. Fig. 4.8 shows the effect of various surface active cutting fluids in reduction of chip contraction. The various curves are between coefficient of chip contraction (K) and uncut chip thickness (t_2).

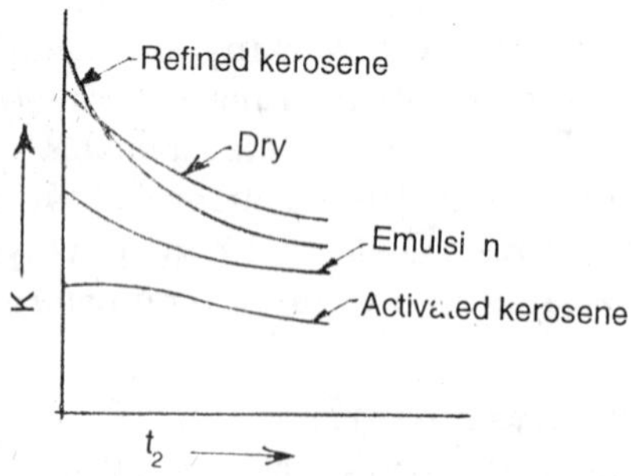

Fig. 4.8

4.16. Benefits Achieved with the Use of Cutting Fluids

The various benefits achieved by using cutting fluids are as follows :

(*i*) *Increased tool life*. By the use of cutting fluids the cutting temperature is reduced and therefore, tool life gets increased.

(*ii*) *Better surface finish*. By using cutting fluids better surface finish can be obtained.

(*iii*) *Lower tool forces*. By using cutting fluids, the coefficient of friction between chip and tool face is reduced and this reduces the tool forces.

(*iv*) Finished surfaces are protected from corrosion.

(*v*) Better dimensional stability of work piece is obtained.

4.17. How coefficient of friction is reduced

The fluid that finds its way between the asperities between chip and tool in the vicinity of the tool point is subjected to the following unique combination of conditions :

(1) High local temperatures approaching

(*a*) hardness of the metal cut.

(*b*) the melting point of the chip metal on the high points of the surface asperities.

(2) Highly stresses metal

(3) Smooth surface produced.

Because of these conditions the chip may react with the cutting fluid to form a low shear strength solid lubricant. The thin layer of solid thus formed prevents the formation of a weld between the chip and tool and hence reduces the coefficient of friction between the chip and the tool.

For example when carbon tetra chloride is used as cutting fluid at low cutting speeds, to cut steels, then iron chloride which is an ionic crystal of low shear strength is formed and is not readily displaced from the surface on which it is produced. This prevents the steel chip from welding to the tool face and thus coefficient of friction is reduced.

Carbon tetra chloride as a cutting fluid has the following characteristics :

(*i*) It is effective at low cutting speeds. At high cutting speeds (above 15 mpm) it becomes less effective because of the following reasons :

(*a*) Sufficient fluid may not reach the tool point against the outward moving chip.

(*b*) Fluid that does reach the tool point may not have sufficient time to react to form the friction reducing reaction product.

(*ii*) It is toxic

(*iii*) It is volatile

(*iv*) Its cost is more.

Example 4.1. *Under certain machining conditions the power required is 0.05 H.P./cm³/min. when the cutting speed is 24 metre/minute depth of cut is 6 mm and feed is 0.25 mm/rev. The work is cooled by a flow of 2 kg/min. of coolant having a specific heat of 0.82. If 80% of heat produced is taken away by the coolant, calculate the rise in the temperature of coolant.*

Solution. w = Metal removed per minute

= Feed × Depth of Cut × Cutting speed

= $0.025 \times 0.6 \times 24 \times 100 = 36$ cm³/min.

Horse power consumed in cutting

= $0.05 \times 36 = 1.8$

Heat produced per minute

$$= 1.8 \times 4500 \times \frac{2.34}{10^3} = 19 \text{ kcal.}$$

Heat taken away by the coolant

= $19 \times 0.8 = 15.2$ kcal.

Let, W = Weight of coolant supplied per minute

W × Specific heat × Rise in temperature

= 15.2

∴ Rise in temperature

$$= \frac{15.2}{2 \times 0.82} = 9.3°\text{C. } \textbf{Ans.}$$

Example 4.2. *A machining operation is cooled by soluble oil having a specific heat capacity of 2800 J/kg °C flowing at the rate of 50 litres/min. If 12 kW is being absorbed at the cutting point and 85% of the heat generated is taken away by the cooling oil, determine its rise in temperature. (1 litre = 0.9 kg).*

Solution. Assuming all the power to be dissipated as heat at the cutting point we have

Heat generated/min. = 12 kW

= 12,000 J × 60 s

= 720,000 joules

Heat taken away by the coolant

= $0.85 \times 720{,}000$

= 612,000 joules

Heat taken up by the coolant

= Mass × Sp. heat × Rise in temp.

= (50 × 9.0) × (2800) × (Rise in temp.) J

612,000 = 50 × 0.9 × 2800 × Rise in temp.

Rise in temperature

= 4.9°C. **Ans.**

Example 4.3. *Compare the cooling, lubricating and anti-welding properties of the following cutting fluids :*

(i) Water *(ii) Mineral oil*
(iii) Fatty oil *(iv) E.P. cutting oil.*

Solution. The properties are compared are follows :

Cutting fluid	*Cooling properties*	*Lubricating properties*	*Anti-welding properties*
Water	Excellent	Poor	Poor
Mineral oil	Fairly good	Good	Fair
Fatty oil	Fair	Excellent	Fair
E.P. cutting oil	Fair	Good	Excellent

Example 4.4. *Describe the cutting fluids used for the following metal cutting operations stating the main requirements placed on the cutting fluids.*

1. For Cast Iron : *(i) Finish and form machining of cast iron (reaming, tapping etc.)*

2. For Steels : *(i) Rough machining*

(a) at low cutting speed

(b) at high cutting speed.

(ii) Rough and finish machining of high strength and heat resisting steels and alloys

(iii) Finish and form machining

(a) at low and medium cutting speeds

(b) at high cutting speeds.

3. Rough and finish machining of high strength and heat resisting steels and alloys.

Solution. The selection of cutting fluids for various machining operations for different types of metals and alloys depends on many factors. Some of these factors are as follows :

(*i*) Rate of heat released

(*ii*) Contact pressure and temperature

(*iii*) Types of machining operations

(*iv*) Wear of tools.

Table 4.2 indicates the cutting fluids used for various machining operations.

Table 4.2

Machining operation	*Typical conditions in contact area*	*Main requirements of cutting fluid*	*Suggested cutting fluid*
(*i*) Rough machining at			
(*a*) Low cutting speed	Low heat release rate	Lubrication	Mineral oils sulphurised oils
(*b*) high cutting speed	High heat release rate	Cooling action	Water base emulsions
(*ii*) Finish and form machining of steels at			
(*a*) low and medium cutting speeds	Low heat release rate	Lubrication	Straight oils sulphurised oils
(*b*) high speeds	High heat release rate	To reduce cutting temperature	Emulsions with 5 to 10% emulsifying oil
(*c*) of cast iron	Abrasive wear of tool	Lubrication and flushing action	Kerosene
(*iii*) Rough and finish machining of			
(*a*) high strength and heat resisting steels (*b*) alloy steels	High temperature and high pressure	High resistance to normal pressure	Emulsions containing surfactant additives.

Example 4.5. *Name the commonly used cutting fluids for machining of*

(*i*) *Brass*

(*ii*) *Bronze*

While carrying out (a) Turning (b) Milling (c) Drilling (d) Tapping.

Solution. The commonly used cutting fluids are as follows :

Material	*Turning*	*Milling*	*Drilling*	*Tapping*
Brass	Mineral oil + 10% fatty oil	Soluble oil (96% water)	Soluble oil (75% to 90% water remaining mineral oil)	10 to 20% lard oil with mineral oil
Bronze	Soluble oil	Soluble oil	Soluble oil	20% lard oil and 10% mineral oil

Example 4.6. *During orthogonal cutting of a mild steel work piece the following data was obtained* :

Cutting force	= *900 N*
Thrust force	= *670 N*
Cutting speed	= *2 m / s*
Underformed chip thickness	= *0.26 mm*
Width of cut	= *2.8 mm*
Chip thickness ratio (cutting ratio)	= *0.32*
Bach Rake angle of tool	= *zero degree*
Length of contact between chip and tool	= *0.8 mm*

Determine : (a) Heat generated due to shearing

(b) Maximum temperature along the tool face.

Solution.

r = Chip thickness ratio
= 0.32

α = Back rake angle
= 0 degree

V = Cutting speed
= 2 m/s

F_H = Cutting force
= 900 N

F_V = Feed (Thrust) force
= 670 N

b = Width of cut
= 2.8 mm = 0.0028 m

H = Total heat generated during cutting
$= F_H \times V = 900 \times 2 = 1800$ J/S

H_1 = Rate of heat generated by friction between chip and tool

$$= P \times V_C$$

where V_c = Velocity of chip relative to tool

$= r \times v$

$= 0.32 \times 2$

P = Frictional force

$= F_V$ = as rake angle is zero

$H_1 = 670 \times 0.32 \times 2$

$= 428$ J/S

H_2 = Heat rate from shearing

$$H = H_1 + H_2$$

$$1800 = 428 + H_2$$

$$H_2 = 1372 \text{ J/S}$$

$$T = T_1 + T_2 + T_3$$

where T = Maximum temperature along tool face

T_1 = Temperature rise of material passing through primary deformation zone

T_2 = Temperature rise of material passing through the secondary deformation zone

T_3 = Initial temperature of the workpiece

R = Thermal Number

L = Length of heat source divided by chip thickness

$$= \frac{L_1}{t_2}$$

where L_1 = Length of contact between chip and tool = 0.8 mm.

$$r = \frac{t_1}{t_2}$$

where t_1 = Underformed chip thickness = 0.26 mm

t_2 = Chip thickness after cutting

$$t_2 = \frac{t_1}{r} = \frac{0.26}{0.32}$$

$$L = \frac{L_1}{t_2}$$

$$L = \frac{0.8 \times .32}{.26} = 0.98$$

$$R = \frac{\rho \,.\, C \,.\, V \,.\, t_1}{K}$$

where ρ = Density of steel = 7200 kg/m^3 (Assume)

C = Specific heat capacity = 500 J/kg K.

K = Thermal conductivity = 43.5 J/Sm k

$$t_1 = \frac{0.26}{1000} \text{ m} = .00026$$

$$R = 7200 \times 500 \times 2 \times \frac{0.26}{1000} \times \frac{1}{43.5} = 43$$

$$T_1 = \frac{(1-p) \times H_2}{\rho \,.\, C \,.\, v \,.\, t_1 \,.\, b}$$

where p = Proportion of shearing heat conducted into the workpiece

= 0.1

$$T_1 = \frac{(1-0.1) \times 1372}{7200 \times 500 \times 2 \times 0.00026 \times 0.0028}$$

= 235.5°C.

It is the mean temperature rise in the primary deformation zone and since it is a temperature difference can be expressed in either centigrade (°C) or degree Kelvin (°K).

T_4 = Average temperature rise of the chip resulting from secondary deformation (Frictional heat source)

$$= \frac{H_1}{\rho \,.\, C \,.\, V \,.\, t \,.\, b}$$

$$= \frac{428}{7200 \times 500 \times 2 \times 0.00026 \times 0.0028}$$

$$= \frac{428}{5.24} = 81.7°\text{C}$$

Now $$\frac{R}{L} = \frac{43}{0.98} = 43.87$$

The value of $\frac{T_2}{T_4}$ depends on the values of $\frac{R}{L}$ and width of secondary deformation zone.

A typical value of $\frac{T_2}{T_4} = 4.2$ when $\frac{R}{L} = 43.87$

$$\frac{T_2}{T_4} = 4.2$$

$$T_2 = 4.2 \times T_4 = 4.2 \times 81.7 = 343°\text{C}$$

T_3 = Initial temperature of work piece

$$= \text{Room temperature} = 25°\text{C (say)}$$

$$T = T_1 + T_2 + T_3$$

$$= 235.5 + 343 + 25 = 603.5°\text{C}.$$

PROBLEMS

4.1. (*a*) What are the sources of heat generation in metal cutting ?

(*b*) Show with the aid of a simple sketch the areas of heat generation that occur when using a single point cutting tool on a lathe.

4.2. (*a*) State the functions of a cutting fluid.

(*b*) What are the essential properties of a cutting fluid ?

4.3. Explain the following types of cutting fluids :

(*a*) Water based cutting fluids.

(*a*) Straight or neat oil based cutting fluids.

4.4. Write short notes on the following :

(*a*) Selection of a cutting fluid.

(*b*) Application of cutting fluid.

(*c*) Maintenance of cutting fluid.

4.5. Describe the effect of cutting fluid on cutting speed and tool life.

4.6. Explain the cutting fluid penetration during metal cutting.

4.7. How does a lubricant and cutting fluid differ from each other ?

4.8. Describe tool friction.

4.9. (*a*) State the characteristics of a lubricant used in metal cutting.

(*b*) Name the commonly used lubricants.

4.10. Explain the effect of cutting fluids on chip contraction.

4.11. Write short notes on the following :

(*i*) Benefits achieved with the use of cutting fluids.

(*ii*) E.P. cutting oils.

5

Surface Finishing Processes

5.1. Surface Finish

A fine surface can be taken to mean which has a greater degree of smoothness than is customarily produced by normal cutting methods. More accurately a tool does it work the less rough is the surface produced. The selection of the method by which a surface is to be produced will depend on a large number of variables ranging from the physical limitations imposed by the material and the duties to be imposed on the surface to the commercial considerations of output. It has been observed that limits of surface finish are primarily governed by the machine and the setting of the tool.

Surface finishing processes for machined surface may be classified into two groups, namely those employing hardened steel tools such as burnishing, scraping and filing and those employing abrasives such as grinding, honing, laping, superfinishing and polishing.

5.1.1. Grinding

It is a metal cutting process that employs an abrasive tool called grinding wheel. The cutting elements of grinding wheel are grains of abrasive material having high hardness and a high heat resistance. They have sharp edges and are held together by bonding materials. Grinding provides high accuracy and a good surface finish. Therefore it is used as a finishing operation. This process removes comparatively little material usually from 0.25 mm to 0.5 mm. Tolerances as small as 0.0025 mm can be obtained by commercial grinding.

During grinding temperature rises with the increased wear of grains which may lead to distortion of workpiece structural changes and crack formation in the ground surface. Hence an abundant flow of coolant is commonly used in grinding. The coolant also slows down softening of wheel bond which is due to heating.

The various cutting fluids used in grinding steel are as follows :

(*i*) A one per cent solution of soda ash with 0.15 per cent sodium nitrite.

(*ii*) A two per cent aqueous solution of powdered soap.

(*iii*) A 3.5% aqueous solution of a neutral paste type emulsion with an oleinic acid base.

Cast iron and copper are often ground dry. Aluminium is ground by using kerosene with or without the addition of mineral oil as coolant.

The grinding process has certain specific features as follows :

(*i*) As the abrasive grains are some distance apart a grinding wheel has an interrupted cutting edge and not a continuous one as on a milling cutter.

(*ii*) A grinding wheel can be self sharpening during the course of the grinding process.

(*iii*) The process of chip removal by a grain takes place in a very short period.

(*iv*) Due to the pyramidal and rounded shape of the cutting element of the abrasive grains, the thickness and width of the uncut chip are inter-related in grinding.

A grinding wheel can be compared to a milling cutter both having the following similarities :

(*i*) Both have a number of cutting edges, each cutting edge having adequate rake and clearance angles.

(*ii*) Each cutting edge is in action only for a short time.

(*iii*) The chip formation process in grinding is similar to cutting by the tooth of a milling cutter. The chip has the same structure and appearance as obtained in milling. Adequate chip space is available for a free cutting action. In the case of a grinding wheel the chip space is available between bonded abrasive particles.

The process of grinding is dependent upon the following inherent properties of the grinding wheel :

(*i*) Type of abrasive

(*ii*) Size and distribution of grits

(*iii*) Amount and type of bond material

(*iv*) Volume of pores relative to that of grits and bonds.

5.2. Abrasive Materials

Materials used as the cutting grains are of two types :

(*a*) Natural abrasives.

(*b*) Artificial or manufactured abrasives.

Natural Abrasives. They include sand stone, diamond, corundum and emery. The principal component of corrundum and emery is natural aluminium oxide (alumina). Corrundum is composed of about 85% aluminium oxide and 15% iron oxide. Emery contains 60% aluminium oxide and 40% iron oxide. The relative abrasive action of each substance depends upon the properties of aluminium oxide.

Diamond abrasive wheels are used extensively for sharpening carbide and ceramic cutting tools. Diamonds are also used for truing and dressing other types of abrasive wheels. Because of their high cost, diamonds are used only when other cheaper abrasives will not produce the desired result.

Artificial Abrasives. They include silicon carbide (SiC) and aluminium oxide (Al_2O_3). Silicon carbide is made by charging an electrical furnace with silica sand, coke, salt and sawdust. A temperature of over 2300°C is maintained for several hours obtained by passing heavy current through the charge and a solid mass of silicon carbide results. After the furnace has cooled the mass of crystals is removed, crushed and graded to various desired sizes. Silicon carbide is very hard (though less than boron carbide and diamond). It has high heat resistance and excellent cutting properties. Two types of silicon carbide is available, namely black and green. The black silicon carbide is of lower quality and contains about 95% SiC. Green silicon carbide is somewhat harder and has a high grinding capacity and contains at least 97% SiC.

Green silicon carbide is mainly used for sharpening carbide tipped cutting tools.

Aluminium oxide abrasive is the crystalline form of aluminium oxide (Al_2O_3). It is produced in an arc furnace from bauxite, iron filings and small amount of coke. The mass of aluminium that is formed is crushed and the particles are graded to size. It is softer than silicon carbide but it is considerably tougher and is a more general purpose abrasive. Common trade names for aluminium oxide abrasives are Alundum and Aloxite.

The physical properties of the material to be cut dictate the kind of abrasive to be selected. As a general guide silicon carbide is used for grinding brittle materials and materials of low tensile strength such as cemented carbides, cast iron, ceramics and low tensile strength metals including brass, soft bronze and copper. Aluminium oxide having less brittle grains is used for tougher and higher strength material such as steel, wrought iron, hardened steel, alloy steel and hard brass and bronze.

In general the physical properties of aluminium oxide compared with silicon carbide are as follows :

(*i*) Silicon carbide is harder than aluminium oxide.

(*ii*) Aluminium oxide can withstand greater stresses than silicon carbide.

(*iii*) Aluminium oxide is more tough than silicon carbide.

(*iv*) Aluminium oxide wheels are generally used for grinding high tensile strength and tough materials whereas silicon carbide wheels are used to grind low tensile strength and non-metallic materials.

5.2.1. Abrasive Grain Size

Abrasive materials are crushed in ball mills and screened for classification into different sizes. The size of abrasive grain required in a grinding wheel depends on the following factors :

(*i*) Amount of material to be removed.

(*ii*) Finish desired.

(*iii*) Hardness of material being ground.

The grit or grain size of an abrasive is denoted by a number representing the number of meshes per inch of the screen through which the grains of crushed abrasives are passed for grinding. The standard grains sizes for grinding wheels are represented in Table 5.1.

Table 5.1

Grit Designation	*Grain Size or Grit Number*						
Coarse	10	12	14	16	20	24	
Medium	30	36	46	54	60		
Fine	80	100	120	150	180		
Very fine	220	240	280	320	400	500	600

The coarser grit will remove the stock at a faster rate and finer finish will require a finer grit.

Sizes from 240 to 600 are designated as flour sizes. These are primarily used for lapping and honing stones.

5.2.2. Bonds

Bonding materials are used as binders to hold the abrasive particles in place. The firmness with which the grains are held in the wheel and the strength of wheel itself in which large centrifugal forces are developed in rotation depend on the bonding material. The bonding material determines whether the wheel is rigid or flexible. It also determines the force that is required to dislodge an abrasive particle from the wheel which plays a major role in the cutting action.

Six types of bonding materials are commonly used.

(*i*) **Vitrified Bonds.** Vitrified bond is made of clay and water. The abrasive grains and clay are thoroughly mixed together with sufficient water to make the mixture uniform. The material is formed into a wheel usually by pressing and then these wheels are dried. They then are fired in a kiln which results in the bonding material becoming hard and strong. Vitrified bonds are used most extensively. Vitrified abrasive wheels have a high production capacity, and are moisture proof.

About 75% of grinding wheels have vitrified bonds.

(*ii*) **Resinoid Bond.** Resinoid bonding is produced by mixing abrasive grains with synthetic resins. Resinoid bonded wheels are strong, elastic and permit high peripheral speeds but are destroyed by alkaline cooling fluids. This can be avoided by impregnating the wheel with paraffin. These wheels normally operate at surface speeds in the region of 3000 m/min. They are particularly suitable for use in grinding steel, cast iron and malleable iron castings.

(*iii*) **Shellac Bond.** Shellac bonded wheels are made by mixing the abrasive grains with shellac in a mixer. After the mixture has been rolled or pressed into desired wheel shapes, they are then hardened by baking for several hours at about 160°C. Thin wheels that are strong but possess some elasticity have shellac bond. They can produce high polish and are used in grinding such parts as camshafts and mill rolls.

(*iv*) **Rubber Bond.** A rubber bond is essentially a mixture of rubber softened by gasoline and sulphur (30%). A rubber bonded wheel has high strength and elasticity and is moisture proof. They are commonly used for snagging work in foundries and for thin cut-off wheels.

(*v*) **Silicate Bond.** This bond is produced by mixing abrasive grains with silicate of soda (water glass). The mixture is given the desired wheel shape and baked at about 260°C for a day or more. This silicate bonded wheels are soft, comparatively weak and have low production capacity. Such wheels has limited applications.

(*vi*) **Oxy Chloride Bond.** This bond is produced by mixing abrasive grains with oxide and chloride of magnesium.

Different types of bonds used in grinding are represented by different symbol as shown in Table 5.2.

Table 5.2

Type of bond	*Symbol*
Vitrified bond	*V*
Resinoid bond	*B*
Shellac bond	*E*
Rubber bond	*R*
Silicate bond	*S*
Oxy chloride bond	*O*

5.2.3. Grade

Grade or hardness indicates the strength with which the bonding material holds the abrasive grains in the grinding wheel. The easier a grain is torn out of the bond, the softer the wheel and *vice versa*. The degrees of hardness are specified by the use of letters of the alphabet. Different grades of grinding wheels are shown in Table 5.3.

Table 5.3

Soft	*A*	*B*	*C*	*D*	*E*	*F*	*G*	*H*		
Medium	*I*	*J*	*K*	*L*	*M*	*N*	*O*	*P*		
Hard	*Q*	*R*	*S*	*T*	*U*	*V*	*W*	*X*	*Y*	*Z*

The grinding wheel of required grade should be selected for each grinding job. The selection of a particular grade of wheel is largely governed by the nature of work, its composition, size and hardness. Hard wheels are used for softer materials and *vice versa*.

5.2.4. Structure

It indicates the spacing between the abrasive grains or in other words density of the wheel. Structure of grinding wheel is designated by a number. The higher the number the wider the spacing. It is observed that the tendency for burns to appear on the ground surface is reduced when a wheel of more open structure is used. Table 5.4 indicates the two types of structure with their numbers.

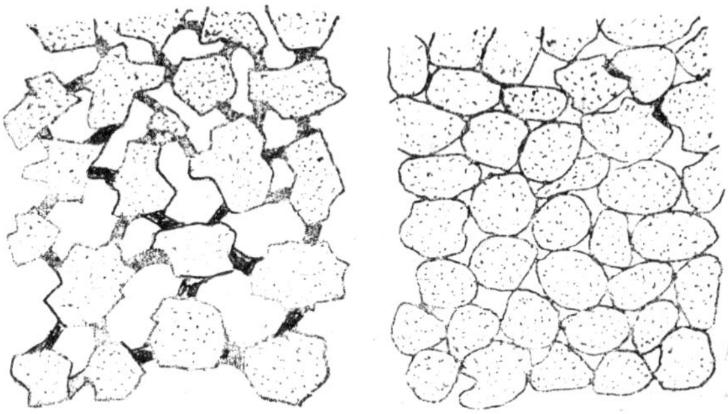

Fig. 5.1

Fig. 5.1 shows open and dense structure.

Table 5.4

Structure	*Symbol*							
Dense	1	2	3	4	5	6	7	8
Open	9	10	11	12	13	14	15	or more

5.2.5. Marking system of grinding wheels

The Indian Standards Institution (IS : 551—1954) has specified a standard system of marking the grinding wheels. According to this system the following elements are represented in a definite order :

1. Abrasive
2. Grain size of Grit
3. Grade
4. Structure
5. Bond.

In addition to this manufacturer may add some symbol to indicate the abrasive used.

Apart from the above information diameter of grinding wheel, its thickness and bore diameter should also be mentioned.

A grinding wheel with the markings 300 × 30 × 35 W A 36 M 5 S 17 will have the following specifications :

Wheel diameter = 300 mm
Wheel thickness = 30 mm

Bore diameter = 35 mm

W—Manufacture's symbol for abrasive used (Use optional)

A—Abrasive (Al_2O_3)

36—Grain size

M—Grade

5—Structure

S—Bond (silicate bond)

17—Manufacturer's symbol for the type of grinding wheel (Use optional)

5.3. Grinding Wheel Cutting Action

During cutting action of a grinding wheel the spacing of the abrasive particles and the effect of the bonding material which holds them in the wheel are very important. Each exposed grain constitutes a small cutting edge thus providing a multiplicity of cutting edges, some having positive rake angles and others having negative rake angles. Each cutting edge acts exactly the same as any other cutting edge under similar conditions with chips being formed (Fig. 5.2). As the cutting edges are small therefore the chips produced are also small. Feed and depth of cut should also be small. In order to achieve close tolerances and excellent surface finish large number of cutting edges, small depth of cut and small feed should be used.

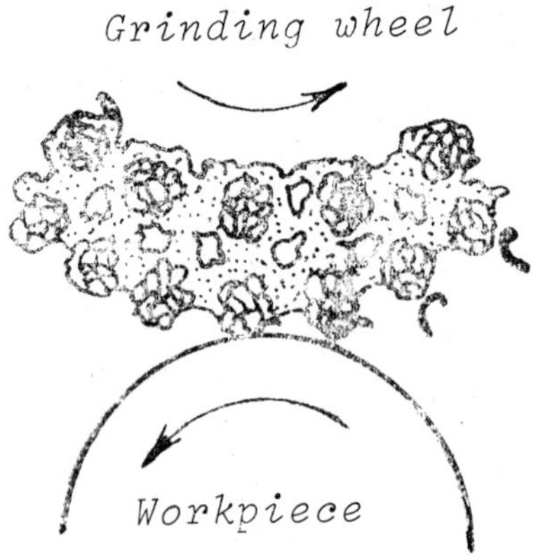

Fig. 5.2

5.4. Grinding Wheel Selection

In order to achieve optimum results the proper grinding wheel should be selected for a given job. The shape of grinding wheel should be such that it permits proper contact between wheel and the surface to be ground. The size of the grinding wheel depends so spindle speed available on the grinding machine and the cutting speed for the wheel. The grinding wheel should be of proper abrasive, grain size, structure grade and bond. Various factors on which the selection of grinding wheel depends are as follows :

(*i*) Properties of material to be ground such as material, hardness, strength and toughness. Hard dense materials require a relatively soft grade of wheel, hard brittle materials require fine grain or closely spaced abrasives very hard material such as tungsten carbide require widely spaced abrasive wheel to permit rapid release of worm abrasive particles since the material ground is as hard as abrasive. Aluminium oxide wheels are commonly used for materials of high tensile strength, where the materials is neither very brittle nor easily penetrated such as carbon, alloy and high speed steels and wrought iron and tough bronzes. Silicon carbide wheels are used for materials of low tensile strength such as brasses, aluminium, glass and marble.

(*ii*) Amount of material to be removed.

(*iii*) Type of surface finish desired.

(*iv*) Dimensional accuracy required.

(*v*) Rigidity of the grinding machine.

(*vi*) Method and type of grinding.

(*vii*) The area of contact between the work and the wheel. According to IS : 1249—1958, the following grinding wheels are recommended for different materials :

Table 5.5

Material to be grounded	*Cylindrical grinding*	*Surface grinding*	*Internal grinding*
	Specification of grinding wheels.		
Hardened Steel	A 60 LV	A 46 KV	A 24 JV
Soft Steel	A 54 MV	A 46 MV	A 46 JV
Cast Iron	C 46 KV	C 46 JV	C 36 JV

5.5. Shapes of Grinding Wheels

Grinding wheels are manufactured in various standard shapes. Different shapes of grinding wheels are as shown in Fig. 5.3. Straight, recessed on one side and recessed both sides wheels are used primarily for grinding external or internal cylindrical surface and for plain surface grinding. The cylinder shaped wheel is used for producing flat surfaces the grinding being done with the end face

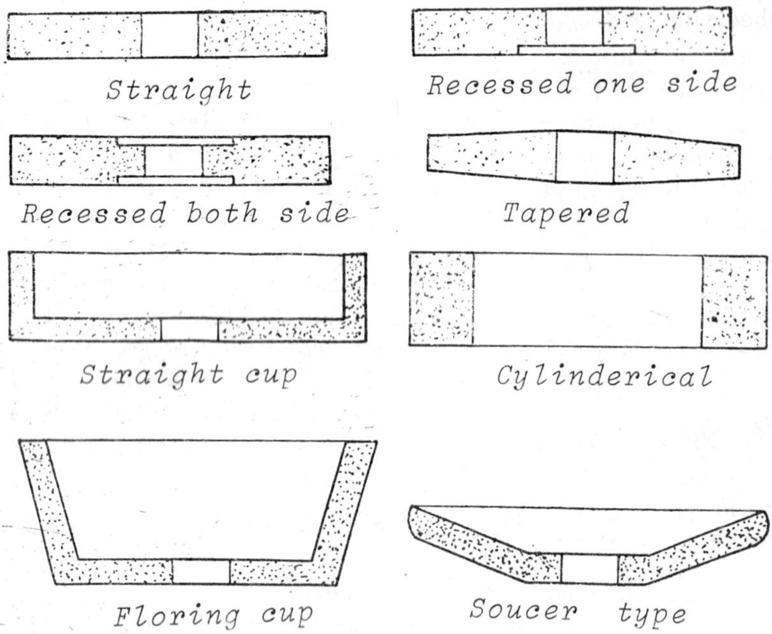

Fig. 5.3. Standard grinding wheel shapes.

of the wheel. Straight cup wheel is used for grinding flat surfaces by traversing the work fast the end or face of the wheel. Flaring cup wheel is used for tool sharpening. Grinding wheels tapered on two sides are used for grinding the gear teeth and threads. Dish type are used for grinding tools saws. Straight grinding wheels can be obtained with a variety of standard faces some of these are shown in Fig. 5.4.

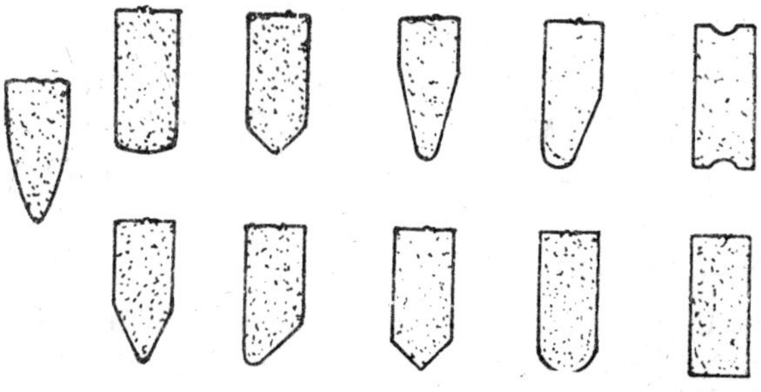

Fig. 5.4. Standard shapes of grinding wheel faces.

5.5.1. Mounted wheels and points

They are small grinding wheels of different shapes. They are attached to metal shanks that can be inserted in the chucks of portable high speed electric motors. Fig. 5.5 shows some mounted wheels and points.

Fig. 5.5. Mounted points.

5.6. Types of Grinding Machines and Processes

Grinding machines can probably be best classified according to the type of surfaces they are used to produce. In order to bring the job to the required shape, size and surface finish the surplus stock is removed either by feeding the job against the revolving wheel or by forcing the revolving wheel against the job. According to the quality of surface finish produced grinding machines are classified into two groups :

(*i*) Rough grinders.

(*ii*) Precision grinders.

Rough Grinders. These grinders are used to produce rough surfaces and the accuracy in dimensions is not high. The various grinders used for rough grinding are swing frame grinders, bench grinder and portable grinder. Pedestal types or swing frame grinders, are usually used for snagging. Snagging is a type of rough grinding that is done in a foundry to remove fins, gates, risers and rough spots from castings preparatory to further machining. Sometimes portable grinders are also used for this purpose. Portable grinders may be either electrically or pneumatically driven and are obtainable in a wide variety.

Precision grinding. Precision grinders are used to obtain accurate dimensions and fine finish, precision grinders according to the type of surface produced are classified as follows :

(*i*) Cylindrical grinders.

(*a*) Centre type

(*b*) Centreless

(*c*) Chuck type.

(*ii*) Internal grinders.
- (*a*) Chuck type
- (*b*) Planetary (work stationary)
- (*c*) Centreless.

(*iii*) Surface grinders.
- (*a*) Reciprocating table
  - (*i*) Horizontal spindle type
  - (*ii*) Vertical spindle type
- (*b*) Rotating table
  - (*i*) Horizontal spindle type
  - (*ii*) Vertical spindle type.

(*iv*) Tool and cutter grinder
- (*a*) Universal
- (*b*) Special.

Precision grinding machines should be used with care and be operated by skilled personnel, such machine can be operated economically only if they have high use factor. As these machines are used to produce products that have close dimensional tolerances they must be constructed very accurately. Their frames should be heavy and rigid to assure permanency of alignment. Rotating parts should be accurately balanced to avoid vibration. Spindles should be mounted in very accurate bearings usually of the preloaded ball bearing type. Controls should be provided in order that all movements that determine dimensions of the workpiece can be made with accuracy. The abrasive dust produced during grinding should not enter between the moving parts.

5.6.1. Cylindrical grinders

Centre type cylindrical grinders are quite commonly used to produce external cylindrical surfaces (Fig. 5.6). It is equipped with head-stock and tail-stock. The workpiece is mounted and rotated between centres. The grinding wheel rotates. Grinding wheel and the workpiece move in the opposite direction at their point of contact. The depth of cut is determined by the feed of the wheel or workpiece. Provision is made to transverse the workpiece with respect to wheel. In large grinders the wheel is reciprocated because of the massiveness of work. The cylindrical grinder is provided with two tables. The upper table may be swivelled about a centre point for taper grinding. The lower table slides on ways on the bed and provides traverse of the work past the grinding wheel.

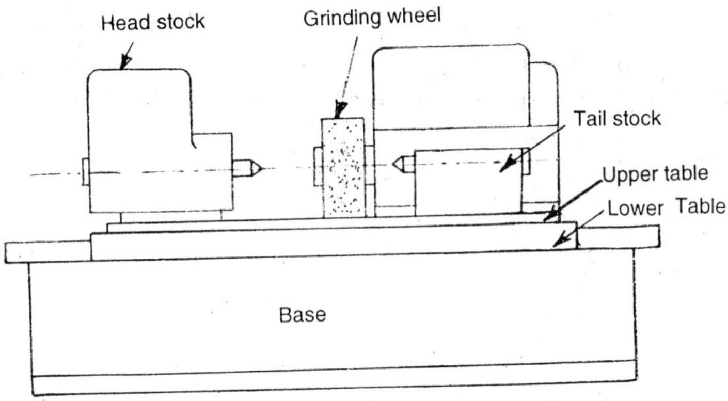

Fig. 5.6. Centre-type cylindrical grinder.

In cylindrical grinding two types of grinding is carried out :

(*i*) Traverse grinding

(*ii*) Plunge grinding.

In traverse grinding the work is reciprocated as the wheel feeds to produce cylinders longer than the width of wheel face. In plunge grinding the wheel is fed to the workpiece rotating in a fixed position and grinding is carried out on workpiece in a length equal to or shorter than the width of grinding wheel. This method is used in grinding for relatively short work and especially in form grinding. The output is very high in plunge grinding. Fig. 5.7 shows traverse grinding and plunge grinding is shown in Fig. 5.8.

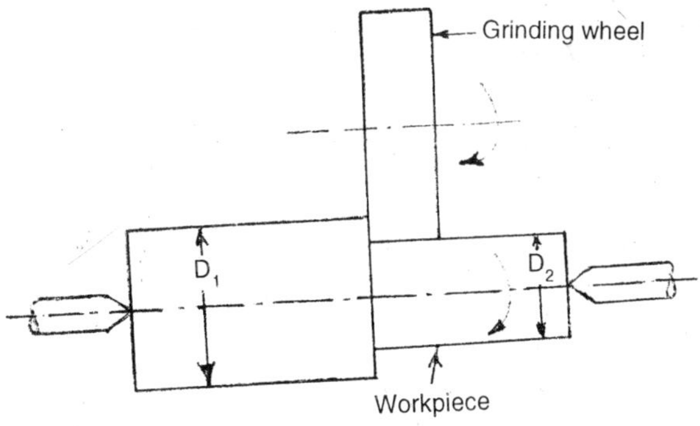

Fig. 5.7. Traverse grinding.

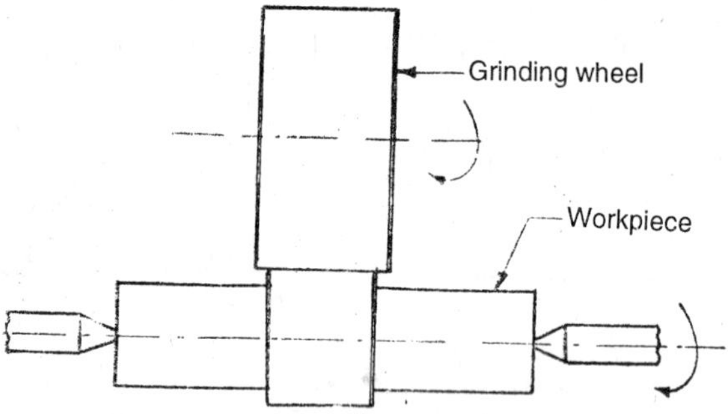

Fig. 5.8. Plunge grinding.

5.7. Depth of Cut

It is the thickness of metal removed by the grinding wheel in one traverse stroke (lengthwise)

$$t = \text{Depth of cut} = \frac{D_1 - D_2}{2}$$

where D_1 = Diameter of workpiece before grinding

D_2 = Diameter of workpiece after grinding.

In finish grinding depth of cut is taken as 0.005 to 0.015 mm per stroke. Other conditions being equal the best surface finish is obtained in grinding with higher speeds of wheel rotation, lower rates of traverse, and smaller depths of cut.

5.8. Feed

In cylindrical grinding feed is the longitudinal movement of the workpiece per revolution.

$$f = \text{feed in mm per workpiece revolution.} = K_1 B$$

where B = Face width of wheel in mm

K_1 = Constant

= 0.4 to 0.6 for finish grinding

= 0.6 to 0.9 for rough grinding

Work or table traverse in metre/minute

$$= \frac{f \times N}{1000}$$

where N = Workpiece speed in R.P.M.

5.9. Cutting Speed

It is relative speed of wheel (V_1) and the workpiece. It is expressed in m/sec.

$$V = \text{Cutting speed} = V_1 = \frac{\pi D N_1}{1000 \times 60}$$

where D = Diameter of grinding wheel in mm.

N_1 = Speed of wheel in R.P.M.

5.10. Machining Time

Machining time in traverse cylindrical grinding is given by the formula

$$T = \text{Machining time}$$
$$= \frac{L.h}{N.ft} . K$$

where L = Length ground in mm

h = Allowance on each side in mm.

f = Longitudinal feed in mm/rev.

N = R.P.M. of workpiece

t = Depth of cut (Rate of infeed per stroke) in mm.

K = Accuracy factor

= 1.1 for rough grinding

= 1.4 for finish grinding.

Fig. 5.9 shows an internal cylindrical grinder. It uses a chuck to hold the work with the grinding wheel revolving the table moves from right to left causing the wheel to enter the work and grind its internal surface.

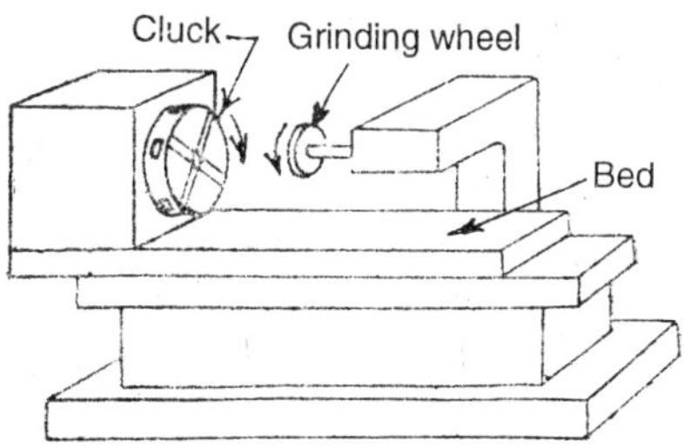

Grinding machine

Fig. 5.9

5.11. Surface Grinders

Surface grinding is used mainly to machine flat surfaces. It can be performed either with the periphery of a straight wheel or the face of a cup, cylinder or segmental wheel. A surface grinder uses a magnetic chuck mounted on table to hold the workpieces. There are two basic types of surface grinding machines differing in movement of their tables and the orientation of the grinding wheel spindles.

1. Reciprocating surface grinders
   (*i*) Horizontal wheel spindle and reciprocating table.
   (*ii*) Vertical wheel spindle and reciprocating table.
2. Rotary surface grinders.
   (*i*) Horizontal spindle and rotary table.
   (*ii*) Vertical spindle and rotary table.

Reciprocating table surface grinder. The most common type of surface grinding machine is the one having a reciprocating table and horizontal spindle (Fig. 5.10). The table is mounted on horizontal way and can be reciprocated longitudinally either by hand wheel or by hydraulic powers. Cross feed is given by moving the wheel head in and out. Infeed is controlled by a hand wheel that lowers the grinding wheel towards the work. In such grinders usually the grinding wheel is mounted directly on the motor spindle. The size of the grinder is designated by the dimensions of the working area of table.

Reciprocating table surface grinder with vertical spindle (Fig. 5.11) is primarily used for production type work. In this grinder the wheel diameter should exceed the width of surface to be machined.

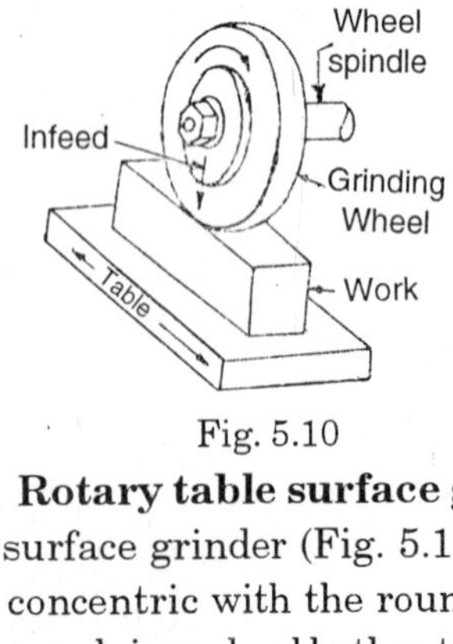

Fig. 5.10

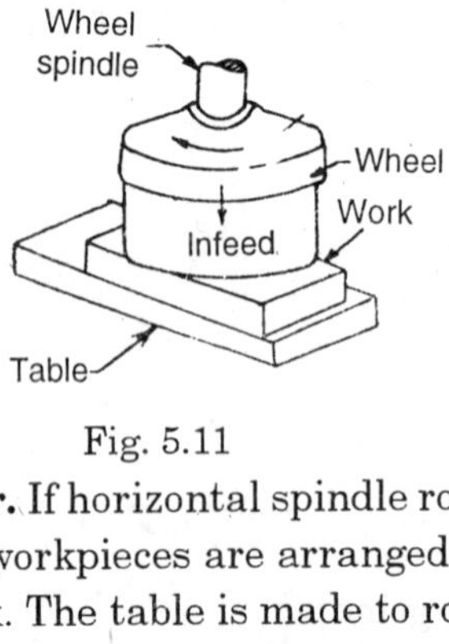

Fig. 5.11

Rotary table surface grinder. If horizontal spindle rotary table surface grinder (Fig. 5.12), the workpieces are arranged in a circle concentric with the round chuck. The table is made to rotate under revolving wheel both rotating in opposite direction. In vertical spindle rotary table surface grinder (Fig. 5.13) a cup wheel is used. Vertical feed to the wheel is given by moving wheel head.

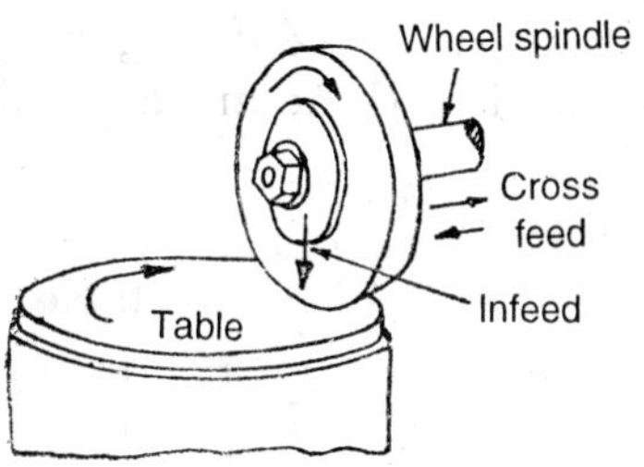

Fig. 5.12

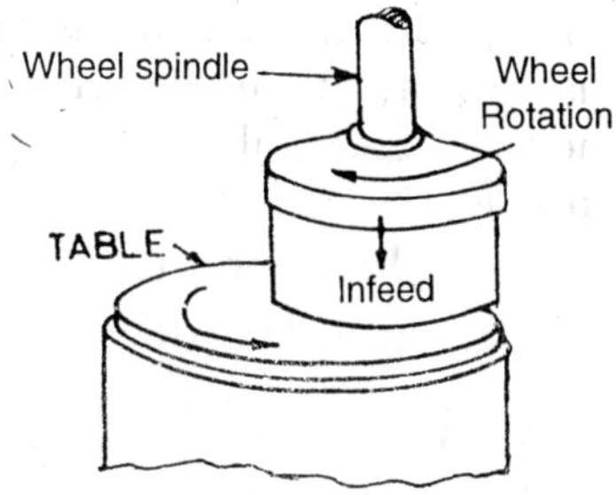

Fig. 5.13

5.12. Tool and Cutter Grinder

This grinder is used to sharpen cutting tool like milling cutters, drills, hobs, reamers taps and broaches. The depth of cut in this grinder is quite small as the grinding is carried out dry to give the operator a good view. Generally cup and dish shaped grinding wheels are used in this machine. The wheels used are soft and cool cutting. For a carbide tipped tools diamond impregnated wheels are used.

5.13. Centreless Grinding

Centreless grinding makes it possible to grind both external and internal cylindrical surfaces without the necessity of the workpiece being mounted between centres in a chuck. The principle of centreless external grinding is shown in Fig. 5.14. In centreless

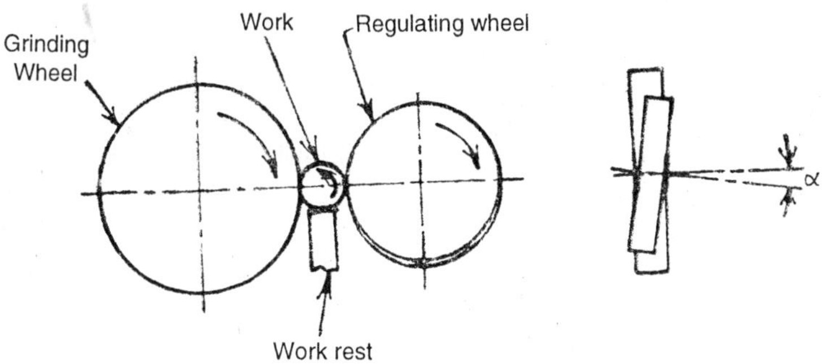

Fig. 5.14

grinding two wheels are used. The larger wheel called grinding wheel operates as regular grinding speeds and does the actual grinding. The small wheel called regulating wheel is mounted at an angle to the plane of grinding wheel. The work with its both ends freely supported on a vee formed by the work rest, rotates between the grinding and the regulating wheels. The grinding wheel is driven by an electric motor and rotates at a maximum surface speed of about 1850 metres per minutes. Normally, the regulating wheel speed range may lie within 33 to 130 metres per minute. The regulating wheel does not act as a cutting tool but it is mainly responsible for controlling the speed of rotation and longitudinal motion of the work. The wheels rotate clockwise and the work driven by the regulating wheel and having approximately the same peripheral speed rotates counter-clockwise. Axial traverse of the work is controlled by varying the inclination of the regulating wheel. The axial feed is approximately calculated by the formula :

$$f = \pi DN \sin \alpha.$$

where f = Feed in mm/minute.

D = Diameter of regulating wheel in mm.

N = R.P.M. of regulating wheel.

α = Angle of inclination of the regulating wheel.

Centreless grinding is carried out in three different ways :

(*i*) Through feed grinding.

(*ii*) Infeed grinding.

(*iii*) End feed grinding.

5.13.1. Through feed grinding

Through feed grinding is normally used for grinding plain cylindrical workpieces. In this process the work is automatically fed through continuously between the grinding wheel and the regulating wheel which have already been set with a particular gap. The grinding starts as soon as the work enters the grinding wheels and grinding of work is complete as soon as it comes out of the wheels. Since the work has to remain outside the wheels before and after grinding operation, suitable supports or guides are provided. (Fig. 5.15 *a*).

5.13.2. Infeed centreless grinding

In this process the work rest and the regulating wheel are retracted so that the work can be put in position and removed, when grinding is completed. When the work is in position the regulating wheel is fed inward until the desired diameter is obtained. The work does not move axially as in through feed but is kept supported against an end stop. This arrangement permits multiple diameters and curved parts to be ground (Fig. 5.15 *b*).

5.13.3. End feed centreless grinding

This process is used for grinding taper work. Both the wheels are tapered and thus produce tapered workpieces. In this process the work is feed from one side until it reaches the stop. Fig. 5.15 (*c*) shows the work being ground by the end feed method.

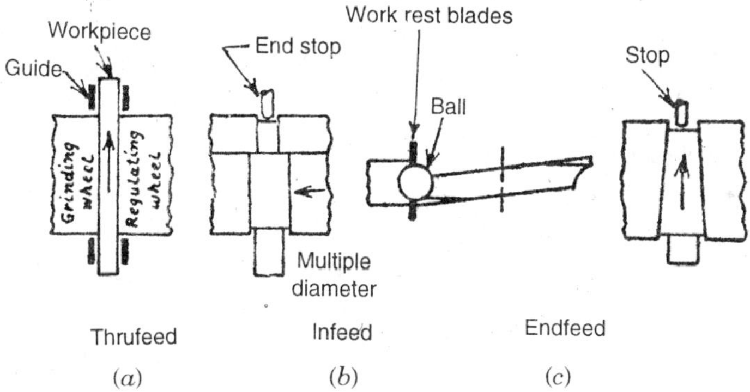

Fig. 5.15

5.13.4. Advantages

Various advantages of centreless grinding are as follows :

(*i*) Work chucking and its centring is not required. This saves setting time. Further errors associated with centering are absent and thus grinding allowance can be reduced.

(*ii*) The work-piece is supported rigidly during the operation and therefore no deflection takes place during grinding. This allows heavier cuts to be taken resulting in economical grinding.

(*iii*) It is very rapid process. Frequently it can be made automatic.

(*iv*) Very little skill is required for the operator.

(*v*) A fairly wide range of components can be ground.

(*vi*) Large grinding wheels can be used so that wheel wear is minimised.

(*vii*) Excellent accuracy and fine surface finish can be achieved as there is no distortion of workpiece during grinding.

In comparison with cylindrical grinders, centreless grinders have the following advantages :

(*i*) their output is higher due to the reduction in work handling time ;

(*ii*) work of very small diameter can be ground (external grinding) ;

(*iii*) concentric surfaces can be ground to high precision ;

(*iv*) less skill is required to operate centreless grinders ;

(*v*) less grounding allowance is required because the workpiece centres itself during operation ;

(*vi*) higher grinding speeds and feeds can be employed, and more metal can be ground off per revolution of the workpiece as there is no danger of bending the work ;

(*vii*) more stable dimensions can be maintained in each lot of workpieces.

5.14. Mounting of Grinding Wheel

To ensure efficient and safe operation, the grinding wheel should be firmly clamped on the spindle, properly balanced, tested for strength and reliably enclosed by a guard. Before mounting the wheel should be checked for cracks because they may not be seen. For this sound the wheel cracks. If the wheel is not cracked, it will give off a dull ringing sound. The wheel should be fit freely on the sleeve. One flange on each side of the wheel should be provided. Washers of rubber card board or leather from 0.5 to 3 mm thick are to be inserted between flanges and the wheel so that any unevenness of the wheel surface is balanced and a tight joint is obtained. Both flanges should be of same diameter and flange diameter should be at least equal to the half of the grinding wheel diameter. The nut is then tightened to hold the grinding wheel firmly (Fig. 5.16). To avoid serious accidents the wheel should be enclosed during operation by a safety guard made up of steel. The guard should be sufficiently strong reliably clampled to the grinder and should protect the operator against splashing cutting fluid. When first starting the wheel, the operator should stand aside and allow the wheel to come to the speed before attempting any grinding.

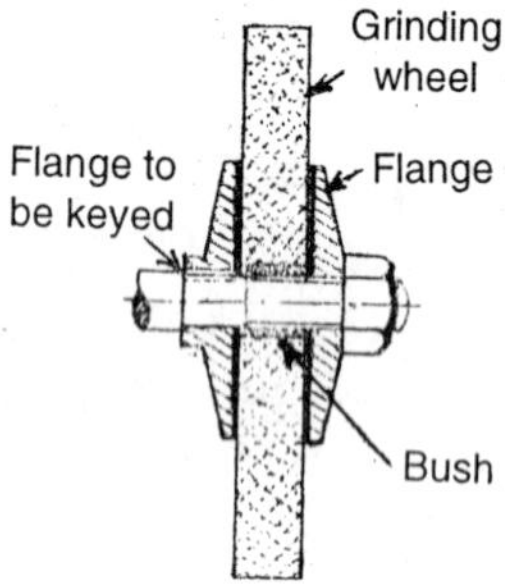

Fig. 5.16

5.15. Dressing and Truing

Grinding wheels must be occasionally dressed or trued to remove dull grains of abrasive and metal particles to resorb the original shape and accuracy of the wheel face.

During grinding operation the grains of the wheel are subjected to wear and the wheel loses its cutting capacity. Along with grain wear another factor that reduces the cut properties of a grinding wheel is the loading of the voids between the grains with the waste material of the grinding process such as sintered metal dust, abrasive grit and particles of bonding material. A worn and loaded wheel ceases to cut properly. This requires sharpening of grinding wheel in order to restore sharp cutting edges and to unload the grinding wheel.

Dressing removes the worn grains and the waste products of grinding. Dressing is carried out by a steel dressing tool consisting of irregularly shaped hardened steel discs that are free to rotate on an axle. The tool is held at an angle against the rctating grinding wheel and moved across its face. The revolving points of the desks remove the foreign particles that have become lodged between the grains and also remove or fracture dulled grains thus producing sharp edges. The other method of dressing is called crush dressing. In this method a hard steel crushing roll having the same contour as the part to be ground is forced against the grinding wheel, while it is revolving usually quite slowly. The crushing action fractures and dislodges some of the abrasive grains thus exposing sharp edges and at the same time imparting a desired shape to the grinding wheel. Dressing may also be carried out by a diamond dresser.

Truing. Truing of grinding wheel is carried out to restore the correct geometric shape of the wheel which has been lost due to non-uniform wear. Truing makes the face of the wheel concentric and the sides plane and parallel. Truing is carried out by means of a diamond dresser. The dresser is being held at an angle of 10° to

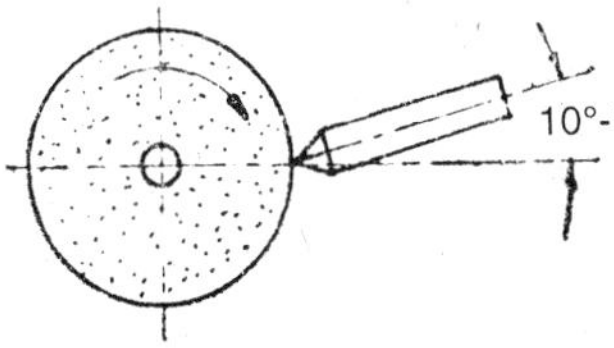

Fig. 5.17

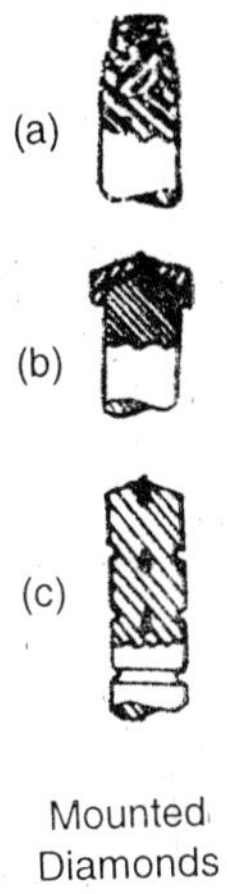

Fig. 5.18

15° to the wheel face (Fig. 5.17). Diamond wheels are not dressed, they are trued when their shape is no longer sufficiently accurate. Metal bonded diamond wheels are trued with a green silicon carbide dressing stick having a vitrified bond. Fig. 5.18 shows mounted diamonds for truing grinding wheels. During grinding of hard materials the abrasive grains dull more quickly than in grinding soft materials. Therefore wheel for grinding hard materials should lose its grains rapidly. Thus softer grade wheels are used for grinding hard materials and harder grade wheels for soft materials.

5.16. Grinding Wheel Balancing

All the wheels should be tested for balance periodically. Because of high rotative speeds involved, a slight unbalance will produce vibrations that will cause waviness in the work surface. In addition unbalance may cause the wheel to break with the probability of serious damage and injury. Balancing is usually done in the static position of wheel by shifting the position of weights on one of the mounting flanges of wheel. Poor balance may be detected by the vibrations set up in the machine, poor finish and difficulty in maintaining size.

5.17. Operating Speeds and Feeds

The surface speeds of grinding wheels are generally high. Table 5.6 shows some typical grinding operations and the average values of wheel surface speeds. The amount of feed for rough grinding varies from 0.025 to 0.1 mm and for finish grinding from 0.005 to 0.01 mm.

Table 5.6

Type of grinding	*Surface speed (metre per min.)*
Surface grinding	1200—1800
Cylindrical grinding	1600—1950
Centreless grinding	1500—1800
Tool and cutter grinding	1300—2000
Snagging (Resinoid bonded wheel)	1800—2200

5.18. Theory of Grinding

During grinding the grinding wheel starts removing the material as soon as it comes in contact with the workpiece. As shown in Fig. 5.19 when an abrasive grain starts to enter the workpiece at K, the depth of cut is zero and it increases gradually as the wheel and the work revolve. As usually wheel rotates at higher speed than

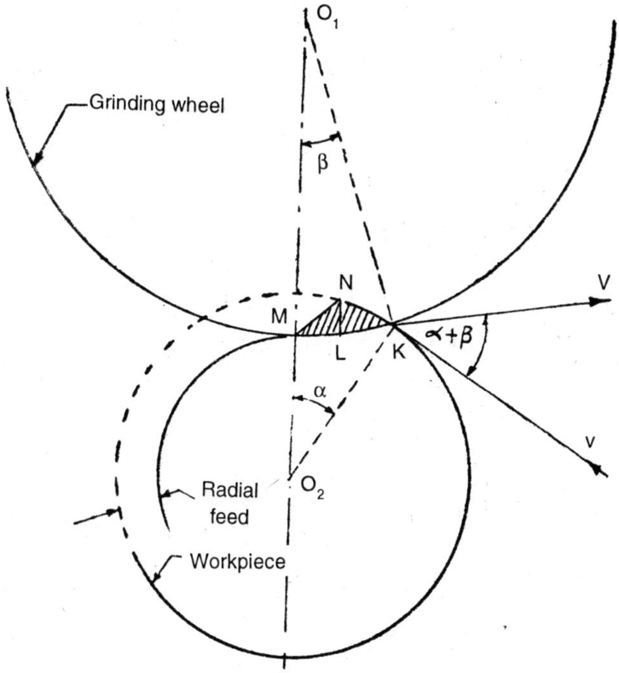

Fig. 5.19

the work the point of maximum cut depth is almost at the point where the wheel leaves the work. Area KMN is the chip with its maximum thickness of NL.

Let D_1 = Diameter of wheel.

D_2 = Diameter of workpiece.

V = Surface velocity of wheel.

v = Surface velocity of workpiece.

T = Time taken by a grain on grinding wheel to move from K to M.

f = Radial feed.

Arc $KM = V \times T$.

During this time a point on workpiece at A will be able to move only up to N.

Arc $KN = v \times T$

By ignoring the very small amount of curvature which occur, KLN may be treated as a right angled triangle, the right angle at L.

$$NL = KN \sin(\alpha + \beta) = vT \sin(\alpha + \beta).$$

If n = number of grits per unit length of wheel circumference, then the maximum chip thickness per grit or grain depth of cut (t) is given by

$$t = \frac{NL}{n(\text{Arc } KM)} = \frac{vT \sin(\alpha + \beta)}{n \cdot V \cdot T}$$

$$= \frac{v}{nV} \sin(\alpha + \beta)$$

Now from $\Delta\, O_1O_2K$

$$O_1O_2^2 = O_1K^2 + O_2K^2 - 2\, O_1K \times O_2K \cos \angle\, O_1KO_2$$

$$\left(\frac{D_1}{2} + \frac{D_2}{2} - f\right) = \left(\frac{D_1}{2}\right)^2 + \left(\frac{D_2}{2}\right)^2 - 2\,\frac{D_1}{2} \cdot \frac{D_2}{2} \cos[180 - (\alpha + \beta)]$$

$$= \left(\frac{D_1}{2}\right)^2 + \left(\frac{D_2}{2}\right)^2 + \frac{D_1D_2}{2} \cos(\alpha + \beta)$$

Neglecting f^2 as compared to D_1 and D_2 and on simplification, we get

$$\frac{D_1D_2}{2} - D_1f - D_2f = \frac{D_1D_2}{2} \cos(\alpha + \beta)$$

$$\cos(\alpha + \beta) = 1 - 2f\left[\frac{D_1 + D_2}{D_1D_2}\right]$$

$$\sin(\alpha + \beta) = \sqrt{1 - \cos^2(\alpha + \beta)}$$

$$= \sqrt{1 - \left[1 - 2f\left(\frac{D_1 + D_2}{D_1D_2}\right)^2\right]}$$

$$= \sqrt{1 - \left[1 + \left\{2f\left(\frac{D_1 + D_2}{D_1D_2}\right)\right\}^2 - 2 \times 2f\left(\frac{D_1 + D_2}{D_1D_2}\right)\right]}$$

Now neglecting $\left\{2f\left(\frac{D_1 + D_2}{D_1D_2}\right)\right\}^2$, we get

$$\sin(\alpha + \beta) = 2\sqrt{\frac{D_1 + D_2}{D_1D_2}}\, f$$

$$\therefore \qquad t = \frac{v}{nV} \sin(\alpha + \beta) = \frac{v}{nV}\, 2 . \sqrt{\frac{D_1 + D_2}{D_1D_2}}\, f$$

$$t = \frac{2v}{nV} \sqrt{\frac{D_1 + D_2}{D_1D_2}} \cdot f$$

Let F = Force on individual grits of grinding wheel.

The force F is proportional to the area of the chip formed which is proportional to the square of grain depth of cut

$$F \propto t^2$$

$$\propto \left(\frac{2v}{nV}\right)^2 \frac{D_1 + D_2}{D_1 D_2} \cdot f \propto \left(\frac{v}{V}\right)^2 \frac{D_1 + D_2}{D_1 D_2} \cdot f$$

$$\frac{2}{n} = \text{constant.}$$

The above expression shows that the grits will break from the wheel if the force exceeds bond strength and also increase in work speed will be more effective in breaking the grits than increasing the radial feed.

5.19. Grinding Wheel Wear

In the grinding process the grains of abrasive are subjected to wear and the grinding wheel loses its cutting capacity.

There are two types of grinding wheel wear :

(*i*) **Attritious wear.** During grinding when the active grains make repeated contact with the work piece, the sharp edges are worn away, producing flat areas or wear scars on the grains. This type of wear is called attritious wear.

(*ii*) **Fracture wear.** When grinding process continues, the forces on the active grains become sufficiently large either to fracture the grain or to tear it from the wheel bond. This type of wear is called fracture wear.

Fig. 5.20 shows the progress of total grinding wheel wear as measured by the total volume (V_1) of grinding wheel material worn with respect to total volume (V_2) of material ground.

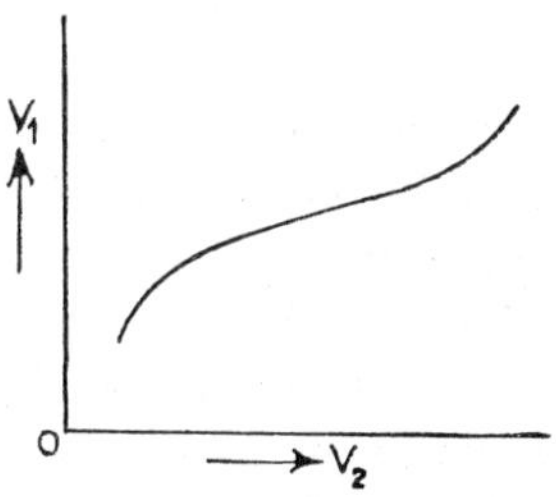

Fig. 5.20

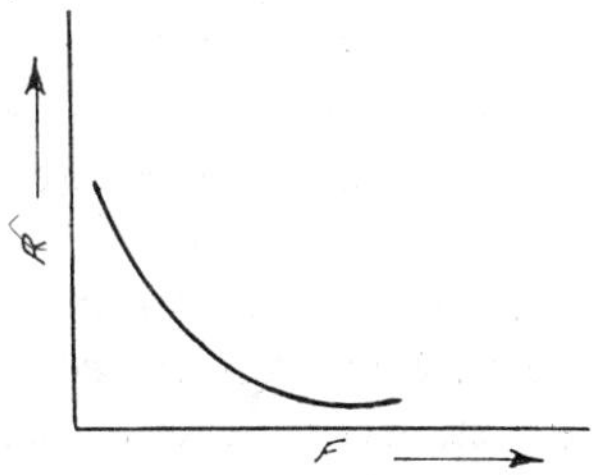

Fig. 5.20 (*a*)

5.19.1. Grinding ratio

The grinding ratio (R) is defined as follows :

$$R = \frac{V_2}{V_1}$$

where V_1 = Rate of grinding wheel wear

V_2 = Rate of metal removal.

A worn grinding wheel ceases to cut and its cutting capacity can be restored by dressing which may be described as sharpening operation. It is observed that it is sufficient to remove a layer of dulled grains 0.08 mm deep to restore the cutting capacity of a grinding wheel.

A high grinding ratio is desirable. Fig. 5.20 (*a*) shows the variation of grinding ratio (R) with thrust force (F) acting during grinding.

5.20. Grinding Temperature

In grinding there is rise in temperature due to the resistance to deformation during shearing of the chips as well as the frictional resistance encountered in the chip tool interface. The temperature changes arising from the grinding process may relate to

(*i*) the mean grit temperature (T)

(*ii*) the mean temperature at or just below the ground surface (T_s).

The grit temperature is found as follows :

$$T = A.E.\sqrt{\frac{V.t}{K.P.C.}}$$

where A = A constant depending on wheel work pair

E = Total specific energy of grinding

V = Surface velocity of grinding wheel

t = Maximum grit depth of cut

K = Thermal conductivity of material

P = Density of job material

C = Specific heat of job material.

The rate of wheel wear depends upon the total grit temperature (T). The surface temperature (T_s) is determined by calculating the shear zone temperature. The severe temperature gradients in the work surface during grinding tend to produce very high residual stresses. Surface damage and residual stresses can be minimised by reducing the time of contact by using higher work speed, by providing small depth of cut and by using good cutting fluid.

5.21. Power Required for Grinding

During grinding size of the chips removed depends upon the grit size used in grinding wheel. A fine grit should be used for finishing operations as it will remove finer chips and leave a smoother surface finish.

Fig. 5.21 shows a surface grinding operation. F and R are the component of forces acting on all the grits in contact with the workpiece.

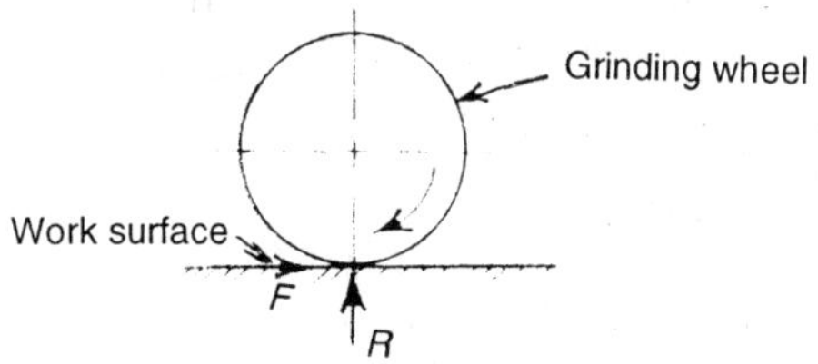

Fig. 5.21

P = Power required for grinding
$= F \times V$ Watts

where F = Tangential force upon wheel in Newtons.
V = Wheel speed in m/sec.
H = Power required per mm^3 of metal removed per second
$= \frac{P}{W}$ J/mm^3

where W = Volume of metal removed per second $= t \times b \times v$.
where t = Depth of cut (mm)
b = Width of cut (mm)
v = Work speed (mm/sec).

Example 5.1. *Calculate the power required per mm^3 of metal removed per second for a surface grinding operation using the following data :*

Wheel speed	$= 20\ m/s$
Work speed	$= 0.18\ m/s$
Tangential force	$= 84\ N$
Depth of cut	$= 0.018\ mm$.
Width of cut	$= 14\ mm$.

Solution.

F = Tangential force = 84 N
V = Wheel speed.
P = Power required.
$= F \times V = 84 \times 20 = 1680$ Watts.
t = Depth of cut = 0.018 mm.

b = Width of cut = 14 mm

v = Work speed = 0.18 m/sec = 180 mm/sec.

W = Volume of metal removed per sec

$= t.b.v = 0.018 \times 14 \times 180$

$= 45.36 \text{ mm}^3$.

H = Power required per mm^3

$$= \frac{P}{W} = \frac{1680}{45.36}$$

$= 37 \text{ J/mm}^3$.

Example 5.2. *(a) Define the following :*

(i) Abrasive grain size.

(ii) Grade of a grinding wheel.

(b) During external cylindrical grinding, the following observations were made :

Diameter of work piece	*= 40 mm.*
Diameter of grinding wheel	*= 240 mm.*
Wheel velocity	*= 16 m / sec.*
Work velocity	*= 14 m / min.*
Wheel depth of cut	*= 0.03 mm*

Grains are 0.5 mm apart.

Calculate grain depth of cut.

Solution. (*a*) **Size of grain.** The size of abrasive grain used in a grinding wheel is designated by a number corresponding to number of openings per unit length in the screen used to size the grain. Since a number however generally indicates only an average grain size, so in sizing the grain a finite number of screen are used.

Grade. The grade of hardness of a grinding wheel indicates the relative strength of the bond which holds the abrasive grains in place. Wheel grade is indicated by letters A to Z, A being the softest wheel and Z the hardest. The effective grade of the wheel depends strongly on the speed of wheel and other grinding variables and whether a cutting fluid is used.

(*b*) D_1 = Diameter of grinding wheel

= 240 mm.

D_2 = Diameter of workpiece

= 40 mm.

v = Surface velocity of workpiece

= 14 m/min = 0.23 m/sec = 230 mm/sec.

V = Wheel velocity = 16 m/sec.

= 16000 mm/sec.

f = Radial feed.

= Wheel depth of cut = 0.03 mm.

n = Grit spacing or grains per mm.

$$= \frac{1}{0.5} = 2$$

t = Grit depth of cut

$$= \frac{2.v}{n.V.} \sqrt{\frac{D_1 + D_2}{D_1.D_2}} \times f$$

$$= \frac{2 \times 230}{2 \times 16000} \sqrt{\frac{240 + 40}{240 \times 40}} \times 0.03$$

= 0.00043 mm.

5.22. Polishing

It is surface finishing process by which scratches and tool marks are removed with a polishing wheel. The workpiece is brought in contact with the revolving wheel that has been charged with a very fine abrasive. Polishing wheels are made of canvas, leather felt or paper. Tolerances of 0.025 mm or less can be obtained in machine polishing.

5.23. Buffing

It is also a surface finishing process and is used to produce a lustrous surface of attractive appearance. In this very little amount of material is removed. In this process also the workpiece is brought in contact with the revolving wheel. Buffing wheels are made up of felt or cotton. Powdered abrasives are applied to the surface of the wheel. The abrasive may consist of iron oxide, chromium oxide, emery etc.

5.24. Lapping

Lapping is the process of producing an extremely accurate highly finished surface. Lapping is carried out by means of lapping shoes called laps. The laps are made up of soft cast iron, copper, lead and brass. The lap material is always softer than the material to be finished. Fine abrasive particles are charged (caused to become embedded) into the lap. Silicon carbide, aluminium oxide and diamond dust are the commonly used lapping powders. Oil and thin greases are used to spread the abrasive powders. As the charged lap is rubbed against workpiece surface, the abrasive particles in the surface of the lap remove small amounts of material from the workpiece surface. Thus it is the abrasive that does the cutting and the soft lap is not worm away. The material removed by lapping is usually less than 0.025 mm.

Lapping can be done either by hand or by special machines. In hand lapping the lap is flat similar to a surface plate. The lap has a carefully turned surface with a series of grooves in it. Grooves are provided to collect the excess abrasive and chips. The surface of lap is charged with a fine abrasive. The work is moved across the surface of the lap using reciprocating rotary motion. Fig. 5.22 shows how one surface of a hardened steel part may be finished on a flat cast iron lap. Fig. 5.23 shows a squaring lap in which the edge of the steel part is lapped at right angles to the bottom surface.

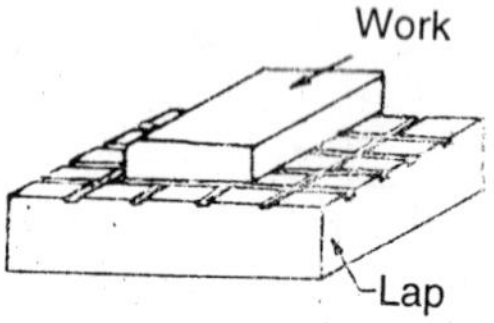

Fig. 5.22

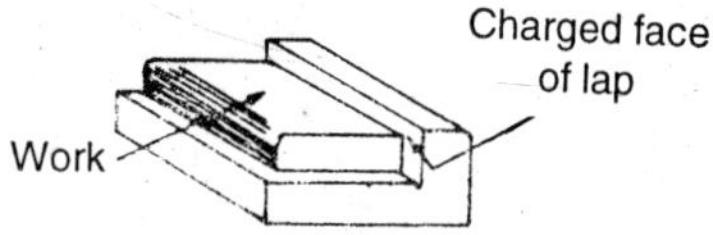

Fig. 5.23

Machine lapping consists of two flat abrasive laps. The two labs called upper and lower laps rotate in the opposite direction (Fig. 5.24). Work holder can take a number of workpieces which are merely pushed around by the work holder and are not clamped in any way.

The nature of relative motion in lapping depends upon the shape and other features of the surface being lapped. Slightly differing motions are imparted to the workpiece and the lap so that the path of abrasive grains of lap is not repeated on the work. Laps are made from cast iron, soft steel copper, brass and hard wood. Lapping machines, are of general purpose and single purpose types, are available. The single purpose types include machines for lapping valve seats, crankshaft, crank pins and journals, cam shafts, gears etc. Cylindrical and flat surfaces are generally finished in general purpose machines.

In lapping the results depend upon the following factors :

(*i*) Type of lapping medium or abrasive material. For example, aluminium oxide is used for improved surface finish whereas silicon carbine is used for rapid stock removal.

(*ii*) Type of lap material.

(*iii*) Speed and pressure of lapping motion. In lapping speeds between 1.5 to 4 m/sec are commonly used.

(*iv*) Material to be lapped. This factor affects the surface finish and non ferrous metals require finer grit size to produce proper surface finish.

5.25. Honing

Honing is an abrading process mostly used for finishing internal cylindrical surfaces such as drilled or bored holes. Removal of metal by honing involves the use of a number of bonded abrasive stones called hones. Honing stones are formed by bonding abrasives like aluminium oxide or silicon carbide in vitrified or resinoid bond. Material like sulı hur, resin or wax can be added to the ponding agent to improve the cutting action.

Although honing can be done by hann as in finishing the faces of cutting tools it is more often done with special equipment. The honing stones are usually held in a honing head. Controlled light pressure is used to hold the stones against the work surface. The honing stones (hones) can be forded radially outwards as desired. Single and multiple spindle honing machines are available in both vertical and horizontal spindle types. For honing single, internal cylindrical surfaces a procedure where in a machine rotates the hone is used quite often the workpiece being manually held and reciprocated over the hone.

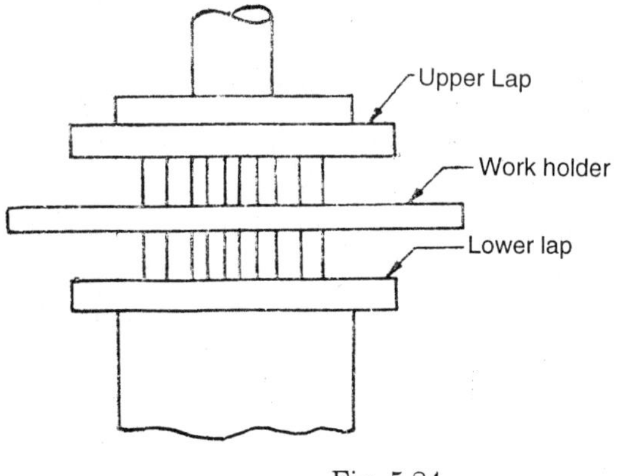

Fig. 5.24

Fig. 5.25

Honing is both a sizing and finishing operations. The primary function of honing is to remove scratches remaining from grinding and the amount of metal removed usually is less than 0.125 mm. Geometrical error in a cylindrical bore corrected by honing is shown in Fig. 5.25.

From 100 to 1,000 times more abrasive grains participate in the cutting process in honing than in grinding ; the cutting speed is only 1/50 to 1/120 of the wheel speed. The pressure of the abrasive tool on the surface being honed is only from 1/6 to 1/10 of that in grinding, and is within 2 to 9 kg per sq. cm (usually 2 to 6 kg per sq. cm). The low cutting speed in honing and the comparatively low pressure provide for a relatively ture in the cutting zone. This enables a better obtained.

Depending upon the diameter being honed and the size of the abrasive sticks, the honing tool may hold from 1 to 12 sticks (in one row). Honing is employed for finishing, not only plain cylindrical surfaces, but surfaces with keyways, splines, ports of various shapes, etc. Tapered surfaces and certain types of flat and contoured surfaces can also be honed.

In addition to the high class of surface finish it produces, honing also corrects certain errors in the geometrical features of the surface, such as taper, out-of-roundness, barrel shape of holes, etc.

5.25.1. Honing tool

Fig. 5.25 (*a*) shows a honing tool. The spring is used to actuate the expanding cones. The honing tool rotates continuously in one direction and simultaneously reciprocates axially. Feed-out (or feed-in) is accomplished by periodical expansion of the sticks in machining internal surfaces or periodical compression of the sticks (bringing them closer together) in machining external surfaces, for each full stroke of the honing tool.

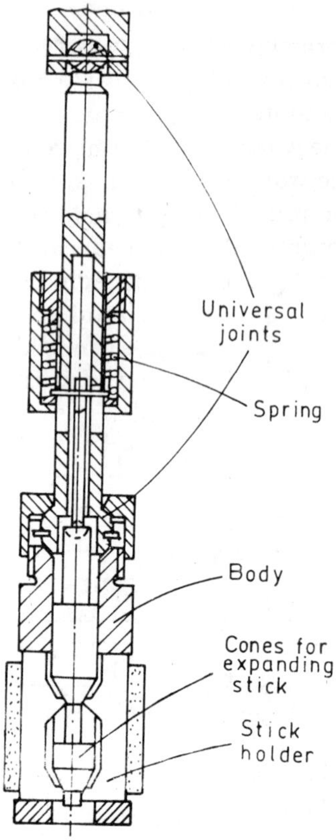

Fig. 5.25 (*a*)

5.26. Super Finishing

It is an abrasive process for removing smear metal, scratches and ridges produced by machining and grinding operations and other surface irregularities from parts that are to have highly finished surface. It is used for producing an extremely high quality of surface finish and is used for removing very small amount of stock. The amount of metal removed is generally 0.005 to 0.0025 mm. Therefore, to achieve such a close dimensional accuracy grinding is generally employed prior to super finishing. In super finishing an abrasive stick is retained in a suitable holder and applied to the surface of the workpiece with a light pressure. As compared to honing super-finishing is done at much lower speed and super finishing is largely used for finishing outside surfaces whereas honing is mostly used for finishing inside surfaces.

Fig. 5.26 shows the principle of super finishing process. The abrasive block reciprocates across the work with a similar amount of over run at each end of stroke. At the same time the work rotates about its axis. These two motions produce a high degree of accuracy. The work is flooded with lubricant during cutting. In this operation the work rotates at a surface speed of about 10 metres per minute for roughing and from 20 to 30 metre per minute for finishing operations.

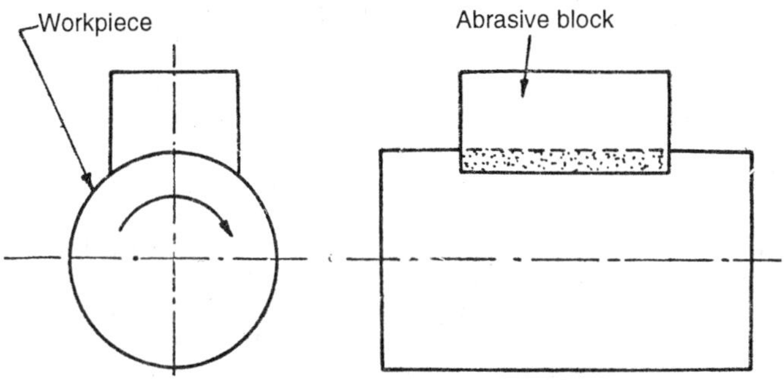

Fig. 5.26

Super-finishing is compared with honing as follows :

(*i*) Super-finishing uses very high controlled pressure.

(*ii*) Super-finishing uses rapid short strokes.

(*iii*) It uses controlled stroke paths so that a single grit never traverses the same path twice.

(*iv*) Copious amounts of low viscosity lubricant—coolant floods over the surface is used.

The abrasives used are aluminium oxide for materials of high tensile strength such as carbon, alloy and high speed steels and materials of considerable hardness. Silicon carbide abrasives are preferable for low tensile materials such as cast iron aluminium brass and materials such as brake linings. Bonded diamond dust is used for finishing cemented carbide tools.

5.27. Specific Energy for Grinding

The energy per unit volume of metal removed or specific energy for surface or internal or external grinding is given by the following relation

$$E = \frac{HV}{U.b.d}$$

where E = Specific energy

H = Tangential force between grinding wheel and work piece

V = Surface speed of grinding wheel

U = Table speed

b = Width of each cut

d = Wheel depth of cut.

Example 5.3. *The circumference of a regulating wheel on a centreless grinder is 300 mm and its R.P.M. is 400. Determine the angle of regulating wheel to achieve a through feed of 830 cm per minute.*

Solution. The feed (f) of the work is given by

f = S.N. sin α

N = R.P.M. of feed wheel

α = Angle of inclination of the regulating wheel.

Now f = 830 cm per minute

S = 300 mm = 30 cm

N = 400 R.P.M.

$840 = 30 \times 400 \times \sin \alpha$

$\alpha = 4°$. **Ans.**

PROBLEMS

5.1. Define the term grinding.

5.2. Describe the various types of abrasives in grinding wheels.

5.3. (*a*) What is a bond ? Name six types of bonds used in grinding wheel manufacture.

(*b*) Describe vitrified, shellac and resinoid bonds.

5.4. (*a*) What is a grinding wheel ?

(*b*) Differentiate between grain, grade and structure of a grinding wheel.

5.5. (*a*) What is the difference between wheel dressing and wheel turning ?

(*b*) Sketch two types of mounted diamonds for wheel turning.

5.6. Write short notes on the following :

(*a*) Grinding wheel selection

(*b*) Cutting action of grinding wheel

(*c*) Shapes of grinding wheels

(*d*) Mounted wheels and points.

5.7. Differentiate rough grinder and precision grinder.

5.8. Make a neat sketch of centre type cylindrical grinder and explain its operation.

5.9. Make a neat sketch of chuck type internal cylindrical grinder and explain its operation.

5.10. (*a*) What is surface grinding ?

(*b*) Make a neat sketch of horizontal wheel spindle and reciprocating table surface grinder and explain its operation.

5.11. (*a*) What is centreless grinding ?

(*b*) Make a neat sketch of centreless grinder and explain its operation.

(*c*) State the advantages of centreless grinding.

5.12. Write short notes on the following :

(*a*) Mounting of grinding wheel

(*b*) Grinding wheel balancing

(*c*) Marking system of grinding wheel.

5.13. Write short notes on the following :

(*a*) Lapping (*b*) Honing

(*c*) Super-finishing (*d*) Polishing and buffing

(*e*) Tool and cutter grinder.

5.14. Describe the following :

(*a*) Grinding wheel wear (*b*) Grinding temperature

(*c*) Power required for grinding.

5.15. Define the following :

(*i*) Grinding ratio

(*ii*) Specific energy for grinding.

5.16. Sketch and describe a honing tool.

6

Chatter and Surface Finish

6.1. Chatter and Vibrations in Machining

Sometime a machine tool can vibrate due to the cutting process itself. In such conditions the exciting force is not coming from an outside element, it is supplied by the cutting process itself. These types of vibrations are self induced vibrations and generally called as machine tool chatter. Chatter is the resonant vibration of the cutting tool, workpiece or the machine tool. It is often so severe that machining must be discontinued and the cutting conditions changed. Its severity is determined by the periodic vibration in the cutting forces and vibrational frequencies such as those of the work, tool and tool support etc. Chatter produces the following effects :

(*i*) It increases wear of the cutting tool and machine tool and dis-adjusts the joints in the fixture and machine tool.

(*ii*) Vibration of the machine-tool-workpiece system deteriorates the surface finish and accuracy.

(*iii*) It reduces tool life.

(*iv*) Heavy vibrations make it necessary to reduce the rate of metal removal and sometimes tool operation becomes very difficult.

Elimination of chatter is essential to preserve workpiece quality and to protect tool life. Presence of chatter necessitates a reduction in the cutting speeds of 10 to 15% when high speed steel tools are used. Chatter tends to occur when damping or dynamic stiffness is small.

Production of chatter depends upon the following factors :

(*i*) Design of machine tool.

Rigidity of the machine tool and the cutting system has a great deal to do with chatter proneness.

(*ii*) Type of workpiece material.

(*iii*) Type of cutting operation.

(*iv*) Type and design of fixturing.

(*v*) Geometry of cutting tool.

(*vi*) Feed, speed and depth of cut.

6.1.1. Vibrations in machine tool

Most machine tools vibrate because of mechanical defects. Such defects are always present. A well designed and well built machine tool operates smoothly because the defects are small but when defects are large, vibrations become excessive.

Different parts of machine tool structure are subjected to loading in different ways because of the following reasons :

(*i*) Changes in workpiece and cutter diameter.

(*ii*) Direction of feed.

(*iii*) Varying depth of cut.

Further the moving parts of machine tools do not always move at the same velocity because of wide range of feed and speed combinations.

This results in a vibratory system having a very complex dynamic behaviour. The vibrations produced affect the machine tool, cutting tool and workpiece.

Vibrations in a machine tool occur due to the following reasons :

(*i*) Un-balanced of rotating parts.

(*ii*) Misalignment of coupling and bearing.

(*iii*) Defective drive (belt, chain gear drive).

(*iv*) Interference in gears.

(*v*) Self induced vibrations because of cutting process (tool chatter) is generated and changes its magnitude.

(*iv*) Hydraulic forces.

(*vii*) Aero dynamic forces.

(*viii*) Mechanical looseness or insufficient rightness of fasteners.

Each cause of vibration generates a force which is changing in either its direction or its magnitude. It is the force which causes vibrations and resulting vibrations characteristics will be determined by the manner in which force is generated and changes its magnitude.

Mechanical vibrations of engines, machines, structures etc. produce side-effects with high level of noise and ending with mechanical failure.

Vibration measurement and analysis leads to the early detection of component deterioration. The vibration level can be reduced by changing faulty machine components or repairing them by balancing, aligning etc. The level at machine vibrations as measured at specific points after certain fixed number of operating hours can be used as an indication of machine condition.

6.2. Types of Vibrations

In metal cutting two types of vibration may take place.

(*i*) Forced vibrations.

(*ii*) Self excited vibrations.

1. **Forced vibrations.** Forced vibrations are produced by the cyclic vibrations in the cutting forces such as

(*i*) Variable forces acting on the system as a result of interrupted cutting.

(*ii*) Centrifugal forces of inertia of unbalanced rotating masses.

(*iii*) The impact forces caused by manufacturing errors on the working surfaces of components of the mechanism for transmitting motion.

(*iv*) Rough spindle bearing.

The forced vibrations can result in an increasing amplitude of vibration and is called regenerative chatter (Fig. 6.1).

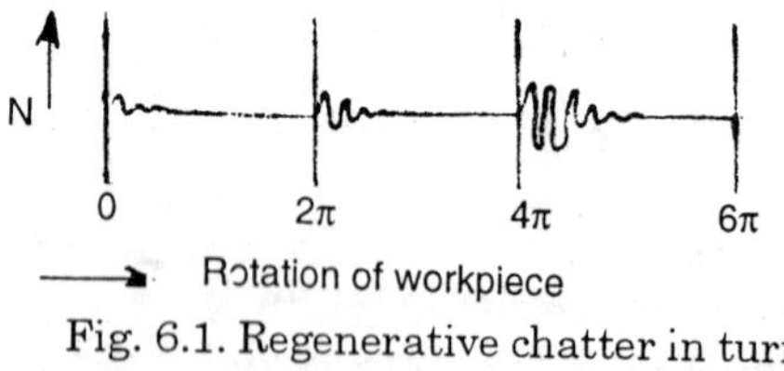

Fig. 6.1. Regenerative chatter in turning.

Forced vibrations which are produced under the action rhythmically varying force on the cutting tool such as RPM of unbalanced pulley spindle, workpiece have a frequency corresponding to the frequency of vibrating agent which may be quite different from natural frequency of vibrating members. Forced vibrations cause problems for finishing operations such as grinding, finish boring, finish turning etc.

2. **Self excited vibrations.** Thes vibrations take place due to the following reasons :

(*i*) Variability of the force of friction between the flowing chip and the tool and between the tool and work.

(*ii*) Non-uniform work hardening of the layer being cut across its thickness.

(*iii*) Instability of the built up edge which leads to changes in the cutting angle and the cross-sectional area of the uncut chip in the cutting process.

Other factors which produce vibrations are as follows :

(*i*) Faulty bearings.

(*ii*) Imperfect balancing.

(*iii*) Faulty meshing of gears.

(*iv*) Weak structure of machine tool.

(*v*) Machine tool over-loaded.

(*vi*) Machine tool mounted on a faulty foundation.

6.3. Factors Affecting Chatter

(*i*) **Rigidity of the system.** Higher the rigidity of the machine tool workpiece system and smaller the clearance between its members the less favourable the conditions for the origination of vibrations.

(*ii*) **Stiffness of work support.** The intensity of chatter increases with the distance from the point of support. The work support should be quite rigid. Moreover hang of tail stock spindle reduces the rigidity and gives rise to more vibrations.

(*iii*) **Stiffness of tool.** The cutting tool should be firmly clamped with a minimum of overhang beyond the point of support. The more the tool overhang from tool holder, the greater the vibrations.

(*iv*) **Cutting speed.** Vibrations first increase and then decrease with and an increase in cutting speed.

(*v*) **Nose radius.** Vibrations increase with an increase in the nose radius of the tool.

(*vi*) **Workpiece material.** In machining steels especially of tough grades heavier vibrations are produced than in machining materials like cast iron.

(*vii*) Faulty bearings also cause vibrations.

(*viii*) Vibrations may be produced by weak structure of machine tool, overloading of machine tool and machine tool mounted on a faulty foundation.

(*ix*) Faulty meshing of gears also sometime produce vibrations.

6.4. Types of Vibratory Systems

Chatter during machining produces three types of systems :

(i) Statically stable system.

(ii) Statically stable but dynamically unstable.

(iii) Statically and dynamically stable system.

In machining self induced vibrations may be considered as free vibrations with negative damping. The negative damping increases the amplitude of vibrations (Fig. 6.2). A statically stable system in one in which displacement from the equilibrium position sets up a force tending to bring the system back to equilibrium position. A system with positive damping conditions are dynamically stable (Fig. 6.3). A dynamically stable system is also statically stable

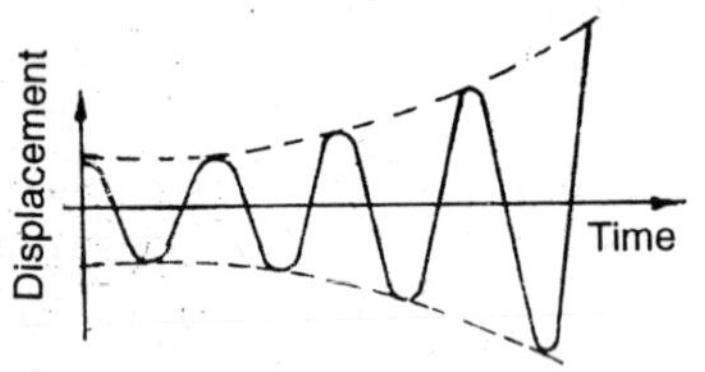

Fig. 6.2

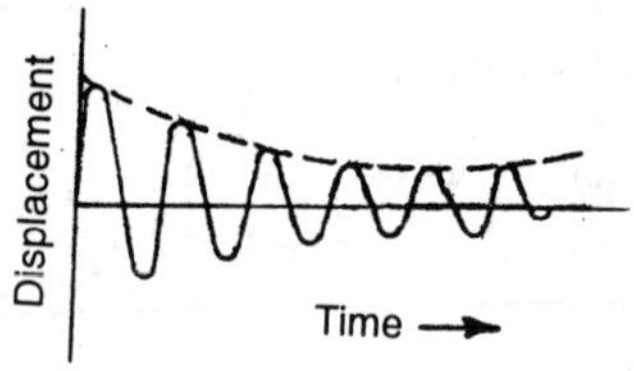

Fig. 6.3

under normal conditions. Machine tools are statically and dynamically stable. However they may become unstable through the effect of cutting process. The machine tool designer should know the magnitude and frequencies of the disturbing forces likely to occur during the operation of the machine tool so that he is able to design the machine such that the natural frequencies of the various parts of the structure do not approach the forcing frequencies.

6.5. Elimination of Chatter

It is desirable to reduce chatter in order to improve workpiece surface finish and to protect the machine tool. Self excited vibrations are more severe than the forced vibrations. Chatter can be reduced by the following methods :

(i) Chatter can be reduced by the use of special devices such as vibration dampers which impede the development of vibrations by increasing the forces of resistance in the machine fixture tool workpiece system.

(ii) Rigid installation of machine tool on its properly prepared foundation reduces the vibrations.

(iii) The use of cutting fluids sometimes helps to reduce vibrations.

(*iv*) The machine tool should be dynamically balanced to limit the unbalanced forces produced during its operation.

(*v*) The site where the machine tool is to be installed should be quite for away from the vibration causing machines such as presses, forging hammers, compressors etc.

6.6. Vibration Isolation

Vibrations produced during operation of a machine tool should be reduced below the permissible level of vibrations to keep the machine tool in good condition, to increase the productivity and to achieve better precision (accuracy) on workpiece surface. Some of the methods used to reduce vibrations are as follows.

(*a*) Elastic vibration isolators are being widely used now-a-days in the installation of machine tools that have dynamic action on the surroundings. Machine tool can be easily installed on vibration isolators and a better quality of surface finish can be obtained from machine tool. Vibration isolators can be made up of the following materials :

(*i*) Cork.

(*ii*) Felt.

(*iii*) Rubber.

(*iv*) Steel springs.

(*v*) Plastic pads.

(*iv*) Pneumatic isolators.

Cork is used in the form of slabs. Cork slabs are placed either directly under the base of machine or under the concrete foundation. It is an effective isolating medium against vibrations, shock and sound. Felt is used in the form of small pads. It is generally placed under the machine to be supported. Rubber pads have the advantage of enduring compression as well as shear.

Steel springs are preferred over other materials as their properties are known more precisely than other materials.

For machines moving at a steady speed the degree of isolation is determined by the ratio (r) defined as follows :

$$r = \frac{\text{Operating frequency of machine}}{\text{Natural frequency of foundation}}$$

By choosing a suitable natural frequency it is possible to find degree of isolation which obviously depends upon the environmental conditions of the site.

(*b*) Vibrations can be reduced by perfectly balancing the rotating equipment of the machine tool. The machine tool should be so installed on the floor that there are no vibrations. Proper isolation of vibration helps to achieve the following objectives :

(*i*) Longer bearings life.

(*ii*) Longer machinery maintenance costs.

(*iii*) Improved working conditions for the workers.

(*iv*) There will not be any vibrations in the building structure.

(*v*) Improved plant layout.

Fig. 6.3 (*a*) shows a method of isolating the machine vibrations.

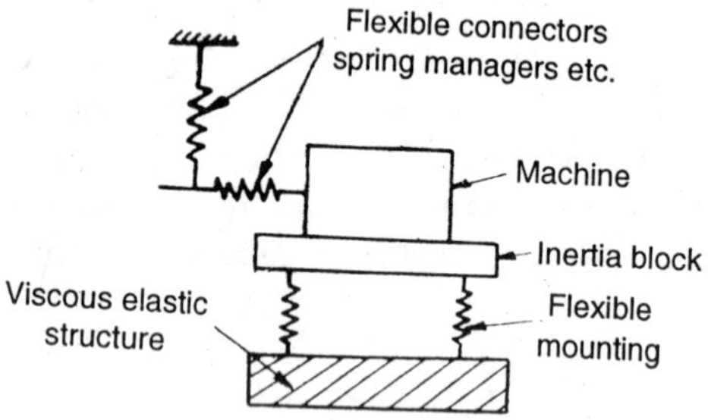

Fig. 6.3 (*a*)

(*c*) Vibration damping helps in reducing vibration by absorbing energy in the form of friction. In vibrations isolating system damping can be provided in the following ways :

(*i*) Fluid damping.

(*ii*) Solid damping.

(*iii*) Sliding friction damping.

Fluid damping is provided by dashpot mechanism and in it the resisting force increases with the velocity of motion. Solid damping is provided due to internal friction of solid material. An example of sliding friction damping is built up of leaf spring in which friction is created due to slipping of leaves against each other when the spring oscillates.

(*iv*) Vibrations can be reduced by replacing or repairing defective parts of a machine. Unbalanced rotors, gears, pulleys etc. try to produce vibrations and should be repaired in time.

6.6.1. Vibration measurement in machine tools

Vibration measurement gives valuable information about the condition of the machine tool which otherwise can only be obtained by stripping the machine down and carrying out a mechanical inspection. Some of the vibration instruments are as follows :

(*i*) Vibrometer,

(*ii*) Analyser,

(*iii*) Vibration recorder,

(*iv*) Vibration monitor.

Vibrometer gives the overall vibration values to assess the vibration severity of the machine vibration and it measures vibration as displacement in microns. Velocity in mm/s and acceleration in m/sec^2. Analyser is useful for segregation of overall vibration into components at various frequencies whereas vibration recorder is used to record the data obtained by analyser. It is coupled along with the vibration analyser. Vibration monitor is used to measure vibrations of bearings of selected strategically machinery continuously.

Measurement of vibration level of a machine helps in judging the condition of machine and thus helps in deciding when and where a repair is required. Measurement and analysis of machine vibrations either continuously or intermittently also help in the successful maintenance of the machine.

6.6.2. Effects of vibrations

Most of the mechanical defects in a machine tool are positively reflected in the form of vibrations. The amount and type of vibration is proportional to the severity and type of defects. The effects of vibrations can be considered on the machine tool, workpiece, tool life and cutting conditions.

(*i*) **Effects of vibrations on machine tool.** Due to vibrations the various parts of machine tool start vibrating and if frequency of vibrations approaches the natural frequency of vibrations of that part, the amplitude of vibrations will be quite high and the part may even break.

(*ii*) **Effect of vibration on tool life.** Vibrations if present reduce the life of cutting tool by about 70 to 80%.

(*iii*) **Effect of vibration on work piece.** Due to vibrations the surface finish and dimensional accuracy are affected.

(*iv*) **Effects of vibrations on cutting conditions.** Due to vibrations the cutting speed does not remain constant. The chip thickness as removed by the cutting tool also does not remain constant and due to this, the cutting forces also vary.

6.7. Surface Finish

The quality of machined surface is characterised by the accuracy of its manufacture in respect to the dimensions specified by the designer. Every machining process leaves its evidence on the surface that has been machined. This evidence is in the form of finely spaced micro irregularities left by the cutting tool (Fig. 6.4). Each kind of cutting tool leaves its own pattern that can be indentified. This pattern is called surface finish or surface roughness. Whenever two machined surfaces come in contact with each other, the quality of the mating surfaces plays an important role in the performance and wear of the mating parts. A good surface finish is desirable. Some degrees of roughness which may be extremely small is always present on any surface because of the following reasons :

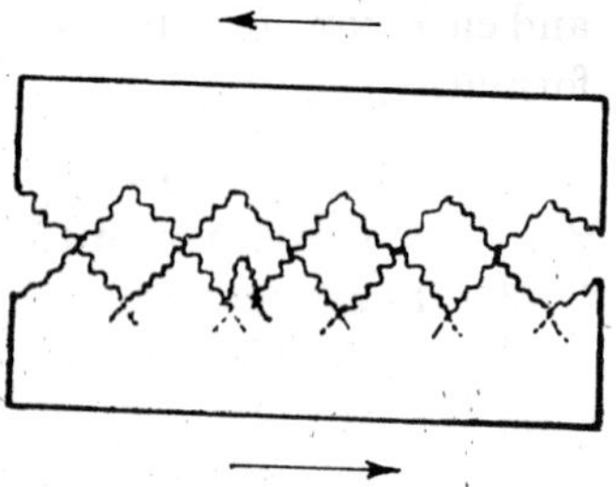

Fig. 6.4. Contact of micro-irregularities.

(*i*) Metals are not absolutely homogeneous. Some portions may be harder than others and may cause the cutting tool to deflect or spring away from the cut surface.

(*ii*) Most metals are of crystalline structure. When metal is cut, some of the crystals are sheared through while others are torn loose from the adjoining crystals.

(*iii*) Minute particles or chips may cling to the edge of tool and scratch the surface of the workpiece.

6.8. Factors Affecting Surface Finish

The various factors that contribute to the quality of surface finish are as follows :

1. Machining variables

(*a*) Cutting speed.

(*b*) Feed.

(*c*) Depth of the cut.

(*a*) **Effect of cutting speed.** Increase in cutting speed improves the surface finish due to the continuous reduction in built up edge (Fig. 6.5). The curve *A* represents the machining of steels except high alloy grade steels. In the beginning the surface roughness increases when cutting speed changes from V_1 to V_2. This is due to the beginning of built up edge formation which reaches its maximum value at the cutting speed V_2. Then the formation of built up edge is reduced due to the rise in temperature and at cutting speed V_2 it almost disappears. This reduces the height (*H*) of micro-irregularities. With further increase in cutting speed the surface roughness continues to decrease. There is almost no hump on the curve *B* obtained in machining high alloy steels, non-ferrous metals and cast iron. This is due to the completed absence of built up edge formation.

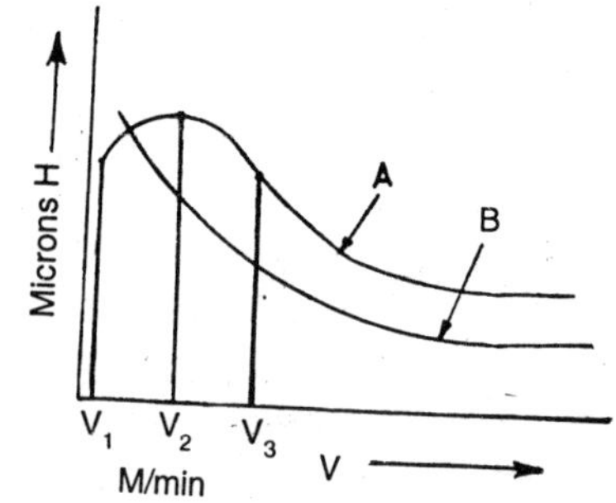

Fig. 6.5

(*b*) **Effect of feed.** Increase in feed rate deteriorates surface finish. It is observed that a rate of feed (*f*) in the range from 0.12 to 0.15 mm per revolution has a negligible effect on the height (*H*) of irregularities but further increase in the feed rate increases surface roughness. Fig. 6.6 shows the variation of feed with height of micro-irregularities when different cutting fluids are used.

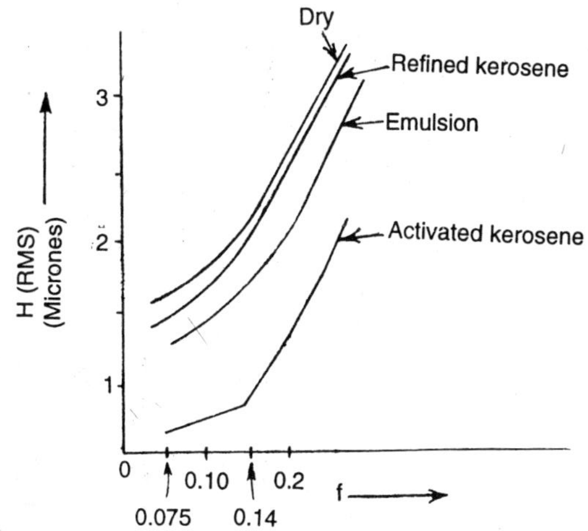

Fig. 6.6

(*c*) **Effect of depth of cut.** Increase in depth of cut deteriorates surface finish.

2. **Tool geometry.** The effect of tool geometry on surface finish is as follows :

(*a*) **Nose radius.** Increase in nose radius improves surface finish. There is an appreciable improvement in surface finish upto 0.3 mm nose radius. Higher value of nose radius produces less improvement in surface finish and on the other hand it causes chatter during machining.

(*b*) **Rake angle.** Increase in rake angle of tool improves surface finish.

(*c*) **Relief angle.** An increase in the relief angle adversely affects surface finish but the effect is, on the whole, small.

(*d*) **Side cutting edge angle.** An increase in side cutting edge angle improves surface finish largely because of the reduced chip thickness but the degree of improvement depends upon the rigidity of the work and its mounting.

(*e*) **Cutting edge.** The height of the micro-irregularities of the cutting edge effects the micro geometry of the machined surface. The jags on the cutting edge are reproduced directly on the ridges of the machined surface, increasing their height. Therefore cutting edge of the tool should be carefully ground and lapped to reduced the micro-irregularities of the cutting edge.

3. Accuracy of bearings.
4. Method of chip removal.
5. Quality of machine tool.
6. Nature of work material.
7. Chatter or vibrations of machine tool.

An increase in cutting speed, an increase in rake angle and the application of a suitable lubricant would lead to an improvement in the quality of the machined surface.

6.9. Surface Finish Terminology

Surface texture includes roughness, waviness, lay, flow etc. as shown in Fig. 6.7.

(*a*) **Roughness.** Roughness consists of surface irregularities which result from the various manufacturing process. These irregularities combine to form surface texture.

(*b*) **Roughness height.** Roughness height is the height of irregularities with reference to an average line. It is measured in millimetres.

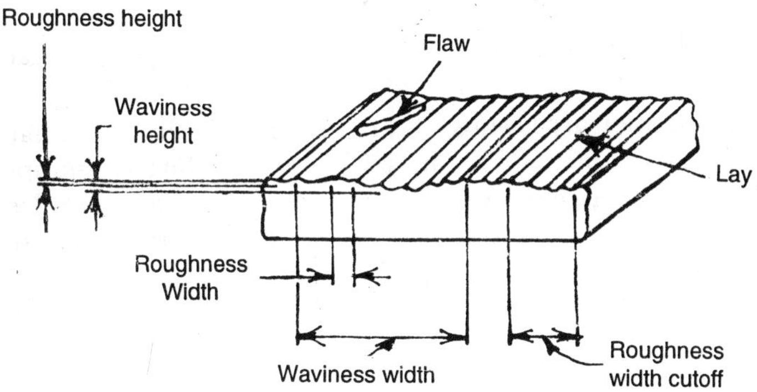

Fig. 6.7

The value of roughness height is expressed in two ways.

(*i*) Arithmetical average value or centre line average value.

(*ii*) Root mean square (r.m.s.) value.

In most cases the arithmetical average value of roughness height is used. Occasionally the root mean square (r.m.s.) value is used.

The r.m.s. is obtained by taking the square root of the sum of the squares of y measurements divided by the number of y measurements. In terms of the measurements indicated in Fig. 6.8 the average and r.m.s. values are calculated as follows.

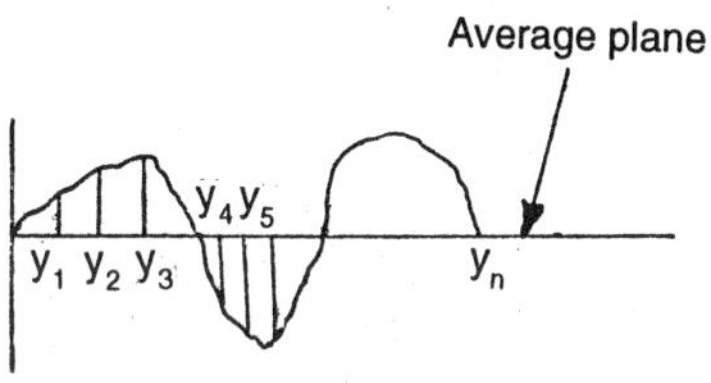

Fig. 6.8

$$\Sigma y_n = y_1 + y_2 + y_3 + \ldots y_n$$

The centre line average (CLA) value or Arithmetical average (*AA*) height is given by

$$AA = \frac{\Sigma y_n}{n}$$

where n is the total number of vertical measurements.

The r.m.s. (root mean square) value is obtained as follows :

$$\text{r.m.s.} = \sqrt{\frac{y_1^2 + y_2^2 + y_3^2 \ldots y_n^2}{n}}$$

Table 6.1 shows some of the r.m.s. ranges for the various machining process in micro inches. The better the surface finish the small is the number of micro inches.

Table 6.1

Process	*r.m.s. range* (10^{-6} *inch*)
Lapping, honing, polishing	2—10
Grinding	5—150
Milling, turning, shaping	20—300
Drilling	75—200
Broaching	10—60
Reaming	8—50
Sawing	250—1000
Blanking	30—100
Forging	100—400
Sand casting	500—1000

(*c*) **Roughness width.** Roughness width is the distance parallel to the normal surface between successive peaks or ridges which constitute the predominate pattern of the roughness. It is stated in millimetres.

(*d*) **Roughness width cut off.** It is the greatest spacing of repetitive surface irregularities so to be included in the measurement of average roughness height. It should always be greater than the roughness width in order to obtain the total roughness height rating. It is expressed in millimetres.

(*e*) **Lay.** It is the direction of predominant surface pattern produced and reflects the machining method.

(*f*) **Waviness.** This refers to the irregularities which are outside the roughness width cut off values. It may be result of work deflecting during machining, working and vibration.

(*g*) **Waviness width.** It is the maximum permitted variation in waviness height. It is measured in millimetres.

(*h*) **Waviness height.** It is the peak to valley distance. It is also expressed in millimetres.

(*i*) **Flaws.** Cracks, scratches and ridges are called flaws. They are not regularly recurring and are imperfections outside the regular pattern of surface texture.

The ISO recommended arithmetical mean roughness values and grade numbers for the specification of surface roughness are indicated in Table 6.2.

Table 6.2

Roughness grade number	*Roughness value* (μm)
N_1	0.005
N_2	0.25
N_3	0.1
N_4	0.2
N_5	0.4
N_6	0.8
N_7	1.6
N_8	3.2
N_9	6.3
N_{10}	12.5
N_{11}	25
N_{12}	50

6.10. Ideal Surface Roughness

The ideal surface roughness represents the best possible finish which may be obtained for a given tool shape and feed and can only be approached if built up edge, chatter, inaccuracies, in machine tool movement etc. are eliminated. Ideal surface finish for the turning operation where a sharp corner tool is used is shown in Fig. 6.9 and where a tool having nose radius is shown in Fig. 6.10.

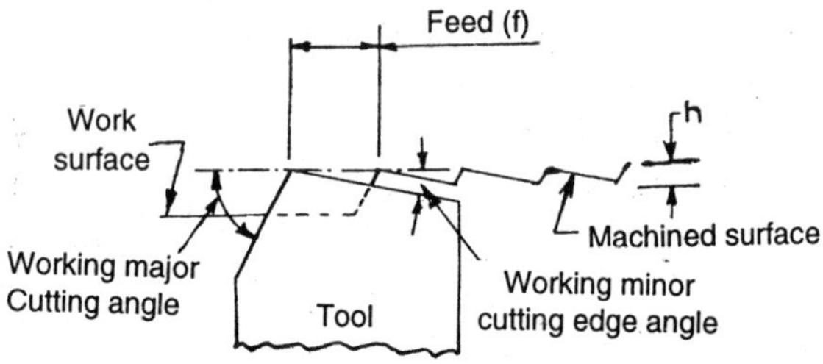

Fig. 6.9

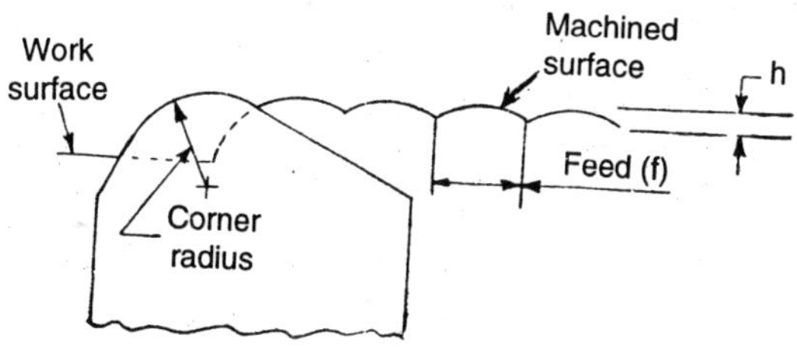

Fig. 6.10

For a sharp corner tool (Fig. 6.9) the roughness is extremely sensitive to changes in minor cutting edge angle.

Let ψ = Minor cutting edge angle.

θ = Working major cutting edge angle.

f = feed in mm/revolution.

h = Ideal value of surface roughness.

$$= \frac{f}{\cot \theta + \cot \psi}$$

For a rounded corner tool (Fig. 6.10) the ideal value of surface roughness is given by

$$h = \frac{f^2}{8r}$$

where r = Nose radius in mm.

6.11. Measurement of Surface Roughness

Surface finish is measured by different method using different units of measurement. The commonly used methods are as follows :

(*i*) Comparison with roughness standards.

(*ii*) Interferometry method.

(*iii*) Profilometer.

(1) **Comparison with roughness standard.** In this method flat and cylindrical sample surfaces finish machined by the common workshop processes and then calibrated are used as a basin of comparison. The thumb or fingernail is moved along the surface of workpiece and a mental note taken of the amount of resistance and the depth of irregularities. The thumb or fingernail is then moved across a series of sample surfaces acting as standards. The standard surface which gives approximately the same roughness feeling as that of workpiece indicates the roughness of the workpiece. This method depends upon individual judgment and lacks precision on this account but it is relatively cheap to apply and is a convenient method for general purposes.

(2) **Interferometry method.** This method is useful for viewing very highly finished surface. In this method the finished surfaces are seen through a microscope which incorporates interferometer.

(3) **Profilometer.** It is used to obtain an enlarged tracing of the surface irregularities. It has a sharp diamond stylus on the end of arm. The stylus is moved across the surface being measured and the stylus follows the contours of irregularities. As the stylus passes

over the surface it rises and falls by amounts proportional to surface roughness.

The relative displacement is highly magnified electronically and results presented either as a surface finished graph or as a roughness value. The stylus is required to be slided with respect to a datum set up by the skid (Fig. 6.11).

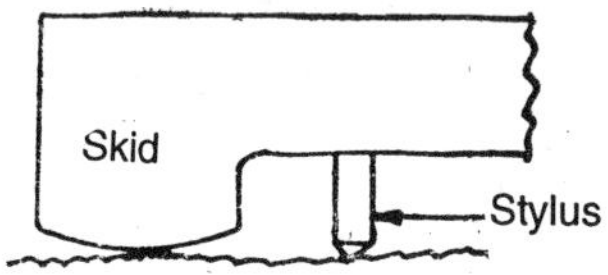

Fig. 6.11

6.12. Surface Finish Representation

Surface finish is either denoted as per IS : 3073—1967 by the symbol ∇ (mean height of the surface irregularities in microns both above and below a mean line) or by the symbol $^{n}\surd$ (root mean square height of the surface irregularities *n* indicating the value in micro inches). The two systems compare with each other as follows :

Type of finishing operation	*Representation as per IS : 3073—1967*		*Corresponding value in micro inches*
	Symbol	*Value in microns*	
Rough Machining	∇	8—25	250—1000
Fine Machining	∇ ∇	1.6—8	63—250
Grinding Finish	∇ ∇ ∇	0.025—1.6	2—63
Lapping	∇ ∇ ∇ ∇	< 0.025	< 2

According to Indian standards the surface roughness is expressed in terms of *CLA* value denoted by R_a.

Fig. 6.12 shows representation of surface roughness.

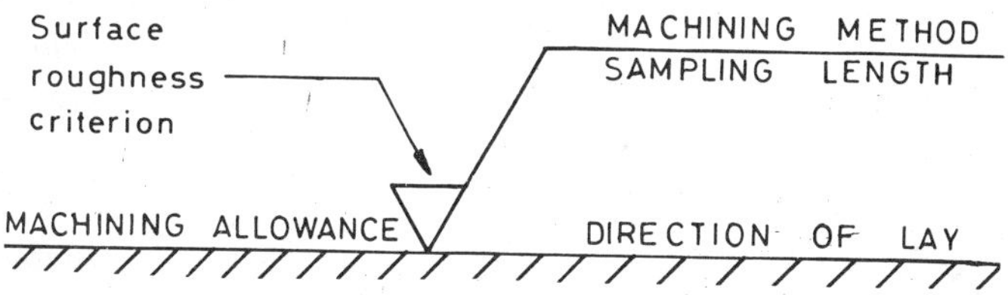

Fig. 6.12

Fig. 6.13 shows a typical value of R_a as 0.16 with a cut off length of 0.40 and direction of lay perpendicular and method of machining as lapping.

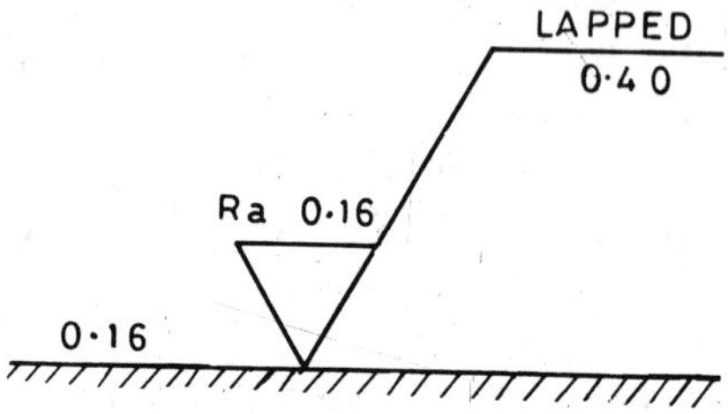

Fig. 6.13

The direction of lay is represented by the following symbols :

⊥ Lay perpendicular to the line representing the surface to which the symbol is applied

= Lay parallel to the line representing the surface to which the symbol is applied

X Lay angular in both directions to the line representing the surface to which the symbol is applied

R Lay approximately radial relative to the centre of the surface to which the symbol is applied

M Lay multidirectional.

6.13. Units of Surface Roughness

The following units are generally used :

Micro inch (μ-in) $= 10^{-6}$ inch

Micro (μ-m) metre $= 10^{-6}$ metre = Micron

Nanometres (nm) $= 10^{-9}$ metre (USA/France) = 0.001 μ-m.

Surface roughness values in microns for different manufacturing processes are indicated in Table 6.3.

Table 6.3

Manufacturing Process	*Surface Roughness (Microns)*
Turning	0.32 to 25
Drilling	1.6 to 22
Milling	0.32 to 25
Shaping	1.6 to 25
Surface grinding and cylindrical grinding	0.063 to 5
Lapping	0.012 to 0.013
Honing	0.025 to 0.42
Broaching, reaming	0.4 to 3.2
Boring	0.4 to 6.4

Table 6.4 indicates the average surface roughness value (R_a) in microns obtainable by different manufacturing methods.

Table 6.4

Manufacturing Method	*Surface Roughness*
Sand casting	6.3—12.5
Die casting	0.8—3.2
Forging	3.2—25
Extrusion	0.8—6.3
Rolling	0.8—3.2
Flame Cut	25—50
Hack Saw Cut	6.3—50
Bandsaw, Chipping	3.2—50
Filing	1.0—12.5
Emery Polish	0.4—1.6
Abrasive Belt	0.1—6.3
Fibre Wheel brushing	0.2—0.8
Cloth buffing	0.05—0.1
Shell Milling	3.2—25
Drilling	6.3—25
Planning & Shaping	1.6—12.5
Face Milling	1.6—12.5
Turning	1.6—12.5
Boring	1.6—6.3
Reaming	0.8—6.3
Cyl. Grinding	0.4—3.2
Centreless Grinding	0.4—3.2
Internal Grinding	0.4—3.2
Surface Grinding	0.4—3.2
Broaching	0.8—3.2

Super Finishing	0.1—0.4
Honing	0.1—0.4
Lapping	0.05—0.4

6.14. Regenerative Chatter

The most common type form of self induced vibration is regenerative chatter. This self induced chatter occurs because most cutting operations involve overlapping cuts, and although a system might be basically stable, the forced vibration resulting from the machining of the wavy surface from the previous stroke or revolution of the workpiece or tool can amplify the previous vibration. Thus, in practice, if the dynamic stability of a turning operation is being studied by, say, gradually increasing the back engagement (depth of cut) chatter will occur because of regenerative effects before true dynamic instability occurs.

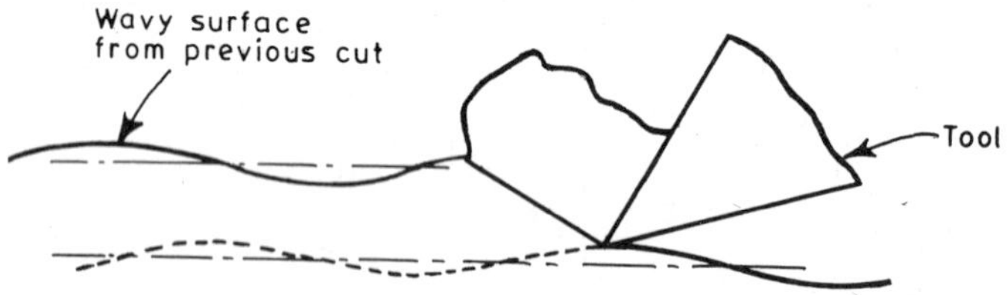

Fig. 6.14

In order to study the regenerative-chatter phenomenon it is necessary to consider the combined effects of wave removing and wave generating. These effects are illustrated in Fig. 6.14.

H = Mean value of undeformed chip thickness.

PROBLEMS

6.1. (*a*) What is chatter in machine tools ?

(*b*) What are the effects of chatter ?

6.2. Describe the following types of vibrations :

(*a*) Forced vibrations. (*b*) Self-excited vibrations.

6.3. Describe the factors that affect chatter.

6.4. Write short notes on the following :

(*i*) Types of vibratory systems.

(*ii*) Elimination of chatter.

(*iii*) Vibration isolation.

6.5. (*a*) What do you understand by surface finish ?

(*b*) Explain the factors which affect the surface finish.

6.6. Define the following :

(*a*) Roughness height.

(*b*) Arithmetical value of surface roughness.

(*c*) R.M.S. value of surface roughness.

(*d*) Roughness width.

(*e*) Waviness width.

(*f*) Waviness height.

(*g*) Flaw.

(*h*) Lay.

6.7. Discuss the methods of measuring surface roughness.

6.8. Write short notes on the following :

(*a*) Surface finish representation.

(*b*) Units of surface roughness.

6.9. Sketch and describe a method to isolate vibrations in a machine tool.

6.10. Write short notes on the following :

(*a*) Vibration measurement in rotating machine tool.

(*b*) Effects of vibrations in machine tool.

(*c*) Causes of vibrations in a machine tool.

(*d*) Regenerative chatter.

7

Basic Features and Kinematic Requirements of Machine Tools

7.1. Machine Tool

A metal cutting machine tool is defined as a power driven machine capable of producing various shapes in metal by cutting away the surplus material. The principle used in all the machine tools is one of the generating the surface required by providing suitable relative motions between the cutting tool and the workpiece. The metal removed by the cutting tool is called chip and will vary in size, shape and form according to the type of material being cut, the cutting tool angle and the position of the tool relative to the workpiece. The surface produced by the cutting process is called machined surface. The accuracy of construction and operation of a machine tool is very necessary feature, because tools reproduce and multiply their own errors.

In a metal cutting machine tool the energy is expended in deformation of material for producing finished surfaces. The purposes of any machine are as follows :

(*i*) To produce surfaces.

(*ii*) To trace formed surfaces.

(*iii*) To provide a finish to a given surface.

The general design of the machine tool takes care of the maximum cutting forces like tangential, axial and radial forces, weight of structures etc., and bending moment and torque produced by them. Bed forms the vital part of the machine tool on which table and other relevant parts of the machine tool move. It is therefore evident that the bed should be sufficiently strong and rigid. Further it should be easier to remove the chips produced during machining. Keeping in view of the strength and rigidity and removal of chips, box type construction of the bed is normally used. Beds of the machine tools are generally made from cast iron or steel. Grey cast iron with some percentage of nickel and chromium is preferred. Beds may be produced by casting or fabricated from steel plates. However, casting is a faster process.

Guide ways or slide ways on which work or tool with their relevent units move should be strong and should have long life. The surfaces of the guide way should be perfectly machined so that it maintains good amount of accuracy and precision. Slide ways may be made from cast iron or steel. The slide ways should have a hardness of 50—55 HRC.

The shaft and spindles should be so designed that they can take axial, bending and twisting loads. The bearings should be so selected that they can resist static and dynamic loads.

A machine tool requires variety of speeds and feeds. This is provided by a suitably designed gear box.

While choosing the drive motor for the machine tool the maximum cutting speed, feed and circulation of the lubricating oil are to be taken into account.

The machine tool should have high productivity and precision. This can be achieved by making the machine tool strong rigid and by making it free from vibrations.

Careful maintenance increases the life and efficiency of the machine tool. A thorough weekly cleaning is essential for any machine tool in continuous use. A general survey of the lubricating system may be restricted to the observation of oil level marks, refilling the oil periodically, and to daily lubricating of all openly moving mechanisms and links and guide ways. The oil filter and pumps should be cleaned once in a year. The ball bearings of the motor require cleaning and refilling with grease once every year. The machine tool before being sent for sales should be tested properly.

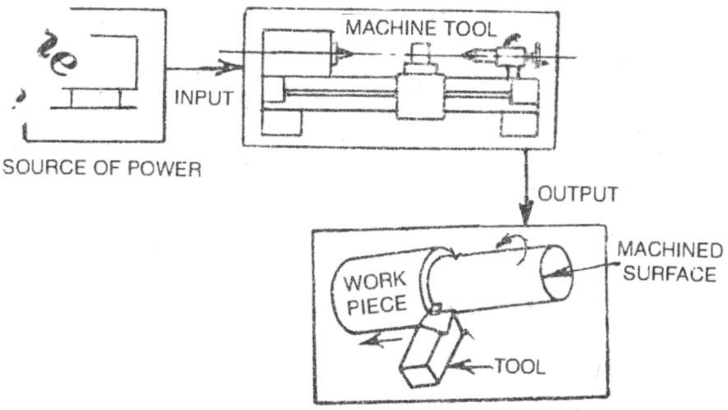

Fig. 7.1 (*a*)

Fig. 7.1 (*a*) shows schematically the power input to machine tool and output from the machine tool in the form of finished workpiece.

7.1.1. Characteristics of machine tool

A machine tool intended for cutting metals at high speed should possess the following characteristics :

(*i*) It should be powerful.

(*ii*) It should be capable of operating at high speeds.

(*iii*) It should be rigid (vibration proof).

(*iv*) It should be durable.

(*v*) It should be safe in operation.

(*vi*) The machine tool should provide facilities for reducing not only the machining time but the handling time as well.

(*vii*) It should have good lubrication facilities.

(*viii*) There should be reliable and rapid clamping of the workpiece and tool.

(*ix*) It should have well balanced rotating parts.

(*x*) It should be simple in design and should have good appearance.

(*xi*) Its cost of manufacturing and operation should be low.

(*xii*) There should be safety and convenience of controls such as

(*a*) Rotating and moving parts should be shielded with hoods.

(*b*) The worker should be protected from chips, abrasives dust and coolant by means of screens, shields etc.

(*c*) The machine tool control system should be automated to as large as possible.

7.1.2. Objectives of machine tool

The basic objectives of a machine tool are as follows :

(*i*) Precision

(*ii*) Productivity.

Precision means the accuracy with which a job can be manufactured on a machine tool. Productivity means the volume of materials removed per minute from the workpiece. More the volume of material removed, more will be the productivity of the machine tool.

Precision depends on static stiffness and strength of the machine tool whereas productivity depends on the dynamic stiffness of the machine tool. During operations the machine tools are subjected to static or dynamic loads, the latter having periodic or impact characteristics. These loads are associated with the cutting process and/or movements of the machine tool members.

It is desireable to examine the cumulative static and dynamic characteristics of the machine tool as well as the corresponding characteristics of individual elements of which the machine tool is made.

Machine tool vibration has detrimental effect on tool life which, in turn, lowers down the productivity and increases the cost of production. It is therefore desireable that a machine tool should be free from vibrations. For example when it is found that vibration is being transmitted from the foundation the machine tool can be isolated from the ground so that no appreciable vibration is transmitted. This is done by supporting the machine tool on springs and dampers as shown in Fig. 7.1 (*b*).

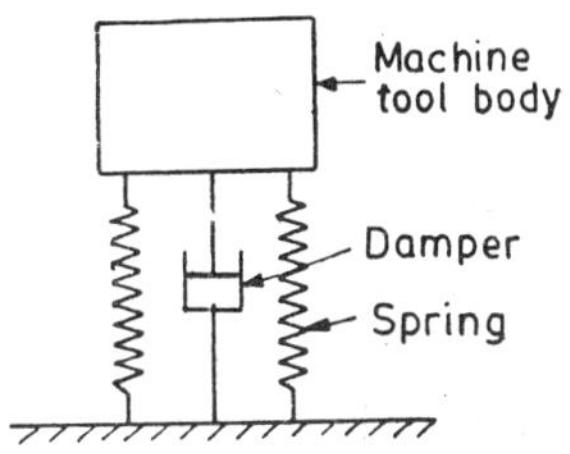

Fig. 7.1 (*b*)

While analysing the dynamic behaviour of machine tools, rigidity and stability are two important characteristics to be considered. Dynamic rigidity (stiffness) is defined as the ratio of amplitude of vibratory force considered harmonic to the vibratory displacement at a given frequency. It is the measure of machine tool's resistance to vibration. Dynamic stability indicates that the masses of a distributed system oscillate with decreasing amplitudes towards the original state of equilibrium.

7.1.3. Production capacity

The production capacity (Productivity) of a machine tool can be increased as follows :

(*i*) By decreasing machining time. This is achieved by :

(*a*) increasing cutting speed or feed.

(*b*) machining several workpieces simultaneously.

(*c*) concentrating a number of cutting tools in each station.

(*ii*) By decreasing handling time. This is achieved by :

(*a*) reducing idle number of operations.

(*b*) increasing the speed of idle strokes.

(c) arranging rapid approach or withdrawal of tools or workpieces.

(iii) By introducing automatic tool changing and bar feeding devices.

(iv) By using machine tools having good rigidity and strength.

7.1.4. Stiffness and rigidity of machine tools

The stiffness of a machine tool may be defined as the load per unit deformation. Stiffness should be considered from the following points of view :

(i) Static stiffness against deformation under static loads.

(ii) Dynamic rigidity behaviour during vibrations under pulsating and inertia forces.

Amongst the static deformation the more important are caused by bending and torsional loads because these produce misalignments and displacements of the guiding elements which affect the working accuracy of machine tools. Following forces produce such loading and deformation conditions :

(i) Weight of workpiece

(ii) Cutting force

(iii) Weight of moving parts of the machine tool.

Dynamic rigidity of a machine tool is defined as the ratio of amplitude of vibratory force considered harmonic to the vibratory displacement at a given frequency. It is the measure of machine tool's resistance to vibrations.

A machine tool consists of a number of elements. These elements experience deformation during operation of the machine tool and therefore can be looked upon as elastic bodies (springs) with a certain stiffness (spring constant for a designer it is necessary to examine the cumulative static and dynamic characteristics of the machine tool as well as the corresponding characteristics of the individual elements of which the machine tool is made. The machine tool should be therefore checked for

(i) Static stiffness

(ii) Dynamic stiffness.

$$K = \text{Static stiffness of an element of machine tool} = \frac{P}{Y}$$

where P = Force

Y = Displacement.

The behaviour of an individual element of machine tool under static loading can be examined from the force displacement relationship. The machine tool consists of a large number of elements and its behaviour is of interest in as much as it affects the parameters of machining and the quality of the machined surface. This can be assessed by means of the following two quantities :

1. Static stiffness with respect to the workpiece accuracy. This is a cross stiffness (K_1)

$$K_1 = \frac{P}{Y_1}$$

where P = Resultant cutting force acting between the cutting tool and workpiece

Y_1 = Relative displacement normal to the machine surface.

Higher value of K_1 will give better accuracy during machining because relative cutter workpiece displacement perpendicular to machine surface will be less.

2. Static stiffness with respect to dynamic stability (K)

$$K = \frac{P}{Y}$$

It is also the cross stiffness.

P = Resultant cutting force

Y = Relative displacement relative normal to the surface of the cut.

This displacement determines the variation of the chip thickness which is of maximum significance for stability of the machine tool against chatter vibration.

The dynamic stiffness depends on the frequency of the force

$$K_d = \frac{P_d}{Y_d}$$

where K_d = Dynamic stiffness

P_d = Dynamic force

Y_d = Displacement.

It will vary with a change in the frequency of the force.

$$C_d = \text{Dynamic compliance} = \frac{Y_d}{P_d}.$$

It is desirable to analyse the static and dynamic stiffness of the machine tool separately.

7.1.5. Precision

A good surface finish of parts produced on a machine tool is desirable. The following factors affect the accuracy of finished components made on a machine tool :

(*i*) Cutting tool geometry

(*ii*) Strength and stiffness of machine tool

(*iii*) Machining variables like :

(*a*) cutting speed

(*b*) feed

(*c*) depth of cut

(*iv*) Accuracy of bearings

(*v*) Vibrations in machine tool

(*vi*) Nature of workpiece material

(*vii*) Methods of chip removal.

7.1.6. Productive time

The various factors of productive time are as follows :

(*i*) *Set up time* : This includes :

(*a*) preparatory time to get tools

(*b*) time to arrange tools on machine.

(*ii*) *Handling time* : This includes :

(*a*) time for loading and unloading of workpieces and tools

(*b*) time for measurements.

(*iii*) *Down time* : This includes

(*a*) time lost in break downs

(*b*) time lost in sudden minor accidents.

(*iv*) Machining time.

7.2. Classification of Machine Tools

The principal type of machine tools on which cutting tools are used in the modern workshop might be classified as follows :

(*i*) Planer, shaper

(*ii*) Lathe

(*iii*) Milling machine

(*iv*) Drilling, tapping and reaming machines

(*v*) Broach, saw

(*vi*) Grinders and polishers

(*vii*) Gear and thread cutting machines.

The above mentioned machine tools may further be classified according to the following criteria :

(*i*) Degree of specialisation

(*ii*) Weight

(*iii*) Degree of accuracy.

(*i*) **Degree of specialisation.** In respect of their degree of specialisation the machine tools can be referred to one of the following groups :

(*a*) **General purpose (Universal) machine tools.** They are designed for performing a great variety of machining operations on a wide range of workpieces. They are employed chiefly in piece and small lot production and for repair jobs.

(*b*) **Single purpose machine tools.** They are designed for performing a single definite machining operation. They may be readily set up for machining different sized parts of the same type. Machine tools used for machining crankpins of crankshafts, for turning the cam contours on camshafts are included in this type.

(*c*) **Specialised machine tools.** These machine tools are used to machine a certain definite workpiece by making the necessary changes in their construction. This group includes unit built machine tools.

(*d*) **Special machine tools.** These machine tools are meant for performing a certain definite operation in machining a certain definite workpiece. Specialised and special machine tools find application in large lot and mass production.

(*ii*) **Weight.** According to weight machine tool can be classified as follows :

(*a*) **Light weight machine tools.** They weigh up to one ton.

(*b*) **Medium weight machine tools.** Their weight varies from 1 to 10 tons.

(*c*) **Heavy weight machine tools.** They weigh over 10 tons.

(*iii*) **Degree of accuracy.** According to the degree of accuracy achieved the machine tools are classified as follows :

(*a*) Standard accuracy.

(*b*) Above standard accuracy.

(*c*) High accuracy.

(*d*) Precision machine tools.

(*e*) High precision or machine tools.

General purpose machine tools are standard accuracy machine tools. Above standard accuracy machine tools are similar to standard accuracy machine tools except that higher requirements are made to the accuracy with which the critical parts are manufactured as well as to the quality of assembly and adjustments. High accuracy machine tools have certain units that are specially designed with the aim of maintaining the high accuracy standards. In the manufacture of precision machine tools the accuracy requirements are still higher than the high accuracy machine tools. High precision machine tools are intended for making the parts which determine the accuracy of high accuracy machine tools and precision machine tools.

7.3. Control Systems of Machine Tools

Machine tools are fitted with various control systems meant to generate controlling movements which are essential for carrying out a machining process in accordance with the technical specifications of the part being machined. Two main functions of control systems are as follows :

(*i*) Changing speeds and feeds.

(*ii*) Providing the working and auxiliary motions in the desired sequence necessary for machining a particular part.

In addition, the machine tools are provided with safety controls to prevent damage to the machine tool and cutting tool during operation.

Machine tool controls may be of the following types :

(*i*) Mechanical

(*ii*) Hydraulic

(*iii*) Electrical.

The control system of a machine tool is defined as the control of the machining process. This is accomplished by transmitting instructions or commands from a transmitter through a chain of transmitting elements to the operative member which receives the commands at the required time and is activated to perform the required machining process.

The various elements of machine tool control system are indicated in Fig. 7.1 (*c*).

Manual control makes use of levers, hand wheels and push buttons etc. whereas mechanical control is by cams, drums, clutches etc. and electrical control makes use of limit switches. Electronic control uses punched card, tape and magnetic tape.

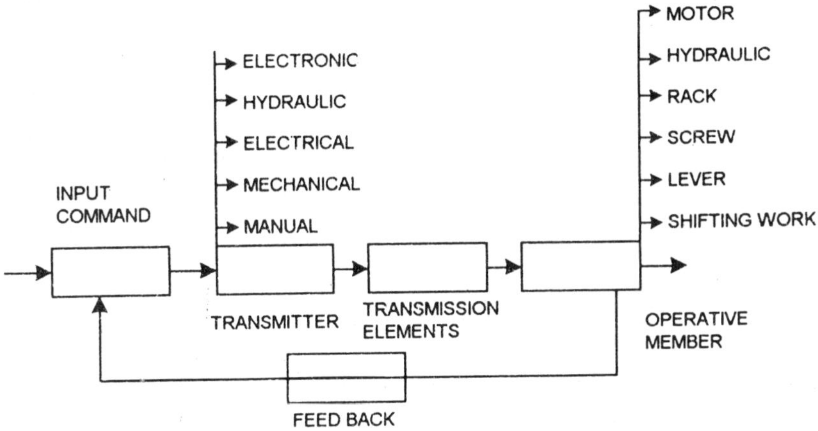

Fig. 7.1 (*c*)

Feedback may be by

(*i*) Visual

(*ii*) Electrical/Electronic servos observation.

Machine tool control system performs the following functions during machining by the machine tool :

(*i*) Positional controls.

(*ii*) Control of speeds, feeds and depth of cut.

(*iii*) Change over from one set of conditions to another set.

(*iv*) Controls for safety.

Machine tool control system should possess the following requirements :

(*i*) Ease of handling.

(*ii*) Ensuring safety to operator and machine from anticipated control movements.

(*iii*) To minimise machining time.

(*iv*) Simplification of the varieties of designs of handles, levers, push buttons, and other control elements.

7.4. Safety and Convenience of Machine Tool Controls

Convenient controls protect the machine tool operator from excessive fatigue and thus contribute towards safety. Machine tool controls should be simplified and made convenient. The control system should be rationally selected and should be automated to as large extent as possible. Safety of machine tools is ensured by following control measures :

(*i*) Shielding the rotating and moving parts of machine tools with hoods.

(*ii*) Providing reliable clamping for workpiece and tools.

(*iii*) Protecting the machine tool operator from chips, abrasive dust and coolant by means of screens, shields etc.

(*iv*) Providing devices for safe handling of large and heavy workpieces.

(*v*) Providing reliable earthing of the machine tool.

7.5. Cutting Motion in Machine Tool

In order to obtain the required shape on the workpiece it is necessary that the cutting edge of the cutting tool should move in a particular manner with respect to the workpiece. There are two types of motions in a machine tool.

(*i*) Working motion

(*ii*) Auxiliary motion.

Working motion. In machine tools the working motions are powered by an external source of energy such as electrical or hydraulic.

The process of chip removal is effected by the working motions of machine tool (formative motions) which are transmitted either to the cutting tool, or to the work or to both simultaneously. Working motions of a machine tool are of the following types :

(*a*) Primary cutting motion or Drive motion.

(*b*) Feed motion.

Both primary cutting motion and feed motion is specified by speed or feed rate.

Primary cutting motion. It provides for cutting the chip from the blank at the cutting speed equal to the velocity with which the chip leaves the work. The most commonly used types of primary cutting motions are of two types :

(*i*) Rotary primary cutting motion.

(*ii*) Reciprocating primary cutting motion.

Rotary primary cutting motion. Rotary motion may be transmitted either to the work as in lathe group of machine tool or

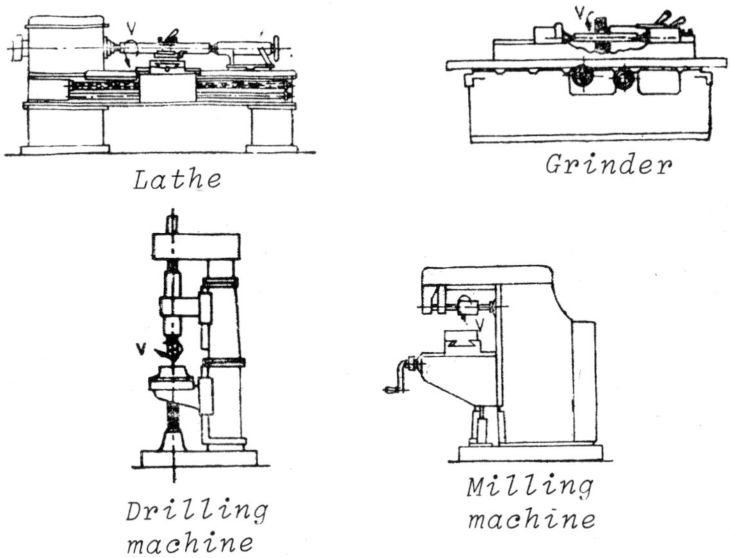

Fig. 7.1

to the tool as in grinding machine, drilling machine of milling machine. Fig. 7.1 shows the machine tools with rotary primary motion.

The cutting speed (V) of a rotary cutting motion is given by

$$V = \frac{\pi D \, . \, N}{100} \text{ m/min.}$$

where D = Diameter of surface being machined or of the rotating tool. (mm)

N = R.P.M. of workpiece of tool.

Reciprocating primary cutting motion. This type of motion is used in shapers, planers, slotters, power hacksaws and broaching machines. This motion can be transmitted to the tool as in shaper and slotter or to the work as in planer.

Fig. 7.2 shows machine tools with a reciprocating primary cutting motion. In machine tools using reciprocating primary cutting motion be cutting takes place periodically.

In such machine tools the cutting cycle consists of a working stroke during which the tool cuts the chips and the idle or returns stroke during which the tool or work returns to its initial position.

The speed of return stroke should be kept higher than that of working stroke in order to reduce the non-productive time in machining. The average value of cutting speed (V) is determined as follows :

$$V = \frac{L(K+1)N}{1000\,K} \text{ metre per min.}$$

where L = Length of working stroke in millimetre.

N = Number of full strokes per minute. One full stroke includes a working stroke and a return stroke.

$K = \frac{T_1}{T_2}$ where T_1 and T_2 indicate the time required for working stroke and return stroke respectively.

In Fig. 7.2, V_1 indicates cutting speed during working stroke and V_2 indicates the speed during return stroke.

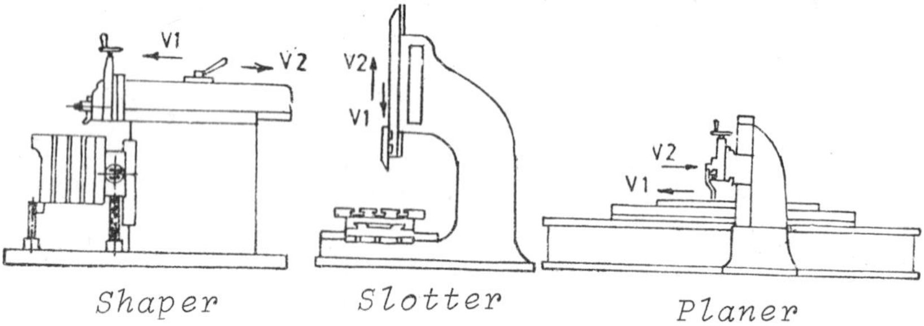

Fig. 7.2

The primary cutting motion of certain machine tools may be of a more complex nature. It can also be a combination of rotary and reciprocating motions.

Feed motion. The rate of feed or speed of the feed motion is substantially less than the cutting speed. The feed motion enables the cutting process to be extended to the whole surface to be machined on the work. Other conditions being equal, the rate of feed determines the cross sectional area of the chip. The accuracy of the primary cutting motion depends mainly on the design of the main spindle, while the accuracy of feed motion depends upon the design of the bed.

Table 7.1 indicates working motions for some of the machine tools.

Table 7.1

S. No.	*Machine Tool*	*Working motions*
1.	Lathes and Boring Machines	(*i*) Drive motion—rotary motion of workpiece. (*ii*) Feed motion—translatory motion of cutting tool in axial or radial direction.
2.	Drilling Machine	(*i*) Drive motion—Rotary motion of drill. (*ii*) Feed motion—Translatory motion of drill.
3.	Grinding machine	(*i*) Drive motion—Rotary motion of grinding wheel. (*ii*) Feed motion—Rotary, Translatory motion of workpiece.
4.	Shaper, Planer Slotter	(*i*) Drive motion—Reciprocating motion of cutting tool. (*ii*) Feed motion—Intermittent translatory motion of workpiece.
5.	Milling Machine	(*i*) Drive motion—Rotary motion of cutter. (*ii*) Feed motion—Translatory motion of workpiece.

Auxiliary Motion. The auxiliary motions do not take part in the process of formation of the required surface but are none the less necessary to make the working motions to fulfil their assigned function. The various types of auxiliary motions in machine tools are as follows :

(*i*) Engaging and dis-engaging of working motions.

(*ii*) Changing the speed of drive and feed motions.

(*iii*) Clamping and un-clamping of workpiece.

The auxiliary motions may be carried out manually or they may be automated in automatic machine tools.

7.6. Forces in Machine Tool

The various forces which tend to deform the machine tool parts or workpiece are as follows :

(*i*) Static loads such as weight of machine tool and its various parts.

(*ii*) Dynamic loads such as the forces caused due to rotating or reciprocating masses.

(*iii*) Cutting forces.

(*iv*) **Friction forces.** The forces are usually taken proportional in machine tool design to the normal load of the friction surfaces lubrication conditions and sliding velocity.

7.7. Process Capability of a Machine Tool

The process capability of a machine tool depends upon its rigidity which is defined as its capability to resist deformation produced due to the introduction of cutting forces generated during machining. A machine tool must possess static as well as dynamic rigidity so that it is able to produce jobs within high degree of accuracy consistently over a long period of time.

A machine tool is a group of links (elements) connected in sequence by joints which constitute a closed dimensional circuit. The inherent quality of the element system controls the accuracy and is known as process capability of the machine tool. Process capability can be improved by using following techniques :

(*i*) By changing rigidity of links.

(*ii*) By reducing range of cutting force.

(*iii*) By reducing number of links.

7.7.1. Compliance of machine tool

Compliance of a machine tool is the reciprocal of rigidity. Static compliance is defined as ratio of displacement of force. The compliance of a centre lathe is calculated as follows :

Fig. 7.2 (*a*) shows a shaft being turned on a centre lathe.

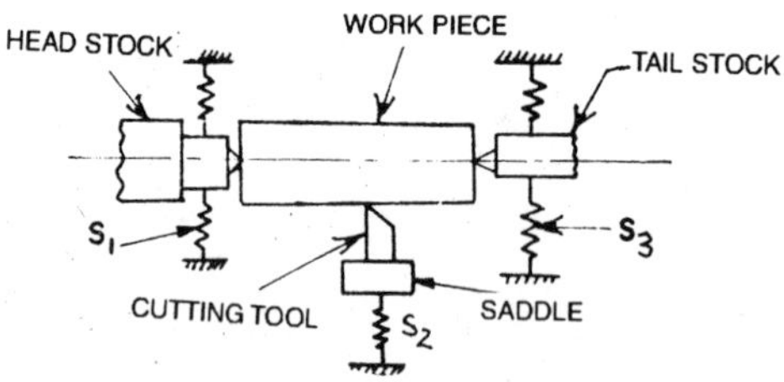

Fig. 7.2 (*a*)

S_1 = Rigidity of head stock

S_2 = Rigidity of saddle

S_3 = Rigidity of tail stock

Y_1 = Deflection at head stock

Y_2 = Deflection at cutting point

Y_3 = Deflection at tail stock

Y_4 = Deflection of the saddle.

The deflection curve under cutting load (F_y) is shown in Fig. 7.2 (*b*)

$$Y_2 = Y_1 + (Y_3 - Y_1) \times \frac{x}{L} \quad ...(1)$$

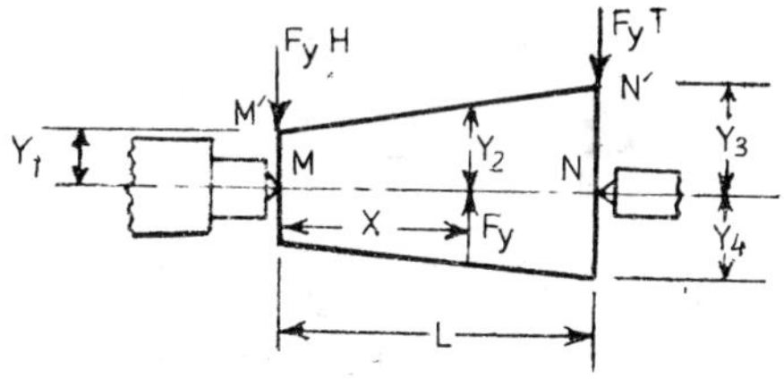

Fig. 7.2 (*b*)

L = Length of workpiece.

x = Distance of the cutting tool tip from the head stock end.

Now
$$y_1 = \frac{F_{yH}}{S_1}$$

$$y_3 = \frac{F_{yT}}{S_3}$$

$$F_{yH} = F_y \times \frac{L - x}{L}$$

$$F_{yT} = F_y \times \frac{x}{L}$$

From equation (1)

$$y_2 = \frac{F_{yH}}{S_1} + \left(\frac{F_{yT}}{S_3} - \frac{F_{yH}}{S_1} \right) \times \frac{x}{L}$$

$$= \frac{F_y}{S_1} \times \frac{L-x}{L} + \frac{x}{L}\left[\frac{F_y}{S_3} \times \frac{x}{L} - \frac{F_y}{S_1} \times \frac{L-x}{L} \right]$$

$$= \frac{F_y}{S_1}\left[\frac{L-x}{L} \right]^2 + \frac{F_y}{S_2}\left(\frac{x}{L} \right)^2$$

Let Y = Deflection of machine tool at cutting point

$$= Y_4 + Y_2$$

$$= \frac{F_y}{S_2} + \frac{F_y}{S_1}\left(\frac{L-x}{L} \right)^2 + \frac{F_y}{S_3}\left(\frac{x}{L} \right)^2$$

$$= F_y \left[\frac{1}{S_2} + \frac{1}{S_2}\left(\frac{L-x}{L} \right)^2 + \frac{1}{S_3}\left(\frac{x}{L} \right)^2 \right]$$

S = Rigidity of machine tool

$$= \frac{F_y}{Y} = \frac{1}{\frac{1}{S_2} + \frac{1}{S_1}\left(\frac{L-x}{L}\right)^2 + \frac{1}{S}\left(\frac{x}{L}\right)^2}$$

$$C = \text{Compliance of machine tool} = \frac{1}{S}$$

$$= \frac{1}{S_2} + \frac{1}{S_1}\left(\frac{L-x}{L}\right)^2 + \frac{1}{S_3}\left(\frac{x}{L}\right)^2.$$

The machining accuracy which includes both profile as well as dimensional accuracy is determined by machine tool compliance.

The representative total compliance value for some of machine tools is indicated in Table 7.1. (A).

Table 7.1 (A)

Machine Tool	*Description*	*Compliance (Micron / kgf)*
Centreless grinding machine	—	1
Lathe (workpiece clamped in chuck)	(*i*) H = 200 mm (*ii*) H = 300 mm (*iii*) H = 400 mm	1.5 1.2 0.57
Lathe (workpiece clamped between centres)	(*i*) H = 200 mm (*ii*) H = 300 mm (*iii*) H = 400 mm	0.75 0.52 0.38
Automatic bar lathe	Screw type	0.2—0.3
Vertical milling machine	—	0.4
Vertical turning and boring mill	—	0.35

7.8. Essential Requirements of a Machine Tool

A machine tool should possess the following requirements :

(*i*) **Low cost.** The initial cost of the machine tool as well as the cost of production should be low.

(*ii*) **High accuracy.** The machine tool should be capable of producing high quality products at highest possible speed.

(*iii*) **High useful life.** The machine tool should render a trouble free service while retaining its accuracy for longer period.

(*iv*) **Low maintenance cost.** The maintenance of machine tool should be easy and maintenance cost should be low.

(*v*) **Reliability.** The machine tool should retain accuracy over period of its life.

(*vi*) **Ease of operation.** It should be easy to operate the machine tool.

(*vii*) **High production capacity.** It is defined as the ability of machine tool to machine a definite number of workpieces in unit time.

(*viii*) **Appearance.** The appearance of machine tool is receiving much attention in recent years. If the machine tool being developed has an advantageous design layout *i.e.* if its units and component assemblies are properly positioned in relation to each order will have a sufficient good shape from the point of view of design principles. The appearance can be further improved by redesigning the intersections of external sources, the surface of the covers etc. These measures however should have no adverse effects on the operational features of the machine tools.

(*ix*) **Safety.** Reliable protection for the operator not only against accident but against excessive fatigue as well is a must in modern machine tool.

(*x*) **Ease of manufacture.** It should be easier to manufacture and assemble various parts of machine tool.

7.9. Selection of Machine Tool

Each machine tool is used to perform particular type of machining operation or operations such as turning, drilling, boring, facing, shaping, milling, broaching, grinding etc. The selection of a machine tool depends upon the following factors :

(*i*) The type of product required.

(*ii*) Degree of accuracy desired. The machine tool should be selected based on the accuracy desired on the job. It is not desirable to select the most accuracy machine tool available in the market for a less accurate job as this will increase the cost of production.

(*iii*) Amount of metal to be removed.

(*iv*) Size of workpiece.

(*v*) Quantity of products required.

7.10. General Requirements of Machine Tool Design

The requirements of a machine tool design are as follows :

(*i*) High productivity.

(*ii*) High accuracy of components manufactured.

(*iii*) Safety and convenience of controls.

(*iv*) Simplicity of design. (*v*) Low cost of manufacturing.

(*vi*) Low cost of operation. (*vii*) Good appearance.

7.11. Basic Features of a Machine Tool

A machine tool is fundamentally an assembly of following basic elements (Fig. 7.3) :

(*i*) Bed, structure of frame.

(*ii*) Slides and slide ways.

(*iii*) Spindles and spindle bearing.

(*iv*) Power units.

(*v*) Transmission linkage.

(*vi*) Work holding and tool holding elements.

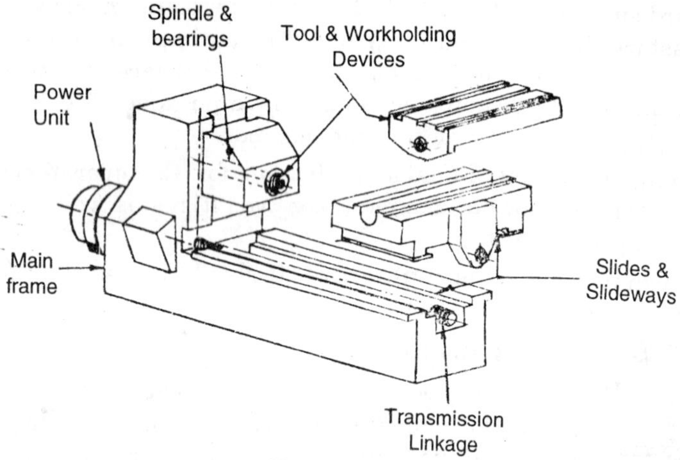

Fig. 7.3

7.12. Bed, Structure or Frame

Machine tools parts such as beds, bases, columns, carriages, tables etc. are known as machine tool structures. Following are the essential requirements of structures for their satisfactory performance.

(*i*) The machine tool structures should be made of proper materials.

(*ii*) They should have high static and dynamic stiffness.

(*iii*) All important mating surfaces of the structures should be machined with a high degree of accuracy to provide the desired geometrical accuracy.

Depending upon the function structures are divided into following groups :

(*i*) Beds and bases on which the various sub-assemblies are mounted.

(*ii*) Box type housings in which individual units are assembled such as spindle head, speed box housing.

(*iii*) Parts used to support the cutting tool and work piece such as table, carriage, tail stock and knee.

Bed is the main element which acts as a base for the rest of the units. Bed is usually made from cast iron has more compressive strength, is a cheap material and can absorb the vibrations set up during machining. The bed has one or more slideways cast as an integral part of it and for this cast iron has an advantage that it can be easily machined, has ideal wearing properties and if required a hard surface can be produced by the induction hardening process. Cast iron possesses vibration proof characteristics.

Modern welding developments have made it possible to produce fabricated steel structures as an alternative to cast iron and in many cases with advantage in regard to cost, lightness and time saving. Fig. 7.4 shows a section of a fabricated lathe bed.

The different types of sections having same cross sectional area and outer parameter which are commonly used for beds are shown in Fig. 7.5.

Fig. 7.4

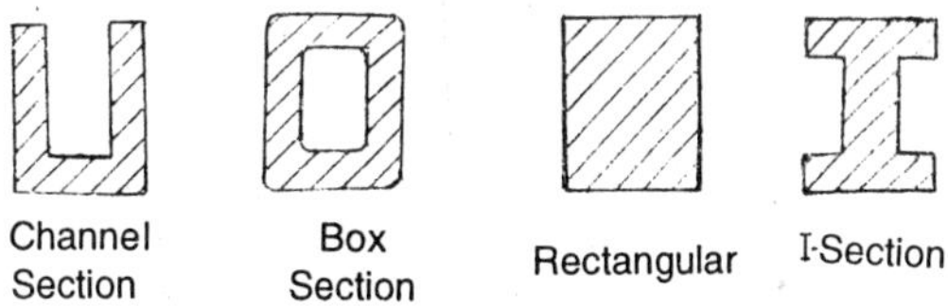

Fig. 7.5

It is observed that box section is more suitable as it is strong in bending and torsion, and can be easily produced. To avoid massive sections in castings carefully designed systems of ribbing are used to offer the maximum resistance to bending and torsional stresses.

Beds, bases, columns and frames of machine tools are generally made from cast iron because of the following advantages possessed by cast iron :

(*i*) It has high compressive strength.

(*ii*) It can be easily cast into intricate shapes.

(*iii*) It has better capacity to absorb vibrations.

(*iv*) It possesses good lubricating properties due to the presence of free graphite in it.

(*v*) It can be machined to a fairly high degree of accuracy and provided a fine surface finish.

(*vi*) It can be easily alloyed with elements like nickel, chromium, molybdenum etc. to increase its hardness.

(*vii*) The cost is fairly low.

However, cast iron can not be easily welded. Therefore, the fabricated structures are made from mild steel which can be easily welded.

Two basic types of ribbing are as follows :

(*a*) Box ribbing.

(*b*) Diagonal ribbing.

The box formation is convenient to produce, apertures in the walls permitting the positioning and extraction of cores. Diagonal ribbing provides greater torsional stiffness and permits swarf to fall between the sections. It is quite commonly used for lathe beds. Fig. 7.6 shows box ribbing and Fig. 7.7 shows diagonal ribbing. Diagonal ribbing is quite commonly used in medium and large size machine tools.

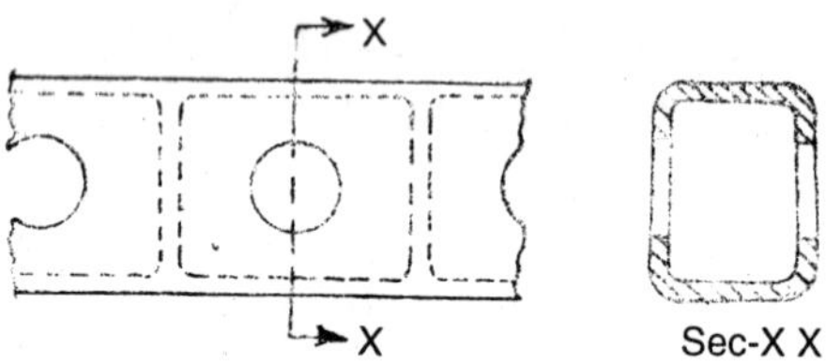

Fig. 7.6

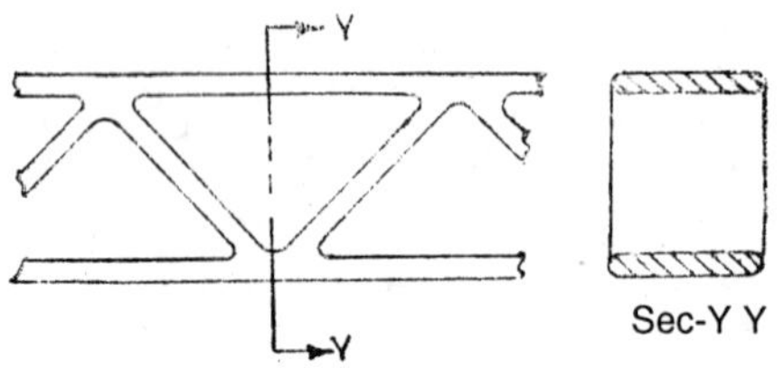

Fig. 7.7

Box type section has the highest torsional stiffness and is best suited in terms of strength and stiffness. The stiffness of machine tool structures life beds, frames, columns etc. can be improved by using ribs and stiffners. The effect of ribs and stiffners depends, to a large extent, upon how they are arranged. Stiffners may be arranged in following two ways :

(*i*) Diagonal stiffners.

(*ii*) Vertical stiffners.

To obtain high surface finish the machine tool should be free from vibrations. Besides other factors the design of the bed influences the vibration characteristics of the machine tool. By controlling the following factors with regard to the design of the machine tool structure, the vibrations can be reduced.

(*i*) By arranging machine tool structure to have natural frequencies which do not coincide with those of the cutting action.

(*ii*) The natural frequency is given by

$$w_n = \sqrt{\frac{k}{m}} \text{ radian/sec.}$$

where w_n = Natural frequency

k = Static stiffness of the structure = $\frac{P}{y}$

P = Straining force.

y = Deformation in the direction of force.

m = Mass.

Since natural frequency is proportional to the square root of the static stiffness, therefore the static stiffness of the structure should be as high as possible. Further to obtain high frequencies an attempt should be made to reduce the mass to the minimum.

(*iii*) The material of the structure should be capable of absorbing vibrations.

Fig. 7.7 (*a*) shows typical cross-section of the table of a machine tool.

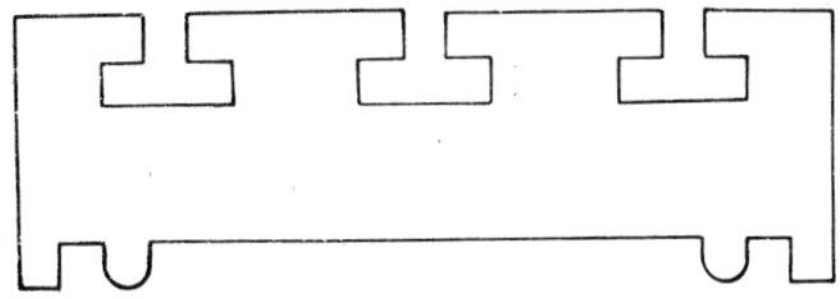

Fig. 7.7 (*a*)

Repair of a machine tool bed may be carried out by the following three methods :

(*i*) Scraping (*ii*) Planing

(*iii*) Grinding.

7.13. Procedure to Design a Machine Tool Structure

Following factors should be considered while designing a machine tool structure :

(*i*) Decide materials for structure.

(*ii*) Decide manufacturing process such as

(*a*) Cast (*b*) Fabricated.

(*iii*) Type of structure

(*a*) Close (*b*) Open.

(*iv*) Forces acting on structure which can cause bending and twisting.

(*v*) Take into account weight of structure, weight of workpiece etc.

(*vi*) Nature of vibrations to be generated during working.

(*vii*) The structure should have sufficient stiffness and strength.

7.13.1. Use of reinforcing ribs or stiffness in lathe beds

The strength and rigidity of lathe beds with parallel and diagonal ribs depends upon the following factors :

(*i*) Number of ribs. (*ii*) Arrangements of ribs.

(*iii*) Thickness of main number of bed beam.

(*iv*) Ratio of depth and length of the bed.

(*v*) Ratio of width and length of the bed.

Fig. 7.8 shows a typical section of lathe bed. Fig. 7.9 shows a cross-section of a cast iron bed for a heavy lathe.

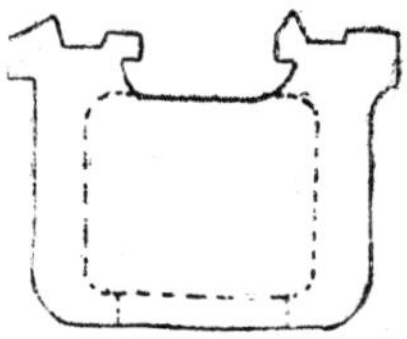

Fig. 7.8

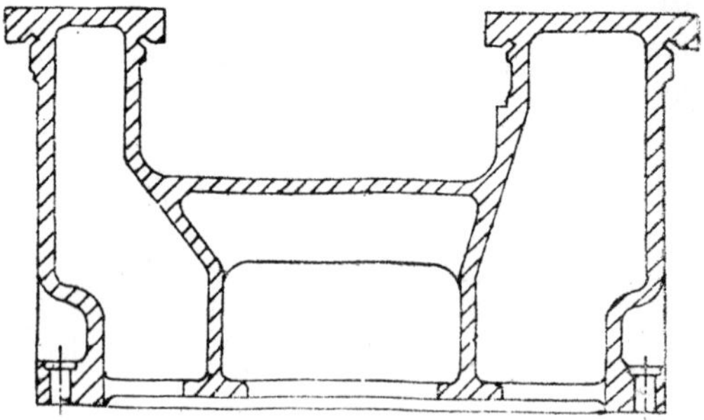

Fig. 7.9

The main requirement made to the bed, base or column of a machine tool is that it maintains the proper relative positions of the units and parts mounted on it over a long period of service under all specified working conditions. The beds, bases or column should satisfy the following requirements :

(*i*) They should have sufficient strength and rigidity.

(*ii*) It should be easier to manufacture them.

(*iii*) Their cost should be low.

(*iv*) Minimum amount of metal should be used during their manufacture.

The configuration of bed (base and column etc.) is determined by the following factors :

(*i*) By the arrangement of ways on bed for various units of machine tool.

(*ii*) By weight, dimensions and length of stroke of main units and parts.

(*iii*) By the necessity of housing various mechanisms inside the bed.

(*iv*) By the various openings, apertures etc. to be provided in the bed walls.

7.13.2. Forces to be considered for machine tool structures design

While designing a machine tool structure the following forces should be taken into account :

(*i*) *Cutting force.* This force depends on the following :

(*a*) Work-piece material.

(*b*) Machining parameters like feed, depth of cut, cutting speed etc.

(*c*) Wear of cutting tool.

(*ii*) *Friction force.* This is considered proportional to the normal force on the contacting surface. Coefficient of friction may be taken as follows :

μ = Coefficient of friction

= 0.001 for steel for rolling friction

= 0.002 for C.I. for rolling friction

= 0.002 – 0.05 under conditions of liquid friction

= 0.03 – 0.2 under conditions of semi-liquid conditions

= 0.2 – 0.35 under dry friction.

(*iii*) Forces of reaction.

(*iv*) Inertial forces due to vibrations and transient processes during speeding up and braking.

(*v*) Forces due to mass of structure, workpiece, fixtures and clamping devices.

The machine tool should be designed based on following :

(i) Designing for bending stiffness.

(ii) Designing for torsion stiffness.

(iii) Checking dimensions for strength due to bending and torsion.

Machine tool beds are analysed as bars subjected to bending and torsion whereas machine tool columns experience following :

(a) Bending in two perpendicular planes. The deflection due to bending of column is determined by analysing the column as a centilever fixed at the base.

(b) Shearing in two perpendicular planes.

(c) Torsion.

The effect of holes and apertures on the torsional stiffness of column should be taken into account. Machine tool bases are designed as plates on an elastic foundation. The dimensions are determined from the consideration that the maximum deflection due to load acting on plate should not exceed the specified limits. The machine tool rectangular tables are treated as rectangular plates of constant thickness. Cross rails, arms, arms should be designed for torsion and bending.

7.14. Slides and Slide Ways (Guide Ways)

A slide is a moving element providing a straight line movements to a workpiece or a tool holder at a controlled feed rate. A slide way gives accurate guiding constrains to the slide and may contain some form of adjustment to eliminate play between the two members as wear takes place. The following points should be considered while designing slide ways :

(i) Provision should be made for effective lubrication. Slide ways may be lubricated intermittently through grease or oil nipples, a suitable method where movements are frequent and speeds low or the slide ways may be lubricated continuously *e.g.* by pumping through a metering valve and pipe work to the point of application, the film of oil introduced between the surface must be extremely thin to avoid the floating of slide.

(ii) **Protection.** The slide ways should be maintained in good order. This is achieved as follows :

(a) By providing protective guards to prevent accidental damage.

(*b*) Possibility of chips getting entrapped should be minimum. It is desirable to have a form of slide ways which does not retain chips such as the inverted vee type.

(*iii*) **Accuracy.** The slide ways should be accurately manufactured so as to provide the accurate alignment under working load and to provide the required motion to slide smoothly. The required accuracy and finish of slide ways are obtained by suitable machining technique. The general tolerance for straightness of machine tool slide ways is 0—0.02 mm for 1000 mm.

(*iv*) **Deformation.** Deformation due to cutting forces should be minimum.

Grey cast iron is most commonly used materials for slide ways. It is employed when the slide ways are made integral part with the bed and correspondingly with the travelling units. The wear resistance of cast iron slide ways can be increased by surface hardening performed with flame or induction hardening. Steel slides are also used. They in the form of strips are either welded to a steel bed or they are secured by screws to a cast iron bed. Fig. 7.10 shows a lathe bed with hardened steel slides secured to the bed.

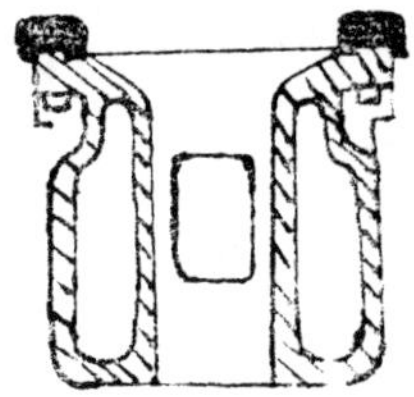

Fig. 7.10

The actual shape of the slide way depends upon the following factors :

(*a*) Load to be carried.

(*b*) Degree of accuracy required.

(*c*) Direction of cutting forces.

(*d*) Position of the element which is used for transmission.

(*e*) Type of machine.

The common types of slide ways are as follows :

(*a*) Flat slide way.　(*b*) Vee and flat slide way.

(*c*) Dovetail slide way.　(*d*) Roller slide way.

(*i*) **Flat slide ways.** Fig. 7.11 shows flat slide ways. They possess a larger load carrying capacity suitable for the larger type of machine. They provide a large areas of contact, thus wear is kept to a minimum. It is easier to manufacture such slide ways and the geometric feature of these slide ways can be easily checked. On the other hand they have the following disadvantages :

(*a*) They require devices for adjusting the clearances.

(*b*) They have tendency to accumulate dirt.

(*c*) They retain the lubricant comparatively poor.

(*ii*) **Vee and flat slide ways.** Vee ways are more difficult to manufacture than flat ways but are capable of self adjustment *i.e.* clearances are automatically eliminated under the action of load. It has no tendency to accumulate dirt. The drawback of the inverted vee type slide way is the lack of bearing surface which results in rapid wear.

For lathe bends both flat and inverted vee slide ways are commonly used. Fig. 7.12 shows a combination of vee and flat slide ways. It is simple to manufacture and is easily rescraped when wear has taken place.

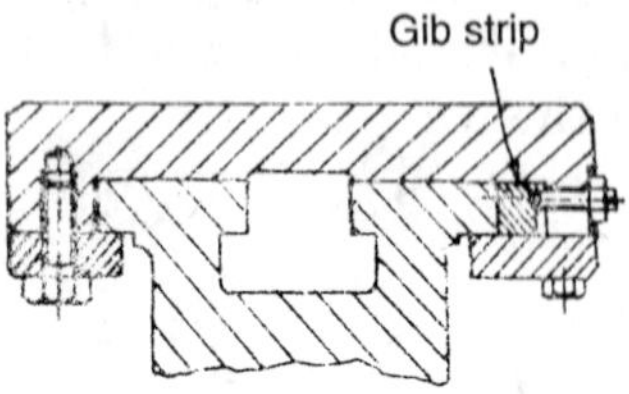

Flat slideway

Fig. 7.11

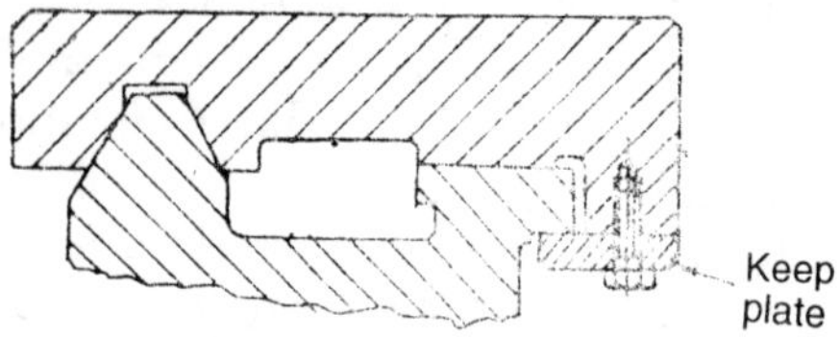

Vee & Flat Slideway

Fig. 7.12

(*iii*) **Dovetail slide ways.** They occupy small space. They are commonly used where the cutting forces tend to produce upward movement of slide thus causing vibrations. The gib strip can be adjusted so that the two elements of the slide are a good sliding fit. This type of slide ways are used in centre lathe cross slide and compound slide. (Fig. 7.13)

(*iv*) **Roller and ball slide ways.** In this system (Fig. 7.14) rollers retained in a brass cage interposed between the sliding members. This arrangement reduces the friction between the two members of the slide because rolling friction is substituted for sliding friction. Roller slide ways can be used to move heavy loads positively and accurately.

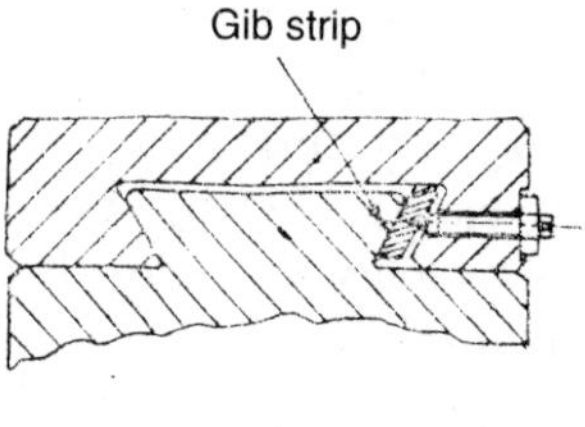

Dovetail slideway

Fig. 7.13

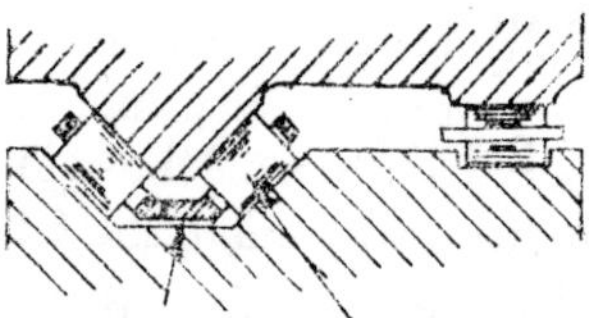

Fig. 7.14

Fig. 7.14 (*a*) shows ball slide ways in which steel balls are inserted between sliding surfaces.

They have the following positive features :

(*i*) Low friction (*ii*) High stiffness

(*iii*) Uniformity of motion (*iv*) High velocity of motion.

In these guide ways the contact of rolling elements with guide way surfaces occurs over a point or a line. It is therefore necessary that the guide way material has high contact strength to be able to transmit large loads through small contact area.

Both roller and ball slide ways are also called anti-friction slide ways (guide ways). Materials that are commonly used for making antifriction guide ways are as follows :

(*i*) spindle steel with HRC 60—62

(*ii*) low carbon structural steel case hardened to a depth of 0.8 to 1 mm.

7.14.1. Classification of guide ways

The various types of guide ways are classified as follows :

1. By kind of friction. Sliding, rolling, and combination types :

(*i*) Sliding and rolling guide ways. They are used in metal cutting tools. Their main features are :

(*a*) Long travels
(*b*) Wide speed ranges (from fine feed rates to considerable main motion)
(*c*) High accuracy.

(*ii*) Sliding guides :

(*a*) Sliding guides are used in metal forming machines and are subjected to great axial loads.
(*b*) Sliding guides are used for cross heads (slides) in piston-type engines with typically high speeds, elevated temperature and loads acting in a single plane.

(*iii*) Sliding and rolling guides used in instruments where loads are insignificant and accuracy requirements are quite essential.

2. By kind of motion

(*i*) Main motion (in the direction of cutting, operating at high speeds)

(*ii*) Feed motion (relatively low speeds)

(*iii*) Auxiliary motion (for positioning the units stationary in the process of machining).

3. By the path of motion

(*i*) Straight motion guide ways

(*ii*) Circular motion guide ways

(*iii*) Curvilinear motion guide ways

4. Location of path of motion in space

According to the location of path of motion in space guide ways are of following types :

(*i*) Horizontal

(*ii*) Vertical

(*iii*) Inclined.

5. Position features

(*i*) Guide ways made integral with machine frames, housings, or other components

(*ii*) Attached guide ways which may be fastened or abrasive bonded in the form of plates, strips etc. Attached guide ways of bronze, zinc alloys and plastics are used for work tables, slides and other shorter ways in heavy and N.C. machine tools.

(*iii*) Frame and column slide ways can also be coated with wear resistant materials such as

(*a*) a uniformly deposited hard chromium plating 25—50 micron thick HRC 68—72

(*b*) sprayed molybdenum coating HRC 65.

6. Geometric form

(*a*) Open type slide ways

(*b*) Closed type slide ways

7.14.2. Slide ways working conditions

Slide ways should be subjected to proper pressure, sliding velocities and lubrication.

(*i*) *Permissible pressure.* The maximum permissible pressure on feed motion ways with the most commonly used cast iron on cast iron sliding pair is as follows :

(*a*) 25 to 30 kg/cm^2 in medium size general purpose machine tools

(*b*) 10 to 15 kg/cm^2 in heavy machine tools

(*c*) 100 to 130 kg/cm^2 in the slides of heavy machines with a bronze on cast iron sliding pair.

(*ii*) *Sliding speed.* The sliding speed commonly used is as follows :

(*a*) up to 1.5 m/s in the main-motion slide ways of planing and shaping machines

(*b*) up to 10 m/s in vertical boring machines

(*c*) 0.1—0.3 m/min in feed motion slide ways.

(*iii*) *Wear rate.* Swarf abrasive grits, scales and other machining wastes drastically increase the wear rate and friction losses in slide ways.

(*iv*) *Lubricating oil temperature.* The working temperature of the lubricating oil is normally close to the room temperature.

7.14.3. Oil for slide ways

To reduce friction force in slide ways use should be made of slide way oils. The grade and viscosity are selected depending on the operating conditions such as

(*i*) Sliding speed

(*ii*) Pressure

(*iii*) Slide way protection against dirt

(*iv*) Motion uniformity

(*v*) Positioning accuracy requirements

(*vi*) Spatial arrangement of the slide ways

For slide ways substantially free from dirt and with scant lubrication, industrial oils of higher viscosity should be used. Greater loads and lower sliding speeds also call for oils of higher viscosity.

Where exposure of dirt is considerable and lubrication is meagre, the lower viscosity industrial oils should be used.

7.14.4. Friction in slide ways

In slide ways following three types of friction may take place

(*i*) Boundary friction

(*ii*) Fluid friction

(*iii*) Mixed (simultaneously boundary and fluid) friction.

The influence of various factors on friction in slide ways is as follows :

(*i*) *Pressure.* Pressure at very low speeds (less than 30 mm per minute) has little effect on coefficient of sliding friction. However at higher speeds coefficient of sliding friction rises with pressure since increased pressure impedes the development of the hydrodynamic pressure.

(*ii*) The viscosity of oil at every low speeds hardly affects coefficient of sliding friction. At higher speeds the increase in viscosity results in significantly reduced coefficient of sliding friction.

(*iii*) The frictional characteristics are substantially improved with the use of hydraulic relief method where by oil pressure takes up part of the external load.

The coefficient of static and sliding friction in uniformly loaded hydraulically relieved slide ways at speed less than 50 mm per minute is approximately determined as follows :

$$f_h = f\left(1 - \frac{P_h}{P}\right)$$

where f_h = Coeff. of friction for hydraulically relieved slide ways

f = Coefficient of friction under same conditions without hydraulic relief.

P_h = Hydraulic relief force

P = External load.

7.14.5. Accurate positioning of slide ways

Following means are used for improving the uniformity of motion and the accuracy of positioning of slide ways (guideways) :

(*i*) Change over to fluidfriction (hydro static) ways

(*ii*) Using proper lubricating oils

(*iii*) Use of rolling guides.

(*iv*) Application of slide ways relieved pressure (hydraulically, mechanically and pneumatically).

(*v*) Raising of the stiffness of the drives and gear trains.

(*vi*) Use of special high stiffness drive systems.

(*vii*) Use of damping devices in feed drives.

(*viii*) Improvement in quality of manufacture of slide ways and using proper materials for slide ways

(*ix*) Proper installation of machine tools.

7.14.6. Classification of rolling guides

Rolling guides are classified as follows :

(*i*) *By geometrical form*. The rolling guides are of two types :

(*a*) prismatic (*b*) cylindrical

(*ii*) *By the method of rolling*. Rolling guides may be

(*a*) without preloading

(*b*) partly preloading
(preload adjusted in a horizontal direction)

(*c*) fully preloaded.

Rolling guides without preloading are much simpler and cheaper in manufacture. Preloaded rolling guides are hardened and are designed for high stiffness and high tilting moments.

(*iii*) *Rolling guides with balls.* The ways are flat, prismatic or cylindrical in cross-section. They are suitable for smaller loads. They are made of hardened steels.

(*iv*) *Rolling guides with rollers.* They can take up high load. Their load carrying capacity is 20 to 30 times greater than that of ball type rolling guides of the same dimensions. The stiffness of these guides is about 2.5 to 3.5 times the stiffness of rolling guides with balls. In these guides made of hardened steel ways the length and diameter are related as follows

$$r = \frac{L}{D} = 1.5 \text{ to } 2$$

where L = Length of roller
D = Diameter of roller.

The force of friction becomes smaller with greater diameter of rolling elements and lower working load.

7.15. Requirements of Guide Ways

Requirements of a slide way are as follows :

(*i*) It should be strong

(*ii*) It should possess sufficient stiffness

(*iii*) There should be less wear

(*iv*) The pressure distribution should be uniform

(*v*) It should provide good guidance

(*vi*) There should be less friction.

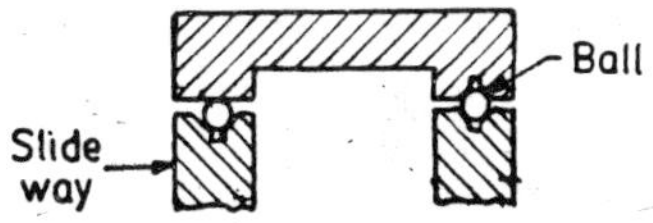

Fig. 7.14 (*a*)

7.15.1. Design criteria for slide ways

Slide ways are designed based on the following :

(*i*) *Wear resistance.* It is governed mainly by the maximum pressure acting on the mating surfaces. This condition may be expressed as

$$f_m \leq f_p$$

where f_m = Maximum pressure acting on mating surfaces

f_p = Permissible value of maximum pressure.

(*ii*) *Stiffness.* In this case the deflections of the cutting edge in directions that significantly influence the machining accuracy should not exceed the permissible deflection

$$\delta_m \leq \delta_p$$

where δ_m = Maximum deflection at the cutting edge

δ_p = Permissible deflection at the cutting edge.

Slide ways should be oiled from time to ensure their proper functioning.

The coefficient of friction between the sliding surfaces at a particular instant of time depends on the time period elapsed since the last oiling. Fig. 7.14 (*b*) shows the variation of coefficient of friction (μ) with times (*t*).

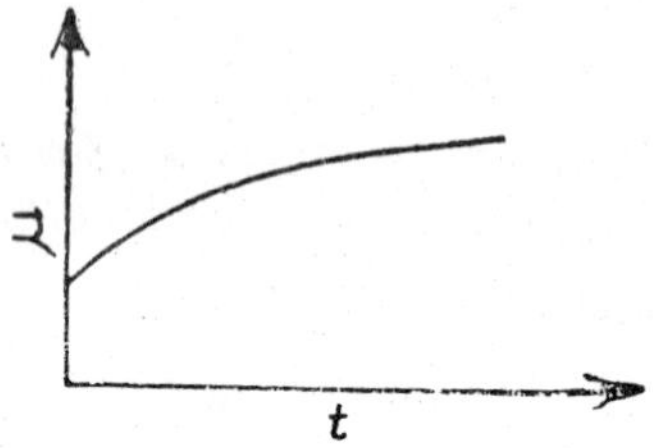

Fig. 7.14 (*b*)

7.15.2. Machine tool columns

Columns support spindle head and knee-table unit. The principal design requirements of columns are same as those of beds *i.e.* high static and dynamic stiffness. The columns are made of thin-walled circular or box sections. The number and size of holes and openings is kept as small as possible and the section is strengthened by means of stiffners. Generally the area of columns section gradually increases as we move from the top towards the base.

In general machine tool columns are subjected to following type of loads :

(*i*) Torsion

(*ii*) Bending in two perpendicular planes.

(*iii*) Shearing in two perpendicular planes.

The dimensions of the column cross-section should be such that the total deflection due to various loads is within permissible limits. The deflection due to bending of column is determined by analysing the column as a cantilever fixed at the base.

The deflection (δ) due to shearing of column is calculated as follows :

$$\delta = \frac{K.P.L.}{C.A.}$$

where P = Shearing force

L = Distance from base of the section where deformation is to be found

C = Shear modulus for material of column

A = Area of cross-section

K = Coefficient distribution of shearing displacement.

7.16. Materials of Beds and Guides

The materials used for beds, frames and guides should possess the following properties.

(*a*) Easy fabrication (*b*) Strength

(*c*) Damping capacity (*d*) Wear resistance.

The materials commonly used for machine tool structures (beds, frames etc.) are cast iron and steel.

Whether the structures should be made from cast iron or steel depends on the following factors :

(*i*) Material properties

(*a*) Strength—Steel has higher strength than cast iron.

(*b*) The unit rigidity of steel under tensile, torsional and bending loads is higher.

(*c*) Cast iron has higher inherent damping properties.

(*ii*) Manufacturing of structures :

(*a*) Welded structures made of steel can have much thinner walls as compared to cast structures.

(*b*) A welded structure can be easily repaired and improved whereas any corrections in a cast structure are much more difficult.

(*iii*) Economy—The cost of structure should be low. In welded structures cost of material, welding, machining, welding fixture etc. has to be considered and in cast structures, the cost of material, casting, machining pattern etc. has to be considered.

(a) It is observed that cast iron should be preferred for making complex and heavy structures and steel should be preferred for smaller sized structures.

(b) Combined welded and cast structures are becoming popular.

Slide ways are made of cast iron and low carbon of low alloyed steels. Grey cast iron is cheap but does not have good wear resistance. The wear resistance of grey cast iron slide ways (guide ways) can be considerably improved by proper heat treatment. The wear resistance of cast iron slide ways can be further improved by applying hard coatings such as chrome plating of slide way with a 25-50 micron layer provides a hardness of HRC 70 and this increases the life of slide ways considerably. Steel slide ways are manufactured separately and then attached to the bed.

Semi-steel with nickel and chromium is a suitable slide way material. The bed is flame hardened by heating the top surface above the critical temperature and then quenching in a moderate rate.

Sometimes plastic slides are also used and backed by cast iron or steel pieces. The various advantages of plastic guides are as follows :

(i) Low friction (ii) Less wear

(iii) Uniform pressure (iv) Easy fabrication.

However plastic guides have less strength and hardness and can be used for low speed-range.

Table 7.2 indicates the allowable maximum pressure (p) in sliding guides.

Table 7.2

Material	*Type of duty*	*y* *(kg/cm²)*
Steel	Low velocity lathes	30—40
Cast Iron	High velocity traverses	2—4
	Special purpose machines	5—7
	Planers	10
	Low velocity lathes and milling machines	26—30

7.17. Wear Resistance of Guides

Following factors are responsible for causing high rate of wear of slide ways :

(*i*) Uncovered slide ways : such slide ways will get worn out because of swarf, dirt etc.

(*ii*) Poor lubrication.

(*iii*) Frequent stops and reversal of work tables or tool slides.

(*iv*) Non-uniform use of slide ways along the length.

The period over which a machine tool can maintain its original accuracy depends on the wear resistance of guides. The wear resistance of guides depends on the following factors :

(*i*) Material and its hardness

(*ii*) Pressure on guides

(*iii*) Sliding velocity (*iv*) Surface finish

(*v*) Friction (*vi*) Lubrication.

Cast iron with a pearlitic structure is wear resistant besides having good mechanical properties. Inserted steel guides having hardness of about HRC 63 are being used widely. Plastic guides have also been introduced. Guides having accurate surface finish have more wear resistance. To reduce wear of guides the pressure over them should be uniformly distributed and the pressure should be within permissible limits. Friction should be minimum.

Friction and hence wear can be reduced by

(*i*) Lubrication of sliding surfaces

(*ii*) By using ball and roller guides

(*iii*) By protecting the guides from dust etc.

7.18. Life of Guide Ways

Life of guide ways should be more. Following methods help in increasing life of guide ways :

(*i*) By using proper material

(*ii*) By providing proper heat treatment

(*iii*) By using proper lubrication

(*iv*) By using proper configuration

(*v*) By providing proper clearance between guide ways and the parts sliding on it.

7.18. (*a*) Working Life of rolling guides

Rolling guides are finding ever increasing application in modern machinery and equipment. Rolling guides offer significant advantages such as

(*i*) Low friction force

(*ii*) Good positioning repeat ability on reversals

(*iii*) Accuracy maintained over time

(*iv*) Moderate lubrication requirements.

Rolling guides provide a very high uniformity of motion of machine components stick slip occurs only if pre load is excessive or the quality of rolling guides is poor. The accuracy of positioning of machine components in rolling guides defined by the deviation from the specified position amounts to 0.1—0.2 microns provided the drive is rigid enough.

Rolling guides are mainly because of the following reasons.

(*i*) *By mechanical impurities.* Metal chips getting into the guides disrupt contact between the mating parts and cause

(*a*) slip and jamming of the rollers.

(*b*) scores and brinelling of cast iron ways

Abrasives produce wear of ways and inadequate supply of coolant brings about considerable fretting wear.

(*ii*) *Slip of rolling bodies.* The slip of rolling elements results from the defects of the cage and from the use of small diameter rollers (needle rollers). Guides with rolling bodies in cages assume more uniform motion.

Rolling guides have long service life at small loads and at low speeds. For high speed and high load applications rolling guides should be back calculated for surface layer fatigue strength. Surface roughness has considerable effect on rolling guide performance. Better surface finish reduces friction and improves stiffness and wear resistance.

7.18. (*b*) Friction in Rolling guides

In rolling guides the force of friction is made up of two components as follows :

(*i*) Frictional force under no load

(*ii*) Frictional force proportional to load.

The frictional force under no load conditions results from the friction of rolling elements against the cage and from viscous friction associated with the lubricant.

The frictional force proportional to load is determined mainly by rolling friction as such and friction due to the difference in velocities at the contact.

$$F = \text{Friction force} = S + \frac{\mu}{r} \times N$$

where S = Initial friction force on one surface of guide (Kgf)

μ = Co-efficient of friction
= 0.001 for hardened steel ways
= 0.0025 for cast iron ways.
r = Radius of rolling element (cm)
N = Normal force on guide way surface (Kgf)

The friction force becomes smaller with greater diameter of rolling elements and lower working load (or preload).

Fig. 7.14 (*c*) shows variation of friction force (*F*) and normal force (*S*).

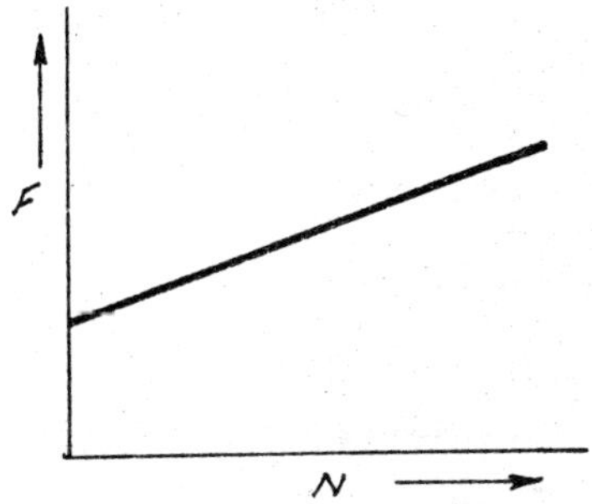

Fig. 7.14 (*c*)

The variation of friction force (*F*) and speed of motion (*V*) is indicated in Fig. 7.14 (*d*).

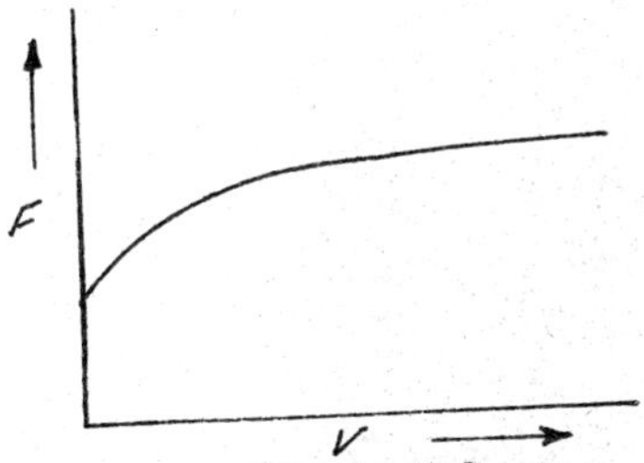

Fig. 7.14 (*d*)

7.18. (*c*) Methods of improving functioning of Slide ways

The service properties of slide ways can be improved by the following methods :

(*i*) To provide favourable frictional conditions :

This can be achieved as follows :

(*a*) Using hydrostatic ways with a high rigidity oil film.

(*b*) Using automatically controlled hydrostatic ways that ensure an extremely high rigidity of the film in the specified load range.

(c) Using lubricating system utilising both hydrostatic and hydrodynamic lift.
(d) Using combined sliding and rolling guides.
(e) Using proper lubricant.
(f) Using proper materials for slide ways.

(ii) To provide adequate protection to guide ways.
(iii) To use optimal cross-section of slide-ways.
(iv) To use optimal surface finishes.

7.18.1. Basic principles of design for rigidity

The operating properties of a machine tool depends on degree of rigidity of its individual units and parts. The rigidity of a mechanical element is defined as follows :

$$S = \text{Degree of rigidity or stiffness}$$

$$= \frac{\rho}{x} \text{ kg/mm}$$

where ρ = Load, kg

x = Extension (deformation), mm

$$S = \frac{A \cdot E}{L}$$

where A = Area of cross-section of the element, mm^2

L = Original length of element, mm

E = Modulus of elasticity, kg/mm^2.

Similarly, stiffness in torsion for a shaft subjected to twisting moment (T) is found as follows :

$$S_t = \text{Stiffness in torsion}$$

$$= \frac{T}{\theta} \text{ kg mm/radian} = \frac{G \cdot I}{L}$$

where G = Modulus of rigidity

I = Polar moment of inertia of shaft

θ = Angle of twist in shaft in radian.

Analysis for rigidity is particularly important for ensuring the adequate accuracy of components produced on the machine tools.

7.18.2. Basic principles of design for strength

While designing a machine tool elements for strength, the induced stresses in the machine tool elements should be compared with allowable stresses. The strength conditions is therefore as follows :

$$\sigma_1 \le \sigma \quad \text{or} \quad \tau_1 \le \tau$$

where σ_1 and τ_1 are induced tensile or compressive and induced shear stress respectively.

σ and τ are allowable tensile or compressive stress and shear stress respectively

$$\sigma = \frac{\sigma_y}{n} \quad \text{and} \quad \tau = \frac{\tau_y}{n}$$

where σ_y = Yield stress in tension or compression

τ_y = Yield stress in shear

n = Factor of safety.

7.18.3. Static and dynamic stiffness

A machine tool consists of a large number of elements and its behaviour is of interest in as much as it affects the parameters of machining and the quality of the machined surface.

It is desirable to examine the cumulative static and dynamic characteristics of the machine tool as well as the corresponding characteristics of individual elements of which the machine tool is made.

A machine tool consists of a large number of elements and these elements experience deformation during operation of the machine tool and therefore can be looked upon as elastic bodies (springs) with a certain stiffness (spring constant).

To analyse the behaviour of structures under static loading, two types of static stiffness may be considered :

(*i*) Static stiffness with respect to the work piece accuracy.

(*ii*) Static stiffness with respect to dynamic stability.

Dynamic stiffness will depend on the frequency of the applied force.

The stiffness of machine tool structures can be improved by using ribs and stiffners in proper arrangement.

7.18.4. Basic design procedure of machine tool structures

The common design strategy for machine tool structures is based on the following :

(*i*) Design for bending stiffness

(*ii*) Design for torsional stiffness

(*iii*) Strength due to bending and torsion.

While designing the following forces should be taken into account :

(*i*) Cutting force (*ii*) Friction force

(*iii*) Force of reaction

(*iv*) Forces due to mass of structures, workpiece fixtures and clamping devices

(*v*) Inertial forces due to vibrations.

While designing the following forces should be taken into account :

(*i*) Cutting force (*ii*) Friction force

(*iii*) Force of reaction

(*iv*) Forces due to mass of structures, workpiece fixtures and clamping devices

(*v*) Inertial forces due to vibrations.

7.19. Spindles and Bearings

Spindles. Machining accuracy depends to a considerable extent in many types of machine tools upon the rotational accuracy of the spindle which transmits motion to the cutting tool or to the work. Generally machine tool spindles are made up of alloy low carbon steel heat treated to give a case hardened surface. Such a spindle possesses resistance to wear combined with a tough core for strength in torsion. Where high precision spindles with maximum stability are required such as spindles for external grinding machines Nitralloy is used. Spindles of heavy machine tools are made of manganese steel with subsequent normalisation or hardening followed by high tempering. Spindles are made hollow with a tapered hole at the front end for receiving the centring element (spindle nose). In case of lathe spindle the external screw threads are cut at nose end to receive the chuck or face plate on it. Fig. 7.15 shows a spindle of lathe machine.

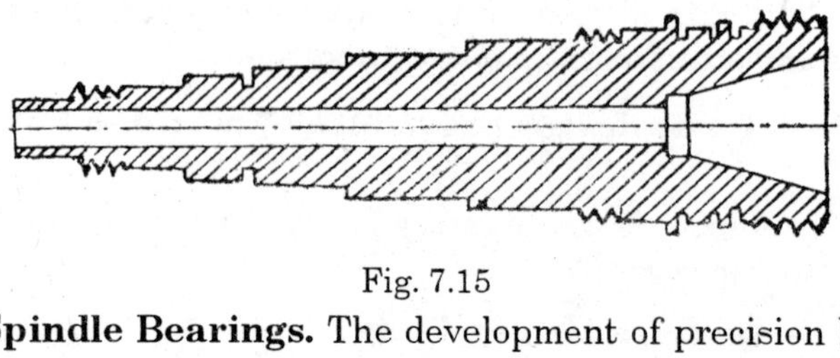

Fig. 7.15

Spindle Bearings. The development of precision bearings for machine tools is a pre-requisite for the development of precision machine tools. The geometrical accuracy and surface finish of a machined component depend largely on the quality of spindle bearings used in the machine tool. The necessity of maintaining an accurate and suitable location of the axis of the rotating spindle at any given speed and load has long been appreciated. Sustained efforts to realize this requirement in practice have resulted in the development of a number of different types of bearings.

The purpose of spindles is not merely that of transmitting power but in doing so without introducing vibrations which may affect the accuracy of the work. Whatever type of bearings are used, the spindles mounting must be rigid so that short stiff spindles should be the aim. If this is not attainable, then an extra bearing may be the solution. It is preferable that a spindle should be relieved of bending stresses and that the drive should be one of pure torque. For precision work, the machine tool spindle bearings must fulfil the following requirements :

(*i*) They should provide minimum deflection under varying loads.

(*ii*) They should provide maximum truth of running under loads of different magnitude and direction.

(*iii*) They should provide maximum temperature variation throughout the speed range.

(*iv*) They should possess adjustability to obtain minimum radial and axial slackness.

(*v*) They should provide simple and convenient assembly.

(*vi*) They should have sufficiently long service.

The spindle unit of a machine tool performs the following functions :

(*i*) To clamp the cutting tool or workpiece.

(*ii*) To centre the workpiece or cutting tool.

(*iii*) To impart rotary or rotary-cum-translatory motion to the cutting tool or workpiece.

Spindle unit should fulfill the following requirements :

(*i*) The spindle unit (spindle and spindle bearings) must have high static stiffness. Machining accuracy is influenced by bending, axial as well as torsional stiffness.

(*ii*) The spindle unit should have high dynamic stiffness.

(*iii*) The spindle should rotate with a high degree of accuracy.

(*iv*) The spindle unit should have a fixture which provides quick and reliable centering and clamping of cutting tool or workpiece.

(*v*) The spindle and spindle bearings should have sufficient wear resistance.

7.20. Materials of Spindles

In machine tool spindle design the critical design parameter is not strength but stiffness. Stiffness is primarily determined by the modulus of elasticity. Although strength of alloy steels is more than plain carbon steels but modulus of elasticity is more or less equal. Therefore costly alloy steels may not be used for making spindles. Following steels are recommended for making spindles :

(*i*) For normal accuracy spindles C 1045 steels, hardened and tempered to HRC 30.

(*ii*) For above normal accuracy spindles steel 5140 (AiSi).

HRC 50—55, induction hardened.

(*iii*) For spindles of precision machine tools.

Low alloyed steel 5120 (AiSi)

HRC 55—60 case hardened.

7.21. Lubrication of Bearings

Machine tool bearings are lubricated with mineral oils having a viscosity selected to suit conditions of operation such as :

(*i*) A light oil (low viscosity oil) for high speed bearings with a fine clearance fit between shaft and bearing.

(*ii*) A heavy oil (high viscosity oil) for heavily loaded low speed bearings.

The spindle oil should possess the following properties :

(*a*) It should be non-corrosive.

(*b*) It should not readily oxidise.

(*c*) It should have high cooling effect.

Depending on the conditions of operation a bearing may be run.

(*i*) Dry. (*ii*) Partially lubricated.

(*iii*) Fully lubricated.

When the bearing runs dry, a metal to metal contact exists and wear rate is quite high. The coefficient of friction lies between 0.15 to 0.4 according to the materials in contact. In partial lubrication the bearing elements are not completely separated by an oil film but some oil or grease is present. The coefficient of friction is generally between 0.02 to 0.1. In fully lubricating bearings the bearing surfaces are completely separated by an oil film. In such bearings friction is minimum and wear is almost eliminated.

7.22. Selection of Bearings

The various considerations in the selection of bearings are as follows :

(*i*) *Direction of load relative to bearing axis*. The various loads which a bearing may be required to meet are :

(*a*) Axial thrust. (*b*) Radial load.

(*c*) Combination of axial thrust and radial load.

(*ii*) *Intensity of loads*. Ball bearings can sustain considerable loads. Roller bearings with their line contact are preferred for severe conditions and shock loads.

(*iii*) Speed of rotation.

(*iv*) Thermal stability.

(*v*) *Shaft stiffness*. Rigid bearings are used for stiff well aligned shafts and self aligning bearings are used for shafts subjected to flexure or misalignment.

(*vi*) Class of accuracy of the machine.

7.23. Types of Bearings

Both sliding and rolling friction bearings are used in spindle supports.

The various types of bearings used are as follows :

1. Rolling bearings.

(*i*) Ball bearings.

(*ii*) Roller bearings.

2. Plain bearings.

7.24. Rolling Bearings

Fig. 7.16 shows a ball bearing whereas a cylindrical roller bearing is shown in Fig. 7.17 and a taper roller bearing is shown in Fig. 7.18. Taper roller bearings have a wide field of usefulness especially in connection with machine tool spindles, gear shafts etc. where high axial and radial forces are combined. One of the method

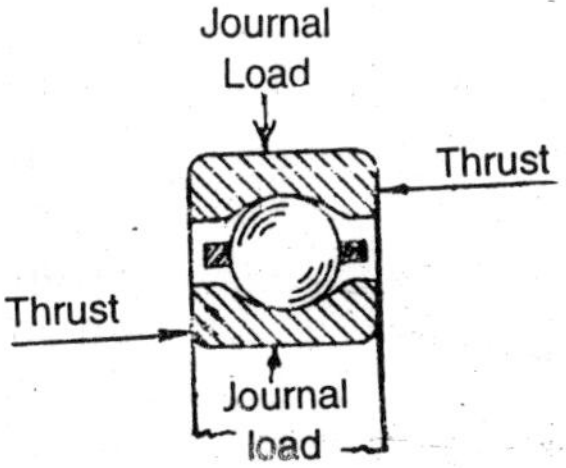

Fig. 7.16

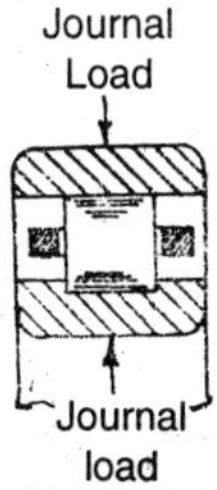

Fig. 7.17

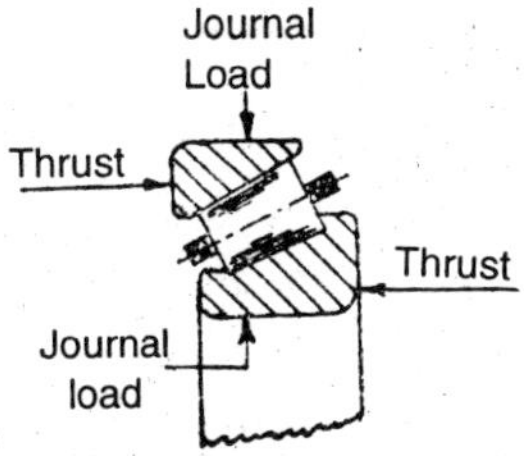

Fig. 7.18

of increasing the accuracy of ball or roller bearings in the spindle is preloading *i.e.* they are fitted with very slight interference fits which take up all radial play between the bearing and spindle leaving the only deflections to be those due to elastic stressing.

This eliminates the clearance between the bearing rings and the balls or rollers and in addition sets up elastic deformation that improves the total rigidity of the spindle unit. Angular contact ball bearings or tapered roller bearings installed in pairs are preloaded by adjustments made during assembly without the need of special devices.

The distinguishing features of anti-friction bearings (ball bearings and roller bearings) as compared to sliding bearings are as follows :

(*i*) Low starting resistance.

(*ii*) Low frictional moments and heat generation.

(*iii*) High load capacity per unit width of bearing.

(*iv*) Less consumption of lubricants.

(*v*) Easy maintenance.

Ball bearings are less proof to heating and permit larger speeds. They are less sensitive to small alignment errors. However ball bearings have higher load capacity. While choosing the type of antifriction bearings following factors should be considered.

(*i*) Radial and axial run out of spindle.

(*ii*) Radial and axial stiffness of spindle unit.

(*iii*) Heat generation.

(*iv*) Thermal deformation of spindle.

(*v*) Maximum permissible speed.

7.25. Plain Bearings

A plain bearing is formed when a shaft rotates in a bush, lines or the bore of a housing. The plain bearings are of the following types :

(*a*) Journal bearing.

(*b*) Thrust bearing.

(*c*) Combination of journal and thrust bearing.

Journal bearing is capable of carrying radial loads whereas the thrust bearing is capable of carrying axial load.

Fig. 7.19 shows the behaviour of a shaft (journal) in a plain bearing with the clearance. Space filled with oil and the load acting as shown, when the journal is at rest position the oil will drain from

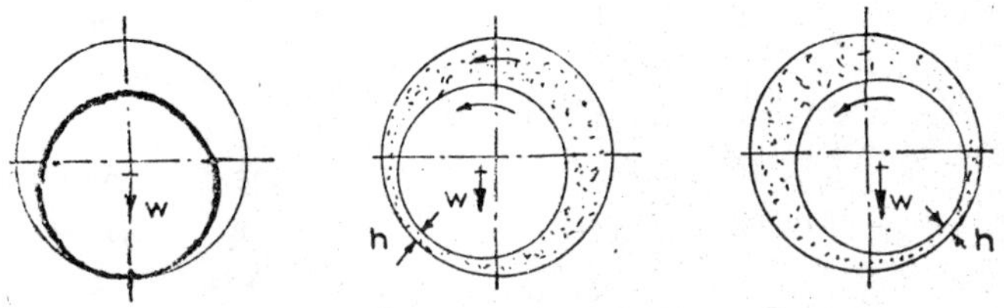

(a) (b) (c)

Fig. 7.19

the bearing leaving the shaft in metal to metal contact with the bearing as shown at Fig. 7.19 (*a*). As shaft starts to rotate, it rolls upto the left and a thin film of oil substitutes the metal to metal contact [Fig. 7.19 (*b*)]. As the speed increases the oil drawn under pressure through friction caused by shaft rotation forces the journal to the right and balances the external load Fig. 7.19 (*c*).

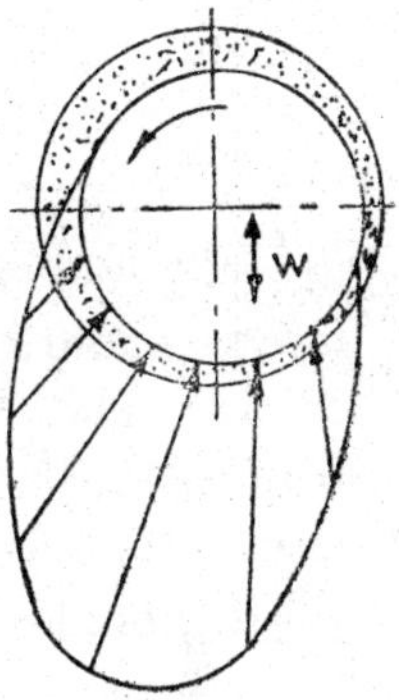

Fig. 7.20

The value of minimum film thickness (h) depends on load W. Higher is the load W, small will be the value of h. Fig. 7.20 shows relative magnitude of pressures normal to the surface of a plain bearing spindle.

7.25.1. Comparison of plain and rolling bearings

1. The frictional loss is greater in plain bearings than in rolling bearings.

2. Plain bearings are used where simplicity and cheapness is required, or where a high standard of precision is not essential.

3. Rolling bearings need reduced torque for starting from rest.

4. Rolling bearings are more reliable.

5. The rolling bearings can be easily lubricated.

6. Maintenance cost of rolling bearings is low.

7. Rolling bearing can be easily replaced.

7.26. Hydrostatic (externally pressurised) Bearings

These bearings have provisions for supplying oil from an external source at considerable pressure to several pockets in the bearings (Fig. 7.21). The oil flows out through the clearances between a shoulder of the spindle and the end of the bearing. Hydrostatic bearings can operate under fluid friction conditions even at the slowest speed of rotation such bearings are particularly suitable for applications involving heavy loads at low speeds.

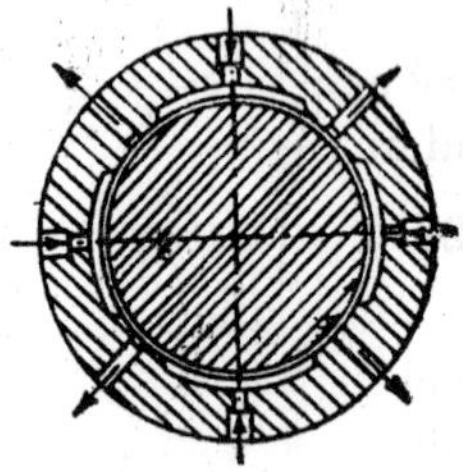

Fig. 7.21

7.27. Bearing Metals

Bearing metal should possess the following properties :

(*i*) It should have high compressive strength so that it can resist the bearing pressure.

(*ii*) It should have low coefficient of friction.

(*iii*) It should have high thermal conductivity so that heat produced due to friction is dissipated easily.

(*iv*) It should be able to resist the temperature without loosing strength.

(*v*) It should be *wear resistant.*

(*vi*) It should maintain a continuous oil film.

(*vii*) It should be able to embed in itself any dirt or grit present in lubricating oil.

(*viii*) It should be shock resistant.

The various bearing metals are classified as follows :

(*i*) Copper base bearing metals.

(*ii*) Tin base bearing metals.

(*iii*) Lead base bearing metals.

(*iv*) Cadmium base bearing metals.

Copper Base Bearing Metals. Copper base bearings metals contain copper 85% and tin 10% and the remaining is zinc and lead. These alloys are stronger and harder and are used for heavy loads.

Tin Base Bearing Metals. The most commonly used alloy is babbit metal which contains 85% tin, antimony 10% and copper 5%. It has low coefficient of friction and is used where bearings are subjected to higher pressure and load.

Lead Base Bearing Metal. It contains lead, tin, antimony and copper. Lead may be 10 to 30% and antimony 10 to 15%. Bearings of this metal are used for light loads.

Cadmium Base Bearing Metal. It contains cadmium 95%, very small amount of irridium. It has more compressive strength and has more favourable properties at higher temperature.

7.28. Power Units

The electric motor is universally adopted power unit for machine tool. There may be only one motor from which other movement are transmitted or there may be a main motor with separate drive motor for individual element such as a coolant pump motor or a feed movement motor. The basic lathe is shown in Fig. 7.3.

7.29. Transmission Element

They are used to transmit and control the essential movement from the motor. They include the drives to the spindle and the feed drives. They are of the following types :

(*a*) Mechanical

(*i*) Pulleys (*ii*) Belts
(*iii*) Screws and nuts (*iv*) Gears

(*b*) Hydraulic

(*c*) Pneumatic.

Slide movement is usually controlled by a lead screw and nut arrangement which may be hand driven or power driven.

7.30. Work Holding and Tool Holding Elements

Different machine tools use different types of work holding devices such as three or four jaw chucks are used on a lathe and vices in drilling and shaping machines. Tool holders are designed to suit a particular type of tool.

If the material of different parts of the machine tool has been correctly chosen with due regard for the operating conditions, and design calculations have been done with sufficient accuracy, such factors as *wear resistance* of the elements that primarily affect performance (ways, spindle journals in sleeve bearings, sleeve and antifriction spindle bearings, lead screws and nuts, etc.) will be less and a suitably long *service life* will be ensured.

7.31. Kinematics in Machine Tools

Kinematics is the branch of science related to position and movement. The kinematic functions to be performed by any machine tool are as follows :

(*i*) To transfer motion and power from the input shaft to the output spindle.

(*ii*) To transfer motion from rotation to translation or reciprocation or *vice versa*.

Such transformation of motions are obtained by a chain of higher pairs or lower pairs comprising the drive of machine tools.

Alignments are closely related to the kinematics of a machine both as regards straight line and accuracy of rotation about a fixed axes. The machine tool must be capable of maintaining it, alignment under conditions of (*i*) static loading and (*ii*) dynamic loading. A machine tool is fundamentally a mechanism which produces linear motion by slides and angular motion by spindles all accurately aligned relatively to each other.

7.32. Geometric Forms of Engineering Components

The components produced by machine tools are essentially combination of mainly the following geometric forms :

(*i*) Cylinder (*ii*) Cone

(*iii*) Sphere (*iv*) Flat surface

(*v*) Helical surface.

In order to produce these geometric forms on a machine tool surplus material must be cut away as chips or swarf. This requires that the machine tool be capable of reproducing controlled movements of workpiece or tool or both in such a way that the required geometrical spaces are obtained.

7.33. Methods of Production of Surfaces

The required machined surface is produced by forming or by generating or by a combination of these two fundamental methods.

The various methods of producing geometrical surfaces are as follows :

(*i*) Forming (*ii*) Generating

(*iii*) Copying (tracing) (*iv*) Tangent tracing.

A geometrical surface is usually defined as the trace obtained in the motion of one geometrical generating line called the generatrix and along other geometrical generating line called the directrix. A cone is an example of ruled surface where the generatrix rotates along a directrix with one of its end fixed at a point called vertex (Fig. 7.22).

The relative motion of the geometrical lines in producing surfaces are called formative motions. Real surfaces can be shaped on metals or other materials with the help of auxiliary bodies having auxiliary real surfaces, lines and points called auxiliary material elements.

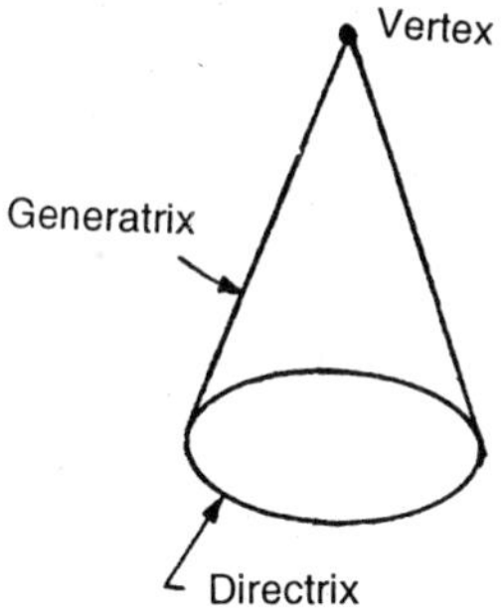

Fig. 7.22

In forming the shape of work produced is direct replica of the cutting tool. Milling of the teeth of a straight spur gear by an involute shaped cutter. Fig. 7.23 is an example of forming. In generating the surface produced is the locus or envelope of a large number of successive relative positions between the tool and the work. An example of this is the production of cylindrical shape on a lathe where the work is rotated and the tool movement is controlled so that the tool travels in a path parallel to the axis of the work producing a cylindrical shape (Fig. 7.24).

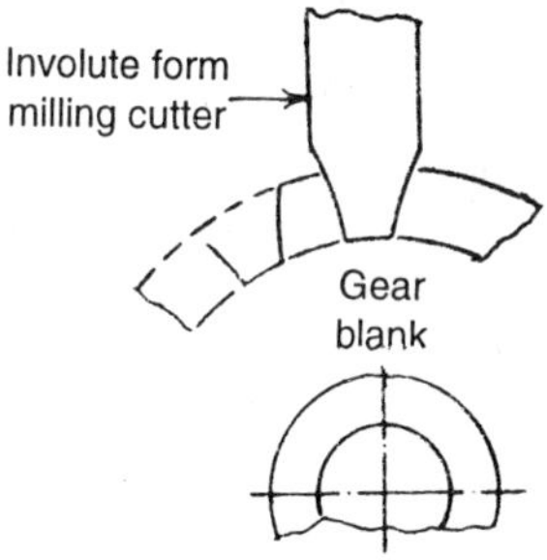

Forming

Fig. 7.23

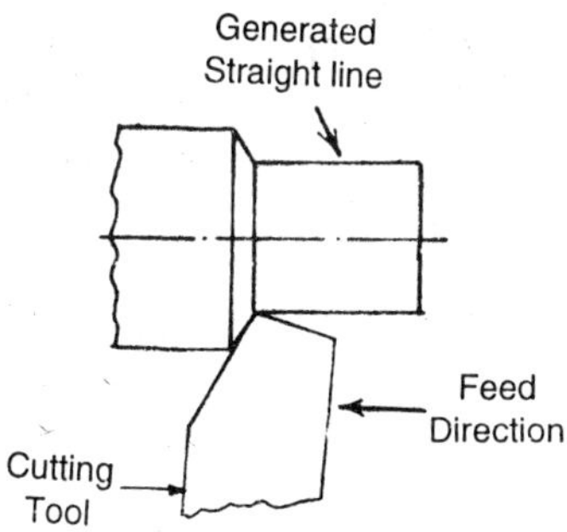

Generating

Fig. 7.24

The forming and generating principles are of importance in the kinematic design of machine. In a machine part requiring a linear motion the machine tool must produce a motion which is straight and in a definite relationship to the work and tools. Similarly for a part requiring an angular motion there must be rotation about a straight axis.

There is one more system called copying which is used for producing more complicated shapes, the shape of the work being a replica of a master component, or accurately made model or template.

In tracing the material point of auxiliary element (cutting tool) produces a line or path being formed as the trace left behind (Fig. 7.25). The tangent tracing is one in which the line being formed is tangent to a series of supplementary auxiliary lines produced by the material point (Fig. 7.26).

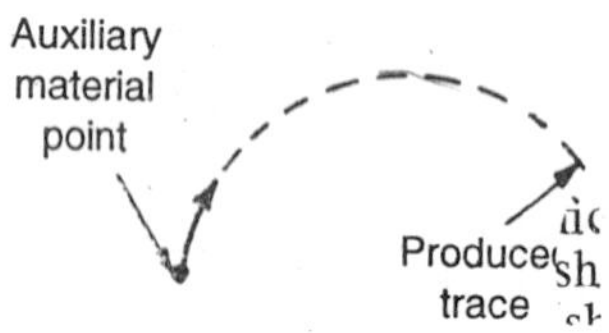

Fig. 7.25

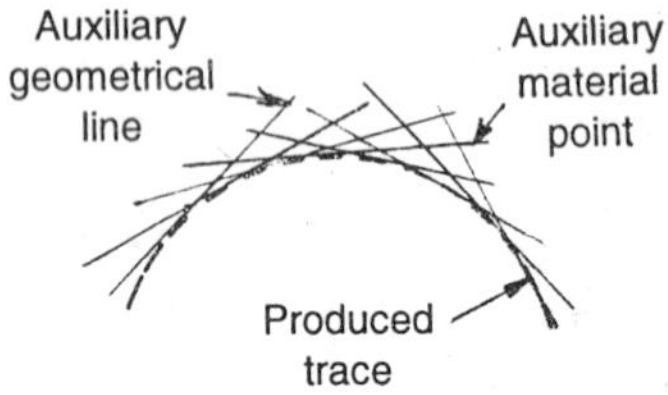

Fig. 7.26

Table 7.3 indicates the inter-relation between processing methods and methods of geometrically shaping the surfaces.

Table 7.3

Processing method	*Formative tool*	*Type of auxiliary element*	*Method of obtaining geometrical generating lines*		*Number of formative motions*
			Generatrix	*Directrix*	
Metal cutting (machining)	Cutting edge	Line or point	Tangent	Generating tangent or tracing	1 to 3
Casting	Foundry moulds	Surface	Forming	Forming	0
Gear hobb-ing	Hob	Line or point	Generation	Tracing	2
Blanking	Dies	Line	Forming	Tracing	1
Grinding	Grinding wheel	Line of point	Tangent	Generating tracing or tangent	2 or 3
Wire draw-ing	Die	Line	Forming	Tracing	1
Die forging	Dies	Surface	Forming	Forming	0
Rolling	Rolls	Line	Forming	Generating	1

7.34. Comparison of Forming and Generating

A profile on a component can be formed or generated.

Forming and generating are compared as follows :

(*i*) In forming the accuracy of work profile is entirely dependent upon the accuracy of the form tool profile whereas in generating the work profile is independent of the tool shape and tool cutting angles.

(*ii*) Form tools do not cut efficiently and long profile can cause chatter and poor surface finish. But long profiles can be easily generated with better surface finish.

(*iii*) It is easier to generate internal profile than to form it.

(*iv*) It is difficult to produce complex form tools and secondly they are expensive. Equipment used in generating is usually expensive in the first instance but proves to be economical on production work because of lower variable cost and higher quality of work.

(*v*) Tool should be set correctly both in forming and generating.

7.35. Degrees of Freedom

A body in space (Fig. 7.27) has six degrees of pure movement as follows :

(*i*) Linear movement along any one of the three conventional axes *XX*, *YY* or *ZZ*. Thus the body has three degrees of freedom by means of axial translation.

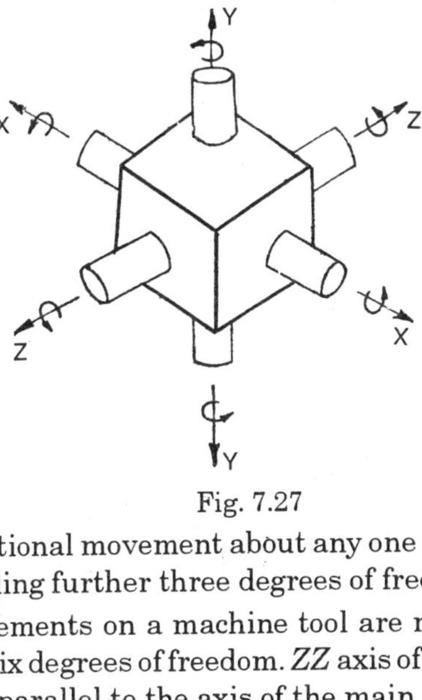

Fig. 7.27

(*ii*) Rotational movement about any one of the axes *XX*, *YY* or *ZZ* thus providing further three degrees of freedom.

All movements on a machine tool are made up from one or more or these six degrees of freedom. *ZZ* axis of motion on a machine tool is usually parallel to the axis of the main spindle. The *XX* axis is, if possible, arranged horizontally and parallel to the work holding surface. The *YY* axis obviously has to be mutually perpendicular to the other two axes.

A body will be constrained from movement by six locations suitability applied and which take into consideration kinematic principles. The removal of one location will then permit one degree of freedom, the removal of two locations will permit two degrees of freedom and so on.

7.36. Trends in the Development of Modern Machine Tools

A machine tool should have highest possible productive capacity under the condition that the necessary and adequate machining accuracy is ensured. To achieve this number of most essential special trends used in modern machine tools are as follows :

(*i*) The power of main drive is increased to increase the speeds of the cutting and feed motions in order to reduce machining time and to operate simultaneously a number of cutting tools.

(*ii*) More extensive systems of infinitely variable (stepless) speeds and feed are being applied enabling the optimum cutting conditions to be set up and changes as required without stopping the machine. This also reduces the machining time.

(*iii*) Machine tools are being equipped with a great variety of auxiliary devices whose aim is to reduce the part of the handling time. Some of such devices are as follows :

(*a*) Devices for facilitating blank loading and removal of the finished workpiece.
(*b*) Devices for quickly changing cutting tools.
(*c*) Machanized fixtures for rapidly changing the position of the work.

(*iv*) The static and dynamic rigidity of machine tools and their vibration proof properties are being increased.

(*v*) The working cycle is being automated to set up a positive working pace constant for the given set up for the purpose of reducing the handling time and to ensure required machining accuracy irrespective of the skill of the operator.

(*vi*) Multi-tool machine tools such as multi-tool lathes, multi-spindle drilling, milling and boring machines are being used.

(*vii*) Machine tool controls are being simplified mainly by automation of the working cycle.

(*viii*) There is a wide ever-increasing application of electrotechnic, electronics hydraulics and pneumatics for performing various functions.

7.36.1. General requirements of machine tool design

A machine tool should fulfill the following requirements :

(1) *High productivity.* It is achieved by following methods :

(*i*) By cutting down machining time

(*ii*) By cutting down non-productive time

(*iii*) Using automatic machines.

(2) *Accuracy.* Accuracy of producing components can be obtained by following methods :

(*i*) By using accurate guiding elements

(*ii*) By using short kinematic trains

(*iii*) By increasing static and dynamic stiffness of machine tool structure

(*iv*) By reducing thermal deformations during machining.

(3) Simplicity in design

(4) Safety and convenience of controls.

Safety of controls is achieved by taking following measures :

(*i*) Shielding the rotating and moving parts of machine tools

(*ii*) Providing reliable clamping devices for workpiece and tool

(*iii*) Providing devices for safe handling of heavy workpieces

(*iv*) Using reliable earthing of machine tool.

(5) Good appearance

(6) low cost of

(*a*) manufacturing

(*b*) operation

(7) Easier installation.

7.37. Maintenance of Machine Tool

Proper maintenance of machine tool helps to extract trouble-free service from it. Planned and timely maintenance helps to reduce the breakdown time of the machine tool thereby increasing its availability which ultimately results in better efficiency and higher productivity with the same capital investment and manpower. Time and money spent on planned maintenance will always pay high dividends. Hence the maintenance if carried out at right time in the right quantum at the right cost by the right personnel will go a long way in reducing the cost of production and increasing productivity.

The following steps can be taken to stiffen the assemblies of metal-cutting machinery under repair :

1. Spindle assembly with sliding bearings :

(*a*) ensuring regular geometric shape, accurate dimensions, and high quality of the spindle journal working surfaces and the bearing supporting surfaces ;

(*d*) replacing the spindle sliding bearings with preloaded antifriction bearings ;

(*c*) improving the accuracy and quality of machining the surfaces of the centre sockets and centres.

2. Headstock :

(*a*) mating thoroughly the headstock bearing surfaces to the bedways ;

(*b*) ensuring intimate mating of the end faces of the attachment bolt heads ;

(*c*) tightening the bolts adequately.

3. Carriage :

(*a*) fitting properly the machine guides, clamping straps and wedges ;

(*b*) adjusting the carriage screws and nuts ;

(*c*) installing a stronger carriage structure.

7.38. Machine Tool Efficiency

The efficiency of the machine tool depends on the energy lost due to friction. The horse power of machine tool should be higher than horse power required at the cutter.

Table 7.4 shows efficiency of the some types of machine tools.

Table 7.4

Type	*Efficiency (%)*
Direct drive spindle	90
One belt drive	85
Two belt drive	70
Geared head	70

7.39. Quality and Performance of a Machine Tool

The real criterion of a machine tool is the accuracy of the work, it produces over a long period.

The quality and performance of a machine tool depends upon the following factors :

(*i*) *The technical standard of design*. In developing a machine tool it is necessary to test the prototype thoroughly to ensure that the design meets the requirements aimed at.

(*ii*) *Materials*. The use of correct materials, proper manufacture of components and assembly are quite essential to get quality and proper output from the machine tool. Hardness of important parts like bed of the machine tool should be checked at different points of the guide ways to make sure that the hardness is uniform. Important parts should be stress relieved after rough machining.

(*iii*) *Inspection*. To maintain quality rigid inspection is required in all the stages. In sub-assembly all the units are assembled and tested before it is given for final assembly. During sub-assembly it is checked in every stage. After the machine is assembled, it is put to running test to check noise, heat, working accuracy and free movement of levers, etc. The tests should be conducted at stabilised temperature of the machine.

(*iv*) *Appearance*. The machine should be suitably painted. Painted surfaces should be uniformly bright. Sharp edges and projections on castings should be removed. Irregularities on surfaces should be covered. Parts like levers, screws and nuts which are liable to be tarnished by exposure should be electroplated.

(*v*) To produce a standard quality of machine tool there should be a code which should acts as a guideline to the manufacturer.

(*vi*) To produce good quality of machine tools, skilled labour should be used for the production of components and assembly unit.

Example 7.1. *Calculate breadth and length of guide way for a total load of 450 kg. The viscosity of lubricant is 0.015 kg sec/m^2 and slide is moving with a transverse rate of 3.5 m/min. The minimum film thickness is 0.01 mm. The permissible pressure is 1.8 kg/cm^2.*

Solution. The maximum possible load (P) that can be sustained by a guide is given by the relation,

$$P = \frac{0.133\, Z V B^3}{h^2}$$

where P = Maximum possible load in kg

Z = Absolute viscosity = 0.015 kg sec/m^2

V = Velocity of sliding = 3.5 m/min. $= \frac{35}{60}$ m/sec.

B = Breadth

h = Minimum film thickness = 0.01 mm

$= 0.01 \times 10^{-3}$ metre

$$450 = \frac{0.133 \times 0.015 \times 3.5 \times B^3}{(0.01 \times 10^{-3})^2}$$

$$B = 0.07 \text{ m} = 7 \text{ m}$$

$$A = \text{Area} = L \times B$$

$$L \times B = \frac{P}{p}$$

where p = Permissible pressure

$= 1.8 \text{ kg/cm}^3$

$$L \times B = \frac{450}{1.8}$$

Length, $$L = \frac{450}{1.8 \times B} = \frac{450}{1.8 \times 7} = 35.7 \text{ cm.}$$

Example 7.2. *Discuss the factors which help in achieving high productivity and high accuracy from machine tools.*

Solution. Following factors help in achieving high productivity :

(*i*) Cutting down machining time.

(*ii*) Cutting down non-productive time.

(*iii*) Machining with more than one tool simultaneously.

(*iv*) Using automatic machines, transfer lines and N.C. machine tools.

Machining time can be reduced by using high cutting speeds and feed rates. The application of stepless, mechanical, hydraulic and electrical drives also help in reducing machining time. Non-productive time can be reduced by using jigs and fixtures which help in reducing clamping and unclamping time.

Higher accuracy of components manufactured on machine tools can be achieved by following measures :

(*i*) Improving geometrical accuracy of machine tools. This is achieved by using accurate guide ways, power screws etc.

(*ii*) Improving the kinematic accuracy of machine tools.

(*iii*) Increasing static and dynamic stiffness of machine tool structures. Higher the static stiffness of machine tool structures, the smaller will be its deformation due to the cutting forces and hence higher will be the accuracy of machining. A high dynamic stiffness reduces the vibrations during machining and this helps in obtaining better accuracy.

(*iv*) Minimising the thermal deformation between the tool and workpiece during machining.

PROBLEMS

7.1. Define a machine tool. Classify the machine tools.

7.2. Explain the following for a machine tool :

(*a*) Primary cutting motion

(*b*) Feed motion.

7.3. What are the essential requirements of a machine tool ?

7.4. Name the basic features of a machine tool. Briefly explain any three.

7.5. Write short notes on the following :

(*a*) Selection of machine tools.

(*b*) Forces in a machine tool.

7.6. (*a*) What is a slide way ?

(*b*) What are the points to be considered while designing slide ways ?

(*c*) Name the materials commonly used for slide ways.

(*d*) Make neat sketches of three different forms of slide and slide ways. Briefly explain them.

7.7. Give three reasons why cast iron is the material mainly used for the production of machine beds.

7.8. Illustrate how a dovetail slide way system eliminates all degrees of freedom except one linear movement required for slide movement.

7.9. Describe the following types of bearings used in machine tool spindles :

(*i*) Ball and roller bearings.

(*ii*) Plain bearings.

(*iii*) Hydrostatic bearings.

7.10. Write short notes on the following :

(*a*) Lubrication of bearings. (*b*) Selection of bearings.

(*c*) Bearing materials. (*d*) Maintenance of machine tools.

(*e*) Stiffness and rigidity of machine tool.

(*f*) Wear resistance of guides.

7.11. What are the advantages and disadvantages of plain and rolling bearings ?

7.12. What are kinematics of a machine tool ?

7.13. Write short notes on the following :

(*a*) Generating, forming and copying.

(*b*) Degree of freedom.

7.14. Write a note on "The Trends in the Development of Modern Machine Tools".

7.15. Why box section is more suitable for beds of machine tools ?

7.16. Prove that compliance (*c*) of a centre lathe is given by

$$C = \frac{1}{S_2} + \frac{1}{S_1}\left(\frac{L-x}{L}\right)^2 + \frac{1}{S_3}\left(\frac{x}{L}\right)^2$$

where S_2 = Rigidity of saddle
S_1 = Rigidity of head stock
S_3 = Rigidity of tail stock
L = Length of workpiece
x = Distance of cutting tool tip from head stock end.

7.17. Write short notes on the following :

(*a*) Process capability of a machine tool.
(*b*) Compliance of a machine tool.
(*c*) Types of forces in a machine tool.
(*d*) Spindle unit functions and requirements.

7.18. Discuss the basic objectives of a machine tool.

7.19. Write short notes on the following :

(*a*) Productivity of a machine tool
(*b*) Precision
(*c*) Productive time
(*d*) General requirements of machine tool design.

7.20. Discuss the design criteria for slide ways.

7.21. Describe the design procedure for machine tool structures.

7.22. Describe the following for a machine tool :

(*i*) Column of a machine tools
(*ii*) Spindle of machine tool.

7.23. Write short note on :

(*i*) Control systems of machine tool
(*ii*) Safety and convenience of controls
(*iii*) Static and dynamic stiffness of machine tools
(*iv*) Design criteria of machine tool structures.

7.24. Discuss general requirements of machine tool design.

7.25. Write short notes on the following :

(*a*) Working life of rolling guides
(*b*) Friction in rolling guides
(*c*) Methods of improving the functioning of slide ways.

8

Kinematic Drives of Machine Tools

8.1. Drive

Machine tool drives are used to transmit motion from power source to the operative element of the machine tool. The general requirement for the machine tool drives is that they should have provision for regulating the speed of travel of the operative elements. The regulation may be in discrete steps or it may be stepless *i.e.* continuous. The former are called stepped drives and latter are called stepless drives.

The transmission systems for cutting and feed motions constitute drive and are obtained by a chain of higher pairs. Machine tool drives can be classified according to :

(*i*) Source of power.

(*ii*) Transmission system.

(*iii*) Nature of motion produced.

The machine tools are universally driven by electric motors and further transmission is obtained by any of the following methods :

(*a*) Mechanical drives using belts, gear trains, chains, lead screw and nut etc.

(*b*) Hydraulic drive.

(*c*) Electrical drive.

In mechanical drives the transmission of motion from external source to the operative element can take place through mechanical elements such as gears, belts, chains etc. Mechanical drives may be of stepless type or stepped type but hydraulic drives and electrical drives are invariably stepless in nature.

Mechanical transmission is used for transmitting rotary as well as translatory motion to the operative element. Hydraulic transmission is used in machine tools for providing rotary as well as translatory motion, although the latter application is more common. Hydraulic transmission, as a rule, provides stepless regulation of speed and feed rate.

Machine tool drive basically consists of the following :

(*i*) an electric motor.

(*ii*) a transmission arrangement.

Selection of drives depend upon the following factors :

(*i*) Surface finish and accuracy desired.

(*ii*) Production time.

(*iii*) Simplicity of design with respect to maintenance, repair and control.

(*iv*) Power to weight ratio.

(*v*) Optimum efficiency.

8.1.1. Individual drive and group drive

Each machine tool may be driven individually by its own motor called Individual drive or may be driven by a belt from a line shaft called Group drive which supplies power to other machine tools also. Further transmission is either mechanical (belts, gears, etc.) electrical or hydraulics.

Group drive is more economical in fixed charges, power consumption and maintenance. The main draw-back of group drive is that in case of breakdown all machine tools in the group become idle. Further in group drive layout of machine tools is controlled by the position of line shaft. Individual drive has the following advantages :

(*i*) Layout is simple and better utilisation of floor space is achieved.

(*ii*) Cleanliness and lighting of shop are improved.

(*iii*) Machine tools requiring wide variations in speed can be run efficiently.

Modern practice favours the use of individual drive. Machine tool drives may be classified as follows :

(*i*) *Main drive.* It is responsible for carrying out major machining operation like cutting, forming etc. Adjustable speed is the desirable feature of this drive.

(*ii*) *Feed drive.* It is used to feed the tool into work piece and *vice versa.*

(*iii*) *Transverse drive.* It is used for positioning the tool with respect to work.

Choice between group drive and individual drive depends upon the following factors :

(*i*) Initial cost.

(*ii*) Operating cost.

(*iii*) Machine tool requirement.

8.1.2. Electric motors for machine tool drives

The majority of the machine tool drives are made suitable for operation on standard 3 phase 50 cycle 400/440 volts, A.C. supply. Selection of electric motors depend on the following factors :

(*i*) The capacity of motor.

(*ii*) The power supply such as A.C. or D.C.

(*iii*) The electrical characteristics of motors such as starting characteristics, running characteristics and speed control.

(*iv*) Mechanical features like mounting enclosures transformation of drive, noise level; type of cooling.

(*v*) Cost.

(*vi*) The motor should be capable of delivering load, torque requirements and temperature rise of the motor should be within safe value.

(*vii*) Overload capacity.

Squirrel cage induction motors are the most popular choice due to their simplicity robustness and low cost. They can be made available with a wide variety of operating characteristics. In general speed regulation is good. A.C. commutator motors have infinitely variable speed over a wide range but their cost is high. D.C. machines are used where wide range of speed variation is required. D.C. shunt motors with field and/or armature control are very commonly used on main drives of machine tools. For traverse drives D.C. series or compound wound motors are preferred.

Following types (Table 8.1) of electric motors are recommended for machine tools of different types.

Table 8.1

Machine Tool	*Type of Motor*
1. Lathe	
(*a*) Main drive and feed drive	(*i*) Multispeed squirrel cage
	(*ii*) Adjustable speed D.C. motor
(*b*) Traverse drive	(*i*) D.C. series
	(*ii*) High slip squirrel cage motor
2. Shapers, slotters	(*i*) Constant speed squirrel cage motor
3. Planers	(*i*) Multispeed squirrel cage
	(*ii*) D.C. adjustable voltage
4. Drilling machines	(*i*) Constant speed squirrel cage motor
	(*ii*) D.C. shunt motor
5. Milling machine	(*i*) Squirrel cage
	(*ii*) D.C. shunt
6. Presses, forging machines	(*i*) High slip squirrel cage
	(*ii*) D.C. compound wound
7. Power saw	Constant speed squirrel cage.
8. Grinder	
(*a*) Wheel	(*i*) Constant speed squirrel cage
	(*ii*) Adjustable speed D.C.
(*b*) Traverse	(*i*) Constant speed squirrel cage

The power rating of the electric motor for a general purpose machine tool is calculated as follows :

$$P_m = \frac{P_C}{\eta} \text{ kW}$$

where P_m = Power rating of electric motor in kW

P_C = Total power required for removing metal, kW

η = Coefficient of efficiency of the drive.

The value of P_C is found as follows :

$$P_C = \frac{F_Z \cdot V}{6120} \text{ kW}$$

where F_Z = Cutting force in kg

V = Cutting speed in m/min.

The value of η is found as follows :

$$\eta = \eta_1, \eta_2, \eta_3, \ldots\ldots, \eta_r$$

where $\eta_1, \eta_2, \eta_3, \ldots, \eta_r$ are the coefficient of efficiency of the individual transmissions involved in transmitting motion from the motor to the operative element.

Table 8.2 indicates the values of coefficient of efficiency for various transmission systems.

Table 8.2

Transmission System	*Coefficient of efficiency*
Ball or roller bearing	0.99
Spur gear drive	0.98
Helical gear drive	0.97
Bevel gear drive	0.96
Belt drive with flat belt	0.98
Belt drive with V belt	0.96

8.2. Strength and Power of Machine Tools

The power capacity of a machine tool depends on strength and rigidity of machine tool. A heavy machine tool uses a high power motor whereas a light machine tool is equipped with a small motor. The electric motor power should be more than that required at the cutting zone. There should be minimum loss of power.

The specific power is the value of required for per cubic centimetre per minute of stock removal. It depends on the following factors :

(*i*) work piece material

(*ii*) type of operation

(*iii*) rake angle of cutting tool

(*iv*) size of cut and speed.

Table 8.3 indicates specific power or average values of kW per cubic centimetre per minute of stock removal for some of the materials for different machining operations.

Table 8.3

Workpiece material	*Machining Operations*			
	Turning	*Shaping*	*Drilling*	*Milling*
Steel (medium)	0.07	0.07	0.08	0.09
Cast iron (soft)	0.015	0.02	0.03	0.04
Aluminium	0.01	0.15	0.025	0.03
Brass	0.01	0.01	0.025	0.035

8.3. Machine Tool Spindle Speeds

To machine work of any diameter D at a cutting speed V, the spindle speed is given by

$$N = \frac{1000\,V}{\pi D} \text{ R.P.M.}$$

where D is in mm and V is in metre per minute. Since the cutting speed is taken constant for a particular work tool pair, the spindle speed must vary as the work diameter changes. The spindle speeds can be obtained by two types of drives :

(*i*) Stepped drive.

(*ii*) Stepless drive.

In stepped drive the output spindle speeds are obtained in a fixed number through single or multiple stages. Whereas in stepless drives infinitely variations of output speeds over a certain range can be obtained in single or multiple stages.

Fig. 8.1 shows the stepped drive with three steps output in single stage whereas Fig. 8.2 shows stepless output in single stage with infinite steps.

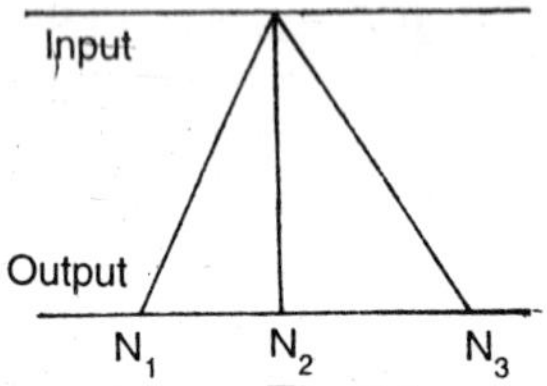

Fig. 8.1

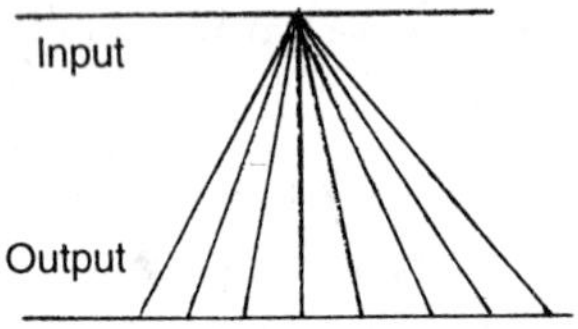

Fig. 8.2

In a stepped drive the following factors should be decided first :

(*i*) Maximum spindle speed (N_{max}).

(*ii*) Minimum spindle speed (N_{min}).

(*iii*) Number of spindle speed steps (n).

(*iv*) The number of stages in which the steps are to be obtained.

The extreme values of spindle speeds can be determined for machine tools if the extreme diameters to be cut are known and also maximum and minimum cutting speeds have been established for the given diameter

D_{max} = Maximum diameter of workpiece

D_{min} = Minimum diameter of workpiece

V_{max} = Maximum cutting speed.

V_{min} = Minimum cutting speed.

R_n = Range ratio of spindle speeds = N_{max}/N_{min}

Now, $$N_{max} = \frac{1000\ V_{max}}{\pi D_{min}}$$

$$N_{min} = \frac{1000\ V_{min}}{\pi D_{max}}.$$

Therefore the minimum spindle speed is dependent upon the maximum diameter of work that can be accommodated and on the minimum cutting speed

$$R_n = \frac{N_{max}}{N_{min}} = \frac{1000\ V_{max}}{\pi D_{min}} \times \frac{\pi D_{max}}{1000\ V_{min}}$$

$$= \frac{V_{max}\ D_{max}}{V_{min}\ D_{min}} = R_v\ R_d$$

where $R_v = \dfrac{V_{max}}{V_{min}}$ and $R_d = \dfrac{D_{max}}{D_{min}}$.

R_v is called ratio of cutting speeds and R_d is called ratio of workpiece diameters. The recommended values of range ratio (R_n) for some of the machine tools are indicated in Table 8.4.

Table 8.4

Machine Tool	R_n
Grinding machines	1—10
Shaper, planer, slotter	10
Automatic lathes	8—10
Drilling machines	20—30
Milling machines	30—50
Centre lathe	40—60

Spindle speeds generally form a series which may be any one of the following types :

(*i*) Arithmetical progression (A.P.)

(*ii*) Geometrical progression (G.P.)

(*iii*) Logarithmic progression (L.P.)

If spindle speeds were in arithmetic progression, the steps between on spindle speed and the next would be too far apart at low speeds and too close together at high speeds whereas spindle speeds in geometric progression provide a more even range of cutting speeds at each step as illustrated below.

Let the range of n spindle speeds be $N_1, N_2, N_3 \ldots N_n$ where N_1 is the minimum spindle speed and N_n is the maximum spindle speed. For any given spindle speed a change in work diameter will produce a proportionate change in cutting velocity. Let the cutting velocity limits be V_{max} and V_{min}.

$$\text{At } N_1, \text{ Max. diameter of work} = \frac{1000\, V_{max}}{\pi N_1}$$

$$\text{Min. diameter of work} = \frac{1000\, V_{min}}{\pi N_1}$$

$$\text{At } N_2, \text{ Max. diameter of work} = \frac{1000\, V_{max}}{\pi N_2}$$

$$\text{Min. diameter of work} = \frac{1000\, V_{min}}{\pi N_2}$$

$$\text{At } N_3, \text{ Max. diameter of work} = \frac{1000\, V_{max}}{\pi N_3}$$

$$\text{Min. diameter of work} = \frac{1000\, V_{min}}{\pi N_3}.$$

Now for constant cutting velocity, minimum diameter at N_1 R.P.M. will be same as the max. diameter as N_2 R.P.M.

$$\frac{1000\, V_{min}}{\pi N_1} = \frac{1000\, V_{max}}{\pi N_2} \text{ and so as}$$

$$\frac{V_{max}}{V_{min}} = \frac{N_2}{N_1} = \text{constant ratio} = \frac{N_3}{N_2} = \frac{N_4}{N_3} \cdots \frac{N_n}{N_{n-1}}.$$

This is a series in geometric progression. Therefore, the spindle speeds are arranged in geometrical progression.

Let ϕ = constant ratio or common ratio

$$\phi^{n-1} = \frac{N_2}{N_1} \times \frac{N_3}{N_2} \times \frac{N_4}{N_3} \cdots\cdots \frac{N^n}{N^{n-1}} \qquad \ldots(1)$$

$$\phi = \sqrt[n-1]{\frac{N_n}{N_1}} = \sqrt[n-1]{R_n}$$

where R_n is the range ratio of spindle speed variation.

For a G.P. the useful value of ϕ lies between 1 and 2, *i.e.* $1 < \phi \leq 2$. In the great majority of general purpose machine tools with. stepped speed variation the commonly used values of ϕ are 1.12, 1.26, 1.41, 1.58, 1.78, or 2.

These numbers belong to Renard Series and are known as Preferred Numbers.

8.4. Ray Diagram

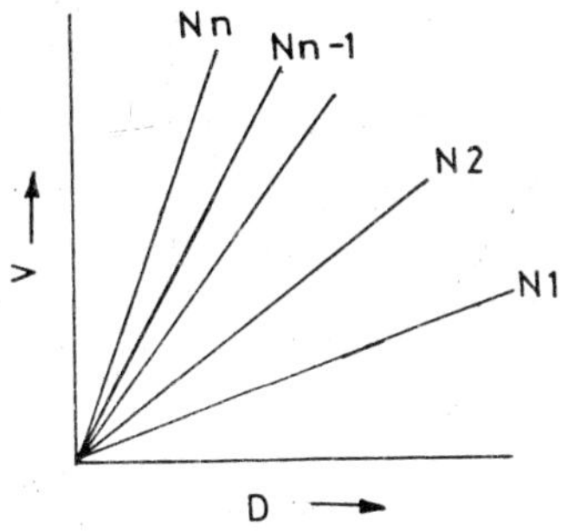

Fig. 8.3. Ray diagram.

For constant speed N the relation between cutting speed V and work diameter D is a straight line. Graphically the relation between V, D and N is represented by Ray Diagram shown in Fig. 8.3.

8.5. Speed Spectrum

The maximum and minimum values of cutting speed (V) in a machine tool is decided by the following two factors :

(*i*) Minimum life of cutting tool for maximum velocity (V_{max}).

(*ii*) Lowest economically justifiable velocity (V_{min}),

$$V = \frac{\pi DN}{1000} \text{ m/min.}$$

where D = work dia. in mm

N = R.P.M.

For a constant value N

$$V \propto D.$$

This gives a straight line graph. As shown in Fig. 8.4, the maximum diameter that can be machined at N_1 revolution per minute should not be more than D_1 and should not be less than D_2. If diameter becomes less than D_2, then the maximum and economical velocity is N_2, where $N_2 > N_1$ and so on. This is shown in speed spectrum for geometric progression in Fig. 8.4. The speed spectrum

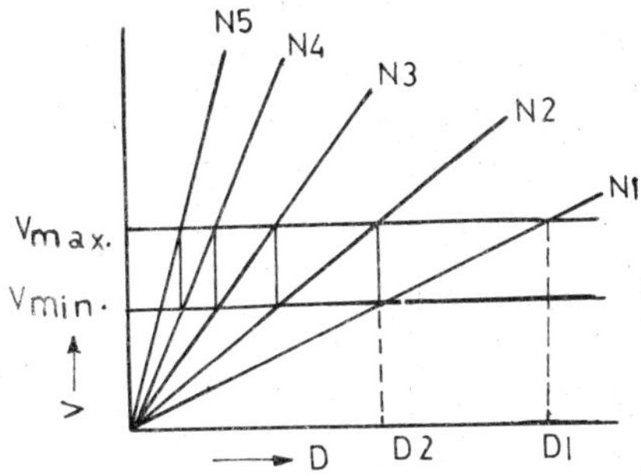

Fig. 8.4. Speed spectrum in geometric progression.

shows that speed loss is constant at all diameters and there is less crowding at higher speeds. N_5 is greater than N_4, N_4 is greater than N_3 and so on.

If the spindle speeds were arranged in arithmetic progression, the speed spectrum will be as shown in Fig. 8.5. In this case it is observed that speed loss becomes a function of diameter and is larger at lower speeds. It is further observed that there is considerable crowding of speeds at higher speeds.

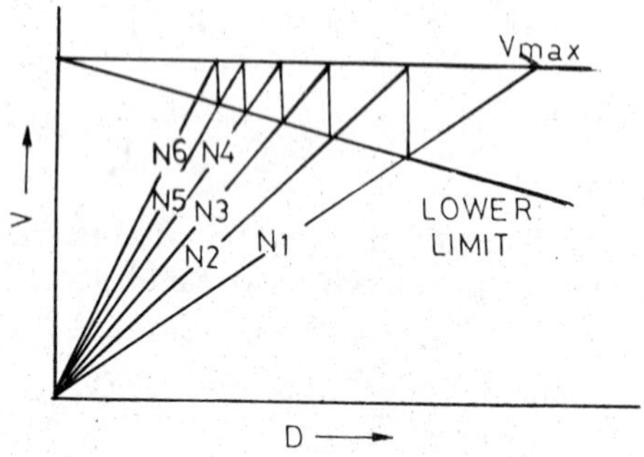

Fig. 8.5. Speed spectrum in Arithmetic progression.

8.6. Standard Values of Common Ratio

The adoption of standardised spindle speeds is of considerable help in production engineering. Standard value of ϕ have been established for standard series of spindle speeds. Generally a series is chosen such that after p number of terms, each figure is doubled and after y number of terms another figure becomes 10 times as shown in Fig. 8.6.

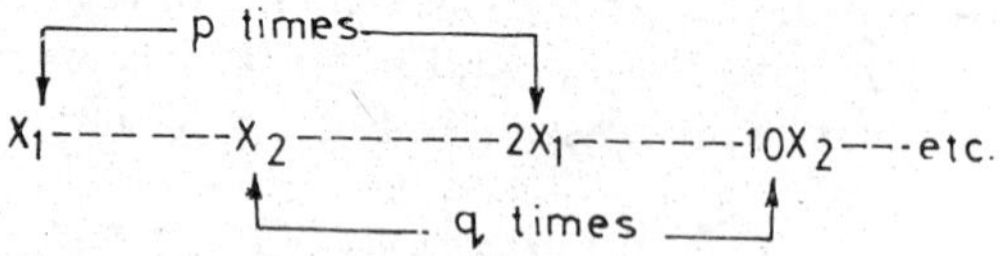

Fig. 8.6

$$\therefore \quad 2x_1 = x_1.\phi^p$$

$$10x_2 = x_2.\phi^q$$

From (1) $\phi = \sqrt[p]{2}$

From (2) $\phi = \sqrt[q]{10}$

or $\phi = \sqrt[p]{2}$

$$\phi = \sqrt[q]{10}$$

Solving this equation the standard values of ϕ are

$$\phi_1 = \sqrt[1.5]{2} = \sqrt[5]{10} = 1.6 \quad \phi_2 = \sqrt[3]{2} = \sqrt[10]{10} = 1.26$$

$$\phi_3 = \sqrt[6]{2} = \sqrt[20]{10} = 1.12 \quad \phi_4 = \sqrt[12]{12} = \sqrt[40]{10} = 1.06.$$

Table 8.5 indicates the typical values of common ratio (ϕ) for some of the machine tools.

Table 8.5

Machine Tool	ϕ
(*i*) General purpose machine tools	
(*a*) Large	1.26
(*b*) Medium	1.41
(*c*) Small.	1.58
(*ii*) Heavy duty machine tools and automats	1.12

8.7. Number of Spindle Speed Steps

It is good practice to select a number of speed steps (n) having the factors 2 and 3 so that $n = 2 A_1 3A_2$ where A_1 and A_2 are whole numbers. This requirement is met by the values n = 2, 3, 4, 6, 8, 9, 12, 16, 18, 24, 27, 32, 36.

The most frequently used values are

n = 3, 4, 6, 8, 12, 18 and

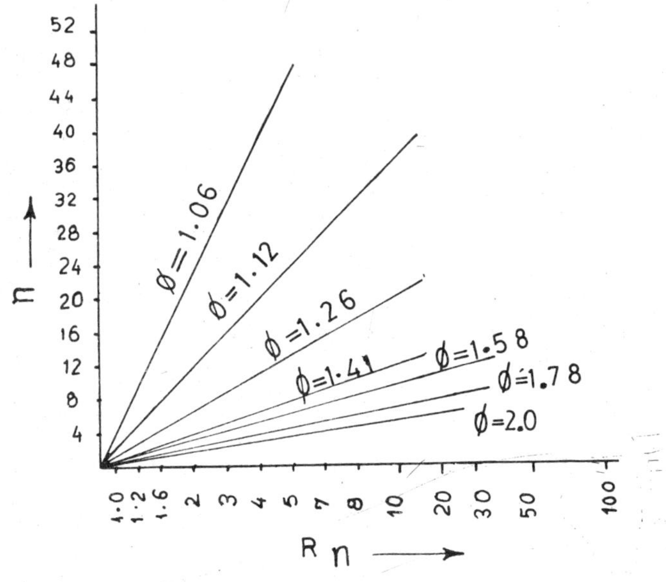

Fig. 8.7

The number of spindle speed steps are obtained by cluster of gears comprising 1, 2 or 3 gears or by pulley blocks of 2, 3 or 4 pulleys.

The number of spindle speed steps (n) is related to the range ratio R_n and common ratio ϕ by the following expression :

$$n = 1 + \frac{\log R_n}{\log \phi} = \frac{\log (R_n \phi)}{\log \phi}$$

The value of n calculated from the above formula is rounded off to a whole number after which the range ratio variation R_n is correspondingly changed.

Fig. 8.7 shows the relationship between speed range ratio (R_n), number of speed steps (n) and common ratio (ϕ) of the speed series.

The value of R_n and n depends upon the following factors :

(*i*) Purpose of the machines tools.

(*ii*) Nature of the manufacturing process.

(*iii*) Type of cutting tools to be used.

(*iv*) Required degree of versatility of the machine tool.

(*v*) Properties of work piece material.

8.8. Principle Kinematic Relationship in the Spindle Drive

The kinematic chain of transmission in the spindle drive should provide a gradation of spindle speeds in a geometrical series with the selected progression ratio ϕ and the given maximum speed (N_n) and minimum speed (N_1).

Spindle speeds can be obtained in two ways :

(*i*) By a single transmission group, *i.e.* by making arrangements between sets of simple gear trains arranged on two shafts. By this method any series of spindle speeds can be produced by selecting the corresponding series of transmission ratio for the gear trains of the group.

(*ii*) By consecutive engagement of transmission groups, the drive being through a compound gear train. This will produce a geometrical series of speeds. This method has the following advantages :

(*a*) Number of spindle speed. Steps can be increased.

(*b*) Number of simple gear trains required to obtain the speeds is reduced.

Because of these advantages the machine tools use spindle speeds in geometrical series.

8.9. Number of Spindle Speed Steps

Number of spindle speeds (n) is obtained by consecutive engagements of transmission groups. The number of spindle speeds is calculated as follows :

$$n = S_a.S_b.S_c \ldots\ldots S_z$$

where S_a, S_b, S_c etc. represent the number of simple gear trains in each consecutive group. For example for the drive shown in Fig. 8.8.

$$n = S_a.S_b.S_c = 3 \times 3 \times 2 = 18.$$

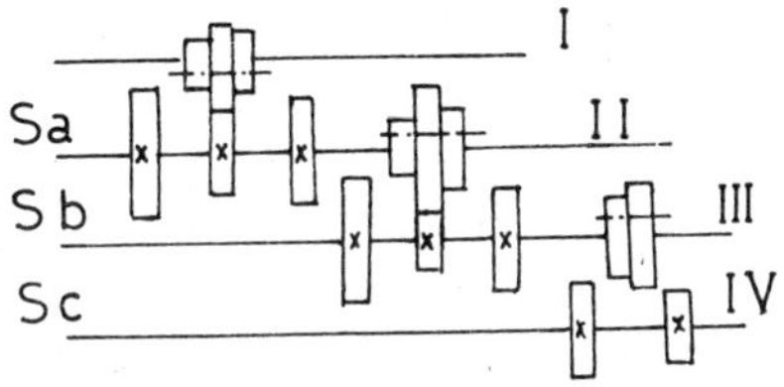

Fig. 8.8

8.10. Range Ratio of Speed Variation in a Drive

Any regularity in the series of spindle speeds is the result of a similar regularity in the series of transmission ratio (r) in the drive. When consecutive gear trains of transmission are engaged, the total transmission ratio of the drive is equal to the product of the transmission ratio of the simple trains that make up the drive.

Let r_{max} = Maximum transmission ratio of the drive.

r_{min} = Minimum transmission ratio of the drive.

$r_{a_{max}}, r_{b_{max}}, r_{c_{max}}$, represent the maximum transmission ratio of the transmission groups S_a, S_b, S_c etc. respectively.

$r_{a_{min}}, r_{b_{min}}, r_{c_{min}}$ represent the minimum transmission ratio of transmission groups S_a, S_b, S_c respectively.

The $r_{max} = r_{a_{max}}, r_{b_{max}}, r_{c_{max}}$, etc.

$r_{min} = r_{a_{min}}, r_{b_{min}}, r_{c_{min}}$, etc.

$\therefore$ R_n = Range ratio of the drive

$$= \frac{N_{max}}{N_{min}} = \frac{r_{max}}{r_{min}} = R_a, R_b, R_c \text{ etc.}$$

where R_a, R_b, R_c are the range ratios of the individual transmission groups.

The limiting maximum range ratio (R_{lim}) in a two shaft group transmission system is

$$R_{tim} = \frac{r_{max,\, lim}}{r_{min,\, tim}} = 8.$$

8.11. Limiting Transmission Ratios

It is a common practice to limit the transmission ratio of gears in a gear box in order to avoid excessively large diameters of the driven gears and a consequent increase in the radial overall dimensions of the drive. The commonly used values of transmission ratio are as follows :

For spur gear $r_{min} = \frac{1}{4}$; $r_{max} = 2/1$

For helical gears $r_{min} = \frac{1}{4}$

$$r_{max} = \frac{2.5}{1}.$$

For feed gear boxes (with slow gearing and small diameter gears).

$$\frac{1}{5} \le r \le \frac{2.8}{1}.$$

8.12. Speed Structure Diagram

This diagram is developed from the kinetic arrangement of the drive to represent speeds at output as well as intermediate shafts of a gear box. In this diagram shafts are shown by vertical equidistant and parallel lines. The speeds are plotted vertical on a logarithmic scale with log ϕ as a unit. Transmission engaged at definite speeds of the driving and driven shafts are shown on the diagram by rays connecting the points on the shaft lines representing these speeds. The transmission ratio is expressed in the form of ϕ_m, when m is the number of intervals between the horizontal lines spanned by the corresponding ray. If the speeds are written from the bottom to the top in the increasing order of magnitude then for transmission ratio $r > 1$, the ray is inclined upward and for $r < 1$ that is for reduction transmission the ray is inclined downward and for $r = 1$, the ray is horizontal. Fig. 8.9 shows a ray diagram for driving shaft I and driven shaft II which has maximum speed N_8 and minimum System N_1.

For transmission engaged at $N_I = N_6$ and $N_{II} = N_3$ the ray is inclined upward ($N_I = N_6$ means the speed of shaft I is N_6 and $N_{II} = N_8$ indicates that the speed of shaft II is N_8) N_8 being greater than N_6. In this case the transmission ratio (r) is ϕ^2 as there are two intervals between N_6 and N_8. For transmission engaged at $N_I = N_6$

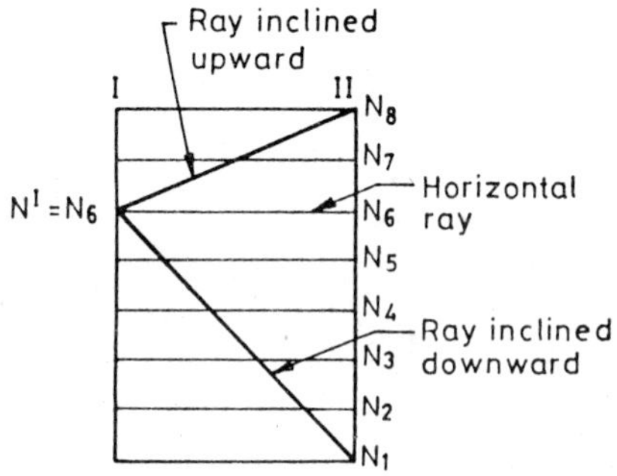

Fig. 8.9

and $N_{II} = N_6$ the ray is horizontal and in this case $r = \dfrac{1}{\phi_0}$. For transmission engaged at $N_I = N_6$ and $N_{II} = N_1$ the ray is inclined downwards and the transmission ratio is less than one and is given by $r = \dfrac{1}{\psi^m} = \dfrac{1}{\psi^5}$, as there are five intervals between N_1 and N_6.

Speed structure diagrams are of two types :

(*a*) Wide diagrams or open diagrams.

(*b*) Narrow diagrams or crossed diagrams.

These groupings indicate the distributive connection between input and output point. The distributive system is open when paths do not cross each other and the distributive system is crossed if the paths cross each other.

Fig. 8.10 shows the possible open diagrams for a spindle to have six speeds for a three shaft gear box. I is driver shift, II is intermediate shaft and III is driven shaft. Fig. 8.11 shows crossed speed structure diagrams for a spindle having six speeds.

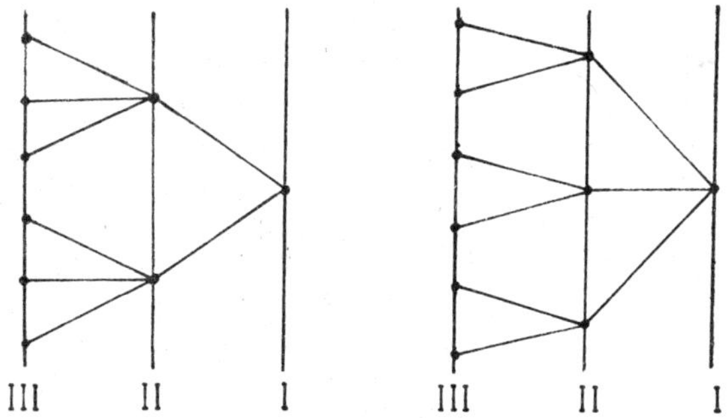

Fig. 8.10

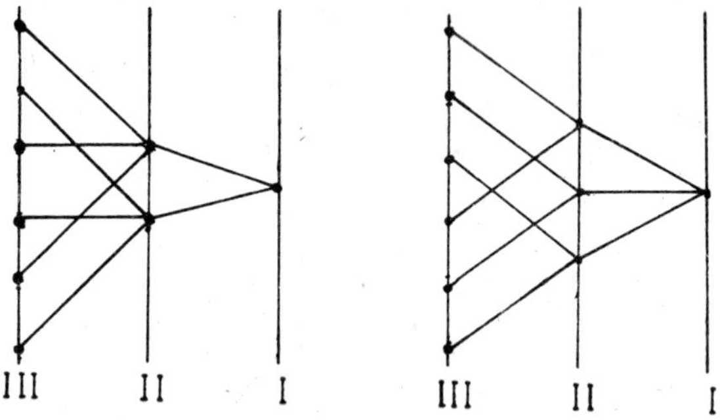

Fig. 8.11

Speed diagrams may also be classified as follows :

(*i*) Unilateral speed diagrams.

(*ii*) Bilateral speed diagrams.

In unilateral speed diagrams the speed changes in one direction only as shown in Fig. 8.11(A) whereas in bilateral speed diagrams the speed changes take place in both direction as shown in Fig. 8.11(B).

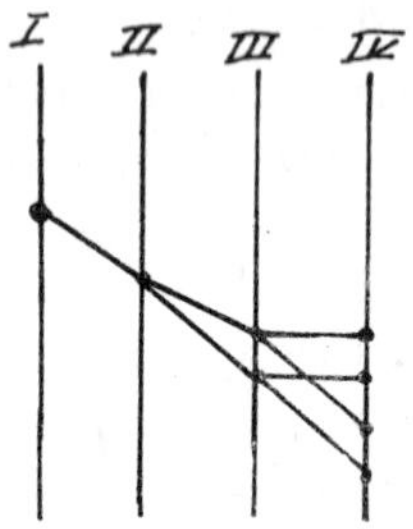

Fig. 8.11 (A)

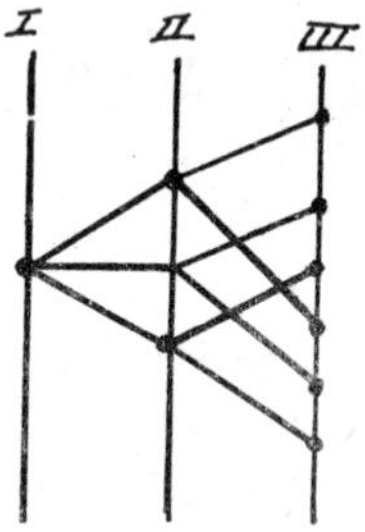

Fig. 8.11 (B)

The structure diagrams may be either open (*O*) or cross (*X*) type. Fig. 8.11(C) shows a typical open type structure diagram for a four speed gear box whereas Fig. 8.11(D) shows a closed type structure diagram for four speed gear box with two stages.

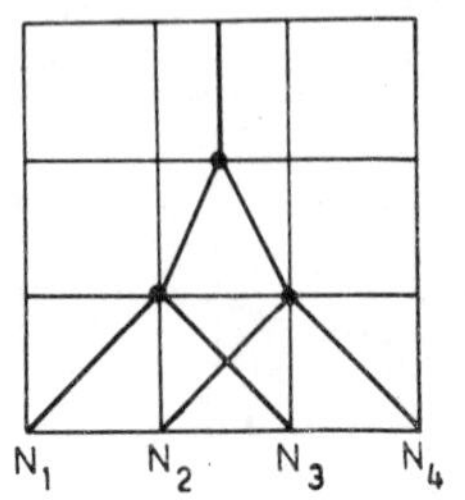

Fig. 8.11 (C)

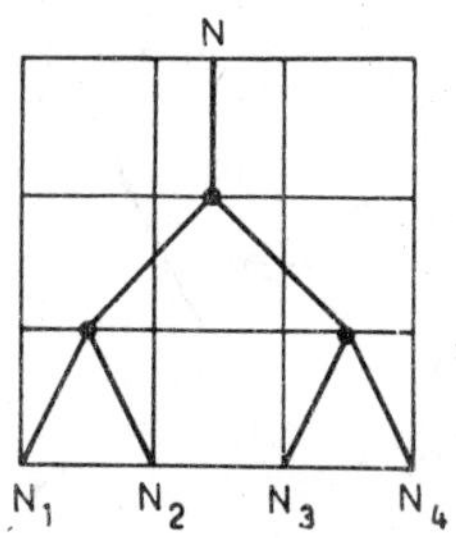

Fig. 8.11 (D)

8.13. Basic Rules for layout of Gear Boxes having Sliding Clusters

The rules applied while designing gear boxes with sliding clusters are as follows :

(*i*) The transmission ratio (r) in a gear box is limited by

$$\frac{1}{4} \le r \le \frac{2}{1}$$

(*ii*) For stable operation the range ratio (R) of any stage should not be greater than 8.

(*iii*) One set of gears must be completely disengaged before the other set begins to come into mesh.

(*iv*) The axial gap between two adjacent gear must be equal to at least two gear width. Fig. 8.12 shows a 2-step stage. The distance space requirement along the axis is $4C$, where C indicates the width of one gear.

(*v*) The sum of teeth of mating gears in a given stage must be the same for same module in a clustered set.

Consider the two step stage of gears shown in Fig. 8.12.

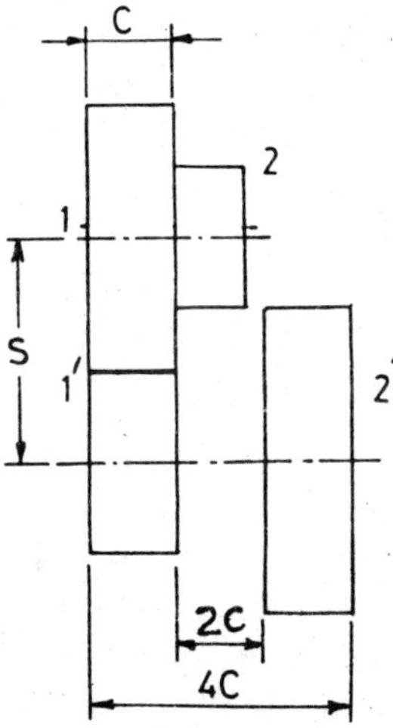

Fig. 8.12

Let T_1 = Number of teeth on gear 1 (driven)

T_1' = Number of teeth on gear 1' (driver)

T_2 = Number of teeth on gear 2 (driver)

T_2' = Number of teeth on gear 2' (driven)

R_1 = Pitch circle radius of gear 1

R_1' = Pitch circle radius of gear 1'

R_2 and R_2' be the pitch circle radius of gear 2 and 2' respectively.

S = Centre distance

m = Module of gear set.

Now $$m = \frac{2R_1}{T_1} = \frac{2R_1'}{T_1'} = \frac{2R_2}{T_1} = \frac{2R_2'}{T_2'}$$

$$R_1 = \frac{T_1}{2}$$

$$R_1' = \frac{mT_1}{2}$$

$$R_2 = \frac{mT_2'}{2}$$

$$R_2' = \frac{mT_2'}{2}$$

$$S = R_1 + R_1' = R_2 + R_2'$$

$$= \frac{m}{2}(T_1 + T_1') = \frac{m}{2}(T_2 + T_2')$$

$$\therefore \quad T_1 + T_1' = T_2 + T_2'$$

(*vi*) The minimum difference between the number of teeth of adjacent gears must be 4.

(*vii*) The minimum number of teeth on smallest gear in drives should be greater than or equal to 17.

(*viii*) Least number of shafts, gears and levers should be used.

(*ix*) Gear box should be of minimum possible size. Both radial as well as axial dimensions should be as small as possible.

Fig. 8.12 (*a*) shows a typical method of reducing radial dimensions of speed gear boxes. In this the axes of shafts I and III have been adjusted along the same straight line.

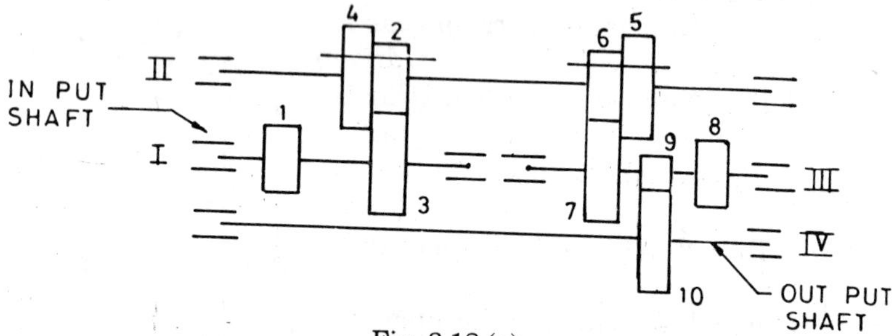

Fig. 8.12 (*a*)

8.13.1. Methods to reduce axial dimensions in speed gear box

In machine tools with traversing spindle head the reduction of axial dimensions of the speed gear box is of great importance because small axial dimensions of the traversing unit are critical from the point of view of stability.

The commonly used methods to reduce axial dimensions of speed boxes are as follows :

(*i*) Using three link gears

(*ii*) Using two link gears

(*iii*) Using one link gear.

Fig. 8.12 (*b*) shows three link gears method

$$S = 7C$$

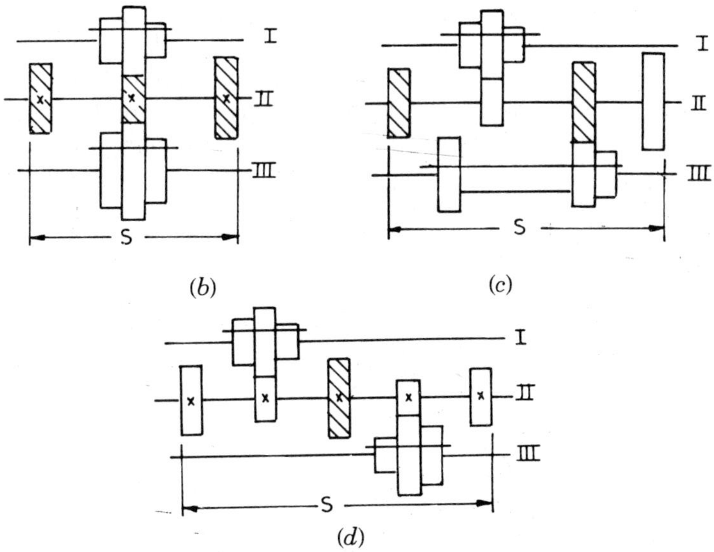

Fig. 8.12

Fig. 8.12 (*c*) shows use of two link gears

$$S = 10C$$

Fig. 8.12 (*d*) shows one link gear method

$$S = 13C$$

where C = Width of one gear

X = Link gear.

Following features related to the functioning of machine tools should be taken into account while designing gear boxes :

(*i*) A friction clutch and brake should be provided on the input shaft in case of machine tools having a large inertia of the driven member. Such machine tools include vertical turret lathes planers etc.

(*ii*) Reversing devices with friction clutches should be provided on machine tools like

(*a*) turret lathes

(*b*) thread cutting lathes

(*c*) radial drilling machines etc.

so that cutting tool can be brought to its initial position. The reversal speed should be nearly 1.5 times more than the cutting speed.

(*iii*) Gear transmissions which do not slide during speed changing should be made helical in order to provide smooth running of the spindle.

(*iv*) In case the spindle head traverses during the working operation then the electric motor should be mounted on the speed box and the transmission from motor shaft to the input shaft of the speed box should be obtained using a clutch or gear pair.

8.14. Shaft Size Calculation

The shafts in a gear box transmit torque from input gear to output gear. Shaft diameter (d) is calculated as follows :

$$\text{H.P.} = \frac{2\pi NT}{4500}$$

where H.P. = Horse power transmitted

T = Torque in kg-m

N = R.P.M.

$$T = \frac{\pi}{16} \cdot f_s \cdot d^3 \approx 0.2\, f_s\, d^3$$

where f_s = Permissible shear stress (Torsional) in kg/cm^2.

Taking into account bending and to provide sufficient rigidity, the value of f_s is assumed 120 kg/cm^2 for mild steel shaft.

$$T = 0.2 \times 120 \times d^3 = 24\, d^3$$

$$\therefore \qquad d = \sqrt[3]{\frac{T}{24}}\,.$$

8.15. To Determine Module for Gears

The module (m) for a gear is calculated as follows :

Let T = Torque transmitted in kg-mm

D = Pitch circle diameter

R = Pitch circle radius

T_1 = Number of teeth

m = Module in mm

F = Tangential force acting at the pitch points transmitted by the gear.

$$F = \frac{T}{R}\,;\; m = \frac{D}{T_1}$$

$$D = mT_1$$

$$R = \frac{mT_1}{2}$$

$$F = \frac{T}{R} = \frac{2T}{mT_1}.$$

Also the value of F for tooth strength is given by

$$F = B.m.C \text{ (kg)}$$

where B = Width of gear in mm

C = Material constant

= 2 for Mild steel = 1 for Cast iron.

Now $\frac{B}{m} = Y ; B = m.Y$

where Y is constant.

The value of Y varies from 8 to 15 and the commonly used value for machine tools is 10.

$$\therefore \quad F = BmC$$

$$F = mY.mC = m^2.Y.C$$

$$m = \sqrt{\frac{F}{YC}}$$

The following modules in mm have been recommended by I.S.I.

1, (1.115), 1.25, (1.375), 1.5, (1.75), 2, 2.25, 2.5, (2.75), 3, [3.25], 3.5, [3.75], 4, 4.5, 5, 5.5, 6, [6.5], (7), 8, (9), 10, (11), (12), (14) 16, (18), 20.

Modules given in round brackets should be given second choice and those given in square brackets should be given third choice.

The rest of the values are preferred modules which should be normally used.

8.16. Kinematic Functions of Machine Tools

Every machine tool is required to perform one or more of the following kinematic functions :

(*i*) To transfer motion from input to output spindle

(*ii*) To transform motion from rotation to translation or reciprocation or *vice-versa*.

8.16.1. To determine number of teeth on gears

The number of teeth of gears depend on transmission ratio. They are determined after plotting the speed chart of gear box.

It is recommended that $T_{min} \geq 20$ in speed boxes

≥ 16 in feed boxes.

However minimum number of teeth (T_{min}) can be calculated using the following formula.

$$T_{min} = 2A \times \frac{1 + \sqrt{1 \pm G(2 \pm G)\sin^2\alpha}}{(2 \pm G)\sin^2\alpha}$$

where A = Tooth addendum coefficient

G = Transmission ratio

α = Pressure angle

Table 8.5 (A) indicates minimum number of teeth for different values of G, A and angle α.

Table 8.5 (A)

G	$\alpha = 20°$ $A = 0.8$	$\alpha = 20°$ $A = 1$
1 : 1	10	13
1 : 2	12	15
1 : 3	12	15
1 : 4	13	16
1 : 5	13	16
1 : 10	14	17

Example 8.1. *A machine spindle is to operate on ferrous metals at 30 m/min and is required to have 5 speeds. The spindle can accommodate H.S.S. Cutters ranging from 10 to 60 mm diameters. Determine the following :*

(a) Spindle speeds.

(b) Plot a graph between cutting velocity and cutter diameter for each spindle speed and calculate the range of cutting velocity for : (i) 12 mm dia. cutter (ii) 36 mm diameter cutter.

Solution.

Let N_1 = Minimum speed of spindle

N_n = Maximum speed of spindle

V = Cutting speed = 30 m/min.

D_{max} = Max. diameter of cutter in mm

D_{min} = Min. diameter of cutter in mm

$$N_1 = \frac{1000 \times V}{\pi . D_{max}} = \frac{1000 \times 30}{\pi \times 60}$$

$$= 159.2 \text{ say } 160 \text{ R.P.M.}$$

$$N_n = \frac{1000 \times V}{\pi . D_{min}} = \frac{1000 \times 30}{\pi \times 10}$$

$$= 955.4 \text{ say } 956 \text{ R.P.M.}$$

n = Number of spindle speed = 6

ϕ = Common ratio

$$= \sqrt[n-1]{\frac{N_n}{N_1}} = \sqrt[5]{\frac{956}{160}} = 1.43.$$

The various speeds are shown in Table 8.6.

Table 8.6

Speed ratio	N_1	N_2	N_3	N_4	N_5	N_6
Spindle speed	160	229	328	469	671	956
Cutter diameter (V = 30 m/min)	59.71	41.72	29.2	20.38	14.24	9.98

From Fig. 8.13.

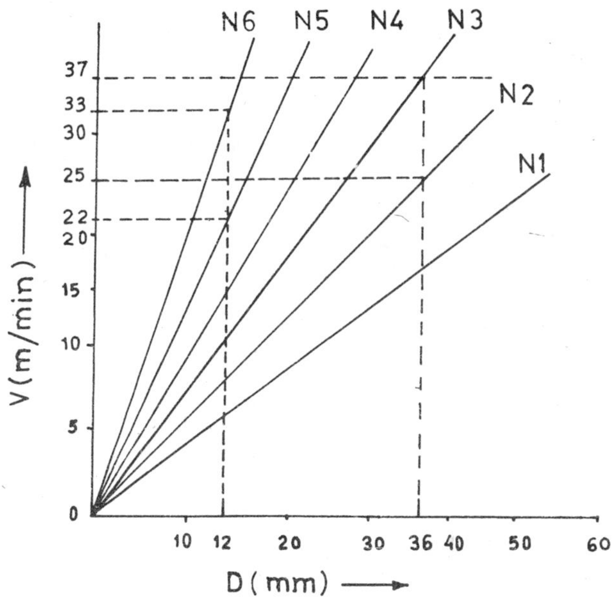

Fig. 8.13

For 12 mm diameter

$$V_{max} = 33 \text{ m/min.}$$

$$V_{min} = 22 \text{ m/min.}$$

Range $= 33 - 22 = 11$ m/min.

For 36 mm diameter

$$V_{max} = 37 \text{ m/min.}$$
$$V_{min} = 25 \text{ m/min.}$$

Range $= 37 - 25 = 12$ m/min.

Example 8.2. *A machine tool spindle is to have six speeds and is to run at a maximum speed of 768 R.P.M. and a minimum speed of 24 R.P.M. Calculate the spindle speeds.*

Solution.

$$N_1 = \text{Min. speed} = 24 \text{ R.P.M.}$$
$$N_n = \text{Maximum speed}$$
$$= 768 = \text{R.P.M.}$$
$$n = \text{Number of spindle speeds} = 6$$
$$\phi = \text{Common ratio}$$
$$= \sqrt[n-1]{\frac{N_n}{N_1}} = \sqrt[5]{\frac{867}{24}} = 2$$

∴ Spindle speeds are as follows :

24, 48, 96, 192, 384, 768.

Example 8.3. *A solid steel gear having 24 teeth is to transmit a maximum torque of 17 kg-m. Determine the module and width of gear.*

Solution. F = Tangential force

$$= \frac{T}{m(T_1/2)}$$

where m = Module in mm

T = Torque in k-mm = 1700 kg-mm

T_1 = Number of teeth = 24

$$F = \frac{17{,}000 \times 2}{m \times 24} = \frac{34{,}000}{m \times 24} \quad ...(1)$$

Also $F = m^2.Y.C$

$$m^2 Y.C. = \frac{34{,}000}{m \times 24}$$

Now $Y = 10$

$C = 2$ for mild steel

$$F = m^2 \times 10 \times 2 = 20 \text{ m}^2 \quad ...(2)$$

From (1) and (2)

$$\frac{34{,}000}{24 \text{ m}} = 24 \text{ m}^2$$

$$m^2 = \frac{34,000}{480}$$

$$m = \sqrt[3]{\frac{34,000}{480}} = 4.14 \text{ mm}$$

$$\approx 4.5 \text{ mm (Nearest standard value)}$$

$$B = mY = 4.5 \times 10$$

$$= 45 \text{ mm. } \textbf{Ans.}$$

Example 8.4. *A 4 speed (2 × 2) gear box is required to be designed for transmitting 8 H.P. with speed ranging from 300 R.P.M. with φ = 1.2. Select on optimum ray diagram and hence calculate gear sizes module and width of gears. Calculate the shaft sizes and sketch the gear box. The gears made up of mild steel.*

Solution. The optimum ray diagram for the gear box is shown in Fig. 8.14.

Various speeds at the output shaft are as follows :

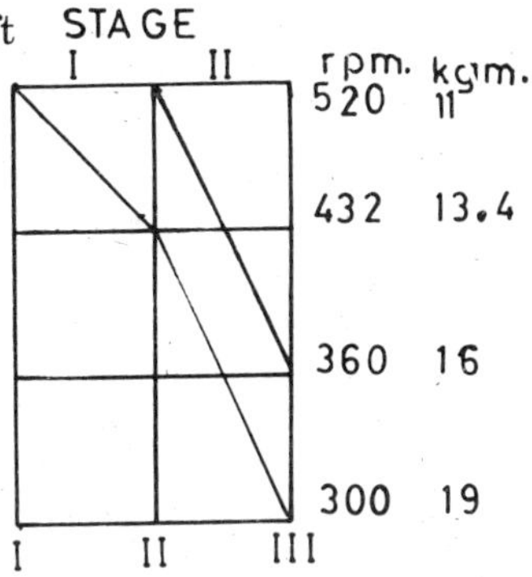

Fig. 8.14

$$N_1 = 300 \text{ R.P.M.}$$

$$N_2 = 300 \times 1.2 = 360 \text{ R.P.M.}$$

$$N_3 = 360 \times 1.2 = 432 \text{ R.P.M.}$$

$$N_4 = 432 \times 1.2 = 520 \text{ R.P.M.}$$

$$\text{H.P.} = \frac{2\pi NT}{4500}$$

$$T' = \text{Torque at } N'$$

$$= \frac{\text{H.P.} \times 4500}{2\pi N_1}$$

$$= \frac{8 \times 4500}{2\pi \times 300} = 19.0 \text{ kg-m}$$

$$T' = \text{Torque at } N_2$$

$$= \frac{\text{H.P.} \times 4500}{2\pi \times N_2}$$

$$= \frac{8 \times 4500}{2\pi \times 360} = 16 \text{ kg-m}$$

$$T''' = \frac{\text{H.P.} \times 4500}{2\pi N_3}$$

$$= \frac{8 \times 4500}{2\pi \times 432} = 13.4 \text{ kg-m}$$

$$T''' = \frac{8 \times 4500}{2\pi \times 520} = 11 \text{ kg-m.}$$

Stage I r_1 = Transmission ratio

$$= 1/1.2$$

$$r_2 = \frac{1}{1.2^{\circ}} = \frac{1}{1}$$

The number of teeth are found as follows :

Transmission ratio (*r*)	*Transmission ratio rationalised and expressed in the form* f/g	$f+g$
$r_1 = \frac{1}{1.2}$	$\frac{1}{1.2} = \frac{5}{6}$ ($f = 5, g = 6$)	11
$r_2 = \frac{1}{1.2^{\circ}} = \frac{1}{1}$	$\frac{1}{1}$	2

Least common multiple (K) of $f + g$, *i.e.* 11 and 2 is 22

$$K = 22$$

$$r_{min} = \frac{5}{6} = \frac{f_{min}}{g}$$

$$\therefore \quad f_{min} = 5$$

$$\frac{f_{min}}{f_{min} + g} = \frac{5}{5+6} = \frac{5}{11}$$

If smallest number of teeth is to be greater than 17

$$EK \frac{f_{min}}{f_{min} + g} \geq 17$$

$$E \times 22 \times \frac{5}{11} = 17$$

$$E = \frac{17 \times 11}{22 \times 5} = 1.7 \approx 2 \text{ (say)}$$

E is the multiple taken such that it is an integer and greater than 1

$$EK = 2 \times 22 = 44$$

Teeth on gear 1 and 1′ are found as follows :

$$T_1 = \text{Number of teeth gear 1}$$

$$= EK \frac{f_1}{f_1 + g_1} = 44 \times \frac{5}{11} = 20$$

$$T_1' = \text{Number of teeth on gear } 1'$$

$$= EK \frac{g_1}{f_1 + g_1} = 44 \times \frac{6}{11} = 24$$

Teeth on gear 2 and 2′ are found as follows :

$$T_2 = EK \times \frac{f_2}{f_2 + g_2} = 44 \times \frac{1}{1+1} = 22$$

$T_2' = T_2 = 22$ as they are to have same speed.

d_1 = Diameter of shaft I

$$= \sqrt[3]{\frac{\text{Torque } (T^{iu})}{24}}$$

(as T^{iu} = 11 kg m = 1100 kg-cm is the torque transmitted by the shaft I).

$$d_1 = \sqrt[3]{\frac{1100}{24}} = 3.5 \text{ cm} = 35 \text{ mm}$$

d_2 = Diameter shaft II

$$= \sqrt[3]{\frac{T^{iu}}{24}} = \sqrt[3]{\frac{1340}{24}}$$

$$= 3.8 \text{ cm} = 38 \text{ mm}$$

(The max. torque transmitted by shaft II is 1340 kg-cm)

Stage II

Transmission ratio (r)	*Transmission ratio rationalised and expressed in the form f/g*	$f + g$
$r_3 = \frac{1}{\phi^2} = \frac{1}{(1.2)^2}$ $= \frac{1}{1.44}$ $\approx 1/1.5$	$\frac{1}{1.5} = \frac{2}{3}$	5
$r_4 = \frac{1}{\phi''} = \frac{1}{1.2°}$ $= 1/1$	1/1	2

K the least common multiple of $f + g$, *i.e.* 5 and 2 is 10

$$K = 10$$

$$r_{min} = \frac{2}{3} = \frac{f_{min}}{g}$$

$$\therefore \quad f_{min} = 2$$

$$\frac{f_{min}}{f_{min} + g} = \frac{2}{2+3} = \frac{2}{5}$$

If smallest number of teeth is to be 17

$$EK \times \frac{f_{min}}{f_{min} + g} = 17$$

$$E \times 10 \times \frac{2}{5} = 17$$

$$E = \frac{17 \times 5}{20} \approx 5$$

$$EK = 5 \times 10 = 50$$

T_3 = Number of teeth on gear 3

$$= EK \times \frac{f_3}{f_3 + g_3} = 50 \times \frac{2}{5} = 20.$$

T_3' = Number of teeth on gear 3′

$$= FK \times \frac{f_3}{f_3 + g_3} = 50 \times \frac{3}{5} = 30$$

T_4 = Number of teeth on gear 4

$$= FK \cdot \frac{f_4}{f_4 + g_4} = 50 \times \frac{1}{2} = 25$$

T_4' = Number of teeth on gear 4′

$= T_4 = 25.$

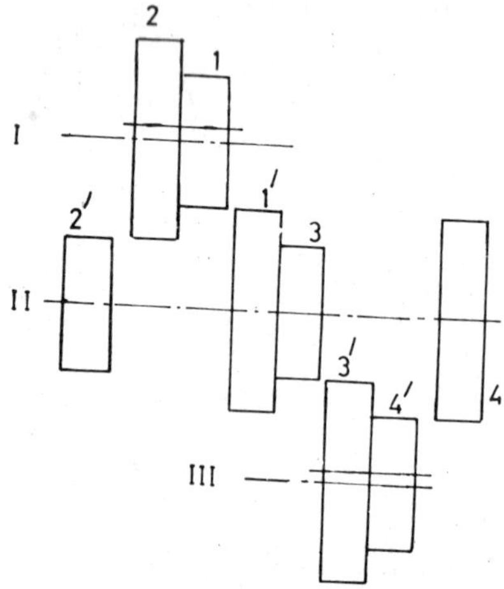

Fig. 8.15

The gear box is shown in Fig. 8.15.

d_3 = diameter of shaft

$$= \sqrt[3]{\frac{1900}{24}} = 4.4 \text{ cm}.$$

As the maximum torque transmitted by shaft III is 1900 kg cm.

To calculate Module (m)

Max. torque = 1900 kg-cm = 19,000 kg-mm.

Max. torque ray provides the value of the force acting at the gear teeth.

$$F = \frac{19,000}{m \times \frac{T_3}{2}} = \frac{19,000}{m \times \frac{30}{2}}$$

$$= \frac{38,000}{30\,m} = \frac{3800}{3\,m}$$

$$E = m^2.Y.C$$

$$\frac{3800}{3m} = m^2.Y.C = m^2 \times 10 \times 2$$

Assuming $Y = 10$ and $C = 2$ for mild steel gears

$$\frac{3800}{3m} = 20\text{ m}^2$$

$$m^3 = \frac{3800}{60}$$

$$m = \sqrt[3]{63.3} = 3.98\text{ mm}$$

Assume $m = 4$ mm (Nearest Standard Value)

B = Width of gear

$$\frac{B}{m} = Y$$

$$B = mY = 4 \times 10 = 40\text{ mm.}$$

Example 8.5. *A 4 speed (1 × 4) gear box is required to be designed with speed ranging from 45 R.P.M. with $\phi = 1.25$. Determine the number of teeth of gears.*

Solution. The optimum ray diagram is shown in Fig. 8.16.

The speeds of driven shaft II are as follows :

$$N_1 = 45\text{ R.P.M.}$$

$$N_2 = 45 \times 1.25 = 56\text{ R.P.M.}$$

$$N_2 = 56 \times 1.25 = 70\text{ R.P.M.}$$

$$N_4 = 70 \times 1.25 = 88\text{ R.P.M.}$$

This means that input shaft I will run at 88 R.P.M. and with the help of gears the speeds (N_1, N_2, N_3 and N_4) will be obtained on driven (output) shaft II.

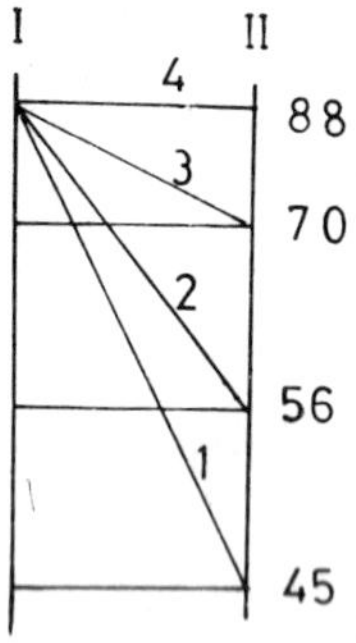

Fig. 8.16

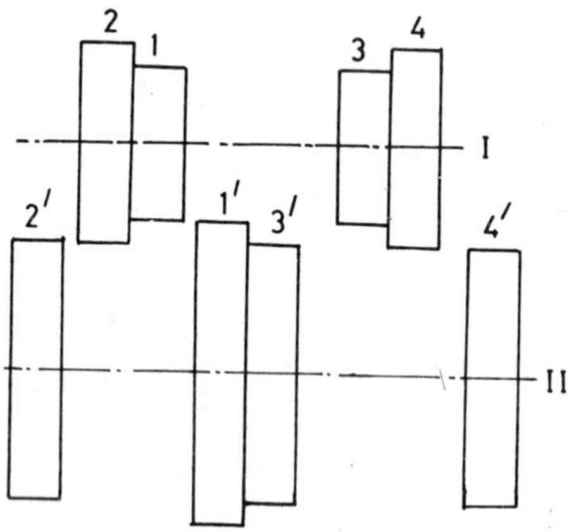

Fig. 8.17

The transmission ratio (r) of ray 1 when speed is reduced from 88 R.P.M. to 45 is $\frac{1}{\phi^3}$ or $\frac{1}{(1.25)^3}$ and the transmission ratio of ray 2 when speed is reduced from 88 R.P.M. to 56 R.P.M. is $1/\phi^2$ or $\frac{1}{(1.25)^2}$. Similarly the transmission ratio of ray 3 when speed is reduced from 88 to 70 R.P.M. is $\frac{1}{\phi}$ or $\frac{1}{1.25}$ and transmission ratio of ray 4 when speed at input shaft and output shaft is same, *i.e.*, 88 R.P.M. The transmission ratio is $\frac{1}{\phi^\circ}$ or $\frac{1}{1.25^\circ} = \frac{1}{1}$.

The number of teeth for the gears of gear box (Fig. 8.17) are calculated as follows :

The least common multiple (K) of $f + g$, *i.e.* 3, 5, 18 and 2 is 90. (See Table 8.7)

$$K = 90$$

$$r_{min} = \frac{1}{2} = \frac{f_{min}}{g}$$

$$\therefore \quad f_{min} = 1$$

$$\frac{f_{min}}{f_{min} + g} = \frac{1}{1+2} = \frac{1}{3}$$

If the smallest number of teeth is to be greater than 17

$$EK \cdot \frac{f_{min}}{f_{min} + g} \geq 17.$$

Table 8.7

Transmission ratio (r)	*Transmission ratio rationalised and expressed in the form f/g*	$f + g$
$r_1 = \frac{1}{(1.25)^3} \approx \frac{1}{2}$	$\frac{1}{2}$ ($f = 1, g = 2$)	3
$r_2 = \frac{1}{(1.25)^2} \approx \frac{1}{1.5}$	$\frac{1}{1.5} = \frac{2}{3}$	5
$r_3 = \frac{1}{1.25}$	$\frac{1}{1.25} = \frac{8}{10}$	18
$r_4 = \frac{1}{1.25^0} = \frac{1}{1}$	$\frac{1}{1}$	2

Where E is a multiple taken such that it is an integer and greater than 1

$$E \times 90 \times \tfrac{1}{3} = 17$$

$$E = \frac{17 \times 3}{90} \approx 1$$

$$EK = 1 \times 90 = 90$$

T_1 = Number of teeth on gear 1

$$= EK \cdot \frac{f_1}{f_1 + g_1} = 90 \times \frac{1}{1 + 2}$$

$$= \frac{90}{3} = 30$$

T_1' = Number of teeth on gear 2

$$= EK \cdot \frac{g_1}{f_1 + g_1} = 90 \times \frac{2}{3} = 60$$

T_2 = Number of teeth on gear 2

$$T_2 = EK \times \frac{f_2}{f_2 + g_2} = 90 \times \frac{2}{5} = 36$$

T_2' = Number of teeth on gear 2′

$$= EK \cdot \frac{g_2}{f_2 + g_2} = 90 \times \frac{3}{5} = 54$$

T_3 = Number of teeth on gear 3

$$= EK \cdot \frac{f_3}{f_3 + g_3} = 90 \times \frac{8}{18} = 40$$

$$T_3' = \text{Number of teeth on gear } 3'$$
$$= EK \times \frac{g_3}{f_3 + g_3} = 90 \times \frac{10}{18} = 50$$
$$T_4 = \text{Number of teeth on gear } 4$$
$$T_4 = EK \times \frac{f_4}{f_4 + g_4} = 90 \times \frac{1}{2} = 45 = T_4'.$$

8.17. Method of Obtaining Different Speeds of Spindle

A wide range of spindle speeds is required in order that a machine tool is adaptable for cutting different types of metals having different properties using varying grades of cutting tools on work-pieces of different diameters. The various methods used for obtaining different speeds of machine tool spindle are as follows :

(*i*) By fitting a cone pulley to the head stock.

(*ii*) By geared mechanism.

(*iii*) By using a variable speed electric motor.

(*iv*) By hydraulic operation.

Any of these methods can be combined to simplify the transmission without reducing the number of speeds available.

8.18. Cone Pulley Arrangement

In this arrangement a cone pulley fitted to the head stock is driven through a counter shaft by an electric motor (Fig. 8.18). The number of speeds obtained depend upon the number of steps on the cone pulley. The various direct speed are obtained by changing the driving belt to the different steps on the cone pulley. A cone pulley with three steps produces three direct speeds of the spindle.

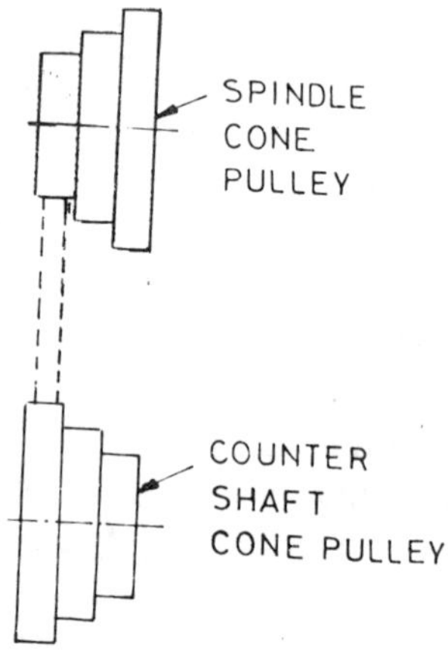

Fig. 8.18

8.19. Cone Pulley Drive by Back Gears

In order to obtain larger number of speeds the head stock is equipped with a cone pulley and back gears. Spindle carries a sleeve over it which is a loose fit (Fig. 8.19). The cone pulley is firmly secured to the sleeve. A pinion P_1 revolves with the cone pulley. A lock pin L engages the gear G_1 with the cone pulley. Back gears G_2 and P_2 are fastened to the quill which revolves on the shaft S at the ends of which the bearings are eccentric with the remaining part of the shaft on which the quill revolves. When speed change is desired, the back gears are pulled in by means of back gear handle H. When the back gears are in the lock pin is out the power and is transmitted from a pinion P_1 to back gear G_2 and then to pinion P_2 and finally to the spindle. A lathe with three steps on cone pulley and with back gears would have six spindle speeds three direct speeds and three indirect speeds through back gears.

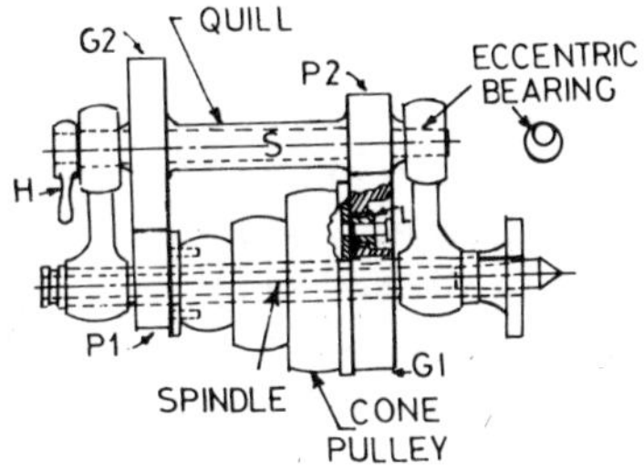

Fig. 8.19

8.20. Speed Gear Boxes

The construction of a speed gear box is intimately linked with the whole structure of the spindle drive. A speed gear box should possess the following requirements :

(*i*) It should provide the designed series of spindle speeds.

(*ii*) It should transmit power of an amount dictated by the purpose of the machine tool.

(*iii*) It should provide smooth silent operation of the transmission and accurate vibrationless rotation of the spindle.

(*iv*) It should have simple construction. This is characterised to a considerable extent by the total number of shaft gears, clutches bearing and control system components.

(*v*) Mechanism of speed gear boxes should be easily accessible so that it is easier to carry out preventive maintenance and to make the adjustments in bearing clutches etc.

The speed gear boxes can be built in two ways :

1. **On basis of general layout**

(*a*) *Gear boxes built into the spindle head (or head stock).*

These gear boxes have the following advantages :

(*i*) They provide a more compact spindle drive.

(*ii*) There is higher concentration of controls.

(*iii*) They are easy to assemble.

Disadvantages :

Such gear boxes have the following disadvantages :

(*i*) Heat produced in the gear-box may heat that spindle head.

(*ii*) Vibration from the gear box may be transmitted to the spindle.

These gear boxes are commonly used in medium and heavy machine tools.

(*b*) *Gear boxes with a divided drive.* In such gear boxes the gear box and spindle head or head stock are designed as separate units and the gear box is linked to the spindle head through some type of transmission such as belt transmission. Such gear boxes have the advantages that heat produced in the gear box by friction losses is not transmitted to the spindle head and also the vibrations developed in the gear box do not affect the spindle rotation and the spindle runs smoothly.

2. **On basis of speed changing method**

(*i*) Speed boxes with change gears.

(*ii*) Speed boxes with sliding gears.

(*iii*) Speed boxes with jaw clutches.

(*iv*) Speed boxes with frictional clutches.

8.21. Gear Box Layout

Gear box layout depends upon the general layout of the machine tool, *i.e.* the spatial and dimensional relation between the various units and the spatial relations between the gear box proper and the spindle head (head stock). It also depends upon the purpose of the machine tool and its type and size.

8.22. Screw Cutting on Lathe by Using Change Gears

During screw cutting the spindle of the lathe provides the rotational movement and the lead screw provides the axial movement necessary to generate a helix. Usually a gear train is used as a drive between the spindle and lead screw. Fig. 8.20 shows a simple change gear train in which the idler gear only controls the direction of rotation of the driver and driven gear and does not affect the speed of rotation.

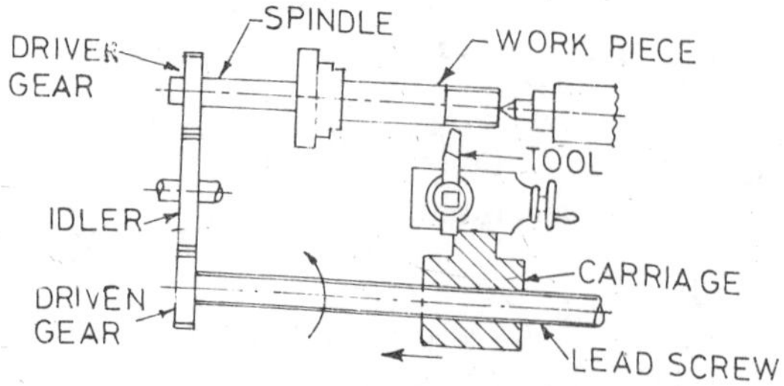

Fig. 8.20. The 'CHANGE' gear train.

8.23. Methods for Changing Speed in Gear Boxes

The following arrangements are made for engaging the various transmissions in gear boxes to change the speeds :

(*i*) Gear boxes with change (slip) gears.

(*ii*) Gear boxes with sliding gears.

(*iii*) Gear boxes with sliding key mechanism.

(*iv*) Gear boxes with friction clutches. Change gears are used when the spindle drive is to be changed over comparatively in frequency for different operations in mass and lot production. The principle drawback of change gears is that a great deal of time is lost in changing speeds. Gear boxes with sliding gears are quite commonly used in general purpose machine tools whereas gear boxes with jaw clutches are commonly used in heavy machine tools. Speed changes by means of friction clutches is used mainly in the group transmissions of small and medium size turret lathes.

Speeds are changed by changing the gears of a group transmission between adjacent shafts with a constant centre distance.

In drives with inverse values of the transmission ratios, the same pair of change gears can be installed in the reverse order. This reduces the total number of gears required for the group transmissions.

Change gears are used in spindle drives where speeds are to be changed infrequently. The drawback of speed changing by change gears is that it is time consuming.

Gear boxes using sliding gears are very commonly used in machine tools. A cluster of two, three or occasionally four gears is arranged to slide on a spline shaft and any of these gears can be made to engage with the corresponding gear on second shaft.

In a three gear cluster the middle gear should be the largest to keep shaft length minimum. The two side gears should be sufficiently small so that their tip diameters are smaller than the root diameter of the middle gear. A four gear cluster is rarely used as it results in excessive shaft length. In lathe feed boxes it is sometimes required to get more than three ratios between a shaft pair. In such cases a pair of cluster gears sliding on the same shaft are used.

The use of multi speed induction motors, mechanical stepless speed variators or DC motors, reduces the complexity of the gear box. Variable speed AC motors with frequency control are nowadays coming into prominance for spindle drives.

8.24. Sliding Gears Arrangement

Sliding gears type gear boxes are quite commonly used because of their reliability and simplicity. They can transmit heavy torque and can run at high speeds. These are widely used in general purpose machine tools. These gear boxes have sliding cluster gears and the gears not participating in the transmission of power to the spindle in a given engagement are not in mesh and are consequently not subject to wear during this time.

Fig. 8.21 shows a sliding cluster of two gears 1 and 2 fitted on a splined shaft 1. The gears 1′ and 2′ are keyed to shaft II. Sliding cluster can be slided along the splined shaft so that at one stage gear 1 and 1′ are in engagement to obtain a particular speed of shaft and then the gear 2 and 2′ can be brought in engagement to obtain second speeds of the shaft II.

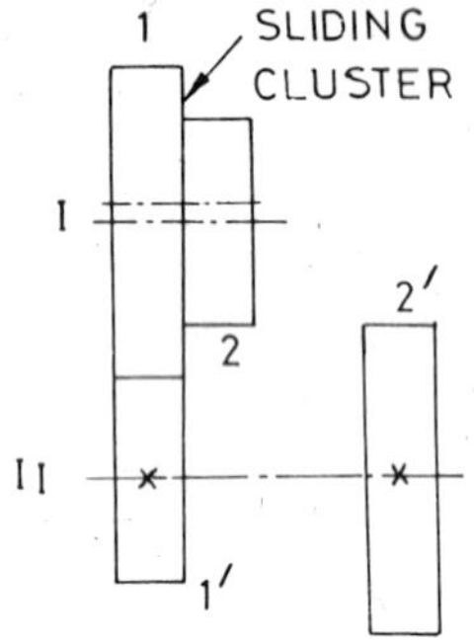

Fig. 8.21

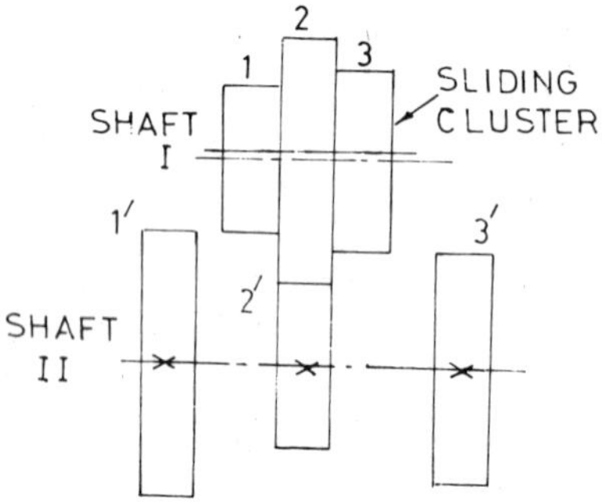

Fig. 8.22

Fig. 8.22 shows a three step sliding cluster which can be moved to bring gear 1 in mesh with gear 1′, gear 2 in mesh with gear 2′ and gear 3 in mesh with gear 3′ to obtained three speeds of shaft II.

Fig. 8 23 shows an all geared head stock in which the different spindle speeu are obtained by shifting the position of gears with the

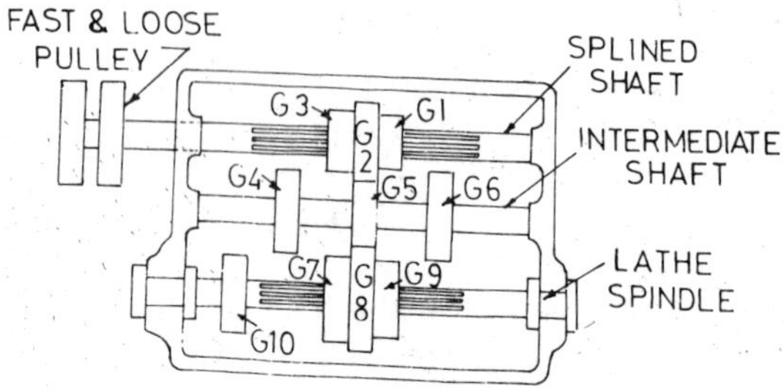

Fig. 8.23

help of a sliding gear mechanism. Such a gear box is designed to give spindle speeds in geometrical progression. A simple design of a nine speed all geared head stock is shown in the above figure. Spur gears G_1, G_2 and G_3 are mounted on the splined shaft whereas gears G_4, G_5 and G_6 are mounted on the intermediate shaft and the lathe spindle carries a cluster (combination) of gears G_7, G_8 and G_9. Power from the driving motor is transferred to the splined shaft through fast and loose pulleys. Gears G_1, G_2 and G_3 can be brought in mesh with spur gears G_4, G_5 and G_6 respectively with the help of a lever and gears G_7, G_8 and G_9 can be brought in contact with gears G_4, G_5 and G_6 respectively with the help of another lever. Finally, the power is thus transferred to lathe spindle which can have nine speeds. Gear 10 called translating gear is used to transmit motion to lead screw and feed shaft.

8.25. Sliding Key Mechanism

This mechanism consists of a hollow shaft into which a slotted rod carrying the key is located and by end-wise movement the rod pulls the key into the key ways of various gears in turn so that any one of a nest of gears is driven by the sliding key.

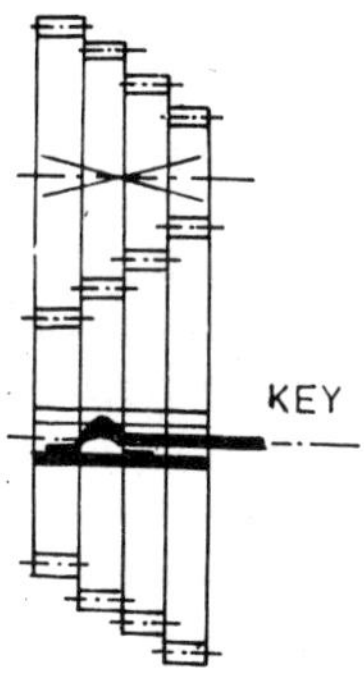

Fig. 8.24

Fig. 8.24 shows a sliding key type gear box. This arrangement is commonly used in feed gear boxes of small and medium size drill presses and turret lathes.

8.26. Feed Gear Boxes

Feed gear box is a part of the feed mechanism. The drive of the feed mechanism may be powered by a separate electric motor or from the head stock spindle through a gear, chain or belt transmission. The feed gear should be arranged near to the working zone especially when the feeds are changed frequently. Feed gear boxes are classified in accordance with the type of geared mechanism, they use to set up the feeds.

(*i*) Feed gear boxes with change gears.

(*ii*) Feed gear boxes with sliding gears.

(*iii*) Feed gear boxes with intermediate gear cones and sliding keys.

(*iv*) Feed gear boxes with gear cone and tumbler gear (Norton type).

(*v*) Feed gear boxes of the Meander type.

The various factors that influence the structure and construction of feed gear boxes are as follows :

(*i*) Purpose of machine tool.

(*ii*) Number of feed steps.

(*iii*) Range of feeds.

(*iv*) Absolute value of rates of feed.

(*v*) Rate at which feeds are to be changed.

(*vi*) Type of feed series (geometrical series or arithmetic series).

(*vii*) Nature of feed motion (continuous or intermittent).

(*viii*) Required accuracy of the feed rates.

(*ix*) Loads applied to the feed gear box.

8.27. Norton Gear Box

In this gear box different speeds of drived shaft are obtained by engaging the tumbler gear with each gear of gear cone fitted on the driving shaft. The sliding gear is keyed the driven shaft and meshes with the tumbler gear which is held in a bracket pivoted on the driven shaft. This gear box (Fig. 8.25) is widely used as feed gear in engine lathes.

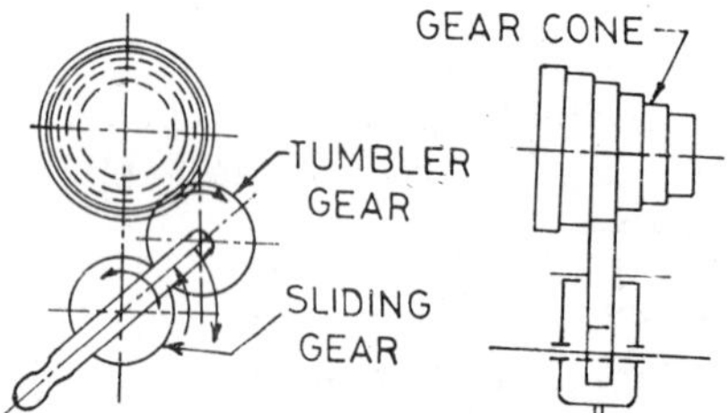

Fig. 8.25

8.28. Feed Gear Box of Meander Type

It is a three shaft mechanism made up of a series of identical double cluster gear and a sliding gear with a tumbler gear (Fig. 8.26). In this gear box all the cluster gears rotate continuously in mesh including cluster gears which do not participate in a particular engagement. If the gears have teeth T_1, T_2, T_0 and T_1, then the following series of transmission ratios (r) are obtained.

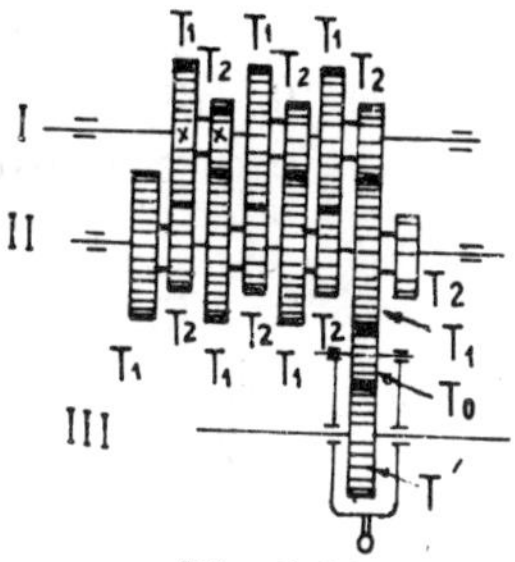

Fig. 8.26

$$r_1 = \frac{T_1}{T_2} \times \frac{T_1}{T'} = k \cdot \frac{T_1}{T_2}$$

where $\frac{T_1}{T'} = k$

$$r_2 = \frac{T_1}{T_2} \cdot \frac{T_2}{T'} = \frac{T_1}{T'} = k$$

$$r_2 = \frac{T_2}{T_1} \times \frac{T_1}{T'} = k \times \frac{T_2}{T'}$$

$$r_4 = \frac{T_2}{T_1} \times \frac{T_2}{T'} = k \left(\frac{T_2}{T_1} \right)^2$$

$$r_5 = \frac{T_2}{T_1} \times \frac{T_2}{T_1} \times \frac{T_2}{T_1} \times \frac{T_1}{T'} = k \left(\frac{T_2}{T'} \right)^3$$

and so on.

8.29. Clutched System

A clutch can be used to transfer power from the driving shaft I to driven shaft II. The clutch (H) can slide on splined shaft. When the clutch (Fig. 8.27) is connected at left the speed (N_2) of driven shaft is given by

$$N_2 = N_1 \times \frac{T_1}{T_1'}$$

where N_1 (R.P.M.) is the speed of shaft I and T_1 and T_1' are teeth on gear I and I′ respectively. Similarly when the clutch is connected to right gear the speed (N_2') of shaft II is given by

$$N_2' = N_1 \cdot \frac{T_2}{T_2'}$$

where T_2 and T_2' are the teeth on gear 2 and 2′ respectively (Fig. 8.28).

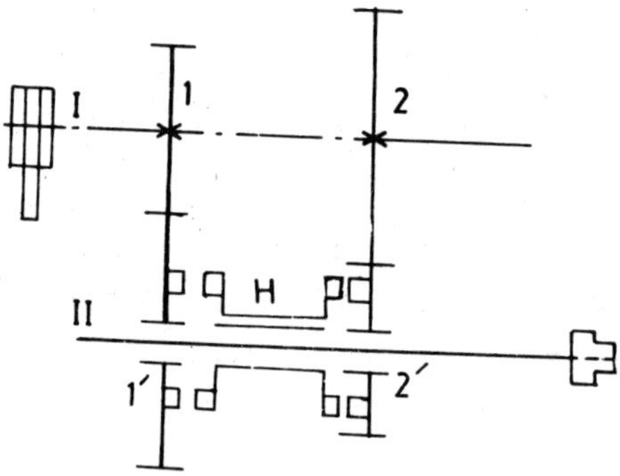

Fig. 8.27

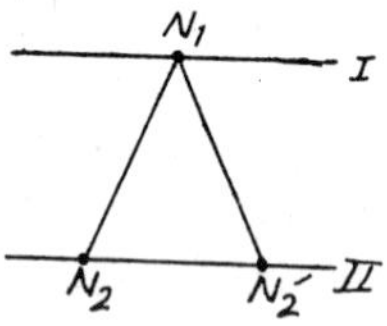

Fig. 8.28

8.30. Ruppert Drive

It is a clutched drive, Fig. 8.29 shows a ruppert drive. This drive uses two clutches (H_1 and H_2) and six gears 1, 1′, 2, 2′, 3 and 3′. It gives four speeds.

When clutch H_1 is towards left and clutch H_2 is also towards left, the output shaft will have one speed. When clutch H_1 is towards right and clutch H_2 is towards left the output shaft II will have second speed. When the clutch H_1 is towards right and H_2 is also towards right the output shaft will have third speed and when clutch H_1 is towards left and clutch H_2 is towards right the output shaft will have fourth speed. A typical ray diagram for this drive is shown in Fig. 8.30.

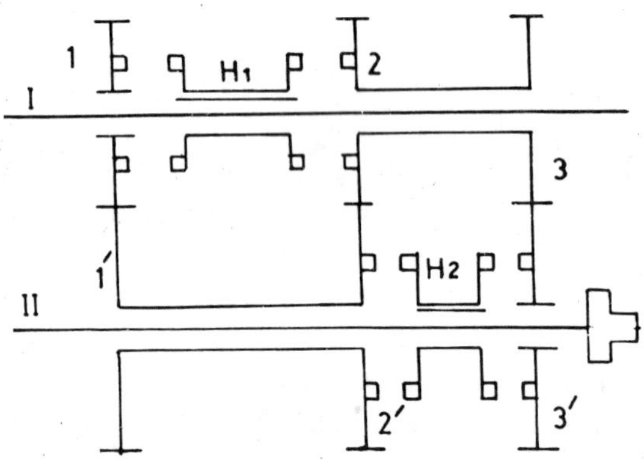

Fig. 8.29

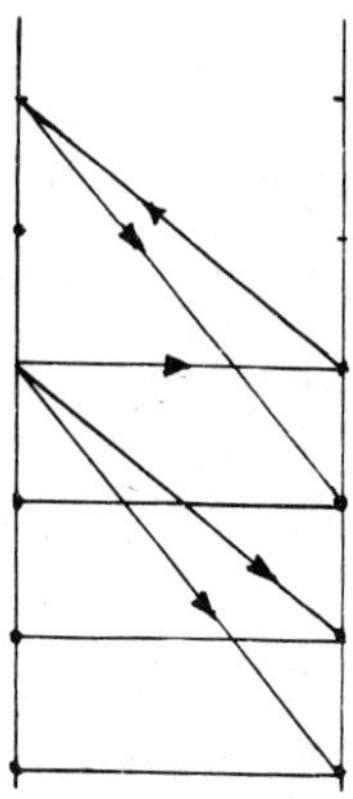

Fig. 8.30

8.31. Feed Drive of a Lathe

The feed drive arrangement of a lathe is shown in Fig. 8.31. The power is transmitted from the head stock spindle to the cone gear shaft through tumbler gear and change gears.

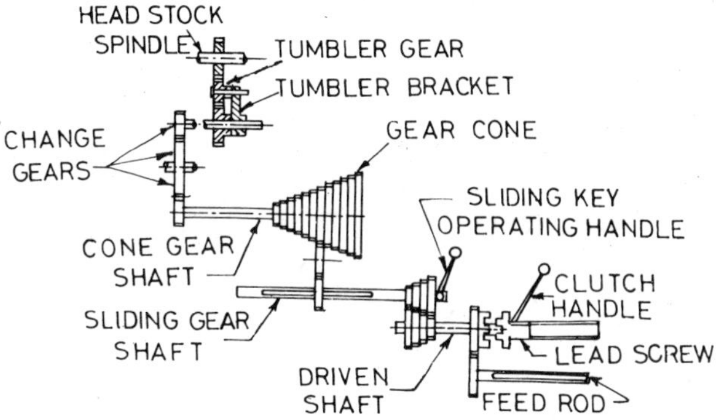

Fig. 8.31

Gear cone has 12 gears and 12 speeds can be obtained on sliding gear shaft with the help of sliding gear. With the help of four gears mounted on sliding gear shaft and sliding key operating handle the driven shaft can be given 48 speeds. Therefore, 48 different feeds can be provided. Lead screw can be engaged or disengaged with the help of clutch. Lead screw should be used when screw cutting is being carried out.

8.32. Pre-optive Gear Box

Such gear boxes are quite commonly used in capstan and turret lathes. In a pre-optive gear box the operator preselects the speed on a dial and then pulls a lever to obtain it. A clutch is operated to get the desired speed without stopping the machine. Thus where frequent speed changes are necessary, this type of gear box is quite helpful. The arrangement of an eight speed gear box is shown in Fig. 8.32 (*a*) and (*b*) shows ray diagram for the same. The speed N_1 is obtained by clutch settings of H_1 to left (H_1L), H_2 to left (H_2L) and

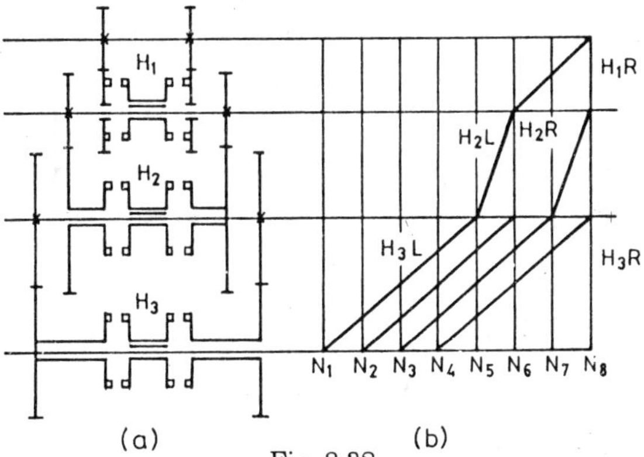

Fig. 8.32

H_3 to left (H_3L) and to obtain speed N_2 clutch settings are H_1 to left, H_2 to right (H_2R) and H_3 to left.

8.33. Infinitely Variable Drives

The infinitely variable (also called variable drive) main and feed drives have found considerable application in modern metal cutting machine tools. The advantages of variable speed drive are as follows :

(*i*) It becomes possible to set up the optimum cutting conditions (speed and feed) with higher accuracy than with a stepped drive.

(*ii*) The speeds can be changed rapidly without stopping the machine. This saves the handling time in machine operation and thus promotes an increase in the production capacity of a machine tool.

(*iii*) A more uniform quality of surface finish is attained.

(*iv*) Variable speed friction drives used in machine tools operate much more quietly than gear or chain drives.

8.34. Types of Infinitely Variable Drives

Various methods are in use for stepless variation of the rates of the working motions. Mechanical, hydraulic and electrical stepless drives are often used to minimise speed loss by having infinite number of speed steps.

8.35. Mechanical Stepless Drives

Most mechanical variable speed drives used in machine tool are of the friction type and therefore their operation involves friction

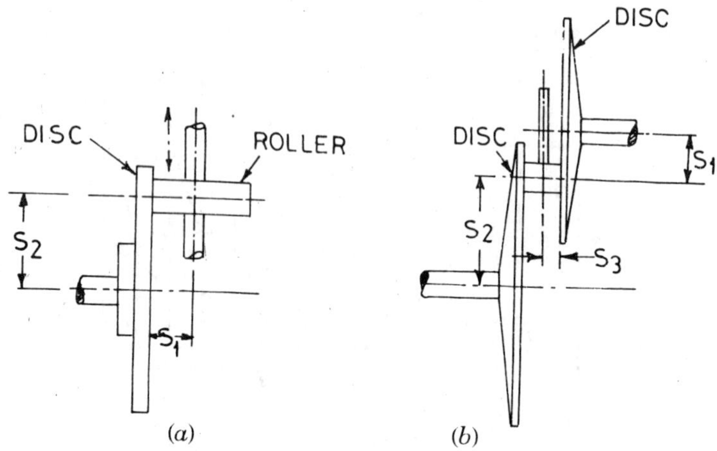

Fig. 8.33

losses. In friction type drives two rolling disc or rollers are passed into line or surface contact. A single discs transmission is shown in Fig. 8.33 (*a*). Motion is transmitted from the roller to the disc. In this system velocity ratio (V.R.) is given by the following relation :

$$\text{V.R.} = \frac{S_1}{S_3}$$

The velocity ratio can be continuously changed by changing the location of roller with respect to disc. Fig. 8.33 shows a double disc transmission system in which the velocity ratio is given by

$$\text{V.R.} = \frac{S_1}{S_2}$$

Fig. 8.34 shows Reeves variable speed transmission system. This system consists of a pair of pulleys connected by a V-shaped belt, each pulley further being made up of two conical discs. These discs can slide along the shaft and rotate with the shaft. In order to adjust the diameter of pulleys the two discs on the shaft are made to approach each other so that diameter is increased or they are made to recede so that diameter can be reduced. In this manner the ratio of driving diameter to driven diameter can be easily changed and therefore any desired speed can be obtained without stopping the machine tool.

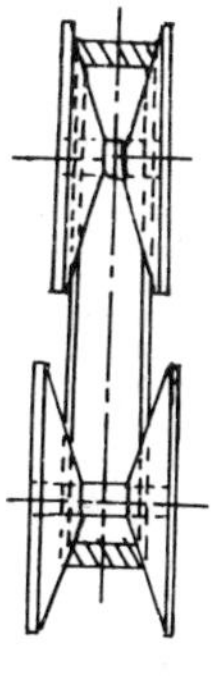

Fig. 8.34

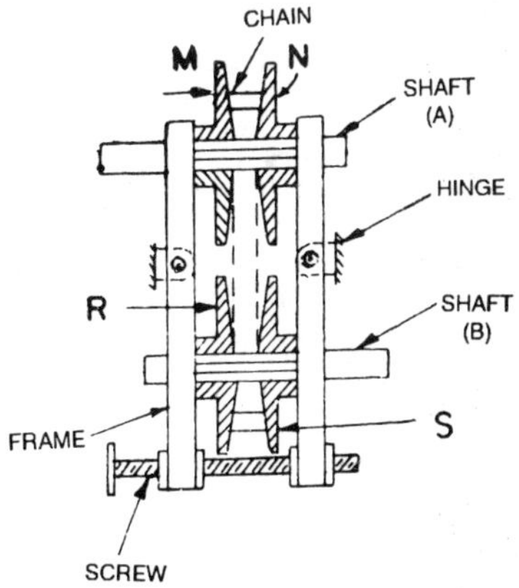

Fig. 8.34 (*a*)

8.35.1. P.I.V. Drive

Positive Infinitely Variable (P.I.V.) drive is a positive torque transmission arrangement. In this system there are two chain wheels, an endless chain, a frame, and a screw. The screw has left hand and right hand threads. The chain wheels have variable pitch circle diameters. One wheel has a pair of cones *M* and *N* and other wheel has a pair of cones *R* and *S*. The cones can be displaced axially and by doing so the effective diameters can be changed and thus the transmission ratios between shafts *A* and *B* are changed. By rotating screw the levered frames get moved thus changing the location of the chain pulley as shown in Fig. 8.34 (*a*).

8.36. Electric Stepless Drives

It is obtained by the electrical motor which is used to drive the various operational movements of machine tools. A 3 phase A.C. motors are commonly used for driving the machine tools. The selection of motor depends upon the starting characteristics, speed adjustment possibilities and power and torque characteristics.

8.37. Hydraulic Drives

Hydraulically actuated machine tools offer great flexibility of speed and feed control, elimination of shock and possess the ability to stall against obstruction thus protecting parts or tools from breakage. Hydraulic actuation also permits slip or slowing up of motion when the cutting tool is over-loaded.

The important elements of a hydraulic transmission are as follows :

(*i*) Pumps
(*ii*) Cylinders
(*iii*) Direction control valves
(*iv*) Pressure valves
(*v*) Throttles.

Hydraulic drives are quite commonly used to obtain infinitely variable rates of rectilinear motion in machine tools. A hydraulic drive is rarely used for rotary motion in a machine tool because of its high cost and low efficiency after wear. The various advantages and disadvantages of hydraulic drives are as follows :

Advantages. (*i*) A hydraulic drive has a wide range of speed variation.

(*ii*) In a hydraulic drive both magnitude and direction of speeds can be easily changed.

(*iii*) A hydraulic drive is smooth and reverses without shock.

(*iv*) A hydraulic drive can be operated by a remote control.

(*v*) A hydraulic drive is self-lubricative by transmission.

(*vi*) Its design is simple and maintenance is easy.

(*vii*) It is quite in operation.

(*viii*) A hydraulic drive has automatic protection against over loads.

Disadvantages. The major drawback of a hydraulic drive is that at low speeds the operation of the hydraulic drive becomes unstable. Secondly, the oil viscosity varies with temperature and may cause fluctuations in feed and speed rates although compensating devices can be introduced to deal with this difficulty.

8.38. Hydraulic Fluids Used in Machine Tool Drives

In hydraulic drives the commonly used fluids are mineral or petroleum oils. Mineral oil has found predominant application in the hydraulic drives of metal cutting machine tools. The oil used should be sufficiently homogeneous as to its chemical composition. The main service property used in selecting and comparing oils is the Viscosity Index which shows the change in the viscosity of an oil with its temperature. An oil with higher viscosity index is preferred. A substantial increase in viscosity index can be achieved by the application of special synthetic oil additives. The hydraulic fluids should not contain matters which are inflammable in nature.

8.39. Elements of a Hydraulic System

The various elements of a hydraulic system are as follows :

(*i*) Pressure producing unit, *i.e.* pump.

(*ii*) The element making use of the pressure, *i.e.* hydraulic motor (cylinder and piston).

(*iii*) Controlling elements such as valves.

(*iv*) Storage and transmission elements such as tank, pipeline etc.

Pumps. The pump develops the pressure or head of the working fluid by expanding mechanical energy. The pressure most commonly used in hydraulic machine tools varies from 5 to 80 kg/cm^2. The various types of pumps used in a hydraulic drive are as follows :

(*i*) Reciprocating pumps

(*ii*) Rotary pumps.

In reciprocating pump the liquid is displaced due to the reciprocating motion of the impelling elements (pistons or plungers).

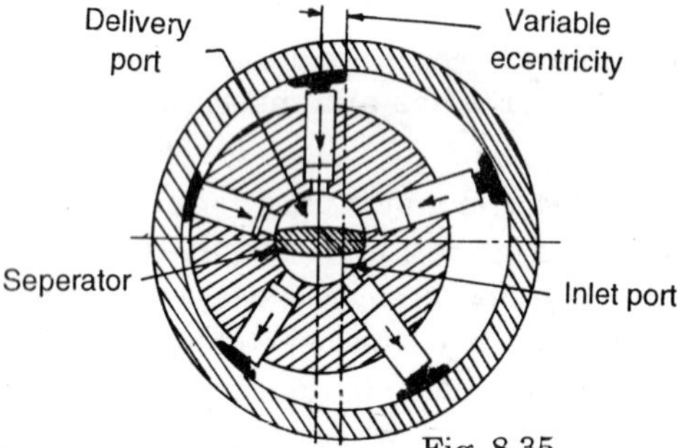

Fig. 8.35

Fig. 8.35 shows a variable delivery plunger pump. Arrows show the direction of piston displacement for the instantaneous position shown. Rotary pumps are of two types :

(*a*) Purely rotary type

(*b*) Rotary piston pumps.

In purely rotary type pumps the impelling elements only rotate such as in screw pump (Fig. 8.36) and gear pump (Fig. 8.37). A screw pump consists of a two worms welded into a common shaft and having right hand and left hand threads. When the worm shaft rotates the liquid supplied to the worms from the right and left flows towards the middle where the discharge pipe is arranged. A gear pump has two gears each with not more than 8 to 12 teeth to ensure a tighter mesh. As the gears rotate the liquid from the suction pipe is caught up by the teeth and is carried between their spaces to the discharge pipe.

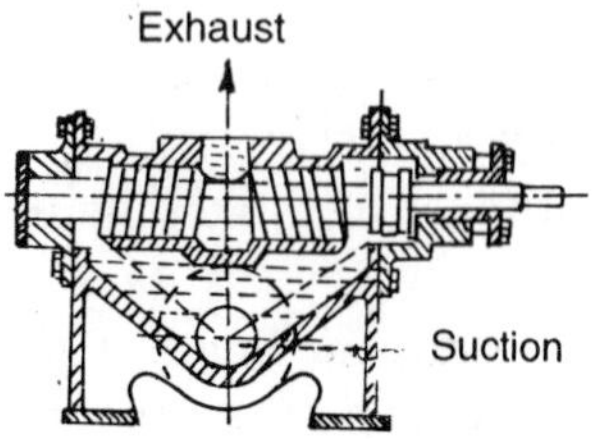

Fig. 8.36

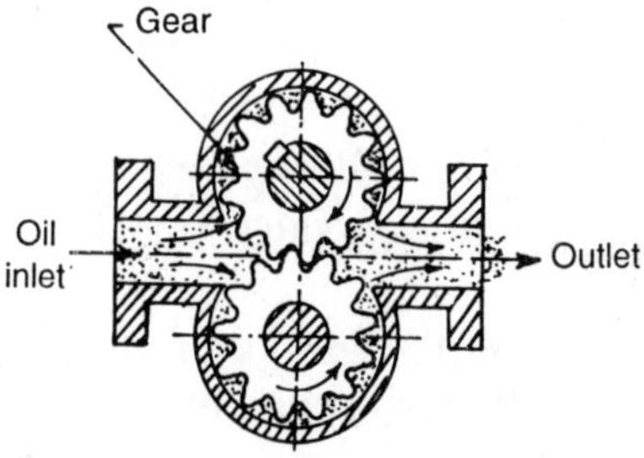

Fig. 8.37

Gear pumps find application in the hydraulic system of machine tools operating at medium and low pressure and at high speeds such as grinders and honing machines. Gear pumps are fixed delivery pumps, *i.e.* they deliver a constant volume at a constant pressure.

In rotary piston pumps the impelling elements (plungers) reciprocate in addition to rotation in respect to the rotary cylinder body.

The selection of a pump depends upon delivery and pressure developed by the pump. The minimum delivery of pumps used in hydraulic drives of machine tool has been taken as 3 litres per minute and maximum delivery as 400 litres/minute.

8.40. Pump Operation Methods

In the hydraulic systems of machine tools pumps may be run both single and dual and in series or in parallel. Series pump operation is used to increase the pressure in the system whereas parallel operation is preferred to increase delivery and to obtain rapid traverse motions such as

(*i*) Rapid approach and withdrawal of an operative unit.

(*ii*) Release of the finished workpiece and clamping of the next black in handling devices.

When a number of pumps run together, a separate circuit for the operation of each pump may be provided or a circuit for the simultaneous operation of pumps may be used.

8.41. Hydraulic Valves

A valve is an apparatus (hydraulic device) mounted in the path of fluid flow and designed for changing the parameters (pressure and volume) of the fluid flowing in the hydraulic system. Each valve has an operative number which is actuated either by an external force (adjustable valves) or by the fluid passing through it (non-adjustable valves). The force acting on the valve changes the cross-sectional area of the opening in the valve and thus the parameters of the fluid are controlled.

Following types of valves are used to control the pressure of the fluid :

(*i*) Relief valves

(*ii*) Safety valves

(*iii*) Reducing valves.

Relief valve maintains a constant pressure at the valve intake by continuously discharging a certain amount of oil back to the tank. Safety valve is used to prevent the pressure from building up above a given maximum value. Safety valves are used in variable displacement speed control circuits. Reducing valves are used to reduce the oil pressure and maintain the reduced pressure at the valve outlet. Flow control is achieved in a constant delivery circuit with the help of throttle valve. Direction control valves are used to change the direction of fluid flow.

8.41.1. Hydraulic Valves Construction

Valves used in hydraulic circuit are of two types :

(*i*) **Sliding type.** It is spool and plate type construction. In this construction the openings are closed or opened by sliding the spool in an axial direction. Fig. 8.37 (*a*) shows sliding type valve construction.

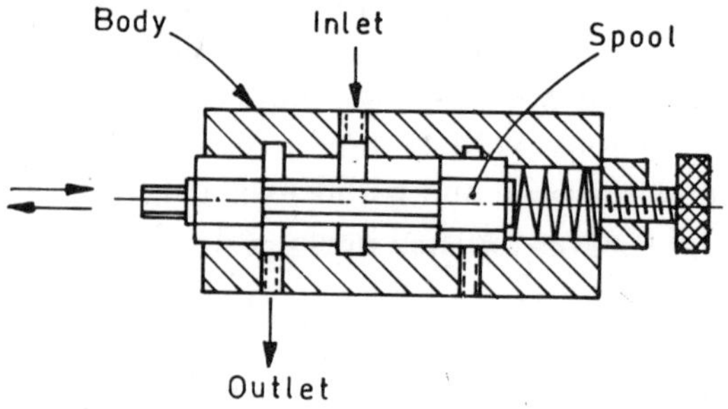

Fig. 8.37 (*a*)

(*ii*) **Sealing type.** In this construction a poppet (as shown in Fig. 8.37 (*b*)) or a ball (as shown in Fig. 8.37 (*c*)) is used to control the valve opening. Packing material is used to prevent leakage.

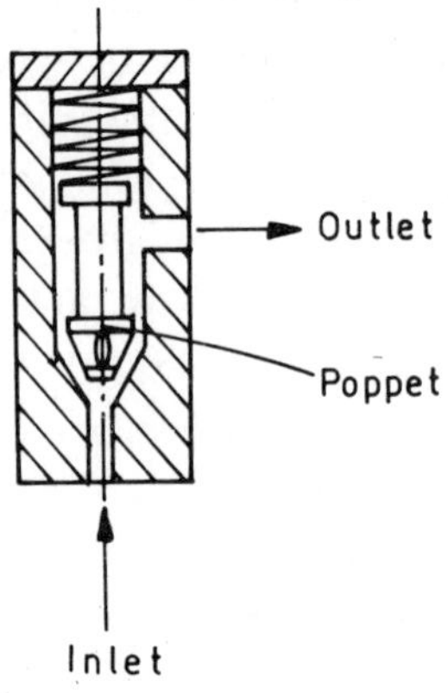

Fig. 8.37 (*b*)

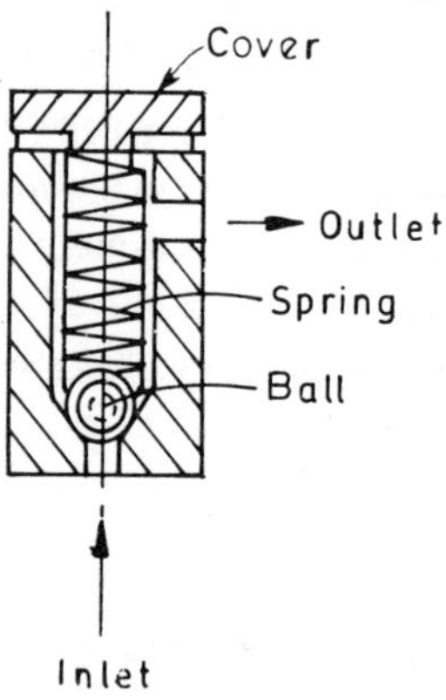

Fig. 8.37 (*c*)

The commonly used valves in a hydraulic circuit are as follows :

(*i*) Pressure control valves.

(*a*) Pressure reducing valves

(*b*) Pressure relief valves.

(*ii*) Flow control valve

(*iii*) Direction control valve.

Some of the valves used in hydraulic circuits are as follows :

(*i*) Throttle valve or Flow control valve

(*ii*) Pressure relief valve

(*iii*) Non-return valve

(*iv*) Pressure reducing valve

(*v*) Direction control valve

(*vi*) Sequence valve.

Throttle Valve or Flow Control Valve

The throttle valve is used to regulate a fluid flow to an adjustable value. Fig. 8.37 (*f*) shows a throttle valve. The fluid entering the valve goes out through an annular gap. This gap is the throttle which can be enlarged or reduced by means of throttling screw.

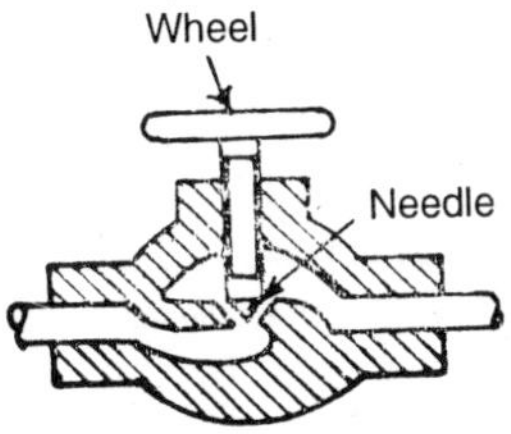

Fig. 8.37 (*d*)

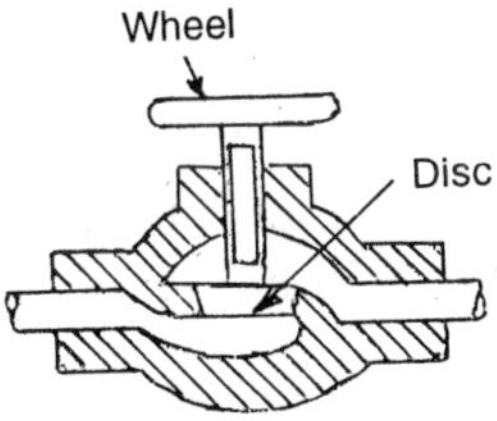

Fig. 8.37 (*e*)

In these valves the area of the constricted passage is varied by displacing a movable member. Fig. 8.37 (*d*) shows a globe valve in which the moving member is a disc whereas in needle valve [Fig. 8.37 (*e*)] the movable member is a needle. Both globe valve and needle valves are throttle valves.

Pressure Relief Valve

It relieves the working pressure at definite present pressure and safe-guard the system against over loading due to high pressure. A pressure relief valve is shown in Fig. 8.37 (*g*). In the initial position the cone is pressed by the compression spring into the mouth of the hole. When the fluid force *P* exceeds the spring pressure, the cone

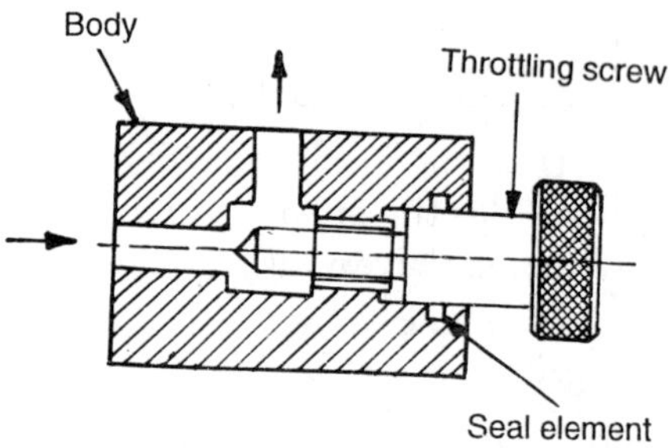

Fig. 8.37 (*f*)

is pushed back and the fluid comes out through the opening. The tension exerted on the cone can be set by means of adjusting screw and compression spring.

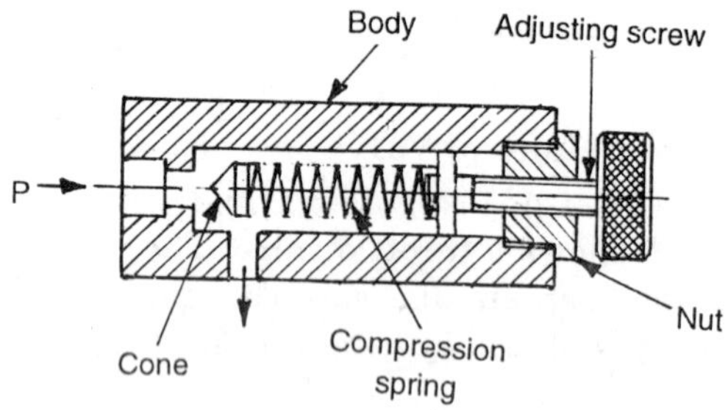

Fig. 8.37 (*g*)

Non-return Valve

It is used to allow the confined fluid to flow in one direction only. The flow in the opposite direction is blocked. A non-return valve is shown in Fig. 8.37 (*h*) when a pressure p, impacts on the

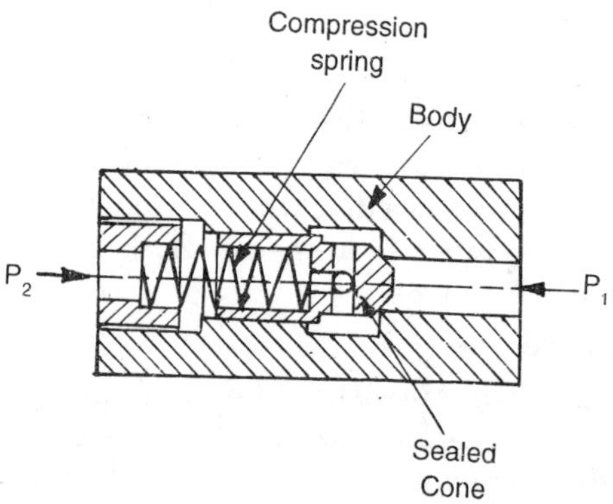

Fig. 8.37 (*h*)

sealing cone it is lifted from its seat and allows the fluid to flow through. The pressure P_1 must, therefore, overcome the low tension of the compression spring then the sealing cone is forced back into its seat by pressure P_2 acting in the opposite direction in addition to spring tension. This will block the flow of fluid. Flow of fluid takes place if,

$$P_1 > P_2 + S$$

where S = spring tension.

Fig. 8.37 (*i*) shows a pressure relief valve using a movable ball. The spring pressure is adjustable by a screw when the pressure

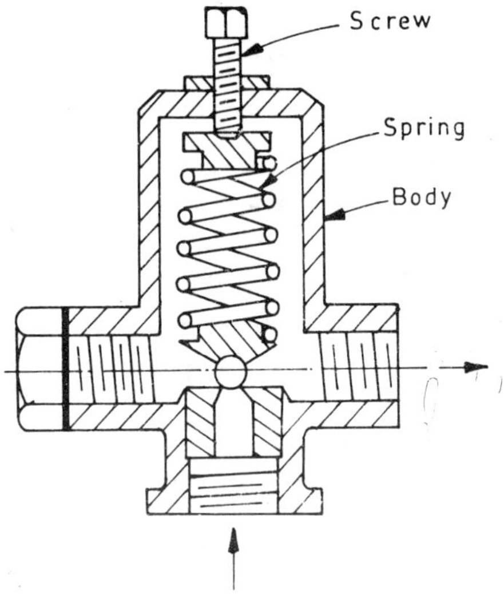

Fig. 8.37 (*i*)

rises beyond the set value, the ball gets lifted from its seat against the spring pressure and the fluid moves out. When fluid pressure gets relieved the spring sets the ball in position and the by-pass is stopped.

Pressure Reducing Valve

The purposes of pressure reducing valve in a hydraulic circuit are as follows :

(*i*) To reduce the pressure in the circuit

(*ii*) To divide the flow from pump into several parallel lines requiring different pressure

(*iii*) To maintain a reduced pressure in a branch circuit.

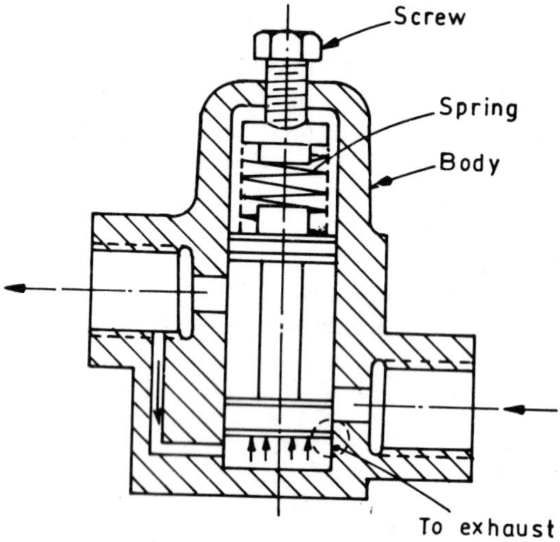

Fig. 8.37 (*j*)

When the liquid at reduced pressure is to be supplied with a restricted volume of flow, the reducing valve is combined with a throttle valve. The throttle valve will be connected either in series or in parallel on the reduced pressure side.

A pressure reducing valve is a open two way valve. It can be of following types :

(*i*) Direct acting valve

(*ii*) Pilot operated direct acting valve.

Fig 8.37 (*j*) shows a direct acting pressure reducing valve. In this valve a spool works against spring pressure to control the secondary line pressure. There are two opening at inlet, one leading to the valve chamber and other to the exhaust. Both openings are partly covered by the spool so that a part of in coming high pressure liquid flows into the chamber and the rest being discharged to the exhaust.

The pressure of the liquid drops in the chamber and the liquid at reduced pressure is supplied to the branch line through the outlet port.

Direction Control Valve

It is used to direct the flow path of fluid in a hydraulic circuit. It can supply fluid to a particular path to bring about an operation while cutting off supply to other path or paths. These valves are of two types :

(*i*) Spool type

(*ii*) Rotary type.

Spool type are commonly used. Rotary type valves find application in machine tool table reversals such as in surface and cylindrical grinding machines. Hydraulic reversing is preferred to mechanical and electrical reversing because of the following reasons :

(*i*) the speed of the response is high

(*ii*) capacity to withstand frequency of reversals is very high.

A direction control valve has one inlet port and a number of outlet ports. Depending on ports provided valve is classified as

(*i*) one way valve

(*ii*) two way valve

(*iii*) three way valve

(*iv*) four way valve

(*v*) multi-way valve.

These valves are further classified according to number of valve positions such as 2-position valve, 3-position valve.

Thus a valve may be 2 position 2 way valve, 2 position 3 way valve, 2 position 4 way valve etc. Fig. 8.37 (*k*) shows a two position 5 way valve. In this valve

P = Centre connection

S_1 and S_2 = Supply ports to openings 1 and 2 of power cylinder

E_1 and E_2 = Exhaust connections.

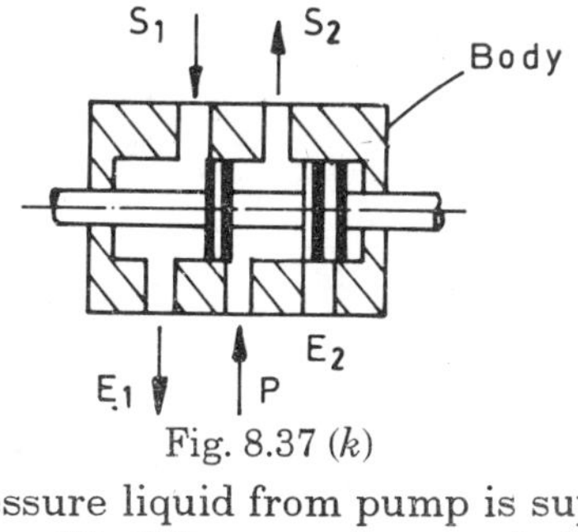

Fig. 8.37 (*k*)

The high pressure liquid from pump is supplied to valve at the centre connection (P). When spool covers both the openings S_1 and S_2, neutral position is obtained and no oil is supplied to power cylinder. When spool is shifted to left exhaust port, E_1 is closed and liquid from pump flow through P to S_1 and to power cylinder port 1. Oil in the cylinder is exhausted to reservoir through cylinder port 2 and through valve from S_2 to E_2. When the spool is shifted to right oil is supplied to power cylinder at port 2 through S_2 and the exhaust is through 1-S_1-E_1.

One Way Direction Control Valve

One way direction control valve is also called check valve. Check valves are of following types :

(*i*) Swing type

(*ii*) Poppet type

(*iii*) Pilot type.

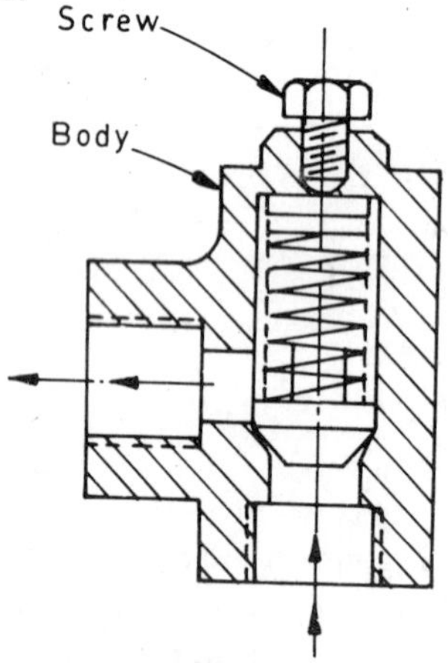

Fig. 8.37 (*l*)

Fig. 8.37 (*l*) shows a right angled check valve. Fluid pressure acting on the poppet will open the valve against spring pressure and flow commences. Reverse flow is not possible.

Two Way Valve

Fig. 8.37 (*m*) shows a two position two way directional control valve. Fig. 8.37 (*n*) shows symbol of this valve.

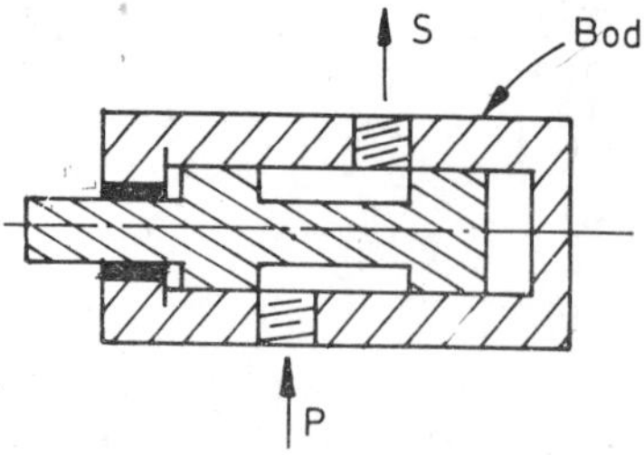

Fig. 8.37 (*m*)

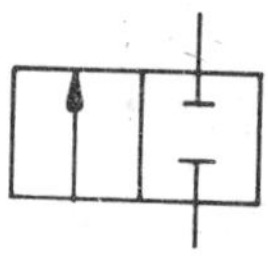

Fig. 8.37 (*n*)

A three way valve will have three ports. Four way valve will have four ports, an inlet port, an exhaust port and two cylinder ports. It may be 2 position 4 way valve or 3 position 4 way valve depending on the spool design.

Sequence Valve

It is used to ensure a particular sequence of operations in the system. It maintains a minimum pressure on the supply (primary) line to bring about the first operation. When first operation is complete the pressure in the line builds up to open the valve to the secondary circuit.

Fig. 8.37 (*o*) shows sequence valve. The spring force holds the spool so that liquid can be supplied to different circuits.

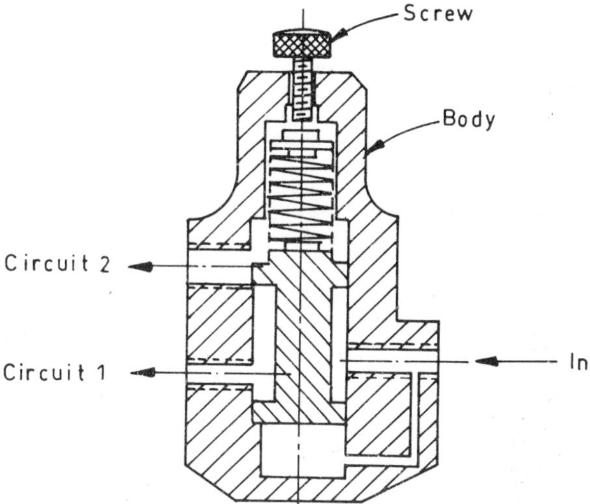

Fig. 8.37 (*o*)

Hydraulic Symbols

They help in drawing of a hydraulic circuit diagram. The various symbols are indicated in Table 8.7.1.

Table 8.7.1

S. No.	*Description*	*Symbol*
1.	Direction of flow (*i*) Non reversible (*ii*) Reversible.	 ——→—— —←→—
2.	Suction or pressure lines carrying fluid	————
3.	Drain line	— — — —
4.	Flexible line rubber hose connection	

5.	Pilot line pipe from a pilot valve to a control valve.	- - - - - - - - - - -
6.	Pipe lines passing but not connected or lines crossing.	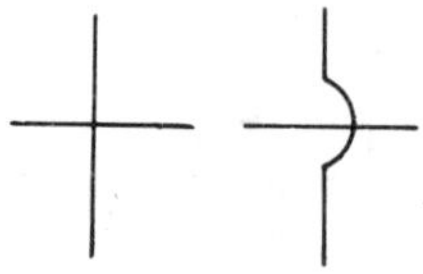 (Preferred)
7.	Connections of fluid lines.	 Tee Junction Elbow
8.	Line to a reservoir— (*a*) end of line above fluid level. (*b*) end of line below fluid level.	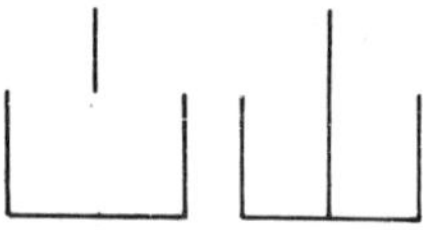 (*a*) (*b*)
9.	Vented pipeline	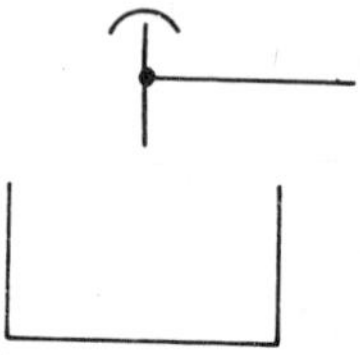
10.	A plug or plugged connection.	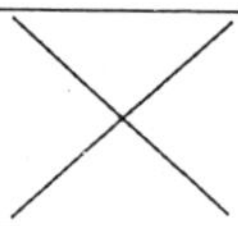
11.	Plugged pipeline	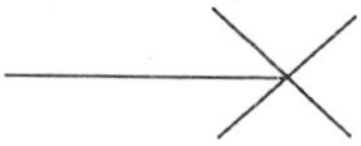
12.	Connection to a pressure gauge or a unit.	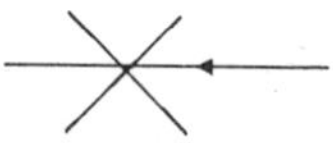
13.	Line with fixed restriction	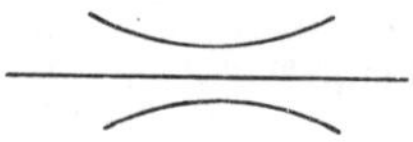

14.	Line with variable restriction	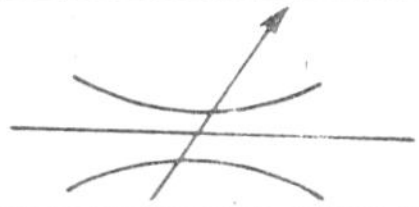
15.	Check valve.	
16.	Filter.	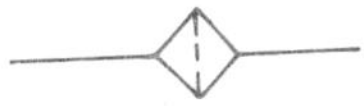
17.	Quick connection with couplings (*a*) without check valve (*b*) with one check valve (*c*) with two check valves.	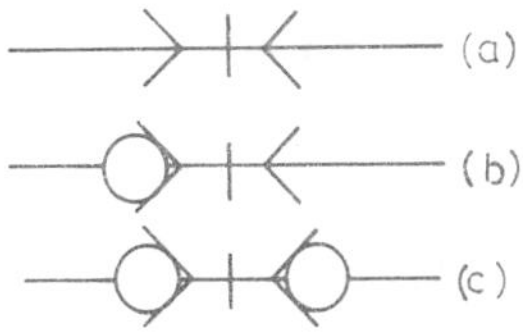
18.	A component enclosure for assembly of several components in a single housing or on a single panel.	
19.	Spring.	
20.	Pressure gauge.	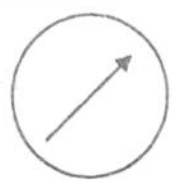
21.	Pressure switch.	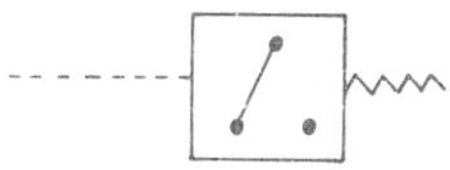
22.	Limit switch.	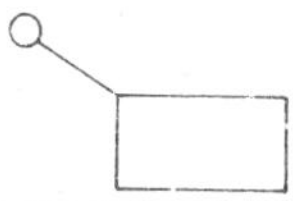
23.	Accumulator—liquid under pressure is stored during an idle period. (*a*) spring loaded (*b*) weighted (*c*) gas-charged (nitrogen).	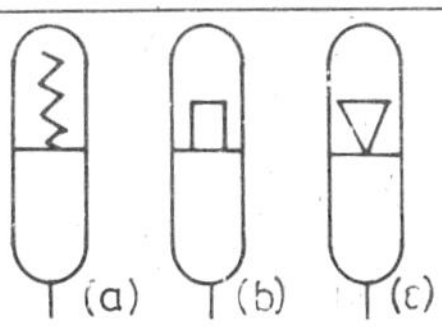

24.	Pressure intensifier.	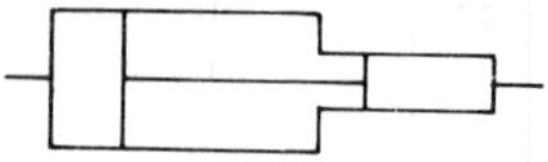
25.	Single-acting Hydraulic Cylinder.	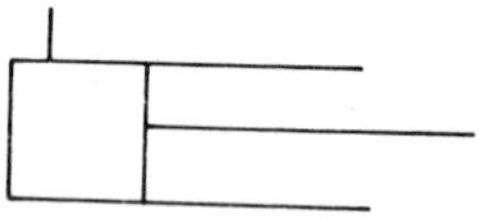
26.	Basic symbol for a valve is a square. The number of squares shows the number of valve positions (*a*) Two squares—Two valve positions (*b*) Three squares—Three valve position.	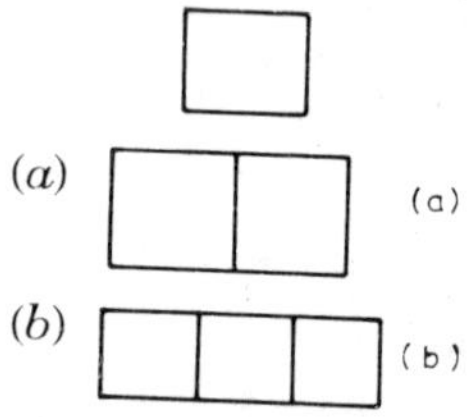
27.	An arrow inside the square shows internal flow.	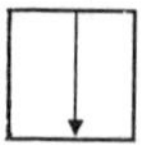
28.	Normally closed single-way valve— Position (*a*)—Non-operating Position (*b*)—Operating.	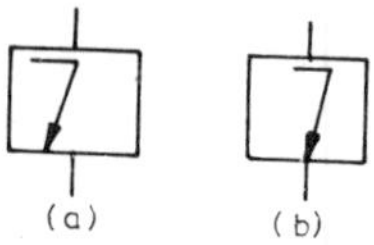
29.	Normally open single-way valve— Position (*a*)—Operating Position (*b*)—Non-operating.	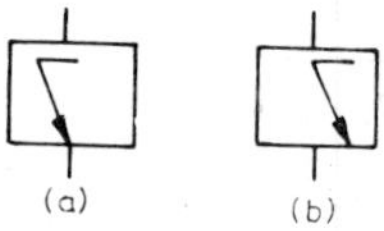
30.	Manual shut off valve.	
31.	Two way valve—with two positions and two connections—normally cpen.	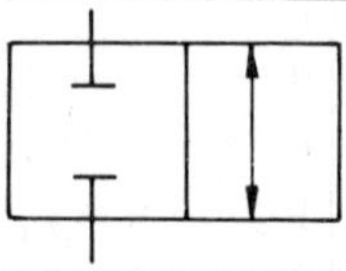
32.	Shut off-valve-with two positions and two connections—spring returned.	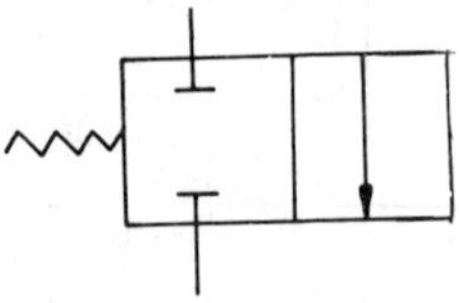

33.	Directional valve—with two positions and three connections. The valve is used— (*i*) to control the flow to give desired motion and (*ii*) to reverse the motion of a hydraulic motor. If the valve is to be spring returned, a spring will be added to this symbol as in 32 above.	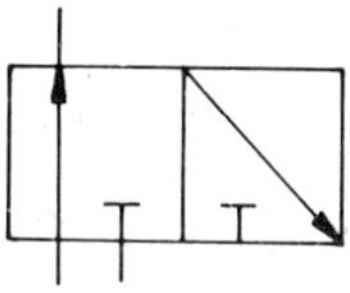
34.	Pressure valve—Pilot operated relief valve to limit the pressure in the flow line.	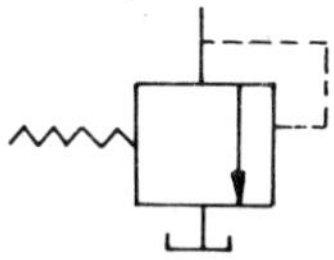
35.	Pressure-reducing valve. The regulator provides operating pressure for the system.	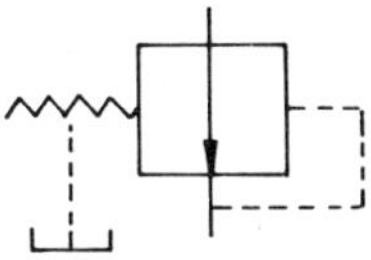
36.	Variable-restriction valve.	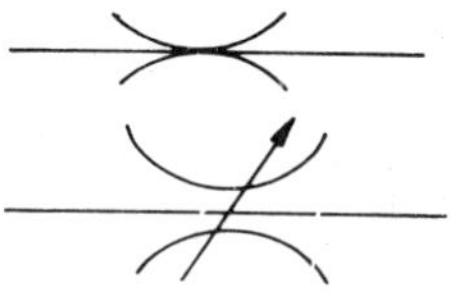
37.	Pressure-compensated adjustable flow control with by-pass.	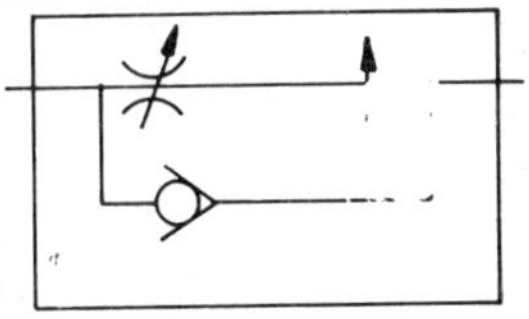
38.	Combination Controls. The various hydraulic symbols can be combined to represent an assembly that performs a function. An assembly is shown by a component enclosure. Internally piloted counter-balance valve with integral check valve.	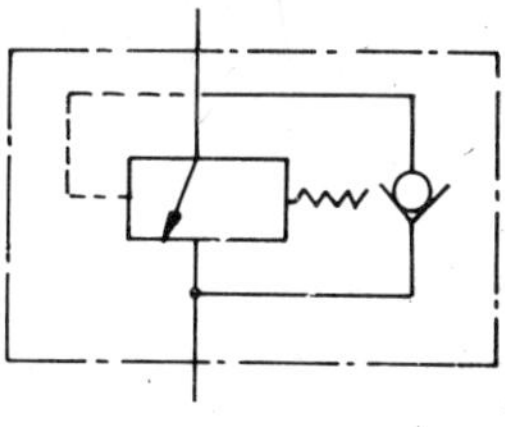

39.	Directional valve—with two positions and four connections. The left-hand square shows the number of connections (four). The right-hand square shows reversibility.	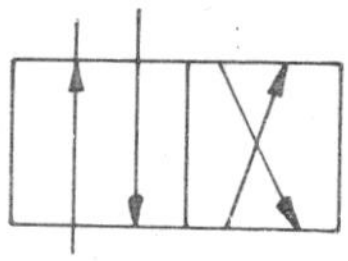
40.	Directional valve—with three positions and four connections. Valve closed when in the centre position. The left-hand square shows the number of lines equal to number of fluid lines of the hydraulic motor. The middle square shows the number of connections. The right-hand square shows reversibility. In the figure, P = pump ; R = reservoir ; M_1 and M_2 = hydraulic motors.	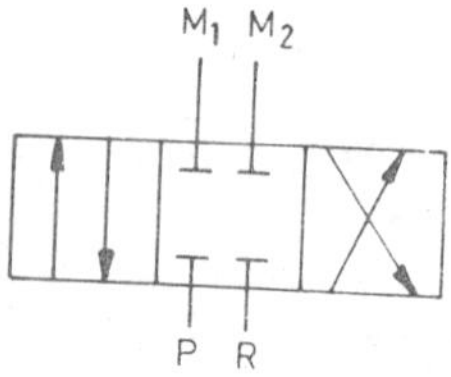
41.	Internal connection in valve housing. Arrow shows the direction of fluid flow.	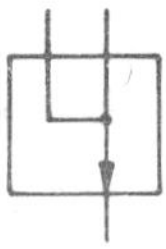
42.	Directional valve—with three positions and four connections. P—connection to pump ; R = connection to reservoir, M_1 and M_2 = connection to hydraulic motors. For all valves—P connects to M_1 and M_2 connects to R or P connects to M_2 and M_1 connects to R. Internal connections shown are : (*a*) Supply and return lines are connected. (*b*) M_1 and M_2 connected to R. P is blocked-off. (*c*) M_1 and M_2 connected to P. R is blocked-off. (*d*) M_1 and M_2 are blocked-off P connnected R.	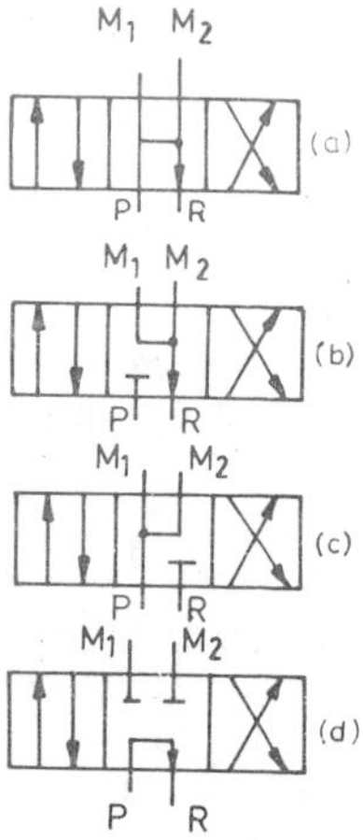
43.	Double acting Hydraulic Cylinder. Sing-end rod.	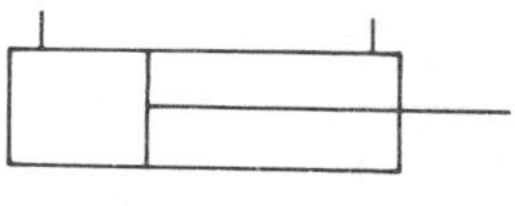

44.	Double acting double-end rod Hydraulic Cylinder.	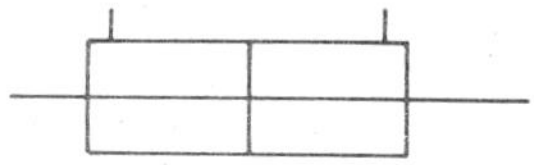
45.	Rotary Hydraulic Motor. (*a*) Fixed displacement, non-reversible, rotation in one direction only. (*b*) Variable displacement.	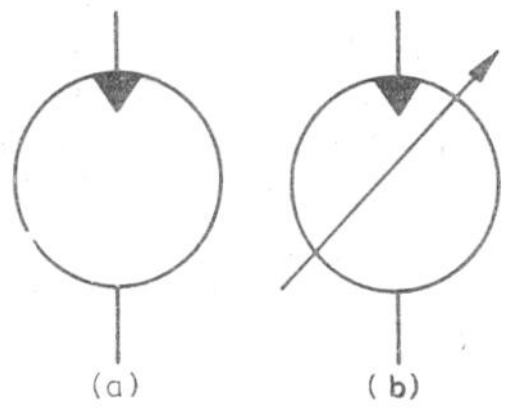
46.	Rotary Hydraulic Motor. (*a*) Fixed displacement, reversible, rotation in both direction. (*b*) Variable displacement, reversible rotation in both direction.	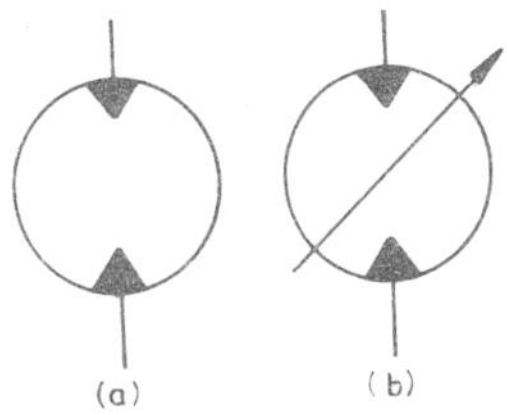
47.	Limited Rotary Hydraulic Motor Oscillator. The output shaft moves back and forth.	
48.	Non-reversible, Single direction Pump— (*a*) Fixed displacement pump. (*b*) Variable displacement pump.	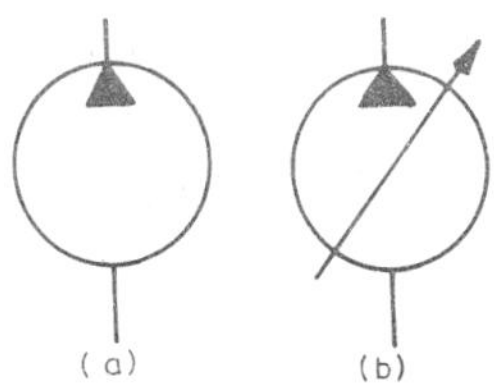
49.	Reversible, two direction pump— (*a*) Fixed displacement pump. (*b*) Variable displacement pump.	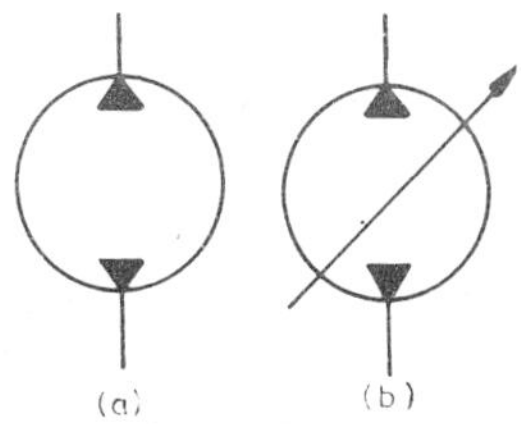

50.	Flexible pipe.	
51.	Pipeline junction.	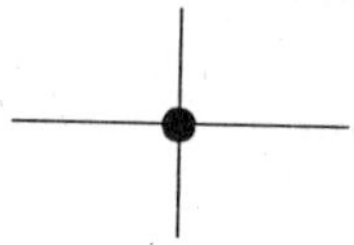

8.42. Hydraulic Circuits

Two types of hydraulic circuits are most commonly used :

(*i*) open circuit

(*ii*) closed circuit.

In open circuit the exhaust oil returns to the reservoir. This methods is preferred because the oil is kept cooler due to the larger volume used. Fig. 8.38 shows an open circuit using fixed displace-

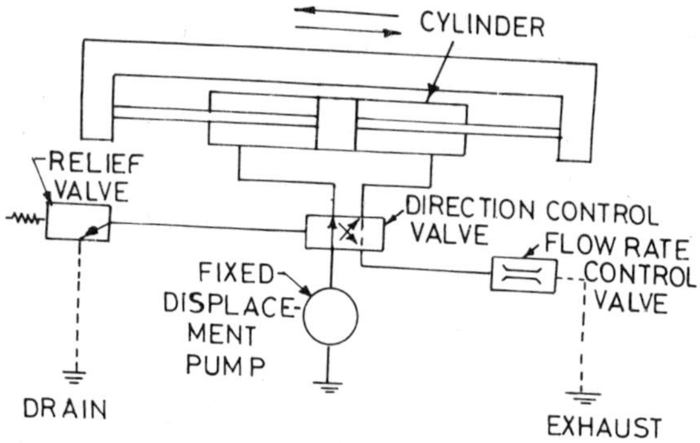

Fig. 8.38

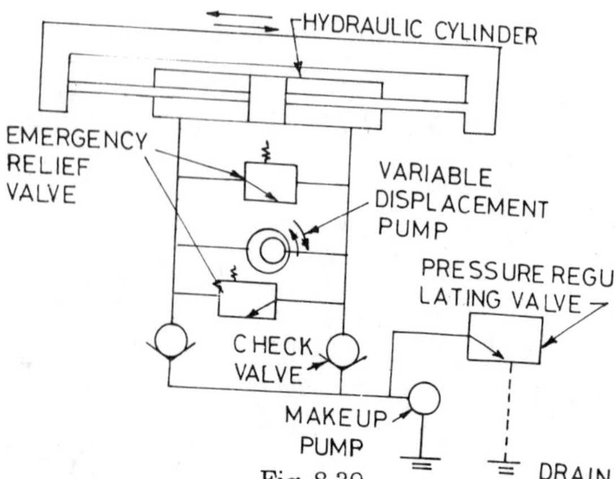

Fig. 8.39

ment pump. The piston speed being controlled by flow rate control valve (throttle valve) in the return line. In a close circuit the exhaust oil returns directly to the pump for re-circulation, leakage being made up by separate supplies.

Fig. 8.39 shows a close circuit using a variable displacement pump to give different rates of table traverse.

8.42.1. Hydraulic cylinders

They are the major component of a hydraulic drive. A piston moves in the cylinder. Based on working of piston, cylinders are of three types :

(*i*) Single acting (Fig. 8.39.1).

(*ii*) Double acting (Fig. 8.39.2) with piston rod on one end.

(*iii*) Double acting (Fig. 8.39.3) with piston rod on both ends.

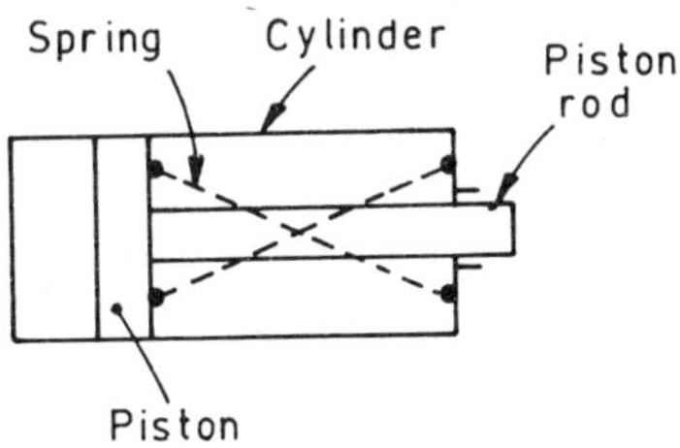

Fig. 8.39.1

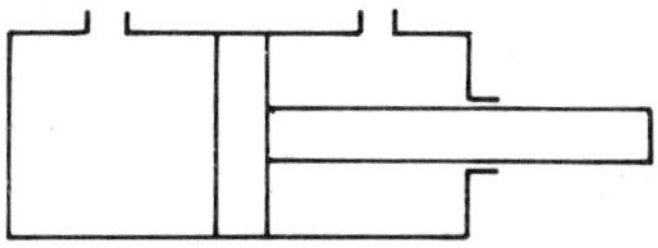

Fig. 8.39.2

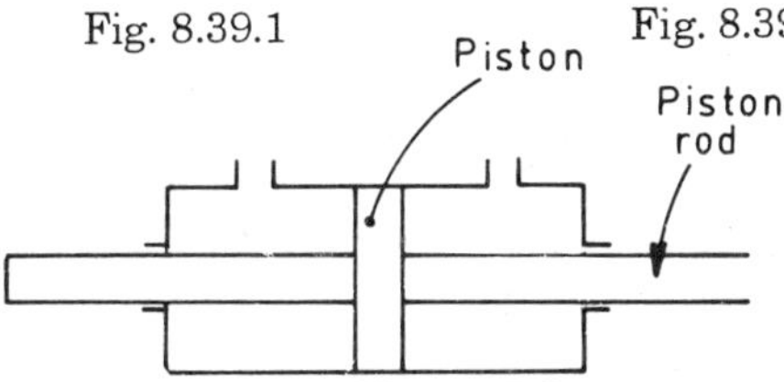

Fig. 8.39.3

8.42.2. Hydraulic motors

They are used for rotary motion. The speed of a hydraulic motor is controlled by changing the amount of fluid through it per unit of time. These are of two types :

(*i*) For rotary motion

(*ii*) For semi-rotary motion.

Fig. 8.39.4 shows a limited rotary vane type motor. It is also called oscillating motor. It has a reversible motion and a limited angle of rotation a maximum up to 330° although a value of 270° is usually not exceeded. These are of two types :

(*i*) Vane type

(*ii*) Piston type.

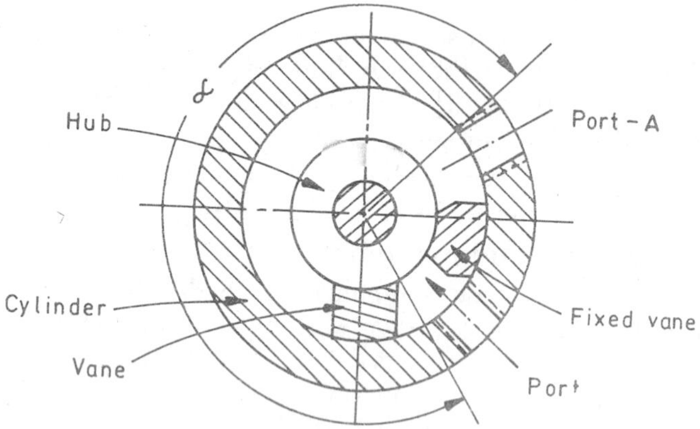

Fig. 8.39.4

Limited rotary motors have extensive application in the feed mechanisms of machine tools, in handling devices of transfer machines to drive chucks in lathes, grinders and other auxiliary mechanisms.

It consists of a rotary hub 1 mounted on a shaft that transmits the motion of the rotary vane. The vane 2 is attached to the rotary hub and they together rotate in a cylinder under the action of unbalanced oil pressure. The hydraulic oil supplied by a pump through a direction flow valve enters at port and causes the vane to move the shaft clockwise. The oil behind the vane is forced out through the port *A* to a drain tank. By changing the position of direction flow valve the oil from the pump is made to enter the port *A* which causes the vane to rotate counterclockwise. The oil behind the vane now drains through the port to the tank. The motor thus supplies an oscillating motion. The fixed vane provides sealing between the two chambers.

8.42.3. Use of flow control valve in hydraulic circuits

Flow control valve (FCV) can be used in a hydraulic circuit in different ways such as

(*i*) metering in circuit

(*ii*) metering out circuit.

As shown in Fig. 8.39.5 the valve is connected between the pump and the cylinder metres the flow into the cylinder during working stroke, called *metering-in* control. Excess fluid from the pump flow back to tank through the relief valve. As shown in Fig. 8.39.6 the valve is connected between the cylinder discharge on exhaust and the tank ; it meters the flow from the cylinder. On the working stroke it thus provides a back pressure which helps in maintaining a more uniform speed of hydraulic motor.

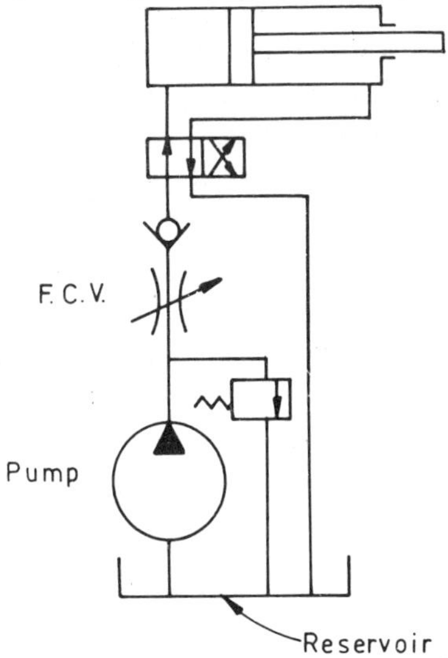

Fig. 8.39.5

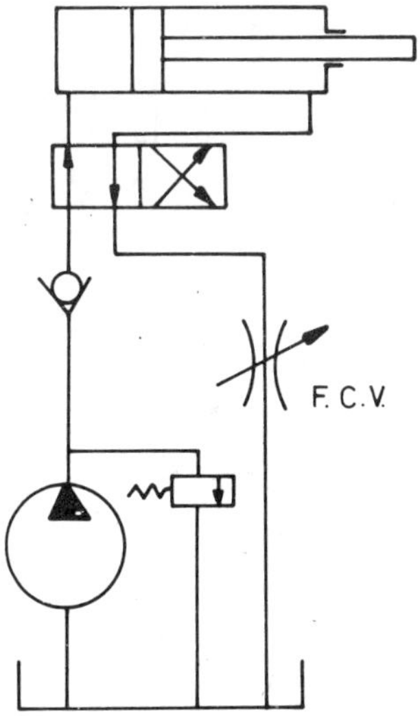

Fig. 8.39.6

8.42.4. Use of relief valve and 2 position 3 way direction control Valve

Fig. 8.39.7 show a typical hydraulic circuit for a power or forming press. A two position 3 way manually operated valve is used to supply and return the process oil from the cylinder.

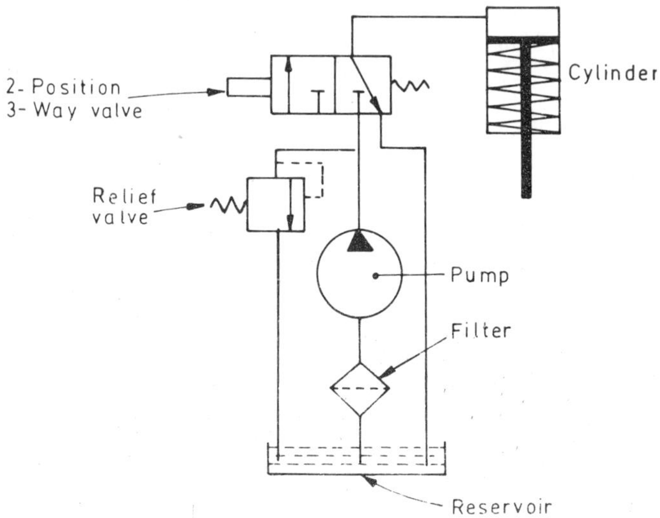

Fig. 8.39.7

8.42.5. Hydraulic systems for feed motion

In hydraulic machine tools the feed motion is achieved by pump and cylinder units. The piston in cylinder gets displaced when the output fluid of the pump is injected into the cylinder.

In order to control the rate of feed in machine tools the commonly used systems are of two types as follows :

(*i*) By controlling the output of a fixed delivery pump by throttles

(*ii*) By variable delivery pumps.

Fig 8.39.8 shows a hydraulic circuit with throttle in the forward pressure line pressure regulating valve keeps pump pressure as constant.

R = Resistance in throttle

P_P = Pump pressure

P_F = Fluid pressure

P_B = Back pressure

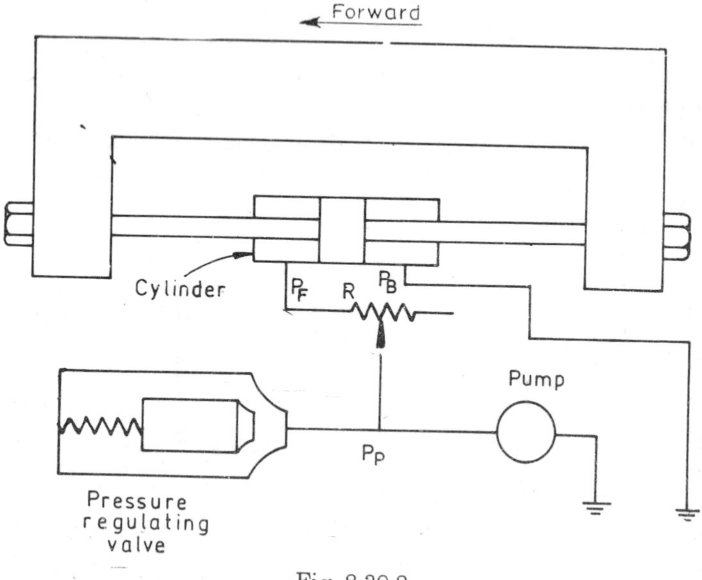

Fig. 8.39.8

Fig. 8.39.9 shows a hydraulic circuit with throttle in the back pressure line. There is an advantage of putting the throttle in the back pressure line as it can take negative work resistance.

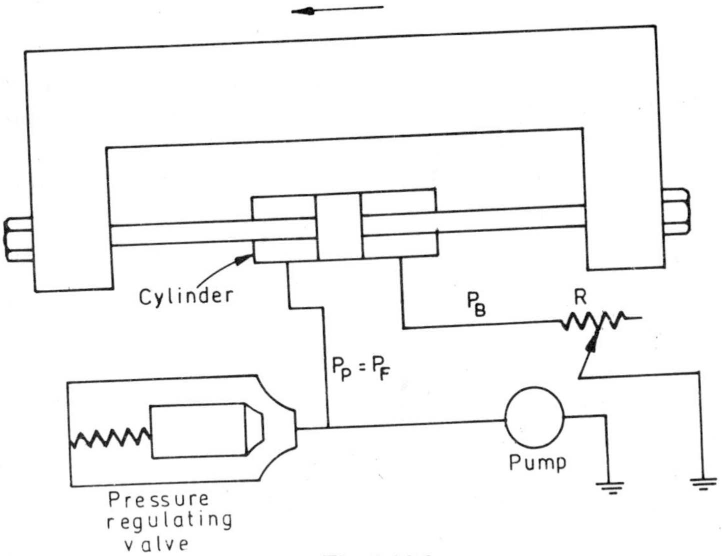

Fig. 8.39.9

8.43. Selection of Drive

The type of drive to be used for a particular machine tool depends upon the following factors :

(*i*) Speed regulation available from the drive

(*ii*) Rigidity of the system

(*iii*) Uniformity in motion

(*iv*) Efficiency of the drive

(*v*) Reliability

(*vi*) Initial cost

(*vii*) Maintenance cost.

8.44. Hydraulic Driver for Shaper

Fig. 8.39.9 (A) shows the hydraulic shaper mechanism. During forward stroke of the ram the oil under pressure is pumped from the reservoir to the right side of the oil cylinder which exerts pressure on the piston. This causes the ram connected to the piston to perform the forward stroke. The oil present on the left side of the cylinder flows through the throttle valve to the reservoir. On the completion of forward stroke of the ram the reversing dog presses the reversing lever and the positions of the valves (*V*) is changed. The oil under pressure is then pumped to the left side of the piston and the ram performs the return stroke and any oil present on the right side of piston flows to the reservoir. On completion of the return stroke the reversing dog operates the reversing lever and position of valves (V) is changed and oil under pressure again flows to the right side of the piston and the forward stroke of ram takes place. This way the cycle continues.

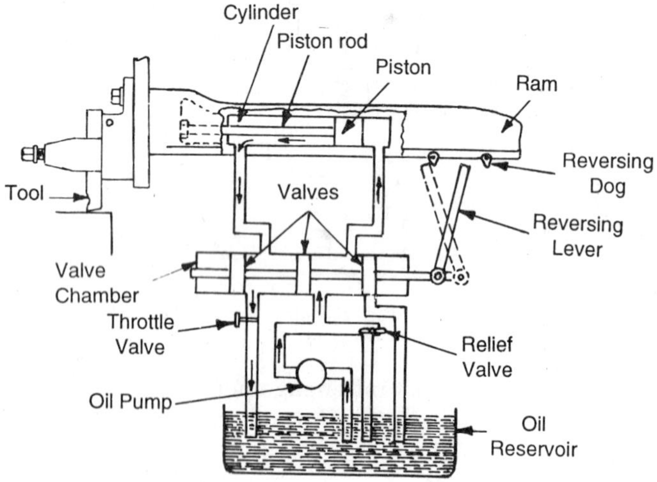

Fig. 8.39.9 (A)

The return stroke of the ram is completed in less time as compared to forward stroke because the constant discharges oil pump, within a fixed period pumps same amount of oil into the right or left hand side of the cylinder and as the left hand end smaller is due to the presence of the piston rod, therefore the oil pressure will be more on the left hand end and piston will be moved back at faster speed. Thus the return stroke will be completed in lesser time.

The throttle valve and relief valves are used to change the cutting speed. When throttle valve is partially closed the excess oil flows to the reservoir through the relief valve and a uniform pressure is maintained during the cutting stroke.

8.45. Hydraulic Drive for Milling Machine

Fig. 8.39.9 (B) shows a typical hydraulic circuit for milling machine. *M* is variable delivery pump controlled by table dogs. Oil is supplied by the gear pump *N* to the pilot valve V_3 for controlling the valves V_1 and V_2 whereby direction and rate of the table movement respectively are determined. The valve V_3 also controls the secondary vertical movement of saddle through pipes *K* and *F* and engagement and disengagement of spindle drive through pipe *R* valve V_4 is used to disengagement some of the secondary movements. The valve *V* is operated by table dogs.

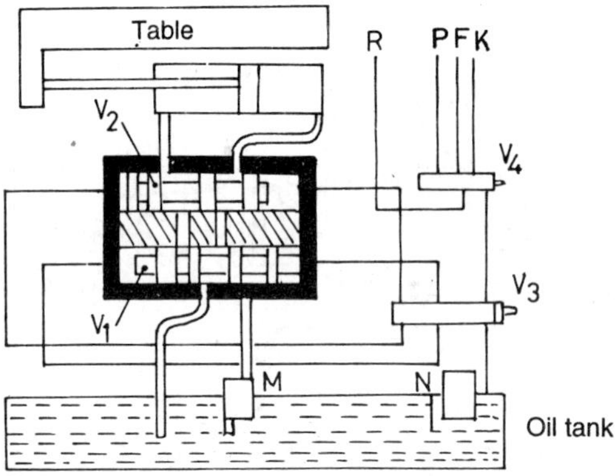

Fig. 8.39.9 (B)

8.46. Clutches

Clutches permit instant engagement and disengagement of the driving and driven shafts. Various types of clutches used in machine tools are as follows :

(*i*) Positive clutch

(*ii*) Friction clutch

(*iii*) Electro-magnetic clutch.

The most commonly used positive clutch is the jaw clutch Fig. 8.39 (*a*). The clutch consists of two halves having projections or so called jaws and recesses. Jaws of one fit into the recesses of other and *vice versa* when the clutch is engaged.

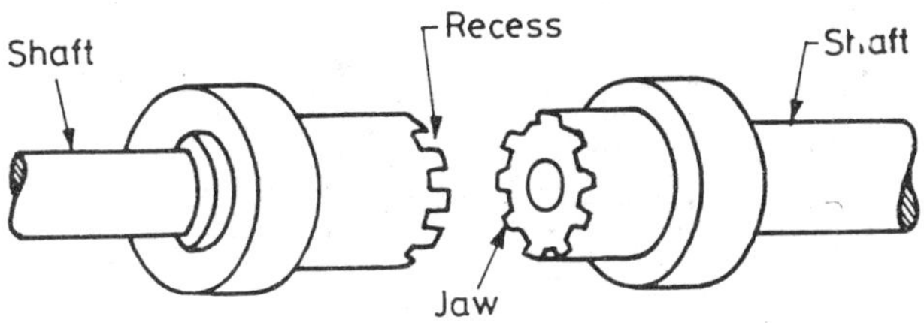

Fig. 8.39 (*a*)

A friction clutch transmits torque by virtue of friction between the two halves. The commonly used friction clutches are of two types :

(*i*) Disc-type friction clutch

(*ii*) Cone-type friction clutch.

Fig. 8.39 (*b*) shows a disc type friction clutch. When the sleeve is moved towards left it exerts an axial force which is multiplied by

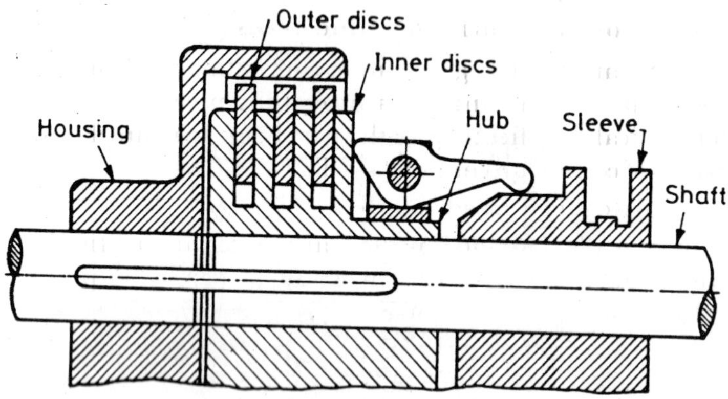

Fig. 8.39 (*b*)

the lever arrangement and applied on the friction discs. The discs get pressed against each other and the clutch gets engaged to transmit rotation between two shafts. Disc type friction clutches have large load carrying capacity with small over all dimensions.

A cone type friction clutch is shown in Fig. 8.39 (*b*). The tapered surfaces of cup and cone are made of materials which have a large coefficient of friction. The clutch gets engaged when the two halves *i.e.* cup and cone are pressed against each other. This clutch is simple in design but the major drawback of this clutch is its large dimensions.

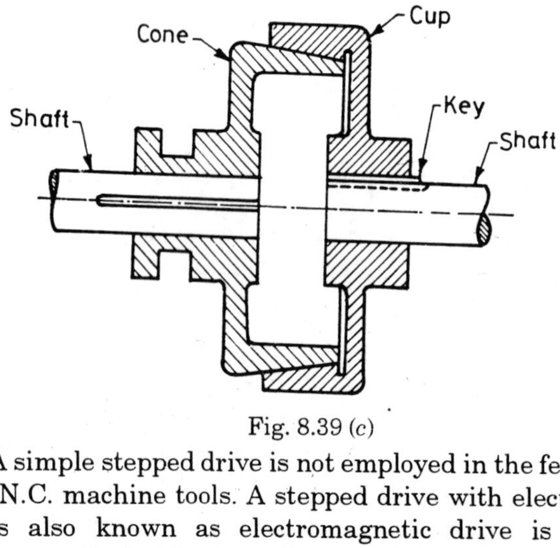

Fig. 8.39 (*c*)

A simple stepped drive is not employed in the feed transmission of N.C. machine tools. A stepped drive with electro-magnetic clutches also known as electromagnetic drive is often used. Electromagnetic clutches permit automatic changing of feed rate.

8.47. Control Systems in Machine Tools

They are used to generate to controlling movements which are essential for carrying out a machining process in accordance with technical specifications of the part being machined. Two main functions of control system are as follows :

(*i*) To change speed and feeds

(*ii*) To provide the working and auxiliary motions in the desired sequence necessary for machining a particular part.

Machine tools are also provided with safety controls to prevent damage to the machine tool and cutting tool during execution of primary auxiliary motions.

Machine tool control system generally consists of the following :

(*i*) a control member to initiate the controlling movements.

(*ii*) a transmission which transmits the controlling movements to the operative member.

(*iii*) an operative member which finally executes the movement.

Automatic control systems can be classified as follows :

(*i*) Mechanical automatic control systems using cams or templates.

(*ii*) Electrical automatic control systems using limit switches and plug boards.

(*iii*) Numerical automatic control systems using punched paper tape, magnetic tape etc.

In mechanical automatic control systems the required sequence of operative movements is programmed on the profile of a cam or template. These systems are simple and reliable. However they are expensive because a new cam or template is required every time when some change in the operative movement is needed.

In electrical automatic control system a definite in built electrical circuit on plug board is used to control a particular movement or operation. The length of travel is controlled by means of switches.

8.47.1. Adaptive Control Systems

The main parameters which cause random variations of the metal cutting conditions are as follows :

(*i*) Changes in workpiece hardness

(*ii*) Changes in machining allowance

(*iii*) Unstable cutting temperature

(*iv*) Changes in deformation of machine tool elastic system.

The random variations are reflected in the changes of

(*i*) Tool wear

(*ii*) Cutting force

(*iii*) Friction force

(*iv*) Cutting temperature.

One or more of which are measured and utilised for an appropriate automatic correction of the controlling parameters so as to maintain stable values of the measured parameters.

The various controlling parameters during machining are as follows :

(*i*) cutting speed

(*ii*) feed

(*iii*) depth of cut

(*iv*) machine tool elastic system consisting of :

(*a*) stiffness

(*b*) damping coefficient

(*c*) mass.

For example tool wear caused due to changes in workpiece hardness can be stabilised by using appropriate value of cutting speed. Similarly due to changes in machining allowance the cutting force may change. The cutting force can be stabilised by controlling the feed rate.

In a metal machining process there are two types of constraints :

(*i*) Process limit constraints regarding

(*a*) Profile shape

(*b*) Surface roughness

(*c*) Power

(*d*) Torque

(*e*) Tool wear.

(*ii*) Process optimisation constraints regarding performance effectiveness which include :

(*a*) Minimum cost

(*b*) Maximum production rate

(*c*) Maximum utilisation of installed capacity

(*d*) Maximum profit.

Adaptive control systems respond to random variations in cutting conditions and correspondingly alter the controlling parameter in order to

(*i*) ensure that the assigned limiting values of process parameters are not exceeded, or

(*ii*) achieve process optimisation from consideration of a performance effectiveness criterion.

Thus there are two types of adaptive control systems :

1. Limit constraint adaptive control systems
2. Process optimisation adaptive control systems.

Fig. 8.40 (*a*) shows a typical limit constraint adaptive control system for a hydraulic tracer semi-automatic lathe in which there

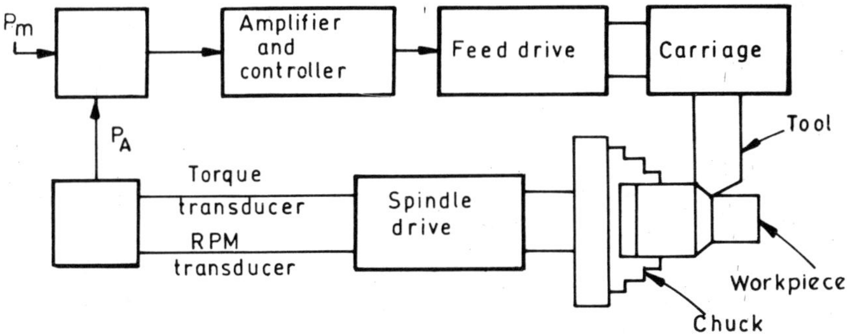

Fig. 8.40. (*a*) Limit constraint adaptive control system.

is a limit constraint on consumed power. The input parameters for the operation of the system are limiting power and maximum feed rate. The torque and r.p.m. of the machine spindle are measured and the actual consumed power (P_A) is compared with the limiting power (P_m). The difference $P_m - P_A$ is amplified and utilized as a controlling signal to regulate the feed rate, which, however, is not allowed to exceed the prespecified maximum value.

Fig. 8.40 (*b*) shows process optimising adaptive control system from the view point of minimum machining cost as the optimising criterion. The minimum machining cost is achieved only at an optimum tool life which calls for a control of the tool wear rate. Direct methods of in-process tool wear measurement are as yet not available, and therefore, some indirect method has to be employed. In the system shown, the tool wear has been estimated through the interface temperature measured by a tool-work thermocouple.

The various symbols are as follows :

TET = Temperature transducer

AWR = Algorithm for wear rate calculation

AFS = Algorithm for optimum feed and speed calculation

DCU = Drive control unit

WP = Workpiece.

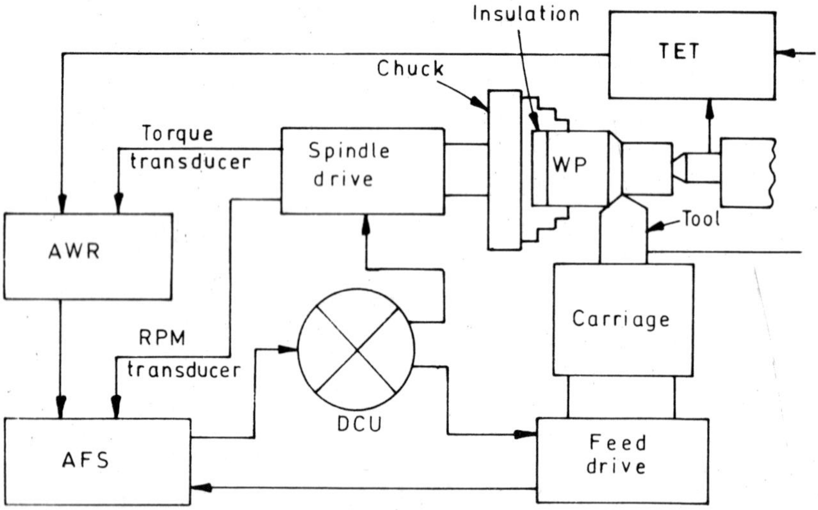

Fig. 8.40. (*b*) Process optimization adaptive control system.

8.48. Gear Boxes with Clutched Drives

Gear boxes using clutches have the following advantages :

1. There is more power availability as compared to draw-key type, Norton or Meander types.

2. Engagement during running is possible using electromagnetic or friction clutches.

3. It enables driving and driven gears to be arranged co-axially leading to compact and efficient gearbox layout.

4. In N.C. machine tools gear boxes are essential for speed control.

Example 8.6. (*a*) *Sketch a hydraulic drive for a horizontal broaching machine.*

(*b*) *Sketch a kinematic structure for a cylindrical grinding machine with hydraulic table feed movement.*

Solution. Fig. 8.40 (*c*) shows a typical hydraulic drive for a horizontal broaching machine in which the broach is pulled through the work piece by a hydraulic force.

Fig. 8.41 shows the kinetic structure for a cylindrical grinding in which table feed movement is achieved hydraulically.

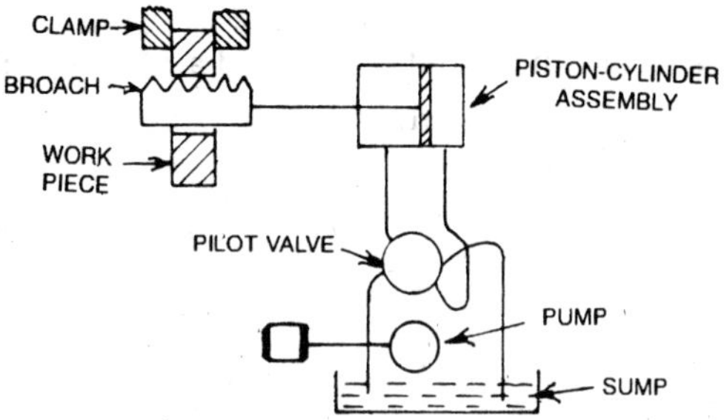

Fig. 8.40 (c)

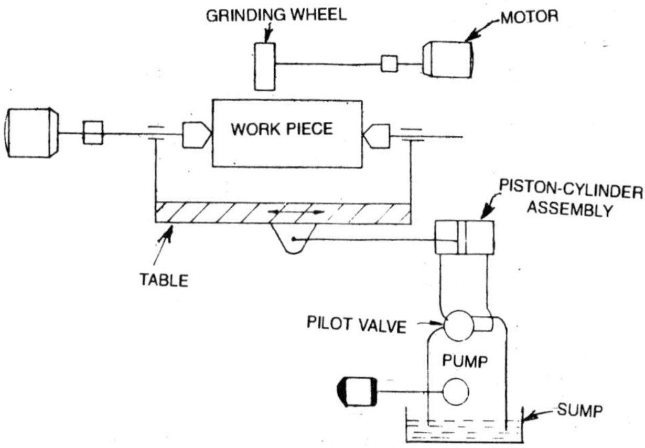

Fig. 8.41

Example 8.6. *Design a nine speed gear box for the head stock of a lathe, the spindle speeds ranging from 28 RPM to 1000 RPM. Draw the structural diagram and show the layout of the gears and connection to motor.*

Solution. Let the speed by in G.P.

$$n = \text{Number of speed steps} = 9$$

$$N_1 = \text{Minimum speed} = 28 \text{ RPM}$$

$$N_9 = \text{Maximum speed} = 1000 \text{ RPM}$$

$$\phi = \text{Geometric progression ratio}$$

$$= \sqrt[n-1]{\frac{N_9}{91}} = \sqrt[8]{\frac{N_9}{N_1}}$$

$$= \sqrt[8]{\frac{1000}{28}} = 1.56'$$

$N_1 = 28$ R.P.M.
$N_2 = 28 \times 1.56 = 43.7$
$N_3 = 43.7 \times 1.56 = 68$
$N_4 = 106$
$N_5 = 165.3$
$N_6 = 258$
$N_7 = 402.5$
$N_8 = 628$
$N_9 = 1000$ R.P.M.

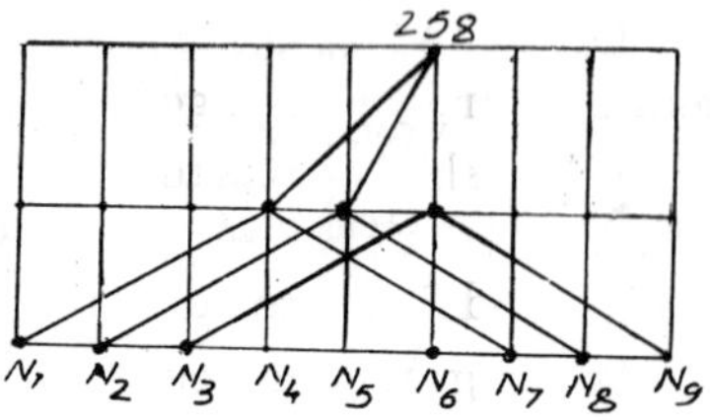

Fig. 8.42

A typical speed diagram (ray diagram) is shown in Fig. 8.42.

$$n = 9 = 1 \times 3 \times 3$$

Let us use a 3 phase 140 R.P.M., 440 V, 50 cycles/sec motor.

D = Motor shaft pulley diameter = 70 mm (say)

D_1 = Diameter of pulley on shaft 1 receiving the drive from motor.

N_1 = R.P.M. of shaft 1 = 258

N = R.P.M. of motor shaft = 1400 R.P.M.

$$\pi D_1 N_1 = \pi D N$$

$$D_1 = \frac{D \times N}{N_1} = \frac{70 \times 1400}{258} = 380 \text{ mm}$$

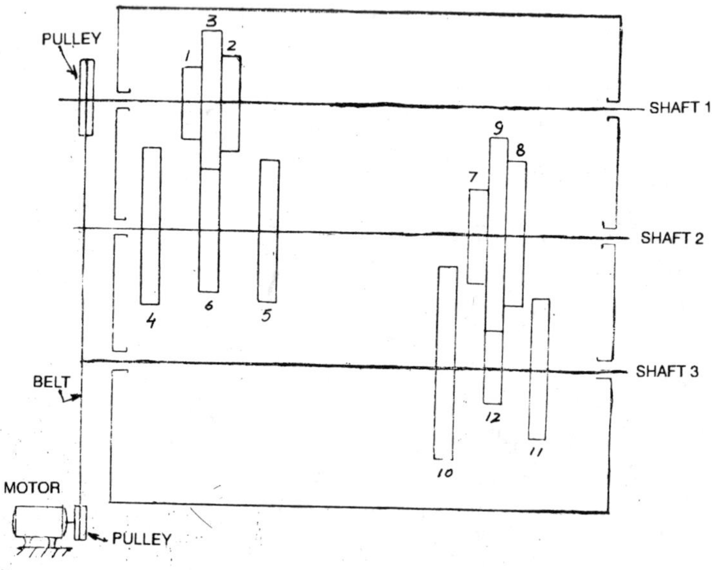

Fig. 8.43

Let T_1, T_2, T_3, T_4, T_5 and T_6 be the number of teeth on gear 1, gear 2, gear 3, gear 4, gear 5 and gear 6 respectively.

When shaft 1 rotates at 258 R.P.M., it is required to obtain 106 R.P.M., 165.3 R.P.M. and 258 R.P.M. on shaft 2. The cluster of gears 1, 2 and 3 is fitted on shaft 1.

When gear 1 comes in contact with gear 4, a speed of 106 R.P.M. is obtained on shaft 2.

$$T_1 = 25 \text{ (say)}$$

$$\frac{T_4}{T_1} = \frac{258}{N_4} = \frac{258}{106}$$

$$T_4 = \frac{27 \times 258}{106} = 61$$

$$T_1 + T_4 = 25 + 61 = 86.$$

When gear 2 comes in contact with gear 5, a speed of 165.3 R.P.M. is obtained on shaft 2.

$$\frac{T_5}{T_2} = \frac{258}{N_5} = \frac{258}{165.3} \quad \text{...(1)}$$

$$T_5 + T_2 = 86 \quad \text{...(2)}$$

Solving (1) and (2), we get

$$T_2 = 34$$

$$T_5 = 52$$

When gear 3 comes in contact with gear 6, a speed of 268 R.P.M. is obtained on shaft 2.

$$\frac{T_6}{T_3} = \frac{258}{258} = 1$$

$$T_6 + T_3 = 86$$

$$\therefore \quad T_6 = T_3 = 43$$

For shaft 2 and shaft 3.

When gear 7 comes in contact with gear 10, the shaft 2 rotates at 258 R.P.M. and shaft 3 rotates at 68 R.P.M.

$$\frac{T_7}{T_{10}} = \frac{68}{258} = 0.263$$

where T_7 = Number of teeth on gear 7

T_{10} = Number of teeth on gear 10.

Let $T_7 = 25$

$$T_{10} = 95$$

$$T_7 + T_{10} = 25 + 95 = 120$$

When gear 8 comes in contact with gear 11, then shaft 2 rotates at 258 R.P.M. and shaft 3 rotates at 258.

$$T_8 = T_{11} = \frac{120}{2} = 60$$

When gear 9 comes in contact with gear 12, the shaft 2 rotates at 258 R.P.M. and shaft 3 rotates at 1000 R.P.M.

$$\frac{T_9}{T_{12}} = \frac{1005}{258} = 3.87$$

$$T_9 + T_{12} = 120$$

$$T_9 = 96$$

$$T_{12} = 24.$$

Structural diagram is shown in Fig. 8.44.

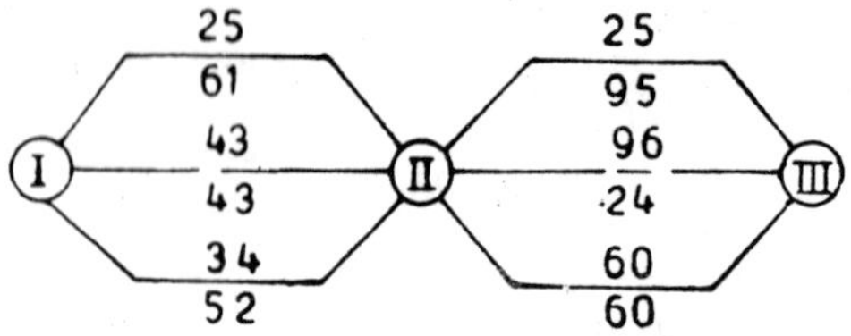

Fig. 8.44

8.49. Flow Chart for Gear Box

Flow chart is used to trace power paths and to indicate stage by stage out puts in a qualitative manner.

Fig. 8.45 shows a gear box for four output speeds and Fig. 8.46 shows flow chart for this gear box.

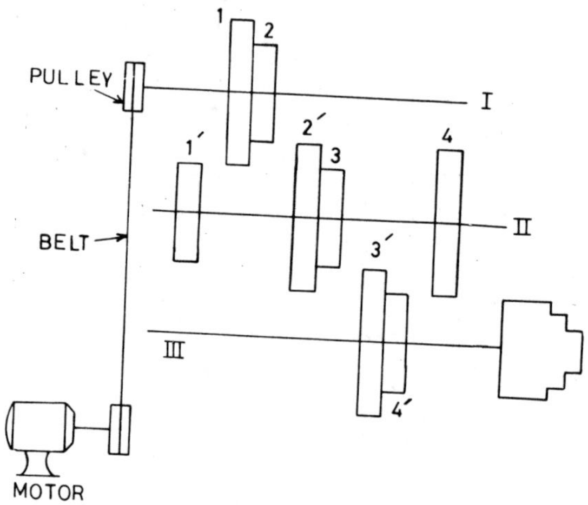

Fig. 8.45

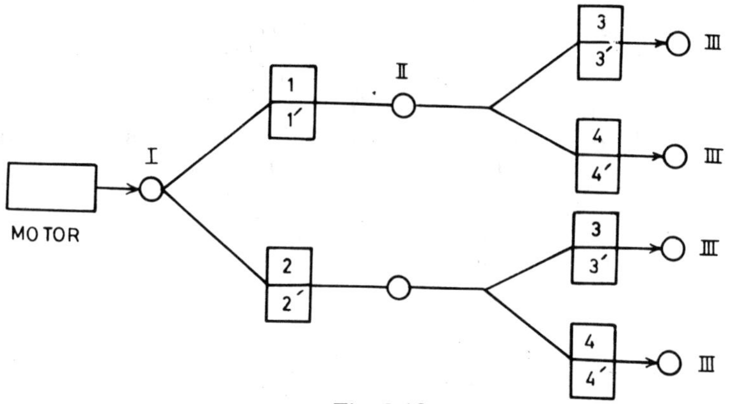

Fig. 8.46

When gear 1 meshes with gear 1′ then the two speech are obtained at output shaft by meshing gears 3 and 3′ and gears 4 and 4′. Similarly when gears 2 and 2′ mesh together two, speeds are obtained by meshing gear 3 with 3′ and gear 4 with 4′.

I = Input shaft

II = Intermediate shaft

III = Output shaft.

Example 8.7. *(a) State the function of throttle valve.*

(b) State the expression for flow rate through a throttle valve.

(c) Name the types of throttle valves.

Solution. (*a*) The function of a throttle valve or flow control valve is to regulate the flow rate in hydraulic circuit by changing the area of constriction at the throat of the throttle. The hydraulic resistance varies with the variation of the orifice. This changes the pressure drop and consequently the rate of fluid flow through the valve.

(*b*) The flow rate (Q) through the valve is given by the expression as follows :

$$Q = \text{Flow rate } (\text{m}^3/\text{sec})$$

$$= K \cdot A \cdot \sqrt{\frac{2gP}{w}}$$

where K = Discharge coefficient and is a function of Reynold number

= 0.72 – 0.74 (Assume)

A = Cross-sectional area at the throat of the throttle (m^2)

P = Pressure drop in the throttle (kg/m^2)

w = Specific weight (kg/m^3)

g = 9.81 m/sec^2.

(c) In throttle valves the construction of flow passage has been obtained by either

(i) translatory motion of a reciprocating device

(ii) rotary movement of restricting device.

Various types of throttle valves are as follows :

(i) Needle type or cone type

(ii) Truncated cone type

(iii) Disc type

(iv) Slot type :

(a) Rotary slot type

(b) Tapered slot type.

Example 8.8. *Sketch typical two arrangements for six speed gear box.*

Solution. Fig. 8.47 (a) shows a six speed (1 × 3 × 2) gear box and Fig. 8.47 (b) shows ray diagram. Another typical arrangement for six speed (1 × 2 × 3) gear box is shown in Fig. 8.47 (c). The ray diagram for this arrangement is shown in Fig. 8.47 (d).

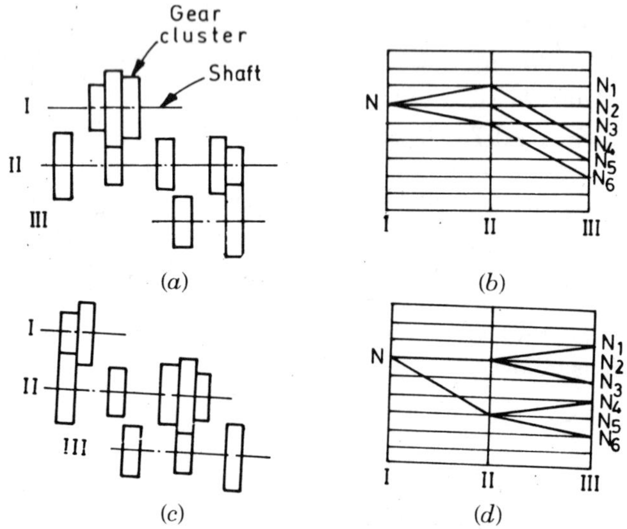

Fig. 8.47

Gear boxes with larger speed ranges and with greater number of steps can be designed by arranging several two axes gear drives (part drives) in series.

The number of steps in a gear box with more than two axes is equal to the product of the numbers of steps of the part drives (intermediate transmissions).

In ray diagrams the speeds plotted vertically on a logarithmic scale and the shafts are shown as vertical parallel lines at equal distance from each other. Distance between consecutive speed lines is constant because of geometric progression. The speed values appear on the logarithmic scale at equal distance and the transmission ratios between two axes are indicated by the vertical distances between the corresponding speed values. As the distances between the axes are shown equal, the slope of the lines joining the speed values on different axes are an indication of the corresponding transmission ratios. The ray diagram shows at a glance the kinematic arrangement, shaft speeds at different stages and torque at various speeds.

PROBLEMS

8.1. What is a kinematic drive ? How is it obtained ?

8.2. Explain stepped drive and stepless drive.

8.3. Explain the following :

(*a*) Ray diagram

(*b*) Speed spectrum in geometric progression.

(*c*) Speed spectrum in arithmetic progression.

8.4. State the basic rules for layout of gear boxes having sliding clusters.

8.5. Explain the following methods of obtaining different speeds of machine tool spindle :

(*a*) Cone pulley arrangement

(*b*) Cone pulley drive by back gears

(*c*) Speed gear boxes.

8.6. Write short notes on the following :

(*a*) Screw cutting on lathe using change gears.

(*b*) Norton gear box.

(*c*) Feed gear box of Meander type.

(*d*) Ruppert drive.

(*e*) Feed drive of a lathe.

(*f*) Infinitely variable drives.

(*g*) Mechanical stepless drive systems.

(*h*) Electric stepless drives.

8.7. Explain hydraulic stepless drives.

8.8. Explain open and closed circuit used in hydraulic drive.

8.9. Write short notes on the following :

(*a*) Hydraulic valves

(*i*) Relief valves (*ii*) Safety valve

(*iii*) Reducing valve.

(*b*) Hydraulic fluids used in machine tool drives.

8.10. The spindle speed change gear for a drilling machine has to comply with the following specifications :

Maximum diameter of drill = 20 mm.

Minimum diameter of drill = 5 mm.

Maximum cutting speed of smallest drill = 28 m/min.

Minimum cutting speed of largest drill = 20 m/min.

Six spindle speed, motor speed = 2800 R.P.M.

Sketch a suitable ray diagram for the layout of the spindle drive and determine the ratios of the gear teeth of the engaging pairs. The H.P. of the machine may be taken as 2 H.P. and the minimum member of teeth on a gear as 17. (*A.M.I.E., 1974*)

8.11. Design the head stock gear box of a turret lathe having arrangement for nine spindle speeds ranging from 34 R.P.M. with $\phi = 1.58$. Only layout and not a full drawing of the gear box should be shown. The H.P. of the machine may be taken at 6 and minimum number of teeth on the gear as 17. The motor rotates at 1410 R.P.M. Draw a suitable and admissible structure developing the corresponding ray diagram and hence select the optimal layout and calculate the gear ratios. (*A.M.I.E., 1975*)

8.12. (*a*) What are the differences between structure diagram and ray diagram ?

(*b*) A six speed gear box is required to be designed for transmitting 10 H.P. with speed ranging from 400 R.P.M. with $\phi = 1.25$.

Select an optimum ray diagram and hence calculate the gear sizes, module and width of gears. Calculate the shaft sizes and sketch the gear box. (*A.M.I.E., 1979*)

8.13. Describe the following :

(*a*) Pre-optive gear box. (*b*) P.I.V. drive.

8.14. Describe individual drive and group drive for machine tools.

8.15. Describe the selection of electric motors for the machine tools drives.

8.16. Describe unilateral and bilateral speed diagrams.

8.17. Write short notes on the following :

(*i*) Speed range ratio.

(*ii*) Common ratio (ϕ) and its standard values.

(*iii*) To determine number of teeth on gears.

8.18. What is a clutch ? Sketch and describe various types of clutches used in machine tools.

8.19. Write short notes on the following :

(*i*) Kinematic functions of machine tool.

(*ii*) Group drive and individual drive of machine tools.

8.20. Discuss control systems in machine tools.

8.21. Describe flow chart for gear box.

8.22. Discuss the general requirements of machine tool design.

8.23. Describe methods to reduce :

(*a*) axial dimensions

(*b*) radial dimension of speed gear boxes.

8.24. Write short notes on the following :

(*i*) Selection of drive for machine tools.

(*ii*) Types of speed boxes.

(*iii*) Types of feed boxes.

(*iv*) Advantages of gear boxes with clutched drive.

(*v*) Types of hydraulic valves.

(*vi*) Any two types of hydraulic circuits.

9

Newer Machining Processes

9.0. Introduction

In recent years a number of new materials have been developed which are being commonly used in space research, missiles and nuclear industry. These materials are more strong, hard, tough, heat and wear resistant and cannot be machined by conventional machining processes. This has led to the development of new metal removing processes called Newer Machining Processes or Unconventional Machining Processes. These processes are not affected by strength hardness, toughness and brittleness of materials and can produce intricate and complicated shapes on the workpiece.

These processes are widely used for :

(*i*) Machining materials which are difficult-to-machine conventionally.

(*ii*) Producing complex surfaces effectively and efficiently.

(*iii*) Producing very high surface qualities.

9.1. Classification

These newer machining processes can be classified into various groups according to the following factors :

1. Type of energy required to shape the materials :
   - (*a*) Chemical
   - (*b*) Electrical
   - (*c*) Thermal
   - (*d*) Magnetic
   - (*e*) Mechanical.
2. Medium for energy transfer :
   - (*a*) Electrons
   - (*b*) Radiation
   - (*c*) Plasma
   - (*d*) Electrolyte
   - (*e*) High velocity.
3. Mechanism of material removal :
   - (*a*) Mechanical erosion
   - (*b*) Ion displacement

(*c*) Vaporisation (*d*) Fusion.

The various newer machining processes are as follows :

(*i*) Electrochemical machining (E.C.M.)

(*ii*) Electrochemical grinding (E.C.G.)

(*iii*) Electrical discharge machining (E.D.M.)

(*iv*) Ultra Sonic machining (U.S.M.)

(*v*) Abrasive jet machining (A.J.M.)

(*vi*) Electron beam machining (E.B.M.)

(*vii*) Lesser beam machining (L.B.M.)

(*viii*) Plasma arc machining (P.A.M.)

(*ix*) Hot machining

(*x*) Electromagnetic forming

(*xi*) Explosive forming

(*xii*) Hydro forming.

These new techniques of machining are quite diverse in nature and differ from each by their characteristics feature of design operation and field of application. However they have the common property of being based on a non-mechanical, physical metal removing phenomenon.

The various advantages of newer machining processes as compared to conventional machining processes are as follows :

(*i*) The physical and mechanical properties of the work material do not predominentally affect the quality of the surface and the productivity of the process.

(*ii*) As there is no physical contact between tool and work therefore the dimensional accuracy achieved is better.

(*iii*) It is not essential that the cutting tool should be made up of material harder than the workpiece material.

(*iv*) Heavy and large machine tools are not required to machine large size workpieces.

(*v*) Simple kinematic motions are required for the different machines.

9.2. Electrochemical Machining (E.C.M.)

It is also called electrolytic machining or anodic cutting. This process is quite commonly used for shaping hard metals or for resharpening of cementing carbide cutting tools. This process is based on principles of Faraday and Ohm. In this process an electrolyte cell is formed by the workpiece (anode) and tool (cathode) in the midst of a flowing electrolyte in a very small gap of 0.025 cm between the two. The metal removal is due to the ion migration towards the tool. The tool is provided with a passage for circulating the electrolyte with sufficient velocity to flush off the metallic ions from the cutting zone. The work is generally kept stationary and the tool is fed in a linear direction. The electrolyte used is generally an aqueous solution of common salt. Sodium nitrate solution is also used. This process is ideally suitable for the production of deep holes and profiled cavities in electrically conducting materials (Fig. 9.1).

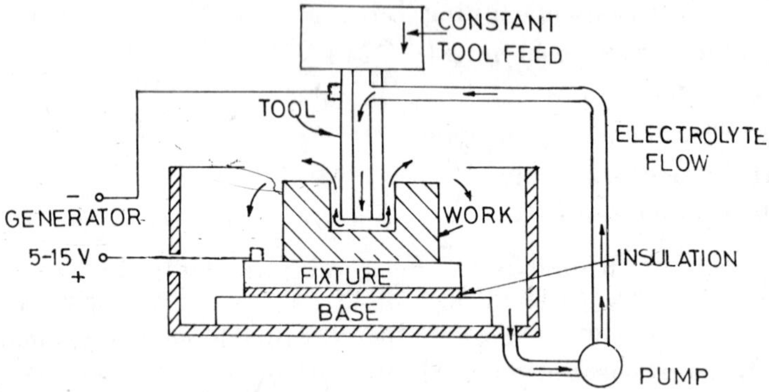

Fig. 9.1. Electrochemical Machining.

The various advantages of this process are as follows :

(*i*) As the tool does not come in contact with the work, therefore tool wear is practically nil.

(*ii*) The metal is removed at a much faster rate.

Electrochemical machining is quite suitable for the following machining operations :

(*i*) To machine through holes of any cross-section.

(*ii*) To machine delicate external shapes such as turbine blades.

(*iii*) To machine blind holes and shaped cavities such as in forging dies.

The materials commonly used in the manufacture of tools are aluminium, bronze, brass, copper and stainless steel.

The electrolyte use perform the following functions :

(*i*) Completes the electric circuit between tool and workpiece.

(*ii*) Allows desirable machining to occur.

(*iii*) Carries away products of reaction from the zone of machining.

(*iv*) Carries away heat generated during chemical reactions.

The electrolyte should have the following properties :

(*i*) High electrical conductivity

(*ii*) Chemical stability

(*iii*) High specific heat and low viscosity.

In *ECM* the electrolyte serves the following two functions :

(*i*) It provides the medium by which electrolysis takes place.

(*ii*) It removes the heat that is generated in the working zone as a result of the flow of a high current through the electrodes and through the electrolyte itself. The quantity of electrolyte flowing should be sufficient to prevent the boiling point of the liquid being reached.

The following two aspects of chemical nature of the electrolyte should be considered.

(*a*) It should not be corrosive.

(*b*) It should not be sufficiently active chemically to cause efficient metal removal.

9.2.1. Metal removal rate

The rate at which the metal is removed from the workpiece in *ECM* is calculated as follows.

$$Z = \eta \cdot \frac{E}{\rho} \cdot I$$

where Z = Volume of metal removed electrolytically per unit time.

E = Electrochemical equivalent of work material.

ρ = Density of the work material.

I = Current

η = Current efficiency *i.e.* fraction of current actually effective in electrolysis.

The tool feed speed is given by

$$V = \frac{Z}{A} = \eta \cdot \frac{E}{\rho} \cdot \frac{I}{A}$$

where V = Total feed speed.

A = Area of work surface exposed to electrolysis.

$\frac{I}{A}$ = Current density.

The current density is limited by the capacity of the supply as well as the capacity of workpiece material, the tool material and the electrolyte to carry the current. The highest metal removal rate by this process varies between 0.3 to 1.4 cubic inch per minute.

9.2.2. Limitations of ECM

(*i*) Tooling cost is more.

(*ii*) The equipment required is very costly.

(*iii*) The electrolyte may attack or corrode some metals.

(*iv*) A cloud of corrosive mist or spray is generally associated with ECM process, especially while using sodium chloride on electrolyte. This may lead to harmful conditions which may affect the operator and contaminate other machines in the adjacent area.

9.2.3. Applications

ECM is quite useful process. Electrochemical machining has been very effectively used for drilling, surfacing, sawing, die sinking, contour machining, multiple hole drilling, etc., in hard metal. For soft metals, only some of the processes are economical, like profiling and multiple hole drilling. The process is also used for deburring of machined components.

9.3. Electrochemical Grinding (E.C.G.)

Electrochemical grinding also known as electrolytic grinding is being widely used for the grinding of tungsten carbide tips. This process is preferred as compared to the conventional grinding because higher metal removal rates are possible by this process. This process is more economical in the use of abrasives which is particularly important if the abrasive is expensive like diamond grit. This process is based on electrochemical machining method. In this process the metal is removed both by electrochemical decomposition and abrasion of metal. In fact 10% of the work metal is removed by abrasive cutting and 90% by electrolytic action. The wheel employed

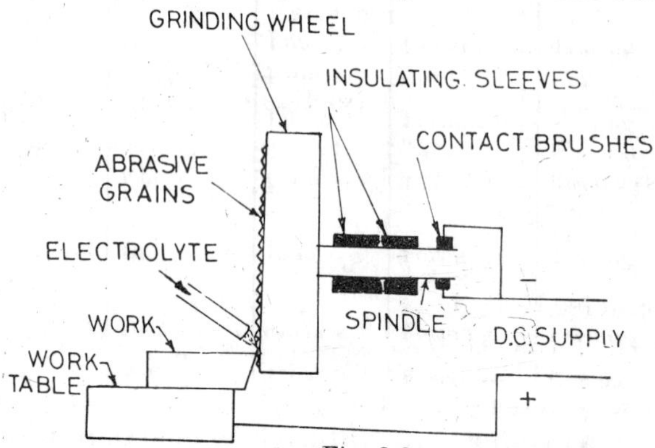

Fig. 9.2

is made of fine diamond particles in metal matrix. The grinding wheel and its spindle are insulated from rest of the machine and are connected to the negative terminal of a low voltage D.C. Supply (Fig. 9.2). The particles of grinding wheel slightly project out from the surface of wheel and come in contact with the workpiece with very little pressure.

During grinding process a continuous stream of non-corrosive salt solution is passed through work and tool which acts both as electrolyte and coolant.

The metal-removal rate can be expressed as

$$Z = Z_1 + Z_2$$

where Z = total metal-removal rate

Z_1 = metal removed electrolytically per unit time

Z_2 = metal removed by mechanical abrasion per unit time.

The value of Z_1 can be obtained from a knowledge of the current flowing, the electrochemical equivalent of the work material, and the current efficiency. For current densities to approximately 1 MA/m^2 (700 A/in^2) the current efficiency can be assumed to be 1.00. Usually in practice Z_1 constitutes 90 per cent and Z_2 10 per cent of the total metal-removal rate Z^4.

In electrolytic grinding the predominance of the electrolytic action reduces wheel wear to a negligible amount and makes it possible to grind hard materials rapidly. Moreover, the wheel can be used for long periods without dressing. The temperature rise and mechanical forces are very small, and hence thermal damage and surface cracks, common in conventional grinding, are eliminated.

Electrolytic grinding has been used very successfully in the grinding of hard materials of an electrically conductive nature. One of the most notable cases of success is in the grinding of carbide-tool tips, where the absence of grinding cracks in the ground tip and the high rate of removal are of great advantage.

9.4. Electrodischarge Machining (E.D.M.)

In this process the metal is removed from the workpiece due to erosion caused by rapidly recurring spark discharges taking place between the tool and work. Fig. 9.3 shows the mechanical set up and electrical circuit for electrodischarge machining.

A thin gap of about 0.025 mm is maintained between the tool and workpiece by a servo system. Both tool and workpiece are submerged in a dielectric. Kerosene is a very common type of liquid dielectric although gaseous dielectrics are also used in certain cases.

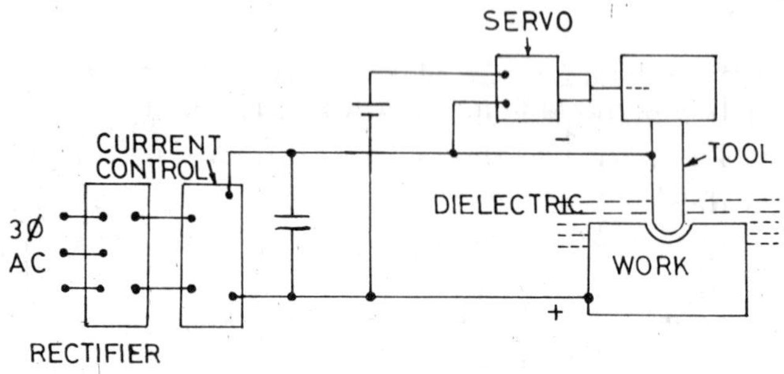

Fig. 9.3

The tool is made cathode and workpiece as anode. When the voltage across the gap becomes sufficiently high it discharges through the gap in the form of a spark in an interval of from 10 to micro seconds. The moment spark occurs sufficient pressure is developed between work and tool as a result of which a very high temperature is reached and at such a high pressure and temperature that some metal is melted and erroded.

This process is used for shaping carbide dies and punches to give any shape or profile.

In *EDM* power supply controls the spark frequency, energy and voltage.

The electrolyte (Dielectric) acts as an insulator or barrier to the current flow. Once the break down voltage of dielectric is reached, a spark is generated by the flow of amperage across this gap.

The dielectric also acts as a coolant during machining. Forcing the coolant through the gap between workpiece and tool removes the particles which are then filtered before the dielectric is re-used.

This method is quite useful to machine cavities or intricate shapes in very hard materials. Blind cavities in dies used in die casting, stamping, forging and injection moulding can be easily produced.

The amount of metal removed from the surface of the work piece is controlled by adjusting the amperage. In *EDM* which removes metal by the process of controlled spark erosion, the tool material should have a high melting point and be a good conductor of heat and electricity.

Advantages

(*i*) The surface finish obtained is very good.

(*ii*) This process can be used for any hard material. Materials like carbide, ceramics can be easily machined by this process.

(*iii*) Loss of metal in machining is very small.

(*iv*) The tool material need not be harder than work material.

Disadvantages

(*i*) Metal removal rate is low.

(*ii*) Power requirement is high.

9.4.1. Tool Wear and Tool Materials

The high rate of tool wear is one of the major difficulties in EDM. The *wear ratio*, defined as the volume of metal lost from the tool divided by the volume of metal removed from the work, varies with the tool and work materials used. For example, with a brass tool and a brass workpiece the ratio is approximately 0.5, while for a brass tool and a hardened-carbon-steel workpiece it is approximately unity and for a brass tool and a tungsten carbide workpiece the ratio may be as high as 3.

High tool-wear rates result in inaccurate machining and add considerably to the expense since the tool electrode itself must usually be accurately machined.

9.4.2. Dielectric Fluid

In EDM process the dielectric fluids commonly used are paraffin oil and transformer oil. Both these fluids are hydrocarbons and it has been found that the hydrogen in these fluids provides the deionizing action necessary for the fluid to become an effective insulator after each discharge.

The dielectric fluid used must remain nonconducing until breakdown occurs ; when the critical voltage is reached, it must break-down rapidly and then deionize rapidly after the condenser has discharged. The latent heat of vaporization of the dielectric fluid must be high so that only a small quantity vaporizes and the spark channel is confined to a small area. The dielectric fluid must have sufficiently low viscosity to flow easily and remove the metal globules effectively from the working zone.

In electrical machining processes such as ECM, Electrolytic grinding and EDM the tool material can be softer than the work material and metal removal rate is independent of the hardness of work material. These are the notable advantages of these processes. One important limitation of these processes is that the work material must be an electrical conductor.

9.5. Ultrasonic Machining (U.S.M.)

In this process the tool is made to vibrate with high frequency on to the work surface in the midst of slurry of abrasive in very fine grit suspended in water. The abrasive used are born carbide, silicon carbide or aluminium oxide. As shown in Fig. 9.4 high frequency current drives a magneto strictive transducer converting electrical energy into mechanical energy. The tool oscillates linearly at ultrasonic frequencies of from 15,000 to 30,000 cycles per second while immersed in a liquid slurry. During cutting the tool performs hammering on abrasive particles which are continuously circulated between the tool and work and thus under the impact of the tool, the abrasive particles perform metal removing operation. The adequate flow of slurry is maintained by a pump. The slurry which is made of abrasive particles suspended in a liquid is fed into the cutting zone under pressure. A concentration of about 30 per cent is the optimum from the point of view of pump design and of achieving adequate penetration. The size of abrasives varies between 200 and 2000 grit. Coarse grades are good for roughing whereas finer grades (say 1000 grit) are used for finishing. To achieve accuracy of high values extre-mely fine grades of 1200 to 2000 grit are used. The tool used is made of a material that is easily machined such as brass or so soft steel. This process can be used to produce holes or cavities in hard and brittle materials. Tool steels, ceramics, cemented carbides, precious stones and gears can be easily machined by this process. The accuracy of the finished profile obtained by this depends upon the tool accuracy but may be as high as 0.003 mm.

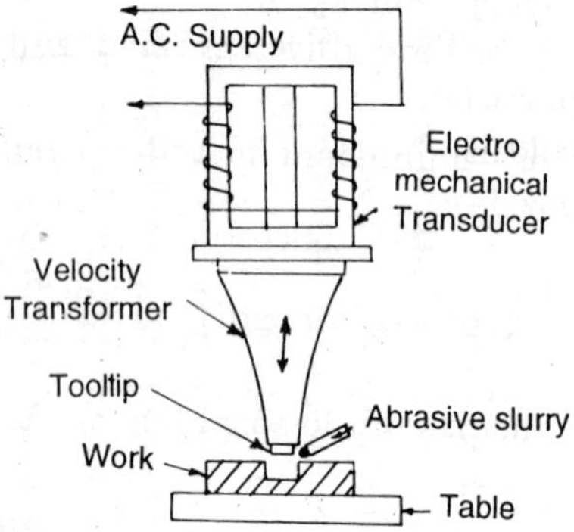

Fig. 9.4

In this process the sonic velocity (V) for a given solid material is calculated by using the following formula :

$$V = \frac{E}{\rho}\left[\frac{m\,(m-1)}{(m^2 - m - 2)}\right]^{1/2}$$

where E = Young's modulus

$\frac{1}{m}$ = Poisson's ratio

ρ = Density of material.

Proper tool material should be selected so that tool does not fail or wear out because of vibrations. Tough maleable materials like alloy steels and stainless steel prove satisfactory.

9.6. Abrasive Jet Machining (A.J.M.)

This process makes use of a focused stream of abrasive particles carried by a high pressure gas (CO_2 or N_2) or air at a velocity of about 200 to 400 m/second. The stream passes through a nozzle and strikes the workpiece as a pressure of about 2 to 8 kg/cm^2

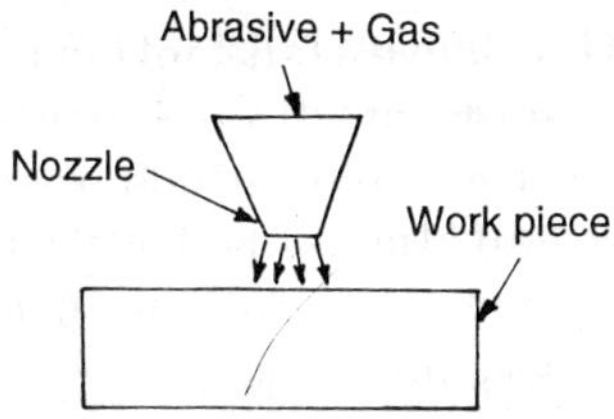

Fig. 9.5

(Fig. 9.5). The material from the workpiece is removed by erosion. The metal removal rate depends upon flow rate and size of abrasive particles. The size of abrasive particles varies from 10 to 50 microns. The abrasive particles should be of irregular shape. The commonly used abrasives are aluminium oxide, silicon, carbide, dolomite and glass. The inside diameter of the nozzle through which the abrasive particles flow is about 0.04 to 0.07 mm and the distance between nozzle mouth and the workpiece is about 0.7 to 1 mm. This process is suitable for machining supper alloys and refractory materials.

Advantages

(*i*) This process can machine thin sections of hard and brittle materials like silicon, mica and ceramics.

(*ii*) Holes of intricate shapes can be produced in the workpiece.

(*iii*) Surface finish obtained is good.

(*iv*) There is no contact between tool (nozzle) and workpiece, therefore, the tool wear is less.

Disadvantages

(*i*) Metal removal rate is low.

(*ii*) A suitable dust collecting system is required.

(*iii*) The abrasive may get embedded into the workpiece surface.

9.7. Electron Beam Machining (E.B.M.)

The electron beam is a stream of negatively charged particles which are generated, accelerated and to some extent focused inside a device called electron gun. An electron gun consists of a cathode which serves as the source of electron, an anode which is kept at ground potential and through which the high velocity electrons pass and a grid cup which is negatively based with respect to the filament. The beam of electron is emitted from the tip of hot cathode. It is accelerated towards the mode by the high potential applied between the anode and cathode.

In this process a high energy beam of electrons from electron gun is focused on the workpiece. This beam heats, melts and vaporises the work material at the point of bombardment. The process is carried out in a vacuum and means are provided to place the workpiece in a sealed compartment (Fig. 9.6). This process is

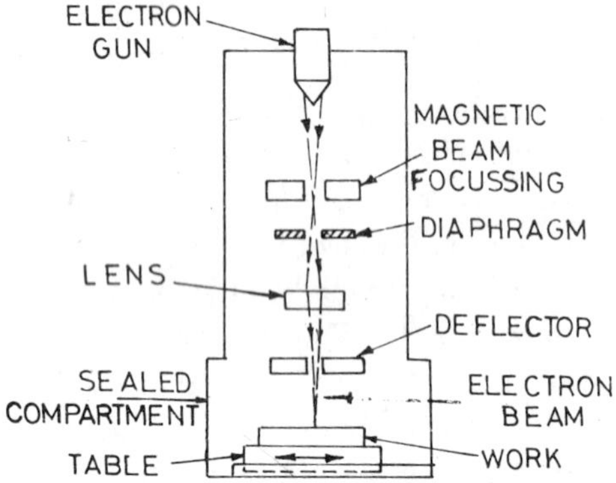

Fig. 9.6

successfully used for drilling holes in difficult materials. The electron beam can be controlled very accurately and machining tolerances of 0.005 mm are possible. This process is quite suitable for materials having a high melting point combined with low thermal conductivity. Although the process does not offer the advantage of high rates of metal removal but it can be used to cut very delicate shapes.

The speed (V) of electron when under control of electric field is given by the relation

$$V = \sqrt{\frac{2e}{m} \times E} \text{ m/sec dynes.}$$

where E = Voltage of electric field in volts

m = Mass of electron in kg

e = Charge of electron in coulomb.

The total power (P) for a beam of current I amperes is given by

$$P = E, I \text{ watts.}$$

The force (F) of the beam from the electron beam on the molten metal is given by the relation

$$F = 0.34 \sqrt{E} \text{ dynes.}$$

9.8. Laser Beam Machining (L.B.M.)

This process uses a laser beam (a narrow beam of coherent, monochromatic light) which is focused on the workpiece by a lens to give extremely high energy density to melt or vaporise any material. A laser usually called ruby rod is used for the production of laser beam. As shown in Fig. 9.7 when electrical energy is discharged into the flash lamp, there is a powerful burst of light and this strikes the Ruby rod and comes out of it in the form of laser beam. This beam is focused on the workpiece by a lens provided in the system.

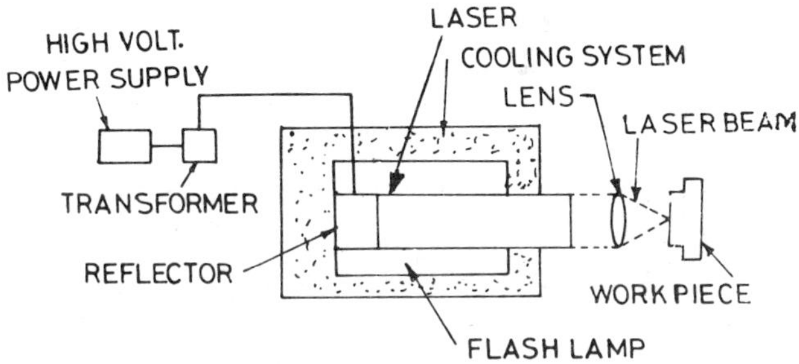

Fig. 9.7

This process is commonly used for micro drilling and micro-welding of materials.

Advantages

(*i*) Laser beam can be focused at one place thereby generating lot of heat.

(*ii*) It is a quicker process.

Disadvantages

(*i*) The input energy requirement is high.

(*ii*) Only thin materials can be machined.

9.9. Plasma Arc Machining (P.A.M.)

This process is based on the formation of a plasma, an ionised conducting gas, by striking of an electric arc between a tungsten electrode and the metal to be cut. In this process an electric arc is produced between a cathodic electrode and an anodic nozzle and then a gas which may be hydrogen, nitrogen or a mixture of these is introduced into the arc chamber. As the molecules of the gas pass through the arc chamber, they absorb energy from the arc and the gas is dissociated into atoms and in some cases into ions. This ionised gas is impinged on the workpiece at a high velocity. The temperature of this hot ionised gas called plasma is about 10,000 to 20,000. The cutting is accomplished by first melting the work surface and then by blasting away the molten metal by plasma (Fig. 9.8), plasma arc cutting is quite commonly used in the cutting of

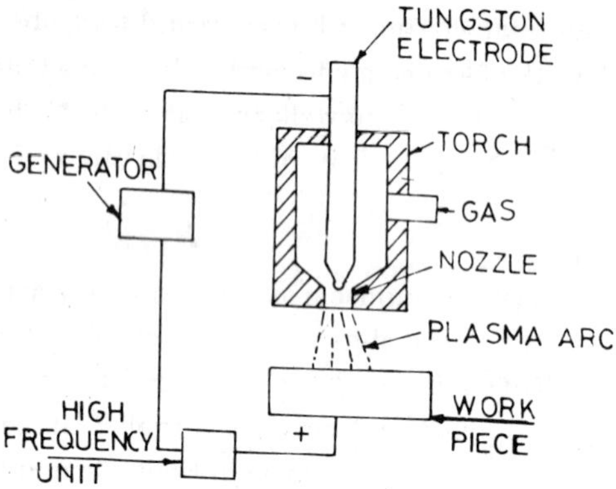

Fig. 9.8

aluminium alloys, copper and highly alloyed steels. Plasma arc cutting process can cut plain carbon shells four times faster than ordinary flame cutting torches. On the machining side, plasma arc has been used for rough turning of very difficult materials.

Advantages

(*i*) In this process only a small shear zone is created in this reducing distortion tendencies.

(*ii*) The surface is smooth.

(*iii*) This process can be used to cut all metals with varying degree of economy and some non-metals can also be cut.

(*iv*) Cleaning and preheating of the workpiece is not required.

(*v*) The metal cutting operation is very fast.

Table 9.1 indicated process capability of some of the non-conventional machining processes.

Table 9.1

Process	*Tolerance (μm)*	*Surface finish CLA (μm)*	*Metal removal rate (mm^3/min)*
ECM	50	0.1—2.5	1500
EDM	15	0.2—12	800
EBM	25	0.4—2.5	1.6
LBM	25	0.4—1.25	0.1
PAM	125	Rough	7500
USM	7.5	0.2—0.5	300

9.10. Hot Machining

In this process the component is heated before being machined. The shear strength of a metal decreases at elevated temperature as compared to that at room temperature. Therefore, the force required on the tool is lower for cutting hot metal as compared to the force required to cut a metal at room temperature. The carbide tools are preferred in hot machining as compared to high speed steel tools because the cutting edge of high speed steel tool gets deformed at higher temperatures. This process is quite commonly used to machine high strength, high hardness and high temperature resistant materials which are difficult to machine by conventional methods.

The application of the correct amount of heat in the required place of workpiece is of maximum importance. The heating method should possess the following requirements :

(*i*) It should be easy to set up and to control.

(*ii*) It should provide a wide range of constant temperature.

(*iii*) Capital cost of the equipment should be low.

(*iv*) The operating cost should be low.

The various methods of heating commonly used are as follows :

(*i*) Furnace heating (*ii*) Flame heating

(*iii*) Induction heating. (*iv*) Arc heating.

In furnace heating the workpiece is heated in a gas or electrical furnace the temperature of which has been raised to that of required for the cutting operation. The workpiece is then removed and is then placed in a vice or fixture on the machine. In flame heating the workpiece is heated by means of a gas flame while it is mounted on the machine. In induction heating, the heating current is induced on the workpiece by transformer action by means of a primary coil which is designed to cover the area to be machined and which is mounted to provide the heat zone in the workpiece. An induction heating set up for milling operation is shown in Fig. 9.9. Induction heating method is easy to control and maximum cleanliness can be maintained in process. Although it is costly method but it is the most efficient method as it heats only a small zone ahead of the tool. Arc heating method is quite suitable for turning and milling operations. In arc heating an arc is struck between the surface and carbon electrodes. Arc heating is used for the machining of refractory and non-magnetic materials which need cutting temperature over 540°C. The main disadvantage of arc heating is the difficulty experienced in maintaining a constant temperature.

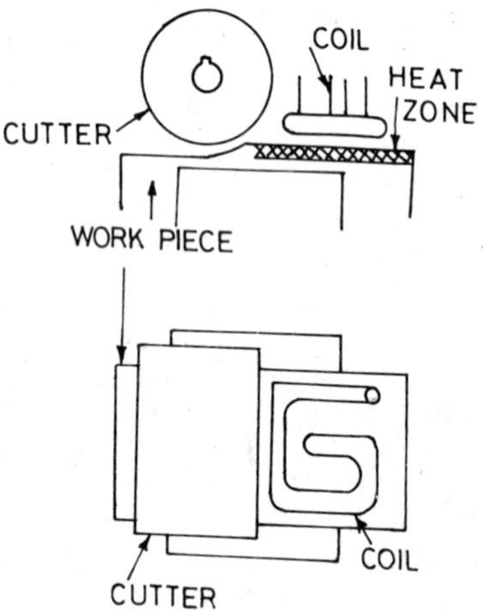

Fig. 9.9

9.11. Explosive Forming

In this process sheet metal is formed to the counter of a prepared die by explosive impact. This process makes use of an explosive which is detonated and its energy transmitted to the workpiece through a fluid. The commonly used fluid is water as it is cheap, convenient to use and has reduced compressibility water also acts as shock dampner. The cylinder contains water. The explosive which is immersed in water and located at a predetermined distance from sheet metal black is detonated and the shock waves generated force and stretch the metal to the shape of the die (Fig. 9.10). It is desirable to exhaust the air from the die before firing the charge because normally the air is trapped between the sides of the die and the component thereby preventing a faithful reproduction of the die form being generated. Die is usually made up of spheroidal graphite iron. This process has been used successfully for forming complex sheet metal parts for jet aircraft engines guided missiles, nuclear and rocket requirements. Another application of this process is to form large paraboidal reflectors for radar installations. Materials like aluminium alloys, copper, low and medium

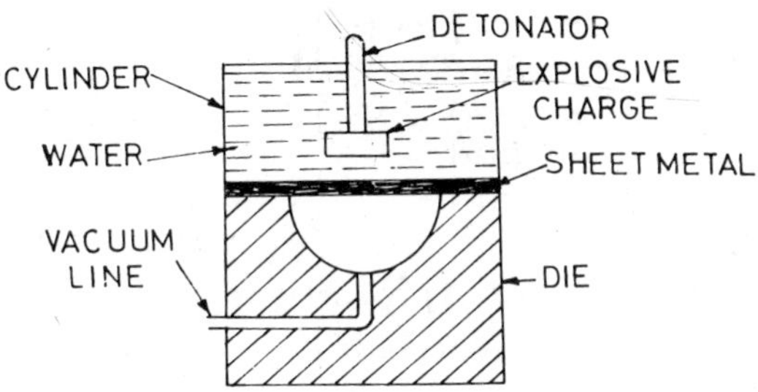

Fig. 9.10

carbon steels, stainless steels, titanium etc. can be easily explosive formed.

Advantages

(*i*) By this process sheet metal is formed into shapes which cannot be produced economically by other conventional processes.

(*ii*) Investment cost in dies is low.

(*iii*) Components can be made to close tolerances.

(*iv*) Tough materials as well as ductile materials can be explosive formed.

(*v*) One die can be used to produce parts in varying thickness.

Disadvantages

(*i*) The process should be conducted at safe and remote places because a lot of sound and noise is produced and precautions are to be taken as explosion hazards exit.

(*ii*) Labour cost is more.

This process is also known as high energy rate forming (HERF).

9.12. Electro Magnetic Forming (E.M.F.)

It is the process of electrically forming conducting metals of moderate thickness by the use of a precisely controlled electromagnetic force. The principle of electromagnetic forming is that when an electric current flows in a conductor, it establishes a magnetic field, also a magnetic flux field can produce an electromotive force in a conductor. As shown in Fig. 9.11 the magnetic field shaper causes the magnetic field to be concentrated at

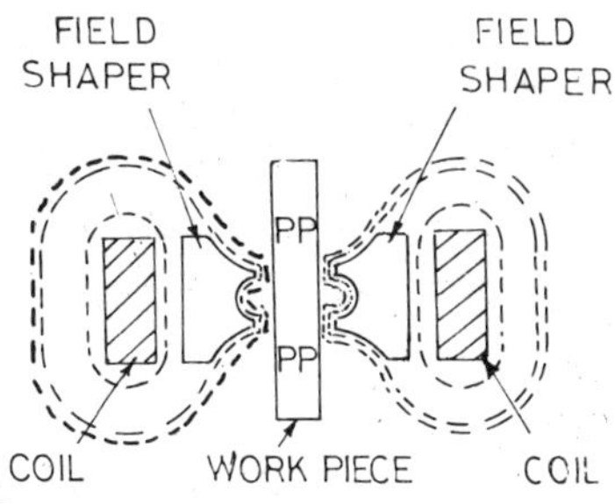

Fig. 9.11

points P with the effect that the workpiece is compressed in those areas. Most suitable materials for this process are those with high electrical conductivity such as copper, silver and aluminium. This process is used for expanding and shaping, tubing, coining and swaging.

Advantages

(*i*) It gives a high rate of production.

(*ii*) It is reliable and controllable.

(*iii*) Maintenance cost is low.

(*iv*) It is a simple and clean process and the component surface does not suffer any contamination.

(*v*) Tools used are simple and there is no tool wear.

9.13. Hydro Forming

This process is used to produce sheet metal components by using a controlled hydraulic pressure. The sheet metal is formed about the punch not by impact but by pressure and is accomplished by hydraulic fluid contained in a cavity in the ram and held by a flexible diaphragm. As shown in Fig. 9.12 (*a*) the blank is placed in the draw ring. Then the upper member is lowered so that the flexible diaphragm is in the contact with the blank [Fig. 9.12 (*b*)]. Then the punch is pushed upward into the die cavity forcing the metal blank to draw in around the punch against the pressure of hydraulic fluid. The sheet metal takes the form of the punch under the application of opposing and increasing forces [Fig. 9.12 (*c*)]. The punch is then lowered and the required component is obtained [Fig. 9.12 (*d*)]. The draw ring is made up of mild steel and punch is made up of cold working steel.

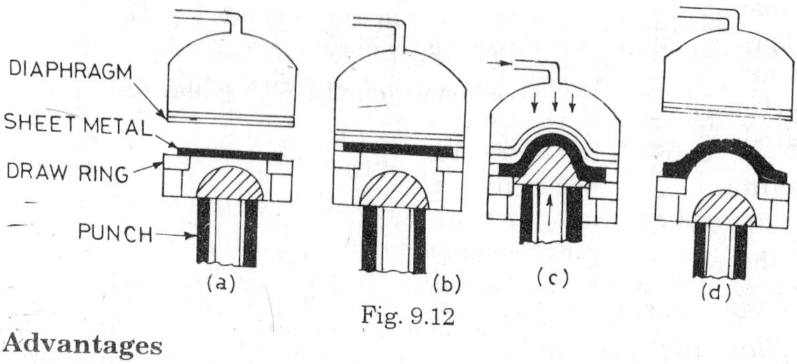

Fig. 9.12

Advantages

(*i*) This process eliminates the need for expensive tooling for deep drawn parts.

(*ii*) In this process the fluid pressure can be controlled easily. The forming of different depths in the same components can be performed easily.

(*iii*) Changes from one metal to another do not affect the tooling.

(*iv*) The process control is easy.

The main drawback of this process is that it cannot be used for large scale production.

9.14. Spark Erosion

Spark erosion is used as a machining operation for a wide range of industrial applications. In this process the cutting tool or electrode is made with negative potential and workpiece with positive potential. Spark is produced between the electrode and the workpiece. Fig. 9.13 shows diagrammatic view of circuit used on spark erosion machines.

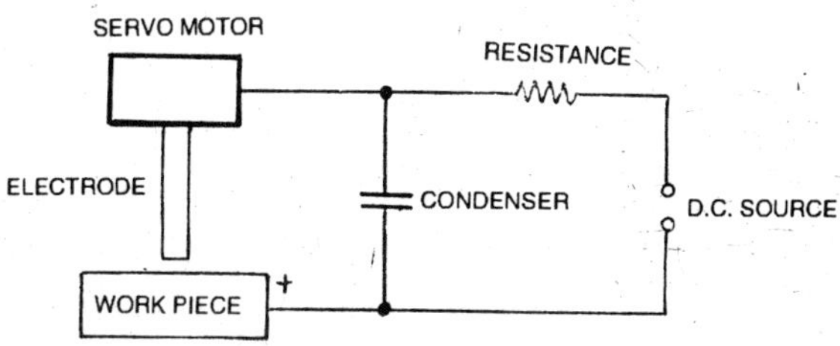

Fig. 9.13

When voltage becomes sufficient high to break the gap between the electrodes, the capacitor is immediately discharged in the form of spark, in the gap, and the capacitor is recharged. The greater the spark the greater will be the size of particles removed from the workpiece. The resistance can be included in the circuit to control the time at which the voltage across the gap begins to increase again. A servomotor is used to provide a controlled feed to the cutting electrode.

Advantages

(*i*) The capital cost of the equipment compares favourably with the more conventional metal cutting machines.

(*ii*) Parts of intricate form can be produced to close tolerances.

(*iii*) As the electrode is not in direct contact with the workpiece, the need for heavy clamping to secure rigidity of the workpiece does not arise.

(*iv*) This process is suitable for shaping of any metal or alloy which is a sufficiently good conductor of electricity.

(*v*) This process is quite suitable for machining hard material which are not normally readily machineable and for shaping or modifying parts like dies, moulds after hardening.

Some of the features of spark erosion, electrolytic (electrochemical) machining and ultra sonic machining can be compared as follows (Table 9.2).

Table 9.2

Feature	*Spark Erosion*	*Ultrasonic machining*	*Electrolytic machining*
Capital cost	Moderate	Moderate	High
Operating labour	Low	Low	Low
Tool cost	Low	Very low	Low
Machine Maintenance	Moderate	Moderate	Moderate
Surface finish and accuracy	Good	Very good	Very good
Power for cutting	High	High	Medium

9.15. Wire-cut Electro Discharge Machining (WEDM)

Fig. 9.14 shows in schematic form the principle of Wire-cut Electro-Discharge Machining process. This process uses a continuously moving very thin copper or brass wire 0.02 to 0.3 mm in diameter as an electrode. This machines the workpiece with electrical discharge like a band saw. The dielectric fluid used is distilled water with constant specific resistance.

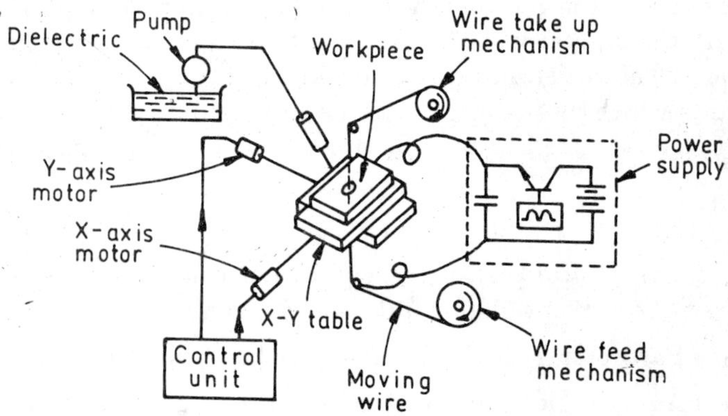

Fig. 9.14

Wire cut EDM machine basically consists of a machine proper composed of a workpiece contour movement control unit (NC unit or copying unit), workpiece mounting table with X and Y axis motion and wire drive section, power supply system which supplies electrical energy to the wire electrode and pump to supply dielectric. The basic principle of metal removal in this process is same as that of EDM but in WEDM instead of a shaped electrode a continuously moving wire acts as the electrode. In WEDM the working zone only is supplied with a jet of dielectric medium instead of submerging the whole workpiece in the dielectric as in case of EDM.

Since a very thin electrode is used, an extremely small amount of discharge energy suffices for one spark and the workpiece is machined under conditions for finishing as specified for conventional EDM.

In this process the wire is passed through a predrilled hole in the workpiece. The electrical power is supplied by the electronic pulse generator, which applies a potential between the wire electrode and the workpiece. The table is moved till the wire is very close to the edge of the hole. The dielectric fluid is supplied into the drilled hole.

The dielectric flow (deionized water) is adjusted, so that no air bubble enters the working zone. The voltage across the spark gap increases linearly, which sets up an electric field across the spark gap. It leads to the breakdown of the spark gap. At this instant, the current from the pulse generator flows across the spark gap. The spark energy heats, melts and vaporizes the material of the workpiece. With vaporizing action the molten material on the workpiece is removed.

9.16. Applications

The WEDM process is quite commonly used in stamping dies, drawing and extruding tools, templates, gauges, cams and plastic molding dies.

9.17. Advantages

Various advantages of WEDM process are as follows :

1. This process can be operated for long time at high production rate.

2. Unskilled operator can carry out machining.

3. The surface finish obtained is of high quality.

4. Electrode wear is negligible. Since the wire electrode is constantly fed during machining, its wear can be practically ignored.

PROBLEMS

9.1. State the reasons responsible for the development of newer machining processes.

9.2. Describe the principle of electro-chemical machining (ECM).

9.3. Describe the principle of electro-chemical grinding (ECG).

9.4. How electro-discharge machining (EDM) is carried out ?

9.5. Explain ultrasonic process (USM).

9.6. Describe the electron beam machining principle (EBM).

9.7. Describe laser beam machining process. State its advantages and disadvantages.

9.8. Describe the principle plasma arc machining (PAM) state its advantages and disadvantages.

9.9. Describe the principle of hot machining.

9.10. What is explosive forming ? Describe it in detail. State its advantages and disadvantages.

9.11. Describe the principle of electro-magnetic forming (EMF).

9.12. Describe the principle of hydro-forming.

9.13. Describe the principle of abrasive jet machining (AJM). State its advantages and disadvantages.

9.14. State the functions of electrolyte in ECM.

9.15. Describe the principle of spark erosion. State the advantages of this process.

9.16. Describe Wire-cut electro discharge machining (WEDM) process.

10

Capstan, Turret and Automatic Lathes

10.0. Introduction

An engine lathe is not preferred for batch and mass production because the time taken for changing and setting the tools and time required for making measurements on the workpiece is quite large. Also a skilled machinist is required to run the engine lathe. For batch or mass production, therefore, it is advantageous if several tools can be mounted in such a manner as to be readily presentable to the work and if possible that several tools can be cutting simultaneously. The feature is possible on turret lathe capstan lathe, screw machines, and other types of semi-automatic and automatic machines.

10.1. Comparison of Turret Lathe, Capstan Lathe and Engine Lathe

These lathes are compared as follows :

(*i*) Turret lathe differs from the engine lathe in that the tail stock of the engine lathe is replaced by a hexagon turret which permits the mounting of multiple tools.

(*ii*) The second difference between engine lathe and turret lathe is the substitution of the square turret of the compound rest. The cross slide is made long enough to permit the mounting of another tool post of square turret at the rear of the slide. The turret may be indexed automatically so that each tool can be presented to the workpiece in rapid succession.

(*iii*) The labour cost required to operate an engine lathe is more than turret and capstan lathe. In turret and capstan lathe the cutting tools required for a particular components are preset to stop by a skilled setter enabling the machine to be operated by an unskilled worker producing components quickly and relatively cheaply.

(*iv*) The overhead changes of turret or capstan lathe are generally more than engine lathe because of higher investment, power and maintenance costs.

10.2. Difference Between Capstan and Turret Lathe

(*i*) In capstan lathe the hexagonal turret is carried on a slide mounted in a saddle bolted to the bed of the lathe (Fig. 10.1) whereas in a turret lathe the hexagonal turret is mounted on a slide directly on the bed (Fig. 10.2).

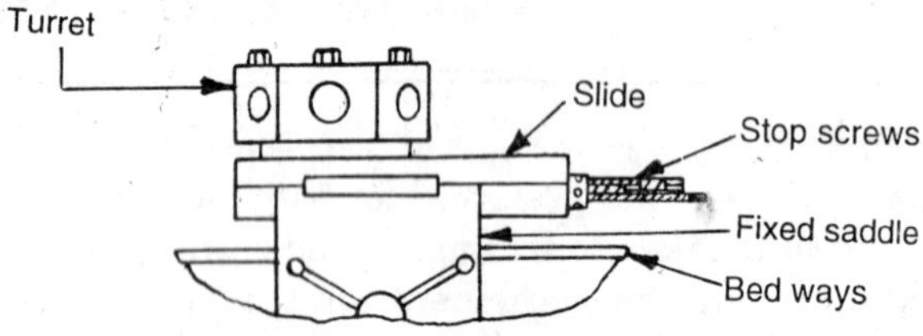

Fig. 10.1

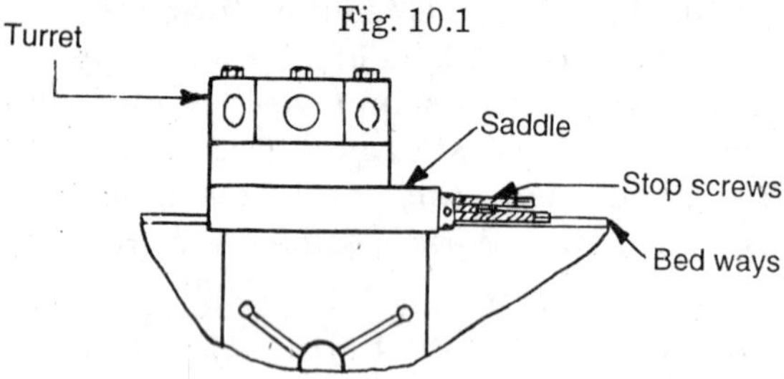

Fig. 10.2

(*ii*) In capstan lathe the turret heat is mounted on a short slide with only a limited amount of travel. In turret lathe the turret saddle bears directly on the bed of lathe and therefore can traverse full length of the bed if required.

(*iii*) A capstan lathe is usually a small or medium size machine whereas the turret lathe is suitable for long and heavy work.

(*iv*) Capstan lathe is suitable for bar work whereas larger and heavier chucking works are generally handled on a turret lathe.

10.3. Principal Parts of a Capstan and Turret Lathes

The various parts of a capstan lathe are shown in Fig. 10.3 and Fig. 10.4 shows the various parts of a turret lathe.

The head stock of turret and capstan lathes houses a speed gear box similar in construction to the same unit as in an engine lathe but providing a narrower range of spindle speed variation and fewer speed steps. One of the chief characteristics of turret head stock is the provision for rapid stopping, starting and speed chang-

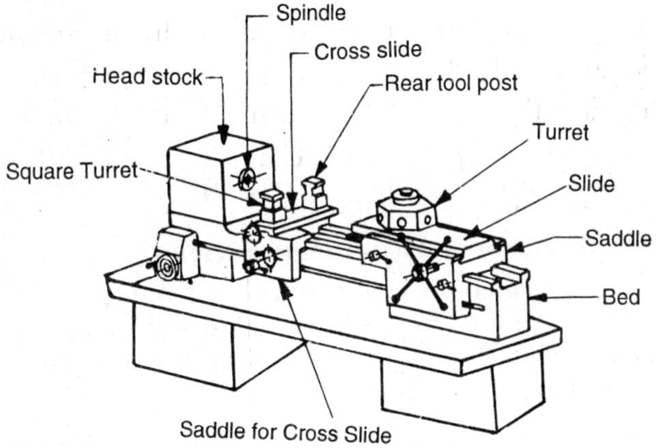

Fig. 10.3

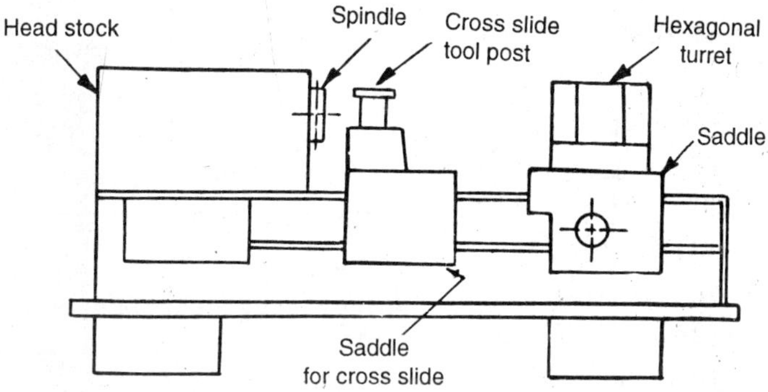

Fig. 10.4

ing in order that the maximum advantage is taken by the operator of the most advantageous cutting speed for any job and at the same time to minimise the loss of time in speed changing, stopping and starting. The bed is a box shaped grey iron casting with a system of well developed internal stiffening ribs. The turret saddle and cross-slide travel along the ways on the top of the bed. The feed gear box may have a device enabling the feeds to be changed without stopping the lathe. The aprons of the cross-slide and turret saddle serve to provide hand and power traverses of these units in the cross and longitudinal directions. The longitudinal and cross feed movement of turret saddle and cross slide are regulated by adjustable stops. These stops enable different tools fitted on the various faces of turret to move by a predetermined amount for performing different operations on repetitive workpieces. The cross slide carriage is of two types :

(i) Reach over type.

(ii) Slide hung type.

The construction of reach over or bridge type of cross slide carriage is more rigid and allows a second tool holder to be mounted at the rear. The slide hung type carriage is generally fitted with heavy duty turret lathe where the saddle rides on the top and bottom guide ways on the front of the lathe bed.

10.3.1. Working and auxiliary motions

The working motions of a turret or capstan lathes provide rotation of spindle carrying workpiece and feed motions for the longitudinal travel of the turret and cross-travel of the cross-slide carrying the cutting tools. Auxiliary motions are as follows :

(i) Swivelling (indexing) of the turret for bringing the tools, consecutively into the cutting motions.

(ii) Feeding out and clamping the bar stocks.

(iii) Rapid approach and withdrawal of the turret, cross slide etc.

10.4. Production Time

The production time for work produced on turret and capstan lathes can be divided into the following sections :

(i) Time for setting up the machine.

(ii) Operating time including chucking, idle movements between cuts, speed and feed changing and replacing tools.

(iii) Actual cutting time.

10.5. Turret Indexing Mechanism

Fig. 10.5 illustrates the principle of turret indexing mechanism. The turret is mounted on a vertical spindle that rotates in suitable bearings in turret slide. An indexing ratchet and index plate are fastened to the spindle. A plunger actuating cam and an indexing pawl are seated in recesses in the bed of the lathe. The plunger and plungers ring are housed in an extension of the turret saddle. The cam has a projecting lug *L* and the plunger carries a projecting plunger pin in such a way that the pin clears the body of the cam but contacts the lug *L*. The pawl has a projecting pin *P* to engage the ratchet. As shown in the figure the turret saddle is in its forward operating position the plunger is seated in a notch of index plate and holds the turret rigidly in position. Then as the turret moves towards the backward position the cam lifts plunger out of the notch in the index plate due to riding of the plunger pin and thus

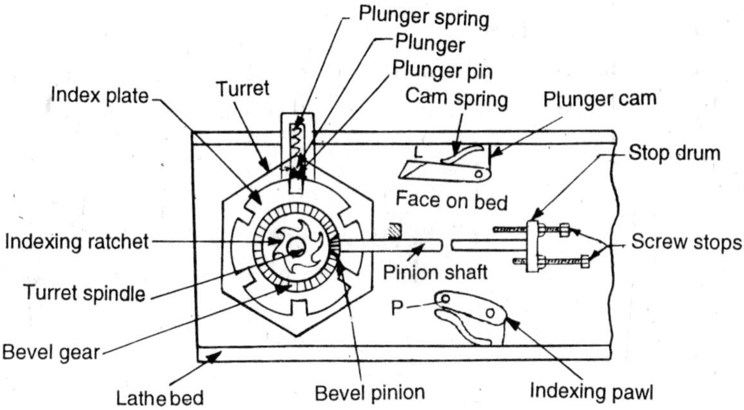

Fig. 10.5

unlocks the index plate. By this time the projecting pin P of pawl makes contact with a tooth of ratchet and causes the ratchet to rotate and thus turret gets rotated through one-sixth of revolution. Then the plunger is forced into the notch by the spring and locks the turret in the new position so that the turret holding the next tool is fed forward. The pawl spring releases the pawl from the ratchet.

The bevel pinion is keyed to a spindle which is attached to the stop drum. During the rotation of turret by one-sixth of revolution the level gear causes the rotation of drum holding six long screws with locknuts. The successive rotation of turret will bring successive stop screw to the working position. The length of the forward stroke of the turret slide is determined by the end of particular screw abutting on a fixed face on the lathe bed.

10.6. Work Holding Devices

The type of work holding equipments for capstan and turret lathes is largely determined by whether the machine is to produce work from bar stock or from separate castings and forgings. The work (castings and forgings) are held with an independent chuck or self-centring chuck. The self centring (universal) chuck is much faster to operate. When component are turned and parted off from a bar fed through the hollow spindle of the machine, a collet chuck is used. The collet may be operated mechanically or automatically (hydraulic or pneumatic). Moving a lever in one direction releases the collet so that bar stock may move forward to expose the required length when it registers against a stop in the hexagon turret. When the lever is moved in the opposite direction the collet is closed. This can usually be done without stopping the rotation of spindle.

A collet chuck should satisfy the following requirements :

(*i*) It should provide concentric clamping with a radial run out not exceeding 0.01 to 0.04 mm.

(*ii*) Reliable holding of stock with normal size errors.

(*iii*) Constant length of bar feed.

(*iv*) Constancy of the plastic properties of the collet.

(*v*) Jaws of collet should have high wear resistance.

The commonly used collets are as follows :

(*i*) Push out type collet with a front taper (Fig. 10.6). It is simple in construction and there is a simple joint between the collet tube and collet. This collet has the disadvantages that a lack of concentricity in clamping exists and the bar stock may slip back.

(*ii*) Drawback type collet with a back taper (Fig. 10.7). This collet is preferred because it ensures proper centring of stock and jamming during bar feed does not take place.

(*iii*) Stationary type collet with a back tapper (Fig. 10.8). This collet also ensures precise bar feed since the collet is not displaced axially in clamping.

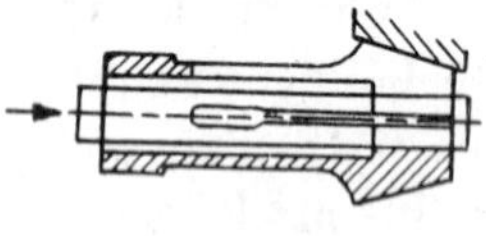

Fig. 10.6

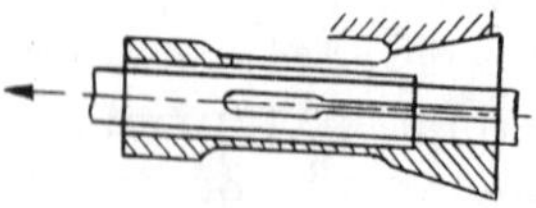

Fig. 10.7

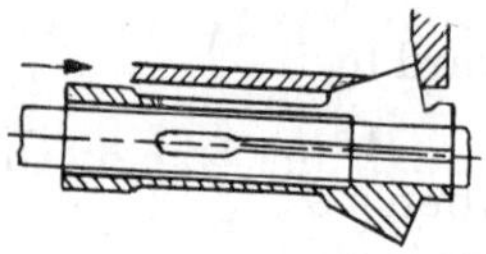

Fig. 10.8

Collets are made from spring steel. The jaws of the collet are expanded slightly so that the bar stock is freely fed out when the collet is open. Fig. 10.9 shows a draw in collet chuck. The chuck is fitted with hand or automatic means for drawing the collet into the chuck. The tapper faces close the collet and cause it to grip the work.

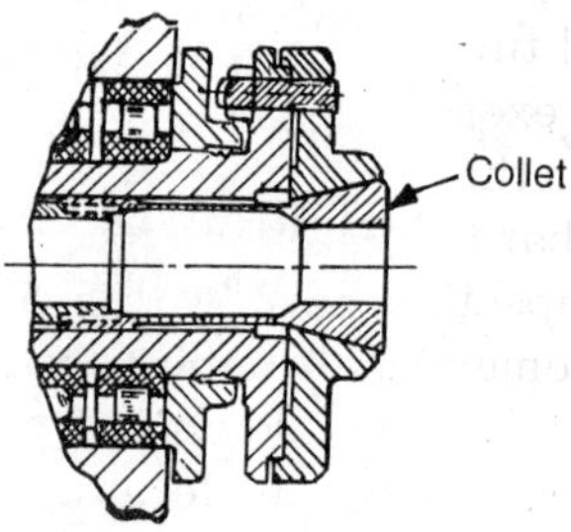

Fig. 10.9

10.7. Bar Feeding Mechanism

There are number of methods used for feeding the bar immediately after the collet releases the work without stopping the machine to reduce the setting time. Fig. 10.10 shows a method in which the bar is fed with the help of wire rope and weight. In this method a guide bar is fixed to the rear of the head stock. A rotating sleeve is mounted on the guide bar to carry the rear end of the bar stock. One end of the wire rope is tied to the sleeve and the other end carries a weight.

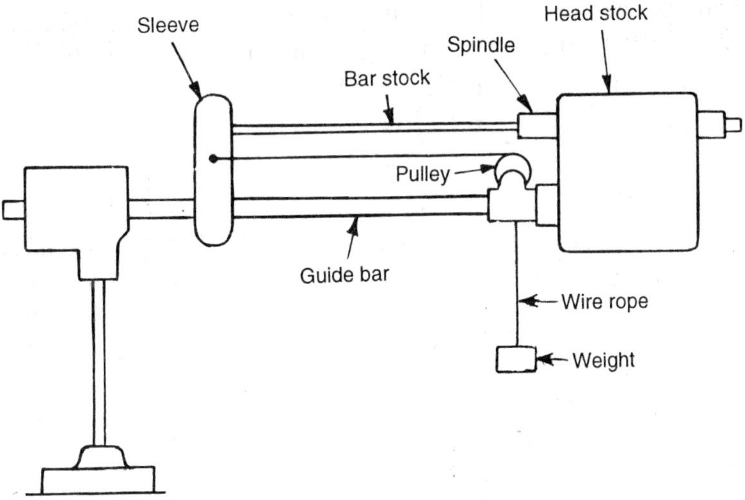

Fig. 10.10

When the chuck opens the bar is automatically pushed forward by the weight and sleeve.

Fig. 10.11 shows the principle of the operation of spring collet when a semi-automatic feeding device is used. In the beginning the bar is clamped in the collet Fig. 10.11 (*a*) then the collet is advanced Fig. 10.11 (*b*) releasing the bar. The feeding finger is a split spring steel tube which grips the bar with a force considerably less than that exerted by the collet but still sufficient to carry the bar forward when the collet is released [Fig. 10.11 (*c*)]. The feeding finger pushes the bar to its farthest position and the collet moves to the left and clamps the bar. Levers on head stock are used to control the movements of both collet and feed finger.

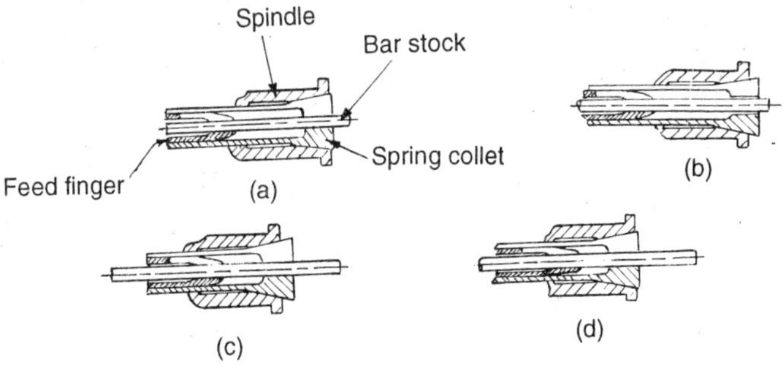

Fig. 10.11

10.8. Economics of Turret Lathe

A turret lathe is economical if the cost of producing a given part on such a lathe including machine and set up costs is less than the cost of producing it on a regular engine lathe. The operator of an engine lathe is paid more than the operator of a turret lathe. But the overhead charges of a turret lathe are more than engine lathe. The choice whether an engine lathe or turret lathe should be used is based on a comparison of the cost of producing parts by both methods.

Example 10.1. *A manufacturing organisation has two alternatives to manufacture the given quantity of a component. A turret lathe and an engine lathe are available. The records show the following data :*

Machine time per component of turret lathe

= 4 minutes

Turret lathe operator rate

= Rs. 3 per hour

Turret lathe overhead including interest on capital

= Rs. 4 per hour

Set up time for turret lathe

= 2 hours

Set up labour rate = Rs. 5 per hour

Machining time per component on engine lathe

= 16 minutes

Engine lathe operator rate

= Rs. 6 per hour

Lathe overhead including interest on capital

= Rs. 2.50 per hour.

How many components would be required in a lot to justify the use of the turret lathe ?

Solution. Let N = Number of components

C_1 = Cost of producing N components on turret lathe

$$= \left[\left(\frac{4}{60}\right) \times (3 + 4)\right] N + 2 \times 5$$

C_2 = Cost of producing N components on engine lathe

$$= N\left(\frac{16}{60}\right)(6 + 2.50)$$

For the cost per component to be equal by the two methods

$$C_1 = C_2$$

$$\left[\left(\frac{4}{60}\right) \times 7\right] \times N + 10 = N\left(\frac{16}{60}\right)(8.50)$$

$$N = 5.5 \text{ or } 6 \text{ components.}$$

Thus a lot of 6 components or more should be done on a turret lathe.

Example 10.2. *A manufacturing company is to manufacture 45 components to fill an order. A turret lathe and an engine lathe are available. The record shows the following data :*

Turret lathe. *Machining time*	= *4 minutes*
Direct labour cost	= *Rs. 3 per hour*
Overhead cost	= *Rs. 4.50 per hour*
Set up time	= *6 hours*
Set up labour rate	= *Rs. 5.50 per hour*
Engine lathe. *Machining time*	= *12 minutes*
Direct labour cost	= *Rs. 4 per hour*
Overhead cost	= *Rs. 2 per hour*
Set up time	= *1 hour*
Set up labour rate	= *Rs. 5 per hour.*

Determine if the job should be done on the turret lathe or engine lathe.

Solution. N = Number of components

C_1 = Cost of producing on turret lathe

$$= \text{Rs.}\left[\left(\frac{4}{60}\right)(3 + 4.50)\,N + 6 \times 5.50\right]$$

C_2 = Cost of producing on engine lathe

$$= \text{Rs.}\left[\left(\frac{12}{60}\right)(4 + 2)\,N + 1 \times 5\right]$$

Break even point occurs when

$$C_1 = C_2$$

$$\left[\left(\frac{4}{60}\right)(3 + 4.50)\,N + 6 \times 5.50\right]$$

$$= \left[\left(\frac{12}{60}\right)(4 + 2)\,N + 1 \times 5\right]$$

$$N = 40.$$

Therefore, the break-even point is 40 components. Thus job of 40 components or more should be done on a turret lathe.

10.9. Turret Lathe Tooling

In setting out the tools to produce any component the use of standard or simple tools should always be considered, because special or complicated tools are expensive. The following factors should be considered during turret lathe tooling :

(*i*) Number of components to be made
(*ii*) Set up time
(*iii*) Work handling time
(*iv*) Machine controlling time
(*v*) Machining time
(*vi*) Tool cost
(*vii*) Set up labour rate
(*viii*) Lathe operator labour rate.

Set up time is the time required by the tool setter to set the various cutting tools and work holders in the turret lathe. Work handling time is the time required for putting work into and removing it from the lathe. Machine controlling time is that required to manipulate the controls which reverse and rotate the turret, and change speeds etc. Machining time is that during which the metal is cut. It should be minimised by using proper tools, feeds and speeds and by using simultaneous cuts.

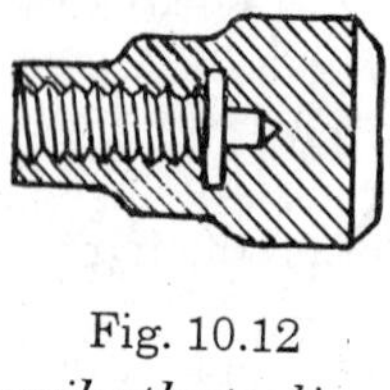

Fig. 10.12

Example 10.3. *Describe the tooling set up required to produce the component shown in Fig. 10.12.*

Solution. Fig. 10.13 shows the sequence of operations for machining the given component. The various operations are as follows :

Operation I

The bar stock is fed against the stock stop provided at station I of the turret and then the collet clamps the bar. Now the turret is

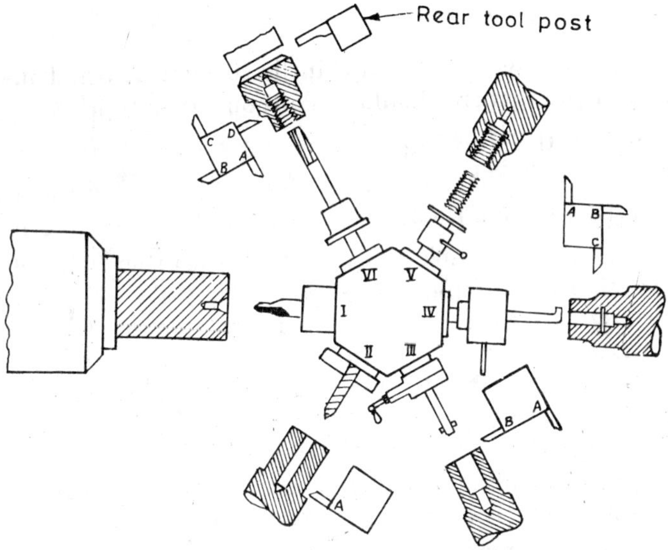

Fig. 10.13

pulled back slightly and end of the bar stock in centre drilled with the help of a retractable combination centre drill counter sink provided in stock stop. The centre drill acts as a guide for the drill at station II of the turret.

Operation II

The hole is produced in the component with the help of a drill and the outside diameter turned with a turning tool. The drill is fitted at station II of the hexagon turret. Front face of the component is finished with the help of facing tool at station *A* of the square turret. Tool at station *A* carries out turning also.

Operation III

Now a boring bar fitted at station III of the hexagon turret is used to enlarge the diameter of drilled hole and a tool fitted at station *B* of square turret is used as a finishing tool for outside diameter of the component.

Operation IV

A recessing tool fitted at station IV of turret is used for cutting the thread recess. The second outside diameter is made with a tool at station *C* of the square turret.

Operation V

A tap provided at station V of turret is used to produce threads.

Operation VI

A reamer is used to fine finish the hole beyond the thread recess. The small outside diameter of the component is finished with a tool fitted at station *D* of the square turret. A parting off tool fitted on the rear tool post is used to part off the component.

10.10. Vertical Turret Lathe

It has a circular table equipped with both removable chuck jaws and T-slots for clamping the work. A cross rail provided on the vertical column carries a five or six sided turret mounted on a slide. The cross rail can be moved be up and down and be fixed at any desired position. The slide carrying the turret can move to and fro along the rail and therefore the position of turret can be adjusted. One or two side heads with square turrets are provided to machine the workpiece from the side. Such latches are designed for chucking type work where the workpiece is too large and heavy.

10.10.1. Automation

Automation is defined as any means of helping the workers perform their tasks more efficiently. By automation the operations are done uniformly and effectively which attain better accuracy and finish. Automation gives an opportunity to the worker to handle more than one machine in a given time. This raises productivity. In automation the human participation is replaced by mechanical or electrical technologies.

Automation is a technology of working in which handling methods, process and design of products are intergrated to utilise economically justifiable mechanisation of thought and effort to achieve automatic and self regulating chain of process. The major part of the automatic operations of a machine tool is covered by automatic drives and controls.

The aim of automation is cost reduction in large scale production technology. The efficiency of a manufacturing facility can be measured in the following three basic ways :

(*i*) Manufacturing cost

(*ii*) Productivity

(*iii*) Profit.

Manufacturing cost involves not only the cost of machining, assembly etc. but is also affected by the efficiency of various manufacturing processes, labour cost and quality of product design. Productivity refers to the efficiency with which labour is utilized and profit is affected by changes in manufacturing costs or productivity.

Labour cost is often the greatest element in the total cost of product and automation helps reducing the labour cost and thus, a decrease in product cost is achieved.

The advantages of automation are as follows :

(*i*) There is an increase in productivity.

(*ii*) The unit cost is reduced as larger number of components can be manufactured in shorter time.

(*iii*) There is an improvement in accuracy.

(*iv*) There is a better resource utilisation.

(*v*) Reduced floor space, maintenance and inventory requirements.

Automation reduces the physical effort required of the operator, frees him of tediously repeated movements and from physical stresses.

The controlling factors which determine the type and the degree to which automation is to be used are as follows :

(*i*) Quantity

(*ii*) Quality.

Quantity means rate of manufacturing the components in a given time.

Automatic machines are preferred for mass production of the components.

Quality means the accuracy with which the components are to be manufactured.

Components with higher quality will be costly. The cost of accurate automatic machine tools is also more.

The various disadvantages of automation are as follows :

(*i*) Initial cost is higher providing additional features in machine tools.

(*ii*) Skilled personnels are required for maintenance of automatic machine tools. This increases maintenance cost.

10.11. Automatic Machines

Automatic machines are used to increase production rate. In such machine both the workpiece handling and metal cutting operations are performed automatically.

Automatic control of the operating cycle is effected with the aid of a cam shaft carrying cams of various shapes linked through a system of levers, gears and other transmissions operative mechanism. The function of the operator is only to inspect a few components after regular intervals and to renew the bar stock when it is exhausted.

The labour cost is minimum in such machines. Machine tools in which automaticity is achieved by mechanical means are productive and reliable. Machine tools with numerical (programmed) control of the operating cycle using stored numerical data or tape or punched cards are an exception among automatic machine tools since they can produce small and medium size components.

10.12. Operating Cycle of Automatic Machine Tools

The operating cycle of automatic machine tools is made of periodically repeated movements of the main and auxiliary working members of machine tool. The main working members of the machine tool participate directly in the cutting process. Movement of main and auxiliary members takes place in a definite sequence, according to definite laws of motion and at definite sections of the paths.

The cycle of automatic machine tools is usually of closed type *i.e.* at the end of the cycle each working member comes to a position which is its initial point in the next cycle.

10.12.1. Types of automatic machines

The classification of the automatic machines depends upon the following factors :

(*i*) Nature of work

(*ii*) Type of blank to be machined

(*iii*) Operation to be carried out

(*iv*) Processing capacity

(*v*) Machining accuracy desired

(*vi*) Design features.

Automatic machines are of two types :

(*i*) Single spindle automatics

(*ii*) Multi-spindle automatics.

10.12.2. Single Spindle Automatics

The commonly used single spindle automatics are as follows :

(*a*) Automatic cutting off machine

(*b*) Swiss type automatic screw machine

(*c*) Turret type automatic screw machine.

10.13. Automatic Cutting off Machine

Such machines can perform operations like facing, form turning chamfering and cutting off. Fig. 10.14 shows the principle of operation of an automatic cutting off machine. Two cross-slides are

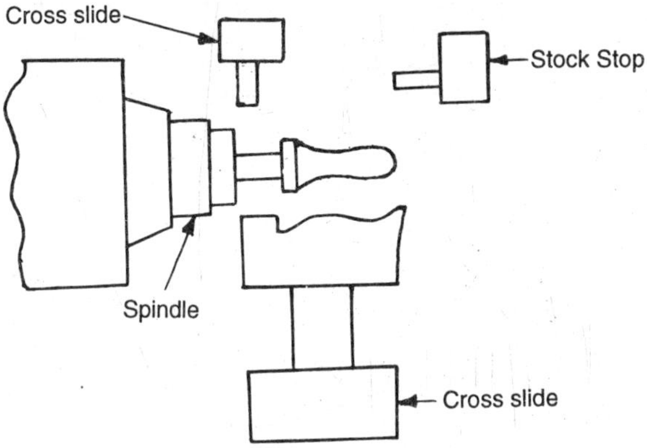

Fig. 10.14

located on the bed at the front end of the spindle. The stock is clamped in the collet chuck of the rotating spindle. A stock stop is provided which is automatically advanced in time with the spindle axis at the end of the cycle. The stock is fed out by the bar feeding mechanism up to the stop. The various operations are carried out by feeding the tools on cross slides which are actuated by cams on a camshaft through a system of levers. These machines are used to produce short components of small diameter and simple shape from bar stock.

Some of the typical parts produced by automatic cutting off machines are shown in Fig. 10.15.

Fig. 10.15

10.14. Swiss Type Automatic Screw Machine

Very accurate machining can be done with these machines. These machines once were used primarily for machining bar stock in making small parts such as screws, bolts, bushings etc. and therefore were called screw machines. But now they are used for producing a wide variety of parts from bar stock. Fig. 10.16 shows the principle of operation of a swiss type automatic screw machine. The bar stock is clamped in rotating spindle in a collet chuck.

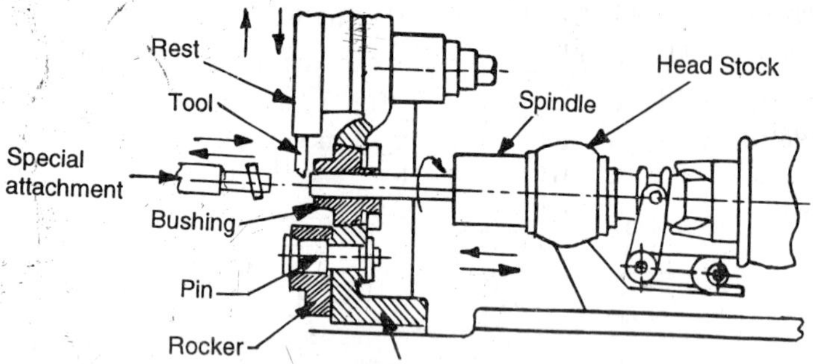

Fig. 10.16

The tool is clamped on rest mounted on a support which moves back and forth in a stationary carriage on the bed of the machine. The tool support is accurated by a rocker arm and lever from a cam controlling radial movements. The head stock can move longitudinally on the bedways. Two or three vertical tool rests arranged radially are provided. Rocker has two tools and can have a rocking motion about the pin. A special attachment is provided on the left hand side of the bed to carry out operations like, boring, drilling, threading etc. The bar stock passes through a guide bushing mounted in tool carriage secured on the bed. Some of the typical parts produced by this machine are shown in Fig. 10.17.

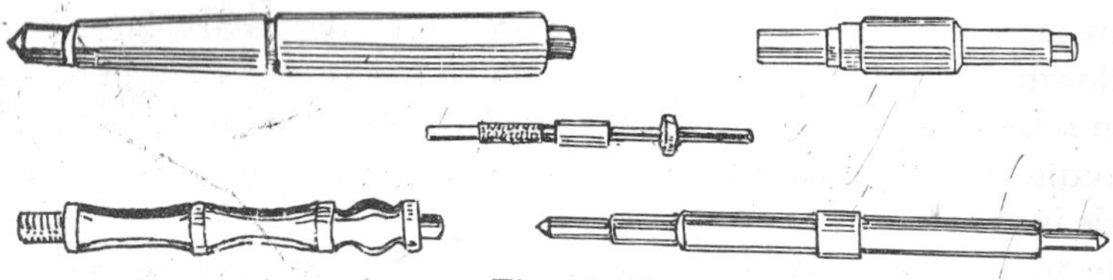

Fig. 10.17

10.15. Turret Type Automatic Screw Machine

They are used to manufacture components from bar stock. In this machine a turret head is provided at the right end of the bed and carries a hexagon turret which can hold six tools. Two cross-slides (front and rear) are provided for cross feeding tools. A vertical slide is provided above the work spindle. A stationary head stock is provided at the left end of the bed and carries a spindle which can rotate in either direction. All these tools are automatically fed at the correct times during the cycles by cams mounted on a cam shaft. The bar stock is advanced to a stop automatically at the beginning of each cycle and then clamped in that position. These tools are fed automatically to carry out different operations. Although these machines were designed for producing screws but now-a-days they are being used to manufacture a wide variety of components.

Cams are used to index, rapid traverse and retract the hexagon turret.

Fig. 10.18 shows the operation of the turret slide. The cam operates a gear segment which further actuates the rack. The rack

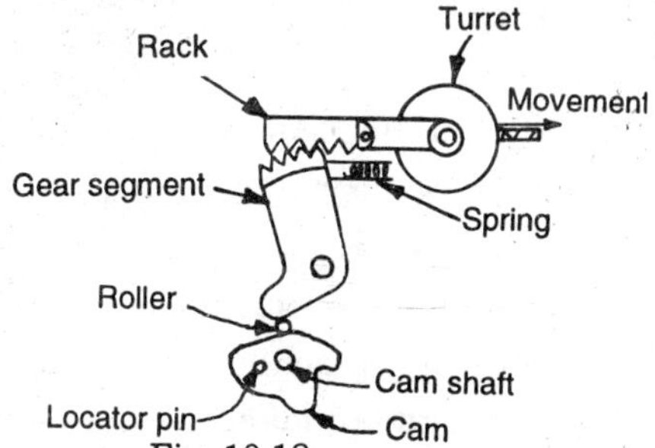

Fig. 10.18

in turn causes the motion of the turret slide. The spring withdraws the slide to its initial position when the roller reaches a low point on the cam.

10.16. Multi-spindle Screw Machines

In these machines a large number of spindle usually four, six or eight are provided. These spindles are carried in a rotatable drum that is indexed in order to bring each spindle successively into a different working position. Each spindle carries a bar of material. A non rotating tool slide holds the same number of tools as there are spindle in order to provide a cutting tool for each spindle. A cross-slide is provided at each spindle position so as to feed a tool from the side to carry out operations like facing, grooving, knurling and cutting off. The bars are loaded into hollow spindles. The tool slide is moved forward and cross-slides moved inward so that the various tools cut simultaneously. All the motions are controlled automatically. On completion of a particular operation the tool slide and cross-slides are moved backward and spindles indexed by one position by rotating the spindle drum so that the next operation can be carried out.

These machines seldom maintain accuracy as good as single spindle machines because of the errors in indexing of the spindles and large number of fittings. The time of production per component is considerably reduced in such machines. These machines are suitable when a very large number of components (say from 2000 to 5000 in a lot) are to be manufactured.

10.16.1. Economics of automatic machines

Automatic machines are used in both mass and large batch production. The cost of production per component is calculated as follows :

$$C = \frac{S}{N} + (R + M) \times T_1 + \left(\frac{R}{N_1} + M\right) T_m + [(R + M)T_2 + A]\frac{T_m}{T}$$

where C = Cost of production per component
S = Cost of setting up the machine
N = Batch size
R = Operator's rate (including overheads)
M = Rate for one machine (including overheads)
T_1 = Loading and unloading time
T_2 = Tool changing time
T_m = Machining time
A = Cost of providing one new cutting edge
T = Tool life
N_1 = Number of machines serviced by operator

Example 10.4. *Calculate the cost per compound to manufacture a batch of 1.8×10^5 components on an automatic machine using the following data :*

Number of machine serviced by one operator	*= 5*
Machine time	*= 32 seconds*
Tool life	*= 4000 seconds*
Tool changing time	*= 60 sec.*
Loading and unloading time	*= 1 second*
Operator's rate	*= 0.1 paisa per sec.*
Rate for one machine	*= 0.13 paisa per sec.*
Cost of providing one new cutting edge	*= Rs. 2*
Cost of setting up the machine (including manufacture of cam etc.)	*= Rs. 600.*

Solution. $N_1 = 5$
$T_m = 32$ seconds
$T = 4000$ seconds
$T_1 = 1$ sec.
$T_2 = 60$ sec.

$$R = 0.1 \text{ paisa per sec.}$$
$$M = 0.13 \text{ paisa per sec.}$$
$$A = \text{Rs. } 2$$
$$S = \text{Rs. } 600$$
$$N = 1.1 \times 10^5$$

$$C = \frac{S}{N} + (R + M)T_1 + \left(\frac{R}{N_1} + M\right) T_m + [(R + M)T_2 + A] \frac{T_m}{T}$$

$$C = \frac{600}{1.8 \times 10^5} \times \left(\frac{0.1}{100} + \frac{0.13}{100}\right) \times 1 + \left(\frac{0.1}{120} + \frac{0.13}{100}\right) + 32 \times \left[\left(\frac{0.1}{100} + \frac{0.13}{100}\right) 60 + 2\right] \frac{32}{4000}$$

$$= \text{Re. } 0.0962 = 0.0962 \times 100$$
$$= 9.62 \text{ paise.}$$

10.16.2. Tool slides of automatic machine tools

Tool slides are the principle working members of automatic machine tool of the lathe type. Manufacturing process and volume of production determine the type of tool slides, their number, arrangement, motion cycles and operative mechanisms (actuating devices).

The tool slides of the single spindle automatic screw machines are classified according to the following features :

(*i*) In respect to arrangement as central (along the spindle axis) and cross slides in the horizontal plane, or vertical, inclined or fan like for the vertical tool slides.

(*ii*) In respect to direction of travel.

(*iii*) In respect to kinematics of their motion as slides with rectilinear travel and rocking slides.

Each tool slide has its independent feed from a special cam.

10.16.3. Methods of increasing production capacity

The production capacity of automatic machine tools can be increased by reducing machining time. Following methods are used to reduce machining time :

(*i*) Machining several workpieces simultaneously.

(*ii*) Employing carbide tipped cutting tools to enable high velocity machining to be used.

(*iii*) Providing independent spindle speeds and rates of feed at each station.

(*iv*) Overlapping working travel motions in time.

(*v*) Reducing the time required to readjust the tools.

(*vi*) Reducing the number of idle travel motions and by increasing the speed of idle travel motions.

10.17. Cam Drives

In automatic and semi-automatic lathes the automaticity is achieved by mechanical means based on cam drives. The cam shaft carries cams of various shapes. When the cam shaft rotates, the cams actuate the various operative mechanisms. Cams are of two types :

(*i*) Plate cams

(*ii*) Cylinder cams.

Plate cams are used to transmit motion with a short stroke and in a plane square to the axis of rotation of cam. Fig. 10.19 shows a plate cam. A cylinder cam is used to transmit motion with a considerable longer stroke and in a plane parallel to or passing through the axis of rotation of the cam. Fig. 10.20 shows a typical cylinder cam.

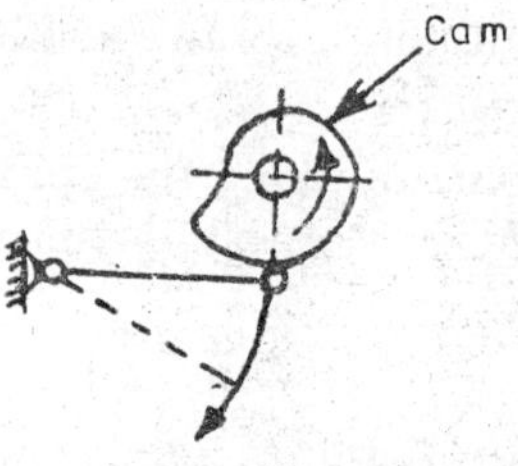

Fig. 10.19

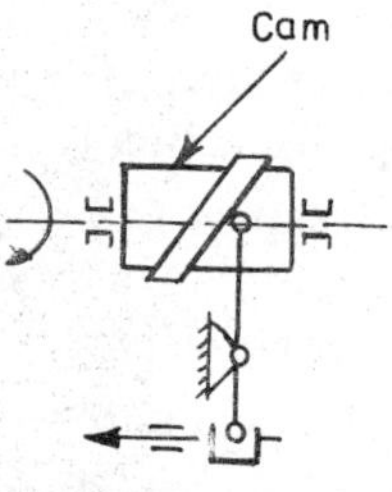

Fig. 10.20

The main advantage of cam mechanisms is that the velocity of the operative element is independent of the design of the driving mechanism and is controlled by the cam profile. The cam mechanism consists of a cam and a follower. The cam mechanism can provide the desired translatory motion if a suitable cam profile is selected. Cam mechanisms are costly and are generally used in automatic machine tools used for mass production of components.

10.18. Layout of Cams

An important operation in the tooling up of automatic lathes is the layout of cams. The layout of cams is dealt with in the following stages :

(*i*) Determine the sequence of operations.

(*ii*) Calculate r.p.m. of the work spindle.

(*iii*) Determine the tools to be used.

(*iv*) Establish the cutting speed according to the material to be machined and operations to be carried out.

(*v*) Determine the travel of each tool.

(*vi*) Determine the feed per revolution of the work spindle for each tool.

(*vii*) Determine the number of revolutions of work spindle for each operation.

(*viii*) Establish the number of revolutions of work spindle required to complete one component.

(*ix*) Determine the hundredth of cam surface for each operation.

(*x*) Draw the tool layout and set of cams.

10.19. Numerical Control of Machine Tools

Numerical control (NC) is considered to be an improved control for machine tools that provides higher productivity. Today industry demands faster production in harder and tougher materials to unprecedented tolerances. Conventional machine tools manual or automatic cannot meet these demands and the answer to the problem has been found in what is called the numerical control of machine tools. This technique saves time, eliminates burdensome tasks and increases overall productivity.

Numerical control is a method of controlling of motions of machine tool components by means of coded instructions in the form of numbers on tapes or punch cards. The information stored in the tapes or cards can be read by automatic means and converted into electrical signals which operate the electrically controlled servo-system. The servo-system permits the slides of the machine tool to be driven simultaneously at the required speed in the required direction to carry out the different operations. Fig. 10.21 shows the scheme of a numerically controlled machine tool.

The programme is recorded on a tape or punch card. Punched tape is then directed to the machine control unit (M.C.U.) which

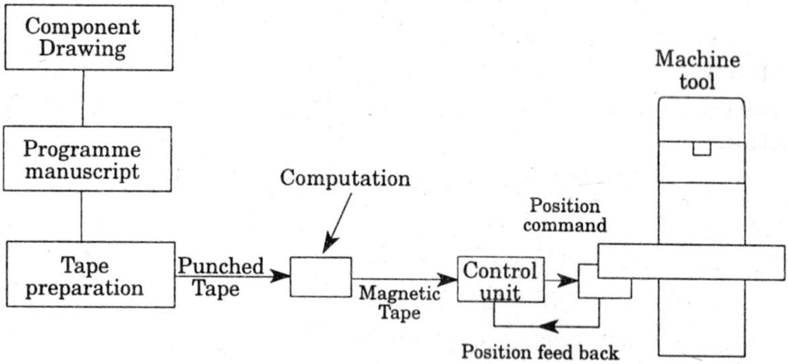

Fig. 10.21

converts the information into electrical signals and sends them to electrically controlled servo-systems which are used to drive the slides of machine tools at the appropriate speed and directions.

Numerical control has caused a virtual revolution in the discrete metal parts manufacturing industry. The success of N.C. has led to a number of extensions of numerical control concepts and technology. Four of the more important developments are as follows :

(*i*) Direct numerical control (D.N.C.)
(*ii*) Computer numerical control (C.N.C.)
(*iii*) Adaptive control (A.C.)
(*iv*) Industrial Robots.

N.C. technology has made it possible to reduce cost of production by reducing the production time. This in turn is mainly directed towards the reduction of non-productive time such as (*a*) set up time, (*b*) work piece handling time, (*c*) tool change time, (*d*) lead time.

Other features of N.C. machine tools are :

(*i*) reduced fixturing
(*ii*) ease of making workpiece design changes
(*iii*) improved accuracy
(*iv*) reduced human error
(*v*) greater manufacturing flexibility.

10.20. Basic Components of an N.C. System

The basic components of an N.C. system are as follows :

(*i*) **Program of instructions.** It is a set of directions which will tell the machine tool what to do. It is coded in numerical or symbolic form on some type of input medium such as one inch wide punched tape.

(ii) **Controller unit also called machine control unit (MCU).** It consists of the electronics and hardware that read and interpret the program of instructions and convert it into mechanical action of the machine tool.

The various elements of MCU are as follows :

(a) Tape reader.

(b) Data buffer.

(c) Signal output channels to the machine tool.

(d) Feed back channels from the machine tool.

(iii) **Machine tool or other controlled process.** It performs the useful work. A machine tool consists of the following :

(a) Work table and work fixtures.

(b) Spindle.

(c) Cutting tools.

(d) Motors and controls for drives.

(e) Other auxiliary equipment needed in machining operation.

10.20.1. The numerical control (N.C.) procedure

During manufacturing on NC machines the following steps should be accomplished.

(i) Process planning. This is listing of the sequence of operations to be performed during manufacturing of a part. This also lists the machines through which the part to be made is routed. Fig. 10.21 *(a)* shows a typical planning sheet. [Fig. 10.21 *(a)* on next page].

(ii) Part programming. The part programmer is responsible for planning the sequence of machining steps to be performed by N.C. system and to document these in a special format.

Part programming is carried out in two ways :

(a) Manual part programming

(b) Computer assisted part programming.

(iii) Tape preparation. A punched tape is prepared based on the instructions listed in part program prepared by part programmer.

(iv) Tape verification. The tape is checked for its accuracy. It is checked by two methods :

(a) To try out the tape on the machine tool to make the part using a foam or plastic as the material for tryout. The errors detected in tape are then removed.

Date	
Dept.	
Prepared By	

Job No. :
Sheet No. :

PLANNING SHEET

Machine tool ....

Operation No.	*Tool number*	*Loading order*	*Tool length offset switch*	*Tool radius correction switch*	*Spindle speed*		*Feed rate*	
					Rev./min.	*Range*	*mm/min.*	*Code*

Fig. 10.21 (*a*)

(b) To run the tape through a computer program which will indicate the contents of the tape and errors in the tape can thus be checked.

(v) *Production.* The corrected tape is then used for manufacturing the parts on the NC machine.

The operator loads the raw material on the machine tool and adjusts the position of the cutting tool relative to workpiece. The N.C. system then takes over and machines the part according to the instructions on the tape.

10.21. Numerical Control (NC) Systems (Control Loops)

The two basic systems of numerical control as follows :

(i) Open loop system (ii) Closed loop system.

Open loop system. This system does not have a feedback device and therefore the actual position of the tool slide or work table is not measured and verified.

As shown in Fig. 10.22 the information is fed from the operator control console to the tape reader which picks off the

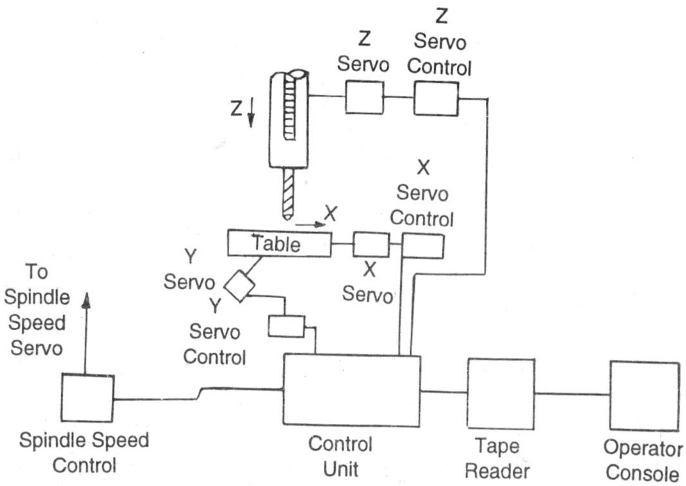

Fig. 10.22

discrete bits of information from the tape and then feeds them to the distribution control unit the information is then directed to the servo control unit for a particular axis (X-axis, Y-axis, Z-axis etc.) control and finally the command is transferred to the servo-motor in the form of electric impulses or signals. The servo-motors control the machine table (slide) movement, the cutter head movement etc.

Closed loop system. This system is generally used because this system ensures that the slides have taken up the desired position (Fig. 10.23). This is done by measuring the actual position

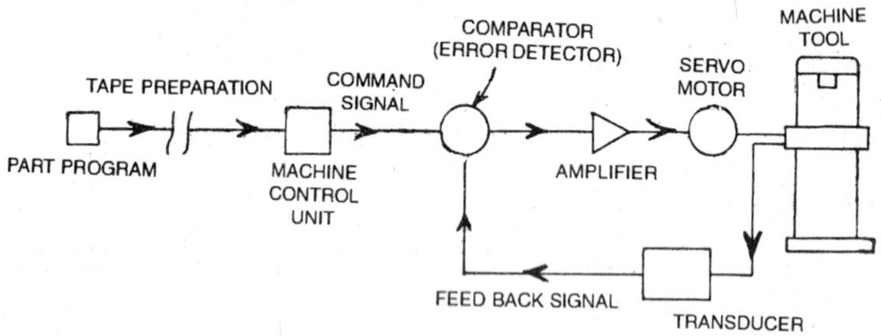

Fig. 10.23

of the slides by transducer attached to each axis. The transducer converts the motion as directed from linear or rotary motion to an electrical impulse. This impulse is fed back to the control unit as a check on the input signal. There should be no difference between input signal and feedback signal. If there is any difference between the two, the correction is made by comparator and then the operation is carried out.

The basic elements of a N/C machine tool system and their functions are carried out by control loops. The command is given by the tape reader through the data processing unit and the drive mechanism carries out the intended work. The drives can be either electrical or hydraulic. The control loop is the link between the command and the drive.

The open loop system is cheaper in investment, maintenance and operation but may become expensive if very high accuracy is required which will demand very specialised equipment.

For contouring N/C systems, closed loop drives are to be preferred for obvious reasons. Straight line contouring can actually be carried out with open loop systems, but in general a closed loop N/C will be more effective, more accurate and more suitable for nearly all operations.

In point-to-point systems, the path of the cutting tool and its feed, while moving from one point to the next one, are without any significance. Therefore, point-to-point systems would require only position loops for controlling the final position of the tool before drilling. In contouring machines both, the path and the feed are important, since operation is based on the ratio of velocities in the various axes of motion. Therefore contouring N/C systems must contain, in addition to the position control velocity of feed-rate control loops as well.

10.21.1. N.C. system for turning

Fig. 10.23 (*a*) shows N.C. system for simple turning on lathe. When part program medium (punched tape) is passed through program reader the coded instructions are transferred into electrical signals which are used to control the various machine tool functions. Punched tape readers commonly used are as follows :

(*i*) Electro-mechanical (*ii*) Photo-electric

(*iii*) Pneumatic.

Buffer storage is a memory device which temporarily retains data.

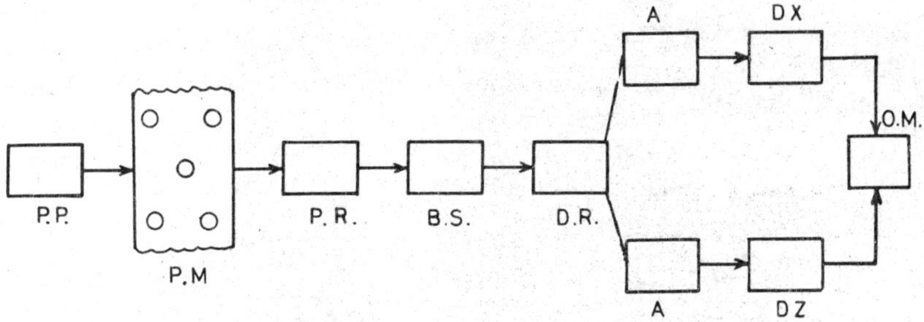

Fig. 10.23 (*a*)

In this figure

P.P. = Part Program

P.M. = Program Medium

P.R. = Program Reader

B.S. = Buffer Storage

D.R. = Decoder

A = Amplifier

D_X = Drive in x-direction

D_Z = Drive in z-direction

O.M. = Operative member.

10.21.2. Servo motor

It receives and acts upon the series of electric command signals from the control unit. The motor response must be accurate to drive the work against the cutting forces.

There are two types of servo motors :

(*i*) High frequency electric servo-motors.

(*ii*) Hydraulic servo motors.

A high frequency servo motor is similar in operation to the normal type of induction motor used upon machine tools at a frequency of 0 Hz. However, a servo motor is operated on a three phase supply at 400 Hz giving full power at 167 revolutions per second.

In hydraulic servo motor fluid is pumped into the motor under frequency which causes the rotor to turn. A hydraulic servo motor of 2.25 kW gives an accuracy of response of 0.005 mm.

10.22. Digital and Analogue Control

Digital control is a system of machine tool control in which the information is numerical information which can change only in discrete amounts. The data are processed in their original digital form and after computation the result is converted into analogue form before being used to drive the slides so that the slides move smoothly and not jump from point to point. Analogue control is a system of machine tool control in which the digital input data are changed to the analogue form which may be voltage or current signal before it is processed. The computation is carried out using the analogue data.

Both use servo-systems which need to have their mechanical output in analogue form because the slides must move smoothly and not jump from point to point.

10.22.1. Axis Selection

Z-axis. It is always the axis of the main spindle. If there are several spindles on a machine, one spindle is selected as the principle spindle and its axis is then considered to be Z-axis. Positive Z movement (+ Z) is in the direction that increase the distance between the workpiece and the tool.

X-axis. It is always horizontal and is always parallel to the holding surface.

If Z-axis is horizontal as in turning centres positive, X-axis (+ X) motion is to the right when looking from the spindle towards the workpiece.

If Z-axis is vertical as in vertical milling machine, the positive X-axis (+ X) movement is identified as being to the right when looking from the spindle towards its supporting column.

Y-axis. It is at right angle to both X-axis and Z-axis. Positive Y-axis movement (+ Y) is always such as to complete the standard 3-dimensional coordinate system.

Rotary Axis. *A*, *B* and *C* are used to identify rotary motion about *X*, *Y* and *Z* axis respectively. Clockwise rotation is designated positive movement and counter clockwise rotation as negative movement.

Positive direction is identified by looking in + *X*, + *Y* and + *Z* directions respectively.

10.22.2. XYZ code

Let $X = 15$

$Y = 20$

$Z = 60$

Depending upon the type of computer, these values may be written as

(*i*) *X* 15 *Y* 20 *Z* 60

or (*ii*) *X* 1500 *Y* 2000 *Z* 6000.

10.22.3. Numerical control programming systems

Numerical control programming can be divided into two main systems as follows :

(*i*) Point to point (PTP) system.

(*ii*) Continuous path system.

Fig. 10.24 (*a*) shows point to point system and Fig. 10.24 (*b*) shows continuous system.

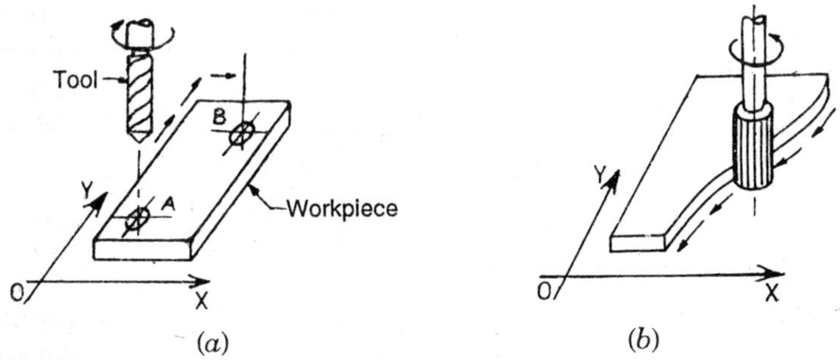

Fig. 10.24

10.23. Point to Point or Positioning System

Point to point control is used in vertical drilling machines, jig, bores and tapping machines. The object of this system is to move a machine tool table (and hence the work) through rectangular co-ordinates according to a programme so that the different machining operations are carried out at the programmed points where the table stop.

10.24. Continuous Path System or Contouring System

In this system tool remains in contact with the work and generates a continuous surface in space. In this system the position of tool relative to the workpiece must be continuously controlled while workpiece is being machined. This system is used in milling machines.

The preparation of part programme for NC machine tools with contouring controls is more complicated than for those with finite positioning controls.

Coordinate positional control is used in drilling, jig boring, turret drilling and milling. Continuous path control is used in milling or flame cutting contours, grooving, boring, and cam milling.

In the contouring systems the simultaneous movements of the tool and workpiece are coordinated to generate the desired profile. Contouring NC machine tools can machine not only straight lines at angle but also complicated profiles. The profile is approximated by elementary straight lines, arcs of circles or segments of parabola to describe the locus of tool cutting edge.

Generally all contouring N.C. machine tools are equipped with a feed back arrangement. Contouring N.C. machine tool are expensive than point to point control principled machine tools.

10.24.1. Part programming (P.P.)

It is the plan proposed for manufacturing a part on N.C. machine tool. Programming can either be done manually or with the help of a computer. But in most cases the program is written manually cailed manual part programming (MPP). Programming involves the detailed step by step listing of operations that the N.C. machine with perform. These steps are written in a definite order and form in what is known as manuscript. One who writes these instructions is designated as part programmer.

While making the part program the programmer first studies the drawing of the part and then decides the sequence of operations, the cutting tool to be used, the path of cutter, speeds, feeds and other necessary information like starting and stopping of the machine etc. The above information is entered in a program sheet in a particular format acceptable by the machine tool control unit combination. The information given on the program sheet is punched on to a paper tape or magnetic tape according to a standard code. This input information punched on the tape is then fed to the machine control unit (MCU).

The program for machining a particular workpiece depends not only upon the workpiece shape and dimensions but also upon the N.C. machine tool on which it is machined. The program for machining a workpiece on one N.C. machine tool may differ from program for machining the same workpiece on another N.C. machine tool because of difference between formats of the machine tools.

Manual programming jobs can be divided into two categories :

(i) Point to point jobs
(ii) Contouring jobs.

Manual part programming is ideally suited for point to point applications.

Manual part programming becomes extremely tedious task and is subject to errors in case of complex workpieces. Therefore for more complex workpieces, computer assisted programming is preferred. This saves time and results in more accurate and more efficient part program. The computer automatically punches the tape in proper tape format for the particular N.C. machine. The part programmer's responsibility in computer assisted part programming consists of the following two basic steps :

(i) Defining the workpiece geometry
(ii) Specifying the operation sequence and tool path.

In addition to part geometry and tool motion statements, the programmer must also provide other instructions to operate the machine tool properly.

10.24.2. Data required for part programming

To prepare the manuscript for manual part programming, the following data is required :

(i) Machine tool specifications
(ii) Specifications of tools
(iii) Specifications of workpiece materials
(iv) Speed and feed tables.

The programmer (person who prepares part program) on obtaining the component drawing decides about the sequence of operations, speeds, feeds for various operations and determines the magnitude of various motions desired. He prepares the planning sheet and writes the instructions in a coded form which is acceptable to the controller of the machine tool.

10.24.3. Input media

The part program is converted into an input medium acceptable to the machine control unit (MCU). The most common types of input media are as follows :

(*i*) Magnetic tape

(*ii*) Punched paper tape

(*iii*) Punched cards

(*iv*) Floppy discs.

10.25. Tapes

Two types of tapes are used in numerical control (NC) of machine tools :

(*i*) Punched paper tape

(*ii*) Magnetic tape.

In punched paper tape a punched hole can represent 1 and absence of hole can represent 0. Punched paper tapes are cheap and are convenient means of transmitting drawing information to computer. In magnetic tapes magnetised spots on tape surface are used. More information can be recorded on magnetic tapes and they can be read at a speed faster than is possible with punched tapes. Magnetic tape is used as the media for storing the input data and the preparation of data confirms to the sequence shown follows :

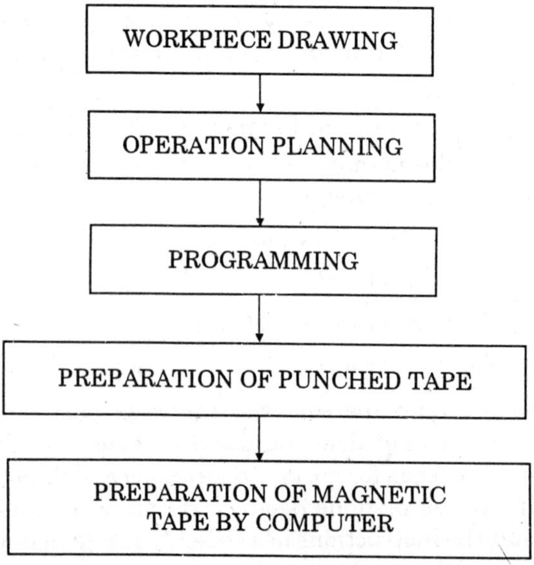

The standard width of paper tape is 25.4 mm. The tape has eight rows of holes plus sprocket holes. Each row of holes lengthwise of the tape is referred to as a channel. Each of the eight channels are numbered 1 through 8.

The code according to which these holes on tape are punched has been standardised by

(*i*) EIA (Electronic Industries Association)

(*ii*) ASCII (American Standard Code for Information Interchange).

(*iii*) ISO (International Standard).

The punched tape as per standard code represents the part program characters on its eight tracks. The tape is usually punched on a teletype machine (a typing-cum-punching machine).

Punched tape is the most commonly used programming medium in N.C. machine tools. These tapes are available in 200 mm diameter rolls and are made of paper, plastics and or a plastic and aluminium sandwich. As compared to magnetic tape the punched tape has the following advantages :

(*i*) Low cost of (*a*) tape
(*b*) program reader
(*c*) perforator.

(*ii*) No hazard of accidental distortion of the coded information.

(*iii*) Ease of detecting damage to the tape.

The programme is punched on the tape on a perforator. The perforator is a key-board instrument like a type writer or computer aided punching machine.

10.25.1. Punched tape readers

Punched tape readers convert the coded instructions into electrical analogues which are utilized for controlling the various machine tool functions.

The commonly used punched tape readers are as follows :

(*i*) **Mechanical (Electrical-mechanical) tape reader.** In this tape reader shown in Fig. 10.24 (*c*) when punched tape is passed through the reader the contact remains open when there is no hole whereas the contact gets closed in case of hole in the tape. The switch remains in ON position in case of hole and switch remains in OFF position when there is no hole in tape.

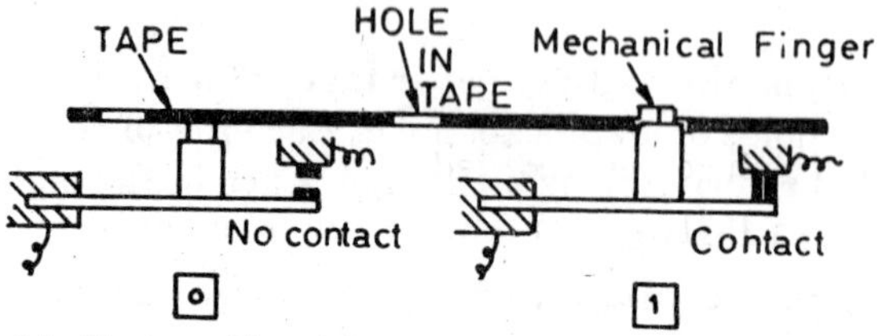

0 indicates off position and 1 indicates on position

Fig. 10.24 (*c*)

(*ii*) **Optical or photo-electrical tape reader.** This reader, works on the principle that if a beam of light falls on a photo-electric cell, the latter generates an electric signal.

When punched tape is fed between a light source and a series of photo-cells and whenever a hole is present in the tape, light is permitted to reach and energise the corresponding photo-cell which converts the light energy into electrical energy to produce a pulse *i.e.* ON position. The pulse is amplified and processed into a form suited to the circuit. When there is no hole, the light from the light source does not reach the photo-cell, and so signal is produced. This position is recorded as OFF. Fig. 10.24 (*d*) shows optical tape reader.

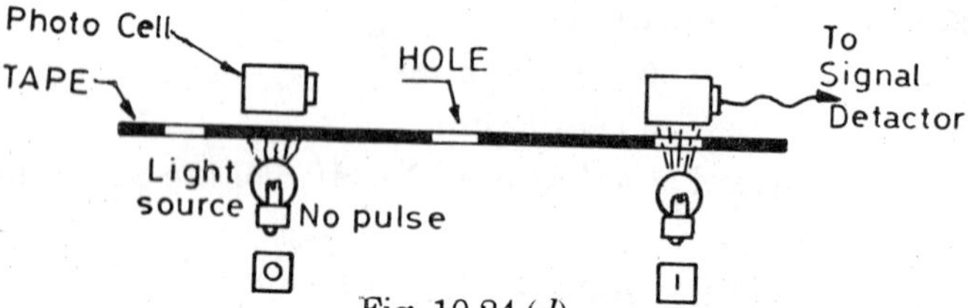

Fig. 10.24 (*d*)

(*iii*) **Pneumatic tape readers.** In pneumatic tape reader, the tape is fed between a series of air jets (8 Nos.), covering the complete pattern of holes which is possible to be punched in a block of information on the tape and tape support plate. The compressed air jets are directed through specially designed tubes which have two openings. The first opening called, main outlet, is near the tape and second opening is connected to a signal detector.

A support plate is used that prevents the tape from being blown away by the compressed air coming from main outlet.

If there is no hole in the tape, the tape covers the main outlet and the free escape of air is restricted and a back pressure is developed in the supply tube. This back pressure is sensed by the signal detector and position is recorded as '0' *i.e.* OFF. But if a hole in the punched tape comes in front of the main outlet, the air is allowed to escape freely and there is no back pressure build up in the supply tube. This loss of back pressure is detected by the signal detector and position is recorded as '1' *i.e.* ON.

Fig. 10.24 (*e*) shows a pneumatic tape reader.

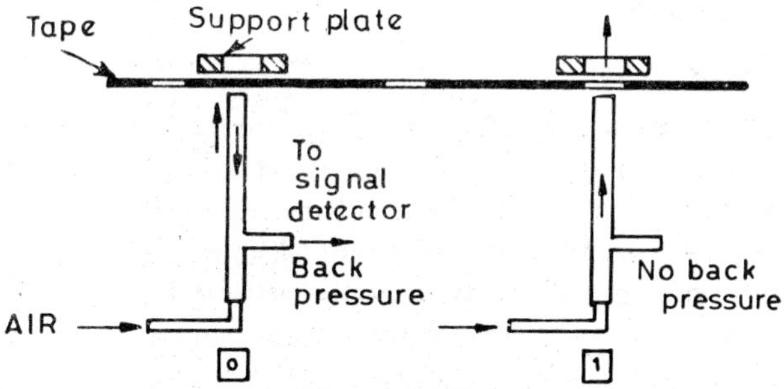

Fig. 10.24 (*e*)

10.25.2. Buffer storage

The information read from the tape is stored into the memory of the control system called buffer storage and is processed by the machine step by step.

10.26. Advantages and Disadvantages of Numerical Control

Advantages. The various advantages of numerical control are as follows :

(*i*) A greater accuracy is achieved.

(*ii*) High production rates are obtained.

(*iii*) Expensive jigs and templates are not needed. This reduces the tooling cost.

(*iv*) Time required for setting up the machine is reduced.

(*v*) The amount of human error is greatly reduced and therefore the scrap rate is decreased.

(*vi*) Programming and tape writing takes much less time than making jigs and fixtures and locating gauges. Also the tapes last longer and require much less space than jigs and fixtures.

(*vii*) Operation of the machine does not require a skilled operator. Except for positioning the workpiece on the table the human element is completely eliminated.

(*viii*) The cutting time of total cycle time is as high as 80% in case of N.C. machines as compared to about 30% in case of conventional machines.

Disadvantages. (*i*) Initial cost of numerical controlled machine tools is high.

(*ii*) Machine tools should be rigidly built than conventional machine tool in order to withstand accelerations dictated by servo controls.

(*iii*) Skilled electronics technicians are needed to maintain the electronic controls.

10.27. Codes

Code is a suitable pattern of performations on the tape to represent each instruction to be imparted to the machine. The elements or symbols of a code are either the absence or presence of a hole punched on the tape or cards. Each combination of holes corresponds to a number which represents the specified displacement of the operative unit of the machine tool.

There are two types of number codes.

(*i*) Binary coded decimal system.

(*ii*) Straight binary system.

Binary coded decimal system can be used both for point to point command system and continuous control system. This system uses an eight channel paper tape 25 mm wide (Fig. 10.24). To ensure positive drive for the tape one more channel of holes is provided for

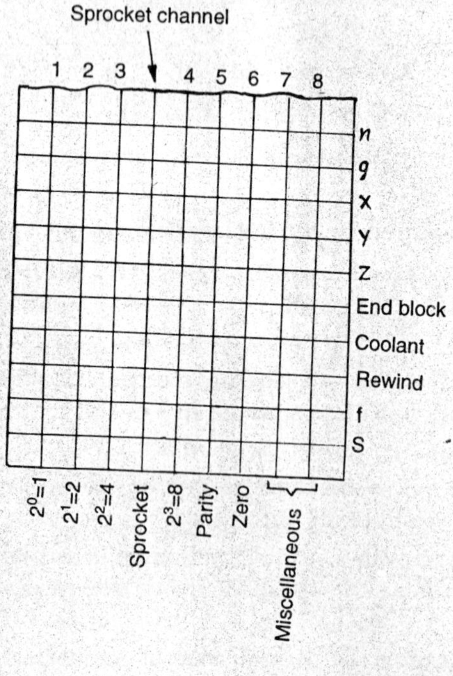

Fig. 10.24

the sprocket channels 1, 2, 3 and 4 are used to represent powers of 2 such as channel 1 is $2^{\circ} = 1$, channel 2 represents $2' = 2$, channel 3 represents $2^2 = 4$ and channel 4 represents $2^2 = 8$. Only an odd number of holes may be punched in each row. If the data requires that an even number of holes be punched into a particular row, another hole should be punched in row 5 which is parity column. Channel 6 is used for zero commands and items such as direction coolant on, coolant off, tape start, tape return are indicated on channels 7 and 8. A particular pattern of holes represents specific command.

Straight binary system is generally used for continuous control. In this system multiple simultaneous motions may be programmed into one row. Therefore, the tape required is much shorter than the length of tape required for binary coded decimal system.

Binary Coded Decimal (B.C.D.) system is quite commonly used in the numerical control of machine tools. The binary representation of numerals 1—9 is as follows :

1 = 0001
2 = 0010
3 = 0011
4 = 0100
5 = 0101
6 = 0110
7 = 0111
8 = 1000
9 = 1001

For example, the number 630 can be represented in BCD system as :

6 = 0110
3 = 0011
0 = 0000

10.28. Machine Control Unit (MCU)

Every N.C. machine tool is fitted with a machine control unit (MCU). The MCU may be mounted on the machine tool itself or it may be housed in a separately standing cabinet like body. The MCU can be considered as a special purpose computer that executes the commands mentioned in the part program *i.e.* the program to manufacture a part on the N.C. machine tool. This program, of course, is in the form of an acceptable input medium like paper tape, and magnetic tape, the paper tape being quite commonly used. The

MCU converts the information from the tape program into the desired command signals used in the actuation system of the machine tool.

10.28.1. Features of modern N.C. machines

Some of the features of modern N.C. machine are as follows :

(*i*) The structure of NC machine tools should be very rigid to withstand heavy cuts and maintain precision and accuracy for a long period.

(*ii*) Large volume of chips are produced during NC machines operation. To transport these chips NC machines are fitted with chip conveyors.

(*iii*) NC machines are equipped with centralized lubrication system with automatic supply in predetermined quantities.

(*iv*) The spindle drive on modern machines is invariably a DC drive in combination with three or four step gear boxes to get a wide range of spindle speeds.

(*v*) The guide ways used in NC machines are hardened and ground flat guide ways or a ground combination of V and flat guide ways.

(*vi*) Automatic tool changer is a common feature on machining centre.

10.28.2. Tool designing for N.C. machines

There is no need of expensive jigs or fixtures for Numerical Control machine tools because of the accuracy built into an N.C. machine. Jigs and fixtures may be clamps and support blocks in most instances. The need for locating the workpiece relative to the zero point selected is important and must be dealt with when planning even simple holding devices.

The tooling problems becomes one of analysing the job, using great care in programming and setting up the machine.

One of the major advantage of numerical control over conventional machining with fixtures is that changes which need to be made can be done quickly by correcting the tape. It is easier and less expensive than re-working a fixture or scrapping a fixture and making a new one.

10.28.3. Automatic tool changer (ATC)

The CNC machines are equipped with automatic tool change facility. This helps the CNC machines to perform a number of operations in a single setting of the workpiece and this will reduce down time in change over from one operation to the next. With the help of A.T.C. the tool is automatically selected and changed based on the tool control function (T-word) in the part program.

Tools are usually stored on drum, chain and egg box type of magazines. To select the correct tool automatically from the magazine and replace it with the one already existing in the machine spindle a tool transfer arm is generally used. This arm shuttles to and fro between the spindle and magazine. The replaced tool carried by the arm can always be returned back to the same fixed place in the magazine. Tool changing time could be as small as four seconds. Tool magazines with upto 60 tools are quite common in our country.

10.29. Development of NC and CNC

This new and increasingly popular method for an automatic control of machine tools has been linked to an industrial revolution. Numerical control (NC) means controlling a process by numbers. The letters, symbols or numbers are recorded in code form on a punched card, punched paper tape or a magnetic tape to carry information regarding all the steps of operations for the manufacture of a workpiece on the machine tool. The numerical control (NC) had its experimental beginning in 1949 at the Servo-mechanism Laboratory of Massachusetts Institute of Technology (M.I.T.) where the initial research project was carried out sponsored by Parson's Corporation and United States Air Force. Between 1955 and 1960 about 500 NC machines were installed in U.S.A. Japan entered the NC commercial scene during mid 60's and by 1971 its NC production was as good as USA. Then countries like USSR, West Germany, U.K. and France also started manufacturing NC machine tools.

In India, in the early 1970's the first indigenously developed NC lathe was built. The Indian machine tool manufacturers after going through the teething troubles and gaining confidence to build NC machines came out in 1979 with a CNC (Computerised numerical control) lathe, a slant bed CNC lathe and vertical machining centres. Around 1982, a horizontal machining centre with automatic tool changer, CNC boring machine, CNC vertical turning machines and CNC travelling wire-cut EDM machines were developed. It is expected that CNC machines would account for at least 25% of all the machines tools produced in India by 1993. At present the number of NC machine tools in India is very small. By 1986 there were about 136 indigenous NC machine tools in operation. In order to increase production of NC/CNC machines tools in our country it is essential to impart training in NC and CNC and to invest in R and D to master the technology of designing and building NC and CNC machine tools with minimum dependence on external sources. With the growth of electronics NC holds a greater promise for the future manufacturing in India.

10.30. Computer Numerical Control (CNC) of Machine Tools

NC systems used on machine tools can be broadly classified as follows :

(*i*) Hard wired or conventional NC

(*ii*) Computer numerical control (CNC) or soft wired NC.

Since 1970, CNC systems have been increasingly replacing the common hard wired MCU. The CNC concept attempts to accomplish as many as possible control functions within computer soft ware. In computer numerical control system a dedicated stored program computer is used to perform all the basic NC functions as per the control program stored in the memory of the computer. Thus machine control data comes direct from the computer memory and not from the continuously read tape in case of hard wired NC system. Fig. 10.25 shows the general configuration of CNC system.

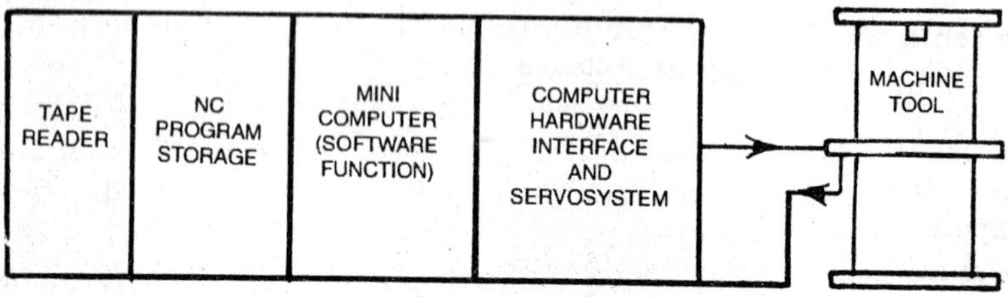

Fig. 10.25

Mini computer together with the associated software now performs the MCU functions of data decoding, control buffering, feed rate control, interpolation and position control.

10.31. Feature of CNC System

CNC system possesses the following special features which make it more popular :

(*i*) In NC system part programming becomes too tedious for complex shaped workpieces whereas in CNC the part programming becomes easy for complex jobs.

(*ii*) It is possible to modify and edit the part program at all stages.

(*iii*) Part program can be stored in the computer memory. The CNC then operates directly from these memories and use of tape reader is greatly reduced.

(*iv*) Part program can be generated directly from an existing part.

(*v*) Flexibility, increased capability and reliability together with reduction in cost and higher productivity make CNC and popular system.

10.32. Functions of CNC

The principal functions of CNC (Computer Numerical Control) are as follows :

(*i*) *Machine tool control.* This involves conversion of the part program instructions into machine tool motions through the computer interface and servo system.

(*ii*) *In-process compensation.* This involves the dynamic correction of the machine tool motions for changes or errors which occur during processing.

(*iii*) *Improved programming and operating features.* It helps in achieving the following :

(*a*) Editing of the part programs at the machine.

(*b*) Graphic display of the tool path to verify the tape.

(*iv*) *Diagnostics.* The N.C. machine tools are complex and expensive systems. The complexity increases the risk of the components failures which lead to system down time. CNC machines are often equipped with a diagnostics capability to assist in maintaining and repairing the system.

10.32.1. Recirculating Ball Screw and Nut

In conventional machine tools lead screw is used for motion transmission.

It has two disadvantages :

(*i*) High friction between lead screw and the nut

(*ii*) Poor power transmission efficiency and inaccuracy due to back lash.

In CNC machines the lead screw arrangement is not used because of above mentioned drawbacks.

To overcome these problems recirculating ball screw and nut arrangement shown in Fig. 10.25 (*a*) is used in CNC machines. Here again the approach is to replace sliding friction by rolling friction. The screw thread is a hardened and ground ball race in which the steel ball in the nut circulate. The balls rotate between the screw and the nut and at some point the balls are returned to start of the thread in the nut. The rigidity of the drive system and positioning accuracy can be further improved by pre-loading the nut assembly.

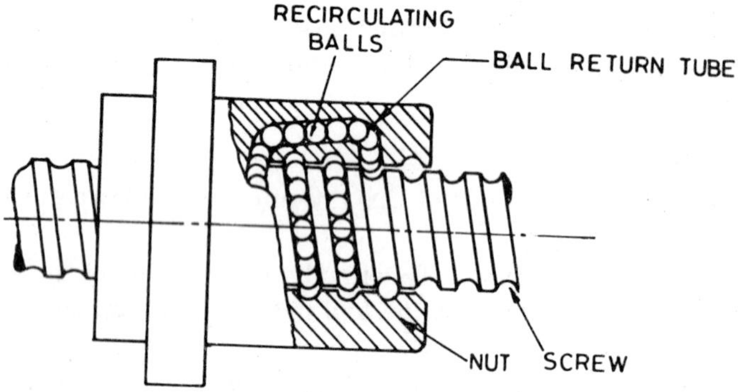

Fig. 10.25 (*a*)

Rigid mounting techniques for bearings are also employed to overcome the problems of backlash.

Various advantages of using recirculating ball screw and nut assembly are as follows :

(*i*) Reversibility

(*ii*) Minimum wear and longer life

(*iii*) High efficiency.

(*iv*) **Stick-slip eliminated.** The stick-slip phenomenon takes place between two lubricated parts. The lubricant tries to cause the mating elements to stick to each other to resist motion and this causes a jerky motion as the mating elements try to stick and then slip during their relative movement. By using ball screw and nut assembly the stick slip phenomenon gets eliminated because sliding metal to metal contact gets substituted by rolling contact.

10.33. Advantages of CNC

The various advantages of CNC are as follows :

(*i*) *Reliability*. The part program tape and tape reader are used only once to enter the program into computer memory. This results in improved reliability.

(*ii*) *Tape editing*. CNC system enables the correcting and optimising (such as speeds, feeds, tool path) the tape during tape try out at the site of machine tool. Thus, CNC permits editing modification of program at all stages.

(*iii*) *Units coversion*. Tapes prepared in units of inches can be converted into International system (S.I.) of units.

(*iv*) *Program display*. As all the functions are directly controlled by the computer the current state of program can be extensively displayed on a CRT (Cathode Ray Tube).

(*v*) *Control flexibility*. CNC systems programming can modify the control function in the desired manner. Machine sequence operations such as tool changing, spindle control etc. can be altered and controlled easily.

(*vi*) *Program storage*. The system has the capability of entering the program through a take or the key board which is then stored in the computer memory. The CNC system then operates directly from these memories and the use of tape reader is greatly reduced, whenever any program is required to be run for manufacture of a component it is called thereby saving time and eliminating errors due to tape reading.

(*vii*) CNC lends itself easily for adaption to DNC set up or to the integrated manufacturing system. This is so because of the ability of the mini computer to communicate with a larger central computer of the DNC.

(*viii*) Use of CNC machine tools has reduced the process planning time considerably in proto-type fabrication of complicated components. This has also reduced the vast amount of tedious and time consuming manual calculations in tools and fixtures.

10.34. Direct Numerical Control (DNC)

In this system a central computer is used for part programming and for other data processing operations. Part programming data is transferred from central computer to the mini computer by

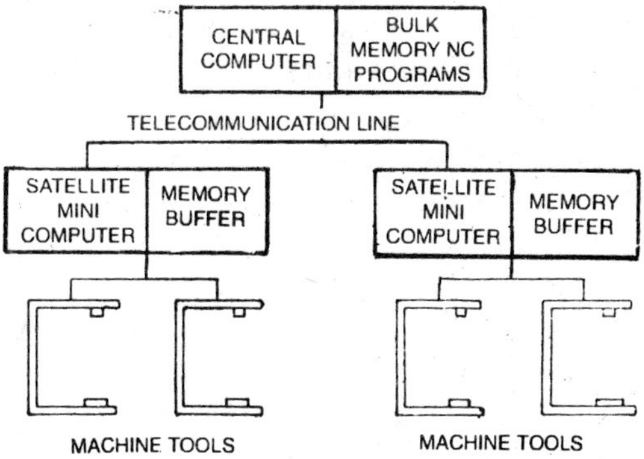

Fig. 10.26

means of telecommunication lines. The mini computer with its own data files can store active programmes and supply to the NC systems as required. The mini computer is assigned to control a group of machine tools. Since a large memory system is required and substantial cabling work is involved interlinking the NC machines to the computer DNC system is expensive and is preferably used in large organisations. Fig. 10.26 shows the general configuration of DNC system. Digital computer is used both in CNC and DNC.

10.35. Major Groups of N.C. Machine Tools

Two major groups of N.C. machine tools are as follows :

(*i*) Machining centres

(*ii*) Turning centres.

10.35.1. Machining centre

It is a sophisticated type of N.C. machine. This machine tool is generally a vertical milling machine with several axes of control and with automatic tool changing facilities. In this machine the tools are usually held in a rotary magazine and tool changes are commanded by the punched tape. Therefore, with this machine a complicated workpiece can be completely machined on all faces except the base through a combination of milling, drilling, boring, facing, reaming and tapping operations. Machining centre is quite useful for batch production of components.

A machining centre appears to be the most capable and versatile N.C. metal cutting tool. N.C. machining centres are generally designed for long hours of continuous operation and thereby accurate performance and productivity are expected to be sustained over long period of time. These centres are of massive construction in order to have enough stiffness so that minimum deviations take place due to large cutting dynamic forces and due to thermal effects because of heat generated from large amount of chips removed. Complex jobs are tackled by modern machining centres having simultaneous control of 3 or 4 linear and 2 or 3 rotary movements as well as positioning capability.

The horizontal turning centre (H.T.C.) is a most useful productive machine for :

(*i*) milling (*ii*) contouring

(*iii*) drilling (*iv*) tapping

(*v*) reaming.

10.35.2. Block and words in N.C. system

In N.C. system the commands are given to M.C.U. through the tape in blocks of data. The blocks are made of a group of words considered a unit and arranged in a definite sequence.

An N.C. word is a collection of characters such as letters, numbers or symbols. Block is a complete N.C. instruction that can be understood by the machine.

10.35.3. Function words

On N.C. machine tools the various functions are represented by words. The important functions with their words representations are as follows :

(*i*) **Sequence number function.** This function identifies a block and it is the first word of block. It is represented by letter N plus three digits.

(*ii*) **Preparatory function.** The preparatory function instructs the machine tool to get prepared for the operation to follow.

Preparatory function is represented by letter G plus two digits. There is a provision for coding a total of 100 preparatory functions from G00 to G99.

Some of the preparatory functions with their word codes are indicated in Table 10.1.

Table 10.1

Code	*Function*
G00	Positioning control
G01	Linear interpolation (Normal dimensions)
G02	Circular interpolation, clockwise
G03	Circular interpolation, anticlockwise
G04	Dwell
G05	Hold—The machine motion stops till the operator intervenes
G06, G07	Unassigned
G08	Acceleration
G09	Decleration
G10	Linear interpolation (long dimensions)
G11	Linear interpolation (short dimensions)
G12	Unassigned
G13 to G16	Prepares system to operate on a particular axis
G17	Selects the *XY*- plane for circular interpolation on a system which can operate in only two directions simultaneously
G18	Selects the *XZ*-plane for circular interpolation
G19	Selects the *YZ*-plane for circular interpolation
G20	Circular interpolation, clockwise direction (large dimensions)
G21	Circular interpolation, clockwise direction (small dimensions)

Code	*Function*
G22 to G29	Unassigned
G30	Circular interpolation, anticlockwise direction, large dimensions
G31	Circular interpolation, anticlockwise direction, small dimensions
G32	Unassigned
G33	Threading mode, constant lead
G34	Threading mode, increasing lead
G35	Threading mode, decreasing lead
G36 to G39	Permanently unassigned to enable the N.C. tool manufacturer to code functions not covered by those specified in this table
G40	Discontinuation of cutter compensation
G41	Cutter compensation—left, cutter to the left of the work surface as seen in the direction of cutter motion
G42	Cutter compensation—right
G43	Cutter offset, inside corner
G44	Cutter offset, outside corner
G45 to G49	Unassigned
G50 to G59	Unassigned and reserved for adaptive control
G60 to G69	Unassigned
G70	Inch programming on N.C. tools which accept dimensions in inches as well as millimetres
G71	Metric programming
G72 to G79	Unassigned
G80	Cancel fixed cycle
G81 to G89	Reserved for fixed cycles such as drilling, counterboring, etc.
G90	Absolute dimension input on a system with provision for both absolute and incremental dimensioning
G91	Incremental dimension input
G92, G93	Unassigned
G94	Feed rate in mm/min (inches/min)
G95	Feed rate in mm/rev (inches/min)
G96	Constant surface speed in m/min
G97	Speed in rev per min
G98, G99	Unassigned

(*iii*) **Dimensional data functions.** The dimensional data is represented by a symbol plus 5—8 digits. The various symbols used are as follows :

X primary *X* dimension
Y primary *Y* dimension
Z primary *Z* dimension
A angular dimension about the *X*-axis
B angular dimension about the *Y*-axis
C angular dimension about the *Z*-axis
U secondary dimension parallel to the *X*-axis

V secondary dimension parallel to the Y-axis

W secondary dimension parallel to the Z-axis

I interpolation parameter parallel to the X-axis

J interpolation parameter parallel to the Y-axis

K interpolation parameter parallel to the Z-axis

(*iv*) **Feed rate function.** Feed rate is expressed by the letter F plus three digits. The digits may represent the feed rate in mm/min or mm/rev or the magic three code equivalent may be used. If there are no digits to the left of the decimal point, then the first digit of magic three code is obtained by substracting from 3 the number of zeros immediately to the right of the decimal point. Table 10.2 shows some values of feed rate and their **magic three code equivalent.**

Table 10.2

Feed rate (mm / min.)	*Magic three Code equivalent*
0.194	319
0.0259	226
0.0078	178

(*v*) **Tool selection function.** The information regarding tool is given by a word prefixed by the letter T and followed by the numerical code for tool position in the tool turret or tool magazine when automatic tool changer (A.T.C.) is used. Each tool pocket on the tool turrent or A.T.C. (automatic tool changer) has a distinct tool number. The T-word in the block specifies which tool is to be used in operation. The tool number for a particular operation is specified as T00 to T99.

(*vi*) **Spindle speed function.** The spindle speed is specified either in revolutions per minute (RPM) or as metres per minute.

If the machine is required to run at 30 mpm the speed will be specified as S30.

(*vii*) **Miscellaneous function.** It is used to specify certain miscellaneous or auxiliary function which does not relate to the dimensional movements of the machine. The miscellaneous functions may be spindle start, spindle stop, coolant ON/OFF etc. These functions are denoted by the letter M plus two digits. Table 10.3 indicates the code of various miscellaneous functions.

Table 10.3

Code	*Function*
M00	Program stop.
M01	Optional stop.
M02	End of program.
M03	Spindle start (clockwise)
M04	Spindle start (anticlockwise)
M05	Spindle stop
M06	Tool change
M07	Coolant on flood cooling
M08	Coolant on (mist cooling)
M09	Coolant off
M10	Clamp (spindle, fixture, slide, etc.)
M11	Unclamp
M12	Unassigned
M13	Spindle start, clockwise direction, coolant on
M14	Spindle start, anticlockwise direction, coolant on
M15	Rapid traverse or feed motion in positive direction
M16	Rapid traverse or feed motion in negative direction
M17, M18	Unassigned
M19	Oriented spindle stop : the spindle stops in a prespecified angular position
M20 to M29	Permanently unassigned
M30	End of tape
M31	Interlock bypass ; temporarily circumvent a normally provided interlock
M32 to M35	Unassigned
M36 to M39	Permanently unassigned
M40 to M45	Gear change
M46, M47	Unassigned
M48	Cancel M49
M49	Bypass override
M50 to M99	Unassigned

(*viii*) **End of block.** The end of block (EOB) symbol identifies the end of instruction block.

10.35.4. Programming formats

The programming format is the method of writing the words in a block of instruction. The commonly used programming formats are as follows :

(*i*) **Fixed block format.** In this format the instructions are always given in the same sequence. All instructions must be given in every block including those instructions which remain unchanged from the preceding blocks. In these formats data is provided in the program and the identifying address letters are not given but the data must be input in a specified sequence and characters within each word must be of the same length.

(*ii*) **Tab sequential format.** In this format instructions in a block are always given in the same sequence as in case of fixed block format and each word is separated by the TAB character. If the word remains same in the succeeding block, the word need not be repeated but TAB code is required to maintain the sequence of words. Since the words are written in a set order, the address letters are not required.

(*iii*) **Word address format.** In this format each data is preceeded and identified by its address letter. For example, Y identifies the Y-coordinate, F identifies the feed rate and so on. If a word remains unchanged, it need not be repeated in the next block. A typical instruction block in word address format will be as follows :

NO10 X0000 Y0000 F 300 S 0600 T 010.00 M13 EOB

N	Sequence number
G	Preparatory function
X	*X*-coordinate
Y	*Y*-coordinate
F	Feed rate
S	Spindle speed
T	Tool address
M	Miscellaneous function
EOB	End of block.

Example 10.5. (*a*) *Write N.C. program for making the component shown in Fig. 10.26 (a).*

Solution.

N010	G71	G90	G94	Metric Mode Absolute system Feed in mm/min
N020	M03	F200	S1200	Spindle start at 1200 RPM feed rate 200 mm/min
N030	G00	X15.00	Y15.00	Move in rapid to point (15, 15)

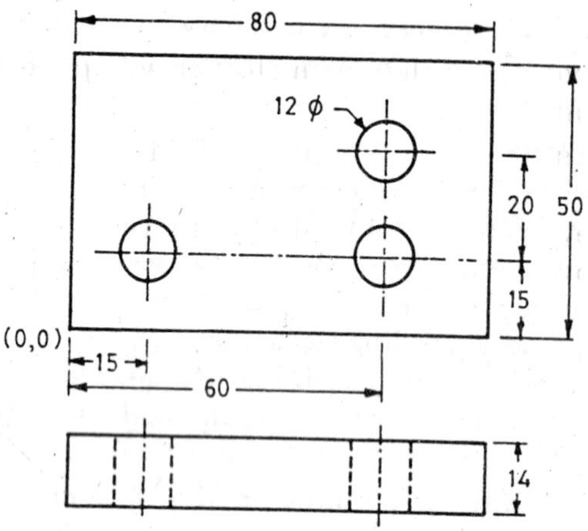

Fig. 10.26 (*a*)

N040	G00	Z3.00		Move in rapid to a point 3 mm above the work-piece
N050	G01	Z-14.00		Drill hole
N060	G00	Z 3.00		Move in rapid to point 3 mm above workpiece
N070	G00	X 60.00		Move in rapid to X = 60
N080	G01	Z-14.00		Drill hole
N090	G00	Z 3.00		—
N100	G00	Y 35.00		Move to Y = 30
N110	G01	Z-14.00		—
N120	G00	Z 20.00		Move in rapid to a point 20 mm above workpiece
N130	G00	X.00	Y.00	(Move in rapid to X0, Y0)

10.35.5. Classification of CNC/NC machine tools

The CNC/NC machine tools are classified on following basis :

1. Based on feed back control

(*i*) Open loop control system

(*ii*) Closed loop control system.

In open loop control system there is no provision to compare the actual position of the cutting tool or workpiece with the input command value.

In closed loop system the actual movement of the machine slide is compared with the input signal. This system makes use of feed back devices. The positional feed back is provided by measuring the slide movements with measuring devices. The position measuring devices used are as follows :

(*a*) Rotary or angular position measuring transducers.

(*b*) Linear position measuring transducers.

Feed back devices are of two type :

(*i*) Velocity feed back to measure and monitor the speed of the drive motor.

(*ii*) Positional feed back to measure and monitor the position or displacement of the machine slide.

Velocity feed back device. A device called tachogenerator is used for velocity feed back. Tachogenerator is simply a generator that gives voltage output which is proportional to its speed. The tachogenerator is normally built in the servo motor case and is directly fitted on the servo motor shaft. The output voltage from the tachogenerator is used as a feed back to monitor the motor speed.

Position feed back device. The displacement of the work table can be established by means of linear grating position measuring transducer shown in Fig. 10.26 (*b*). From the known number of

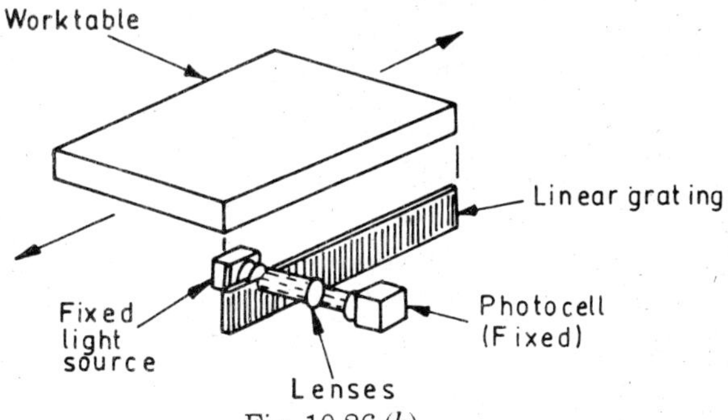

Fig. 10.26 (*b*)

engraved lines per unit length on the linear scale and by counting the number of pulses generated, the work table displacement can be measured.

2. Classification based on control system

NC and CNC control systems are as follows :

(*a*) Point-to-point control systems

(*b*) Straight line control systems

(*c*) Continuous path or contouring control system.

10.35.6. Tool holders

Tool holders used on CNC machine tools should be of quick changing type and should be able to pre-set. This will reduce the tool change time to about 3 to 5 seconds.

Spindle tooling provides an objective connection between the cutting tool and spindle of the machine tool. Fig. 10.26 (*c*) shows a typical spindle tooling holding for an end mill cutter.

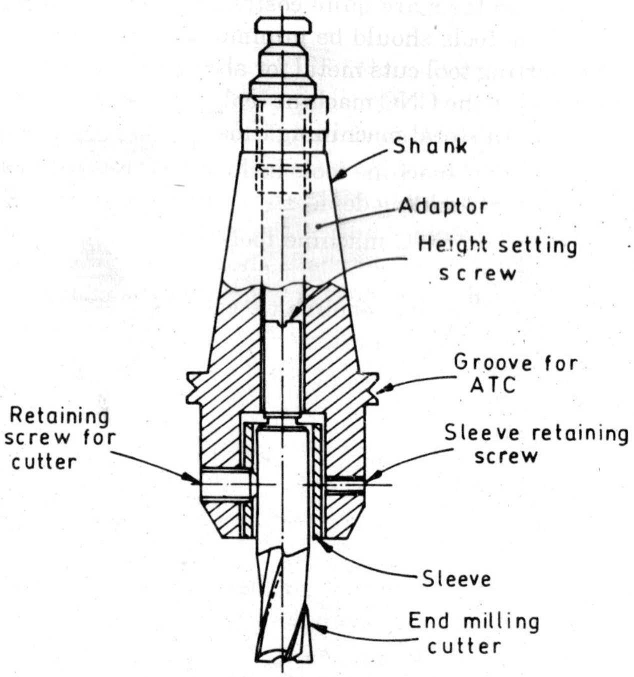

Fig. 10.26 (*c*)

10.35.7. Work holding devices

In CNC machine tools the various machining operations on different surfaces of the workpiece are performed in a single setting, therefore the work holding device should be such that the workpiece should be accessible from different sides. To reduce clamping and unclamping time hydraulic and pneumatic actuation is widely used in work holding devices.

Work holding device should have the following features :

(*i*) It should facilitate quick loading and unloading of the component.

(*ii*) It should be fool-proof *i.e.* it should ensure that workpiece can not be loaded wrongly.

(*iii*) It should provide for easy removal of chips.

(*iv*) It should be possible that the workpiece is accessible from different sides for machining in one setting.

(*v*) The work holding device should not interfere with the cutting tools.

10.35.8. Tooling for CNC machine tools

As CNC machine tools are quite costly, therefore the down time on these machine tools should be minimum. In conventional machine tools the cutting tool cuts metal for about 25% of the total machining time whereas the CNC machine tools are expected to cut metal for 60 to 75% of the total machining time.

The tooling for CNC machine tools includes the cutting tools and the tool and the work holding devices.

The tooling used on CNC machine tools should possess the following requirements :

(*i*) Tooling should be rigid enough to withstand higher cutting forces for high metal removal rates.

(*ii*) Tooling should be capable of being pre-set and re-set in the shortest possible time to keep the down time to minimum.

(*iii*) Tooling should be accurate enough to produce repetitive accuracy on the work surface.

Tooling for CNC machine tools includes the cutting and tool and work holding devices.

With quick, simple and accurate provision of adjusting tools, the non-productive time on the machine can be kept to a minimum.

10.35.9. Types of tools

The commonly used tools are of following types :

(*i*) **Pre-set tools.** Pre-setting of tools is done with the tools held in the tool-holders so that the assembly *i.e.* the tool-holder and cutting tool can be straight way fitted on the machine. Pre-setting of tools in advance reduces machine tool down time and ensures continuity of production.

(*ii*) **Qualified tools.** In qualified tools the position of the cutting edge is guaranteed within close limits of accuracy from a specified datum on the tool-holder. The tool fits into locations on the machine which are accurately positioned relative to known datum positions on the slides. Thus, the cutting edges of a qualified tool will be located in a pre-determined position.

(*iii*) **Semi-qualified tools.** Such tools have three adjustable buttons on the tool shank. These buttons can be adjusted to a qualified dimension and can be used on different machines.

(*iv*) **Indexable inserts.** Indexable carbide inserts are commonly used on CNC machines as compared to brazed tools which are normally not used. Indexable carbide inserts are used to take up higher cutting speed and to minimise tool change time. The indexable inserts of tungsten carbide are further coated with a wear resistant layer of titanium carbide or titanium nitride.

10.35.10. Standard tape control for NC machine

The Electronic Industries Association (EIA) has developed standards to define the physical characteristics of punched tape and tape coding for the industry. The American Standards Code for Information Interchange (ASCII) also developed a perforated tape. The two standard tapes are very much alike in that they are both one inch wide and have provision for eight rows of holes plus the sprocket holes. The main difference is in the parity check. The EIA codes require an odd number of holes on every row across the tape and the ASCII has an even number of holes as a parity check. Most machine control units for NC have EIA tape readers but some are made to read either one.

10.35.11. N.C. programming by scanning and digitizing

Programming may be done directly from a drawing, model, pattern, or template by digitizing or *scanning*. A simple two dimensional part that needs nothing more than positioning operations such as sheet-metal punching or hole drilling can be digitized (given X-Y coordinate locations) from a fully dimensioned drawing. The drawing is placed on the table and an optical reticle or other suitable viewing device connected to an arm or arms is placed over the location points. Transducers are made to identify the location and, upon a signal, transfer it to either a tape punch or other suitable programming equipment. Most digitizing equipment also has auxiliary input to allow the establishment of reference points or the addition of data such as position refinement.

A scanner enables an operator to program complex free-form shapes by manually moving a tracing finger over the contour of a model or premachined part. Overall accuracy of the scanning system from model to tape is ± 0.005 in.

Many digitizing and scanning units have the capability to "edit" or revise the basic data gathered.

10.35.12. N.C. tape parity check

In both ISO and EIA coding system one track is reserved for parity checking. Parity track is a device for error checking and to ensure that the tape has been punched correctly. The ISO code specifies even parity which means that number of holes in any row should be even. The EIA code specifies odd parity and uses track 5 as parity track.

After the punched tape has been prepared, a method is usually provided for checking the accuracy of the tape. Sometimes the tape is checked by running it through a computer programme which plots the various tool movements (or table movements) on paper. In this way, major errors in the tape can be covered. The "acid test" of the tape involves trying out on the machine tool to make the part. Foam or plastic material is sometimes used for this tryout. Programming errors are not uncommon, and it may require about three attempts before the tape is supposed to be correct and ready to use.

10.35.13. CNC machine structure

The design and construction of CNC machine should be such that it meets the following objectives :

(*i*) High precision and repeatability

(*ii*) Reliability

(*iii*) Efficiency.

To meet the above requirements the CNC machine structure should be designed to withstand normal weight consideration. The machine structure should not bend due to heavy cutting forces and should be capable of resisting fluctuation forces produced during machining operation due to higher cutting speeds and feeds.

There should be minimum thermal distorsion in the structure. The machine tool should be provided with an efficient and fool-proof lubrication and cooling system. An efficient arrangement should be provided for easy removal of swarf. Since cutting time is much more in CNC machines, the volume of swarf produced is also more. Therefore swarf should be quickly removed in order to carry out machining operation smoothly.

The swarf removal from the cutting zone is generally taken care of by the design configuration of the machine. Slant bed and vertical bed turning centres have the advantages over flat bed or horizontal bed configuration in that the swarf does not accumulate on the guidways. Similarly horizontal machining centres are advantageous to vertical machining centres. But swarf removal by gravity is not adequate in CNC machines. To supplement the gravity system, multiple coolant jets are arranged around the cutting tool and the coolant, under pressure, takes away the accumulated swarf from the cutting area. Compressed air jets are also used for swarf clearance from the cutting zone.

Continuously operating linear or rotary conveyors are used for removing the swarf from the machine tool. The system is such that the swarf from the cutting zone falls directly on the conveyor and is immediately taken away.

10.35.14. CNC machine program language

The various NC part programming languages are as follows :

(*i*) **APT (Automatic Programmed Tool) language.** This is the most commonly used language. It is a three dimensional language used to direct a tool in a well defined path.

The APT general processor program has a language of about 300 "words". The words are all English-like and have specific meanings. None have more than six letters. Included are such terms as fedrat, cutter, from, point, plane, golft, gorght, circle, poast, etc. Some are descriptions of geometric shapes or patterns and others are instructions regarding tool movements as explained in more detail later.

The part programmer must know the precise meaning and capability of each word and how it can be used before he can expect to write a part-program manuscript.

Most of other APT like languages are either subsets, super subsets or variants of the current APT version available.

There is far less arithmetic required in preparing a manuscript for a computer program than for a manual part since the computer performs the bulk of the mathematical calculations. However, the part programmer must be precise in the use of all words and notations as called for in the APT language.

(*ii*) **NELAPT.** It has been developed by the National Engineering Laboratory, U.K. It is a subset of APT with a few advanced fractures not available in APT.

(*iii*) **EXAPT.** It is extended subset of APT and has been developed by West Germany experts.

10.35.15. Manual part programming sheet

The manual part programming sheet used in N.C. machine tool indicates the various functions and values of X, Y and Z

Manual Part Programming Sheet

Job No. .... Department .... Date ....

N *Seq. No.*	*G Prep. Funct.*	*X* *coor.*	*Y* *coor.*	*Z* *coor.*	*R*	*I*	*J* *value*	*K*	*F* *Feed*	*T* *Tool*	*Q* *Tool Offset*	*M* *Misc. Func.*	*S* *Speed*	*EOB* *End of Block*

coordinates. A typical manual part programming sheet is indicated on page 541.

10.35.16. Post processor for N.C. machine

The post processor is an individual program written to take into account the particular variables of the machine-tool/control-unit combination on which the part will actually be machined. Each machine has its own characteristics, such as indexing table, tool changers, swivelling head, etc. For example, there is no point in having tool-change instructions in a tape program if there is no automatic tool changer on the machine. Most machine-tool and control-unit builders have developed programs and post processors for their particular equipment.

When a programmer writes an APT part-program manuscript, the first computer output will not be the program tape for use on the machine tool. The first output will be what is known as the "CL", which is the abbreviation for "center line" or "cutter line." This merely tells where the center line of cutter, with a given configuration, will have to be located in a rectangular coordinate system to machine a part to the desired geometry as shown in Fig. 10.26 (*d*). An additional step, *post-processing*, is required to adapt

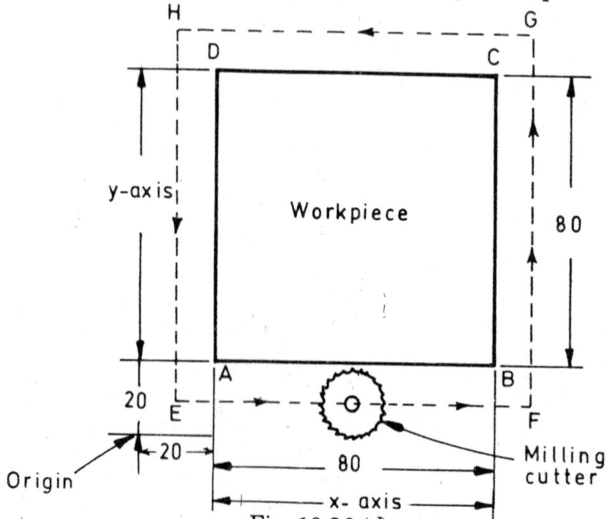

Fig. 10.26 (*d*)

the CL output to the particular machine-tool/control-unit combination which will be used to machine the workpiece. The tape that will be used is a product of the post processor.

The workpiece point locations are as follows, taking cutter diameter as 20 mm.

Point	*X*	*Y*
A	20	20
B	100	20
C	100	100
D	20	100

Programmed point locations will be as follows :

Point	*X*	*Y*
E	10	10
F	110	10
G	110	110
H	10	110

As shown in above figure cutter offset has been made perpendicular to the surface being machined.

Some MCU's have cutter-compensation capabilities to take into consideration the variable diameter of cutting tools or tools that were programmed with one diameter in mind and have been changed or have been resharpened to a smaller diameter.

Example 10.5. (*b*) *Fig. 10.26 (e) shows a component made of mild steel. Write program for making this component on CNC milling machine.*

Solution. A typical part program for making the component is as follows.

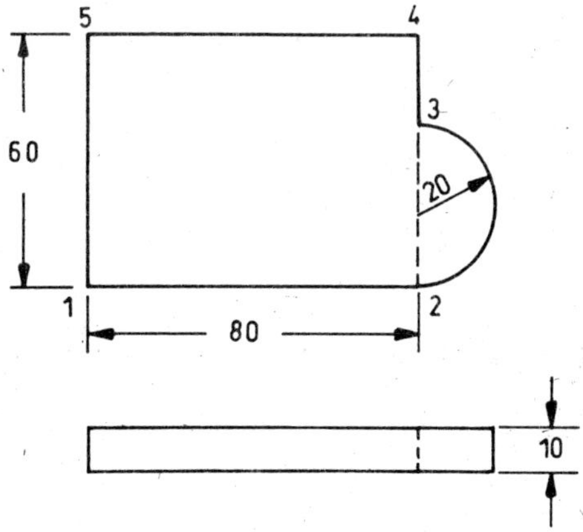

Fig. 10.26 (*e*)

As shown in Fig. 10.26 (*f*)

N01	G90	G40	G80	G21	EOB	
N02	G92	X0	Y0	Z50		
N03	M03	S1000				
N04	G00	G17	X30	Y30		
N05	G00	G42	X40	Y50		Point 1
N06	G01	Z—12	F100			
N07	G01	X130	F40	S1000	M08	Point 2
N08	G03	X130	Y90	R20	F20	Point 3
N09	G01	X130	Y110	F50		Point 4
N10	G01	X50	Y110			
N11	G01	X50	Y50			Point 5
N12	G00	Y30	M09	M05		
N12	G40					
N13	G00	X0	Y0	Z0		
N14	M30					

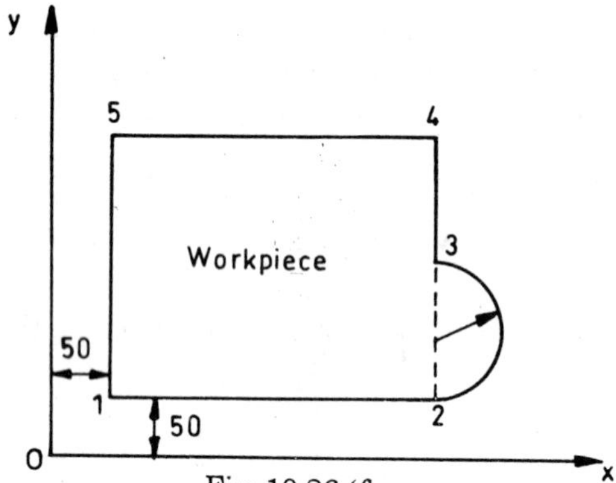

Fig. 10.26 (*f*)

10.36. CAM

Computer Aided Manufacturing (CAM) is gaining wide acceptance in engineering industries for their ability to create major increase in the productivity. In CAM computers are used to aid the manufacturing processes. Computer Aided Design (CAD) and Computer Aided Manufacturing (CAM) were originally developed independently but are now-a-days being integrated into a single system called CAD/CAM system. In CAD/CAM design can be developed and the manufacturing process can be monitored and controlled from start to finish with a single system.

CAM can be defined as the use of computer systems to plan, manage and control of operations of a manufacturing plant through either direct or indirect computer interface with the plant's production resources. Computers also help all functions of management such as process planning, coordination, control of production, inventory, control etc. CNC, DNC and flexible manufacturing systems have number of advantages over traditional methods of manufacturing.

10.37. Transfer Machines

In transfer machines the processing equipment is arranged in order of the sequence of manufacturing operations. Production lines may be non-automatic and semi-automatic and automatic. In automatic transfer machines the operator loads the blanks and usually checks the workpiece.

These machines are provided with some automatic mechanism for moving workpieces from station to station to carry out the various operations. Transferring usually is carried out by the following methods :

(*i*) Rotary transfer system

(*ii*) In-line transfer system.

In rotary transfer system the workpieces are held in fixtures in a continuously rotating table. The rotating table brings the workpieces under different machine (Fig. 10.27). This method is

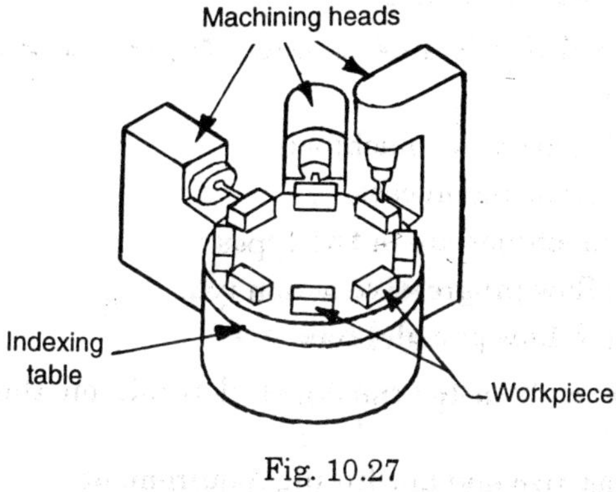

Fig. 10.27

quite compact and permits the workpiece to be loaded and unloaded at a single location without having to interrupt the machining. In the in-line method the workpiece is held in a special pallet or fixture. The fixtures are located and clamped in proper position.

The empty pallets are returned to the starting station by a return conveyor arranged parallel to the main transfer line (Fig. 10.28).

Rotary transfer machines can usually accommodate only six or fewer stations because of restriction on space whereas the size of an in-line machine can be almost unlimited. Sometimes an endless

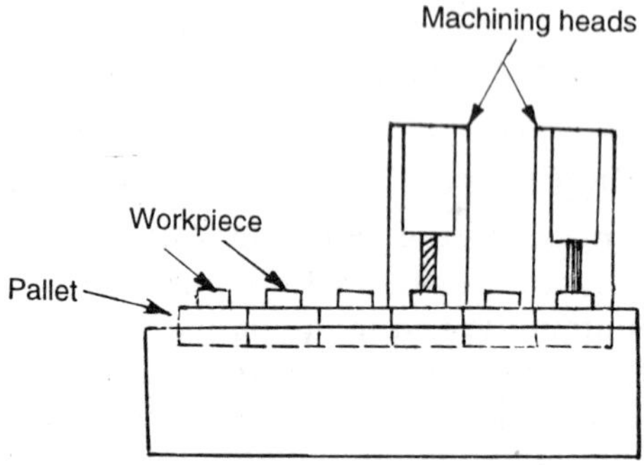

Fig. 10.28

chain that moves intermittently as required is used to transfer workpieces from one station to other station.

The choice of workpieces transferring system depends upon the following factors :

(*i*) Weight of workpiece.

(*ii*) Shape of workpiece.

(*iii*) Nature of manufacturing process.

(*iv*) Machine tool lay-out.

The most efficient transfer machine layout depends upon the following factors :

(*a*) Type of part to be machined.

(*b*) Manufacturing process.

Transfer machines are of two types :

(*i*) Single flow progressive action type

(*ii*) Multiple-flow parallel type.

Selection of transfer machines depends on the following factors :

(*a*) Product size and machining requirements

(*b*) Handling systems used

(*c*) Floor space available.

In multistation in-line transfer machines parts fixed in fixtures called pallets are moved from station to station. Throughout the entire operation they are held in the same fixture. These types of in-line transfer machines are called pallet type transfer machines. After completion of operations the pallets are returned by conveyor to the initial loading station.

Pallets are often carried in conveyors which are indexable.

10.38. Advantages and Disadvantages

The various advantages of transfer machines are as follows :

(*i*) Higher production rates are achieved.

(*ii*) Less floor space is required.

(*iii*) Less number of operations are required.

(*iv*) The quality of products is considerably improved.

(*v*) The length of production cycle is reduced.

Disadvantages

(*i*) The initial cost of transfer machine is high. It is of great importance that the construction of components to be machined on transfer machine should remain stable for sufficient time to justify the cost of such machine.

(*ii*) Much time is required to change over the machine to handle a different shaped components.

(*iii*) A breakdown of one machine means stoppage of whole of production line.

10.39. Economic Comparison of Various Manufacturing Systems

As shown in Fig. 10.28 (*a*) the manufacturing cost per component (*C*) depends largely on batch size (*N*). It is observed that manual system is economical for smaller batch size and numerical control is economical both for small and medium batch production.

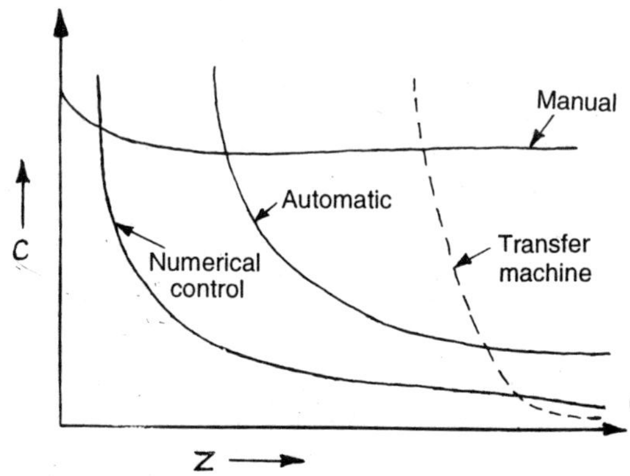

Fig. 10.28 (*a*)

Automatic system is preferred for medium and large size batch production. The transfer machines are preferred for large size batch components.

10.39.1. Time comparison of conventional, CNC and FMS machining methods

Cutting time in CNC ranges from 60 to 75%. In the conventional general purpose machine the cutting time is about 25% of total machining time.

As the CNC machines are very costly, the down time of these machines should be reduced to minimum. In conventional machines the skilled operator is responsible for many inputs to the machine. With increase in complexity of the component the time to produce the component also increases.

In CNC machines there is reduction in production time and human error and there is greater manufacturing flexibility.

There is reduced lead time. Lead times is the time between the receipt of a design drawing by the production engineer and manufacturer being ready to start production on shop floor, including the time needed for planning, design and manufacture of jigs etc.

FMS (Flexible Manufacturing System) enables increased productivity and lower manning levels. There is flexibility to redesign products to meet changes as per marker requirements

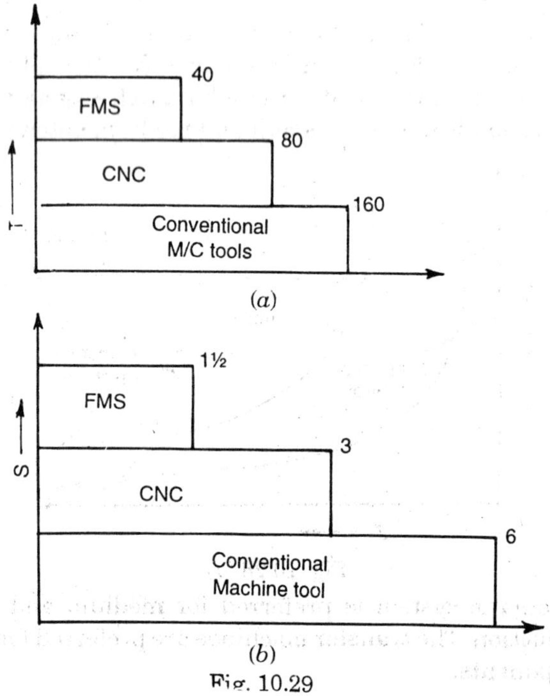

Fig. 10.29

without making further investment. There is overall reduction in manufacturing cost. Reduced inventory and lead times are other features of F.M.S.

Fig. 10.29 (*a*) shows machining time comparism for FMS, CNC and conventional machine tools whereas lead time for these manufacturing methods are compared in Fig. 10.29 (*b*).

T = Machining Time (Hours)

S = Lead Time (months).

10.40. Production Capacity of Automatic Machine Tools

Piece output indicates the main index of production capacity of automatic and semi-automatic machine tools.

$$P = \text{Piece output} = \frac{3600}{T} \text{ pieces per hour}$$

where T = Calculated time in seconds for machining the workpiece

$$= T_S + \frac{T_C}{N}$$

where T_S = Standard time (time per piece) in seconds.

T_C = Set up time in seconds. It is the time for setting up the machine and for demounting the tools after machining one lot.

N = Number of workpieces in one lot.

The value of standard time (T_s) is found as follows :

$$T_S = T_1 + T_2 + T_3 + T_4 + T_5 \text{ seconds.}$$

where T_1 = Machining time in seconds

T_2 = Handling time for moving slides etc., in seconds

T_3 = Servicing time for setting, adjustments, tool changing chip removal etc. for single workpiece in seconds.

T_4 = Fatigue time (seconds) for rest and personal needs of operator

T_5 = Time (seconds) for breakdown, delays etc.

10.41. Computer Application in Production

CAD (computer aided design), CAM (computer aided manufacturing) and robotics have proved to be a boon in increasing productivity CAD assists in the creation, modification and analysis or optimisation of a design whereas CAM helps to plan, manage and control the operations of a manufacturing plant through either direct or indirect computer interface with the plant's production resources.

The computer aided manufacturing techniques have focused on the problem of how to improve the overall productivity and economy of manufacturing. Development of concepts like flexible manufacturing cells and flexible manufacturing systems (FMS) have brought substantial productivity increases by using the computer to increase machine utilisation and rationalise manufacturing processes. Computer aided design techniques help the designer to react speedily to customer needs.

The NC technology has itself undergone revolutionary changes leading to CNC technology.

Overall product cost and quality are governed by the efficiency at every stage from design to dispatch. Realising this, engineers have tried to improve performance and reliability at every stage of manufacture of a product and here is where application of the computer has led to a revolution in manufacturing technology. Computer based manufacturing methods have helped the manufacturing plants to respond to changing market needs faster and also to diversify the range and variety of products.

10.42. N.C. System for Simple Turning

Fig. 10.30 shows a schematic diagram of a Numerical Control (N.C.) system for simple turning operation on a lathe. The information regarding the movement of cutting tool during turning is coded on a program medium like paper tape in the form of holes. The

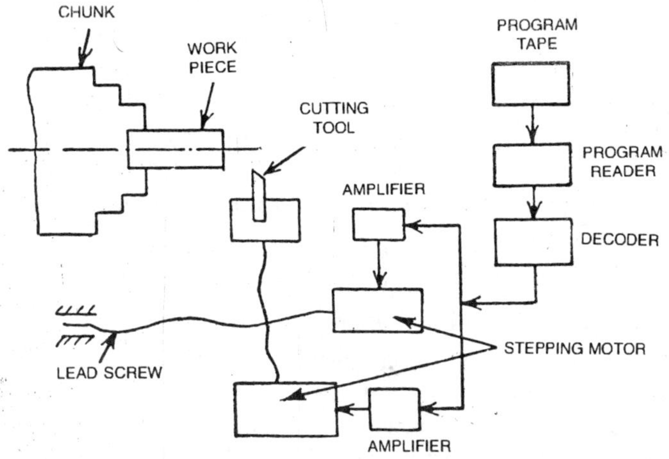

Fig. 10.30

punched tape is passed through a program reader which indentifies the presence or absence of a hole and sends the corresponding information to the decoder. The decoder generates a pulse every time a hole is sensed. The electrical pulses (signals) so generated are amplified by the amplifier and fed to a stepping motor which makes the lead screw to rotate and then translatory displacement of tool is achieved by means of a screw and nut mechanism.

Example 10.6. *Explain the following terms as used in numerical control :*

(*i*) *Absolute system.*

(*ii*) *Incremental system of dimensioning.*

Solution. In N.C. the dimensions of a drawing are measured according to these systems.

In absolute system to the co-ordinates are mentioned in the program with respect to one reference point (Datum).

In incremental system the co-ordinates of a point are mentioned in the program with respect to the previous point.

An absolute system is one in which all position commands are referred to one reference point, which is called the zero point. Absolute systems may be subdivided into an Absolute-Input-Output (AIO) systems and absolute programming systems. By the term *Absolute-input-output,* we mean a system in which both programmed dimensions (the input) and feedback signal (the output) are supplied in an absolute form.

The Absolute-Input-Output systems are using absolute measuring devices as Binary, BCD, or Gray code encoders. It is obvious that these systems are more accurate, since a feedback error cannot exist. On the contrary, when using incremental techniques it can entail a cumulative error of the table positions. In addition, the AIO systems are protected against forced errors, such as power cuts, since the absolute feedback transducer keeps and always indicates the correct position.

When considering an incremental system both the programming and the feedback elements are incremental. A typical feedback device is the rotary encorder which provides sequence of serial pulses.

Fig. 10.31 indicates the typical position of points *A*, *B* and *C* and their co-ordinate are indicated in Table 10.4.

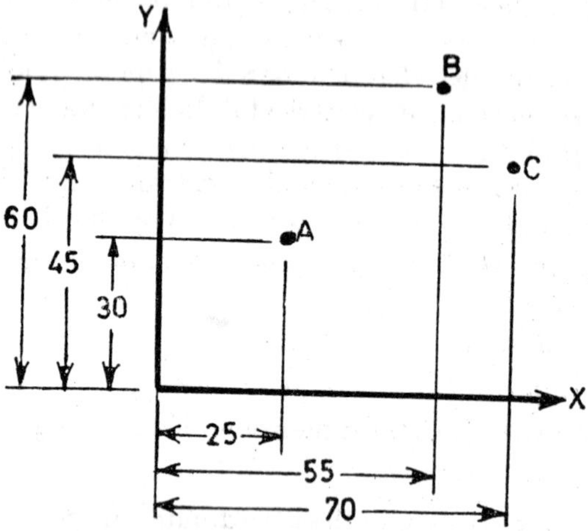

Fig. 10.31

Table 10.4

Point	*X-co-ordinate*	*Y-co-ordinate*
	Absolute System	
A B C	25 55 70	30 60 45
	Incremental System	
A B C	25 30 15	30 30 – 15

Example 10.7. (*a*) *Discuss the economically controlled machines.*

(*b*) *The initial cost of an N.C. turret lathe is Rs. 62500 with a payback period of 3 years. Determine the production cost per component using the following data :*

Operator's wages = Rs. 5 per hour

Tool (fitted with disposable carbide type) cost = Rs. 2 per cutting edge.

Setting time = 70 seconds.

Cost of tape preparation and programming per unit of machining time = Rs. 0.30/sec.

Total cycle time is 280 second out of which 50% is spent an actual chip removal.

100% overhead are applied to the machine and operator. The lathe is run for 2000 hours per year. The batch size is 30.

Solution. (*a*) In NC machines the cost of preparations for machining a batch of components is calculated as follows :

$$C = K \cdot T_m$$

where C = Cost of preparation for machining a batch of components

K = Cost of part programming and tape preparation per unit machining time

T_m = Machining time.

Further the production cost per component (C_p) is found as follows :

$$C_p = \frac{K \cdot T_m}{N} + M\,(T_1 + T_m) + \frac{T_m}{T}\,(M \cdot T_C + C_t)$$

where N = Batch size

T_1 = Loading and unloading and tool advance and tool withdrawal time

T_C = Tool changing time

T = Tool life

C_t = Cost of a sharp tool

M = Total machine and operator rate.

(*b*) Since 100% overheads are applied to the machine and operator, therefore the value of M will be as follows :

$$M = \frac{2 \times 625000}{3 \times 2000 \times 3600} + \frac{2 \times 5}{3600}$$

$$= \text{Re. } 0.06 \text{ per second}$$

Now $T_m = \dfrac{280}{2} = 140$ seconds

N = Batch size = 30

K = Cost of programming and tape preparation pe. unit machining time

= Re. 0.30 per second

T_1 = Loading and unloading, tool advance and withdrawal time

= 140 seconds (assume)

T = Tool life = 280 seconds (assumed)

T_c = Tool changing time

= 70 seconds

C_t = cost of a sharp tool = Rs. 2

C_p = Production cost per component

$$= \frac{K \cdot T_m}{N} + M(T_1 + T_m) + \frac{T_m}{T}(M \cdot T_C + C_t)$$

$$= \frac{0.3 \times 140}{30} + 0.06(140 + 140) + \frac{140}{280}(0.06 \times 70 + 2)$$

$$= 1.4 + 16.80 + 1.21 = \text{Rs. } 19.41.$$

10.42. (*a*) Interpolation in N.C. Machines

It is used to get cutter located from one point to the next. In N.C. machines two types of interpolations are generally used :

(*i*) Linear Interpolation

(*ii*) Circular Interpolation.

For this the preparatory codes are G01 and G02 or G03.

In linear interpolation it is required to provide the coordinates of destination points.

In circular interpolation it is required to provide coordinates of destination points as well as the coordinates of centre of arc with respect to starting point of arc. The data processing unit calculates the radius of the circle of which arc forms the part.

For example, let the cutter be at some point and it is required to proceed to a point (40, 50) along a straight line. Then the program for linear interpolation will be

N10 G01 X40 Y50.

For circular interpolation if it is required to move further along an arc of a circle whose centre is (0, 0) to a point (60, 0) then the program will be

N11 G02 X60 Y0I – 40J – 50

where I, J correspond to the coordinates of the centre with respect to starting point (40, 50).

10.42. (*b*) Code Numbers for Feed and Speed

In N.C. machines the important code numbers for feed (mm/Rev.) and speeds (R.P.M.) according to DIN 260250 VDI 3252 are indicated in Table 10.5 (*a*) and Table 10.5 (*b*).

Table 10.5 (*a*)

Code No.	*Feed (mm/Rev.)*	*Code No.*	*Feed (mm/Rev.)*
00	0 (Rest)	17	0.71
01	0.112	18	0.8
02	0.125	19	0.9
03	0.14	20	1.0
04	0.16	21	1.12
05	0.18	22	1.25
06	0.2	:	:
07	0.224	28	2.5
08	0.25	:	:
09	0.28	50	31.5
10	0.315	51	35.5
11	0.355	52	40
12	0.4	53	45
13	0.45		
14	0.5		
15	0.56		
16	0.63		

Table 10.5 (*b*)

Code No.	*Speed (RPM)*	*Code No.*	*Speed (RPM)*
54	50	71	355
55	56	72	400
56	63	73	450
57	71	74	500
58	80	75	560
59	90	76	630
60	100	77	710
61	112	78	800
62	125	79	900
63	140	80	1000
64	160	81	1120
65	180	:	:
66	200	:	:
67	224	:	:
68	250	:	:
69	280	:	:
70	315	99	fast traverse

Every word is composed of an address letter and a number or a symbol. For example No. 4 means sentence No. 4, F18 means tool movement of 0.8 mm/revolution (refer to code number in Table 10.5 (*a*)) and S65 means spindle speed of 180 R.P.M. (Refer to code number in Table 10.5 (*b*)).

Example 10.7. (*a*) *Compare various machine tools for Increasing variety and Increasing Batch, size.*

Solution. General purpose machine tools are used when variety of components to be made is high but batch size is low. Special purpose machine tools are used for lower variety and higher batch size. Typical comparison of various machine tools are shown in Fig. 10.31 (*a*).

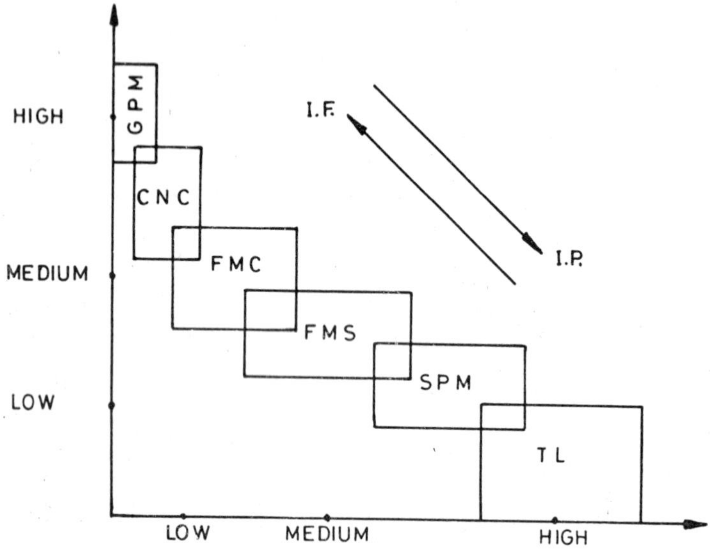

Fig. 10.31 (*a*)

In this Fig. 10.31 (*a*)

V = Increasing variety

S = Increasing batch size

I.P. = Increasing productivity

I.F = Increasing flexibility

GPM = General purpose machine tools

CNC = Computerised numerical control machine tools

FMC = Flexible manufacturing cells

FMS = Flexible manufacturing system

SPM = Special purpose machines

$T.L$ = Transfer lines.

Example 10.7. (*b*) *Write the coordinates of points* P_1, P_2, P_3, P_4 *and* P_5 *according to*

(*a*) *Absolute system*

(*b*) *Incremental system.*

Points are shown in Fig. 10.31 (b).

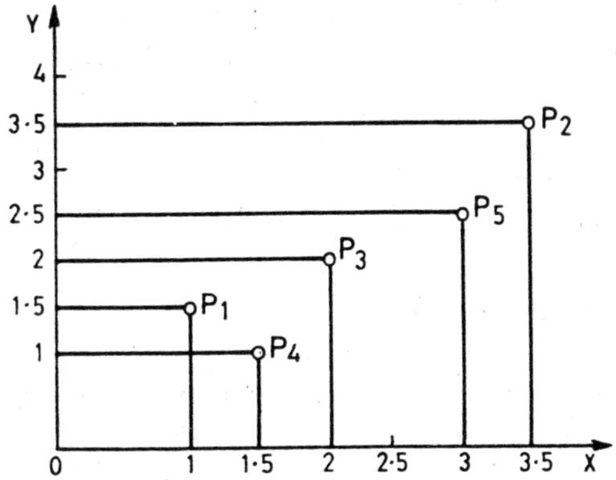

Fig. 10.31 (*b*)

Solution. The coordinates are as follows :

(*a*) Absolute system (Datum O)

Point P_1. $x_1 = 1$

$y_1 = 1.5$

Point P_2. $x_2 = 3.5$

$y_2 = 3.5$

Point P_3. $x_3 = 2$

$y_3 = 2$

Point P_4. $x_4 = 1.5$

$y_4 = 1$

Point P_5. $x_5 = 3$

$y_5 = 2.5$

(*b*) Incremental System

Point P_1. $x_1 = 1$

$y_1 = 1.5$

Point P_2. $x_2 = 3.5 - 1 = 2.5$

$y_2 = 3.5 - 1.5 = 2$

Point P_3. $x_3 = 2 - 3.5 = -1.5$

$y_3 = 2 - 3.5 = -1.5$

Point P_4. $x_4 = 1.5 - 2 = -0.5$

$y_4 = 1 - 2 = -1$

Point P_5. $x_5 = 3 - 1.5 = 1.5$

$y_5 = 2.5 - 1 = 1.5.$

Example 10.7. (*c*) *Write part program for making the component shown in Fig. 10.31 (c) from raw material bar of 25 mm. diameter. Maximum depth of cut being limited to 2mm.*

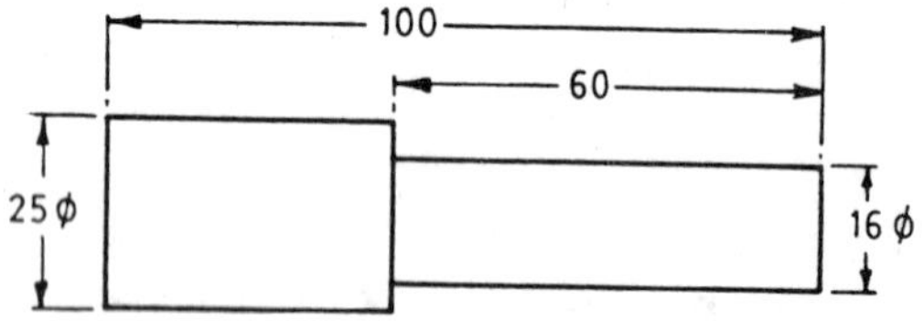

Fig. 10.31 (*c*)

Solution. The 25 mm diameter bar is shown in Fig. 10.31 (*d*)

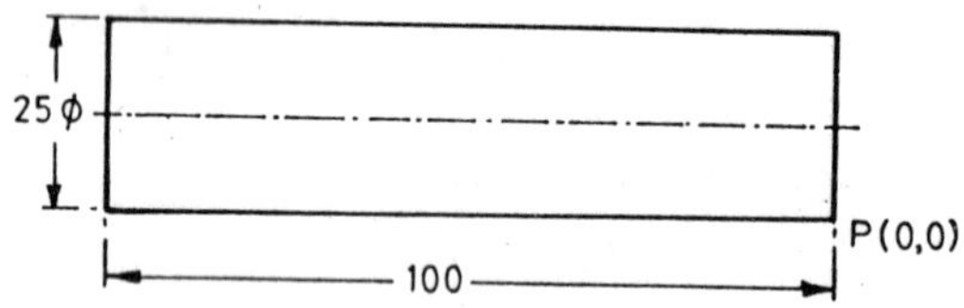

Fig. 10.31 (*d*)

Let us take point *P* (0, 0) as reference point. For point *P*

$$X = 0$$

$$Z = 0$$

where Z = Distance moved parallel to the longitudinal axis of workpiece.

X = Distance moved by the tool perpendicular to the longitudinal axis of workpiece.

Fig. 10.31 (*e*) indicates the positive (+) and negative (–) directions for the values of Z and X with regard to reference point.

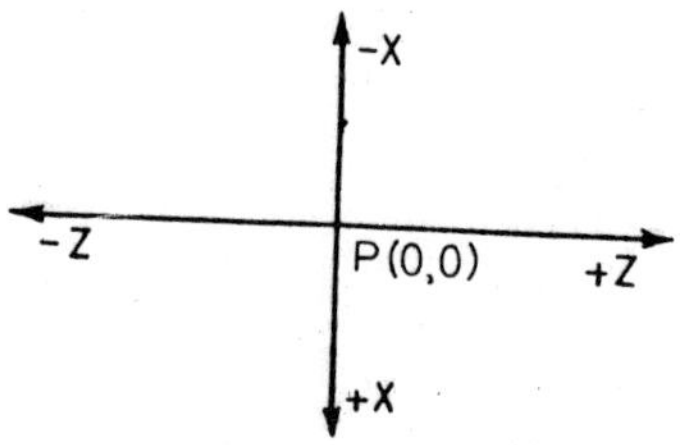

Fig. 10.31 (*e*)

The operations to be carried out will be as follows :

(*i*) Facing

(*ii*) Cleaning

(*iii*) Turning.

Assuming absolute system of coordinates the program will be as follows :

N1	G90	G71	M03	S1000
N2	G01	X—1250	Z00	F200M08
N3	G00	X—1250	Z100	
N4	G00	X0	Z100	
N5	G01	X0	Z—9900	
N6	G00	X 100	Z—9900	
N7	G00	X100	Z100	
N8	G00	X—200	Z100	
N9	G01	X—200	Z—6000	
N10	G01	X0	Z—6000	
N11	G00	X0	Z100	
N12	G00	X—400	Z100	
N13	G01	X—400	Z—6000	
N14	G01	X0	Z—6000	
N15	G00	X0	Z100	
N16	G00	X—450	Z100	
N17	G01	X—450	Z—6000	
N18	G01	X100	Z—6000	
N19	G00	X100	Z500	
N20	M02	M05		

Operation N2 indicates facing, operation N5 indicates cleaning and turning operation starts from N9.

10.43. N.C. Machine Tools Drives

In N.C. machine tools the main drives hardly differ from those used on conventional machine tools. These drives may be simple stepped drives, stepped drives with electromagnetic clutches and stepless drives.

Feed drives for point to point system are somewhat different. A simple stepped drive is not used in the feed transmission of N.C. machine tools. However a stepped drive with electromagnetic clutches also called electromagnetic drive is often used. The electromagnetic clutches permit automatic changing of the feed rate. The feed drive of point to point N.C. machine tools are generally powered by stepping motors. Fig. 10.32 shows a schematic diagram

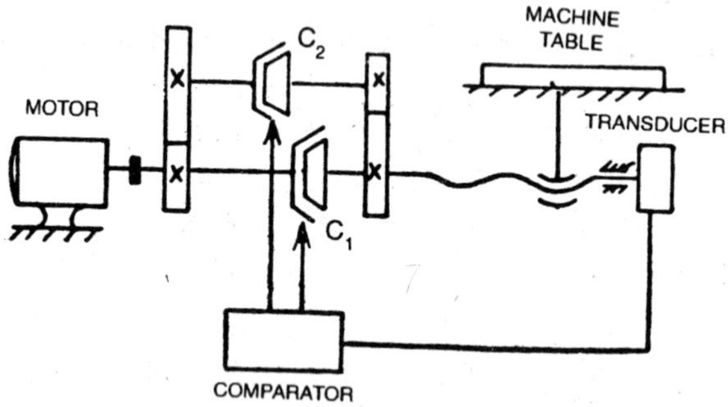

Fig. 10.32

of an electromagnetic feed drive. The drive is powered by a three phase induction motor which may be connected to the bad screw of the machine tool through electromagnetic clutches C_1 and C_2. The clutch C_1 gets engaged during positioning movement and the transducer constantly monitors the displacement of the operative member and sends this information to the comparator. The comparator activates electromagnetic clutch C_2 resulting in a reduced feed rate.

Hydraulic and electrical stepless drives are commonly used in continuous path systems.

10.44. Economics of Numerically Controlled Machines

The cost of manufacturing a component on an N.C. machine tool is made of cost of programming and tape preparation and production cost.

C = Manufacturing cost per component

$= C_1 + C_2$

where C_1 = Cost of part programming and tape preparation per component

C_2 = Production cost = $C_3 + C_4$

C_3 = Machining cost

$= R\,(T + T_1)$

where R = Total machine and operator rate

T = Machining time per component

T_1 = Loading and unloading and tool advance and withdrawl time

$$C_4 = \text{Tooling cost}$$

$$= \frac{T}{T_2} (R \times T_3 + S)$$

where T_2 = Tool life

T_3 = Tool changing time

S = Cost of sharping tool.

Example 10.8. *In an N.C. turret lathe calculate the cost of manufacturing a component when batch size is 20 using following data :*

Initial cost of lathe	*= Rs. 3 × 10⁶*
Payback period	*= 3 years.*
Operator's wages	*= Rs. 8 per hour*
Overheads for machine and operator	*= 100%*
Tool life	*= 600 seconds*
Cost of tape preparation per units of machining time	*= Rs. 4/sec.*

Total cycle time is 300 seconds out which 5% is spent on actual chip removal.

The lathe tools are fitted with disposable carbide inserts costing Rs. 18 per cutting edge tool resetting time is 80 seconds.

Solution. R = Machine rate + Operator rate

$$= \frac{2 \times 3 \times 10^6}{3 \times 50 \times 40 \times 3600} + \frac{2 \times 8}{3600}$$

= Rs. 0.28 per second

C_1 = Cost of part programming and tape preparation

$$= \frac{4 \times 150}{N}$$

where N = Batch size = 20 and machining time is 150 seconds

$$= \frac{4 \times 150}{20} = \text{Rs. } 30$$

C_2 = Production cost = $C_3 + C_4$

C_3 = Machining time cost

$= R\,(T + T_1)$

T_1 = 300 seconds

T = 150 seconds.

Assuming loading and unloading time 150 seconds

$$C_3 = 0.28\ (150 + 300) = \text{Rs. } 126$$

$$C_4 = \text{Tooling cost}$$

$$= \frac{T}{T_2}\ (R \times T_3 + S)$$

$$= \frac{150}{600}\ (0.28 \times 80 + 18) = \text{Rs. } 10.1$$

where T = 150 seconds

T_2 = Tool life = 600 seconds.

T_3 = Tool changing time = 80 seconds.

S = Cost of sharpening the tool

C = 30 + 126 + 10.1

= Rs. 166.1.

10.44.1. The coordinate system in N.C. system

The three primary motions for an N.C. machine are given as X, Y and Z-axis. The primary X motion is normally parallel to the longest dimension of the machine table, Y motion is normally parallel to the shortest dimension of the machine table and Z motion refers to the axis of the driven spindle. Positive Z movement (+ Z) is in the direction that increases the distance between the workpiece and the tool. Fig. 10.32 (a) shows coordinate convention for single column vertical milling drilling and boring machine.

X-axis = Table side to side

Y-axis = Table front to rear

Z-axis = Spindle vertically into workpiece.

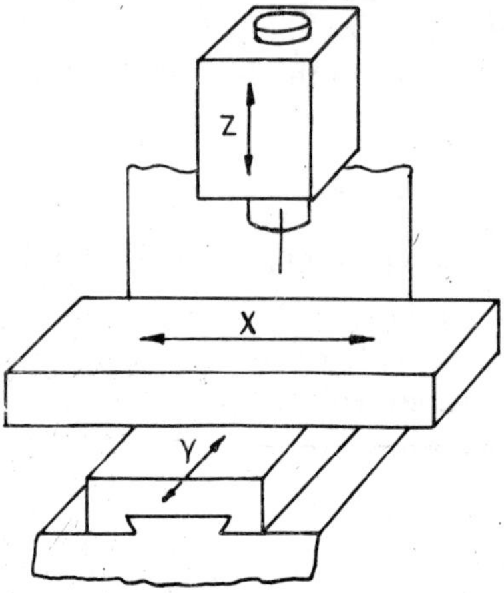

Fig. 10.32 (a)

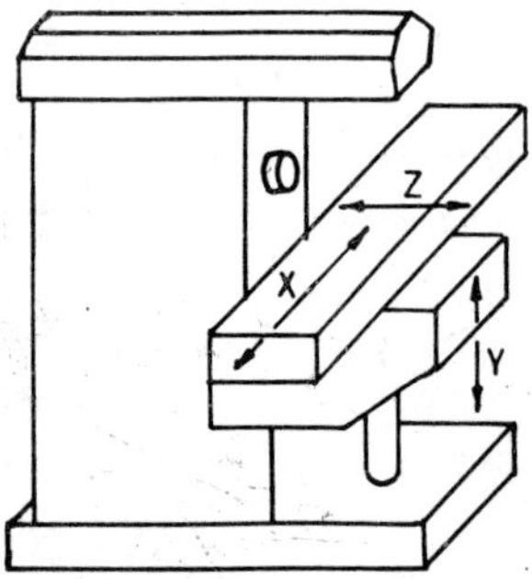

Fig. 10.32 (b)

Fig. 10.32 (*b*) shows coordinate convention for horizontal milling machine.

Fig. 10.32 (*c*) shows coordinate convention for turning machine according to V.D.I. 3255.

Fig. 10.32 (*d*) shows angular movement directions *A*, *B* and *C* about *X*, *Y* and *Z* axis respectively according to VDI 3255.

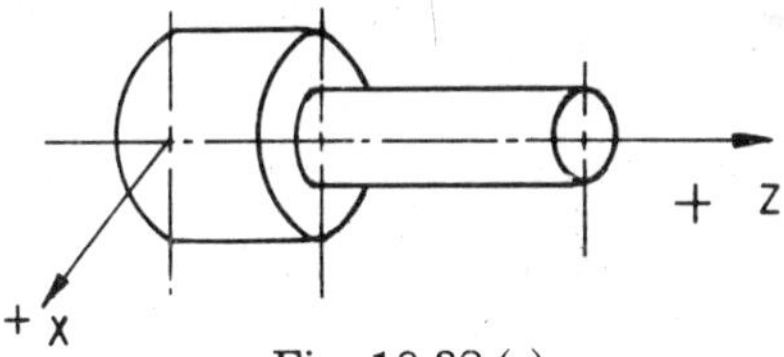

Fig. 10.32 (*c*)

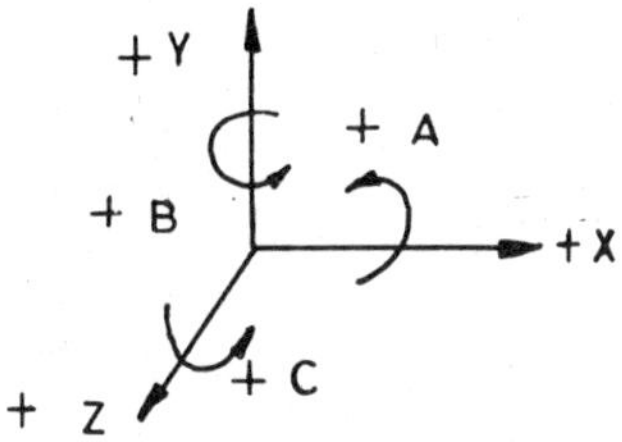

Fig. 10.32 (*d*)

10.44.2. Coordinates and reference points in N.C. machine tools

Reference points should be clearly established so that the workpiece and tool can be brought to the correct position.

Machine datum zero point (MP) is the origin of the machine coordinate system. The workpiece datum zero point (WP) is the origin of workpiece coordinate system. The starting point (SP) indicates the starting point of tool or slide.

Zero System. The point where *X*, *Y* and *Z* axes cross is called zero point. A machine tool may have two types of zero point.

(*i*) *Fixed zero point.* The fixed zero point machine is usually made so that the zero location is at the low left hand corner of *X*-*Y* coordinate on some systems the fixed zero may be moved by means of switches or dials to any where within the full travel range of the machine.

(*ii*) *Floating zero point.* It allows the operator to place the zero at any convenient location without regard to the initial fixed zero point. The operator merely moves the table to the desired location by means of jog buttons. The jog buttons make it possible for the operator to manually move the table to the desired location at feed rates set on the dial. When the table is at the exact desired location, the operator depresses a button which establishes this point as the zero point.

Fig. 10.32 (*e*) shows a comparison between a fixed zero point and floating zero point.

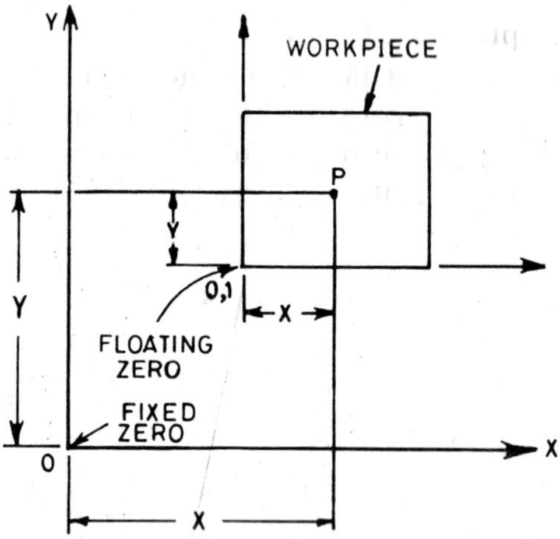

Fig. 10.32 (*e*)

10.45. Laser Machines for Productivity

New concepts in production engineering are required as batch sizes in production are becoming smaller and smaller. Laser machines provide reliability, quality, flexibility, productivity, and above all simplicity in operation particularly for sheet metal processing.

CNC laser processing machines is quite suitable for processing metallic and non-metallic materials such as steel, high temperature resistant materials super alloys, tungsten, molybdenum titanium, ceramic, plastic, wood etc. The machine consists of a rigid welded and stress relieved structure with a table designed specially for the laser processing of sheet metal. The portal carbon-dioxide laser cutting machine can control the laser beam. Salient features of laser machine are as follows :

(*i*) Slides driven by precision linear motion guides and ball-screws.

(*ii*) Motorisation by A.C. servo drives.

(*iii*) Centralised lubrication for slides and ball screws.

(*iv*) *X*-axis movement for forward and backward movement of the work table.

(*v*) *Y*-axis movement for right and left movement of focussing unit.

(*vi*) *Z*-axis movement for up and down motion of the focussing unit.

Example 10.9. *Describe N.C. Coding Systems.*

Solution. The data to CNC system is input in the coded form. The coding is based on two digits 0 and 1. The number system which uses these two digits is called binary. All the data input to the control system is converted into a binary equivalent. A minimum of four digits are required in the binary system to represent any single digit number in the decimal system as indicated in Table 10.6.

Table 10.6

Decimal	*Binary*
0	0000
1	0001
2	0010
3	0011
4	0100
5	0101
6	0110
7	0111
8	1000
9	1001

The binary system uses base 2 whereas in decimal system base is 10.

The values in decimal system can be converted into binary system and vice versa.

10.46. Decimal to binary Conversion

In order to convert decimal number into binary equivalent the decimal number is divided by 2 and remainder is written on side. This forms the right most digit of binary number. The quotients are progressively divided by 2 and remainder is written on the side till the remainder is 1 or 0. The last remainder forms the left most digit of the binary number.

Example 10.10. *To write binary equivalent number of decimal numbers 9 and 5.*

Solution. (*a*) 9 = 8 + 1
= 1000 + 0001
= 1001

(*b*) 5 = 4 + 1
= 0100 + 0001
= 0101.

Example 10.11. *Convert decimal number 57 to binary number.*

Solution. Divide 57 by 2 till remainder is 1 or 0.

2	57
2	28 – 1
2	14 – 0
2	7 – 0
2	3 – 1
	1 – 1

Hence, Binary number is 111001.

Example 10.12. *Write the two instruction blocks when two holes are to be drilled in the job shown in Fig. 10.33. Using C.N.C. machine.*

The holes are to be drilled using a 10 mm drill rotating at 400 RPM when feed rate is 150 mm / min. The G, M and T codes are not to be specified.

Solution. (*a*) In fixed block format the two instruction blocks will be as follows :

N	*X*	*Y*	*F*	*S*	
001	15.00	20.00	150	400	E0B
002	75.00	20.00	150	400	E0B

(*b*) In TAB sequential format the two instruction blocks will be as follows :

001 TAB 15.00 TAB 20.00 TAB 150 TAB 400 E0B

002 TAB 75.00 E0B

(*c*) In word address format the two instruction blocks will be as follows :

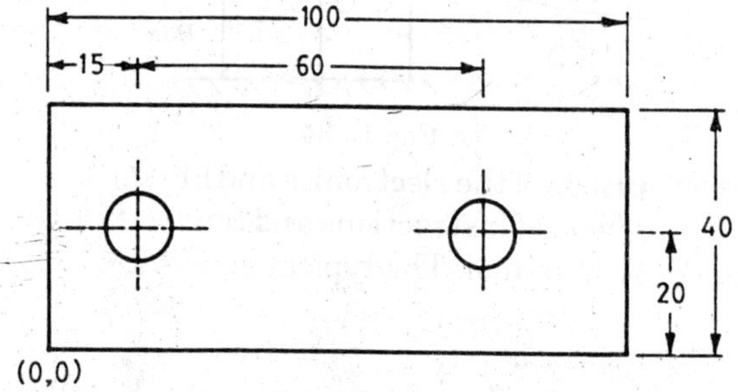

Fig. 10.33

N001	X15.00	Y20.00	F150	S400	E0B
N002	X75.00	E0B			

Example 10.13. *Describe basic components of an N.C. system.*

Solution. Numerical control (NC) can be defined as a form of programmable automation. In N.C. the numbers form a program of instructions designed for a particular component. When component changes the program of instructions also changes. The capability to change the program for each new component is what gives N.C. flexibility.

Not only has N.C. replaced human skills and intuition but also it has made it possible to generate complex machine motions with a degree of precision that is far beyond any human capability.

Three basic components of an N.C. system are as follows :

(*i*) Program of instructions

(*ii*) Controller unit also called a machine control unit (M.C.U.)

(*iii*) Machine tool or other controlled process.

The program of instruction serves as the input to the controller unit which in turn commands the machine tool or other processes to be controlled.

The program of instructions is the detailed step-by-step set of directions which tell the machine tool what to do. It is coded in numerical or symbolic form on some type of input medium that can be interpreted by the controller unit. The program of instructions is prepared by some one called a part programmer. For a machining operation the processing steps involve the relative movement between the cutting tool and the workpiece Fig. 10.34 shows three basic components of a numerical controlled system.

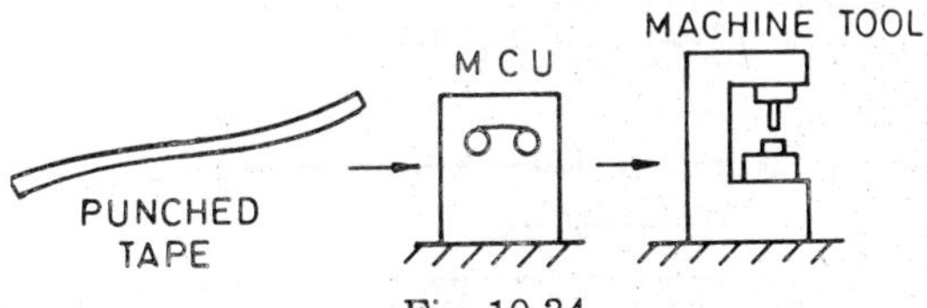

Fig. 10.34

M.C.U. consists of the electronics and hardware that read and interpret the program of instructions and convert it into mechanical actions of the machine tool. The typical elements of M.C.U. are as follows :

(*i*) Tape reader

(*ii*) A data buffer

(*ii*) Signal output channels to the machine tool

(*iv*) Feed back channels from the machine tool

(*v*) Sequence controls

(*vi*) Control panel.

The function of tape reader is to wind and read the punched tape containing the program instructions. The data buffer stores the input instructions in logical blocks of information. A block of information usually represents one complete step in the sequence of processing elements.

The signal output channels are connected to the servo motors and other controls in the machine tool. The machine control unit (MCU) sends the instructions to the machine tool through these channels. The return loop sends back the feed back data to the controller. This will help to check that :

(*i*) Instructions have been properly executed by the machine.

(*ii*) The table and workpiece have been properly located with respect to the tool.

The sequence controls coordinate the activities of various elements of the MCU. The control panel or control console contains the dials and switches by which the machine operator runs the NC system. It may also contain data displays to provide information to the operator.

The duties of the operator are as follows :

(*i*) To start and stop and machine

(*ii*) To load and unload the machine

(*iii*) To change tool. In some machines automatic tool changers are provided. In such machines tools are automatically changed under tape command.

(*iv*) To control the coolant supply.

Modern N.C. machines are generally provided with a micro computer as the controller unit. Such machines are called computer numerical control (CNC) machines.

Fig. 10.35 shows flow chart of numerical control steps.

The positional control function implies that the hand wheel has been replaced by a button which makes it possible to move the table very fast, very slow or by a desired increment as small as a fraction of a thousand of a millimetre.

In N.C. machine tools all the movements of the tool and machine table are automatically controlled by electric motors. The motors used for controlling the speed, feed and depth of cut are either servomotor or stepper motor which enable the user to select any desired speeds and feeds.

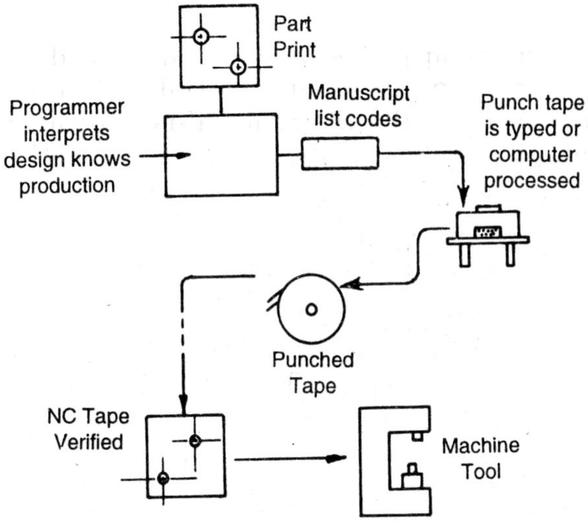

Fig. 10.35

The machine may have a tool magazine so that the tool changing is done automatically. Other functions like machine ON/OFF, coolant on/off etc. are controlled through part programming.

Example 10.14. *What are the special characteristics of automatic machine tools ?*

Solution. Automation leads to higher production rate. Automatic machine tools produce accurate components and idle time during machining is reduced.

Various special elements of an automatic machine tool are as follows :

(*i*) Automatic handling of product between various processing units

(*ii*) Automatic feeding of work stock

(*iii*) Automatic controls

(*iv*) Automatic tool changing

(*v*) Automatic discharge of the product.

Example 10.15. *(a) How machine tools are classified ?*

(b) What are main requirements of machine tools ?

(c) State the factors which affect cutting force during machining.

(*d*) *Name the principal features of construction of machine tools.*

Solution. (*a*) Machine tools are classified in following ways :

(*i*) Based on the type of processing operation

(*ii*) Degree of specialisation :

(A) General purpose machine tools

(B) Special purpose machine tools

(*iii*) Size and weight of machine tools

(*iv*) Accuracy of the machine tool.

A part from this there is a general classification of machine tools based on the following :

(*i*) The shape of the generated surface

(*ii*) The shape of cutter

(*iii*) The nature of relative movement

(*iv*) The type of finish

(*b*) Primary requirements of machine tools are as follows :

(*i*) Within permissible limits the specified accuracy of shape, size and surface finish of the components produced on the machine must be obtainable consistently and as far as possible independently of the operator's skill.

(*ii*) The operational speeds and rates of metal removal provided by the machine must be in accordance with the latest developments in materials and tools and, therefore, ensure the possibility of high productivity. In addition, the design must be such as to enable it to cope with future developments in these matters in order to prevent the machine from becoming obsolete in a short time.

The machining quality depends not only upon the machine tool itself, but also on other factors mentioned below :

(*a*) The tool

(*b*) The tool holder

(*c*) The workpiece and its clamping

(*d*) The cutting conditions.

(*iii*) In order to be competitive in operation, the machine must show a high technical and economic efficiency.

(*c*) The cutting force during machining is affected by the following factors :

(*i*) Cutting speed, feed and depth of cut

(*ii*) Tool geometry and tool material

(*iii*) Tool wear

(*iv*) Hardness of workpiece material

(*v*) Cutting fluid used.

(*d*) The principal features of construction of all types of machine tool consist of following :

(*i*) Principal supporting structure such as supporting frame, bed, column or knee

(*ii*) Holding devices for workpiece

(*iii*) Arrangements for holding and mounting of cutting tools

(*iv*) Provision for kinematic interlink in order to carry out specific and desired operations

(*v*) Source of power

(*vi*) Transmission system.

The transmission system provided for cutting and feed motions are commonly known as drives. The selection of drives depends on the following factors :

(*i*) Production time

(*ii*) Surface finish and accuracy required

(*iii*) Optimum efficiency

(*iv*) Power to weight ratio

(*v*) Minimum cost

(*vi*) Simplicity of design with respect to maintenance, repair and control.

PROBLEMS

10.1. Compare an engine lathe with capstan and turret lathes.

10.2. What is the difference between capstan and turret lathe ?

10.3. Make a neat sketch of a turret lathe, name its parts and describe its operation.

10.4. Make a neat sketch of capstan lathe, name its parts and describe its operation.

10.5. Write short notes on the following :

(*a*) Turret indexing mechanism.

(*b*) Work holding devices for a turret lathe.

(*c*) Bar feeding mechanism of turret lathe.

(*d*) Vertical turret lathe.

10.6. Describe the tooling set up on a turret lathe required to produce the bolt shown in Fig. 10.36.

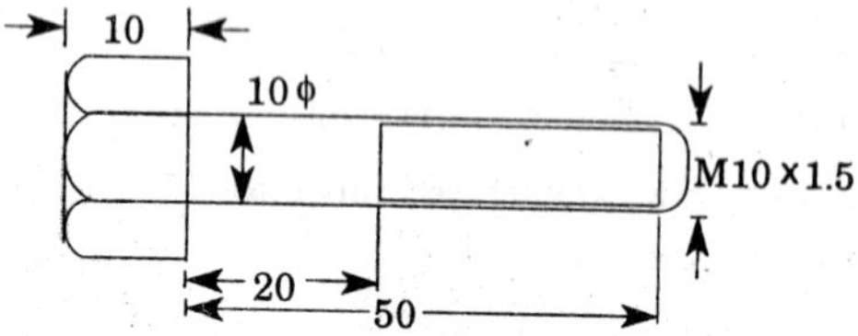

Fig. 10.36

10.7. (*a*) What is an automatic machine ? State the factors which affect the classification of automatic machines ?

(*b*) What are the different types of automatic machines ?

10.8. Describe the following automatic machines :

(*i*) Automatic cutting off machine.

(*ii*) Swiss type automatic screw machine.

(*iii*) Turret type automatic screw machine.

10.9. Write short notes on the following :

(*a*) Multi-spindle screw machine

(*b*) Type of cams used in automatic machine

(*c*) Cam lay-out.

10.10. What is numerical control of machine tools ?

10.11. Explain open loop system and closed loop system of numerical control.

10.12. Write short notes on the following :

(*a*) Digital and analogue control for N.C. machine tools.

(*b*) Point to point numerical control system.

(*c*) Continuous path numerical control. System of NC machine tools.

(*d*) Type of tapes used in numerical control.

(*e*) Codes used in numerical control.

10.13. State the advantages and disadvantages of numerical control machine tools.

10.14. (*a*) What is a transfer machine ?

(*b*) Describe the following types of transfer machines.

(*c*) Rotary transfer machines.

(*d*) In line transfer machines.

10.15. State the advantages and disadvantages of transfer machines.

10.16. Discuss the features of NC machines.

10.17. (*a*) What is automation ?

(*b*) Describe the economics of automatic machines.

(*c*) State advantages and disadvantages of automation.

10.18. Write short notes on the following :

(*a*) Tool slides of automatic machine tools.

(*b*) Methods of increasing production capacity of automatic machine tools.

(*c*) Operating cycle of automatic machine tools.

10.19. Explain the following with reference to NC machine tools :

(*i*) Part programming

(*ii*) Input media

(*iii*) Punched paper tape

(*iv*) Machine control unit (MCU).

10.20. Discuss the development of NC and CNC machine tools.

10.21. Describe CNC machine tools.

10.22. Discuss the various features of CNC that make it more useful.

10.23. Describe :

(*a*) Absolute system

(*b*) Incremental system of dimensioning used in NC.

10.24. Describe DNC system.

10.25. With the help of schematic diagram explain a numerical control system for simple turning operation.

10.26. Write short note on the following :

(*i*) Computer application in production

(*ii*) B.C.D. system for N.C.

10.27. Discuss the cost of manufacturing a component on N.C. machine tool.

10.28. Describe basic components of an N.C. system.

10.29. Write short notes on the following :

(*i*) Functions of CNC system of machine tools

(*ii*) Advantages of CNC system

(*iii*) Data required for part programming

(*iv*) Machining centre N.C. machine tool

(*v*) Computer aided manufacturing (CAM)

(*vi*) Laser machines for productivity.

10.30. Sketch and describe N.C. system for simple turning on lathe.

10.31. Write short notes on the following :

(*i*) Automatic tool changer (A.T.C.) for C.N.C. machines

(*ii*) N.C. procedure

(*iii*) Process planning sheet.

10.32. Discuss the following :

(*i*) Block and words in N.C. system

(*ii*) Function words in N.C. system of machines

(*iii*) Programming Formats.

10.33. Write short notes on the following for CNC machine tools :

(*i*) Tool holders

(*ii*) Work holding devices

(*iii*) Tooling for CNC machine tools

(*iv*) N.C. machine tool structure

(*v*) Manual part programming sheet

(*vi*) Post processor for N.C. machine

(*vii*) N.C. machine program languages.

11

Testing, Maintenance and Erection of Machine Tools

11.1. Testing of Machine Tools

Machine tools are subjected to various tests before they are sent for sales. Since machine tool consists of various parts assembled together such as motor shafts, couplings, gear, clutches, bearings, coolant pumps, and other structures such as columns, beds, gear boxes, tail stock, head stock etc. Certain basic tests are essential for smooth operation of machine tool. Tests also deal with temperature increase in certain parts such as bearings. The rise in temperature in bearings should be within permissible limits. The entire structure of machine tool should be stiff and rigid. The bed of the machine tool is normally made of cast iron to have more vibration proof characteristics. The amplitude of vibrations should be within the desired range.

The accuracy and surface finish of the parts produced by a machine tool depends upon many factors. One of these factors is the accuracy of the machine tools. Therefore, to produce parts economically and accurately it is essential that the machine tool on which the parts are produced is accurate. An inaccurate machine tool cannot produce accurate parts. To check how accurate a machine tool is it very important to test the machine tool to certain accepted standards.

Testing of a machine tool has the following advantages :

(*i*) By testing of a machine tool it can be put in a proper grade or precision class, thereby helping a purchaser to know what he can expect from the machine tool.

(*ii*) Testing helps in preventive maintenance of a machine tool.

(*iii*) Testing helps in determining the condition of the machine tool and hence its useful life.

There are two types of tests :

(*i*) Geometrical tests or Alignment tests.

(*ii*) Practical tests or Performance tests.

Geometrical tests cover the manufactured accuracy of machine tools. They are checks on the relationship of the various elements of the machine tool when it idle and unloaded. Such tests include checking the parallelism of the spindle and of a lathe, squareness of the table movement to the spindle of a milling machine and that the taper hole of a drilling machine is running true. Practical tests are used to check the working accuracy of a machine tool. Both these tests are collectively known as Acceptance Tests.

Testing of a machine tool may be carried out in the following cases :

(*i*) Before a machine is despatched from the manufacturer to the customer.

(*ii*) After a new machine has been installed and levelled.

(*iii*) When a machine has been overhauled.

(*iv*) When a machine is not giving satisfactory performance.

Standards for testing of different machine tools were first published by a German called Dr. Georg Schlesinger in 1927. In our country the various tests have been prescribed by Indian Standard Institute, based on the tests formulated by Dr. Schlesinger. In order to ascertain the condition or performance of a machine tool inspection charts are available which enable the manufacture or inspector to check the various alignments against prescribed limits.

The degree of working accuracy of a machine tool, besides depending on machine tool itself, is also influenced by the following factors :

(*i*) Type of cutting tool and its condition.

(*ii*) Tool material.

(*iii*) Cutting speed, feed and depth of cut.

(*iv*) Material to be machined.

(*v*) Clamping equipment.

(*vi*) Skill of the operator.

11.1.1. Procedure for acceptance test

Acceptance tests cover the grade of accuracy of the machine tool and also its working accuracy.

The following procedure is followed while carrying out acceptance tests :

(*i*) The machine tool is set up and the principal horizontal and vertical planes and axes are checked with a spirit level.

(*ii*) Guiding and bearing surfaces of bends are checked for the following :

(*a*) Parallelism

(*b*) Flatness

(*c*) Straightness.

(*iii*) The various components of the machine tool are checked for movements in different directions.

(*iv*) The main spindle is tested for :

(*a*) Concentricity

(*b*) Axial slip

(*c*) Accuracy of axis.

(*v*) Working tests are carried out on the machine tool to check whether the machine tool produce finished components within the specified limits of accuracy.

Acceptance tests include primary trials and idle run, test, performance test under load, checking whether the machine tool complies with the accuracy standards, and tests to determine the rigidity and vibration proof properties in metal cutting.

The following points are considered in the acceptance test :

(*i*) The levelling test to ascertain the straightness and parallelism of the slide ways is to be done. Dial indicators, test mandrels straight edges, gauge blocks, spirit levels are used for this test. The allowable tolerance is 0.02 mm for a length of 1000 mm.

(*ii*) When the cutting operation is taking place on the machine, certain amount of vibrations are noted. Therefore, machine is to be tested properly whether the amplitude of vibration is within the desired range. Vibration test can be conducted by using transducer which senses the mechanical vibrations and converts into electrical signal which is fed into amplifier which amplifiers the signal.

(*iii*) The operating temperature of bearings should be limited to 80 to 90°C. If the temperature is increased then artificial cooling is to be provided.

Acceptance charts are prepared for the machine tool tests which specify the type of tests and the range of allowable or permissible limits of deformation, deflection, amplitude of vibrations etc.

11.2. Testing Equipment

The various tools and equipment used for carrying out the acceptance tests are as follows :

(*i*) *Dial gauge.* The dial gauge should have clearly readable gradations on sufficiently large dial. It need not be finer than 0.001 mm.

(*ii*) *Spirit level.* Both horizontal and frame type spirit levels are used. It should have a sensitivity varying from 0.03 to 0.05 mm per metre for each division.

(*iii*) *Straight edge and squares.* They are used to check straightness or flatness. They are made up of cast iron or steel. They should have a strong ribbed construction with wide bearing surfaces.

(*iv*) *Test mandrels.* They are used to check the true running of the spindle of the machine tools. They are accurately turned hardened and ground. A test mandrel is so chosen in length and diameter that the deflection due to its weight is negligible.

The test mandrels may have either a taper shank for being fitted in the nose of the machine spindle or a round shank for being held between the centres.

(*v*) Autocollimeter.

(*vi*) Micrometer.

Test charts are compiled for each type of machine tool giving details of tests to be carried out and permissible errors. They are extensively used as guide-lines for conducting tests.

11.3. Order of Test

The test is carried in the following order :

(*i*) Accuracy of the machine tool itself :

(*a*) Levelling.

(*b*) Erecting and setting up.

(*c*) Testing the guiding and bearing surfaces.

(*d*) Testing the axes and surfaces in relation to other important units and components.

(*ii*) Accuracy of finished workpiece.

(*iii*) Power consumption.

11.4. Test Chart for General Purpose Parallel Lathes

As per IS 1878 (Part 1) 1971 some of the tests carried out to check the accuracy of general purpose lathes with swing over bed up to 800 mm are as follows :

[For complete details refer IS : 1878 (Part 1) 1971]

(See Table on next page)

11.5. Maintenance of Machine Tools

The machine tool users expect a machine tool to produce accurate workpiece within specified limits not only when it is new but throughout its working life. For this reason the wear of the machine tool must not exceed certain limits and parts which become fault due to wear or other damages must be replaced or repaired without delay.

The direct object of machine tool maintenance is to delay the deterioration which takes place and to avoid disruption to the production programme. Improved maintenance would reduce machine tool down time and lead to higher productivity and subsequent lower the production cost. Good maintenance is in fact good management.

Maintenance can be defined under three main headings as follows :

(*i*) Preventive maintenance.

(*ii*) Corrective maintenance.

(*iii*) Reconditioning.

Timely inspections and repairs keep the metal cutting machine tools in working order. Productivity of labor, product quality and cost depend upon the condition of processing equipment.

The lack of timely preventive maintenance may cause troubles and premature failure of machine tools which in turn may disturb the entire production process.

The accuracy of a repaired or reconditioned machine tool depends mainly on the restoration of base parts to their original geometric accuracy and relative positions.

11.6. Preventive Maintenance

The aim of preventive maintenance is to reduce wear and tear and to prevent to disruption to production. Lubrication is generally considered to be the heat of preventive maintenance of machine tools. All moving parts are subject to sliding or the rolling friction and in both the cases the lubrication is must. Depending upon the

Geometrical Tests

Part Name	*Object*	*Measuring Instrument*	*Permissible deviation*	*Figure*
1. Bed	Straightness of carriage slide ways (*a*) In longitudinal direction	Spirit level	0.02 mm per 1000 mm	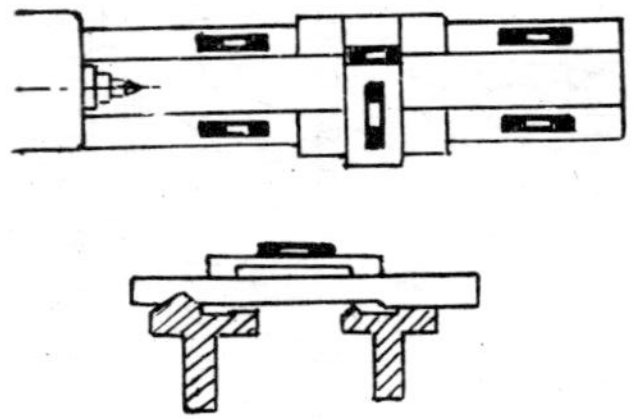
	(*b*) In transverse direction	Spirit level	0.04 mm per 1000 mm	Fig. 11.1
2. Carriage	Straightness of carriage in a horizontal plane	(*a*) Dial gauge and test mandrel	0.02 to 0.03 mm per 1000 mm	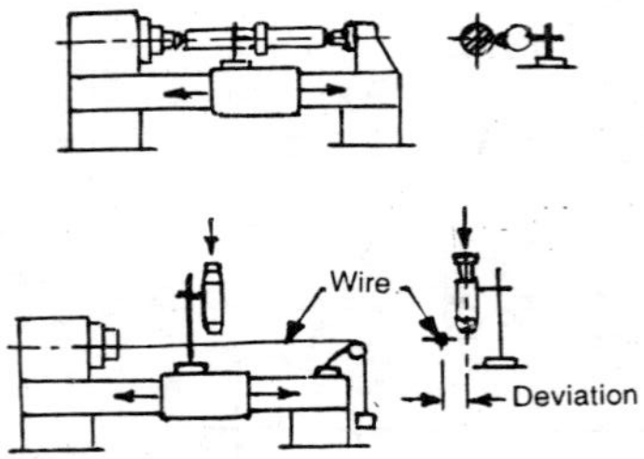
		(*b*) Taut wire and microscope		Fig. 11.2

Part Name	*Object*	*Measuring Instrument*	*Permissible deviation*	*Figure*
3. Head stock spindle	Parallelism of spindle axis to the carriage movement (*a*) In horizontal plane (*b*) In vertical plane when maximum value of L is 300 mm	Dial gauge and mandrel	(*a*) 0.015 per 300 mm free and end of mandrel inclined towards tool only (*b*) 0.02 per 300 mm free end of the mandrel inclined upward only	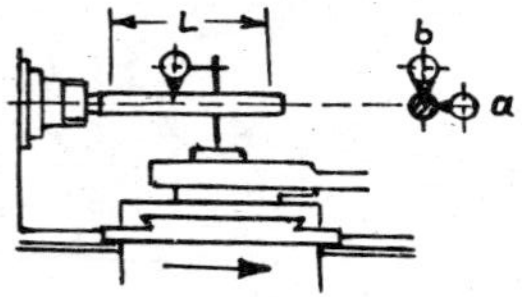 Fig. 11.3
4. Centres	Difference in height between head stock and stock centres	Dial gauge and test mandrel	0.06 mm per 1000 mm. Tail Stock centre higher than head stock centre.	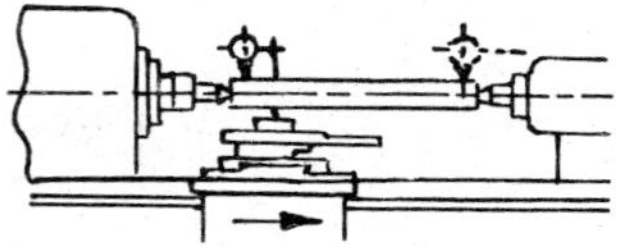 Fig. 11.4
5. Tool slide	Parallelism of the longitudinal movement of the tool slide to the spindle axis	Dial gauge and test mandrel	0.04 mm per 300 mm free end of the mandrel inclined upward only.	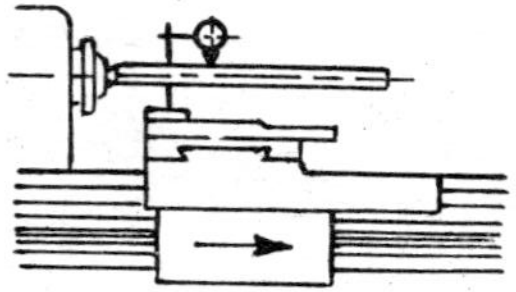 Fig. 11.5

Practical Test

Nature of test	*Cutting condition*	*Check to be applied*	*Measuring instrument*	*Observations*	*Permissible deviation*	*Figure*
Turning of- cylindrical test piece held in chuck	Machining of two diameters and cylinder over a maximum length of $S = 20$ mm	(*a*) Roundness (*b*) Cylindricity	Micro-meter	Test pieces to be finish machined on the two collars in one pass of the tool	(*a*) 0.01 mm (*b*) 0.04 for $L = 300$ mm	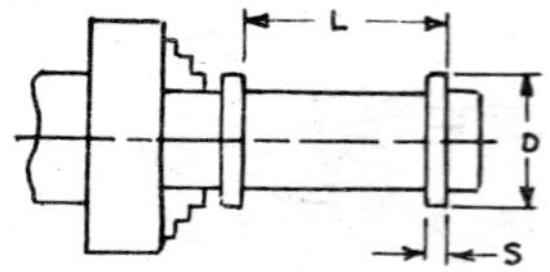 Fig. 11.6

lubrication methods used in the machine tool, lubrication schedules are formed.

In machine tools there are certain points which if not checked periodically not only reduce the efficiency of the machine but tool also may lead to major break-down. Therefore, regular inspection of such points is quite essential. All wearing parts in the machine tool or the parts subjected to fatigue are replaced normally before failing in a preventive maintenance system.

Preventive maintenance is the planned maintenance of machine tools and equipment. A regular planned preventive maintenance consists of a minor and medium repairs and major overhauls. Preventive maintenance plays an important role in achieving reliability in the use of the system. The preventive maintenance programme can account for the most efficient operation of machines which can result in high productivity. Adequate number of the personnel should be used for preventive maintenance. If there are too many maintenance people the cost of keeping them is excessive and if too less the cost of idle time equipment looms large. Fig. 11.7 is between cost (*O*) and number of maintenance personnel (*N*). The total cost is indicated by curve *A* whereas cost of idle personnel is indicated by curve *B* and cost of idle equipment is indicated by curve. *E*. To minimise cost the optimum number of personnel (*P*) should be used.

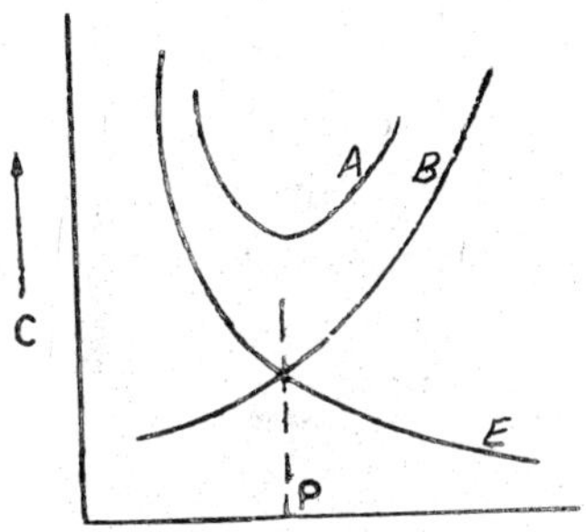

Fig. 11.7

A well conceived preventive maintenance programme should contain the following features :

(*i*) Adequate records covering volume of cost and work.

(*ii*) Inspection frequency schedule.

(*iii*) Proper identification of all items to be included in preventive maintenance programme.

(*iv*) Well qualified personnels for maintenance.

Preventive maintenance is essential to keep the machine in order for production and safety. Reliability safety and above all availability of right machine at right point of time are the other advantages of preventive maintenance.

A proper preventive maintenance schedule should be followed such as under :

(*i*) **Daily Checks**

The following duties should be performed by the operator :

(*i*) To clean the machine.

(*ii*) To check lubricating oil levels and oil flow in sight glasses.

(*iii*) To check coolant level.

(*iv*) To keep the maintenance department informed of even the minor defects noted in the performance of the machine.

(*ii*) **Weekly Checks**

The following checks should be carried out by the maintenance department :

(*i*) To check all lubrication levels

(*ii*) To check coolant.

(*iii*) To check all filters.

(*iv*) To check hydraulic and pneumatic lines.

(*iii*) **Monthly Checks**

(To be carried out by the maintenance department).

(*i*) To check spindle drive belts for wear.

(*ii*) To check hydraulic pumps and hydraulic oil.

(*iii*) To check movement of all axis under manual dial in control.

(*iv*) **Six Monthly Checks**

(*i*) To check machine alignment.

(*ii*) To replace oils and filters.

11.7. Corrective Maintenance

The object of corrective maintenance is to replace the worn part and to carry out repair. The maintenance engineer should regularly inspect the specific elements of the machine in order to determine whether wear has reached the stage when corrective maintenance should be carried out before failure occurs. When inspection shows that corrective action is necessary, the machine tool should be withdrawn from production. It is essential to maintain a record of the nature and cost of all repairs carried out. This will help to bring to light those elements of machines which need improved servicing, more frequent inspection or modification to the machine design. Such records also help in taking the decisions regarding the need for reconditioning and replacement.

11.7.1. Preventive maintenance planning

Preventive maintenance can be defined as planned and coordinated inspections, adjustments, repairs and replacement in maintaining the machines. The purpose is to reduce unscheduled interruption or undue deterioration of operating equipment. It is a scientific way of tackling maintenance problem. It helps in maintaining a reliable production system.

11.7.2. Programme of preventive maintenance

The programme of preventive maintenance of a machine includes the following operations :

(*i*) Cleaning of parts
(*ii*) Lubrication
(*iii*) Application of protective coatings
(*iv*) Repair of cracks and other repairable damages
(*v*) Adjustments
(*vi*) Inspection of state of components
(*vii*) Replacement of worn out/broken components
(*viii*) Analysis of history of behaviour of machine tool and its parts
(*ix*) Preventive maintenance cost calculations.

Cleaning prevents corrosion and abrasion due to dust whereas lubrication reduces friction. Adjustments of alignments or tightening of loose nuts and bolts eliminate undue stresses. Protective coatings guard against rust and corrosion. These actions increase the useful life of parts and therefore constitute an intrinsic part of preventive maintenance.

Whenever there is minor or major fault in the machine tool, it is desireable to pay proper attention at appropriate time to such faults. This will keep the machine tool running and the production loss will be minimum.

A machine tool is stopped due to the following reasons :

(*i*) Breakdown maintenance
(*ii*) Preventive maintenance.

Breakdown maintenance not only brings a serious production hold up but also upsets production flow of the industry. Preventive maintenance is a more scientific way of tackling maintenance problem and is quite commonly used now a days.

Preventive maintenance helps

(*i*) to prolong the life of the machine

(*ii*) to reduce un-expected breakdowns

(*iii*) to improve accuracy of machine tool

(*iv*) to ensure quality and continuity of production.

Preventive maintenance calls for taking an equipment for repair at planned intervals of time so that uncalled for breakdowns can be prevented. These intervals are decided mainly keeping into view the following factors :

(*i*) Complexity of the machine tool

(*ii*) Load conditions

(*iii*) Position of machine.

Repair complexity is a relative index to give a comparative idea of the complexity of a machine and takes into account the mechanical gearing, hydraulic and pneumatic units, guide surfaces and transmission units of machine.

The complexity of machine tool plays a very important role in the maintenance and in deciding the duration of the individual repair and in turn the repair cycle.

Further the spares stock, repair cost and the man power planning depends upon the total complexity of the machine tool.

Although there is no absolute measurement of the repair complexity of a machine but for the purpose of planning, relative figures are decided which give a comparative idea about the repair complexity of the machine.

The concept of repair complexity of a machine tool is used to determine :

(*i*) Maintenance staff

(*ii*) Spares and parts needed for maintenance

(*iii*) Maintenance cost

(*iv*) Percentage breakdowns and hence the efficiency etc.

The average repair complexity (RC) is indicated in Table 11.1.

Table 11.1

S. No.	Time of machine tool	RC
1.	Light machine tool	8
2.	Medium machine tool	9
3.	Heavy machine tool	11
4.	Tools and cutters	7.5

11.7.3. Preventive maintenance repair cycle

Repair cycle of preventive maintenance consists of four stages as indicated below :

(i) Inspection (I)

(ii) Small repair (S)

(iii) Medium repair (M)

(iv) Complete overhaul (C).

For example a typical repair cycle of a centre lathe is given by :

$$C - I_1 - S_1 - I_2 - S_2 - I_3 - M_1 - I_4 - S_3 - I_5 - S_4 - I_6 - M_2 - I_7 - S_5 - I_8 - S_6 - I_9 - C - I_1$$

This means that :

(i) Lathe would be taken up for first inspection I_1.

(ii) After about 6 months the first small repair (S_1) will be carried out.

(iii) First medium repair (M_1) after second inspection (I_2), second small repair (S_2) and third inspection (I_3).

(iv) Second medium repair (M_2) after fourth inspection (I_4), third small repair (S_3), fifth inspection (I_5), fourth small repair (S_4) and sixth inspection (I_6).

(v) Finally the lathe would be taken up for complete overhaul after sixth small repair (S_6) and ninth inspection (I_9).

(vi) The cycle would thus follow same sequence after 9 years (6 × 18 months).

The volume of work to be carried out in each of repair categories (I, S, M, C) is as follows :

1. **Inspection (I)**

(i) To inspect various mechanisms at all speeds and feeds.

(ii) To adjust spindle bearings, clutches, brakes, couplings, lead nut play, clamping devices.

(iii) To tighten nut, bolts and to replace damaged ones.

(*iv*) To change oil and to clean oil and coolant filters and lubricating distributors.

(*v*) To clean chips removers.

2. **Small repair (S)**

(*i*) To dis-assemble some unit (say 2 to 3) of machine tools which are expected to get worn out. For example to dis-assemble Tool post and Apron of a lathe and to replace worn out part and to clean other parts.

(*ii*) To check the working of guide surfaces.

3. **Medium repair**

(*i*) To dis-assemble more units of machine tool such as headstock, tool post, tail stock etc. and to replace worn out parts and to check working of each part.

(*ii*) To grind/scrap the guide surfaces.

(*iii*) To check the machine as per standard accuracy test charts.

4. **Complete overhaul**

(*i*) To dis-assemble every part, to clean the various parts and to replace worn out parts.

(*ii*) To grind or scrap all the guide surfaces.

(*ii*) To check foundation condition and to repair it if required.

11.7.4. Man power planning

Following four main categories of workers are required for maintenance work :

(*i*) Fitters

(*ii*) Machine operators

(*iii*) Oilers, welders etc.

(*iv*) Helpers.

(*A*) For breakdown maintenance

For metal cutting machine tools the number of filters, machine operators and oilers required are calculated as follows :

$$\text{Fitters} = \frac{a}{400}$$

$$\text{Machine operators} = \frac{a}{1650}$$

$$\text{Oilers} = \frac{a}{950}$$

where a = Total repair complexity of the equipment.

(*B*) For preventive maintenance one helper should normally be provided with two fitters.

For various stages of preventive maintenance the typical man hours required per unit of repair complexity are indicated in Table 11.2.

Table 11.2

Preventive maintenance stages	*MH*		
	Fitters	*Machine operators*	*Oilers, Welders etc.*
Inspection (I)	1.0	0.5	0.5
Small repair (S)	5.0	4.0	1.0
Medium repair (M)	20	10	2.0
Complete overhaul (C)	30	20	4.0

where MH = Man hours required per unit of repair complexity.

11.7.5. Preventive maintenance stages for metal cutting equipment

The work to be carried out during various stages of preventive maintenance for metal cutting machines is as follows :

1. **Inspection**

(*i*) To externally inspect pulleys, flywheels, gears, sprockets, friction discs etc. and to tighten the joints.

(*ii*) To open out covers and check the condition of mechanisms.

(*iii*) To regulate :

(*a*) spindle bearings

(*b*) friction and brake tension

(*c*) smooth sliding of tables, slides, saddles, slotter ram

(*d*) belts, chains.

(*iv*) To tighten wedges and clamping plates.

(*v*) To check the condition of guides of the beds, carriages traverse and other friction surfaces.

(*vi*) To check lubricating and hydraulic system and to carry out minor repairs. To replace lubricating oil in reservoirs.

(*vii*) To inspect guards, fencings etc. and to carry out repairs.

(*viii*) To replace worn out parts.

2. **Small repair**

(*i*) To dis-assemble 2 to 3 units of the machine. To clean the parts and to check working of the various parts. For the remaining units of the machine open the covers and clean the parts.

(*ii*) To check working of spindles, and bearings and to replace worn out bearings.

(*iii*) To clean lead screws of slides, carriage, traverses etc. and to replace worn out mating nuts.

(*iv*) To check for proper working of levers, handles and safety mechanisms.

(*v*) To clean and repair scratches and other damages on friction surfaces of bed guides, carriages, slides, traverses, columns etc.

(*vi*) To check and repair the coolant system.

(*vii*) To check for proper functioning of limits, reverses and stoppers.

3. **Medium repair**

(*i*) To dis-assemble the machine partly and to clean and check the working of various parts.

(*ii*) To grind spindle shanks.

(*iii*) To replace worn out bearings, gears, fasteners.

(*iv*) To restore/replace worn out lead screws and nuts of longitudinal and transverse feeds.

(*v*) To replace/restore and scrap regulating wedges and clamping devices.

(*vi*) To check the accuracy of the machine as per accuracy chart.

4. **Complete overhaul**

(*i*) To completely dis-assemble the machine and all its units.

(*ii*) To clean and inspect all parts and to replace worn out parts.

(*iii*) To check lubricating system, hydraulic system, cooling system and to repair them. To replace oil, coolant etc.

(*iv*) To repair or replace guards and fencings.

(*v*) To check the foundation.

(*vi*) To check the machine for accuracy as per accuracy chart.

11.7.6. Machine stoppage during preventive maintenance

In order to carry out preventive maintenance the machine tool is stopped for some time. Table 11.3 indicates the number of days for which a machine can be stopped for preventive maintenance.

Table 11.3

Preventive Maintenance Category	*N*
Inspection	Few hours
Small repair	0.25
Medium repair	0.55
Complete overhaul	1.0

where N = Permissible number of days per unit of repair complexity.

11.7.7. When to replace a machine tool

As the age of machine increases the cost of maintenance rises and operational efficiency of the machine comes down. Requirements of quality and quantity of production make an old machine more or less obsolete in relationship to new demands. These factors are considered while replacing the existing machine at some stage in its life by a new machine.

Therefore a machine tool may be replaced when

(*i*) repair and maintenance cost of machine tool becomes high

(*ii*) the operational efficiency of the machine tool becomes low

(*iii*) the machine tool is not producing components of desired accuracy

(*iv*) power required per unit volume of metal removed becomes high

(*v*) new similar machine tool with better performance is available at reasonable cost.

11.8. Reconditioning

It is the rebuilding of the machine so that it gives the required production. The need to recondition the machine can be determined by the frequency of the corrective maintenance. There is certain life span of every machine tool and component after which it becomes unserviceable inspite the best possible planned and preventive maintenance carried out during its useful life. This is the stage when major overhaul or reconditioning is called for. Thorough inspection of machine tool should be made. The inspection report should indicate the details of the components required to be replaced during reconditioning and the skilled labour required to accomplish the task. A rough estimate of the cost is prepared and generally it is undesirable to recondition the machine tool if the cost of parts to be replaced and repaired exceeds 50% of the prevailing cost of the new equipment. Another very important aspect governing the decision to recondition the machine tool is the time factor. It is very important to estimate the time required to put the machine back in normal operation considering the availability of reconditioning facilities and spares required for replacement. This will give the figures of production loss due to direct or inter related effect on manufacturing process. Sometimes replacement proves to be more economical than to recondition the machine.

The basic principles for maintenance, repair and rebuilding of the machine tools are identical with those for manufacturer of the machine tools. Test charts of machine tool provide best information regarding its accuracy and performance.

The design and manufacture and subsequent industrial application of new models of machine tools is one of the major factors in increasing productivity. Periodic renovation of production capacities is essential to ensure a normal economic growth rate.

11.9. Erection of Machine Tools

A machine tool should give sufficient accuracy and should be reliable. To achieve higher accuracy and productivity the machine tool should have dynamic stability. The performance of a machine tool and its service life depend to a considerable degree upon its proper installation on the foundation which enables the load due to weight of machine tool and mounted workpiece to be uniformly transmitted to a larger area of soil and secondly foundation protects the machine tool against vibrations. Erection of a machine tool means placing it on the foundation. Erection of machine tools should be carried out with maximum care and as per the instructions given in the operating manuals supplied by respective machine tool manufacturers. Poor erection of machine tools causes many problems. Erection of machine tool should be carried out by skilled labour and supervisions. Successful and efficient operation of machine tool depends greatly on erection of machine tools. Some general rules followed during erection of machine tools are as follows :

(*i*) Foundation made for the machine tool should be such that machine tool works vibration free.

(*ii*) Foundation bolts should be placed as per recommendations of machine tool suppliers keeping enough space for final concreting of bolts.

(*iii*) The quality of soil for foundation should be determined. It should be rigid and should not get settled by external pressure.

(*iv*) The machine tool should be isolated from vibration sources by using materials like rubber, cork, springs etc.

After erecting the machine tool perfect levelling of machine tool should be done. It is necessary that the proper alignment is produced when the machine tool is erected on its foundation. The foundation bolts should be tightened evenly and firmly.

11.10. Foundation

Foundation should be strong enough to support the machine tool. The foundation is made up of the following materials :

(*i*) Plain concrete or reinforced concrete.

(*ii*) Masonry of bricks or stones.

(*iii*) Combination of concrete and masonry.

(*iv*) Structural steel.

11.11. General Inspection of Machine Tools

A machine tool having passed the alignment tests should be examined for mechanical defects and limitations. The machine tool should be inspected to ensure that :

(*i*) The machine tool works satisfactorily at all designed feeds and speeds.

(*ii*) The gears, belts, pulleys etc. run quietly at all speeds.

(*iii*) There are no vibrations during cutting operations.

(*iv*) The lubrication system functions properly.

(*v*) The operating levers clear each other in the minimum positions.

(*vi*) Safety devices are fitted on the machine tool to avoid accidents.

11.12. Care and Maintenance of Machine Tools

Machine tools should be handled carefully in order to give good and longer service. The following precautions are essential to maintain a machine tool in good condition :

(*i*) The machine tool should be cleaned frequently.

(*ii*) The electric motor should be protected from dust and moisture.

(*iii*) The guide ways should be protected from foreign materials like chips.

(*iv*) Before starting the work, check whether all levers are in position.

(*v*) All hand lubricating points should be lubricated daily. Poor lubrication causes early wear.

(*vi*) The temperature of the bearings should not exceed the body temperature.

(*vii*) The machine tool should not be over-loaded.

11.13. Lubrication Record Card

A record card of the type shown in Fig. 11.8 (*a*) should be maintained to show that lubrication of the machine tool has been carried out.

LUBRICATION RECORD CARD

Machine Description ...... *Machine No. ....*

Type of oil to be used ....

Date	*Amount Used*		*Servicing Carried Out*	*Serviced By*	*Approved By*
	Oil	*Grease*			

Fig. 11.8 (*a*)

11.14. Corrective Maintenance Record Card

The corrective maintenance record card enables decision to be made regarding the need to withdraw the machine tool from production not only for corrective maintenance record card is shown in Fig. 11.8.

CORRECTIVE MAINTENANCE RECORD CARD							
Machine Description .... *Department*						*Machine No.*	
Date	*Maintenance Breakdown*	*Replacement Parts*			*Down Time Hours*	*Total Cost of Repairs*	*Remarks*
		Ordered	*Received*	*Cost*			

Fig. 11.8

11.15. Replacement Schedule

All wearing parts in the machine, or the parts subjected to fatigue are replaced normally before failing in a preventive maintenance system. A schedule is prepared depending upon the life of the part, the preventive maintenance time and cost, cost of part and the life of other components which may be replaced in the same preventive maintenance cycle.

In making the formats for the lubrication schedules, care should be taken to mention properties like viscosity, non drip property, viscosity index, acid and water contents allowed or any other property which may be important to be considered for better service of the parts to be lubricated. Also the standard oils available in the market confirming to the specifications should be mentioned on the format.

Lubrication is generally considered to be the heart of preventive maintenance of machine tools. All moving parts are subject to sliding or the rolling friction and in both the cases the lubrication is a must.

11.16. Operator Care

No preventive maintenance system can work if the care done by the operator is inadequate.

Operator care includes the following :

(*a*) Cleaning the machine.

(*b*) More frequent lubrication which is not possible for preventive maintenance team.

(*c*) Avoiding over-loading the machine.

(*d*) Avoiding accidents.

(*e*) Keeping the maintenance department informed of even the minor defects noted in the performance of a machine.

11.17. Installation of Machine Tool

While installing a machine tool the following procedure may be adopted :

1. Check the machine tool including all accessories for any damage which might have been caused to any part during transit.

2. Prepare the foundation as per drawing. Foundation should be checked for

(*i*) level at top surface
(*ii*) position of foundation bolts
(*iii*) strength.

3. Lift the machine tool and place it on the foundation after inserting the foundation bolts in the legs of the machine.

4. Check the level of bed of the machine.

5. Tighten nuts on foundation bolts.

11.18. Test Chart for Shaping Machine

Table 11.4 indicates typical test chart for a shaping machine.

Table 11.4

S. No.	*Test to be Applied*	*Permissible Error mm*
1.	Table flat and level in both directions	0.04 per 1,000 mm.
	Column and table slide : Guide surface of ram square with guide surfaces of column in plane through centre of column	0.02 per 300 mm.
2.	Front bearing surface of table slide flat or level	0.03 per 1,000 mm.
3.	Upper guide on table slide square with column ways	0.03 per 300 mm.
4.	Work Table : Upper surface of table square with side clamping surfaces	0.02 per 300 mm.
5.	Incline of table in its transverse movement	± 0.015 per 300 mm.

6.	Upper surface of table parallel with its transverse movement	0.01 per 300 mm.
7.	Movement of ram parallel with work table (table rising at front)	0 to 0.015 per 300 mm.
8.	Movement of ram parallel with T-slots	0.015 per 300 mm.
9.	Movement of ram parallel with side clamping surfaces	0.02 per 300 mm.
10.	Movement of ram parallel with side T-slots (slots rising at front end)	0 to 0.02 per 300 mm.
11.	Side clamping surfaces of table parallel with its vertical adjustment	0.02 per 300 mm.
12.	Guide for table support parallel with transverse movement of table	0.02 per 300 mm.
13.	Table saddle : (for machine equipped with saddle) : Saddle surface square with guide surface of ram (inclined at upper end towards the column)	0 to 0.02 per 300 mm.

Fig. 11.8 shows testing the saddle surface square with guide surface.

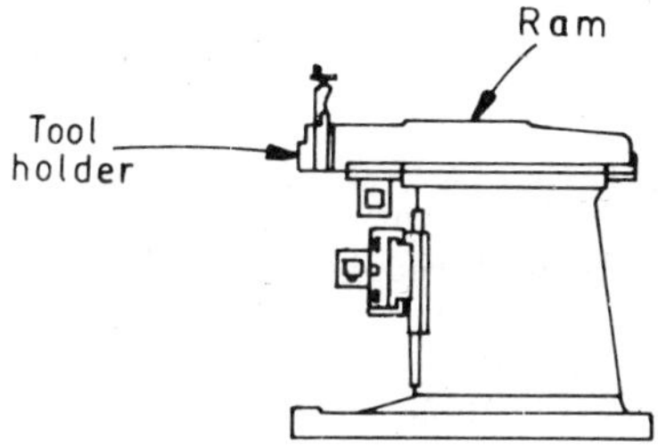

Fig. 11.8

Fig. 11.9 shows a shaper. Shapers are used for machining horizontal, vertical and inclined flat surfaces on small and medium-sized workpieces, for cutting straight slots and grooves, and much less frequently, for machining ruled surface of irregular profile.

In operating a shaper, the work is clamped on the overhanging table while the tool is clamped in the toolholder of the ram which has a horizontal reciprocating motion, as a rule, across the work. Either power or hand cross or vertical feeds can be transmitted to the table which travels crosswise along a rail and vertically with the rail along ways of the column.

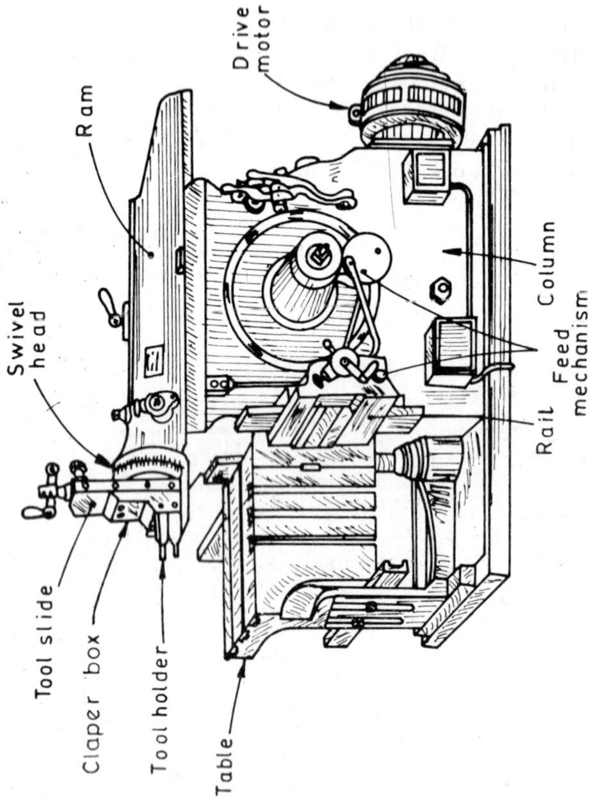

Fig. 11.9

11.19. Test Chart for Radial Drilling Machine

Table 11.5 indicates typical test chart for radial drilling machine.

Table 11.5

S. No.	*Test to be Applied*	*Permissible Error*
1.	Baseplate : Baseplate flat or level in longitudinal direction Ditto, in transverse direction	 0.1 per 1,000 mm. 0.1 per 1,000 mm.

2.	Column : Column square with baseplate in plane through centre line of baseplate (sleeve inclined towards the front side) For machines up to 1,400 mm. (4 ft. 7 in.) length of radial arm (maximum spindle radius) For machines of over 1,400 mm. (4 ft. 7 in.) length of radial arm	0 to 0.2 per 1,000 mm. 0 to 0.3 per 1,000 mm.
3.	Ditto, in plane perpendicular to plane through centre line of baseplate	0.1 per 1,000 mm.
4.	Arm : Arm parallel with baseplate (dipping at outer end) : For machines up to 1,400 mm. (4 ft. 7 in.) length of radial arm For machines of over 1,400 mm. length of radial arm	0 to 0.2 per 1,000 mm. 0 to 0.3 per 1,000 mm.
5.	Saddle ways, flat or level	0.1 per 1,000 mm.
6.	Drilling spindle : Taper of spindle for true running ; maximum amount by which mandrel 300 mm. (12 in.) long may run out	0.03
7.	Spindle square with baseplate in plane through centre line of baseplate (lower end inclined towards column)	0 to 0.2 per 1,000 mm.
8.	Ditto, in plane perpendicular to said plane	0.1 per 1,000 mm.
9.	Feed of spindle sleeve square with baseplate in plane through centre line of baseplate (inclined at lower end towards column)	0 to 0.1 per 300 mm.

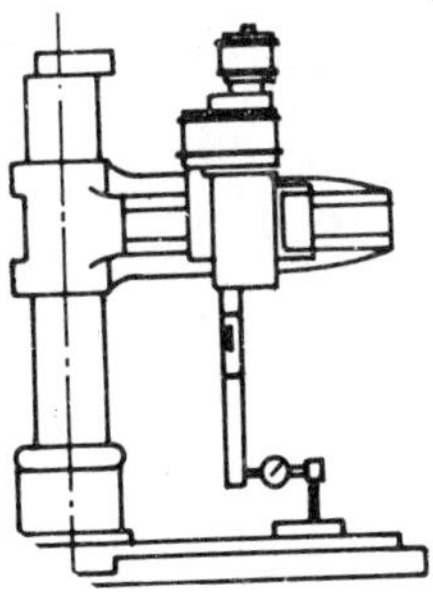

Fig. 11.10

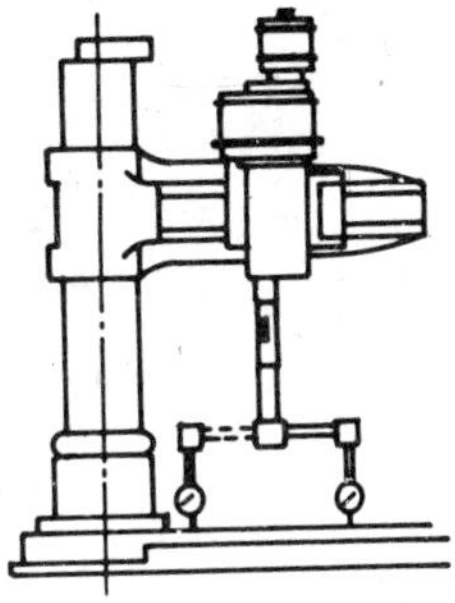

Fig. 11.11

Fig. 11.10 shows checking of taper of spindle for true running and Fig. 11.11 shows testing spindle square with bast plate.

PROBLEMS

11.1. Why testing of machine tool is essential ?

11.2. Describe

(*a*) Geometrical tests (*b*) Practical tests

(*c*) Acceptance test.

11.3. Write short notes on the following :

(*a*) Testing equipment (*b*) Order of carrying out a test

(*c*) Two geometrical tests for a general purpose lathes with swing over bed upto 800 mm.

11.4. What is maintenance of machine tools ?

11.5. Describe the following :

(*a*) Preventive maintenance

(*b*) Corrective maintenance

(*c*) Reconditioning of tools.

(*d*) Erection of machine tools.

11.6. Describe the procedure for acceptance test.

11.7. State the advantages of testing of a machine tool.

11.8. Write short note on :

(*i*) General inspection of machine tool

(*ii*) Lubrication record card

(*iii*) Corrective maintenance record card

(*iv*) Care and maintenance of machine tools.

12

Economics of Machine Tool Selection

12.1. Introduction

The machine tools selected for making a component should be so selected that the cost of manufacturing the component is minimum.

The selection of machine tool mainly depends on the following factors :

(*i*) Size and shape of the component

(*ii*) Material of the component

(*iii*) Accuracy to be obtained

(*iv*) Number of components to be made *i.e.* lot size

(*v*) Quality of the component

(*vi*) Cost of machine tool.

12.2. General Classification of Machine Tools

Machine tools may be broadly classified into three major divisions :

1. General Purpose Machine Tools

They are able to perform many of the metal cutting operations with their range of operation. Some of these machine tools are :

(*i*) Centre lathes

(*ii*) Drilling machines

(*iii*) Shaping, planing and slotting machines

(*iv*) Milling machines

(*v*) Boring machines

(*vi*) Grinding machines.

2. Production Machine Tools

These machine tools are specially designed to enhance the rate of production and to reduce the manufacturing cost. The machine tools like :

(*i*) Multiple head drilling machine
(*ii*) Capstan and turret lathes
(*iii*) Automatic screw machines
(*iv*) Multiple tool lathes
(*v*) Semi-automatic lathes

are production machine tools. Approach to automation mainly depends on volume of production.

3. Special Purpose Machine Tools

There are quite important in reducing manufacturing cost when relativity jobs are manufactured continuously. Machine tools like :

(*i*) Cam shaft grinder
(*ii*) Gear generator

are a few example of these machine tools.

The principle used in all machine tools is one of the generating the surface required by providing suitable relative motions between the cutting tool and the workpiece. The cutting edge or edges on the cutting tool remove a layer of work material.

12.3. Machine Tool Characteristics

Machine tool characteristics such as

(*i*) Speed range
(*ii*) Feed range
(*iii*) Power
(*iv*) Efficiency
(*v*) Size
(*vi*) Accuracy
(*vii*) Rigidity
(*viii*) Cost of machine tool

play an important role in selecting a machine tool to manufacture the given component.

12.4. Optimum Selection

Optimum selection of machine tools to produce the required surface on the workpiece is quite important for economical manufacturing. For example to produce a horizontal surface (Fig. 12.1) on a workpiece a horizontal milling machine (Fig. 12.2) proves to be quite economical.

Similarly a wide variety of operations involving the machining of horizontal, vertical and inclined surfaces can be performed on

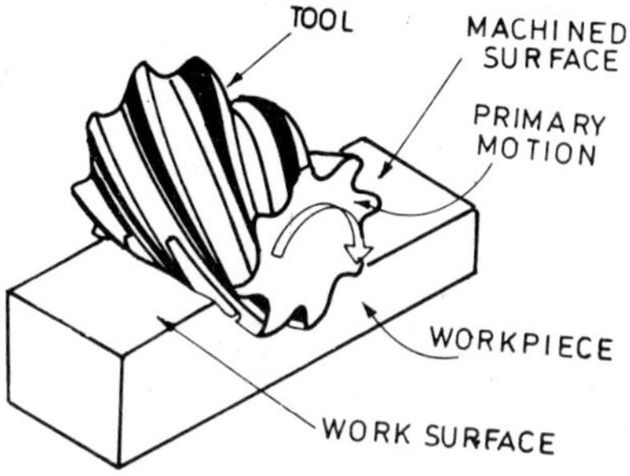

Fig. 12.1

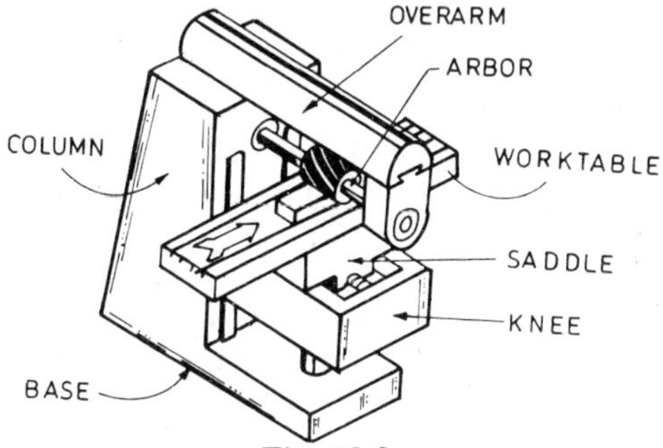

Fig. 12.2

a vertical milling machine (Fig. 12.3). Face milling operation is carried out with the help of knee type vertical milling machine is shown in Fig. 12.4.

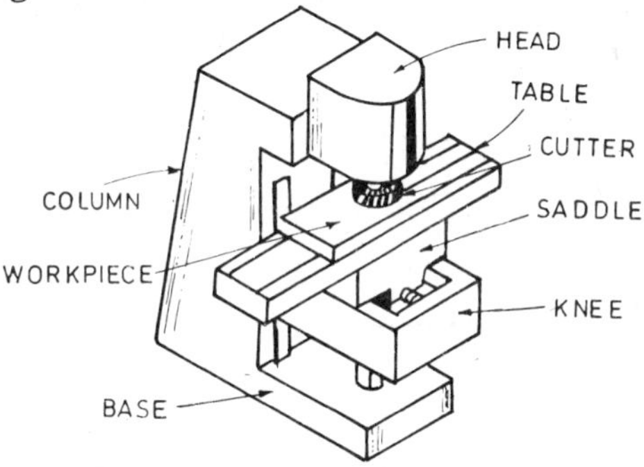

Fig. 12.3

Similarly to cut slots in a workpiece various machine tools which may be used are

(*i*) Shaper

(*ii*) Slotter

(*iii*) Milling machine

(*iv*) Broaching machine.

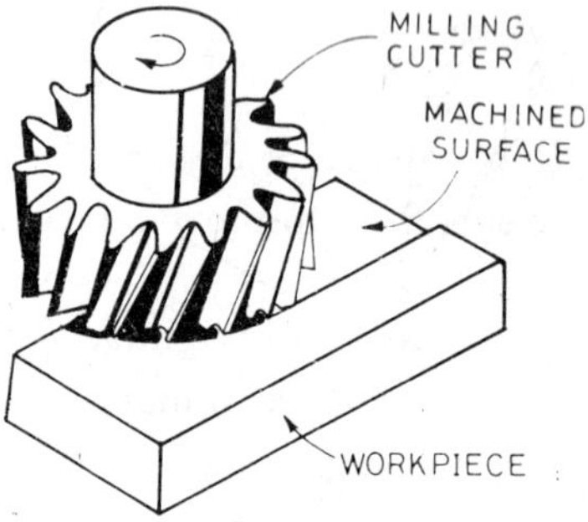

Fig. 12.4

Fig. 12.5 shows a vertical broaching machine and Fig. 12.6 shows broaching action. But for economical machining, the machine tool selected should be such that machining time is minimum, labor cost is minimum while maintaining the desired accuracy.

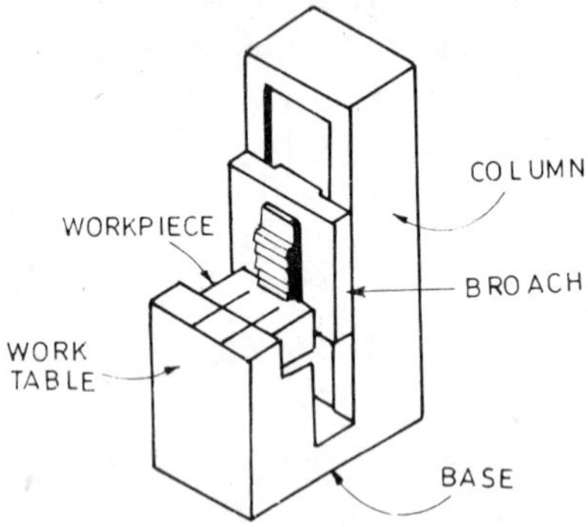

Fig. 12.5

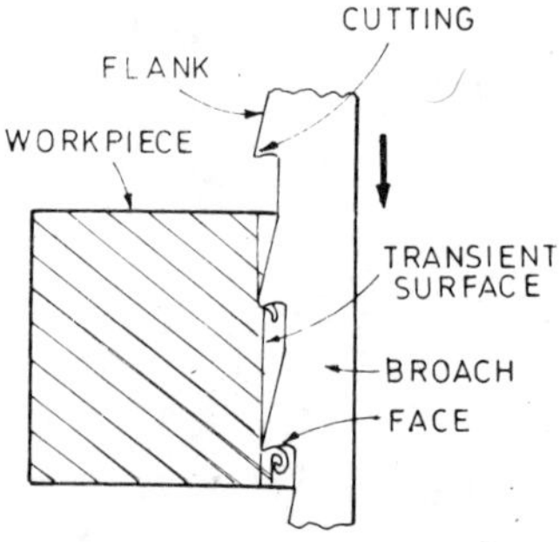

Fig. 12.6

Proper selection of machine tools leads to

(*i*) improved productivity

(*ii*) reduced manufacturing cost.

Profit made by a company is affected by changes in manufacturing costs or productivity.

Modern trends of

(*a*) rising strength of workpiece material

(*b*) higher cutting sheeds of improved cutting tool materials call for :

(*i*) increased power capacity and rigidity of the machine tools

(*ii*) better dynamic performance of machine tools

(*iii*) improved design of bearings etc.

There is a quest for cost reduction and improved rate through introduction of various degrees of automation in machine tools. By automisation of machine tools the production is considerably increased. The machines may be either semi-automatic or fully automatic.

Improved dynamic performance of the machine tool is one of the main requirements since the machine tools are required to produce higher quality work from materials which are becoming more difficult to machine. Vibration of the machines impairs tool-life and often causes excessive wear and idling time. Also high force levels and increased production rates magnify the vibration and chatter problems in machine tools. For high precision machines the requirements for dynamic performance are far more higher than the ordinary machine tools.

For a machine tool

(*a*) the labour cost should be minimum

(*b*) overhead costs should be low.

Whereas transfer machine tools are used exclusively for mass production, the class of machine tools referred to as automatic are used in both mass and large batch production.

12.5. General Considerations for Selection of Machine Tools

The important considerations for the selection of machine tool are as follows :

1. Size and capacity. The machine tool capacity and size depends on the

(*a*) size of workpiece

(*b*) type of machining operations to be carried out

(*c*) holding devices and clearance for tools to be provided

(*d*) amount of metal to be removed.

2. Strength. The machine should have the desired

(*a*) strength

(*b*) stiffness.

3. Power. This depends on power required at the cutting zone. This will depend on

(*a*) workpiece material

(*b*) type of operation

(*c*) cutting tool geometry

(*d*) size of cut and speed.

4. Cost. The cost of the machine tool should be low.

12.6. Methods of Machine Selection

To do same kind of job more than one machines may be available. One machine may have higher technological efficiency due to low operating cost whereas capital outlay of other machine may be high.

Time value of money should be accounted for while comparing machine tools for selection. Time value of money can be accounted for by using the following techniques :

1. Present worth analysis (PW)
2. Equivalent annual cost principle (EAC).

12.6.1. Present worth analysis

In this case the depreciable amount is determined as follows :

$$A = (P - S)\left[\frac{r}{(1+r)^n - 1}\right]$$

where A = Amount set aside per year for the accumulation of the depreciable amount for machine tool at the end of nth year

n = Machine tool life in years

P = Initial cost of the machine tool

S = Salvage value at the end of machine tool life

r = Annual rate of compound interest on the investment capital.

The present worth technique of comparison consists of reducing all the future differences between the alternatives to a single equivalent present sum.

12.6.2. Equivalent annual cost principle (EAC)

This is generally used for machine tools having unequal service life.

Comparison is made between EAC cost

$$\text{EAC} = \text{Equivalent annual cost}$$

$$= P\left[\frac{r(1+r)^n}{(1+r)^n - 1}\right]$$

where P = investment

r = rate of compound interest

n = life of machine tool in years.

12.6.3. Break even analysis

This type of analysis for the selection of machine tools helps in comparing the number of a components that can be economically made on a particular machine. For example, Fig. 12.7 shows a graph between cost of manufacturing the components and number of components for two machines A and B.

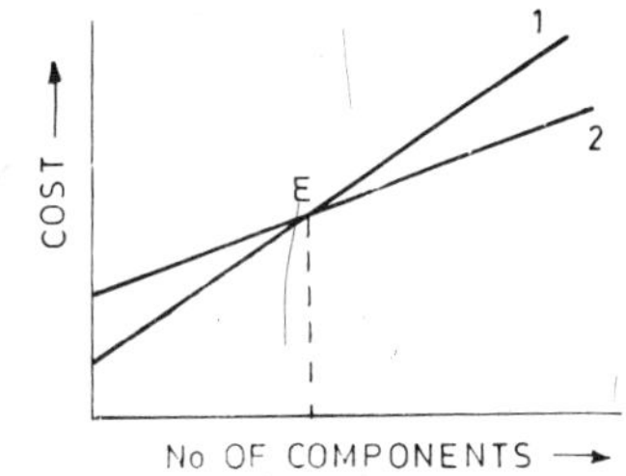

Fig. 12.7

The point (E) is called break even point at which cost of manufacturing is same whether machine 1 is used or machine 2 is used.

However machine 1 is economical if components to be made are less than the components indicated by break even point (E) and machine 2 is more economical if the number of components to be made are more than the number of components indicated by break even point (E).

Q = Number of components at equal cost break even point (E)

$$= \frac{N_1 N_2 (H_2 C_2 + T_2 - H_1 C_1 - T_1)}{N_2 C_1 - N_1 \cdot C_2}$$

where N_1 or N_2 = Number of components per hour subscripts indicating machine 1 and 2

H_1 or H_2 = Number of hours of set up

O_1 or O_2 = Over head charges per hour

R_1 or R_2 = Rate of labour per hour

T_1 or T_2 = Special tools or equipment cost per lot

D_1 or D_2 = Depreciation rate per hour

C_1 or C_2 = Composite rate

$= R + O + D.$

12.7. Economics of Transfer Machines

In transfer machines the workpiece is moved from one station to the other automatically so that various machining processes can be carried out economically.

Let V = Cutting speed

T = Tool life (desired)

T_m = Machining time

$$= \frac{K}{V} \quad \text{...(1)}$$

where K = Distance moved by the tool corner relative to the workpiece during the machining time.

Let V_S = Cutting speed for a tool life T_S. According to Taylor's equation

$$V_S T_S^n = V \cdot T^n$$

$$\left(\frac{T}{T_S}\right)^n = \frac{V_S}{V}$$

$$= \frac{V_S}{K} \times T_m$$

$$T = \left[\frac{V_S T_m}{K}\right]^{\frac{1}{n}} \cdot T_S \quad \text{...(2)}$$

Let N = Number of components to be manufactured

Now $$T_1 = N(T_2 + T_m) + N\Sigma \frac{T_m \times T_3}{T} \quad \text{...(3)}$$

where T_1 = Total time to produce N components

T_2 = Time taken to index the machine and advance and withdraw the tools

T_3 = Tool changing time at any station

Σ = Sum of the terms for the stations on the machine.

Thus,

T_4 = Average production time per component

$$= T_2 + T_m + \Sigma \frac{T_m \cdot T_3}{T} \quad \text{...(4)}$$

Now

Let C_1 = Rate (Cost per Unit time) for each station

C = Total rate for the transfer machine

$= \Sigma C_1$

M = Production cost per component

$$= \Sigma C_1 \cdot T_4 + \Sigma \frac{T_m \cdot C_2}{T} \qquad ...(5)$$

where C_2 = Cost of providing new tool at the station.

Substituting values from equation (2) and (4) in equation (5) we get

$$M = \Sigma C_1 (T_2 + T_m) + T_m^{1-\frac{1}{n}} \left[\Sigma C_1 \Sigma \left(\frac{K}{V_S} \right)^{\frac{1}{n}} \cdot \frac{T_3}{T_S} \right.$$

$$\left. + \Sigma \left(\frac{K}{V_S} \right)^{\frac{1}{n}} \cdot \frac{C_2}{T_S} \right] \qquad ...(6)$$

Equation (6) can now be differentiated with respect to T_m (machining time) to find the machining time (T_p) giving minimum costs

$$T_p = \left(\frac{1}{n} - 1 \right) \Sigma \left(\frac{K}{V_S} \right)^{\frac{1}{n}} \cdot \frac{T_3}{T_S} + \frac{\Sigma \left[\left(\frac{K}{V_S} \right)^{\frac{1}{n}} \left(\frac{C_2}{T_S} \right) \right]^n}{\Sigma C_1} \qquad ...(7)$$

The minimum production cost per component can now be calculated by substituting the value of T_p for T_m is equation (6) and optimum tool life at each station can be obtained from equation (2).

12.8. Efficiency of Manufacturing Facility

Proper selection of

(*i*) manufacturing systems and

(*ii*) machine tools

helps in reducing over all cost of a component.

The efficiency of a manufacturing facility can be measured in three basic ways :

(*i*) Manufacturing cost

(*ii*) Productivity

(*iii*) Profit.

The manufacturing cost involves not only cost of machining, assembly etc. but also cost of moving the components from one machine tool to other machine tool and temporary storage. It can be affected by

(*i*) Efficiency of various manufacturing processes used and the way these processes are integrated or arranged in the factory

(*ii*) Labour costs and

(*iii*) Quality of product design.

Productivity refers to the efficiency with which labour is utilised. It is generally taken to mean the average output per man hour. Profits made by the company will be affected by changes in manufacturing cost or productivity.

Example 12.1. *A 10 mm diameter hole is to be drilled in a soft steel plate with a feed of 0.2 mm/rev. The drill rotate at 400 RPM. Determine the power required if specific power is 0.06 kW per* cm^3 *of metal removed.*

Solution. D = Diameter of hole = 10 mm

f = Feed = 0.2 mm

N = RPM = 400

P = Power required

$$= \frac{\pi}{4} . D^2 . f \times N \times \text{Specific power}$$

$$= \frac{\pi}{4}\left(\frac{10}{10}\right)^2 \times \frac{0.2}{10} \times 400 \times 0.06$$

= 0.37 kW.

Let η = Efficiency of motor

= 0.8 (say)

$$\text{Power of motor} = \frac{0.37}{0.8} = 0.46 \text{ kW.}$$

Example 12.2. *State the factors for production time.*

Solution. The various factors of productive time are as follows :

(*i*) Machining time

(*ii*) Set up time.

The time required to

(*a*) arrange tools on the machine

(*b*) study blue prints

(*c*) handle measuring instruments etc.

(*iii*) **Handling time.** This time includes

(*a*) time for loading and unloading of workpiece

(*b*) time for manipulation of tools and the machine

(*c*) time for checking the size etc.

(*iv*) **Down time.** It includes

(*a*) time loss due to breakdowns

(*b*) sudden accidents time

(*c*) time to obtain tools etc.

Example 12.3. *Two machine tools A and B have the following particulars. Which machine will be economical based on equivalent annual cost (EAC) principle.*

Solution.

	Machine A	**Machine B**
Investment (Rupees)	20,000	40,000
Service life (years)	4	8
Rate of interest	10%	10%

For Machine A

$$\text{EAC} = \text{Equivalent annual cost}$$

$$= P \times \left[\frac{r(1+r)^n}{(1+r)^n - 1}\right]$$

where P = Investment

= Rs. 20,000

r = Rate of interest

= 10%

= 0.1

n = Life of machine tool in years

= 4

$$\text{EAC} = 20000\left[\frac{0.1(1+0.1)^4}{(1+0.1)^4 - 1}\right]$$

$$= \text{Rs. } 6310$$

For Machine B

$$\text{EAC} = P\left[\frac{r(1+r)^n}{(1+r)^n - 1}\right]$$

$$= 40000\left[\frac{0.1(1+0.1)^8}{(1+0.1)^8 - 1}\right]$$

$$= \text{Rs. } 7509$$

As EAC of machine A is less the EAC of machine B therefore machine A will be economical.

Example 12.4. *Determine the number of break even point components for an engine lathe and turret lathe using following data :*

	Engine lathe	*Turret lathe*
Number of components per hour	*3*	*5*
Number of hours of set up	*0.34*	*1.1*
Composite rate (labour + overhead + depreciation rate)	*5*	*4*

No. special tools are required.

Solution. $$Q = \frac{N_1 N_2 (H_2 C_2 - H_1 C_1)}{N_2 C_1 - N_1 C_2}$$

where N_1 = Number of components made on engine lathe per hour = 3

N_2 = Number of components made on turret lathe per hour = 5

C_1 = Composite rate for engine lathe = Rs. 5

C_2 = Composite rate for turret lathe = 4

H_1 = Number of hours of set up for engine lathe = 0.34

H_2 = Number of hours of set up for turret lathe = 1.1

Q = Break even point components

$$= \frac{3 \times 5\,(1.1 \times 4 - 0.34 \times 5)}{5 \times 5 - 3 \times 4}$$

= 3.1 components.

PROBLEMS

1. Discuss general classification of machine tools.
2. What are essential characteristics of a machine tool ?
3. Discuss general considerations for selection of machine tools.
4. Describe various methods of selecting machine tools.
5. Write short note on the following :
   (*a*) Optimum selection of machine tools
   (*b*) Break even quantity for machine tools
   (*c*) Economics of transfer machines
   (*d*) Efficiency of manufacturing facility.

13

Typical Problems

13.1. Process Card

It indicates the type of manufacturing operation and the time taken for this operation and other details as follows :

PROCESS CARD

Item No. .... Date ....

Description .... Quantity ....

Drawing No. .... Material ....

S. No.	*Operation*	*Standard Time*	*Total Time*	*Remarks*

13.2. Turning/Milling Data Sheet

It indicates the following details :

(*i*) Machine tool details

(*a*) Type

(*b*) Make

(*c*) Power

(*d*) Rigidity—Good/Fair/Poor

(*e*) Coolant.

(*ii*) Operation details :

(*a*) Nature

(*b*) Stage—Roughing, semifinishing, finishing.

(*iii*) Workpiece details :
- (*a*) Material
- (*b*) Heat treatment
- (*c*) Hardness
- (*d*) Tensile strength
- (*e*) Surface condition
- (*f*) Tolerance.

(*iv*) Tool details :
- (*a*) Approach angle
- (*d*) Tool holder condition
- (*c*) Tool material.

(*v*) Machining data :
- (*a*) Cutting speed, feed, depth of cut
- (*b*) Metal removal rate
- (*c*) Surface finish
- (*d*) Chips—Broken, long, short, curved ; colour of chips.

13.3. Geneva Wheel Mechanism

Geneva mechanisms are used in Machine tools mainly in indexing devices with a constant angle of periodic rotation. They are commonly used in indexing of spindle carriers in automatic and semi-automatic lathes, and of turrets. They are also used in indexing rotary table of a rotary indexing table transfer machine. Fig. 13.1 shows the principle of geneva indexing mechanism. This mechanism make use of a geneva plate, locking plunger, an indexing plate and a pin. The geneva plate can have any number of slots to suit the number of machining stations. One revolution of the indexing plate

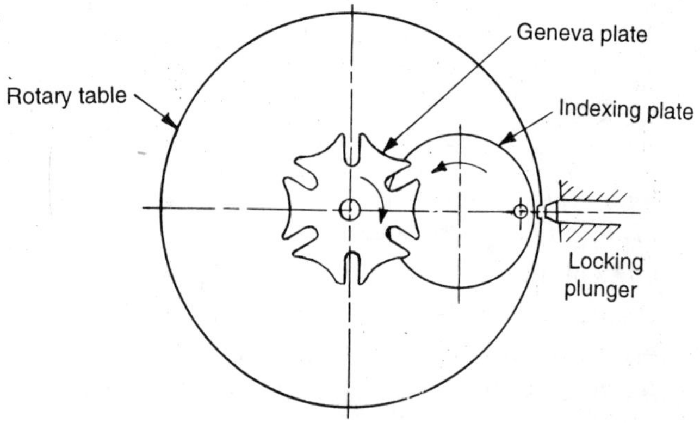

Fig. 13.1

pushes the slotted geneva plate having six equally spaced slots as shown in the Fig. 13.1 through one sixth of a revolution by means of the pin engaging the slot. The locking plunger then engages positively with the table to lock it in position after each indexing.

13.4. Power Consumption for Plain Milling Process

The power in plain milling process is found as follows :

$$P = \frac{K}{\left[f \cdot \sqrt{\frac{d}{D}}\right]^n}$$

where P = Power = $\frac{\text{kW}}{\text{cm}^3}$

K = Material constant

= .02 – 0.03 for mild steel

f = Feed per tooth = $\frac{F}{Z \cdot N}$

Z = Number of teeth on cutter

N = RPM

F = Feed rate, mm/min.

d = Depth of cut, mm

D = Cutter diameter, mm

n = 0.28 for mild steel

= 0.4 for bronze.

13.4.1. Production systems

Production systems can be grouped under three headings depending upon the quantities of parts being manufactured within the system.

They are as follows :

(*i*) Job production

(*ii*) Batch production

(*iii*) Mass production.

(*i*) *Job Production*. This is the manufacture of single (one off), or very few products to a customer's individual specification and orders may not always be repeated. Shipbuilding is an example of job production.

(*ii*) *Batch Production*. This is the system of production where parts are manufactured in fixed quantities called 'batches'. The batches may be small, medium or large in number, each batch containing a number of identical articles. The determination of an optimum batch size is important, and economic factors may have to be taken into account. The great advantage of batch production is the flexibility of the system which is responsive to quick changes of plan brought about by internal or external circumstances, *e.g.*, sudden cancellation of an order. The use of general purpose machines with skilled operators and support staff allows such flexibility. Much quick and inventive jig and tool design help in easy manufacturing.

(*iii*) *Mass Production or Flow Production*. This is the type of production system in which large quantities of identical parts are continuously manufactured and/or assembled. The fixed costs incurred in setting up such a high rate production system are large, and can only be justified by a correspondingly high rate of demand. Flow production is associated with special purpose machines, tools, fixtures, inspection devices, and handling and positioning devices such as robots. Such an automatic system lends itself to control through the medium of a computer, the term *automation* having been coined to describe it. In a flow production system the plant and equipment is arranged in a flow-line layout.

13.5. Copying Systems for Machine Tools

A copying system is used to reproduce a form on the workpiece from a template within the limits of accuracy required. Many copying systems are available for almost all types of machine tools, some built as an integral part of the machine tool while some are fitted as an attachment. The copying systems are of the following types depending upon the power used by the system :

(*i*) Hydraulic copying system.

(*ii*) Mechanical copying system.

(*iii*) Electric copying system.

(*iv*) Pneumatic copying system.

Fig. 13.2 shows the principle of operation of a hydraulic copying system for a lathe. In this system when the lathe saddle traverses along the bed the stylus follows the template the stylus is always kept in contact with the template by spring pressure. When the stylus while following the template moves to the right, the spool also move to the right and the oil to the left of the piston flows out and then oil flows to the right of the piston and pushes the piston to the left. Thus the tool slide and tool will move to the left reproducing

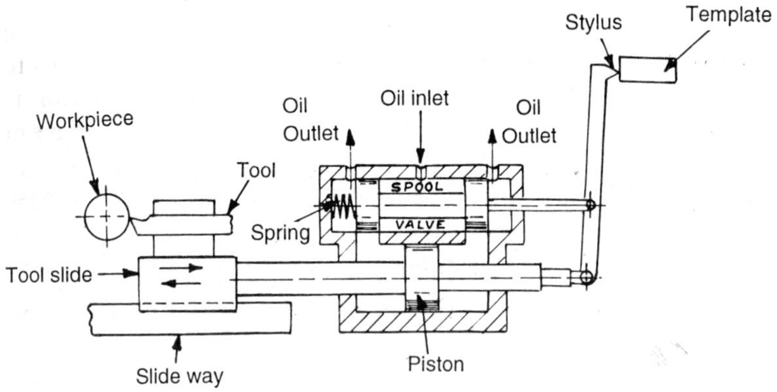

Fig. 13.2

the template shape upon the workpiece. The accuracy of the system depends upon the accuracy with which the spool valve is manufactured.

13.6. Slotted Arm Quick Return Mechanism

The mechanism is generally used in shaping machine. In shaper the cutting operating is carried out only in forward stroke and backward stroke is idle. It is, therefore, desirable that return stroke should be completed as quickly as possible and this is achieved by using quick return mechanism shown in Fig. 13.3. In

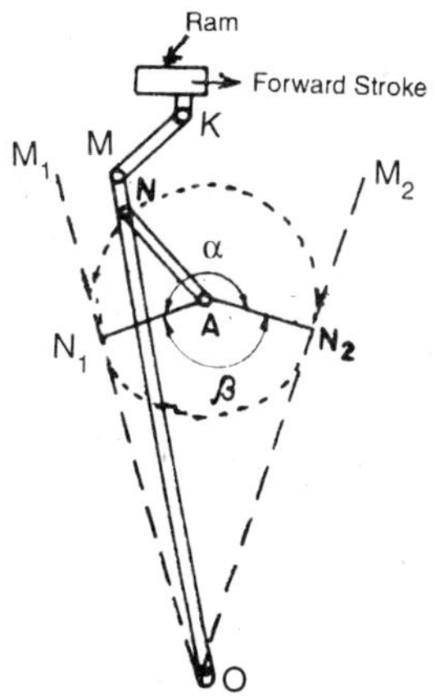

Fig. 13.3

this mechanism the crank AN rotates about centre A. The link OM can rotate about O. It has a slot through which a block N can slide. When the crank rotates about A link OM oscillates about centre O between its ultimate position OM_1 and OM_2. The oscillating motion of *OM* makes the ram to reciprocate through link *MK*. During clockwise movement the forward stroke is constituted from the crank positions AN_1 to AN_2 and return stroke is from AN_2 to AN_1. The ratio of forward to return stroke is equal to the ratio of angle α and β.

Fig. 13.4 shows kinematic configuration of slotted arm analysis for maximum forward and return velocity

V_1 = Maximum forward speed

V = Velocity of crank m/min = $2\pi RN$

L = Length of slotted arm

S = Stroke length

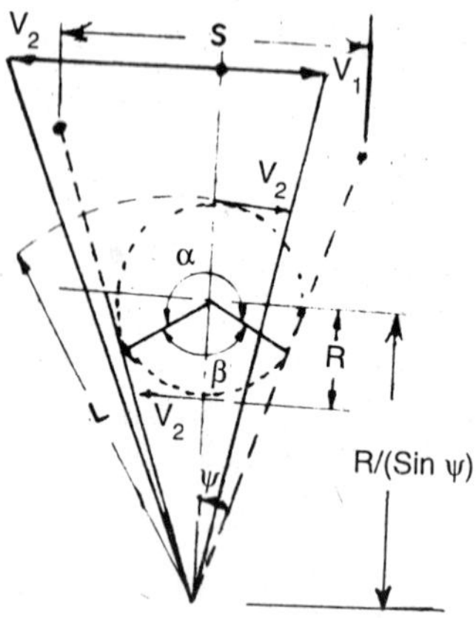

Fig. 13.4

The value of V_1 is given by

$$\frac{V_1}{V} = \frac{L}{\left(\dfrac{R}{\sin\psi} + R\right)}$$

where R = crank radius in metre

N = crank R.P.M.

Now $\sin\psi = \dfrac{S}{2L}$

$$\frac{V_1}{V} = \frac{L}{\left(\dfrac{R \times 2L}{L} + R\right)} = \frac{LS}{R(2L + S)}$$

$$V_1 = V \times \frac{LS}{R(2L+S)} = \frac{2\pi RN \times LS}{R(2L+S)}$$

$$= \frac{\pi N \times LS}{S + \dfrac{S}{2}}$$

Again V_2 = Maximum return speed

$$\frac{V_2}{V} = \frac{L}{\left(\dfrac{R}{\sin\psi} - R\right)}$$

$$V_2 = \frac{2\pi RN \,.\, L}{\left(\dfrac{R \times 2L}{S} - R\right)}$$

$$= \frac{\pi NL \,.\, S}{L - \dfrac{S}{2}}$$

$\therefore$ Q = Maximum quick return ratio

$$= \frac{V_2}{V_1} = \frac{\pi NLS}{L - S/2} \times \frac{L + S/2}{\pi NLS}$$

$$= \frac{2L+S}{2L-S}.$$

Example 13.1. *In a slotted arm quick return mechanism for a shaping machine the maximum quick return ratio is 3/2 and design stroke is 400 mm. Calculate the value of maximum quick return ratio when stroke is 180 mm.*

Solution. Q = Maximum quick return ratio = 3/2

L = Length of slotted arm

S = Stroke = 400 mm.

We know that

$$Q = \frac{2L+S}{2L-S}$$

$$Q\,(2L - S) = 2L + S$$

$$L = \left(\frac{Q+1}{Q-1}\right) \times \frac{S}{2}$$

$$= \left(\frac{3/2+1}{3/2-1}\right) \times \frac{400}{2} = 1000 \text{ mm.}$$

When S = 180 mm.

$$Q = \frac{2L + S}{2L - S} = \frac{2 \times 1000 + 180}{2 \times 1000 - 180}$$
$$= 1.19.$$

Example 13.2. *While machining a workpiece on a shaper a quick return ratio of 3 / 2 is obtained. If the workpiece is 200 mm long and is machined at a cutting speed of 18 metres per minute, calculate R.P.M. of crank.*

Solution. Q = Quick return ratio

$$= \frac{3}{2}.$$

V = cutting speed = 81 m/min

L = Length of workpiece (stroke length)

= 200 mm.

N = R.P.M. of crank

The cutting speed is given by

$$V = \frac{N.L.(1 + 1/Q)}{1000}$$

$$18 = \frac{N \times 200 \times (1 + 2/3)}{1000}$$

$$N = 54 \text{ R.P.M.}$$

13.7. Fellow's Gear Shaper

Gear shapers may be automatic and semi-automatic. They are used to cut external and internal spur and helical gears, cluster gears, gear racks etc. In gear shaping machines the cutting tool is either a rack type cutter [Fig. 13.5 (*a*)] or a rotary type cutter [Fig. 13.5 (*b*)].

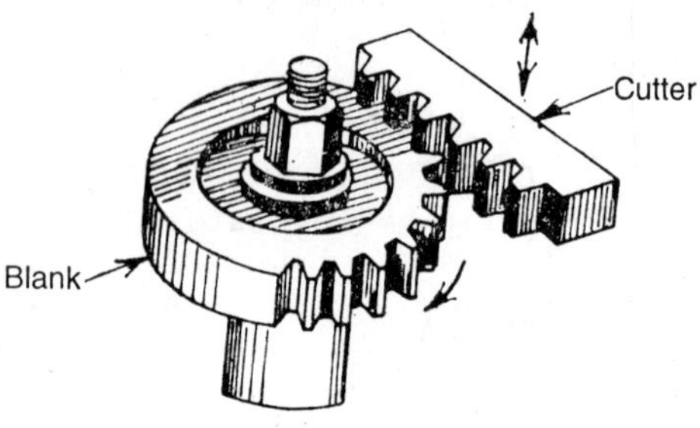

Fig. 13.5 (*a*)

Fellow's Gear shaper uses a rotary type cutter. This gear shaper has the following motions (Fig. 13.6).

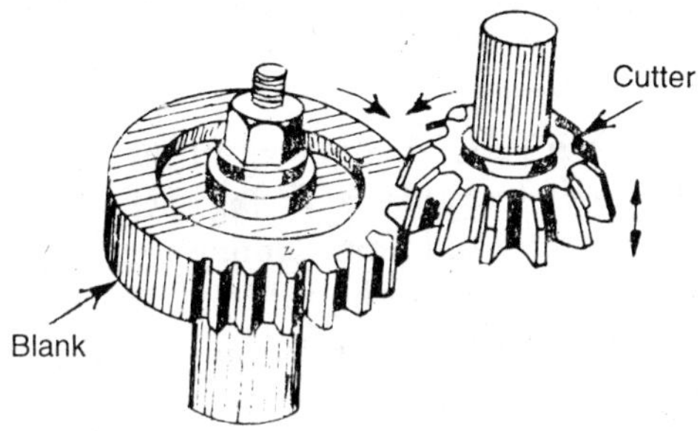

Fig. 13.5 (*b*)

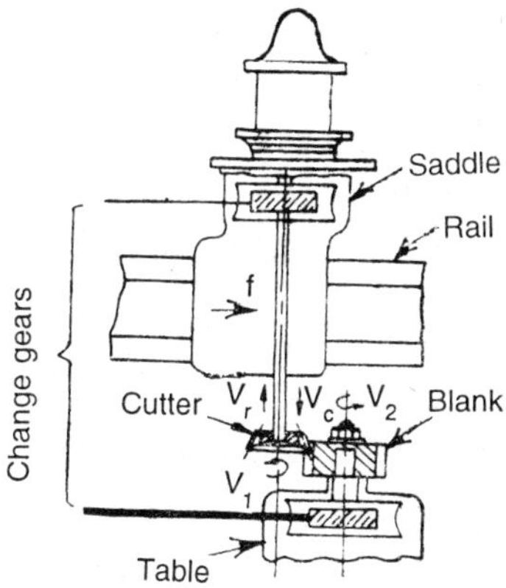

Fig. 13.6

(*i*) The straight line primary cutting motion (V_o) achieved by travel of cutter only in one direction during cutting stroke and return (V_r) of cutter to initial position during return stroke.

(*ii*) To obtain circular feed (indexing motion) there is continuous rotation of shape cutter at speed V_1 and gear blank at V_2. Change gears are used to co-ordinate the speeds of cutter and blank in such a manner that in one revolution of cutter blank makes T_c / T_g where T_c is the number of teeth on cutter and T_s is the number of teeth on gear to be cut.

(*iii*) The feed in motion (*f*) which may be radial or circular of cutter is obtained by travel of cutter axis in a direction towards the blank axis with reciprocation of cutter and, circular feed. The feed in motion comes stops automatically when the cutter has fed into the required depth of teeth while the cutting motion continues till the gear blank makes one revolution so that all the teeth get cut. Then the machine is automatically stopped. There can be one, two or three passes to cut the gear.

(*iv*) The table with the blank is withdrawn from the cutter or the cutter is withdrawn from blank during each return stroke. This is done to prevent rubbing and consequent intensive wear of cutting edges and damage to gear to tooth profile.

Example 13.3. *The force on the cutting tool of a planning machine is 800 kg and the table of the machine, makes a total of 300 forward and return strokes per hour of length 1.8 metre. The friction resistance on the forward (cutting) stroke is 60 kg. Calculate the power required neglecting friction on the return stroke. If the table is driven by hydraulic pressure on a piston 80 mm diameter, determine the hydraulic pressure on the piston.*

Solution. N = Number of cutting strokes per second

$$= \frac{300}{60 \times 60} \times \frac{1}{2} = \frac{1}{24}$$

$$\text{Speed of table} = 1.8 \times \frac{1}{24} = \frac{3}{40} \text{ metre per second}$$

$$W_1 = \text{Work done in cutting}$$
$$= \text{Cutting force} \times \text{Speed}$$
$$= 800 \times \frac{3}{40}$$
$$= 60 \text{ kg-m per sec.}$$

$$W_2 = \text{Work done against friction}$$
$$= \text{Friction force} \times \text{Speed}$$
$$= 60 \times \frac{3}{40} = 4.5 \text{ kg-m per sec.}$$

$$W = \text{Total work done}$$
$$W = W_1 + W_2 = 60 + 4.5$$
$$= 64.5 \text{ kg-m per sec.}$$

$$\text{H.P.} = \frac{64.5}{75} = 0.86$$

Let p = pressure on the piston (kg/cm^2)

A = Area of piston

$$= \frac{\pi}{4} D^2 \text{ (cm}^2\text{)}$$

where D = Diameter of piston in cms.

Total force on piston

$$= 800 + 60 = 860 \text{ kg.}$$

$$p \times \frac{\pi}{4} D^2 = 860$$

$$p \times \frac{\pi}{4} 8^2 = 860$$

$$p = 17 \text{ kg/cm}^2. \textbf{ Ans.}$$

Example 13.4. *A medium carbon steel black is to be machined with a high speed steel tool bit on a crank shaper. The ratio of return time to cutting time is 2 : 3 and feed is 0.25 mm per stroke. If the width of blank is 100 mm, length of stroke is 150 mm and cutting speed is 25 metre per minute determine the following :*

(*a*) *Machining time,*

(*b*) *Return speed.*

Solution. V_1 = Cutting speed

V_2 = Return speed

B = Width of block

L = Length of stroke

f = Feed.

Cutting stroke time (T_1)

$$= \frac{L}{v_1} = \frac{150}{25 \times 1000}$$

$$= 0.006 \text{ minute.}$$

T_2 = Return time,

$$\frac{T_2}{T_1} = \frac{2}{3} \text{ (Given)}$$

$$T_2 = \frac{2}{3} \times T_1 = \frac{2}{3} \times 0.006 = 0.004 \text{ minute.}$$

Total time per cycle (T_3)

$$= T_1 + T_2$$

$$= 0.006 + 0.004 = 0.01 \text{ minute}$$

Number of cycles required (N)

$$= \frac{B}{f}$$

$$= \frac{100}{0.25} = 400$$

T = Total machining time

$$= T_3 \times N = 0.01 \times 400$$
$$= 4 \text{ minutes. } \textbf{Ans.}$$

$$V_2 = \text{Return speed} = \frac{3}{2} V_1 = \frac{3}{2} \times 25$$
$$= 37.5 \text{ metre per min. } \textbf{Ans.}$$

13.8. Transfer Devices in Automatic Machine Tool Systems

Transfer device is a mechanism used to move the workpieces from station to station while maintaining their orientation. Transfer devices place the workpieces at the required point and at the required time so that working operations can be performed at each station.

Advantages of using transfer devices are as follows :

(*i*) Cycle time for production is reduced.

(*ii*) Productivity of machine tools is increased.

(*iii*) Number of operators required is reduced.

Tranfer devices are of two types :

(*i*) In-line transfer devices

(*ii*) Rotary transfer devices.

In-line transfer devices are used to move the workpieces in a straight line path as shown in Fig. 13.7 for an In-line transfer machine.

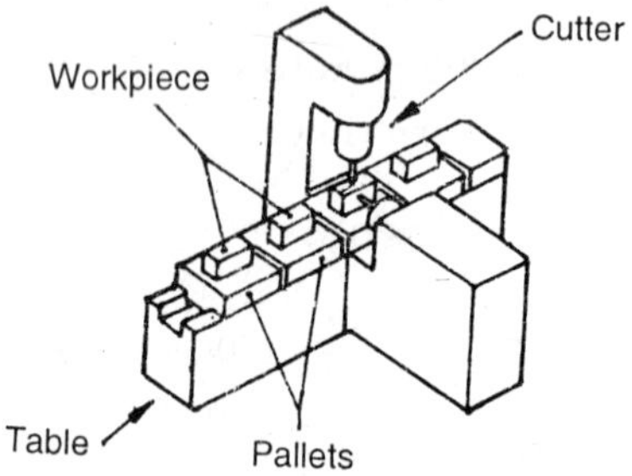

Fig. 13.7

The in-line transfer devices are of two types as follows :

(*i*) Pallet-type transfer machines

(*ii*) Plain-type transfer machines (also called non-pallet type).

Fig. 13.8 shows a typical in-line transfer device. In this transfer device the workpieces are loaded at a point remote from the work station and then through a drive unit transferred to work station.

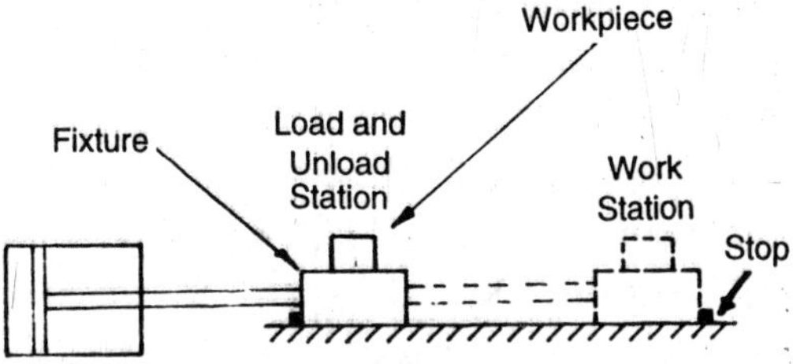

Fig. 13.8

In rotary transfer devices around a rotary table a number of workstations are located where both horizontal and vertical machines perform the required machining operations. In such devices the principal element is the rotary mechanism for the table which is indexed periodically. Fig. 13.9 shows a pawl and ratchet type of indexing operated from a hydraulic cylinder and Fig. 13.10 shows pawl and ratchet whereas Fig. 13.11 shows a Geneva Indexing mechanism for rotary table. In-line transfer devices can be used to feed heavy workpieces whereas rotary transfer devices are used to move less heavy workpieces and when total number of operations required are rather less.

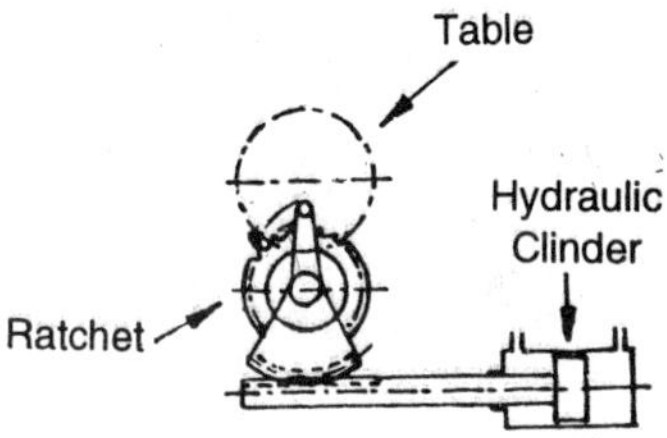

Fig. 13.9

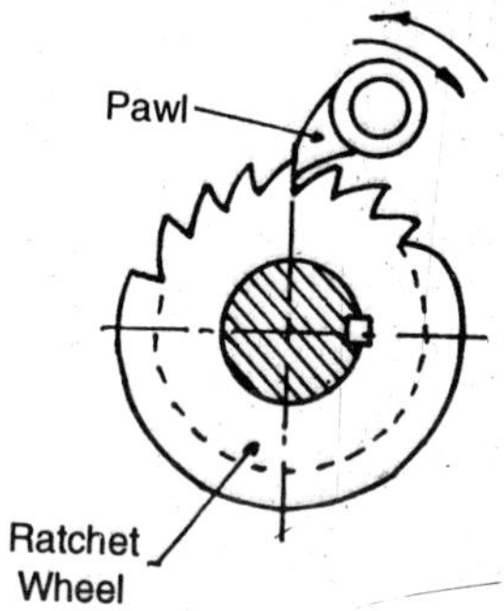

Fig. 13.10

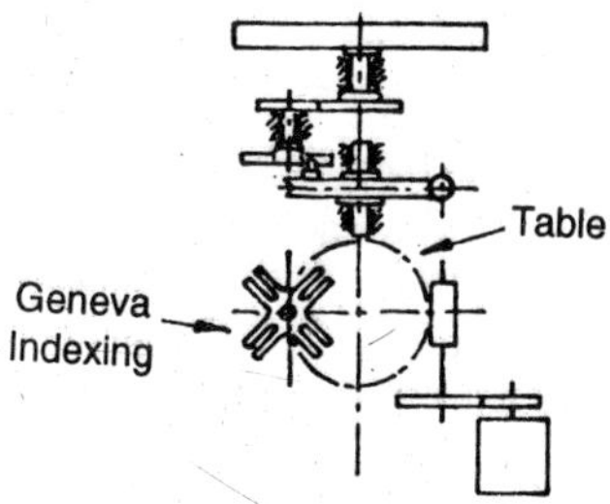

Fig. 13.11

In rotary transfer devices the rotary mechanisms for the table which are indexed periodically are of two types :

(*i*) Pawl and ratchet type of indexing.

(*ii*) Geneva-indexing mechanism.

Choice of transfer devices depends on the following factors :

(*i*) Number of operations required

(*ii*) Size and weight of workpieces

(*iii*) Desired rate of production

(*iv*) Forces to be applied at various work stations

(*v*) Type of transfer device such as

(*a*) Pneumatic

(*b*) Hydraulic

(*c*) Electric

(*d*) Combination of two or more types.

13.9. Pawl and Ratchet Drive

It is used to obtain intermittent motion of the operative element of a machine tool.

In some machine tools it is required that the relative position between the cutting tool and workpiece should change periodically. This requirement is generally essential in :

(*i*) machine tools with a reciprocating primary cutting motion, *e.g.*, shaping machines in which the workpiece must be fed intermittently upon completion of one full stroke of the cutting tool, and

(*ii*) machine tools with reciprocating feed motion, *e.g.*, grinding machines, in which the workpiece must be infed intermittently after each half or full stroke of the reciprocating table.

Fig. 13.12 shows a pawl and ratchet gear mechanism. It consists of a pawl mounted on an oscillating pin. During each oscillation the pawl turns the ratchet through a particular angle. The ratchet wheel is linked to the machine tool table through a net and screw transmission.

The pawl and ratchet convert the continual and uniform rocking motion of the pawl carrier bracket into the intermittent rotary motion of the table traverse lead screw. This intermittent movement of the screw is essential to ensure that the table only moves on the return stroke and remains stationary on the forward stroke.

For a particular nut-and-screw pair of some **constant** **transmission ratio**, the feed of the table during each oscillation **depends**

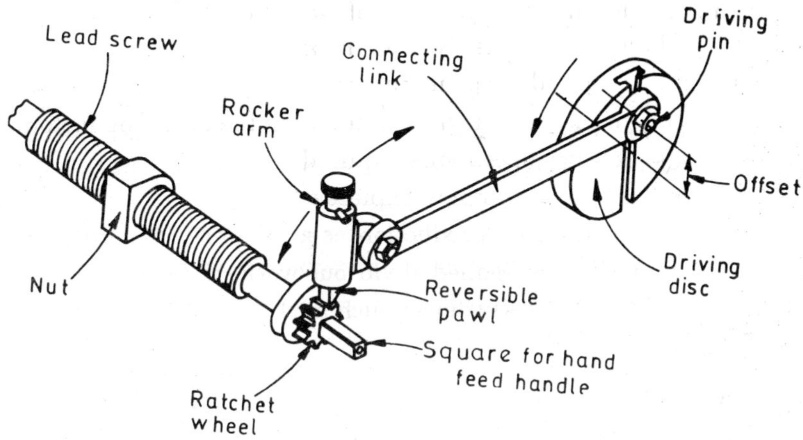

Fig. 13.12

upon the swing of the oscillating pawl. Generally, the rotation of the ratchet wheel in one stroke of the pawl should not exceed 45°.

The rate of traverse is controlled by the amplitude of the rocking motion of the pawl carrier bracket.

The driving disc rotates at same speed as the stroke wheel. The driving pin is adjustable in tee slot to vary feed per stroke. Offset of the driving pin determines the feed per stroke. In this mechanism, traverse rate is determined as follows :

Traverse rate (mm/double stroke)

$$= \frac{\text{Lead of traverse screw}}{\text{Number of teeth on ratchet wheel}} \times \text{increment per double stroke.}$$

Example 13.5. *Calculate the traverse rate for a shaping machine equipped with a 6 mm lead traverse screw and a 30 teeth ratchet wheel, when set to an increment of three teeth per double stroke. If the machine is running at 50 double strokes / min, calculate the time to traverse across 28 mm.*

Solution. Traverse rate $= \frac{6 \text{ mm}}{30 \text{ teeth}} \times 3$ teeth

$= \textbf{0.6 mm/double stroke}$

Time to traverse across 24 mm at 50 double strokes/min

$$\text{Time taken} = \frac{\text{width of component}}{\text{traverse rate} \times \text{number of double strokes/min}}$$

$$= \frac{28}{0.6 \times 50} = \frac{14}{15} \text{ min} = \textbf{56 seconds}.$$

13.10. Unit-Built Machine Tools

Unit-built machine tools are special machine tools consisting of standard units.

Such machines find application in the multiple-tool machining of various workpiece (mostly of the housing type) in large-lot and mass production. They are extensively employed in plants manufacturing automobiles and agricultural machinery.

Unit-built machine tools are designed for such operations as drilling, boring, threading and, less frequently, for milling surfaces.

Advantages ensuing from the proper application of unit-built machine tools include : (*a*) a substantial reduction in the time required to design and manufacture a special machine tool ; (*b*) high production capacity due to multiple-tool machining and a minimum amount of handling motions ; (*c*) comparatively low manufacturing cost ; (*d*) reduction in the costs of machining workpieces on the machine tool due to the high productivity and simple servicing ; (*e*) a more readily automated machining cycle ; and (*f*) the possibility of using some of the standard units again if changes are made in the product being manufactured.

In cases when an established assortment of parts is being manufactured, it is possible to design unit-built machine tools that can handle several similar parts of different sizes by changing over from part to part.

Unit-built machine tools can operate as individual machines or they can be components of automatic transfer machines or automated production lines.

13.10.1. Principal units of unit built machine tools

Usually a unit built machine tool consists of the following parts :

1. Bed
2. Column
3. Power units
4. Multiple spindle heads
5. Fixtures for locating and holding the workpiece
6. Fixture base.

In some cases, the beds or columns are mounted on sub-bases which are also standard units. If several workpieces are to be machined consecutively, stationary fixture is replaced by a movable two-position fixture or by a revolving table on which are mounted fixtures for locating and clamping the workpiece.

Unit-built machine tools with a hydraulic drive of the operative units use standard hydraulic control panels to control the operating cycle.

Fig. 13.13 shows a three way multiple spindle drilling machine.

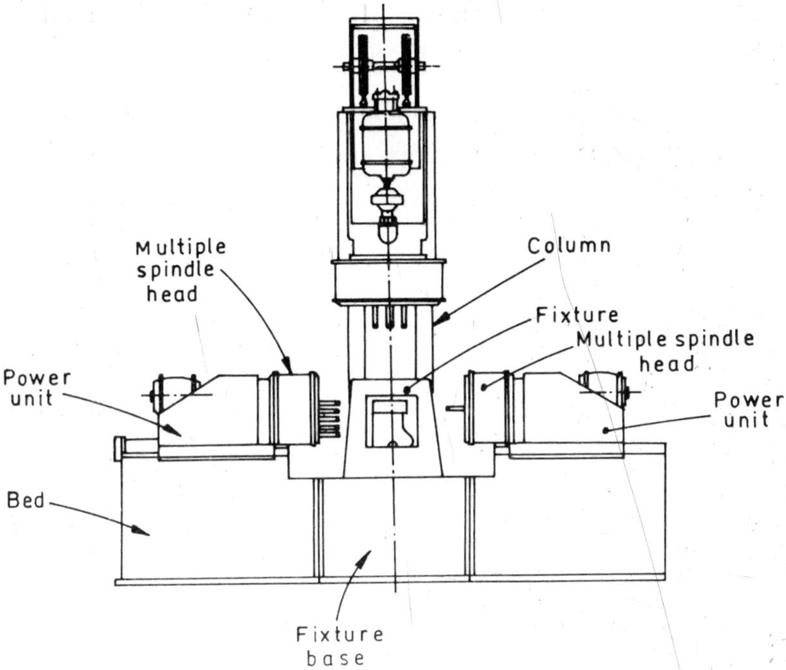

Fig. 13.13

The various parts of unit built machine tool are described as follows :

1. Standard beds, sub-bases and columns. They are castings or weldments of box shape with ways for the travel of the power unit. Special nonstandard beds are of welded steel plate construction as a rule, and have separate hardened steel ways secured by screws. In many cases, the ways are designed in the from of a saddle that is mounted on the welded bed after it is completely machined.

2. Multiple spindle heads. They accommodate the tool spindles and transmit rotation from the output shaft of the power unit to the spindles.

Standard multiple-spindle heads consist of housing, intermediate plate, front, and rear covers. Standardized spindles, shafts and gears are mounted in the bores of the housing and intermediate plate. Central gear meshes with a gear mounted on the output shaft of the power unit. The components of the head are assembled through the opening in housing. The rear conver has holes for securing the head to the housing of the power unit.

A size range of spindle heads has been standardized. The component castings of the heads are manufactured to the standardized dimensions and stored as stock. The holes for the bearings are bored in each particular case to suit the workpiece that is to be machined by the machine tool.

3. Fixtures. The fixtures or jigs for locating and holding the workpiece are designed in accordance with the size and shape of a definite workpiece, and the type of machining operation to be performed. Therefore, they cannot be standardized. The workpiece is located in the fixture by rest buttons, pads, locating pins, V-blocks, etc.

4. Power units. They are of two types :

(*i*) Self contained type

(*ii*) Separate feed type.

Power units may be *self-contained* or *separate-feed* types.

Self-contained standard power and feed units are ones that impart both rotary and feed motions to the cutting tool, and can be mounted on the machine tool in any required working position.

The separate-feed type of power unit imparts only rotary motion to the cutting tool, the drive of the feed motion being arranged separately in the bed (or column) of the machine tool.

Special thread-cutting power units with reversible spindles are used for threading operations.

The feed motion in a power unit may be obtained by :

(*a*) travel of the power unit housing which carries the spindle head ;

(*b*) travel of a quill containing the rotating spindle with the cutting tool, the housing being stationary.

Power units can operate with a wide range of different feed and traverse cycles. The simplest cycle is one in which the unit travels back and forth at the same speed.

13.11. Gear-Cutting Machine Classification

They are classified according to the following features :

(1) The type of machining and tool used : into gear hobbers, gear shapers, gear planers, gear broaching machines, gear-shaving machines, gear grinders, gear lappers, gear-tooth honers and gear-tooth rounding machines.

(2) Purpose : into machines for cutting spur and helical gears, worm wheels, herringbone gears, gear racks, straight bevel gears, and curved-tooth bevel gears.

(3) The finish of the machined tooth surfaces : into machines for roughing the teeth, for finishing the teeth, and for microfinishing the active surfaces of the teeth.

13.12. Gear Shapers

They are used to cut gears. Semiautomatic and automatic gear shapers cut external and internal spur and helical gears, cluster gears, flanged gears, toothed clutches, gear racks, ratchet wheels, cams, etc.

In this general type of gear-cutting machine, the cutting tool resembles either a gear rack, called a *rack-type cutter* (Fig. 13.14), or a gear, called a *rotary gear shaper cutter* (Fig. 13.15). Gear

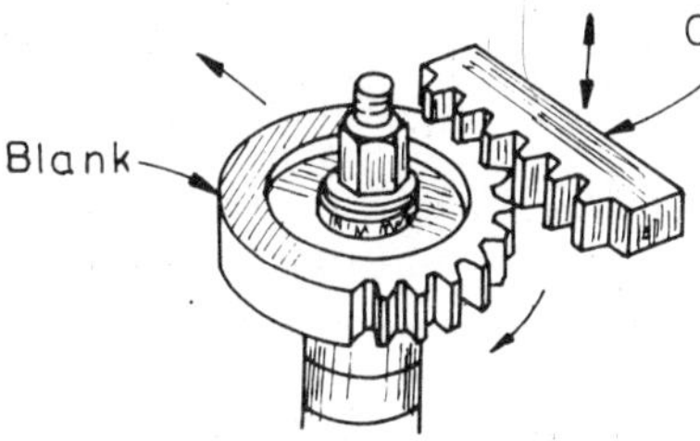

Fig. 13.14

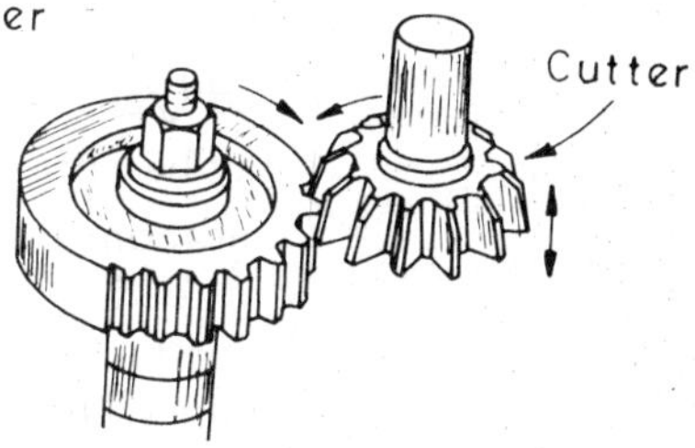

Fig. 13.15

shapers using a rotary cutter have found much wider application because they have a higher output (the cutting process is not interrupted to index the blank) and can perform all the operations done in hobbers, except for cutting worm wheels. They can additionally cut internal gears by the generating principle. The output of gear shapers is less than that of hobbers. They are indispensable, however, for such jobs as cutting internal gears of practically any diameter, as well as cluster gears in which the distance between the gear rims is not sufficient for the required overtravel of a hob.

13.13. Robots

In the industrial world, robots are performing hazardous and monotonous tasks with tireless precision.

The rapid progress in the fields of electronics and computers has added momentum to the R & D activity in the field of robotics.

Robotics is a branch of technology which concerns all problems of robot design, development and application.

Robots play an important role in flexible manufacturing systems in industrial productions.

13.13.1. Types of robots

Robots are classified as follows :

1. *Classification Based on Level of Sophistication*

On the basis of sophistication robots are classified according to their generation. These are :

(*i*) **First Generation Robots.** Most of the industrial robots currently being used belong to this group. These are simple programmable robots.

(*ii*) **Second Generation Robots.** These robots have capability to understand the environment by acquiring data.

(*iii*) **Third Generation Robots.** Intelligent robots of the future with characteristics as yet hardly understood.

2. *Classification Based on Manipulative Function*

Robots can be grouped under three major headings from this point of view. These are as follows :

(*i*) Pick and place robots,

(*ii*) Special purpose robots, and

(*iii*) Universal robots.

3. *Classification Based on Manipulator Geometry*

Industrial robots are sometimes classified according to the geometry of the main functional unit, *viz.*, the manipulator arm. Generally four types of robots are there under this classification :

(*i*) Cartesian or *XYZ*,

(*ii*) Cylindrical,

(*iii*) Polar, and

(*iv*) Jointed arm.

Fig. 13.16 shows cartesian type manipulator arm.

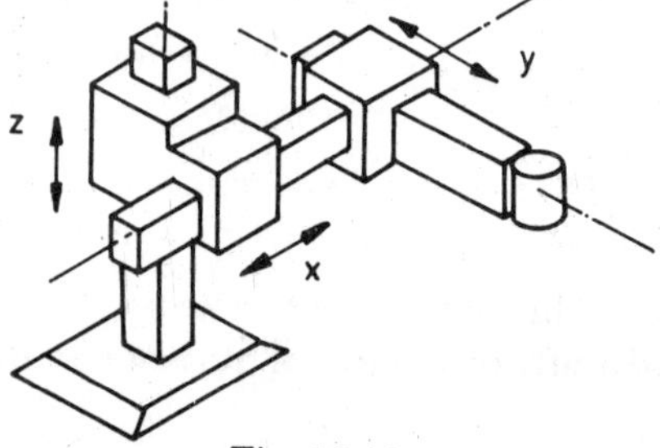

Fig. 13.16

4. *Classification Based on Motion Characteristics*

When robots are classified according to the motion characteristics of the arm, they fall into the following two categories :

(*i*) Point-to-point (PTP) robots capable of taking the end effector from one point to another without attaching any importance to the path ; and

(*ii*) Continuous-path (CP) robots where the tool moves along a desired path.

5. *Classification Based on Type of Control*

According to the control system used for moving the arm, industrial robots can be classified into two main groups :

(*i*) Non-servo controlled robots which do not employ feedback control for their drive units making them cheaper but at the same time less expensive ;

(*ii*) Servo controlled robots sense the arm configuration and this information is feedback to the controller for comparison with the desired position. Higher accuracy can be achieved but costs of such systems are more.

13.13.2. Elements of robot system

Fig. 13.17 shows a commercial robot system and its basic elements.

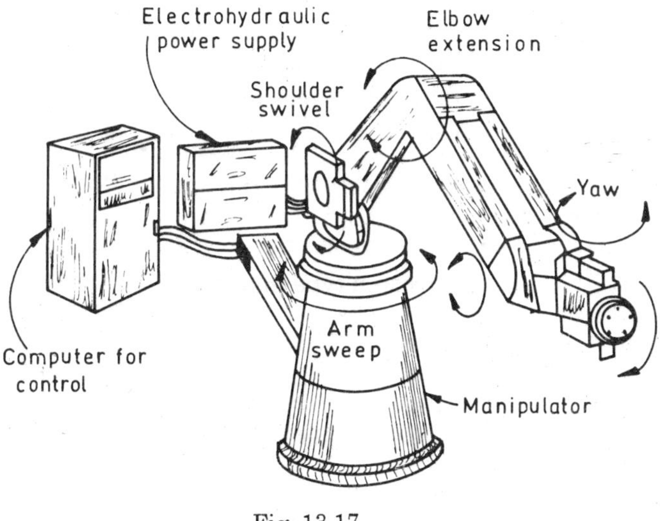

Fig. 13.17

1. *Manipulator*. This is the most obvious part of the robot to an observer and this chiefly comprises of a base, an arm and a wrist.

Within the manipulator are the mechanical parts—links, power joints, transmission system, and internal sensors that execute robot's movements.

2. *Controller*. This is the 'brain' of a robot. It performs three major functions such as :

(*i*) Storing, sequencing and, for more sophisticated robots, positioning of data in memory ;

(*ii*) Initiating and stopping the motions of the manipulator.

Two basic components of the controller are :

(*a*) the hardware, and

(*b*) the software.

3. *Sensors*. In case of intelligent robots sensing of the environment is essential. Different types of external sensors including vision can be incorporated.

4. *Energy Source*. Movement of the manipulator arm requires energy and this is supplied by the source of energy. Depending on the load range and the type of application—electrical, hydraulic or pneumatic drives can be used. For small to medium range of the work load, electrical drive is most suitable, whereas hydraulic system is used for higher work loads. Pneumatic systems are suitable for systems where accuracy requirements are less.

5. *End Effector*. This is the tool which directly interacts with the job, and depending on the type of work an end effector can be a gripper, a spray painting gun, a welding torch etc.

13.13.3. Operational unit

Operational unit of a robot constitutes of (*i*) articulated mechanical system (AMS), (*ii*) actuators, and (*iii*) transmission system. An operational unit is controlled by a computer which receives commands from the operator and is continuously fed with data regarding the joint variables. In case of intelligent robots the environment is also sensed. To feed back data, AMS is provided with sensors (called internal sensors) which indicate the position and velocity of the end effector (EE), whereas external sensors are provided for sensing the environment.

13.14. MACHINE TOOL INSTALLATION

Machine tools are installed on foundation with the aid of

(*i*) levelling pads

(*ii*) wedges

(*iii*) shoes.

With the machine being held down by means of foundation bolts. The machine-toll bed is secured on the foundation by means of foundation anchor bolts, which are placed into special pockets in the foundation and grouted with cement mortar or higher grades of concrete as shown in Fig. 13.18.

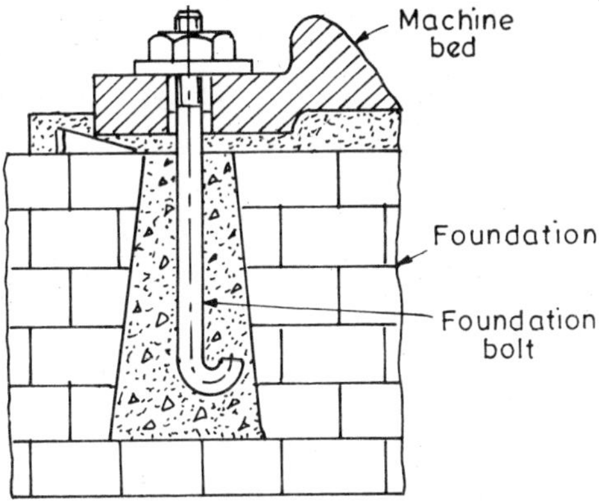

Fig. 13.18

Foundations for machine tools sensitive to shocks and vibrations are specially separated by means of various shock absorbers.

The installation directly on a concrete shop floor is permitted for machine tools weighing up to 15 tons with beds of medium and high rigidity, excluding machine tools operating under dynamic loads (*e.g.*, shapers, slotters, etc.), and also machine tools sensitive to vibrations, such as jig borers.

The thickness of a concrete foundation block is calculated from the condition of its strength and is taken as not less than 150 mm. Most machine tools of medium size and normal accuracy (about 90-95% of the total) used in engineering industries are now installed on common shop concrete floors

13.15. COMPUTER INTEGRATED MANUFACTURING (CIM)

It is an interdisciplinary science applied to manufacturing. It involves the amalgamation of information science with automated manufacturing. This concept is represented below :

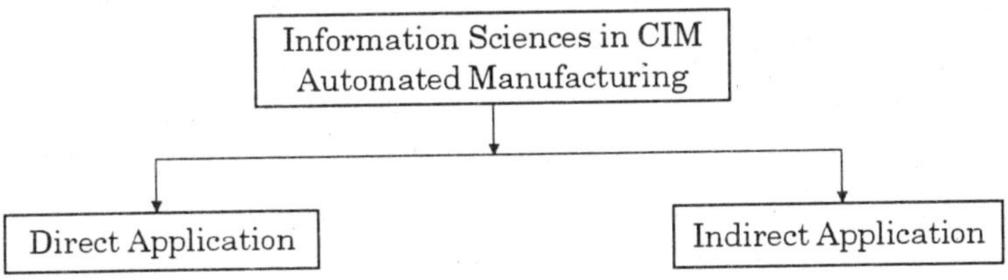

Direct application. In this method, computer or a network of computers monitor and control the hardware in a manufacturing plant, such as machine tools, inspection machines, robots and automated guided vehicles which physically transform or transport or assemble components.

Indirect application. In this method, the followings are included :

(*i*) Computer Aided Design (CAD)
(*ii*) PPC
(*iii*) Inventory Control
(*iv*) Marketing/Sales, Factory Management
(*v*) Manufacturing resources planning (MRP-II)
(*vi*) Just in time (JIT) techniques
(*vii*) Optimized production technology (OPT).

The growth of CIM in developed countries has been phenomenal. The recent studies indicate the growth of CIM in the form of FMS around the world. A typical CIM set up involves the versatile FMS cells comparising NC machines with material integration provided by an automated material handling system. A robot plays an important role in the CIM model. The tasks such as welding, spray painting, machine loading, material handling and assembly are carried out by robots on the floor shops of factories. The recent advances in machine vision and expert systems have made robots versatile and integral part of factory automation. Robots are synonymous with high productivity. The major incorporators in CIM are the USA and Japan.

The only FMS installed in our country is in a Heavy Alloy Penetrator Project (HAPP) at Trichy. This system has intelligent CNC Work Centre, integrated with a tool management system and loading/unloading gantry. Robots and other hardwares for CIM are being developed at Bhabha Atomic Research Centre for nuclear applications. In the developing countries, a rapid change over to CIM has seen that overheads are lessened and profits increased.

13.16. ECM METAL REMOVAL

Metal removal rate (MRR) can also be entressed as follows :

According to Faradays first law of electrolysis, mass of ions liberated by the substance (M) is given by

$$M = EIT$$

where E = Constant called electrochemical equivalent of the substance

I = Current flowing through the electrolytic cell in amperes

T = Time in second.

According to Faraday's second law of electrolysis

$$M = \frac{W}{V}$$

where M = Equivalent weight of material dissolved or deposited.

W = Atomic weight of material in gm

V = Valency of metal dissolved.

Also $$E = \frac{1}{F} \cdot \frac{W}{V}$$

Therefore, $$M = EIT$$

$$= \frac{1.W}{F.V} \cdot I \cdot T$$

where F = Faraday's constant = 96500 coulomb = 26.8 amp hours

$$MRR = \text{Metal removal rate} = \frac{M}{A \cdot \rho \cdot T} \text{ cm/min.}$$

where A = Machined area in cm^2

ρ = Density of workpiece in gm/cm^3

$$MRR = \frac{W.IT}{FV} \times \frac{1}{A.\rho.T}$$

$$= \frac{W.I}{F.V.A.\rho} \text{ cm}^3\text{/min.}$$

Example 13.1. *In an ECM process for machining iron it is desired to obtain a metal removal rate of 2 cm^3/min. Determine the amount of current required for the process, assuming that At. wt. of iron = 56 gm, valency at which dissolution occurs = 2, density of iron = 7.8 gm/cm^3 and Faraday's constant = 1609 amp-min.*

Solution. W = Atomic weight of iron = 56 gm

V = Valency of iron dissolution = 2

ρ = Density of iron = 7.8 gm/cm^3

F = Faraday's constant = 1609 amp-min.

$M.R.R.$ = Metal removal rate = 2 cm^3/min.

$$M.R.R. = \frac{IW}{Fv\rho} \text{ cm}^3\text{/min}$$

$$2 = \frac{I \times 56}{1609 \times 2 \times 7.8}$$

$$I = \frac{1609 \times 2 \times 7.8}{56}$$

$$= 896.4 \text{ amperes.}$$

13.17. PREFERRED NUMBERS AND SELECTION OF COMMON RATIO

The preferred numbers are the numbers of a G.P. series containing the number 1 and the common ratio being any one of the following quantities :

$(10)^{1/20} = 1.12,$

$(10)^{2/20} = 1.25,\ (10)^{3/20} = 1.41,$

$(10)^{4/20} = 1.12,$

$(10)^{5/20} = 1.78,\ (10)^{6/20} = 2$

denoted by $R\ 20, R\frac{20}{2}, R\frac{20}{3}, R\frac{20}{4}, R\frac{20}{5}, R\frac{20}{6}$.

where R denotes Renard Series.

In order to allow also for speed changes due to changes of motor, the ratio 2 must be available.

As $\sqrt[3]{2} \simeq \sqrt[10]{10} \simeq 1.25$, this condition is also satisfied in the normal range

$$\left(R\frac{20}{2},\ \phi = \sqrt[10]{10}\right).$$

The various properties of the different common ratios are given in Table 13.1.

Table 13.1

ϕ / *Progression Ratio*	*ISA Standard*	$\sqrt[E]{2}$	$\sqrt[E]{10}$	*ISA Designation*	*Maximum speed loss* $\left(\frac{\phi - 1}{\phi}\right) 100$
1.06	—	$\sqrt[12]{2}$	$\sqrt[40]{10}$	—	5
1.12	1.12	$\sqrt[6]{2}$	$\sqrt[20]{10}$	*R*20	10
1.26	1.25	$\sqrt[3]{2}$	$\sqrt[10]{10}$	*R*20/2	20
1.41	1.40	$\sqrt[2]{2}$	$\sqrt[20/3]{10}$	*R*20/3	40
1.58	1.60	$\sqrt[15]{2}$	$\sqrt[5]{10}$	*R*20/4	40
1.78	—	$\sqrt[12]{2}$	$\sqrt[4]{10}$	—	45
2	2	$\sqrt[1]{2}$	$\sqrt[20/6]{10}$	*R*20/6	50

In both the cases of geometric and arithmetic progressions it is found that the width of the diameter range increases with workpiece diameter. Arithmetic progression reduces the possibility of working at economic cutting speeds. Geometric progression is generally accepted from kinematic and design point of view. The G.P. series also leads to minimum manufacturing costs over the life of the machine if all speeds and feeds are equally probable.

13.18. STANDARD FEEDS AND SPEEDS

Table 13.2 indicates standard feeds for various values of progression ratio (ϕ).

Table 13.2

$\phi = 1.12$	$\phi = 1.25$	$\phi = 1.4$			$\phi = 1.6$	$\phi = 2$		
1	1		1		1		1	
1.12				11.2				
1.25	1.25	0.125				0.125		
1.40			1.4					
1.60	1.5			16	1.6			16
1.80		0.18						
2	2		2				2	
2.24				22.4		0.25		
2.50	2.6	0.25			2.5			
2.10			2.8					31.5
2.85	3.15			31.5				
3.55		0.355						
4	4		4		4		4	
4.50				45				
5	5	0.5				0.5		
5.60			5.6					
6.30	6.3			63	6.3			63
7.10		0.71						
8	8		8				8	
9				90				
10	10	1.0			10	1.0		

Table 13.3 indicates standard speeds for various values of progression ratio.

Table 13.3

Basic Range R = 20	*Range R 20/2*	*Range R 20/3*			*Range R 20/4*		*Range R 20/6*		
φ = 1.2	φ = 1.25	φ = 1.4			φ = 1.6		φ = 2		
100				1000					
112	112	11.2				112	11.2		
125									
140	140			1400	140				1400
160		16							
180	180		180			180		180	
200				2000					
224	224	22.4			224		22.4		
250			250						
280	280			2800		280			2800
315		31.5							
355	355		355		355			355	
400				4000					
450	450	45				450	45		
500			500						
560	560			5600					5600
630		63							
710	710		710			710		710	
800				8000					
900	900	90			900		90		
1000			1000						

13.19. LEE AND SHAFFER SLIP LINE FIELD

In metal cutting Lee and Shaffer slip line field theory is based on theory of plasticity for ideal rigid materials. According to this theory shear occurs on a single shear plane and the chip is stress

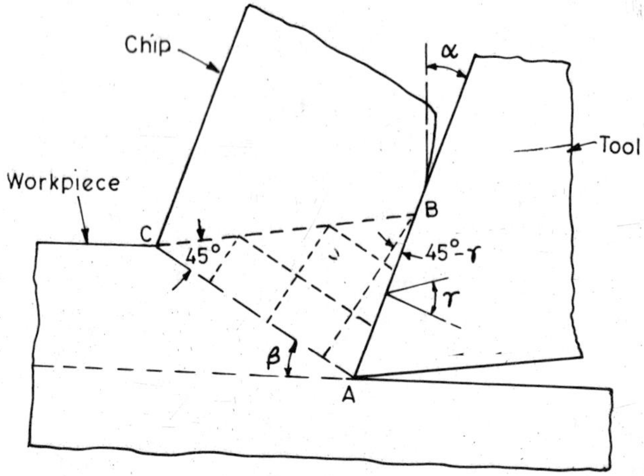

Fig. 13.19

free. The slip line diagram proposed by Lee and Shaffer is shown in Fig. 13.19. The resultant cutting force is inclined at an angle γ to the normal to the tool rake face. The deformation zone is contained in the triangular region *ABC*. Plane *AC* is shear plane. The plane *CB* is stress free and hence the slip lines meet this line at 45°. One set of the slip lines are inclined at (45° – γ) to the tool rake face.

As shown in figure

$$\angle CAB = 45° + \gamma$$

$$\beta + \angle CAB = 90 + \alpha$$

$$\beta + 45 + \gamma = 90 + \alpha$$

$$\beta + \gamma - \alpha = 45°$$

where β = Shear angle

α = Rake angle of tool

γ = Friction angle of the tool face.

13.20. MECHANISMS FOR STRAIGHT MOVEMENT

In machine tools following mechanisms are mainly used to produce straight movement :

(*i*) Rack and pinion transmissions

(*ii*) Worm and rack transmissions

(*iii*) Lead screw and nut transmissions

(*iv*) Can mechanisms

(*v*) Hydraulic devices

(*vi*) Solenoid type electromagnetic devices.

Rack-and-pinion transmissions are used for the principal movement, the feed movement, and various auxiliary movements.

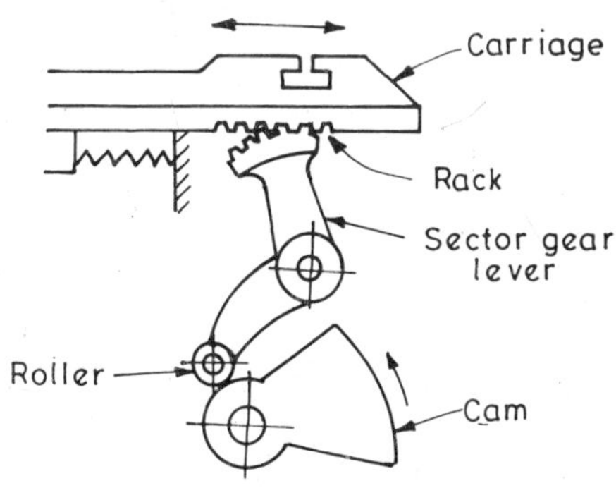

Fig. 13.20

Worm-and-rack transmissions are of two types : one with the worm arranged at an angle to the rack, which enables the diameter of the gear wheel driving the worm to be increased for smoother movement ; the other with the worm parallel to the rack, when the rack forms a part like a long nut incomplete (segment-like) in cross section. The operating conditions of this transmission are more favourable than those of the rack-and-pinion.

Cam mechanisms converting rotating movement into straight movement are employed mainly in automatic machine tools. There are cam mechanisms with disc cams and cylindrical cams.

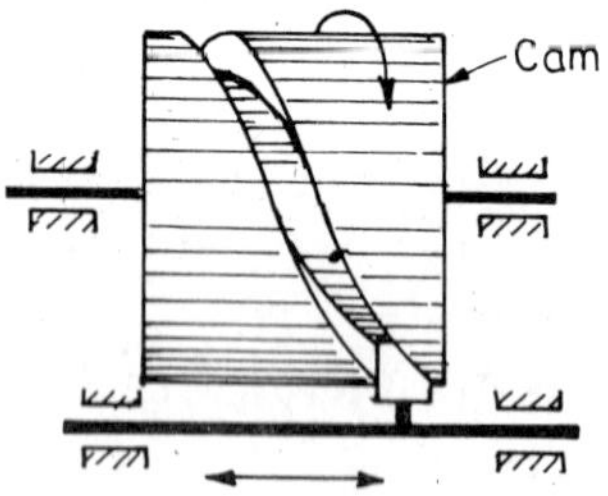

Fig. 13.21

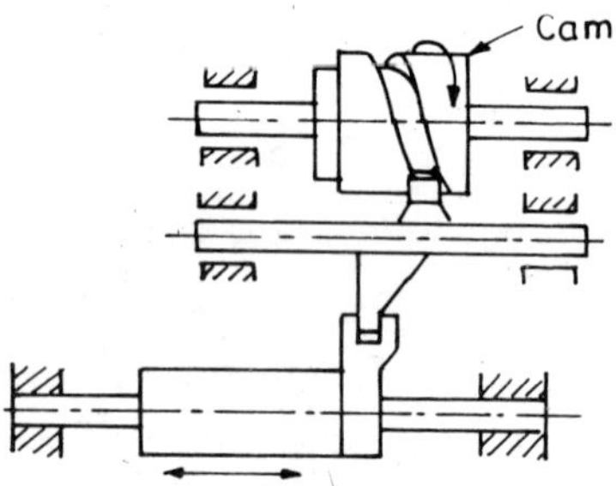

Fig. 13.22

Fig 13.20 shows the scheme of a disc cam mechanism. When rotated, cam transmits motion through roller and the sector gear lever to the rack of the carriage, which produces the reciprocating motion according to the cam profile. Fig. 13.21 and Fig. 13.22 present cam mechanisms with cylindrical cams.

13.21. SHARPENING MILLING CUTTER

Milling cutter sharpening is carried out in following order such as first the tooth faces are ground, then the external surface

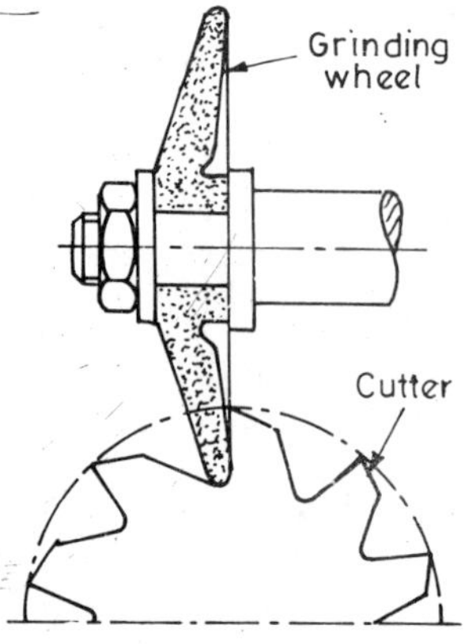

Fig. 13.23

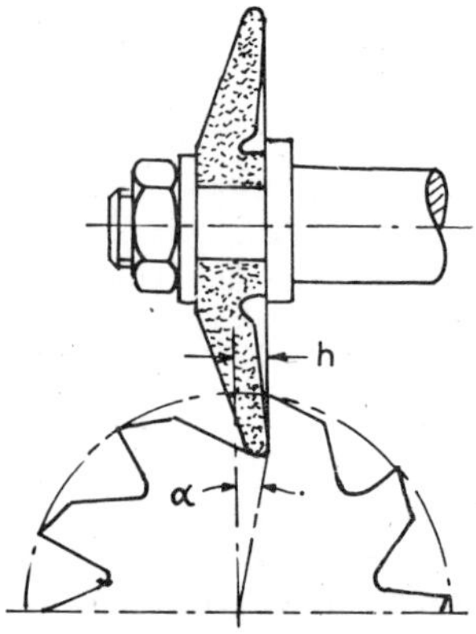

Fig. 13.24

and finally the lands. As a rule, only the land is ground when the cutter is resharpened after it has been in operation.

The tooth faces of straight-tooth profile-sharpened cutters are ground with a dish wheel. If the cutter has a zero rake (α) angle the face of the wheel is in a plane passing through the axis of the cutter (Fig. 13.23) while if $\alpha > 0$ (Fig. 13.24) the tool face is offset by the amount

$$h = \frac{D}{2} \sin \alpha$$

where D = cutter diameter

α = rake angle

h = offset.

Example 13.2. (*a*) *Discuss the functions of structural diagram and speed chart for a gear box.*

(*b*) *Sketch a typical twelve speed gear box.*

(*c*) *Sketch a typical three speed gear box.*

Solution.

(*a*) **Structural diagram.** *Structural diagram* is a graphical representation of the drive arrangement in general form. It provides the following data on the drive :

(*i*) The number of transmission groups (a transmission group is a set of gear trains arranged on two consecutive shafts) ;

(*ii*) The number of transmissions in each group ; the relative order of the groups in the compound transmission train ;

(*iii*) The order of kinematic arrangement of the groups, *i.e.*, their characteristics and the relation between the transmission ratios ;

(*iv*) The speed range ratio of each group and of the whole transmission ;

(*v*) The number of speed steps of each shaft in each group.

Speed chart. It is used to determine the specific values of all the transmission ratios and speeds of all the shafts in the drive. It is constructed according to the kinematic diagram of the drive.

Fig. 13.24 (*a*) shows a typical structural diagram.

Let ϕ = common ratio.

To construct a structural diagram, a series of parallel straight lines are drawn horizontally representing the speeds on a logarithmic scale. Then a series of vertical lines are drawn approximately equidistant from each other. Each zone between two adjacent vertical lines is allotted to a transmission group in the order of the

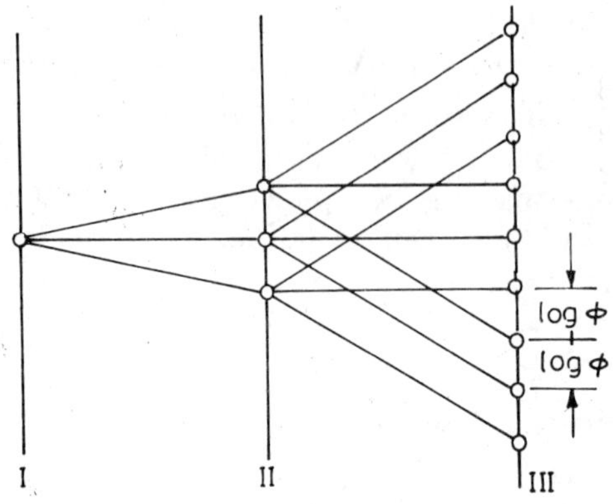

Fig. 13.24 (*a*)

arrangement of the groups along the train of transmission. Group characteristics of all the groups are determined. On the left vertical line of the first zone we plot a point symmetrically in respect to the horizontal lines. Opposite this point, on the right vertical line of the first zone, we plot as many points as there are transmission in this group. These points are then connected with the point on the left line with straight lines. This is continued to the last zone. Structural diagram indicates the relationships between the transmission ratio of the group transmissions but does not give the actual values.

(*b*) A twelve speed gear box is shown in Fig. 13.25. The gearing diagram is shown in Fig. 13.25 (*a*) and structural diagram is shown in Fig. 13.25 (*b*).

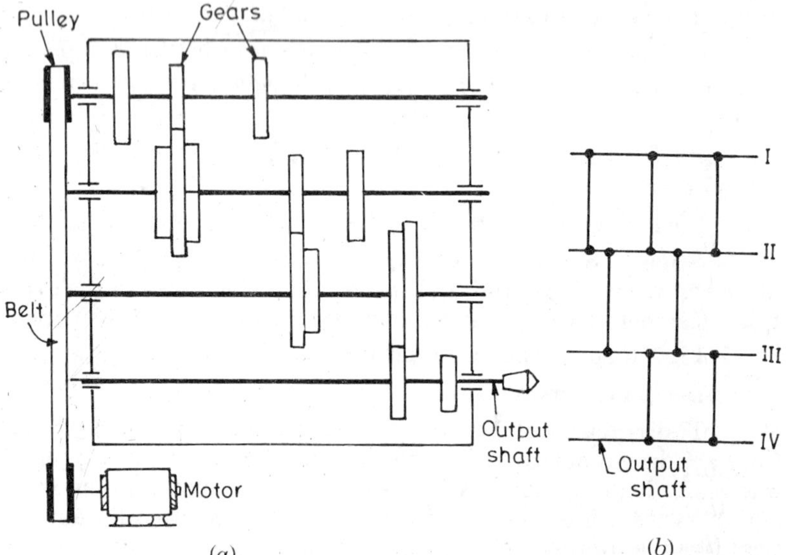

(*a*) (*b*)

Fig. 13.25

Fig 13.26 shows a typical three speed gear box spindle speeds. If sliding gear with teeth z_1 is engaged with claw clutch output spindle is driven directly by pulley with the gear transmission out of action. In this case the spindle speed is equal to the drive pulley speed.

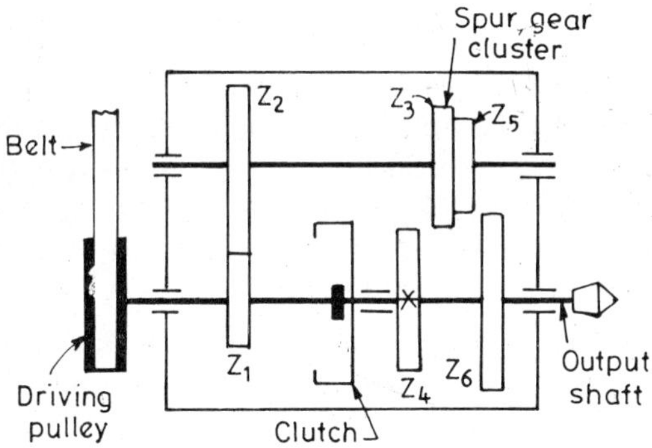

Fig. 13.26

When sliding gear z_1 is disengaged from clutch and meshed with gear wheel z_2, two more spindle speeds can be obtained by engaging gear cluster z_3-z_5 alternately with gear wheels z_4 and z_6

$$n_2 = n_p \frac{z_1}{z_2} \cdot \frac{z_3}{z_4} \; ; \; n_3 = n_p \frac{z_1}{z_2} \cdot \frac{z_5}{z_6}$$

where n_p = Drive pulley speed in RPM

n_2 and n_3 = Second and third step spindle speeds respectively in RPM.

Example 13.3. (*a*) *How do you classify gear boxes.*

(*b*) *Sketch a typical separate drive unit gear box.*

Solution. (*a*) According to the layout gear boxes can either

(*i*) be built into the spindle head or head stock or

(*ii*) can have a separate drive.

Gear boxes can be distinguished by

(*i*) mode of speed change

(*ii*) constructional arrangement

As to the mode of speed change the gear boxes may utilise

(*i*) sliding gears

(*ii*) claw clutches

(*iii*) friction clutches

(*iv*) magnetic clutches

(*v*) composite gear change

(*vi*) pick off gears.

The selection of a particular speed change mechanism depends on the following :

(*i*) purpose of machine tools

(*ii*) frequency of speed change

(*iii*) duration of working movement.

The advantage of sliding-gear transmissions is that they are capable of transmitting high torque, being comparatively small in radial dimensions claw clutch gear boxes feature small axial displacement needed for speed changing, less engagement force as compared with sliding gear mechanisms.

Friction and magnetic clutches in the gear box provide quick and smooth engagement of gears on the run and under load. Pick off gears are used in machine tools for mass and batch production.

(*b*) For some models of lathes, turret lathes and millers the spindle head (head stock) and the speed gear box are arranged as separate units connected by a belt transmission as shown in Fig. 13.27. When higher spindle speeds are needed, clutch is engaged

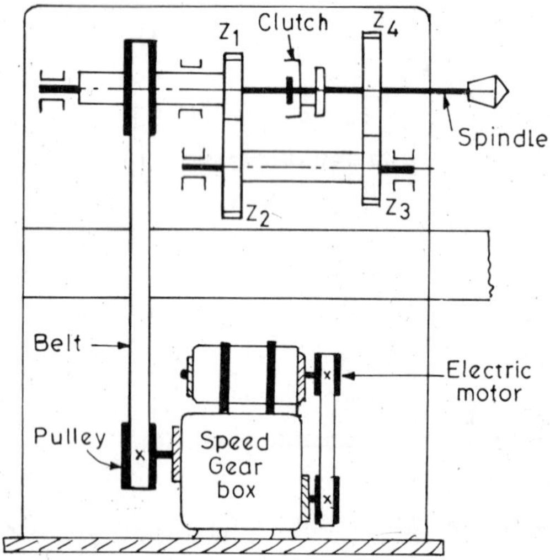

Fig. 13.27

with the pulley through gear wheel with teeth z_1 fixed on it, sliding gear cluster z_2-z_3 is disengaged from gears z_1 and z_4, so that rotation is transmitted to spindle directly from speed gearbox through belt transmission. When lower spindle speeds are required the clutch is disengaged, the cluster meshes with gear wheels z_1 and z_4 transmitting the rotation from the gearbox and belt transmission to the spindle.

The use of a separate drive in combination with spindle relieved of belt tension provides smooth spindle rotation and is more common in precision machine tools.

Example 13.4. *Sketch a typical six speed gear box for speeds ranging from 160 to 500 RPM.*

Determine driven pulley diameter if driving pulley (motor shaft pulley) rotates at 1000 RPM and is 150 mm in diameter.

Solution. N_1 = Minimum speed = 160 RPM

N_6 = Maximum speed = 500 RPM

n = Number of speed steps = 6

ϕ = Common ratio

$$= \sqrt[n-1]{\frac{N_6}{N_1}}$$

$$= \sqrt[5]{\frac{500}{160}}$$

$$= 1.26$$

Thus speeds will be as follows :

N_1 = 160 RPM

N_2 = 160 × 1.26 = 200 RPM

N_3 = 250 RPM

N_4 = 315 RPM

N_5 = 400 RPM

N_6 = 500 RPM.

Fig. 13.28 shows kinematic diagram for six speed gear box.

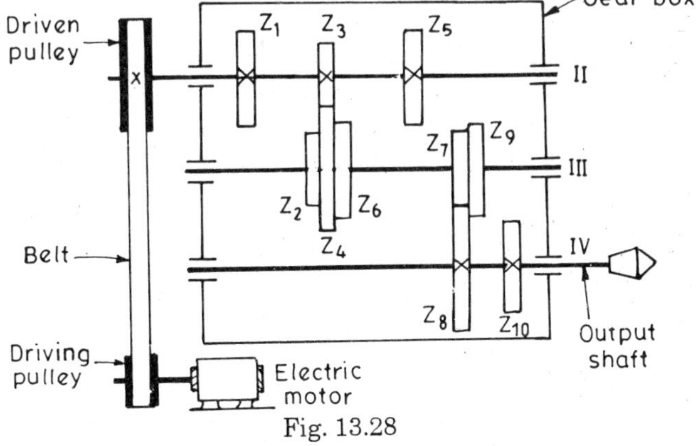

Fig. 13.28

Gears with teeth Z_1, Z_2, Z_3, Z_4 ...... Z_{10} are used. Shaft I is motor shaft. Gear box has three shaft namely shaft II, shaft III and shaft IV. Two types of structural diagrams are shown in Fig. 13.29 and Fig. 13.30. The speed charts are shown in Fig. 13.31 and Fig. 13.32.

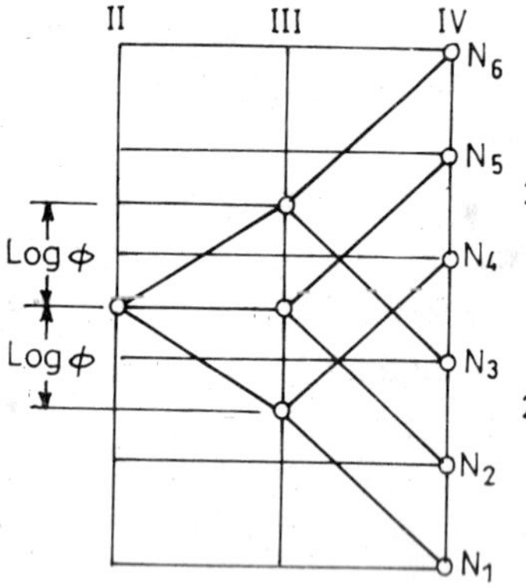

Fig. 13.29

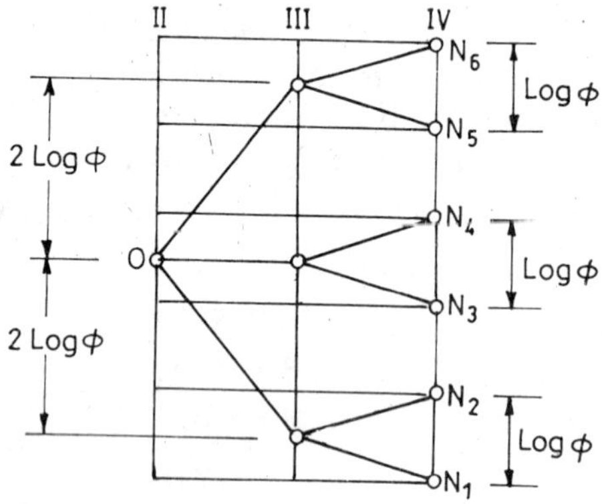

Fig. 13.30

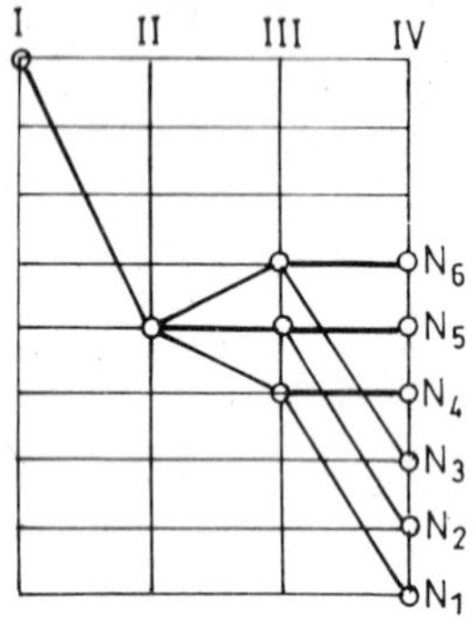

Fig. 13.31

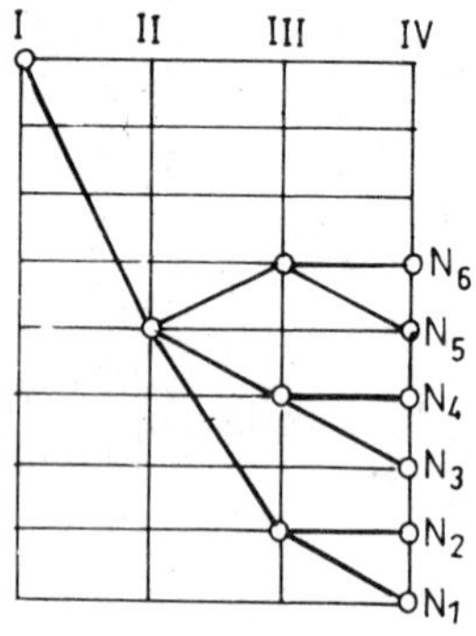

Fig. 13.32

Let D_1 = Driving pulley (motor shaft pulley) diameter

= 150 mm

N_1 = RPM of driving pulley = 1000

D_2 = Diameter of driven pulley

N_2 = RPM of driven pulley on shaft II

= 500 RPM.

$$\pi D_1 N_1 = \pi D_2 N_2$$

$$\pi \times 150 \times 1000 = \pi \times D_2 \times 500$$

$$D_2 = 300 \text{ mm.}$$

Example 13.5. *Define cutting speed in shaper.*

Solution. The cutting speed for shaper is given by the relation.

$$V = \text{Cutting speed}$$
$$= \frac{N \times L\,(1+R)}{1000} \text{ m/min}$$

where N = No. of strokes/min
= RPM of bull gear
L = Length of cutting stroke in mm

$$R = \frac{t_2}{t_1}$$

where t_1 = Time of forward stroke
t_2 = Time of return stroke

$$= \frac{2}{3}.$$

Example 13.6. *While machining a steel plate on shaper the length of stroke is 240 mm and number of strokes per minute is 27. If ratio of return to cutting time is 2 : 3, calculate the cutting speed.*

Solution.

N = Number of strokes/min = 27
L = Length of stroke
= 240 mm
R = Ratio of return stroke time to cutting stroke time

$$= \frac{2}{3}$$

$$V = \text{Cutting speed}$$
$$= \frac{N\,.\,L\,.\,(1+R)}{1000}$$
$$= \frac{27 \times 240\left(1+\frac{2}{3}\right)}{1000}$$
$$= 10.8 \text{ m/min.}$$

Example 13.7. *During machining of a mild steel flat plate 500 × 800 mm on a shaper, the cutting speed is 12 m per minute, ratio of return time to cutting time is* $\frac{2}{3}$, *clearance at end of stroke is 18 mm and feed is 2 mm. Determine the time for completing one* *complete cut. Also calculate metal removal rate of feed is 4 mm and depth of cut is 3 mm.*

Solution. Keep 800 mm parallel to stroke

$$L = \text{Stroke length}$$
$$= 800 + 2 \times \text{clearance}$$
$$= 800 + 2 \times 18 = 836 \text{ mm.}$$
$$W = \text{Width of workpiece}$$
$$= 500 \text{ mm}$$
$$f = \text{Feed}$$
$$= 2 \text{ mm}$$
$$R = \text{Ratio of return time to cutting time}$$
$$= \frac{2}{3}$$
$$V = \text{Cutting speed} = 12 \text{ m/min.}$$
$$T = \text{Time for one complete cut}$$
$$= \frac{L(1+R)}{1000 \times V} \times \frac{W}{f}$$
$$= \frac{836\left(1 + \frac{2}{3}\right) \times 500}{1000 \times 12 \times 2}$$
$$= 29.8 \text{ minutes.}$$

Metal removal rate (MRR)

$$= N \,.\, L \,.\, d \,.\, f$$

where d = Depth of cut

$= 3$ mm

f = Feed

$= 4$ mm

$$V = \frac{N \,.\, L(1+R)}{1000}$$
$$12 = \frac{N \times 836\left(1 + \frac{2}{3}\right)}{1000}$$
$$N = 8.6$$
$$M.R.R = N \,.\, L \,.\, d \,.\, f$$
$$= 8.6 \times 836 \times 3 \times 4$$
$$= 86275 \text{ mm}^3\text{/min.}$$

PROBLEMS

13.1. Write short notes on the following :

(*i*) Process card

(*ii*) Turning/milling data sheet

(*iii*) Geneva wheel mechanism

(*iv*) Power consumption for plain milling process

(*v*) Fellow's gear shaper.

13.2. Show that for an oscillating mechanism for a shaper the maximum quick return ratio (Q) is given by

$$Q = \frac{2L + S}{2L - S}$$

where L = Length of slotted lever

S = Stroke length.

13.3. Write short notes on the following :

(*a*) Transfer devices in automatic machine tools

(*b*) Copying systems for machine tools

(*c*) Pawl and ratchet drive

(*d*) Unit built machine tools.

13.4. Describe principal units of unit built machine tools.

13.5. Write short notes on the following :

(*a*) Gear cutting machine classification

(*b*) Gear shapers

(*c*) Robots.

13.6. Discuss basic elements of a commercial robot.

14

Objective Type Problems

1. Tick mark the correct answer :

(*A*) The metal cutting wedge is fundamental to the geometry of

(*a*) Head tools only

(*b*) Power driven tools only

(*c*) Sheet metal cutting tools only

(*d*) All cutting tools.

(*B*) Continuous chips are formed when cutting

(*a*) Brittle materials

(*b*) Ductile materials

(*c*) Amorphous plastic materials

(*d*) Free cutting non-ferrous alloys only.

(*C*) The rake angle of a cutting tool :

(*a*) Controls the chip formation

(*b*) Prevents rubbing

(*c*) Determine the profile of tool

(*d*) Determine whether the cutting action is oblique or orthogonal.

(*D*) Back rake angle for H.S.S. single point cutting tool to machine free cutting brass is

(*a*) 15° (*b*) 0°

(*c*) 5° (*d*) 10°.

2. In the list of processes given below tick (√) mark the chip removal processes

(*a*) Die casting (*b*) Extruding

(*c*) Forging (*d*) Rolling

(*e*) Broaching.

3. In the list of processes given below tick (√) mark the non-chip removal processes

(*a*) Grinding (*b*) Spinning on lathe

(*c*) Thread cutting (*d*) Drilling
(*e*) Milling.

4. State whether the following statements are true or false :

(*a*) For a given cutting speed cemented carbide tool removes more work material than H.S.S. tool

(*b*) Optimum rake angle of a tool is not a function of the properties of work material

(*c*) Cemented carbide is more tough than high speed steel

(*d*) In oblique cutting, the cutting edge of tool is not perpendicular to the cutting, direction

(*e*) Chip reduction coefficient is always more than unity

(*f*) Larger value of chip reduction coefficient indicates poor machinability

(*g*) Grinding wheel is a single point cutting tool

(*h*) Decreasing wedge angle of tool reduces mechanical strength of tool.

5. Fill in the blanks :

(*a*) The point angle of twist drill to machine steel is ......

(*b*) The cutting speed of H.S.S. twist drill to machine grey cast iron is ......

(*c*) The cutting speeds of H.S.S. milling cutter to machine aluminium is ......

6. Tick mark the correct answer :

(*A*) A twist drill has its point thinned in order to

(*a*) Reduce the hole diameter
(*b*) Increase the rake angle
(*c*) Locate in the centre punch mark
(*d*) Reduce the axial (feed) pressure.

(*B*) A reamer is used to correct the

(*a*) Size and roundness of a drilled hole
(*b*) Size and position of a drilled hole
(*c*) Finish and position of a drilled hole
(*d*) Finish and depth of a drilled hole.

(*C*) An oversize hole is produced by a drill if

(*a*) Lips of drill are of unequal length
(*b*) Feed is too high
(*c*) Insufficient coolant is used
(*d*) Cutting speed is too high.

(*D*) Cemented carbide tipped tools can machine metal even when their cutting elements get heated up to the temperature

(*a*) 1650°C (*b*) 1400°C

(*c*) 1000°C (*d*) 1800°C.

(*E*) Cemented carbide tools are usually provided with

(*a*) Positive back rake angle

(*b*) Neutral back rake angle

(*c*) Negative back rake angle.

7. State whether the following statements are true or false :

(*a*) The rates of feed and cutting speeds for twist drill are lower than for most other machining operations

(*b*) Like any other cutting tool the twist drill must be provided with correct tool angles

(*c*) A twist drill produces a hole of fine finish and accurate size

(*d*) No cutting fluids are used for carbide tipped milling cutters.

8. Tick mark the correct answer :

The time taken to drill hole through a 20 mm thick plate at 300 R.P.M. and at a feed of 0.2 mm/revolution is

(*a*) 15 seconds (*b*) 12 seconds

(*c*) 20 seconds.

9. State the usually recommended value of rake angle for machining aluminium with cutting tools made up of

(*a*) High speed steel tool (*b*) Cemented carbide tool

(*c*) Diamond tool.

10. Two major factors which determine the r.p.m. of milling cutter are the material being cut and

(*a*) Number of teeth in cutter

(*b*) Diameter of cutter

(*c*) Time allowed to complete the job

(*d*) Depth of cutter.

11. Mark against each statement according to the key given below :

Mark A—If the condition produces discontinuous chips

Mark B—If the condition produces continuous chips

Mark C—If the condition produces built up chips

(*i*) Brittle materials and slow cutting speeds.

(*ii*) Ductile materials and high depth of cut

(*iii*) Ductile materials with coarse feed
(*iv*) Ductile materials with fine feed
(*v*) Mild steel with sharp cutting edge of tool
(*vi*) Mild steel with high cutting speed
(*vii*) Mild steel with low rake angle.

12. Friction between chip and tool may be reduced by
(*a*) Increased sliding velocity
(*b*) Increased shear angle
(*c*) Use of low tool finish.

13. State whether the following statements are true or false :
(*a*) Aluminium oxide abrasives are used for grinding high tensile strength materials
(*b*) Silicon carbide abrasives are used for grinding low tensile strength materials
(*c*) Selection of grinding wheel does not depend on the work piece material
(*d*) Fine grain wheels are used to grind soft ductile materials
(*e*) Hard and brittle materials and finishing cuts require dense structure in grinding wheel
(*f*) Grade of grinding wheel is denoted by a number
(*g*) Structure of grinding wheel is denoted by alphabets.

14. State whether the following statements are true or false :
(*a*) Machinability index implies the degree of easiness in machining
(*b*) Free cutting steel cannot be easily machined
(*c*) Heat resisting steels possess low machinability
(*d*) Cast iron does not permit as high a cutting speed as structural carbon steel
(*e*) A most machinable metal one which permits fastest removal of largest amount of material per grind of the tool
(*f*) For the same amount of applied force orthogonal cutting removes more metal
(*g*) For the same amount of metal removal the shear stress induced in orthogonal cutting is more than in oblique cutting
(*h*) In orthogonal cutting the cutting edge of the tool remains inclined to the direction of the work feed.

15. The studs used as a coolant in general machine shop consists of :
(*a*) A solution of detergent and water

(*b*) A straight mineral oil
(*c*) An emulsion of oil and water
(*d*) A chemical solution.

16. State whether the following statements are true or false :
(*a*) A cutting fluid should have low conductivity
(*b*) Use of cutting fluids promotes a better surface finish.

17. State whether the following statements are true or false :
(*a*) The structure of a grinding wheel indicates the relative spacing of grains in the wheel
(*b*) The grade of a grinding wheel indicates the relative strength of the bond which hold the abrasive grains in place
(*c*) About 75% of grinding wheels have vitreous bonds
(*d*) Super-finishing is used to remove more metal than honing
(*e*) Coolant is not required during super-finishing
(*f*) Corundum contains more aluminium oxide than emery.

18. Select the suitable peripheral speeds for following grinding operations given in column *A* from the column *B* and indicate in the space provided

A — *Type of grinding operation*		*B* — *Speed in metres/min*
(*i*) Cylindrical grinding	☐	(*a*) 1200—1800
(*ii*) Internal grinding	☐	(*b*) 2700—4800
(*iii*) Snagging off hand grinding with vitrified wheel	☐	(*c*) 600—1800
(*iv*) Surface grinding	☐	(*d*) 1600—1950
(*v*) Rubber, shellac and resinoid bonded wheel.	☐	(*e*) 1500—1800

19. Match the words of column *A* with the words of column *B* and fill in the space provided

Column A		*Column B*
(*i*) Emery	☐	(*a*) To machine external cylindrical surfaces
(*ii*) Silicon carbide	☐	(*b*) Artificial abrasive
(*iii*) Surface grinding	☐	(*c*) To machine flat surfaces
(*iv*) Centre type cylindrical grinding	☐	(*d*) Natural abrasive
(*v*) Symbol used for silicate bond	☐	(*e*) E

(*vi*) Symbol used for shellac bond. ☐ (*f*) S

20. State whether the following statements are true or false :

(*a*) Cast iron is often ground dry

(*b*) The workpiece is supported between the centres during centreless grinding

(*c*) Surface grinder is used to grind flat surfaces.

21. Milling cutter is sharpened on :

(*a*) Tool and cutter grinder (*b*) Centreless grinder

(*c*) Cylindrical grinder (*d*) Surface grinder.

22. State whether the following statements are true or false :

(*a*) Ordinarily the surface finish improves with cutting speed.

(*b*) An increase in back rake angle of a cutting tool deteriorates surface finish

(*c*) Some degree of roughness which may be extremely small is always present on any machined surface.

23. Arrange the following machining processes in the increasing order of good surface finish

Milling, filling, hand grinding, drilling, surface grinding, lapping, sawing, super finishing, turning.

24. State whether the following statements are true or false :

(*a*) Grey cast iron is the most commonly used material for slide ways

(*b*) The clearance adjustment of dovetail slide ways is difficult

(*c*) Spindles of machine tool are generally made solid

(*d*) In generating the work surface produced is independent of the shape of the tool.

25. State the degrees of freedom possessed by the parts given below, indicate translation by T and rotation by R.

(*a*) Single point tool operating in lathe tool post

(*b*) Arm of radial drill

(*c*) Plug gauge in component bore.

26. The common ratio ϕ for spindle speeds in G.P. series is given by

(*a*) $\frac{1}{4} \le \phi < 2$ (*b*) $1 \le \phi \le 2$

(*c*) $1 \le \phi \le 8$.

27. In machine tool drives, the modulus for gears are usually selected between

(*a*) $10 \ge m \ge 1$ (*b*) $2 \ge m \ge 1$

(*c*) $20 \ge m \ge 1$.

28. State whether the following statements are true or false :

(*a*) Plain cylindrical bearings have high stiffness and good load carrying capacity.

(*b*) Ball bearings have comparatively high frictional losses than plain cylindrical bearings

(*c*) The spindle oil used for lubrication should be corrosive in nature

(*d*) Rolling bearings have less maintenance cost

(*e*) Gear pumps used in hydraulic system are of fixed delivery type.

29. Gear pumps used in hydraulic system are used for

(*a*) Low and medium pressure

(*b*) Medium and high pressure

(*c*) Low and high pressure.

30. Fill in the blanks :

(*a*) A gear pump can be used to obtain as high as .... pressure in the hydraulic drive of machine tools

(*b*) Multiple piston pump can be used to obtain a maximum pressure of ...... in a hydraulic drive

(*c*) The pressure most commonly used in hydraulic machine tool ranges from ...... to ......

31. Electron beam machining (E.B.M.) process is quite suitable for a material having

(*a*) High melting point and high thermal conductivity

(*b*) High melting point and low thermal conductivity

(*c*) Low melting point and low thermal conductivity

(*d*) Low melting point and high thermal conductivity.

32. Idnentify the following tools as single point cutting tools or multi-point cutting tools

(*i*) Twist drill

(*ii*) Grinding wheel

(*iii*) Roughing tool of shaper

(*iv*) Parting tool in lathe

(*v*) Milling cutter

(*vi*) Reamer.

33. Emery is a

(*a*) Artificial abrasive

(*b*) Natural abrasive

(*c*) Type of cloth.

34. Grinding is
(*a*) Metal fusing operation (*b*) Metal powdering operation
(*c*) Metal finishing operation.

35. Grinding is done wherever
(*a*) Other machining operations cannot be carried out
(*b*) A large amount of material is to be removed
(*c*) High accuracy is required.

36. Name the abrasives to be used (Aluminium oxide or Silicon carbide) to grind the following materials :
(*a*) Steels (*b*) Cast iron
(*c*) Aluminium (*d*) Wrought iron
(*e*) Copper (*f*) Non-metallic materials
(*g*) Bronze.

37. Laser beam machining process is used to machine
(*a*) Thicker materials
(*b*) Thinner materials
(*c*) Heavier materials.

38. The size of abrasive grains in a abrasive a jet machining varies from
(*a*) 60 to 100 microns (*b*) 10 to 50 microns
(*c*) 1 to 5 microns.

39. In collet the included angle of taper is usually
(*a*) 50° (*b*) 30°
(*c*) 20° (*d*) 10°.

40. State whether the following statements are true or false :
(*a*) The head stock remains stationary in a swiss type automatic screw machine
(*b*) Collets are used when the components are to be produced from bar stock
(*c*) The overhead charges of an engine lathe are more than a turret lathe
(*d*) Multi-spindle automatic screw machines maintain better accuracy than single spindle automatic screw machines
(*e*) Silicon carbide is most efficient when used for grinding softer materials
(*f*) Aluminium oxide is efficient when used for grinding hard materials.

41. State four properties of work material which affect the cutting tool life.

42. State three requirements which should be fulfilled for ideal all gear drives.

43. State three conditions for the formation of continuous chips with built up edges.

44. The Young's modulus of carbide tools is about

(*a*) Three times than for steel

(*b*) Six times than for steel

(*c*) Nine times than for steel

(*d*) None of the above.

45. Twist drills are usually considered suitable for machining holes having a length less than

(*a*) Two times their diameter

(*b*) Five times their diameter

(*c*) Ten times their diameter.

46. A hard grade grinding wheel is suitable for grinding

(*a*) Hard materials

(*b*) Soft materials

(*c*) Both hard and soft materials

(*d*) None of the above.

47. The relative motion of workpiece in planning is

(*a*) Rotary (*b*) Translatory

(*c*) Rotary and translatory (*d*) None of the above.

48. The accuracy obtained by the grinding process can be of the order of

(*a*) 0.25 mm (*b*) 0.025 mm

(*c*) 0.00025 mm.

49. In quick return mechanism of shaping machine the ram stroke length is proportional to

(*a*) Slotter arm length (*b*) Crank length

(*c*) Ram length (*d*) None of the above.

50. The usual ratio of forward and return stroke in quick return mechanism of shaping machine is

(*a*) 3 : 2 (*b*) 6 : 8

(*c*) 3 : 1.

51. Name the materials used for making laps and lapping media in lapping process.

52. State the height in microns of irregularities resulting in surface profile during the following microfinishing processes :

(*a*) Grinding (*b*) Honing

(*c*) Lapping (*d*) Superfinishing.

53. Name the materials which can be easily machined by ultrasonic machining process.

54. Describe the various types of costs of engineering products. The cost of engineering products can broadly be grouped as follows :

(*a*) Direct costs (*b*) Indirect costs.

Direct costs are the costs of material and labour. Indirect costs or overhead costs can be sub-divided as under :

(*i*) Works overheads such as wages of works superintendents, foremen, inspectors, storekeepers etc. and costs of depreciation of machines, costs of cutting oil, cost of heating lighting etc.

(*ii*) Office overheads such as cost of wages of all office staff, postage, legal expenses etc.

(*iii*) Sales overheads such as cost of sales staff, advertising etc. Costs may be more conveniently grouped as follows :

(*a*) Fixed costs (*b*) Variable costs.

Fixed costs includes depreciation cost, interests, cost of tooling, setting up etc.

Variable cost includes directs labour cost, material cost and part of indirect costs which will vary as production varies.

55. The amount of metal removed by honing process is less than

(*a*) 0.125 mm (*b*) 0.225 mm

(*c*) 0.015 mm.

56. In ECM process normal current requirement is

(*a*) 800 amps/cm^2 of workpiece area

(*b*) 100 amps/cm^2 of workpiece area

(*c*) 200 amps/cm^2 of workpiece area.

57. The voltage applied between tool (cathode) and workpiece (anode) in E.C.M. process is

(*a*) 30—50 V (*b*) 3—20 V

(*c*) 60—90 V (*d*) None of the above.

58. Name the electrolytes used in ECM process.

59. *Statements :*

(*i*) With carbide tools better cutting conditions can be achieved with negative rake and high cutting speeds.

(*ii*) In metal cutting it is always desirable to obtain a shortest possible shear plane because for a fixed shear strength reduction in shear plane area reduces the shearing force required to produce sufficient stress.

60. Name H.S.S. commonly used for making tools.

61. The diameter (D) of a plain milling cutter is approximately related to arbor diameter (d) as

(*a*) $D = 2.5\ d$ to $3\ d$ (*b*) $D = 4.5\ d$ to $6\ d$

(*c*) $D = 1.5\ d$ to $2\ d$.

62. State whether the following machining operation are forming or generating or a mixture of each :

(*a*) Milling a keyway using an end milling cutter

(*b*) Drilling a hole using a twist drill

(*c*) Finish shaping a flat surface using a broad tool.

(*d*) Face milling on flat surface.

63. *Statements :*

(*i*) The larger the cutting angle and the smaller the thickness of uncut chip, the more tightly the chip will curl (the smaller its radius of curvature will be)

(*ii*) The use of cutting fluids reduces the radius to which the chip curls.

(*iii*) An increase in nose radius leads to greater chip contraction.

(*iv*) Greater the cutting angle (or smaller the positive rake angle) the greater is chip contraction.

64. State the factors which affect the chip contraction.

65. Name four fine finishing operations.

66. Name the cutting fluids used for machining, the following metals :

(*i*) Cast iron

(*ii*) Mild steel and free cutting steel

(*iii*) Aluminium and aluminium alloys.

67. State whether the following statements are true or false :

(*a*) A cutting tool with large back rake angle is weak and tool point may break off readily.

(*b*) A cutting tool with negative back rake angle has better heat conductivity.

(*c*) Negative back rake angles are specially provided on cemented carbide tipped tools because the comented carbide possesses very high compressive strength and comparatively very low tensile and shear strengths.

(*d*) Nose radius provided on cutting tool imparts strength to the cutting point.

(*e*) Manually operated machine tools are economical for smaller batch size production.

(*f*) Transfer machines are economical for larger batch size production.

(*g*) During drilling the chips produced are removed automatically out of drill hole by helical flutes.

68. Suggest the electric motors for the drive of the following machine tools :

(*i*) Lapping machine

(*ii*) Rotary shears

(*iii*) Main drive of a boring machine.

69. State the accuracy that can be achieved on NC machines.

70. *Statements :*

(*a*) There is MCU in CNC

(*b*) CNC facilities part programming of complex shaped parts

(*c*) MCU converts the information from the tape program into the desired command signals.

71. Name the commonly used actuation systems in N.C. equipment.

72. Classify the manufacturing plants in terms of production volume.

73. Fill in the blank :

(*i*) In spark erosion workpieces has ...... potential. (Positive, negative)

(*ii*) The surface finish obtained by spark erosion is ...... as compared to ultrasonic machining. (High, low).

74. State the type of twist drill to be used for machining the following material :

(*a*) Laminated plastics (*b*) Brass

(*c*) Cast Iron (*d*) Steel

(*e*) Copper

(*f*) Aluminium alloy cutting long chips.

75. Name the three regions in which heat is generated during metal cutting.

76. The type and number of bearings to be used for spindles of machine tool depend on

(*a*) Type of spindle (*b*) Type of machine tool

(*c*) Load on the bearing (*d*) None of the above.

77. State the basic requirements of a machine tool drive.

78. State the common requirements of machine tool spindle supports.

79. State three factors which influence the stiffness of hydrodynamic bearings.

80. *Statements :*

(*a*) Forced vibrations in machine tools are most often caused by cyclic variations in the cutting forces.

(*b*) In planer the relative motion between cutting tool and work is rectilinear.

81. Define (*a*) cutting oils (*b*) emulsions.

82. H.S.S. cutting tools are generally provided with

(*a*) Positive rake angle

(*b*) Negative rake angle.

83. Cemented carbide and ceramic cutting tools are usually provided with

(*a*) Positive rake angle (*b*) Negative rake angle.

84. State the initial information required for designing a speed gear box.

85. The range ratio (R_n) of spindle speeds in speed gear boxes of machine tools, is related to range ratio of cutting speed (R_v) and range ratio of workpiece diameters (R_d) as

(*a*) $R_n = R_v \times R_d$ (*b*) $R_n = R_v + R_d$

(*c*) $R_n = R_v - R_d$ (*d*) None of the above.

86. Define the following for a speed gear box.

(*i*) Range ratio of spindle speeds (R_n)

(*ii*) Range ratio of cutting speeds (R_v)

(*iii*) Range ratio of workpiece diameters (R_d).

87. Give reasons for the following statements

(*a*) C.I. is commonly used for making machine tool structures.

(*b*) Use of disposable ceramic tools reduces the machining cost.

(*c*) Metallic workpieces with high hardness have poor machinability).

88. State five factors which restrict the use of plastic slide ways.

89. State four factors which commonly contribute to the natural surface roughness of a workpiece.

90. Name the materials which can be easily machined by cemented carbide tools.

91. State whether the following statements are true or false :

(*i*) In a cutting tool with positive rake angle the direction of thrust is towards tip of tool.

(*ii*) In a cutting tool with negative rake angle the thrust is directed into the body of the tool.

92. State three applications of negative rake carbide tools.

93. What is the difference between forming and generating of surfaces ?

94. State three demerits of N.C. control machine tools.

95. Define the factors of productive time.

96. Why cast iron and bronze are usually milled dry ?

97. What will happen if the frequency of vibration coincides with the natural frequency of any mode of machine tool ?

98. The quantity of metal removed (Q) per unit time in rotational metal cutting operations is given by

(*a*) $Q = 1000\, f.t.\, V$ mm^3/min (*b*) $Q = f.t.\, V$ mm^3/min

(*c*) $Q = \dfrac{f\,.\,t\,.\,V}{1000}$ mm^3/min (*d*) None of the above.

where f is feed (mm), t is depth of cut (mm) and v is cutting speed (m/min).

99. State four applications of each of the following D.C. motors :

(*i*) Shunt motors (*ii*) Series motors

(*iii*) Compound motors.

100. State whether the following statements are true or false :

(*i*) D.C. shunt motor runs practically at constant speed at almost all loads.

(*ii*) D.C. series motor has the characteristic of decreasing speed for increasing load.

(*iii*) D.C. series motor is well suited for lighter starting torque.

(*iv*) Three phase induction motor can either be squirrel cage or phase wound.

(*v*) In three phase induction motor starting torque is low because resistance in the armature circuit can not be added.

(*vi*) In CNC machine tool structure close type structure is used.

101. State three main requirements of machine tools.

102. Coefficient of friction in anti-friction guide ways is

(*a*) High (*b*) Low.

103. State two characteristics of tool material in E.D.M.

104. Name the types of working motions in a machine tool.

105. The common ratio (ϕ) used for automats is

(*a*) 1.26 (*b*) 1.41

(*c*) 1.12 (*d*) None of the above.

106. Name three materials commonly used for making slide-ways.

107. *Statements :*

(*i*) Point to point N.C. system is generally used in drilling and boring machines

(*ii*) Contouring N.C. machine tools are expensive than those operating on point to point control principle.

(*iii*) A punched tape is most widely used programming medium in N.C. machine tools

108. Name three programming medium in N.C. machine tools.

109. Numerically controlled systems with a feed back device are known as

(*a*) open loop systems (*b*) closed loop systems.

110. Short answer questions :

(*a*) Compare group drive and individual drive of machine tools.

(*b*) Classify machine tool structures

(*c*) Part program in N.C. system.

111. Carbon tetra chloride is used as cutting fluid at

(*a*) Low cutting speeds

(*b*) High cutting speeds.

112. *Statements :*

(*a*) High speed steel high in cobalt has the ability to retain its hardness at high temperature

(*b*) The machining accuracy which includes both profile as well as dimensional accuracy is determined by machine tool compliance.

113. Classify rolling guides based on geometrical form.

114. (*a*) In rolling guides the friction force becomes smaller with greater diameter of rolling elements.

(*b*) In rolling guides operating under light loads the resistance to motion is determined mainly by sliding friction.

115. In Taper roller guide ways the taper on roller is

(*a*) 0.5 to 1 μm (*b*) 2 to 4 μm

(*c*) 6 to 8 μm (*d*) None of the above.

(1 μ m = 1 micron)

116. State the coolants used for milling the following materials :

(*i*) Steel and brass (*ii*) Cast iron and bronze.

117. State the reasons for the following :

(*a*) Limited use of diamond tools

(*b*) Why low values of rake angle are recommended for diamond tools ?

118. State the commonly used rake angle of cutting tool while turning aluminium

(*a*) H.S.S. tool (*b*) Cemented carbide tool

(*c*) Diamond tool.

119. State two main requirements of slide ways materials.

120. *Statements :*

(*a*) Longitudinal oil grooves sharply lower the hydrodynamic load carrying capacity of the guide ways

(*b*) In slide ways the hydrostatic friction takes place where a special lubricating system provides separation of the slide way mating surfaces by an oil film of high rigidity.

121. Name three factors that contribute to the rise of hydro-dynamic pressure in slide ways.

122. State the drawbacks of stick-slip phenomenon during motion of machine tool slides on slide ways.

123. *True or false statements :*

(*i*) By jogging the operator brings the tool to the reference position and sets this position through the control panel as (0, 0, 0) or the reference desired by the programmer.

(*ii*) A block corresponds to one line of instruction on the part program.

124. *Fill in the blanks :*

(*a*) In N.C. machine tools the motors used to control, speed, feed and depth of cut are ......

(servo motors, electric motors)

(*b*) The rotary movement about x-axis is designated by ......

(A, B, C)

(*c*) The ...... axis of motion is always the axis of the main spindle of the machine. (Y-axis, Z-axis)

(*d*) Circular profiles can be produced on a CNC lathe using ...... codes. (G80, G81, G02, G03)

125. Name two typical elements of M.C.U. of N.C. machine tools.

126. Classify NC/CNC machines based on control systems.

127. *Fill in the blanks :*

(*a*) In conventional machines, the cutting tool cuts metal for about ...... % of the total machining time.

(b) In CNC machine tools the cutting time is about ...... % of total machining time.

128. Name three types of actuation systems used in N.C. machines.

129. In CNC machines the rotary movements about x, y and z axis are represented by

(a) A, B, C respectively (b) P, Q, R respectively

(c) x', y', z' respectively (d) None of the above.

130. Circular interpolation on CNC machine can be carried out using

(a) G02 (b) G03

(c) G02 or G03 code.

131. Nitriding process of surface treatment for steel tools is used for tools taking

(a) light cuts (b) medium cuts

(c) heavy cuts.

132. At very low cutting speeds the tool wear is due to

(a) plowing action (b) transfer.

133. State the ways in which machine tools can be classified.

134. State general requirements of a machine tool.

135. State five requirements of a cutting tool.

136. Name three materials which are commonly machined by cast alloy tools.

137. What are the basic requirements of tool materials used for the efficient rough machining of steel ?

138. *Statements* (True or False) :

(a) Twist drills are usually considered suitable for drilling holes having a length less than five times their diameter.

(b) Large twist drills are usually provided with a taper shank.

(c) The Z-axis of an N.C. machine is always in line with the axis of the principal spindle of the machine whether axis is vertical or horizontal.

(d) Flank surfaces in single point tool are those which face the workpiece.

In a single point cutting tool there are two flank surfaces

(i) Principal flank surface

(ii) Auxiliary flank surface

(e) In a single point cutting tool face is the surface along which the chip flows out.

139. Milling cutters are broadly classified into how many groups.

140. What is the difference between a reamer and a twist drill ?

141. State disadvantages of N.C. machine tools.

142. Name four arrangement used for speed changing in an all geared drive.

143. State major advantage of hydraulic drives.

144. Define hydraulic drive.

Fill in the blanks (145, 146 and 147)

145. (*a*) In electrolytic grinding 90% of the metal is removed ....

(*b*) For cutting turbine blades ...... machine process is used.

(*c*) Machinability and hardness are ...... related to each other.

146. Name the three main aspects of machinability.

147. Compliance (C) of a machine tool is given by

(*a*) $C = K$

(*b*) $C = \frac{1}{K}$

(*c*) $C = K^2$

(*d*) None of the above

where K = static stiffness.

148. State five characteristics of 3 phase A.C. motor for electrical drive.

Answers

1. (A) (*a*) (B) (*b*)
   (C) (*a*) (D) (*b*).
2. (*e*).
3. (*b*).
4. (*a*) True (*b*) False
   (*c*) False (*d*) True
   (*e*) True (*f*) True
   (*g*) False (*h*) True.
5. (*a*) 118° (*b*) 25—40 metre/min
   (*c*) 180—240 metre/min.
6. (A) (*d*) (B) (*a*)
   (C) (*a*) (D) (*c*)
   (E) (*c*).
7. (*a*) True (*b*) True
   (*c*) False (*d*) True
   (*e*) True.
8. (*e*)
9. (*a*) 35° (*b*) 15°
   (*c*) 0°.
10. (*c*).
11. (*i*) (*a*) (*ii*) (*c*)
    (*iii*) (*c*) (*iv*) (*b*)
    (*v*) (*b*) (*vi*) (*b*)
    (*vii*) (*c*).
12. (*a*).
13. (*b*) True (*b*) True
    (*c*) False (*d*) False
    (*e*) True (*f*) False
    (*g*) False.
14. (*a*) True (*b*) False
    (*c*) True (*d*) True
    (*e*) True (*f*) False
    (*g*) True (*h*) False.
15. (*c*)

16. (*a*) False (*b*) True
(*c*) True (*d*) False
(*e*) False (*f*) True.

18. (*i*) 1600—1950 (*ii*) 600—1800
(*iii*) 1500—1800 (*iv*) 1200—1800
(*v*) 2700—4800.

19. (*i*) (*d*) (*ii*) (*b*)
(*iii*) (*c*) (*iv*) (*a*)
(*v*) (*f*) (*vi*) (*e*)

20. (*a*) True (*b*) False
(*c*) True.

21. (*a*).

22. (*a*) True (*b*) False
(*c*) True.

23. (*i*) Sawing (*ii*) Hand grinding
(*iii*) Filling (*iv*) Turning
(*v*) Milling (*vi*) Drilling
(*vii*) Surface grinding (*viii*) Lapping
(*ix*) Super finishing.

24. (*a*) True (*b*) False
(*c*) False (*d*) True.

25. (*a*) $2T$ (*b*) $1T$, $1R$
(*c*) $1T$, $1R$.

26. (*b*). 27. (*a*).

28. (*a*) True (*b*) False
(*c*) False (*d*) True
(*e*) True.

29. (*a*).

30. (*a*) 30 kg/cm^2 (*b*) 70 kg/cm^2
(*c*) 5 to 80 kg/cm^2.

31. (*b*).

32. Multipoint cutting tools are twist drill, milling cutter grinder wheel and reamer.

33. (*b*). 34. (*c*).

35. (*c*).

36.

Material	*Abrasive used*
(*a*) Steels	Aluminium oxide
(*b*) Cast iron	Silicon carbide
(*c*) Aluminium	Silicon carbide
(*d*) Wrought iron	Aluminium oxide
(*e*) Copper	Silicon carbide
(*f*) Non-metallic material	Silicon carbide
(*g*) Bronze	Silicon carbide

37. (*b*) 38. (*b*)

39. (*b*)

40. (*a*) False (*b*) True
(*c*) False (*d*) False
(*e*) True (*f*) True.

41. The properties of the work material which affect the cutting tool life are as follows :
(*i*) Shear strength of the metal
(*ii*) Coefficient of friction between the chip and the cutting tool
(*iii*) Hardness and strain hardenability of the work material
(*iv*) Micro structure particularly the presence of hard constituents.

42. Requirements to be fulfilled for ideal geared drives are as follows :
(*i*) Least possible gears, shafts and levers are used
(*ii*) It should give sufficient speed changes
(*iii*) Only gears required for power should be engaged at a time.

43. (*a*) Low rake angle (*b*) Low cutting speed
(*c*) High feed.

44. (*a*) 45. (*b*)

46. (*b*) 47. (*b*)

48. (*c*) 49. (*b*)

50. (*a*)

51. In lapping laps are made from the following materials :
(*i*) Cast iron (*ii*) Soft steel
(*iii*) Copper (*iv*) Brass
(*v*) Hard Wood (*vi*) Hardened Steel
(*vii*) Glass.

The lapping media include abrasive flours such a diamond dust, boron, carbide silicon carbide aluminium oxide and emery mixed with an oil or bonding vehicle such as gasoline, kerosene, petroleum, or vegetable oil.

(*a*) 0.9 to 5 (*b*) 0.13 to 1.25
(*c*) 0.08 to 0.25 (*d*) 0.01 to 0.25.

53. Materials with a comparatively low tensile strength such as glass, ceramics etc. can be easily machined by U.S.M. process.
55. (*a*) 56. (*a*)
57. (*b*) 58. NaCl, KCl, $NaNO_3$
59. (*i*) True (*ii*) True.
60. 18—4—1 H.H.S. is commonly used for making cutting tools. It contains
    18% Tungsten
    40% Chromium
    1% Vanadium.
61. (*a*)
63. (*i*) True (*ii*) True
    (*iii*) True (*iv*) True.
64. The main factors affecting chip contraction are as follows :
    (*a*) Geometric elements of cutting tool point (chiefly cutting angle and nose radius)
    (*b*) Cutting variables such as cutting speed and feed
    (*c*) Cutting fluid
    (*d*) Workpiece material
    (*e*) Mechanical properties of workpiece material.
65. (*i*) Lapping (*ii*) Honing
    (*iii*) Precision turning (*iv*) Precision boring.
66. (*i*) Dry machined
    (*ii*) Mineral oil, lard oil, inactive E.P. oil
    (*iii*) Mineral oil, inactive E.P. oil.
67. (*a*) True (*b*) True
    (*c*) True (*d*) True
    (*e*) True (*f*) True
    (*g*) True.
68. (*i*) Adjustable speed D.C. or squirrel cage motor
    (*ii*) D.C. shunt or general purpose squirrel cage motor
    (*iii*) Squirrel cage or adjustable D.C. motor.
69. Positioning accuracy of ± 0.01/300 mm and ± 0.025 mm over the entire transverse and a repeatability of ± 0.005 mm is generally available on present day NC machines.
70. (*a*) True (*b*) True (*c*) True.

71. Following three types of actuation systems are commonly used in NC equipment

(*i*) Electro-mechanical (*ii*) Hydraulic
(*iii*) Pneumatic.

72. In terms of production volume the manufacturing plants are classified as follows :

(*i*) Job shop production (*ii*) Batch production
(*iii*) Mass production.

73. (*i*) Positive (*ii*) low.

74. (*a*) *H* (*b*) *N*
(*c*) *N* (*d*) *N*
(*e*) *S* (*f*) *S*.

75. (*a*) A long shear plane (*b*) Tool chip interface
(*c*) Tool workpiece interface.

76. (*c*)

77. Basic requirements of machine tool drive are as follows :

(*i*) To transmit motion and power from the input shaft to the output spindle, ram, or table.

(*ii*) To convert rotary motion to the translatory or reciprocating motion or *vice-versa*.

78. The common requirements of spindle supports are as follows :

(*i*) Guiding accuracy
(*ii*) High stiffness
(*iii*) Ability to perform satisfactorily under varying conditions of spindle operation
(*iv*) Stability against vibrations
(*v*) Minimum heating.

79. The stiffness of hydrodynamic bearings changes with

(*i*) lubricant viscosity (*ii*) temperature
(*iii*) rotational speed of journal.

80. (*a*) True (*b*) True

81. (*a*) Cutting oils are mixtures of lard, cotton seed or rape-seed oils and mineral oils.

(*b*) Emulsions are usually mixtures of a saluble oil consisting of mineral oil, sodium or potassium base soaps, free fatty acids and glycerine or alcohol with a large proportion of water. Paste cutting compounds are usually solid emulsions of mineral oil, sodium or potassium base soaps and water.

82. (*a*) 83. (*b*)

84. The following information is required initially to design a speed gear box.
   (*i*) Maximum output R.P.M. (N_{max})
   (*ii*) Minimum output R.P.M. (N_{min})
   (*iii*) The number of steps into which the range between N_{max} and N_{min} is divided
   (*iv*) The number of stages in which the required number of steps are to be achieved.

85. (A)

86. $R_n = \dfrac{N_{max}}{N_{min}}$ $R_v = \dfrac{V_{max}}{V_{min}}$

$$R_d = \frac{D_{max}}{D_{min}}$$

where N_{max} = Maximum output RPM of spindle
N_{min} = Minimum output RPM of spindle
V_{max} = Maximum cutting speed
V_{min} = Minimum cutting speed
D_{max} = Maximum workpiece diameter
D_{min} = Minimum workpiece diameter.

87. (A) (*i*) Cast iron has better vibrations damping properties
   (*ii*) Cast iron has better sliding properties.
   (*iii*) Cast iron can be easily cast.
   (B) Because much higher cutting speeds are possible while using ceramic tools.
   (C) Because power consumption and temperature and hence tool wear rate will be more.

88. (*i*) Poor structural stiffness
   (*ii*) Poor wear resistance when contaminated by abrasive dirt
   (*iii*) Low thermal conductivity
   (*iv*) Poor contact rigidity
   (*v*) Tendency to smell by absorbing lubricant.

89. (*i*) The occurrence of chatter or vibrations of the machine tool.
   (*ii*) Defects in the structure of work material
   (*iii*) In accuracies in machine tool movements such as movement of saddle on lathe bed.
   (*iv*) Surface damage caused by chip flow.

90. (*i*) C.I. (*ii*) None ferrous metals
   (*iii*) Non-metallic materials like plastics and marble.

91. (*i*) True (*ii*) True.

92. Negative rake carbide tools, find a particular use in the milling of steel, planer and shaper tools and for facing cuts.

93. In forming, the shape of the surface is a replica of the shape of the cutting tool.

In generating the shape of the surface depends on the direction of motion of the tool with relation to the work and is practically independent of the tool shape.

Generated surfaces are ordinary easier to produce than formed surfaces and can be finished to a higher degree of precision particularly when the work is so hard that abrasive cutting materials must be employed.

94. (*i*) Cost of N.C. machine tools is very high
(*ii*) Special skills in programming maintenance are essential
(*iii*) Down time of N.C. systems is very expensive.

95. Factors of productive time are as follows :
(*i*) **Set up time.** It is the preparatory time to get tools, to do paper work and to arrange tools on the machine.
(*ii*) **Handling time.** It consists of time for measurement, loading and unloading of workpiece.
(*iii*) **Machining time.** It is the time to carry out machining of workpiece.
(*iv*) **Down time.** It is the time lost due to
(*a*) break downs (*b*) waiting for tools
(*c*) minor accidents etc.

96. Because chips tend to mix with the cutting fluid to make a sticky mass that clogs the cutter teeth.

97. It may result in complete or partial destruction of machine tool and decrease its life.

98. (*a*).

99. (*i*) Pumps, lathes, drilling machines, press, planers
(*ii*) Conveyors, trains, cranes, trams
(*iii*) Crushers, compressors, punch presses, refrigeration plants.

100. (*i*) True (*ii*) True
(*iii*) False (*iv*) True
(*v*) True (*vi*) True.

101. (*i*) Precision (*ii*) Productivity
(*iii*) Low cost.

102. (*b*).

121. (*i*) Improved design of slide ways
(*ii*) Better surface finish
(*iii*) Higher viscosity of oil.
122. (*i*) Poor machining accuracy and surface finish
(*ii*) Lower productivity
(*iii*) Additional automatic loading of drive systems.
(*iv*) Shorter life and breakdown of cutting tools.
(*v*) Increased slide way wear rate
123. (*i*) True (*ii*) True.
124. (*a*) Servomotors (*b*) A
(*c*) *z*-axis (*d*) G02 or G03.
125. (*i*) Program reader
(*ii*) Feed back system.
126. Based on control system features the NC/CNC control systems are classified as follows :
(*i*) Point to point control system
(*ii*) Straight line control system
(*iii*) Continuous path or contouring control system.
127. (*a*) 25%
(*b*) 60—75%
128. Three types of actuation systems commonly used in N.C. machine tools are as follows :
(*i*) Electro mechanical
(*ii*) Hydraulic
(*iii*) Pneumatic
129. (*a*)
130. (*c*)
131. (*c*)
132. (*a*)
133. Machine tools can be classified in different ways as follows :
(*i*) Based on the type of processing operations
(*ii*) Degree of specialisation
(*iii*) Accuracy of the machine tool
(*iv*) Size and weight of the machine.
Apart from this there is a general classification of machine tools based on the following :
(*i*) The shape of generated surface
(*ii*) The shape of cutter
(*iii*) The type of finish

(*iv*) The nature of relative movement between workpiece and cutter.

134. (*i*) Accuracy : Accuracy produced should be high.

(*ii*) Rate of metal removal : It should be maximum.

(*iii*) Economical : Machine tool should have economical efficiency.

Machining quality depends on the various factors as mentioned below :

(*i*) Cutting tool

(*ii*) Tool holder

(*iii*) Workpiece and its clamping

(*iv*) The cutting conditions.

135. Five major requirements of a cutting tool are as follows :

(*i*) High wear resistance

(*ii*) High hardness.

The property of retaining hardness at the elevated temperature is known as hot hardness.

(*iii*) More toughness

(*iv*) Low coefficient of friction between tool and chip.

(*v*) Easier manufacturing of tool.

136. (*i*) Cast iron

(*ii*) Malleable iron

(*iii*) Hard bronzes.

137. The basic requirements for a tool material used for efficient rough machining of steels are as follows :

(*i*) More toughness

(*ii*) Superior wear resistance.

Cemented tungsten carbides coated with titanium carbide, titanium nitride and titanium dioxide are the common materials used for such tools. The thickness of coating varies between 5 to 8 microns.

138. (*a*) True

(*b*) True

(*c*) True

(*d*) True

(*e*) True.

139. Milling cutters are broadly classified into two groups :

(*i*) Plain milling cutters

(*ii*) Face milling cutters.

In plain milling cutters the cutting edges are at the periphery of the cutter and may be arranged either parallel to the axis of rotation or helically, the axis of the cutter is parallel to the generated surface.

In a face milling cutter such as an end mill cutter the teeth are on the one end as well as on the periphery. During cutting the axis of rotation in end or face milling is perpendicular to the generated surface. Each tooth of a milling cutter resembles a single point cutting tool.

140. Reaming operation is intended for finishing a previously drilled hole. The reamer is similar to a drill but has several cutting edges and straight flutes. It is intended to remove a small amount of work material only but it considerably improves the accuracy and surface finish of a hole.

141. The disadvantages of N.C. system are :
   (*i*) The initial cost of numerical control machines is higher than for conventional machines.
   (*ii*) Electronically trained personnel are required to service the equipment.
   (*iii*) Additional floor space is required for this equipment.
   (*iv*) Personnel must be trained in the programming and operations of this equipment.

142. The commonly used arrangements for speed changing in an all geared drive are as follows :
   (*i*) Sliding key method
   (*ii*) Tubular gears
   (*iii*) Use of claw clutches
   (*iv*) By using clusters of gears.

143. The major advantage of the hydraulic drives is that they supply a constant uniform torque over a wide range of speeds and the variation in speed can be brought about easily. This is not so with mechanical means.

144. Hydraulic drives are the hydraulic power utilising elements that use hydraulic energy supplied by the pumps and convert it again into mechanical energy.

145. (*a*) Electrolytically
   (*b*) ECM.
   (*c*) Directly.

146. Three main aspects of machinability are as follows :
   (*i*) Tool life
   (*ii*) Surface finish

(*iii*) Power required to cut the metal.

147. (*b*).

148. Three phase A.C. motor is commonly used for Electrical Drive of machine tools. The main characteristics of motor are as follows :

(*i*) Starting characteristics
(*ii*) Power and torque characteristics with respect to R.P.M.
(*ii*) Speed adjustment possibilities
(*iv*) Possibility of rapid braking
(*v*) Freedom from vibration.